SPANISH NOW! Level 2

Second Edition

by

Christopher Kendris, Ph.D.

Former Assistant Professor
Department of Spanish and French
State University of New York
Albany, New York

BARRON'S

For my wife Yolanda, my two sons Alex and Ted, my daughter-in-law Tina,
and my four grandsons Bryan, Daniel, Matthew, and Andrew

with love

All inquiries should be addressed to:
Barron's Educational Series, Inc.
250 Wireless Boulevard
Hauppauge, New York 11788

Library of Congress Catalog Card No. 95-39096

International Standard Book No. 0-8120-9324-0

Library of Congress Cataloging-in-Publication Data

Kendris, Christopher.
    Spanish Now! : level 2 / by Christopher Kendris. — 2nd ed.
        p.   cm.
    Includes index.
    ISBN 0-8120-9324-0
    1. Spanish language—Grammar.   2. Spanish language—Textbooks for foreign speakers—English.
I. Title.
PC4112.K44   1996
468.2'421—dc20
                                                                                                95-39096
                                                                                                CIP

PRINTED IN THE UNITED STATES OF AMERICA
15

Table of Contents

Structures and Verbs

Review of Level 1 Topics in Units 1 to 4

Appendix

Vocabulary (Spanish and English Words in One Alphabetical Listing)

Index

Preface to the Second Edition

Spanish Now!, Level 2 contains a variety of exercises for proficiency in the four skills: speaking, listening, reading, and writing. The exercises consist of topics on practical situations, such as meeting people, socializing, giving an oral report, providing and obtaining information, talking about what is in the pictures, expressing personal feelings, asking for help, giving advice, helping others, getting acquainted with announcements and advertisements in newspapers and magazines, travel interest, dialogues, shopping, sports, educational and cultural topics, visits to museums to enjoy Spanish art, and much more. The exercises in the four proficiencies have functional meaning in everyday topics and situations to stimulate the learner to participate in Spanish for communication.

Work Units 1–4 provide essential basic review of Level 1 topics so the student can embrace Level 2 topics with ease and confidence. In this way the student can become actively involved in making progress and in communicating in Spanish, not only with the teacher and peers, but also with people outside the classroom.

In the back pages of the book the student has fingertip access to comprehensive verb tables to master verb forms and a section on definitions of basic grammatical terms with examples in Spanish and English to achieve a better understanding of the elements of sentence structure.

Spanish Now!, Level 2 is a work that reflects my strong desire to make the study of Spanish stimulating for the student of any age by infusing the book with life and vigor. It contains original stories (some of which are humorous), many skits, playlets, sketches, scenes and dialogues. There are many exercises that will please the traditional and the modern teacher because the drills and exercises are imaginative, varied, and entertaining.

This book features evidence of Spanish as a living language used throughout the world. It contains photographs of authentic documents, famous Spanish persons and places, crossword and other word games that tease the brain, simple riddles, proverbs, reproductions of masterpieces of Spanish art, and many other features not found normally in a Spanish textbook. You say that masterpieces of Spanish art belong in a museum? That they are dead? They are dead when a student is not aware of them. They are alive when a student sees them. Some masterpieces of Spanish art are in this book to educate our students so that they can become aware of such great Spanish artists as Goya, Sorolla, Murillo, Velázquez, El Greco, just to mention a few. Have you ever noticed, for example, that in the painting *The Duchess of Alba* by Goya (which is in Work Unit 10), the duchess is pointing to the floor near her feet where the artist signed his name upside down? Take a close look at the delicate detail of her gown and the unusual expression on her face. Personally, I consider this painting the *Mona Lisa* of great Spanish art. Give me one good reason why our students should not have the chance to see Spanish art by great Spanish masters. The few included in this book might very well inspire some of our students to appreciate Spanish art.

The stories and dialogues in this book, for the most part, tell of the adventures of an imaginary Spanish family–Clara and Francisco Rodríguez and their two children, Juana and Pedro, and their dog, Coco. This book makes studying Spanish fun! There is something in it for every teacher and every student of Spanish.

Supplemental materials such as transparencies, cassettes, and other audiolingual software can be used advantageously because this book contains stories, dialogues, and a variety of exercises that give abundant practice in Level 1 and Level 2 reading, writing, and speaking in Spanish.

The language content in this book meets the minimum standards and sequence of a course of study in Spanish Level 2 presented in curriculum guides issued, for example, in 1992 by the New York State Education Department, Bureau of Foreign Languages, and those of the New York City Foreign Language Program for secondary schools.

A separate manual with answer keys to all exercises is provided by the publisher upon request. Two audiocassettes based on this book are also available.

Special thanks go out to my friend and colleague, Dr. Hilda Garcerán de Vall, a teacher of the Spanish language. Her distinguished late husband, Dr. Julio Garcerán, was also a teacher of Spanish. They wrote the book *Guía del idioma español*, published by Las Americas Publishing Company. I deeply appreciate their helpful suggestions while reading the manuscript to make sure that the Spanish contained in this book is *correcto como debe ser.*

I am also grateful for the assistance provided by the Embajada de España, Oficina Cultural, Washington, D.C., for furnishing me with dates, facts, figures, and cultural information in the introduction and elsewhere in this book.

If you have any suggestions as to the improvement of this book in the next edition, please let me know by writing to the publisher.

Christopher Kendris, Ph.D.

About the Author

Dr. Christopher Kendris earned his B.S. and M.S. degrees at Columbia University where he held a New York State scholarship and his M.A. and Ph.D. degrees at Northwestern University. He also earned two diplomas with distinction at the Université de Paris (en Sorbonne), Faculté des Lettres, Ecole Supérieure de Préparation et de Perfectionnement des Professeurs de Français à l'Etranger, and at the Institut de Phonétique (en Sorbonne), Paris. In 1986, he was one of ninety-five teachers in the U.S. who was awarded a Rockefeller Foundation Fellowship for Teachers of Foreign Languages in American High Schools. His fellowship provided for summer studies in Europe in creative ways to teach Spanish and French.

He has taught foreign languages at the College of The University of Chicago as visiting summer lecturer and at Northwestern University, where he held a Teaching Assistantship in French and Tutorial Fellowships in Spanish and French for four years. He has also taught at Colby College, Duke University, Rutgers—the State University of New Jersey, and the State University of New York at Albany. He served as Chairman of the Foreign Languages Department at Farmingdale High School, Farmingdale, New York, where he was also a teacher of Spanish and French. He also worked at The Library of Congress, Washington, D.C. using his language skills.

Dr. Kendris is the author of numerous school and college books, workbooks, and other language guides. Among his most popular works are *501 French Verbs* and *501 Spanish Verbs Fully Conjugated in All the Tenses, How to Prepare for SAT II: French, How to Prepare for SAT II: Spanish* (both books with audiocassettes for listening comprehension test practice with answers), *French Now! Level 1, Write It in French, Write It in Spanish* (both composition workbooks with answers), *Master the Basics: French, Master the Basics: Spanish, Pronounce It Perfectly in French* (with two audiocassettes of listening comprehension including tests with answers), and many others, all of which have been issued by Barron's. He is listed in *Contemporary Authors, Directory of American Scholars*, and in the author volume of *Books in Print.*

Abbreviations Used in This Book

abs. absolute
adj. adjective
adv. adverb
art. article
aux. auxiliary (helping)
ca. circa, about, around + year
cf. compare
cond. conditional
conj. conjunction
def. definite
dem. demonstrative
dir. direct
ed. edition
e.g. for example
etc. and so on, and so forth
excl. exclamation
f., fem. feminine
fam. familiar
ff. and the following
fut. future
i.e. that is, that is to say
imper. imperative
imperf. imperfect
indef. indefinite
indic. indicative
indir. indirect
inf. infinitive

interj. interjection
irreg. irregular
m., masc. masculine
n. noun
neg. negative
neut. neuter
num. numeral, number
obj. object
part. participle
perf. perfect
pers. person
pl. plural
pluperf. pluperfect
poss. possessive
prep. preposition
pres. present
pret. preterit
prog. progressive
pron. pronoun
refl. reflexive
rel. relative
s., sing. singular
sub. subjunctive
subj. subject
superl. superlative
v. verb
WU Work Unit

Introduction

Introduction

Reprinted with permission of United Nations

¡Hola!   **¡Buenos días!**   **¡Hola!**   **¡Buenos días!**   **¡Hola!**   **¡Buenos días!**
Hi!   Hello!   Hi!   Hello!   Hi!   Hello!

    Did you know that there are approximately 400,000,000 Spanish-speaking people all over the world? Spanish is the official language in the following lands: Spain, Argentina, Peru, Chile, Ecuador, Bolivia, Uruguay, Paraguay, Colombia, Venezuela, Costa Rica, Honduras, Guatemala, El Salvador, Nicaragua, Mexico, Cuba, the Dominican Republic, Equatorial Guinea (a republic in West Equatorial Africa, formerly known as Spanish Guinea), and the Philippines, where Spanish is one of the three official languages. According to the 1990 census (*The World Almanac 1995*, p. 600), it is estimated that 17.5 million Americans use Spanish at home and about three-fourths of these Spanish-speaking Americans also speak English. The Hispanic population of New York City is about 1.8 million. **¡Totalmente formidable!**

STRUCTURES AND VERBS

A Child in Ecclesiastical Dress (1660s) by Juan Bautista del MAZO (1612–1667)
Courtesy of The Toledo Museum of Art, Toledo, Ohio

La familia Rodríguez: Presentación

¡Hola! *Hi!*
Somos la familia Rodríguez. Somos cinco en la familia.
We are the Rodríguez family. We are five in the family.

Me llamo Clara Rodríguez. Soy la madre. Tengo un buen esposo. Estoy contenta.
My name is Clara Rodríguez. I am the mother. I have a good husband. I am happy.

Me llamo Francisco Rodríguez. Soy el padre. Tengo una buena esposa. Estoy contento.
My name is Francisco Rodríguez. I am the father. I have a good wife. I am happy.

Me llamo Juana Rodríguez. Soy la hija. Tengo un buen hermano. Estoy contenta.
My name is Juana Rodríguez. I am the daughter. I have a good brother. I am happy.

Me llamo Pedro Rodríguez. Soy el hijo. Tengo una buena hermana. Estoy contento.
My name is Pedro Rodríguez. I am the son. I have a good sister. I am happy.

Me llamo Coco. Soy el perrito. Tengo una buena familia. Estoy contento.
My name is Coco. I am the little dog. I have a good family. I am happy.

KEY WORDS AND PHRASES

buen, bueno, buena *adj.* good
cinco *num.* five
contento, contenta *adj.* happy
en *prep.* in
esposa *n.f.* wife
esposo *n.m.* husband
estar *v.* to be
estoy *1st pers. s., pres. indic. of* **estar**; I am
familia *n.f.* family
hermana *n.f.* sister
hermano *n.m.* brother
hija *n.f.* daughter
hijo *n.m.* son
llamarse *refl. v.* to be named, to be called

madre *n.f.* mother
*me llamo *1st pers., s., pres. indic. of* **llamarse**; my name is... (I call myself...)
padre *n.m.* father
perrito *n.m.* little dog
ser *v.* to be
somos *1st pers., pl., pres. indic. of* **ser**; we are
soy *1st pers., s., pres. indic. of* **ser**; I am
tener *v.* to have
tengo *1st pers., s., pres. indic. of* **tener**; I have

*It is also correct to say **Soy** + your name.

PRESENTE DE INDICATIVO		PRESENTE DE INDICATIVO	
ser (to be)		**estar** (to be)	
Singular		Singular	
1 yo	**soy**	1 yo	**estoy**
2 tú	**eres**	2 tú	**estás**
3 Ud. (él, ella)	**es**	3 Ud. (él, ella)	**está**
Plural		Plural	
1 nosotros (-as)	**somos**	1 nosotros (-as)	**estamos**
2 vosotros (-as)	**sois**	2 vosotros (-as)	**estáis**
3 Uds. (ellos, ellas)	**son**	3 Uds. (ellos, ellas)	**están**

For review of verbs, consult the verb tables beginning on page 448.

EJERCICIOS

I. Conteste las siguientes preguntas con oraciones completas según la presentación de esta lección. (Answer the following questions in complete sentences according to the presentation in this lesson.)

1. ¿Cómo se llama la madre? (What is the mother's name?) _____

2. ¿Cómo se llama el padre? _____

3. ¿Cómo se llama la hija? _____

4. ¿Cómo se llama el hijo? _____

5. ¿Cómo se llama el perrito? _____

II. **Complete las siguientes oraciones según la presentación de esta lección.** (Complete the following sentences according to the presentation in this lesson.)

1. Clara Rodríguez es _____ ; está _____

2. Francisco Rodríguez es _____ ; está _____

3. Juana Rodríguez es _____ ; está _____

4. Pedro Rodríguez es _____ ; está _____

5. Coco es _____ ; está _____

III. **Escriba las seis formas del verbo ser en el presente de indicativo.** (Write the six forms of the verb **ser** in the present indicative.) _____

_____

IV. **Escriba las seis formas del verbo estar en el presente de indicativo.** (Write the six forms of the verb **estar** in the present indicative.) _____

_____

REVIEW EXERCISES SPANISH LEVEL 1

I. **Conteste las siguientes preguntas con oraciones completas.** (Answer the following questions in complete sentences.)

Modelo: ¿Cómo se llama usted?   **Respuesta:** Me llamo Carlos Santiago.
(What is your name?)   (My name is Carlos Santiago.)

1. ¿Cómo se llama usted? _____

2. ¿Cuántos años tiene usted? _____

3. ¿En qué ciudad vive usted? ¿Cuál es la dirección? _____

4. ¿Cuántos días hay en el mes de enero? _____

5. Mencione dos cosas que usted tiene en el bolsillo en este momento. _____

_____

II. **Escriba oraciones completas empleando los siguientes modismos.** (Write complete sentences using the following idioms.)

1. tener hambre: _____

2. tener sed: _____

3. tener prisa: _____

4. tener frío: _____

5. tener calor: _____

III. Escriba oraciones completas empleando los siguientes modismos. (Write complete sentences using the following idioms.)

1. hacer un viaje: _____

2. hacer una pregunta: _____

3. estar bien: _____

4. estar de acuerdo: _____

5. ir de compras: _____

KEY WORDS AND PHRASES

The vocabulary and idioms in the following list appear in the same order as in Exercises I, II, III. If you do not remember the verb forms in the present indicative, refresh your memory by reviewing the verb tables beginning on page 448.

¿Cómo se llama usted? (What is your name?)
¿Cuántos años tiene usted? (How old are you?)
¿En qué ciudad vive usted? (In what city do you live?)
¿Cuál es la dirección? (What is the address?)
¿Cuántos días hay en el mes de enero? (How many days are there in the month of January?)
Mencione dos cosas que usted tiene (Mention two things that you have)

en el bolsillo (in your pocket)
en este momento (at this moment)
tener hambre (to be (feel) hungry)
tener sed (to be (feel) thirsty)
tener prisa (to be in a hurry)
tener frío (to be (feel) cold)
tener calor (to be (feel) warm)
hacer un viaje (to take a trip)
hacer una pregunta (to ask a question)
estar bien (to be (feel) well)
estar de acuerdo (to be in agreement, to agree)
ir de compras (to go shopping)

IV. Pictures. Proficiency in Speaking and Writing.

A. Look at the picture of the child and the little dog on page 1. Describe the scene to your Spanish teacher or a friend of yours in class. You may use your own words or any of the following: **el niño** / the child; **un manto hermoso** / a beautiful robe; **un perrito** / a little dog; **un jarrón de flores** / a vase of flowers; **una mesa** / a table. You may also want to say that **Juan Bautista del Mazo fue un gran artista español** / Juan Bautista del Mazo was a great Spanish artist.

B. Next, look at the pictures of the Rodríguez family at the beginning of this Work Unit. Say a few words in Spanish to your teacher or classmates about **la familia, la madre, el padre, la hija, el hijo, el perrito.** You may use your own words or those given next to the pictures.

C. Now, select either A or B and write in Spanish what you just said in class. Ask your teacher if you may write on the chalkboard.

ESTRUCTURAS DE LA LENGUA

SER AND ESTAR

These two verbs mean *to be* but note the differences in use:
Generally speaking, use **ser** when you want to express *to be*.
Use **estar** when *to be* is used in the following ways:

(a) Health: **¿Cómo está Ud.?** / How are you?
   Estoy bien / I am well.
   Estoy enfermo (enferma) / I am sick.

(b) Location: persons, places, things
   (1) **Estoy en la sala de clase** / I am in the classroom.
   (2) **La escuela está lejos** / The school is far.
   (3) **Barcelona está en España** / Barcelona is (located) in Spain.
   (4) **Los libros están en la mesa** / The books are on the table.

V. Speaking and Writing Proficiencies. Create two dialogues. You can play the part of Tú. Talk in Spanish with one of your friends in class.

A. **Situation:** You are not feeling well today. Your friend, Lola, asks you how you are. Reply in two or more short sentences.

   Lola: ¿Cómo estás?

   Tú: _____

   You may use the following words or your own: **bien** / well; **enfermo, enferma** / sick; **cansado, cansada** / tired.

B. **Situation:** It is your first day in a new school. You want to know where the cafeteria, the library, and the nurse's office are located. Ask your teacher. You may want to use the following words or your own: **dónde** / where; **está** / is located; **están** / are located; **la cafetería** / the cafeteria; **la biblioteca** / the library; **la oficina de la enfermera** / the nurse's office.

   Tú: _____

   La profesora: La cafetería y la biblioteca están en el primer piso (the first floor), **la oficina de la enfermera está en el segundo piso** (the second floor).

(c) State or condition that may change: persons
   (1) **Estoy contento (contenta)** / I am happy.
   (2) **Los alumnos están cansados (Las alumnas están cansadas)** / The students are tired.
   (3) **María está triste hoy** / Mary is sad today.
   (4) **Estoy listo (lísta)** / I am ready.
   (5) **Estoy pálido (pálida)** / I am pale.
   (6) **Estoy ocupado (ocupada)** / I am busy.
   (7) **Estoy seguro (segura)** / I am sure.
   (8) **Este hombre está vivo** / This man is alive.
   (9) **Ese hombre está muerto** / That man is dead.
   (10) **Este hombre está borracho** / This man is drunk.

VI. Speaking and Writing Proficiencies. Create one more dialogue. You can play the part of Tú again. Talk in Spanish with María, a classmate.

Situation: The school day has just ended. Your friend María tells you she is ready to go to the movies. Tell her you're sorry but you're not ready. Your dog is sick, you feel sad, and you have to go home. You may give your excuse in your own words, or you may use the following words, or any of the above in (a), (b), and (c): **lo siento /** I'm sorry; **no estoy listo (lista) /** I'm not ready; **mi perro (perrito) está enfermo /** my dog (little dog) is sick; **estoy triste /** I feel sad; **tengo que ir a casa /** I have to go home.

María: Estoy lista para ir al cine.

Tú: _____

(d) State or condition that may change: things and places
　　(1) **La ventana está abierta** / The window is open.
　　(2) **La taza está llena** / The cup is full.
　　(3) **El té está caliente** / The tea is hot.
　　(4) **La limonada está fría** / The lemonade is cold.
　　(5) **La biblioteca está cerrada los domingos** / The library is closed on
　　　　Sundays.

VII. Friendly Persuasion. Speaking and Writing Proficiencies.

Situation: You are in a Spanish restaurant. You came in from the cold to warm up with a nice cup of hot tea. But things did not turn out the way you had expected. Tell the waiter you feel cold (**tengo frío**) because the door is open (**porque la puerta está abierta**), the windows are open (**las ventanas están abiertas**), and the tea is cold (**y el té está frío**). You may use these words or your own words and ideas.

Tú: _____

_____

(e) To form the progressive present of a verb, use the present tense of **estar** + the present participle of the main verb:

　　Estoy estudiando en mi cuarto y no puedo salir esta noche / I am studying in my room and I cannot go out tonight.

(f) To form the progressive past of a verb, use the imperfect tense of **estar** + the present participle of the main verb:

　　Mi hermano estaba leyendo cuando (yo) entré en el cuarto / My brother was reading when I entered (came into) the room.

VIII. Pictures. Speaking and Writing Proficiencies.

Look at Picture No. 1 below. What is the man doing? / **¿Qué está haciendo el hombre?** Do you want to say that the man is running in the park? Then say, **El hombre está corriendo en el parque.** Or, you may use your own words and ideas.

Picture No. 1

Tú: _____

IX. Pictures. Speaking and Writing Proficiencies.

A. Look at Picture No. 2 below. What is the man doing in the street? / **¿Qué está haciendo el hombre en la calle?** Do you want to say that the man is cleaning the street with a broom? Then say, **El hombre está limpiando la calle con una escoba.** Or, you may use your own words and ideas.

Picture No. 2

Tú: _____

B. Look at Picture No. 2 again. What is the woman doing? / **¿Qué está haciendo la mujer?** Do you want to say that the woman is walking? Then say, **La mujer está caminando.** Or, the woman is taking a walk? If so, then say, **La mujer da un paseo.** You may use these words or your own words and ideas.

Tú: _____

Dos diferencias

Dibujo 1

Dibujo 2

Entre estos dos dibujos existen dos diferencias. ¿Cuáles son?
(There are two differences in these two drawings. What are they?)

Modelo: En oraciones completas, escriba las dos diferencias entre los dos dibujos (In complete sentences, write the two differences between the two drawings.)

Solución: 1. En el primer dibujo, la ventana está abierta. En el segundo dibujo, la ventana está cerrada. (In the first drawing, the window is open. In the second drawing, the window is closed.)

2. En el primer dibujo, el té (el café) está caliente. En el segundo dibujo, el té (el café) está frío (o: no está caliente). (In the first drawing, the tea (coffee) is hot. In the second drawing, the tea (the coffee) is cold (or: is not hot.)

9

X. En oraciones completas escriba las dos diferencias entre los dos dibujos.

Dos diferencias

Dibujo 1

Dibujo 2

Entre estos dos dibujos existen dos diferencias. ¿Cuáles son?

Solución: 1. _____

_____

_____

2. _____

_____

_____

XI. En oraciones completas, escriba las cuatro diferencias entre los dos dibujos.

Cuatro diferencias

Dibujo 1

Dibujo 2

Entre estos dos dibujos existen cuatro diferencias. ¿Cuáles son?

Solución: 1. _____

2. _____

3. _____

4. _____

ARTICLES

Definite Article

There are four forms of the definite article (the) in Spanish. They are as follows:

	Singular	Plural
Masculine	**el**	**los**
Feminine	**la**	**las**

EXAMPLES:

> **el libro** (the book); **los libros** (the books)
> **la pluma** (the pen); **las plumas** (the pens)

A definite article agrees in gender and number with the noun it modifies.

If a noun is masculine singular, you must use the masculine singular form of *the,* which is **el.** If a noun is masculine plural, you must use the masculine plural form of *the,* which is **los.** If a noun is feminine singular, you must use the feminine singular form of *the,* which is **la.** If a noun is feminine plural, you must use the feminine plural form of *the,* which is **las.**

How do you know if a noun is masculine or feminine? See farther on in the beginning of the topic **Nouns.**

If a feminine singular noun begins with stressed **a** or **ha,** use **el,** not **la.** This is done in order to avoid slurring the **a** in **la** with the stressed **a** or **ha** at the beginning of the noun that follows. Actually, that is what happened; the two vowel sounds **a** were not pronounced distinctly because they were slurred and **el** replaced **la.** For example, **hambre** (hunger) is a feminine noun but in the singular it is stated as **el hambre.** NOTE: **Tengo mucha hambre.** And NOTE:

> **el agua** / the water; but**las aguas** / the waters
> **el hacha** / the axe; but**las hachas** / the axes

However, if the def. art. is in front of an adj. that precedes the noun, this is not observed: **la alta montaña** / the high (tall) mountain, **la árida llanura** / the arid (dry) prairie.

Contraction of the Definite Article el

When the preposition **a** or **de** is in front of the definite article **el,** it contracts as follows:

> **a** + **el** changes to **al**
> **de** + **el** changes to **del**

EXAMPLES:

> **Voy al parque** / I am going to the park.
> **Vengo del parque** / I am coming from the park.

But if the def. art. **el** is part of a denomination or title of a work, there is no contraction: **Los cuadros de El Greco** / the paintings of El Greco.

The Definite Article Is Used:

(a) In front of each noun even if there is more than one noun stated, as in a series, which is not always done in English: **Tengo el libro, el cuaderno, y la pluma** / I have the book, notebook, and pen.

(b) With a noun when you make a general statement: **Me gusta el café** / I like coffee; **La leche es buena para la salud** / Milk is good for health.

(c) With a noun of weight or measure: **un dólar la libra; un peso la libra** / one dollar a pound (per pound).

LAS CAMPOCOMIDAS
rápidas·nutritivas·deliciosas

Salchichón Gran Serrano

Chopped Pork

Salchichón Catedral

Lunch

Chorizo Pamplona

Jamon Cocido Extra

Salami

Reprinted with permission of LECTURAS (Ediciones HYMSA), Barcelona

EJERCICIOS

I. Food and Drink. Speaking Proficiency.

Situation: You have accepted an invitation for dinner at a friend's house. Your friend wants to know what kind of meat (**la carne**) you like or don't like. You may want to say that you like sausage and cooked ham / **Me gustan el salchichón y el jamón cocido;** you can say that you don't like pork sausage / **No me gusta el chorizo.** Maybe you prefer **(yo prefiero)** roast beef / **el rosbif;** or lamb / **la carne de cordero.** Your friend also wants to know what you like to drink. Try any of these: milk / **la leche;** tea / **el té;** coffee / **el café;** soda pop / **la gaseosa.** You may use any of these words or your own words and ideas.

II. Pictures. Proficiency in Speaking and Writing.

Look at Picture No. 3 below. Where are these people? / **¿Dónde están estas personas?** What are they doing? / **¿Qué están haciendo?** Are they happy? Sad? / **¿Están contentas? ¿Están tristes?**

Tell your best friend in your Spanish class that these people are in a restaurant / **Estas personas están en un restaurante;** they are eating / **están comiendo;** and they are happy / **y están contentas.**

You may also want to say that the woman is the mother, the girl is the daughter, and the man is the father / **la mujer es la madre, la muchacha es la hija, y el hombre es el padre.**

You may use the Spanish words suggested above or you may use your own words and ideas. After you talk about the picture, write what you said on the lines below.

Picture No. 3

Tú: _____

_____

(d) In front of a noun indicating a profession, rank, title followed by the name of the person: **El profesor Gómez es inteligente** / Professor Gómez is intelligent; **La señora García es muy amable** / Mrs. García is very nice; **El doctor Torres está enfermo** / Dr. Torres is sick. But in direct address (when talking directly to the person and you mention the rank, profession, etc.), do not use the definite article: **Buenas noches, señor Gómez** / Good evening, Mr. Gómez.

(e) With the name of a language: **Estudio el español** / I study Spanish.

For examples of when you do not use the definite article with the name of a language, see (b) in the list "The definite article is not used," which follows.

(f) With the name of a subject matter: **Estudio la historia** / I study history.

(g) With the days of the week, when in English we use *on:* **Voy al cine el sábado** / I am going to the movies on Saturday.

(h) With parts of the body or articles of clothing, especially if the possessor is clearly stated: **Me pongo el sombrero** / I put on my hat; **Me lavo la cara todas las mañanas** / I wash my face every morning.

(i) With common expressions, for example: **a la escuela** / to school; **en la iglesia** / in church; **en la clase** / in class; **la semana pasada** / last week; **la semana próxima** / next week.

(j) With the seasons of the year: **en la primavera** / in spring; **en el verano** / in summer; **en el otoño** / in autumn; **en el invierno** / in winter.

(k) To show possession with the preposition **de** + a common noun: **el libro del alumno** / the pupil's book; **los libros de los alumnos** / the pupils' books; **los niños de las mujeres** / the women's children.

Note that when a proper noun is used, the definite article is not needed with **de** to show possession: **el libro de Juan** / John's book; **el libro de María** / Mary's book; **los libros de Juan y de María** / John's and Mary's books.

(l) With names of some cities, countries and continents: **la Argentina, el Brasil, el Canadá, los Estados Unidos, la Habana, la América del Norte, la América Central, la América del Sur.**

(m) With a proper noun modified by an adjective: **el pequeño José** / Little Joseph.

(n) With a noun in apposition with a pronoun: **Nosotros los norteamericanos** / We North Americans.

(o) With an infinitive used as a noun, especially when it begins a sentence: **El estudiar es bueno** / Studying is good. There are some exceptions: **Ver es creer** / Seeing is believing; and other proverbs. But you do not normally use the definite article with an infinitive if it does not begin a sentence: **Es bueno estudiar** / It is good to study. This is a general rule.

(p) When telling time: **Es la una** / It is one o'clock; **Son las dos** / It is two o'clock.

III. Socializing. Proficiency in Speaking and Writing. In the following situations, continue to act the part of Tú. You are talking with friends. After you have practiced speaking, you may write the completed dialogues.

A. Situation: Julio wants to know what you're doing tonight. Tell him in two or more sentences that you're busy; you have to wash the family car and then you have to clean the bathroom.

Julio: ¿Qué haces esta noche?
Tú: _____

You may use your own words or ideas or the following: **Estoy ocupado / ocupada. Tengo que lavar el carro de mi familia...; pues...; tengo que limpiar el cuarto de baño.** Maybe you have other things to do in the evening. If so, use your own words in Spanish.

B. Situation: You meet Felipe downtown. He greets you by saying, Hi! He wants to know where you're going. He says he's coming from the park. Tell him you're going to the park to feed the birds because they are always hungry.

Felipe: ¡Hola! ¿Adónde vas? Yo vengo del parque.
Tú: _____

You may use your own words and ideas or the following: **Voy al parque. Voy a dar de comer a los pájaros porque siempre tienen hambre.**

C. Situation: You are in the school cafeteria talking in Spanish with some students from your Spanish class. You are saying a few things about Mr. Gómez, your Spanish teacher, about Mrs. García, the office secretary, and the school physician, Dr. Torres. You are telling your friends that Professor Gómez is intelligent / **el profesor Gómez es inteligente;** Mrs. García is very nice / **la señora García es muy amable;** and Dr. Torres is absent today because he is sick / **el doctor Torres está ausente hoy porque está enfermo.**

You may use your own ideas and words or the Spanish words used above. Either way, say a few things about persons who have a title in front of their last names, *e.g.,* **el profesor X, la profesora X, la señora X, la señorita X, el señor X, el doctor X.**

Tú: _____

Suddenly, **el profesor Gómez** walks by your lunch table and you say to him, **Buenos días, señor Gómez.** Then **la señora García** stops to greet you and your friends. You say to her, **Buenos días, señora García.**

Tú: _____

IV. **Providing Information. Proficiency in Speaking and Writing.**

A. **Situation:** The next day in Spanish class, your teacher asks all the students, one at a time, to come to the front of the room to tell what courses (**las asignaturas**) they are studying. Now, it's your turn (**Ahora, te toca a ti**).

Here are some school subjects you may want to use in your presentation: **el español** / Spanish; **el inglés** / English; **el francés** / French; **el alemán** / German; **el italiano** / Italian; **la historia** / history; **la química** / chemistry; **las matemáticas** / mathematics. You may use any of the above subjects or any of your choice that are not mentioned here.

Begin your presentation by greeting the students. State your name and say that you are studying five subjects. You may want to begin with the following words:

¡Hola, amigos míos! Bueno, ahora me toca a mí. Me llamo... . Estudio cinco asignaturas. Son: el español, el inglés...

Tú: _____

B. **Situation:** Your friend Julia is writing a report in her Spanish class. She has to find out where each student in class goes every day of the week.

Tell her at least one place you go to every day Monday through Sunday. You may want to say that you go to the supermarket on Mondays / **Voy al supermercado los lunes;** to your friend's house on Tuesdays / **a casa de mi amigo (amiga) los martes;** to the movies on Wednesdays / **al cine los miércoles;** to the swimming pool on Thursdays / **a la piscina los jueves;** to the Star Restaurant on Fridays to work / **al Restaurante La Estrella los viernes para trabajar;** and so on.

You may use the Spanish words above for the places you go to on certain days of the week or you may use your own words and ideas. Either way, help Julia with her report by providing her with information about where you go every day of the week.

Tú: _____

_____

V. Dialogue. Proficiency in Speaking and Writing.

Situation: Your Spanish teacher is trying to encourage you to speak in Spanish by asking you a series of personal questions. After the conversation, write in Spanish what you said on the lines where **Tú** is indicated.

This is a guided dialogue but you may vary your responses. Remember that the speaking and writing proficiency exercises in this book are based on the structures of the Spanish language, and the use of verbs, vocabulary, and idioms presented on the pages that precede these proficiency exercises. You may find the need to review the preceding pages.

La maestra: ¿Te lavas la cara y las manos todas las mañanas?

Tú: Sí, señora. _____
(Tell her you wash your face and hands every morning.)

La maestra: ¿Vas al concierto de la escuela la semana próxima?

Tú: Sí, señora. _____
(Tell her you are going to the concert in school next week.)

La maestra: ¿Te gusta hacer un viaje en el verano con tu familia?

Tú: Sí, señora. _____
(Tell her you like taking a trip in the summer with your family.)

La maestra: ¿Y tu hermano, el pequeño José, ¿cómo está?

Tú: _____
(Tell her that your brother, little Joseph, is fine.)

La maestra: ¿Estudias todos los días?

Tú: Sí, señora. _____
(Tell her that you study every day.)

La maestra: ¿Es bueno estudiar?

Tú: Sí, señora. _____
(Tell her it is good to study. You can also say **El estudiar es bueno.**)

La maestra: ¿Te gusta estudiar?

Tú: Sí, señora. _____
(Tell her you like to study. Tell her that you like to play also. (**Me gusta jugar, también.**)

La maestra: Tú hablas español muy bien.

Tú: _____
(Thank her and tell her she is a good teacher of Spanish. **Muchas gracias, señora Vega. Usted es una buena maestra de español.**)

The Definite Article Is Not Used:

(a) In direct address with the rank, profession, title of the person to whom you are talking or writing: **Buenos días, señora Molina** / Good morning, Mrs. Molina.

(b) After the verb **hablar** when the name of a language is right after a form of **hablar: Hablo español** / I speak Spanish.

(c) After the prepositions **en** and **de** with the name of a language or a subject matter: **Estoy escribiendo en inglés** / I am writing in English; **La señora Johnson es profesora de inglés** / Mrs. Johnson is a teacher of English; **El señor Gómez es profesor de historia** / Mr. Gómez is a teacher of history.

(d) With a proper noun to show possession when using **de: los libros de Marta** / Martha's books.

(e) With an infinitive if the infinitive does not begin the sentence: **Es bueno trabajar** / It is good to work. **Me gusta viajar** / I like to travel. This is a general rule.

(f) With a noun in apposition with a noun: **Madrid, capital de España, es una ciudad interesante** / Madrid, capital of Spain, is an interesting city.

(g) With a numeral that denotes the order of succession of a monarch: **Carlos V (Quinto)** / Charles the Fifth.

(h) With names of some countries and continents: **España** / Spain; **Francia** / France; **México** / Mexico; **Europa** / Europe; **Asia** / Asia; **África** / Africa.

EJERCICIOS

I. **Discriminación de los sonidos. Su profesor de español va a pronunciar una sola palabra, sea la de la letra A, sea la de la letra B. Puntee A o B para indicar que su profesor de español ha pronunciado la palabra de la letra A o la palabra de la letra B.**
(**Sound discrimination.** Your Spanish teacher is going to pronounce one word, either in letter A or letter B. Check A or B to indicate that your Spanish teacher pronounced the word in letter A or letter B.)

Modelo: ■ A. hoy
            ☐ B. hay

He punteado la letra A porque creo que mi profesor de español ha pronunciado la palabra de la letra A. (I have checked the letter A because I believe that my Spanish teacher pronounced the word in letter A.)

1. ☐ A. pero
   ☐ B. perro

2. ☐ A. porque
   ☐ B. ¿por qué?

3. ☐ A. cuando
   ☐ B. cuanto

4. ☐ A. hacia
   ☐ B. hacía

II. **Varias palabras en una sola. Utilizando las letras en la palabra ADVENIR, ¿cuántas palabras puede usted escribir? Escriba diez palabras, por lo menos.**
(**Several words in one.** Using the letters in the word **ADVENIR,** how many words can you write? Write ten words, at least.)

ADVENIR

1. _____   3. _____   5. _____   7. _____   9. _____

2. _____   4. _____   6. _____   8. _____   10. _____

III. **Varias palabras en una sola.** Utilizando las letras en la palabra **ESPAÑA**, ¿cuántas palabras puede usted escribir? Escriba cuatro palabras, por lo menos.
   (**Several words in one.** Using the letters in the word ESPAÑA, how many words can you write? Write four words, at least.)

ESPAÑA

1. _____   3. _____

2. _____   4. _____

IV. **LETRA RELOJ.** Tres palabras se esconden en este reloj: Una palabra de las doce a las cuatro, una palabra de las cuatro a las seis y, por fin, una palabra de las siete a las once.
   (**LETTER CLOCK.** Three words are hiding in this clock: one word from 12 to 4, one word from 4 to 6, and, finally, one word from 7 to 11)

La misma letra puede emplearse en la palabra que sigue. Este reloj no tiene agujas. ¡Es un reloj de palabras! Use la forma de **ser o estar** en el presente de indicativo. (The same letter can be used in the word that follows. This clock has no hands. It's a word clock! Use the form of **ser** or **estar** in the present indicative.)

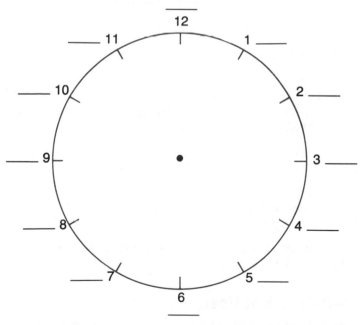

De las doce a las cuatro: Nosotros _____ la familia Rodríguez.

De las cuatro a las seis: Yo _____ el hijo.

De las siete a las once: Yo _____ contento.

The Neuter Article lo

The neuter article **lo** has idiomatic uses, generally speaking.
It is used:

(a) With a masculine singular form of an adjective that is used as a noun: **lo bueno** / the good; **lo malo** / the bad; **lo simpático** / what(ever) is kind.

(b) With a past participle: **lo dicho y lo escrito** / what has been said and what has been written.

(c) With an adjective or adverb + **que,** meaning *how:* **Veo lo fácil que es** / I see how easy it is.

Indefinite Article

In Spanish, there are four forms of the indefinite article (a, an, some, a few). They are as follows:

	Singular	Plural
Masculine	**un**	**unos**
Feminine	**una**	**unas**

EXAMPLES:

un libro (a book); **unos libros** (some books, a few books)
una naranja (an orange); **unas naranjas** (some oranges, a few oranges)

An indefinite article agrees in gender and number with the noun it modifies.

If a noun is masculine singular, you must use the masculine singular form of *a, an,* which is **un.** If a noun is masculine plural, you must use the masculine plural form of *some, a few,* which is **unos.**

If a noun is feminine singular, you must use the feminine singular form of *a, an,* which is **una.** If a noun is feminine plural, you must use the feminine plural form of *some, a few,* which is **unas.**

How do you know if a noun is masculine or feminine? See farther on in the beginning of the topic **Nouns.**

The plural of the indefinite article indicates an indefinite number: **unas treinta personas** / some thirty persons.

The Indefinite Article Is Used:

(a) When you want to say *a* or *an.* It is also used as a numeral to mean *one:* **un libro** / a book or one book; **una pluma** / a pen or one pen. If you want to make it clear that you mean *one,* you may use **solamente** (*only*) in front of **un** or **una: Tengo solamente un libro** / I have (only) one book.

(b) With a modified noun of nationality, profession, rank, or religion: **El doctor Gómez es un médico excelente** / Dr. Gómez is an excellent doctor.

(c) In front of each noun in a series, which we do not always do in English: **Tengo un libro, un cuaderno y una pluma** / I have a book, notebook, and pen. This use is the same for the definite article in a series of nouns.

(d) In the plural when an indefinite number is indicated: **Tengo unos dólares** / I have some (a few) dollars.

The Indefinite Article Is Not Used:

(a) With **cien** and **mil: cien libros** / a (one) hundred books; **mil dólares** / a (one) thousand dollars.

(b) **cierto, cierta** and **tal: cierto lugar** / a certain place; **cierta persona** / a certain person; **tal hombre** / such a man; **tal caso** / such a case

(c) With **otro, otra: otro libro** / another book; **otra pluma** / another pen.

(d) With an unmodified noun of nationality, profession, rank, or religion: **Mi hijo es dentista** / My son is a dentist; **Soy mexicano** / I am Mexican; **Es profesora** / She is a teacher. However, when the subject is qualified, the indefinite article is used.

(e) When you use **Qué** in an exclamation: **¡Qué hombre!** / What a man! **¡Qué lástima!** / What a pity!

(f) With some negations, particularly with the verb **tener,** or in an interrogative statement before an unmodified noun object: **¿Tiene Ud. libro?** / Do you have a book? **No tengo libro** / I don't have a book.

(g) With a noun in apposition: **Martí, gran político y más grande poeta . . .** / Martí, a great politician and greatest poet . . .

V. People. Proficiency in Speaking and Writing.

A. Situation: Today it's your turn to come to the front of the Spanish class to say two or three things about someone you know. It could be a member of your family, your family doctor, dentist, or one of your teachers.

You may use your own words and ideas or the following: **Miguel Santiago es dentista** / Miguel Santiago is a dentist; **es un dentista excelente** / he is an excellent dentist; **¡Qué hombre!** / What a man!; **es muy simpático** / he is very nice; **es mi tío** / he is my uncle; **la hija del doctor Santiago es profesora de español** / Dr. Santiago's daughter is a teacher of Spanish; **¡Qué mujer!** / What a woman!; **es muy simpática** / she is very nice.

B. After you have made at least four statements about one or more people you know, practice writing your statements on the chalkboard, on a sheet of paper, or on the lines below.

1. _____

2. _____

3. _____

4. _____

NOUNS

A noun is a word that refers to a person **(Roberto, Elena, el muchacho, la muchacha),** a thing **(el libro, la pluma),** a place **(la casa, la escuela, el parque),** a quality **(la excelencia, la honra).**

In Spanish, a noun is either masculine or feminine. When you learn a noun in Spanish, you must learn it with the article, for example: **el libro, la pluma; el muchacho, la muchacha; el hombre, la mujer.**

A noun that refers to a male person or animal is masculine in gender, naturally: **el hombre, el toro, el tío, el padre.** A noun that refers to a female person or animal is feminine in gender, naturally: **la mujer, la chica, la tía, la vaca, la madre.** This is easy to understand. What is not so easy to understand for us English-speaking people is that a noun referring to a thing, a place, or a quality also has a gender. You must learn the gender of a noun when you learn the word by using the article with it.

Generally speaking, a noun that ends in **o** is masculine: **el libro.**

Generally speaking, a noun that ends in **a** is feminine; also a noun that ends in **ción, sión, dad, tad, tud, umbre: la casa, la lección, la ilusión, la ciudad, la dificultad, la nacionalidad, la solicitud, la costumbre.**

Generally speaking, a noun that ends in **nte** refers to a person and the gender is masculine or feminine, depending on whether it refers to a male or female person:

el estudiante / la estudiante; el presidente / la presidente

Generally speaking, it is difficult to tell the gender of a noun that ends in **e.** Some are feminine, some are masculine. You must learn the gender of the noun when you learn the word with the definite or indefinite article.

MASCULINE	FEMININE

el aire / air   **la calle** / street
el arte / art   **la clase** / class
el baile / dance   **la fe** / faith
el bosque / forest   **la fuente** / fountain
el coche / car   **la gente** / people
el parque / park   **la leche** / milk

EJERCICIOS

I. El aspecto común. ¿Cuál es el aspecto común de estos objetos? Escriba su contestación con una frase.
(**Common feature.** What do these objects have in common? Write your answer in one sentence.)

Modelo:

un lápiz   **una pluma**   **una tiza**

Respuesta: Son cosas para escribir. (Answer: They are things for writing.)

   1. El aspecto común. ¿Cuál es el aspecto común de estos dibujos? Escriba su contestación con una frase.
(**Common feature.** What do these drawings have in common? Write your answer in one sentence.)

Respuesta: _____

2. El aspecto común. ¿Cuál es el aspecto común de estos dibujos? Escriba su contestación con una frase.
(**Common feature.** What do these drawings have in common? Write your answer in one sentence.)

Respuesta: _____

(**Several words in one.** Using the letters in the word LÁSTIMA, how many words can you write? Write six words, at least.)

LÁSTIMA

1. _____   3. _____   5. _____

2. _____   4. _____   6. _____

Irregular Gender of Nouns

Feminine nouns that end in **o.** Three common ones are:

la mano / hand; **la radio** (**la radio** is the radiotelephonic broadcast that we listen to; **el radio** is the object, the apparatus) / radio; **la foto** / photo (actually, this word is a shortened form of **la fotografía**)

Masculine nouns that end in **a.** Four common ones are:

el día / day; **el clima** / climate; **el drama** / drama; **el mapa** / map

Nouns that end in **ista**

These nouns are generally masculine or feminine, depending on whether they refer to male or female persons:

el dentista, la dentista / dentist; **el novelista, la novelista** / novelist

Plural of Nouns

To form the plural of a noun that ends in a vowel, add **s:**

el chico / los chicos; la chica / las chicas; el libro / los libros
la dentista / las dentistas; el coche / los coches; la clase / las clases

To form the plural of a noun that ends in a consonant, add **es:**

el profesor / los profesores; la flor / las flores; la ciudad / las ciudades

A noun that ends in **z** changes **z** to **c** before adding **es:**

el lápiz / los lápices; la luz / las luces

Sometimes a masculine plural noun refers to both male and female persons:

los padres / the parents, the mother and father
los tíos / the aunt and uncle, the aunts and uncles

23

los niños / the children, the little boy and little girl, the little boys and little girls
los hijos / the children, the son and daughter, the sons and daughters

Generally, a noun that ends in **ión** drops the accent mark in the plural. The accent mark is not needed in the plural because the stress naturally falls on the syllable that contained the accent mark in the singular. This happens because another syllable is added when the noun is made plural: **la lección / las lecciones; la ilusión / las ilusiones**

Generally, a noun that ends in **és** drops the accent mark in the plural. The accent mark is not needed in the plural because the stress naturally falls on the syllable that contained the accent mark in the singular. This happens because another syllable is added when the noun is made plural: **el francés** / the Frenchman; **los franceses** / the Frenchmen

Sometimes the accent mark is kept in the plural in order to keep the stress where it is in the singular. This generally happens when there are two vowels together and one of them is strong and the other weak: **el país / los países**

Some nouns have a plural ending but they are regarded as singular because they are compound nouns; that is to say, the single word is made of two words that combine into one: **el tocadiscos** / the record player; **los tocadiscos** / the record players; **el paraguas** / the umbrella; **los paraguas** / the umbrellas; **el abrelatas** / the can opener; **los abrelatas** / the can openers; **el sacapuntas** / the pencil sharpener.

Generally speaking, a noun that ends in **s** in the singular with no stress on that final syllable remains the same in the plural: **el lunes / los lunes; el martes / los martes**

Generally speaking, a noun that ends in **s** in the singular with the stress on that syllable (usually it is a word of one syllable) requires the addition of **es** to form the plural: **el mes / los meses**

Some nouns that contain no accent mark in the singular require an accent mark in the plural in order to preserve the stress where it fell naturally in the singular: **el joven** / the young man; **los jóvenes** / the young men

Nouns That Change Meaning According to Gender

Some nouns have one meaning when masculine and another meaning when feminine. Here are two common examples:

NOUN	MASCULINE GENDER MEANING	FEMININE GENDER MEANING
capital	capital (money)	capital (city)
cura	priest	cure

Nouns Used as Adjectives

It is common in English to use a noun as an adjective: *a history class, a silk tie, a gold watch*. When this is done in Spanish, the preposition **de** is usually placed in front of the noun that is used as an adjective and both are placed after the noun that is being described:

una clase de historia / a history class (a class of history); **una corbata de seda** / a silk tie (a tie of silk); **un reloj de oro** / a gold watch (a watch of gold)

Also note that the preposition **para** (*for*) is used in order to indicate that something is intended for something: **una taza para café** / a coffee cup (a cup for coffee). However, if the cup is filled with coffee, we say in Spanish: **una taza de café** / a cup of coffee

Nouns Ending in ito or illo

Generally speaking, the ending **ito** or **illo** can be added to a noun to form the diminutive form of a noun. This makes the noun take on the meaning of little or small in size:

un vaso / a glass (drinking); **un vasito** / a little drinking glass; **una casa** / a house; **una casita** / a little house; **un cigarro** / a cigar; **un cigarillo** / a cigarette

To form the diminutive in Spanish, ordinarily drop the final vowel of the noun and add **ito** or **illo: una casa / una casita.** If the final letter of the noun is a consonant, merely add **ito** or **illo: papel** / paper; **papelito** *or* **papelillo** / small bit of paper

At other times, these diminutive endings give a favorable quality to the noun, even a term of endearment:

una chica / a girl; **una chiquita** / a cute little girl. Here, note that before dropping the final vowel **a** to add **ita,** you must change **c** to **q** in order to preserve the hard sound of *K* in **chica; un perro** / a dog; **un perrito** / a darling little dog; **una abuela** / a grandmother; **abuelita** / "dear old granny"

In English, we do something similar to this: drop / droplet; doll / dolly *or* dollie; pig / piggy *or* piggie or piglet; bath / bathinette; book / booklet; John / Johnny; Ann / Annie.

EJERCICIOS

I. Escriba la forma correcta del presente de indicativo de los verbos SER o ESTAR. Estudie la presentación de la familia Rodríguez y las reglas antes de comenzar. (Write the correct form in the present indicative of the verbs **SER** or **ESTAR.** Before beginning, review the presentation of the Rodríguez family, the basic rules of language structure, and the examples in this Work Unit.)

1. ¿Cómo está Ud.?—¿Yo? _____ bien, gracias.

2. Hoy, (yo) _____ enfermo.

3. La escuela _____ lejos.

4. (Yo) _____ el padre. Me llamo Francisco Rodríguez.

5. Barcelona _____ en España.

6. (Yo) _____ la madre. Me llamo Clara Rodríguez. _____ contenta.

7. Juana, ¿por qué _____ (tú) pálida hoy?

8. La ventana _____ abierta.

9. (Nosotros) _____ la familia Rodríguez.

10. El café _____ caliente.

II. En las siguientes oraciones escriba la forma correcta del artículo determinado (definite article) el, la, los, las si es necesario. Antes de comenzar, estudie las reglas de esta lección. (In the following sentences write the correct form of the definite article **el, la, los,** or **las** where necessary. At times, no definite article is needed. Before beginning, review the basic rules of language structure and the examples in this Work Unit.)

1. Tengo _____ libro, _____ cuaderno y _____ pluma.

2. Me gusta _____ café pero _____ leche es buena para _____ salud.

3. Esto cuesta un dólar _____ libra.

4. ¿Por qué está ausente _____ profesor Gómez?

5. Buenas noches, _____ señor Rodríguez.

6. ¿Qué lengua extranjera estudia Ud.?—¿Yo? Estudio _____ español.

7. Me lavo _____ cara todas las mañanas.

8. ¿Dónde están _____ libros de _____ alumnos?

9. ¿Qué hora es? ¿Es _____ una?—No es _____ una. Son _____ dos.

10. ¿Habla Ud. _____ español?—¿Yo? Sí, hablo _____ español.

11. ¿Dónde están _____ alumnas? ¿Están en _____ clase?

12. En _____ verano, me gusta nadar en _____ piscina.

13. ¿Dónde están _____ cuadernos de _____ alumnas?

14. ¿Qué lengua hablan en _____ Brasil? ¿Y en _____ Habana? ¿Y en _____ Estados Unidos?

15. Nosotros _____ norteamericanos tenemos muchos amigos de habla española.

16. Madrid, _____ capital de España, es una ciudad interesante.

17. ¿En qué lengua escribe Ud.?—¿Yo? Escribo en _____ español.

18. Hace mucho frío aquí en _____ invierno y en _____ primavera hace fresco.

19. ¿Estudia Ud. _____ historia?—¿Yo? Sí, estudio _____ historia y me gusta mucho.

20. ¿Dónde está _____ doctor Torres?

III. **En las siguientes oraciones escriba la forma correcta del artículo indeterminado (indefinite article) un, una, unos, unas si es necesario. Antes de comenzar, estudie las reglas de esta lección.** (In the following sentences write the correct form of the indefinite article **un, una, unos, unas** if necessary. Before beginning, study the rules of language structure and the examples in this Work Unit.)

1. En esta clase hay _____ veinte personas.

2. Tengo solamente _____ libro y _____ pluma.

3. Este señor es _____ médico. Es _____ médico excelente.

4. Tengo _____ cuaderno, _____ naranjas y _____ dólares.

5. El hijo del señor Robles es _____ dentista.

6. ¿Es _____ profesora la señora García?

7. Sí, la señora García es _____ profesora excelente.

8. ¿Es Ud. _____ norteamericano?—Sí, soy _____ mexicano.

9. El señor López es muy inteligente. ¡Qué _____ hombre!

26 10. Necesito _____ otro libro y _____ otra pluma.

IV. Escriba la forma correcta del artículo determinado (definite article) el, la, los, las. Antes de comenzar, estudie las reglas de esta lección. (Write the correct form of the definite article **el, la, los, las.** Before beginning, study the rules of language structure and the examples in this Work Unit.)

1. _____ hombre

2. _____ mujer

3. _____ padre

4. _____ madre

5. _____ vaca

6. _____ tío

7. _____ toro

8. _____ presentación

9. _____ ciudad

10. _____ coches

11. _____ fuentes

12. _____ bailes

V. Escriba el plural de las siguientes palabras. (Write the plural of the following words.)

1. el chico _____

2. la chica _____

3. el dentista _____

4. la dentista _____

5. el coche _____

6. el profesor _____

7. la profesora _____

8. la flor _____

9. la ciudad _____

10. el lápiz _____

VI. Escriba el plural de las siguientes palabras. (Write the plural of the following words.)

1. la luz _____

2. la lección _____

3. la ilusión _____

4. el francés _____

5. el país _____

6. el tocadiscos _____

7. el paraguas _____

8. el abrelatas _____

9. el sacapuntas _____

10. el lunes _____

VII. Escriba el singular de las siguientes palabras (Write the singular of the following words.)

1. los países _____

2. las luces _____

3. los lápices _____

4. las flores _____

5. los paraguas _____

6. los martes _____

7. los meses _____

8. los lunes _____

9. los jóvenes _____

10. los tocadiscos _____

VIII. Traduzca las siguientes expresiones. (Translate the following expressions into Spanish. The answers to all these exercises are in this Work Unit.)

1. a history class _____

2. a silk tie _____

3. a gold watch _____

4. a coffee cup _____

5. a cup of coffee _____

6. a Spanish class _____

IX. Traduzca las siguientes palabras. (Translate the following words into Spanish. The answers to all these exercises are in this Work Unit.)

1. a drinking glass; a little drinking glass _____

2. a girl; a cute little girl _____

3. a dog; a darling little dog _____

4. a house; a little house _____

X. Dictado. Escriba las frases que su profesor de español va a pronunciar.
(**Dictation.** Write the sentences that your Spanish teacher is going to pronounce.)

1. _____

2. _____

3. _____

XI. HUMOR. La adivinanza para hoy. (The riddle for today.)
¿Qué hay en el medio de Barcelona? (What is in the middle of Barcelona?)

Solución: _____

XII. La palabra española "la ropa" no significa en inglés "rope" sino "clothes, clothing." (The Spanish word la ropa does not mean "rope" in English but rather "clothes, clothing.")

la ropa / clothes, clothing
la cuerda / rope, cord
La ropa está suspendida en la cuerda. / The clothes are hanging on the line.

Mnemonic Tip	**Cuerda** = cord, rope. The letters **crd** are in **cuerda** and in cord.

¿Cuántos ejemplos puede Ud. decir y escribir? (How many examples can you say and write?)

XIII. En español hay muchas palabras que se escriben y se pronuncian idénticamente, pero tienen distinto significado. (In Spanish there are many words that are written and pronounced identically, but have a different meaning.)

Por ejemplo: (For example:)

sobre *n.m.* / envelope
sobre *prep.* / on, upon

El sobre está sobre la mesa./ The envelope is on the table.

¿Cuántos ejemplos puede Ud. decir y escribir? (How many examples can you say and write?)

XIV. Complete este crucigrama. (Complete this crossword. The missing Spanish words are given in English after each statement. They are all in this Work Unit.)

VERTICALES

1. Mi lápiz no tiene punta. Necesito un _____ . (pencil sharpener)

2. Una casa pequeña es una _____ . (little house)

5. No hay bastante _____ para leer. (light)

6. Mi hermano está estudiando en _____ cuarto y yo estoy estudiando en el mío. (his)

HORIZONTALES

3. Cuando está lloviendo, tomo mi par _____ . (umbrella)

4. Voy _____ parque. (to the)

5. Me gustan _____ flores. (the)

7. Necesito una _____ para café. (cup)

8. Mi madre _____ mi padre son amables. (and)

9. Mi hermano tiene una corbata de_____ . (silk)

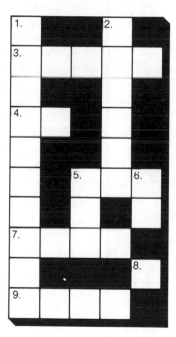

XV. Varias palabras en una sola. ¿Cuántas palabras españolas puede Ud. hallar en el vocablo NOMBRES? Encuentre quince por lo menos. Usted puede utilizar las letras en cualquier orden y añadir signos de acento o tilde, si es necesario, para formar nuevas palabras. Por ejemplo: sé, señor.
Several words in one. How many Spanish words can you find in the word NOMBRES [NAMES]? Find 15, at least. You may use the letters in any order and add accent marks or a tilde (˜), if needed, to form new words. For example: sé [I know], señor [sir, mister].

$$\boxed{\text{N O M B R E S}}$$

1. _____   4. _____   7. _____   10. _____   13. _____

2. _____   5. _____   8. _____   11. _____   14. _____

3. _____   6. _____   9. _____   12. _____   15. _____

XVI. Culture. Appreciation of Spanish Art. Speaking and Writing Proficiency.

Situation: You and your classmates are on a field trip to The National Gallery of Art in Washington, D.C. You are admiring a painting by EL GRECO, a great Spanish artist / **un gran artista español.** It is entitled *The Virgin with Saint Inés and Saint Tecla.*

Look at the picture on the following page. Say aloud a few words in Spanish that come to mind while you appreciate looking at the painting. You may use your own words or, for starters, you may use the following:

Este cuadro de El Greco es magnífico / This painting by El Greco is magnificent. How about a few more adjectives? For example, **impresionante** / impressive; **interesante** / interesting; **espléndido** / splendid; **bello** / beautiful; **gracioso** / gracious; **extático** / ecstatic. Some nouns: **el éxtasis** / ecstasy; **La Virgen** / The Virgin; **el nene** / the baby; **el ángel, los ángeles** / the angel, angels; **las alas** / the wings; **el cordero blanco** / the white lamb; **las manos bellas** / the beautiful hands; **la cabeza de un león** / the head of a lion. A few verbs: **mirar** / to look at; **Yo miro** / I am looking at; **ver** / to see; **yo veo** / I see; **Me gusta mucho** / I like it a lot; **apreciar** / to appreciate; **Yo aprecio muchísimo este cuadro** / I appreciate this painting very much; **admirar** / to admire; **Yo admiro** / I admire. If you want to use other verbs, check them out in the tables of regular and irregular verbs beginning on page 448. Now, practice writing what you said on these lines:

_____

_____

_____

_____

_____

_____

The Virgin with Saint Inés and Saint Tecla by EL GRECO (1541–1614)
Courtesy of The National Gallery of Art, Washington, D.C.

A Girl and Her Duenna by Bartolomé Estaban MURILLO (1617–1682)
Courtesy of The National Gallery of Art, Washington, D.C.

Work Unit 2
Review of Level 1 Topics

Have you ever looked out your window to see what's going on in the streets?

Juana está en la ventana con su madre

Todas las noches Juana trabaja, aprende y escribe sus lecciones después de cenar. Pero esta noche Juana está en la ventana con su madre. Las dos miran lo que pasa en la calle. Es una noche de fiesta en las calles para celebrar el dos de mayo, la guerra de Independencia de España que duró cinco años, de 1808 hasta 1813. Hay un desfile magnífi- co, y hay música. Hay mucha gente en la calle, por ejemplo, muchachas y mujeres hermosas   5
y lindas; hay, también, muchachos y hombres guapos. Juana está loca de curiosidad. Todo el mundo camina, canta, baila, come y bebe.

En la calle, debajo de la ventana, un soldado guapo habla con Juana. El soldado pregunta:

—¿Quiere Ud. bajar y bailar y cantar conmigo?   10
Juana responde:
—En otra ocasión. Todas las noches trabajo, aprendo y escribo mis lecciones.
Juana sonríe y la madre de Juana ríe.
Antes de cerrar la ventana, Juana guiña el ojo y se ríe sin motivo.

KEY WORDS AND PHRASES

año *n.m.* year

antes *adv.* before; **antes de cerrar** before closing

aprender *v.* to learn

bailar *v.* to dance

bajar *v.* to come down

beber *v.* to drink

calle *n.f.* street

caminar *v.* to walk

cantar *v.* to sing

celebrar *v.* to celebrate

cenar *v.* to dine, to have dinner

cerrar *v.* to close

comer *v.* to eat

con *prep.* with; **conmigo** with me

curiosidad *n.f.* curiosity

de *prep.* of, from

debajo de *adv., prep.* below, underneath

desfile *n.m.* parade

después *adv.* after; **después de cenar** after having dinner

dos *num.* two; **las dos** the two, both

durar *v.* to last; **duró** lasted

ejemplo *n.m.* example; **por ejemplo** for example

en *prep.* in, at; **en otra ocasión** at some other time

es *pres. indic., 3d pers., s. of* **ser** it is

escribir *v.* to write

España *n.f.* Spain

esta *dem. adj., f.s.* this; **esta noche** this evening, tonight

estar *v.* to be; **estar loco (loca)** to be crazy

fiesta *n.f.* holiday, celebration, party

gente *n.f.* people; **mucha gente** many people

guapo *adj.* handsome

guerra *n.f.* war

guiñar *v.* to wink; **Juana guiña el ojo** Jane winks

haber *v.* to have (used as an aux. v. to form the seven compound tenses; see appendix)

hablar *v.* to talk, to speak

hasta *prep., adv.* up to, until

hay there is, there are (*idiomatic v. form of* **haber**)

hermoso, hermosa *adj.* beautiful

independencia *n.f.* independence

lección *n.f.* lesson; **sus lecciones** her lessons
lindo, linda *adj.* pretty
lo que *pron.* what, that which; **lo que pasa** what is going on, happening
loco, loca *adj.* crazy
madre *n.f.* mother; **la madre de Juana** Jane's mother
magnífico *adj.* magnificent
mayo *n.m.* May
mirar *v.* to look at, to watch
mis *poss. adj., pl.* my; **mis lecciones** my lessons
motivo *n.m.* motive; **reírse sin motivo** to giggle
mucho, mucha *adj.* much, many
mujer *n.f.* woman
música *n.f.* music
noche *n.f.* evening, night
ocasión *n.f.* occasion (time, opportunity)
ojo *n.m.* eye
otra *adj., f.* other, another; **en otra ocasión** at some other time
para *prep.* for, in order (to)

pasar *v.* to happen; to pass by
por *prep.* for, by; **por ejemplo** for example
preguntar *v.* to ask
que *pron.* that, which
querer *v.* to want, to wish; **¿Quiere Ud. ...?** / Do you want...?
reír, reírse *v.* to laugh; **la madre de Juana ríe** Jane's mother laughs; **Juana se ríe sin motivo** Jane giggles
responder *v.* to answer, to respond, to reply
sin *prep.* without
soldado *n.m.* soldier
sonreír *v.* to smile; **Juana sonríe** Jane smiles
su *poss. adj., s.* her; **su madre** her mother
sus *poss. adj., pl.* her; **sus lecciones** her lessons
también *adv.* also, too
todas las noches every evening
todo el mundo everybody
trabajar *v.* to work
ventana *n.f.* window
vez *n.f.* time; **una vez** one time; **dos veces** two times; **otra vez** again, once again

EJERCICIOS

I. Conteste las siguientes preguntas con oraciones completas. (Answer the following questions in complete sentences.)

1. ¿Dónde está Juana? _____

2. ¿Dónde está la madre de Juana? _____

3. ¿Qué hace Juana todas las noches? _____

4. ¿Qué miran Juana y su madre? _____

5. ¿Qué celebra la gente? _____

6. ¿Qué hay en la calle? _____

7. ¿Qué hace todo el mundo? _____

8. ¿Quién está debajo de la ventana? _____

9. ¿Qué pregunta el soldado a Juana? _____

10. ¿Qué responde Juana y qué hace antes de cerrar la ventana? _____

_____

II. ¿Sí o No?

1. Todas las mañanas Juana trabaja, aprende y escribe sus lecciones. _____

2. Esta noche Juana está en la ventana con su hermana. _____

3. En la calle, hay un desfile magnífico, hay música y mucha gente. _____

4. En la calle, debajo de la ventana, un soldado habla con otro soldado. _____

5. Juana baila con el soldado guapo y los dos cantan, comen y beben. _____

III. Acróstico. Complete cada palabra en español según la lectura.
(**Acrostic.** Complete each word in Spanish according to the reading selection in this Work Unit.)

1. Otra _____ .

2. Juana _____ en la ventana.

3. Esta _____ Juana está en la ventana.

4. Hay, _____ , muchachos y hombres guapos.

5. _____ de cerrar la ventana, Juana guiña el ojo.

6. Es una _____ de fiesta.

7. Juana trabaja, _____ y escribe sus lecciones.

1. V
2. E
3. N
4. T
5. A
6. N
7. A

IV. Community/Neighborhood. Proficiency in Speaking and Writing.

Situation: You are busy doing your Spanish homework in your room when you hear a lot of noise coming from the street. You go to the window, open it, and look to see what's going on.

In several sentences describe the activity in the street. You may use your own words and ideas or the following: **Hay un desfile magnífico** / There is a magnificent parade; **Hay música también** / There is music also; **Hay mucha gente en la calle** / There are many people in the street; **Hay muchachas lindas y mujeres hermosas** / There are pretty girls and beautiful women; **Hay muchos muchachos y hombres guapos** / There are many handsome boys and men; **Todo el mundo camina, canta, baila, come y bebe** / Everybody is walking, singing, dancing, eating, and drinking.

After you have made at least four statements describing the activity in the street, you may write what you said on a sheet of paper and give it to your Spanish teacher, or you may practice writing on the lines below.

1. _____

2. _____

3. _____

4. _____

ESTRUCTURAS DE LA LENGUA

VERBS

A. Introduction

A verb is a word that expresses an action *(to work)* or a state of being *(to think)*. Tense means time. Spanish and English verb tenses are divided into three main groups of time: past, present, and future. A verb tense shows if an action took place (past), is taking place (present), or will take place (future). Here, we will review the present indicative tense.

Spanish verbs are divided into three main conjugations (types) according to the infinitive ending, which can be either **–ar, –er, –ir**. You might say that these endings mean *to* in English: **trabajar** *(to work),* **aprender** *(to learn),* **escribir** *(to write)*. In this unit, we will review all three types in the present indicative.

You must memorize the personal endings for each of the **–ar, –er, –ir** infinitive types. You must also memorize the personal subject pronouns in Spanish because each one must agree with its own personal ending on the verb. These are all given in dark letters in the following chart.

		–AR type	**–ER** type	**–IR** type
Infinitives ⟶		**trabajar** *to work*	**aprender** *to learn*	**escribir** *to write*
		I work; do work; am working.	I learn; do learn; am learning.	I write; do write; am writing
Singular	1. **Yo**	trabaj**o**	aprend**o**	escrib**o**
	2. **Tú** *You* (fam.)	trabaj**as**	aprend**es**	escrib**es**
	3. **Él** *He;* **Ella** *She* **Ud.** *You* (formal)	trabaj**a**	aprend**e**	escrib**e**
Plural	1. **Nosotros-as** *We*	trabaj**amos**	aprend**emos**	escrib**imos**
	2. **Vosotros-as** *You* (fam.)	trabaj**áis**	aprend**éis**	escrib**ís**
	3. **Ellos-as** *They* **Uds.** *You* (formal)	trabaj**an**	aprend**en**	escrib**en**

Rules and Observations

1. To form the present tense of a regular verb ending in **–ar,** drop the **–ar.** What remains is called the *stem.* Add to the stem the personal endings shown in the above chart. They are: **–o, –as, –a; –amos, –aís, –an.** Note that the characteristic vowel in this set of endings is the letter **a,** except for the first person singular, which is **o.** This is the first conjugation type.

2. To form the present tense of a regular verb ending in **–er,** drop the **–er.** What remains is called the *stem.* Add to the stem the personal endings shown in the above chart. They are: **–o, –es, –e; –emos, –éis, –en.** Note that the characteristic vowel in this set of endings is the letter **e,** except for the first person singular, which is **o.** This is the second conjugation type.

3. To form the present tense of a regular verb ending in **–ir,** drop the **–ir.** What remains is called the *stem.* Add to the stem the personal endings shown in the above chart. They are: **–o, –es, –e; –imos, –ís, –en.** Note that these endings are exactly the same as those for the **–er** type verbs explained in par. 2 above, except for the first and second persons plural which are **–imos** and **–ís.**

4. Also note the three possible translations into English for Spanish verbs in the present indicative tense, as shown on the above chart.

V. Providing and Obtaining Information. Proficiency in Speaking and Writing.

A. Situation: You are having a conversation with a friend while standing in line for tickets to a basketball game. Provide your friend with some information. Your friend wants to know when you work (**trabajar**), what you are studying (**estudiar**) in school, if you are learning (**aprender**) any Spanish, what you like to drink (**beber**), and if you can write (**escribir**) in Spanish.

While talking to your friend, use the two **–ar** type verbs, the two **–er** type verbs, and the one **–ir** type verb given above in the present indicative tense. Review the conjugation of these regular verbs in the present tense in the above chart.

Also, review the vocabulary under the reading selection above. There are many verbs and words there that you can borrow. You may use your own words and ideas or the following: **Trabajo todas las noches** / I work every evening; **Estudio español en la escuela** / I am studying Spanish in school; **Aprendo mucho español en la clase** / I am learning a lot of Spanish in class; **Me gusta beber leche, jugo de naranja, té, café y cola** / I like to drink milk, orange juice, tea, coffee, and cola; **Me gusta escribir en español** / I like to write in Spanish.

_____

_____

_____

_____

B. Situation: Now, here's your chance to ask your friend a few questions to obtain some information. You may use your own words and ideas, or those on the preceding pages in this Work Unit, or the following, for example: **¿Cuándo trabajas (tú)?** / When do you work?; **¿Qué estudias en la escuela?** / What do you study in school?; **¿Aprendes español?** / Are you learning any Spanish?; **¿Qué te gusta beber?** / What do you like to drink?; **¿Te gusta escribir en español?** / Do you like to write in Spanish?

_____

_____

_____

B. Some Common Regular Verbs of the First Conjugation Type: –AR

acabar to finish, to end, to complete

aceptar to accept

acompañar to accompany

acusar to accuse

admirar to admire

adoptar to adopt

adorar to adore, to worship

alumbrar to illuminate, to light, to enlighten

amar to love

andar to walk

anunciar to announce

apreciar to appreciate

articular to articulate, to pronounce distinctly

atacar to attack

ayudar to help, to aid, to assist

bailar to dance

bajar to go down

borrar to erase

botar to fling, to cast (away), to throw (away), to launch

buscar to look for, to search

cambiar to change

caminar to walk, to move along

cantar to sing

celebrar to celebrate

cenar to have dinner (supper)

cepillar to brush

cocinar to cook

colocar to put, to place
completar to complete
comprar to buy, to purchase
contestar to answer, to reply
cortar to cut, to cut off, to cut out
cruzar to cross
chariar to chat, to prattle
chistar to mumble, to mutter
declarar to declare
dejar to let, to permit, to allow, to leave (something behind you)
denunciar to denounce
descansar to rest
desear to desire, to want
dibujar to design, to draw, to sketch
dudar to doubt
echar to cast, to fling, to hurl, to pitch, to throw
emplear to employ, to use
enojar to anger, to annoy, to vex
enseñar to teach, to show, to point out
entrar to enter, to go in, to come in
escuchar to listen (to)
esperar to expect, to hope, to wait (for)
estimar to estimate, to esteem, to respect, to value
estudiar to study
explicar to explain
expresar to express
faltar to be lacking, to be wanting, to lack, to miss, to need
formar to form, to shape
fumar to smoke

ganar to earn, to gain, to win
gastar to spend (money), to wear out, to waste
gozar to enjoy
gritar to shout, to scream, to shriek, to cry out
habitar to inhabit, to dwell, to live, to reside
hablar to talk, to speak
hallar to find, to come across
indicar to indicate, to point out
invitar to invite
lavar to wash (something or someone)
levantar to raise (something or someone)
llegar to arrive
llenar to fill
llevar to carry (away), to take (away), to wear
llorar to weep, to cry, to whine
marchar to march, to walk, to function (machine), to run (machine)
matar to kill
mirar to look (at), to watch
nadar to swim
necesitar to need
ocupar to occupy
olvidar to forget
osar to dare, to venture
pagar to pay
parar to stop (someone or something)
pasar to pass (by), to happen, to spend (time)
perdonar to pardon, to forgive, to excuse
pintar to paint
practicar to practice

preguntar to ask, to inquire, to question
preparar to prepare
presentar to present, to display, to show, to introduce
prestar to lend
principiar to begin, to start
proclamar to proclaim, to promulgate
pronunciar to pronounce
quedar to remain
quemar to burn, to fire
regalar to give as a present, to make a present of, to give as a gift
regresar to return, to go back, to regress
reparar to repair, to mend, to notice, to observe
sacar to take out (something), to get
saltar to jump, to leap, to hop, to spring
saludar to greet, to salute
secar to dry, to wipe dry
separar to separate, to detach, to sort, to set apart
telefonear to telephone
terminar to end, to terminate, to finish
tocar to play (musical instrument), to knock (on the door)
tomar to take
trabajar to work
tratar to try, to treat a subject
usar to use, to employ, to wear
viajar to travel
visitar to visit

VI. Reporting Activities. Proficiency in Speaking and Writing.

    A. Situation: Your Spanish teacher wants to know what you and your friends are doing today. You have been asked to go to the front of the class and give a report of six activities that you are doing together.

        Of the above list of commonly used regular **–ar** type verbs, select six and use them in brief sentences. You may use your own words and ideas or any of the following. Either way, state six activities that you are performing today with your friends, for example: **Nosotros buscamos un taxi** / We are looking for a taxi; **Nosotros cantamos canciones españolas** / We are singing Spanish songs; **Nosotros dibujamos varios dibujos** / We are sketching several drawings; **Nosotros escuchamos la música** / We are listening to music; **¡Nosotros lavamos todas las pizarras en todas las salas de clase de esta escuela!** / We are washing all the chalkboards in all the classrooms of this school!

    B. After giving your oral report, you may want to write the six activities on a sheet of paper to give to your teacher. First practice them on the following lines:

1. _____

2. _____

3. _____

4. _____

5. _____

6. _____

C. Some Common Regular Verbs of the Second Conjugation Type: –ER

aprender to learn
beber to drink
comer to eat
comprender to understand
correr to run, to race, to flow
creer to believe

deber to owe, must, ought
depender to depend
leer to read
responder to answer, to respond, to reply
romper to break, to shatter

tañer to pluck, to play (a stringed musical instrument)
temer to fear, to dread
vender to sell

VII. Meeting People. Proficiency in Speaking and Writing.

A. **Situation:** Five parents are visiting your school today. They all speak Spanish. They are with their sons and daughters. They obtained permission from the school principal to drop in on classes in session. They are visiting your Spanish class because they want to know if the students use the language actively. Their children are shy and they would like to see them encouraged to participate in Spanish conversation.

Of the above list of commonly used regular **–ar** and **–er** type verbs, select at least three **–ar** verbs and two **–er** verbs and use them in brief sentences. Remember that you are talking to one parent at a time and you must use the subject pronoun **Usted** (**Ud.,** 3d person, singular) for politeness. You may use your own words and ideas or the following: **¿Desea Ud. hablar español conmigo?** / Do you want to speak Spanish with me?; **¿Practica Ud. la lengua en casa con su hijo (hija)?** / Do you practice the language at home with your son (daughter)?; **¿Lee Ud. español?** / Do you read Spanish?

After the parents and their children leave the classroom, write what you said on the lines below for practice.

B. Begin your statements or questions with a greeting, such as **Buenos días, señor (señora). ¿Cómo está Ud.?**

1. _____

2. _____

3. _____

4. _____

5. _____

D. Some Common Regular Verbs of the Third Conjugation Type: –IR

abrir to open
admitir to admit
añadir to add
asistir to attend
cubrir to cover
cumplir to fulfill, to keep (a promise), to reach one's birthday (use with **años**)
decidir to decide
describir to describe, to sketch, to delineate

descubrir to discover
discutir to discuss
escribir to write
gruñir to grumble, to grunt, to growl, to creak
insistir to insist, to persist
omitir to omit
partir to leave, to depart, to divide, to split
permitir to permit, to admit, to allow, to grant

prohibir to prohibit, to forbid
pulir to polish
recibir to receive
remitir to remit, to forward, to transmit
subir to go up
sufrir to suffer, to endure, to bear up, to undergo
unir to unite, to connect, to join, to bind, to attach
vivir to live

VIII. Family Activities. Proficiency in Speaking and Writing.

Situation: You are having a conversation with a friend. During the course of the conversation, tell your friend three things that you and your brother or sister or parents do at home.

Of the list of commonly used regular **–ir** type verbs on page 40, select at least three and use them in brief sentences. Remember that you are talking about yourself and your brother or sister or your parents. That means you are talking in the 1st person plural using **Nosotros** (we) as the subject of your verb. You may use your own words and ideas or any of the following: **En mi casa, nosotros abrimos las ventanas en el verano cuando hace sol** / In my house, we open the windows in summer when it is sunny; **Los sábados, mi hermano y yo pulimos la mesa en el comedor** / On Saturdays, my brother and I polish the table in the dining room; **Mis padres, mi hermano, mi hermana y yo vivimos en una casita** / My parents, my brother, my sister and I live in a small house.

Practice writing what you said on the chalkboard or on a sheet of paper to give to your teacher or on the these lines:

1. _____

2. _____

3. _____

Personal Pronouns

Subject Pronouns

Examples

Singular
1. **yo** / I
2. **tú** / you (*familiar*)
3. **usted** / you (*polite*)
   él / he, it
   ella / she, it

Yo hablo.
Tú hablas.
Usted habla.
Él habla.
Ella habla.

Plural
1. **nosotros (nosotras)** / we
2. **vosotros (vosotras)** / you (*fam.*)
3. **ustedes** / you (*polite*)
   ellos / they
   ellas / they

Nosotros hablamos.
Vosotros habláis.
Ustedes hablan.
Ellos hablan.
Ellas hablan.

As you can see in the examples given here, a subject pronoun is ordinarily placed in front of the main verb.

In Spanish, subject pronouns are not used at all times. The ending of the verb tells you if the subject is 1st, 2nd, or 3rd person in the singular or plural. Of course, in the 3rd person sing. and pl. there is more than one possible subject with the same ending on the verb form. In that case, if there is any doubt as to what the subject is, it is mentioned for the sake of clarity. At other times, subject pronouns in Spanish are used when you want to be emphatic, to make a contrast between this person and that person, or out of simple courtesy. You must be certain to know the endings of the verb forms in all the tenses (see the entry **Verb Tables** in the Index) in the three persons of the singular and of the plural so that you can figure out the subject if it is not clearly stated. In addition to pronouns as subjects, nouns are also used as subjects. Any noun—whether common (**el hombre, la mujer, el cielo, la silla,** *etc.*) or proper (**María, Juan y Elena, los Estados Unidos,** *etc.*) is always 3rd person, either singular or plural.

Generally speaking, in some Latin American countries **ustedes** (3rd pers., pl.) is used in place of **vosotros** or **vosotras** (2nd pers., pl.).

E. Interrogative Word Order

1. Generally speaking, the subject is placed after the verb when asking a question.

2. An inverted question mark is placed at the beginning of a written question so that the reader knows that a question is about to be asked. A question mark at the end of the question is required, as in English.

EXAMPLES:

Declarative statement	Interrogative statement
(a) **Juana está en la ventana.**	**¿Está Juana en la ventana?**
(b) **Ud. quiere bailar y cantar.**	**¿Quiere Ud. bailar y cantar?**

EJERCICIOS

I. Cambie las siguientes oraciones sustituyendo las palabras *en letras cursivas* por un pronombre personal. (Change the following sentences by substituting the word in italics with a personal subject pronoun, for example, él, ella, ellos, ellas, and so on. Follow the model.)

Modelo: *Juana y su madre* están en la ventana.   *Ellas* están en la ventana.
(*Jane and her mother* are at the window.)   (*They* are at the window.)

A. Verbos con la terminación **–AR**

1. *Juana* trabaja mucho. _____

2. *El soldado* baila bien. _____

3. *La señora* Rodríguez canta bien. _____

4. *Juana y Pedro* estudian las lecciones. _____

5. *María y yo* preparamos la lección. _____

B. Verbos con la terminación **–ER**

1. *Juana y María* aprenden mucho en la escuela. _____

2. *Pablo y Pedro* beben leche todos los días. _____

3. *Cristóbal, Juan y yo* comemos juntos. _____

4. *Los alumnos y las alumnas* comprenden la lección. _____

5. *El niño* teme la oscuridad. _____

C. Verbos con la terminación **–IR**

1. *El profesor* abre la ventana. _____

2. *Las alumnas* reciben buenas notas. _____

3. *María y José* parten hoy. _____

4. *Ud. y Ricardo* escriben las oraciones. _____

5. *Ud., Juan y Cristóbal* viven en la misma casa. _____

II. Cambie las siguientes oraciones sustituyendo el pronombre personal como sujeto entre paréntesis en lugar de las palabras *en letras cursivas*. Cambie el verbo en la forma necesaria. (Change the following sentences by substituting the personal subject pronoun in parentheses in place of the words in italics. Change the verb into the required form. Follow the model.)

> **Modelo:** *Juana* aprende la lección.   (Yo) *Yo aprendo* la lección.
> (*Jane* is learning the lesson.)   (*I am learning* the lesson.)

A. *La señora López* anda despacio.

1. (Yo) _____   6. (Nosotros) _____

2. (Tú) _____   7. (Vosotros) _____

3. (Ud.) _____   8. (Uds.) _____

4. (Él) _____   9. (Ellos) _____

5. (Ella) _____   10. (Ellas) _____

B. *Juanita responde bien.*

1. (Yo) _____   6. (Ud. y yo) _____

2. (Uds.) _____   7. (Él) _____

3. (Tú) _____   8. (Ellas) _____

4. (Ella y él) _____   9. (Tú y yo) _____

5. (Ud.) _____   10. (Uds. y ellos) _____

C. *Carlos y yo* escribimos la lección.

1. (Ud.) _____   6. (Tú) _____

2. (Yo) _____   7. (Ella) _____

3. (Uds.) _____   8. (Él) _____

4. (Nosotros) _____   9. (Vosotros) _____

5. (Ellos) _____   10. (Ellas) _____

III. Conteste las siguientes preguntas en forma afirmativa con oraciones completas. En la respuesta (a) use la palabra Sí. En la respuesta (b) use la palabra también según los modelos. (Answer the following questions in the affirmative in complete sentences. In answer [a] use the word Sí. In answer [b] use the word **también** [also], according to the models.)

Providing and Obtaining Information. Proficiency in Speaking and Writing.

Situation: You are having a good time at María's birthday party where there are many friends and relatives. Her aunt, **la señora Sabelotodo,** (Mrs. Know-It-All) is there. She cannot stop talking. She is constantly asking questions to get information. Help your friends by answering her questions in complete sentences on the lines below.

Modelos: a. ¿Canta Ud. bien? (Do you sing well?)
b. ¿Y Uds.? (And you?)

Escriba: a. Sí, yo canto bien. (Yes, I sing well.)
b. Nosotros cantamos bien, también. (We sing well also.)

A. Verbos con la terminación **–AR**

1. a. ¿Baila Ud. todas las noches? _____

   b. ¿Y Juana? _____

2. a. ¿Borra la profesora la palabra en la pizarra? _____

   b. ¿Y los otros alumnos? _____

3. a. ¿Trabaja María en la clase de español? _____

   b. ¿Y Carlos y Juan? _____

4. a. ¿Tocas tú el piano? _____

   b. ¿Y las muchachas? _____

5. a. ¿Llora la niña? _____

   b. ¿Y los niños? _____

6. a. ¿Espera Juanita el autobús? _____

   b. ¿Y sus amigos? _____

B. Verbos con la terminacion **–ER**

1. a. ¿Aprende Ud. el español? _____

   b. ¿Y los otros alumnos? _____

2. a. ¿Beben leche los niños? _____

   b. ¿Y Andrés? _____

3. a. ¿Come la familia a las ocho? _____

   b. ¿Y Ud.? _____

4. a. ¿Comprende Ud. el español? _____

   b. ¿Y ellos? _____

5. a. ¿Lee María el cuento? _____

   b. ¿Y Uds.? _____

C. Verbos con la terminación **–IR**

1. a. ¿Abre el profesor la puerta? _____

   b. ¿Y tú? _____

2. a. ¿Recibe José buenas notas? _____

   b. ¿Y Cristóbal? _____

3. a. ¿Sonríe el profesor de vez en cuando? _____

   b. ¿Y los otros profesores? _____

4. a. ¿Escribe Ud. cartas? _____

   b. ¿Y nosotros? _____

5. a. ¿Vivimos en la misma casa? _____

   b. ¿Y Miguel y María? _____

IV. Conteste que sí a las siguientes preguntas en oraciones completas, según el modelo.
(Answer the following questions in complete sentences beginning with sí, according to the model answer.)

Providing and Obtaining Information. Proficiency in Speaking and Writing.

Situation: Mr. Rodríguez is having the rooms in his house painted. He is asking the painter many questions and he replies while working. You may participate in the conversation by asking the painter the following questions. Later, for practice, write the answers on the lines below.

Modelo: ¿Toma Ud. leche en el café?   Sí, tomo leche en el café.
(Do you take milk in coffee?)   (Yes, I take milk in coffee.)

1. ¿Trabaja Ud. todos los días? _____

2. ¿Viaja el señor Pérez de vez en cuando? _____

3. ¿Usa Ud. guantes en el invierno? _____

4. ¿Leen los alumnos mucho? _____

5. ¿Vende la casa la familia Rodríguez? _____

6. ¿Corre Ud. a la clase de español? _____

7. ¿Vivimos Juan y yo en la misma casa? _____

8. ¿Reciben Carlos y Carlota buenas notas? _____

45

9. ¿Admite Ud. siempre la verdad? _____

10. ¿Habla Ud. español en la clase de español? _____

V. Componga oraciones en el presente de indicativo empleando los siguientes verbos.
   (Write sentences using the following verbs in the present indicative.)

   1. hablar _____

   2. comer _____

   3. recibir _____

VI. Dictado. Escriba las frases que su profesor de español va a pronunciar.
   (**Dictation.** Write the sentences that your Spanish teacher is going to pronounce.)

   1. _____

   2. _____

   3. _____

GENTE Lecturas

**ROMINA Y ALBANO
celebran sus 14 años de casados en S'Agaró**

VII. Complete la siguiente oración con tantos nombres como Ud. pueda decir y escribir.
(Complete the following sentence with as many nouns as you can say and write, according to the model.)

Modelo:

Yo deseo

un vaso de leche / a glass of milk
una cereza / a cherry
dinero / money
un vaso de agua / a glass of water
tener amigos / to have friends

música / music
paz / peace
felicidad / happiness
la verdad / the truth

VIII. En español hay muchas palabras que se escriben y se pronuncian idénticamente, pero tienen distinto significado. (In Spanish there are many words that are written and pronounced identically, but have a different meaning.)

Por ejemplo:

cocina *n.f.* / kitchen
cocina *3rd pers. sing., pres. indic. of* **cocinar** / to cook

El cocinero cocina en la cocina / The cook is cooking in the kitchen.

presente de indicativo

cocinar / to cook

yo	cocino	nosotros	cocinamos
tú	cocinas	vosotros	cocináis
Ud.		Uds.	
él	} **cocina**	ellos	} cocinan
ella		ellas	

¿Cuántos ejemplos puede Ud. decir, escribir y dibujar? (How many examples can you say, write, and draw?)

IX. En español hay muchas palabras que se escriben y se pronuncian idénticamente, pero un signo de acento es necesario para notar su diferente significado. (In Spanish there are many words that are written and pronounced identically, but an accent mark is necessary to note their different meaning.)

Por ejemplo:

el *def. art., masc., sing.* / the
él *subj. pron., masc., sing.* / he; *also obj. of a prep.* / him (**para él** / for him)

Yo compro el billete para él y tú compras el billete para ella. / I'm buying the ticket for him and you're buying the ticket for her.

¿Cuántos ejemplos puede Ud. decir y escribir? (How many examples can you say and write?)

X. Otro ejemplo (Another example)

¿A ti te gusta el té? / Do you like tea?

XI. En español hay muchas palabras que se escriben y se pronuncian idénticamente, pero tienen distinto significado. (In Spanish there are many words that are written and pronounced identically, but they have a different meaning.)

Por ejemplo:

deber *n.m.* / duty, obligation
deber *v.* / to owe, ought to, should, must

Deber un deber es natural. / To owe an obligation is natural.
Debe de ser tarde. Debo ir. / It must be late. I have to go.

Mnemonic Tip	Deber contains *deb* and so does *debt.*

presente de indicativo

deber / to owe

yo	debo	nosotros	debemos
tú	debes	vosotros	debéis
Ud.		Uds.	
él	} debe	ellos	} deben
ella		ellas	

¿Cuántos ejemplos puede Ud. decir y escribir? (How many examples can you say and write?)

XII. Sharing Information. Proficiency in Speaking and Writing.

A.Situation: You are planning to spend a summer session studying Spanish at the Universidad de Madrid. You are looking for an apartment. Read the newspaper announcement of an apartment vacancy that is given below.

You are sharing this information with Ricardo, a student in your Spanish class, who is also making plans to study Spanish in Madrid. Maybe you can share the apartment with him.

While talking with Ricardo, you may add words and ideas of your own. Refer to the following vocabulary according to your needs while providing responses to the seven questions.

GRAN APARTAMENTO
en Madrid
buena vista del parque El Retiro
2 dormitorios – 2 cuartos de baño
cocina moderna, gran balcón
cerca del Museo del Prado
tel. 12-34-56-78

B.After your conversation with Ricardo, write on the chalkboard or on a sheet of paper what you and he said. You may practice writing on the lines below.

1. ¿En qué ciudad está situado el apartamento? _____

   _____

2. ¿Cuántos dormitorios hay en el apartamento? _____

   _____

3. ¿Cuántos baños hay? _____

   _____

4. ¿Es grande o pequeño el apartamento? _____

   _____

5. ¿Cómo se llama el parque cerca del apartamento? _____

   _____

6. ¿Cómo se llama el museo cerca del apartamento? _____

   _____

7. ¿Cuál es el número de teléfono? _____

   _____

KEY WORDS AND PHRASES

apartamento *n.m.* apartment
balcón *n.m.* balcony
baño *n.m.* bath
buena *adj., f.s.* good
cerca *adv.* near; **cerca del** near the
ciudad *n.f.* city
cocina *n.f.* kitchen
¿Cómo se llama el parque?
    What is the name of the park?
cuál *pron.* what, which
cuántos *adj., m. pl.* how many
cuarto *n.m.* room
del of the **(de + el > del)**

dormitorio *n.m.* bedroom
en *prep.* in; **¿en qué?** in what?
está situado is situated, located
gran, grande *adj.* big, large, great
hay there is, there are
moderna *adj., f.s.* modern
museo *n.m.* museum
número *n.m.* number
o *conj.* or
parque *n.m.* park
pequeño *adj., m.s.* small
teléfono *n.m.* telephone
vista *n.f.* view

Catedral de JAEN (Andalucía) España
Courtesy of Spanish National Tourist Office, New York, N. Y.

La señora Rodríguez está buscando en el guardarropa, Juana está buscando en el tocador y Pedro está buscando debajo de la cama.

*Have you ever looked high and low for some-
thing you lost?*

¿Dónde está mi sombrero?

El señor Rodríguez está buscando su sombrero. La señora Rodríguez está buscando el sombrero en el guardarropa. Juana está buscando en el tocador y Pedro está buscando debajo de la cama.

El señor Rodríguez:	¿Dónde está mi sombrero?	
Juana:	Ahora estoy buscando en el tocador, papá.	5
Pedro:	Y ahora yo estoy buscando debajo de la cama. Estamos buscando en todas partes, papá.	
La señora Rodríguez:	Yo estoy buscando, también, Francisco. Estoy buscando en el guardarropa. ¡Oh! Estoy buscando tu sombrero por todas partes.	
El señor Rodríguez:	Ahora estoy buscando debajo de la silla. Vamos a buscar en la cocina, en la sala, en el cuarto de baño, en el sótano, debajo de la cama, debajo del tocador, en el guardarropa, en el garaje. ¡Por todas partes!	10
Juana:	¡Mira! ¡Mira, papá! ¡Coco se está comiendo tu sombrero! ¡Está debajo del tocador!	15
El señor Rodríguez:	¡Oh! ¡No! ¡Dios mío!	
	(El señor Rodríguez sale del dormitorio.)	
La señora Rodríguez:	¿Adónde vas, Francisco?	
El señor Rodríguez:	Voy al centro para comprar otro sombrero. ¡Caramba!	
La señora Rodríguez:	¡Espera! ¡Espera, Francisco! Voy contigo. Quiero comprar una falda.	20

KEY WORDS AND PHRASES

¿adónde? *adv.* to where? where to?
ahora *adv.* now
al (a + el > al) to the, at the
baño *n.m.* bath
buscar *v.* to look for, to search
cama *n.f.* bed
¡Caramba! *interj.* Darn it!
centro *n.m.* center; **al centro** downtown
cocina *n.f.* kitchen
comprar *v.* to buy, to purchase
contigo with you *(fam.)*
cuarto *n.m.* room; **el cuarto de baño** bathroom
debajo *adv.* under; **debajo de** under, underneath
del (de + el > del) of the, from the

¡Dios mío! *excl.* My God!
¿dónde? *adv.* where?
dormitorio *n.m.* bedroom
en *prep.* in; **en todas partes** everywhere
¡Espera! Wait!
esperar *v.* to wait (for)
está *3d pers., s., pres. indic. of* **estar**; is
está buscando is looking for
está comiendo is eating
estamos buscando we are searching, looking for
estoy buscando I am searching, looking for
falda *n.f.* skirt
garaje *n.m.* garage
guardarropa *n.m.* wardrobe, clothes closet

ir *v.* to go
mi *poss. adj.* my
¡Mira! Look!
mirar *v.* to look (at)
otro sombrero another hat
papá *n.m.* dad
para *prep.* for, in order (to)
por *prep.* for, by, through; por todas partes everywhere
querer *v.* to want
¿quién? *pron.* who?
quiero *1st pers., s., pres. indic. of* querer; I want
sala *n.f.* living room
sale *3d pers., s., pres. indic. of* salir
salir *v.* to leave, to go out

se está comiendo is eating up
señor *n.m.* Mr.
señora *n.f.* Mrs.
silla *n.f.* chair
sombrero *n.m.* hat
sótano *n.m.* cellar
su *poss. adj.* his
también *adv.* also, too
tocador *n.m.* dresser, chest of drawers
tu *poss. adj., (fam.)* your
vamos *1st pers., pl., pres. indic. of* ir; let's go
vamos a buscar let's search
vas *2d pers., s., pres. indic. (fam.) of* ir; you are going
voy *1st pers., s., pres. indic. of* ir; I am going
y *conj.* and

EJERCICIOS

I. Seleccione la respuesta correcta conforme al significado de la lectura en esta lección. (Choose the correct answer according to the reading selection in this Work Unit.)

1. El señor Rodríguez está buscando (a) en el tocador (b) debajo de la cama (c) su sombrero (d) en el guardarropa _____

2. Juana está buscando (a) debajo de la cama (b) en la sala (c) debajo del tocador (d) en el tocador _____

3. Pedro está buscando (a) debajo de la silla (b) en el garaje (c) en el cuarto de baño (d) debajo de la cama _____

4. El sombrero está (a) en el tocador (b) debajo del tocador (c) debajo de la cama (d) en la cocina _____

5. El perrito está comiendo el sombrero debajo (a) de la cama (b) de la silla (c) del guardarropa (d) del tocador _____

II. Responda en español en frases completas. (Answer in Spanish in complete sentences.)

Modelo: ¿Quién está buscando debajo de la cama? (Who is looking under the bed?)
Respuesta: Pedro está buscando debajo de la cama. (Pedro is looking under the bed.)

1. ¿Quién está buscando en el tocador? _____

2. ¿Quién está buscando en el guardarropa? _____

3. ¿Quién está buscando debajo de la silla? _____

III. Acróstico. Complete cada palabra en español.
   (**Acrostic.** Complete each word in Spanish.)

1. cellar

2. other, *m.s.*

3. Look!

4. bath

5. to receive

6. to wait (for)

7. to answer

8. eye

ESTRUCTURAS DE LA LENGUA

Verbs Irregular in the Present Indicative, Including Stem-changing Verbs and Orthographical Changing Verbs

NOTE that the first three forms up to the semicolon are the 1st, 2nd, and 3rd persons of the singular; the three verb forms under those are the 1st, 2nd, and 3rd persons of the plural. The subject pronouns are not given in order to emphasize the verb forms.

SUMMING UP. The following verbs are summed up here because they were used in the reading proficiency selections and in the speaking and writing proficiency exercises in the preceding lessons. They are also used in this lesson, in particular, in the exercises that follow this summing up, and in Work Units that follow. They are arranged alphabetically to help you find—easily and quickly—the verb you need to use. If there are additional verbs you want to use in the speaking and writing proficiency exercises, consult the verb tables beginning on page 448.

---

acordar / to agree (upon)
   acuerdo, acuerdas, acuerda;
   acordamos, acordáis, acuerdan

   This is a stem-changing verb. The **o** in the stem changes to **ue** when stressed.

acordarse / to remember
   me acuerdo, te acuerdas, se acuerda;
   nos acordamos, os acordáis, se acuerdan

   This is a stem-changing verb. The **o** in the stem changes to **ue** when stressed.

acostarse / to go to bed, to lie down
   me acuesto, te acuestas, se acuesta;
   nos acostamos, os acostáis, se acuestan

   This is a stem-changing verb. The **o** in the stem changes to **ue** when stressed.

almorzar / to lunch, to have lunch
   almuerzo, almuerzas, almuerza;
   almorzamos, almorzáis, almuerzan

   This is a stem-changing verb. The **o** in the stem changes to **ue** when stressed.

REVIEW OF STEM-CHANGING VERBS

A. There are many Spanish verbs that change the vowel in the stem when it is stressed. (By stress we mean when you raise your voice on the stem vowel and it is pronounced prominently higher in tone than the other vowels in the word.) This happens frequently in the present tense.

B. The stem of a verb is what is left after we drop the ending of its infinitive form (**–ar, –er, –ir** types).

EXAMPLES:

INFINITIVE	ENDING OF INFINITIVE	STEM	STEM VOWEL		CHANGES TO
*acordar (to agree)	ar	acord	o	>	ue
*contar (to count)	ar	cont	o	>	ue
*pensar (to think)	ar	pens	e	>	ie
*entender (to understand)	er	entend	e	>	ie
*volver (to return)	er	volv	o	>	ue
*sentir (to feel, feel sorry, regret)	ir	sent	e	>	ie
*servir (to serve)	ir	serv	e	>	i

*The forms of these verbs in the present indicative tense are presented later.

REVIEW OF ORTHOGRAPHICAL CHANGING VERBS

A. Orthography is spelling. An orthographical changing verb is a verb that changes in spelling. There are many Spanish verbs that change in spelling in order to keep a certain sound in the verb form as it is in the infinitive.

B. EXAMPLES:

> ***conocer** (to know, to be acquainted with) adds **z** in front of the second **c** in the present tense in order to keep the sound of **s** as it is in the infinitive. In other words, instead of saying **yo conoco**, we say and write **yo conozco**.
>
> ***ofrecer** (to offer) adds **z** in front of **c** in the present tense in order to keep the sound of **s** as it is in the infinitive. In other words, instead of saying **yo ofreco**, we say and write **yo ofrezco**.

Study the rules, examples, and models above before beginning the exercises!

EJERCICIOS

IV. In each of the numbered incomplete statements below, write the required verb form in the present indicative tense of the verb almorzar (to lunch, to have lunch) and the rest of the words in the model sentence.
Refer to the above stem-changing and orthographical changing verbs according to your needs. In this exercise, you are practicing the verb **almorzar.**

Modelo: Yo almuerzo a la una.   (Ellos) Ellos almuerzan a la una.
(I have lunch at one o'clock.)   (They have lunch at one o'clock.)

1. **Tú** _____

2. **Eduardo** _____

3. **Él** _____

4. **Ella** _____

5. **Ud.** _____

6. **Nosotros** _____

7. **Ud. y yo** _____

8. **Ellos** _____

9. **Yo** _____

10. **Ellas** _____

V. Rewrite the sentences given below substituting the appropriate form of the verb in parentheses in the present indicative tense. Keep the same subject.
Refer to the above stem-changing and orthographical changing verbs according to your needs. In this exercise you are practicing the following verbs: **almorzar, conocer, contar, entender, ofrecer, pensar, servir, volver.**

Modelo: María piensa bien.   (entender)   María entiende bien.
(Mary thinks well.)   (Mary understands well.)

1. **(pensar)**   Yo entiendo bien. _____

2. **(volver)**   ¿Almuerzas tú a la una? _____

3. **(contar)**   Ahora yo sirvo. _____

4. **(conocer)**   Yo ofrezco. _____

5. **(almorzar)**   ¿A qué hora vuelven las muchachas? _____

aparecer / to appear, to show up
   aparezco, apareces, aparece;
   aparecemos, aparecéis, aparecen

   This **–cer** verb changes only in the 1st person singular where the **c** changes to **zc.**

cerrar / to close
   cierro, cierras, cierra;
   cerramos, cerráis, cierran

   A stem-changing verb. The **e** in the stem changes to **ie** when stressed.

caber / to fit, to be contained
   quepo, cabes, cabe;
   cabemos, cabéis, caben

   Irregular in the 1st pers. sing. only in this tense.

cocer / to cook
   cuezo, cueces, cuece;
   cocemos, cocéis, cuecen

   A stem-changing and orthographical changing verb. The **o** in the stem changes to **ue** when stressed. Also, this **–cer** verb changes **c** to **z** in front of **o** or **a.**

caer / to fall
   caigo, caes, cae;
   caemos, caéis, caen

   Irregular in the 1st pers. sing. only in this tense. Pres. part. is **cayendo.**

coger / to seize, to grasp, to grab, to catch
   cojo, coges, coge;
   cogemos, cogéis, cogen

   An orthographical changing verb. This **–ger** verb changes **g** to **j** in front of **o** or **a.**

VI. **Change the following verb forms in the present indicative tense using the new subject given in parentheses. You may add additional words if you wish.**
Refer to the above stem-changing and orthographical changing verbs according to your needs. In this exercise you are practicing the following verbs: **aparecer, caber, caer, cerrar, cocer, coger.**

Modelo: Ella aparece. (Yo)   **Escriba:** Yo aparezco.
   (She appears.)   (I appear.)

1. Esta cosa cabe. **(Yo)** _____

2. Nosotros caemos. **(Yo)** _____

3. El alumno cierra el libro. **(La profesora)** _____

4. Yo cierro la ventana. **(Ellos)** _____

5. El niño cae. **(Yo)** _____

6. Yo cuezo en la cocina. **(Mi madre)** _____

7. El sol aparece. **(Yo)** _____

8. Mi hermana coge el libro **(Yo)** _____

9. Nosotros cogemos las manzanas. **(Tú)** _____

10. Uds. cuecen en la cocina. **(Yo)** _____

colgar / to hang
cuelgo, cuelgas, cuelga;
colgamos, colgáis, cuelgan

A stem-changing verb. The **o** in the stem changes to **ue** when stressed.

confesar / to confess
confieso, confiesas, confiesa;
confesamos, confesáis, confiesan

A stem-changing verb. The **e** in the stem changes to **ie** when stressed.

comenzar / to begin, to start, to commence
comienzo, comienzas, comienza;
comenzamos, comenzáis, comienzan

A stem-changing verb. The **e** in the stem changes to **ie** when stressed.

conocer / to know, to be acquainted with
conozco, conoces, conoce;
conocemos, conocéis, conocen

An orthographical changing verb. This **–cer** verb changes **c** to **zc** only in the 1st pers. sing. of this tense.

conducir / to conduct, to lead, to drive
conduzco, conduces, conduce;
conducimos, conducís, conducen

This **–cir** verb changes only in the 1st pers. sing. of this tense where the **c** changes to **zc.**

construir / to construct, to build
construyo, construyes, construye;
construimos, construís, construyen

This **–uir** verb requires the insertion of **y** in front of the regular present tense endings **o, es, e,** and **en**. Pres. part. is **construyendo.**

VII. **Change the following verb forms in the present indicative tense using the new subject given in parentheses. You may add additional words if you wish.**
Refer to the above stem-changing and orthographical changing verbs according to your needs. In this exercise you are practicing the following verbs: **colgar, comenzar, conducir, confesar, conocer, construir.**

Modelo: Isabel cuelga la ropa en el jardín. (Yo)
(Isabel is hanging the clothes in the garden.)

Escriba: Yo cuelgo la ropa en el jardín.
(I am hanging the clothes in the garden.)

1. Nosotros colgamos la ropa en el sótano. **(Yo)** _____

2. Yo comienzo la conversación. **(Ud.)** _____

3. Mis amigos conducen bien. **(Yo)** _____

4. Yo confieso la verdad. **(El chico)** _____

5. Francisca conoce a muchas personas. **(Yo)** _____

6. Nosotros confesamos todo. **(La señora Gómez)** _____

7. Nosotros construimos una casita. **(Mi padre)** _____

8. Tú conoces a Roberto. **(Yo)** _____

9. Los alumnos comienzan el examen. **(Nosotros)** _____

10. Ud. conduce lentamente. **(Yo)** _____

contar / to count, to relate
cuento, cuentas, cuenta;
contamos, contáis, cuentan

A stem-changing verb. The **o** in the stem changes to **ue** when stressed.

costar / to cost
cuesta;
cuestan

An impersonal verb used in the 3rd pers. sing. and plural. A stem-changing verb. The **o** in the stem changes to **ue** because of stress.

continuar / to continue
continúo, continúas, continúa;
continuamos, continuáis, continúan

This **–uar** verb is a stem-changing verb. The **u** in the stem changes to **ú** when stressed.

dar / to give
doy, das, da;
damos, **dais**, dan

An irregular form in the 1st pers. sing. and no accent mark is needed in the 2nd pers. plural.

corregir / to correct
corrijo, corriges, corrige;
corregimos, corregís, corrigen

An orthographical and stem-changing verb. The **g** changes to **j** in front of **o** or **a** in order to keep its original sound of *h*, as in the English word *hello*. Also, **e** in stem changes to **i** when stressed. Pres. part. is **corrigiendo.**

decir / to say, to tell
digo, **dices**, **dice**;
decimos, decís, **dicen**

An irregular form in the 1st pers. sing. Also, the **e** in the stem changes to **i** when stressed. Pres. par. is **diciendo.**

VIII. Change the following verb forms in the present indicative tense using the new subject given in parentheses. You may add additional words if you wish.
Refer to the above stem-changing and orthographical changing verbs according to your needs. In this exercise you are practicing the following verbs: **contar, continuar, corregir, costar, dar, decir.**

Modelo: Nosotros contamos
el dinero. (Yo)
(We are counting the money.)

Escriba: Yo cuento el dinero.
(I am counting the money.)

1. Nosotros continuamos la lección. **(Yo)** _____

2. Rosa y yo corregimos las palabras. **(Yo)** _____

3. ¿Cuánto cuesta el libro? **(los libros)** _____

4. Dolores da la respuesta. **(Yo)** _____

5. Juana dice la verdad. **(Yo)** _____

6. Pablo cuenta la historia. **(Los alumnos)** _____

7. Alicia continúa la lectura. **(Juan y Juana)** _____

8. ¿Cuánto cuestan los zapatos? **(la camisa)** _____

9. Rosa dice mentiras. **(Carmen y José)** _____

60   10. Nosotros damos gracias. **(Yo)** _____

defender / to defend, to protect
def**ie**ndo, defi**e**ndes, defi**e**nde;
defendemos, defendéis, defi**e**nden

A stem-changing verb. The **e** in the stem changes to **ie** when stressed.

dirigir / to direct
diri**jo**, diriges, dirige;
dirigimos, dirigís, dirigen

An orthographical changing verb. The **g** changes to **j** in front of **o** or **a** in order to keep its original sound of **h**, as in the English word *hello*.

devolver / to return (something), to give back (something)
dev**ue**lvo, dev**ue**lves, dev**ue**lve;
devolvemos, devolvéis, dev**ue**lven

A stem-changing verb. The **o** in the stem changes to **ue** when stressed.

doler / to ache, to pain, to hurt, to cause grief, to cause regret
d**ue**lo, d**ue**les, d**ue**le;
dolemos, doléis, d**ue**len

A stem-changing verb. The **o** in the stem changes to **ue** when stressed.

IX. **Change the following verb forms in the present indicative tense using the new subject given in parentheses. You may add additional words if you wish.**
Refer to the above stem-changing and orthographical changing verbs according to your needs. In this exercise you are practicing the following verbs: **defender, devolver, dirigir, doler.**

Modelo: Nosotros defendemos
a sus amigos. (Yo)
(We defend your friends.)

Escriba: Yo defiendo
a sus amigos.
(I defend your friends.)

1. Yo devuelvo los libros a la biblioteca. **(Ud.)** _____

2. La ventana nos defiende del viento. **(Los muros)** _____

3. La directora dirige bien. **(Yo)** _____

4. Me duele la cabeza. **(los brazos)** _____

5. María te devuelve tu libro. **(Yo)** _____

dormir / to sleep
d**ue**rmo, d**ue**rmes, d**ue**rme;
dormimos, dormís, d**ue**rmen

A stem-changing verb. The **o** in the stem changes to **ue** when stressed. Pres. part. is **durmiendo.**

empezar / to begin, to start
emp**ie**zo, emp**ie**zas, emp**ie**za;
empezamos, empezáis, emp**ie**zan

A stem-changing verb. The second **e** in the stem changes to **ie** when stressed.

elegir / to elect, to select, to choose
eli**jo**, eliges, elige;
elegimos, elegís, eligen

An orthographical and stem-changing verb. The **g** changes to **j** in front of **o** or **a** in order to keep its original sound of **h**, as in the English word *hello*. Also, the second **e** in the stem changes to **i** when stressed. Pres. part. is **eligiendo.**

encontrar / to meet, to encounter, to find
enc**ue**ntro, enc**ue**ntras, enc**ue**ntra;
encontramos, encontráis, enc**ue**ntran

An orthographical changing verb. The **o** in the stem changes to **ue** when stressed.

X. Change the following verb forms using the new subject given in parentheses.
Refer to the above stem-changing and orthographical changing verbs according to your needs. In this exercise you are practicing the following verbs: **dormir, elegir, empezar, encontrar.**

> **Modelo:** Nosotros dormimos
> ocho horas cada noche. (Yo)
> (We sleep eight hours
> each night.)

> **Escriba:** Yo duermo
> ocho horas cada noche.
> (I sleep eight hours
> each night.)

1. Siempre tú eliges chocolate. **(Yo)** _____

2. Yo empiezo el trabajo. **(La maestra)** _____

3. Tú encuentras la lección fácil. **(Yo)** _____

4. Yo duermo en un hotel. **(Mi tío)** _____

5. El profesor empieza la lección. **(Tú)** _____

---

entender / to understand
entiendo, entiendes, entiende;
entendemos, entendéis, entienden

A stem-changing verb. The second **e** in the stem changes to **ie** when stressed.

---

escoger / to choose, to select
escojo, escoges, escoge;
escogemos, escogéis, escogen

An orthographical changing verb. This **–ger** verb changes **g** to **j** in front of **o** or **a.**

---

enviar / to send
envío, envías, envía;
enviamos, enviáis, envían

This **–iar** verb changes **i** to **í** in the stem when stressed.

---

estar / to be
estoy, estás, está;
estamos, estáis, están

XI. Change the following verb forms using the new subject given in parentheses.
In this exercise you are practicing the following verbs: **entender, enviar, escoger, estar.**

> **Modelo:** No lo entiendo. (Tú)
> (I don't understand it.)

> **Escriba:** Tú no lo entiendes.
> (You don't understand it.)

1. Mi padre me envía dinero. **(Mis padres)** _____

2. Luis escoge una buena manzana. **(Yo)** _____

3. Yo estoy muy bien, gracias. **(Mis amigos)** _____

4. Alberto no entiende nada. **(José y Elena)** _____

5. Uds. entienden todo. **(Nosotros)** _____

guiar / to guide, to drive, to lead
 guío, guías, guía;
 guiamos, guiáis, guían

This **–iar** verb changes **i** in the stem to **í** when stressed.

huir / to flee, to escape, to run away, to slip away
 huyo, huyes, huye;
 huimos, huís, huyen

This **–uir** verb requires the insertion of **y** in front of the regular present tense endings **o, es, e,** and **en.** Pres. part. is **huyendo.**

hacer / to do, to make
 ha**go**, haces, hace;
 hacemos, hacéis, hacen

Irregular form only in the 1st pers. sing. in this tense, as noted.

ir / to go
 voy, vas, va;
 vamos, vais, van

Pres. part. is **yendo.**

XII. Change the following verb forms using the new subject given in parentheses.
In this exercise you are practicing the following verbs: **guiar, hacer, huir, ir.**

Modelo: Tú no haces nada. (Yo)
(You are doing nothing.)

Escriba: Yo no hago nada.
(I am doing nothing.)

1. Nosotros guiamos bien. **(Yo)** _____

2. Siempre huimos del peligro. **(Yo)** _____

3. Eva va a Madrid en tren. **(Yo)** _____

4. Mis amigos van de compras. **(Nosotros)** _____

5. Yo hago los deberes. **(Los alumnos)** _____

XIII. Advertisements in Newspapers. Proficiency in Speaking and Writing.

Situation: Today in your Spanish Club the students are having fun telling each other what they see in pictures in newspapers and magazines. It's your turn **(Te toca a ti).**

Examine carefully the picture on the next page where four children are enjoying sugar wafers **(los barquillos).** Say something about the children, for example, what they are doing, why they seem to be happy, what they are eating. You may use your own words and ideas or any of the following: **La muchacha y los muchachos están contentos /** the girl and the boys are happy; **comen barquillos deliciosos /** they are eating delicious sugar wafers. You may want to say something about where they are and if it is a nice day: **están en el campo /** they are in the country; **hace buen tiempo, hace sol, es un buen día /** the weather is fine, it's sunny, it's a nice day. Try to use some of the words in the picture or any of the stem-changing and orthographical changing verbs you practiced above. After giving a brief description, practice writing what you said on these lines in at least three simple sentences:

1. _____

2. _____

3. _____

63

VIVA CON SUS HIJOS LA FANTASTICA AVENTURA DE UN VIAJE A DISNEYWORLD

Descubra también que los Barquillos Cuétara "una auténtica gozada" como dicen sus hijos Cuatro "frescos" sabores para elegir: Fres-Nata Fres-Coco, Fres-Lemón y Demecao.

Los Barquillos Cuétara son ligeros y gustan a todos siempre y en cualquier momento y ni usted misma podrá resistir la fresca y deliciosa tentación de su sabor, si los mete en el frigorífico este verano.

Participe en el Concurso y podrá vivir con sus hijos la aventura, fantástica pero real, de un viaje a Disneyworld, al que Cuétara tiene el gusto de invitarle.

Presentaciones:
FRES-COCO: Paquete aluminio 175 grs. y Estuches familiares 1/2 Kg 1 Kg y 1.5 Kg
FRES NATA: Paquete aluminio 175 grs. y Estuche familiar 1/2 Kg.
FRES LEMON Paquete aluminio 175 grs. y Estuche familiar 1/2 Kg.
DEMECAO Paquete aluminio 175 grs. y Estuches familiares 1/2 Kg y 1 Kg

Reprinted with permission of Galletas CUÉTARA, Madrid.

---

jugar / to play
juego, juegas, juega;
jugamos, jugáis, juegan

A stem-changing verb because **u** in the stem changes to **ue** when stressed.

---

morir / to die
muero, mueres, muere;
morimos, morís, mueren

A stem-changing verb because **o** in the stem changes to **ue** when stressed. Pres. part. is **muriendo.**

---

mentir / to lie, to tell a lie
miento, mientes, miente;
mentimos, mentís, mienten

A stem-changing verb because **e** in the stem changes to **ie** when stressed. Pres. part. is **mintiendo.**

---

mostrar / to show, to point out
muestro, muestras, muestra;
mostramos, mostráis, muestran

A stem-changing verb because **o** in the stem changes to **ue** when stressed.

XIV. Change the following verb forms using the new subject given in parentheses.

In this exercise you are practicing the following verbs: **jugar, mentir, morir, mostrar.**

Modelo: Los jugadores juegan
todos los sábados. (Yo)
(The players play every Saturday.)

Escriba: Yo juego
todos los sábados.
(I play every Saturday.)

1. Este chico siempre miente. **(Estos chicos)** _____

2. Nosotros morimos de hambre. **(Yo)** _____

3. El vendedor muestra los zapatos. **(Ellos)** _____

4. José juega al fútbol. **(Uds.)** _____

5. Nosotros mostramos paciencia. **(Yo)** _____

---

negar / to deny, to refuse
n**ie**go, n**ie**gas, n**ie**ga;
negamos, negáis, n**ie**gan

A stem-changing verb because **e** in the stem changes to **ie** when stressed.

---

obtener / to obtain, to get
obten**go**, obt**ie**nes, obt**ie**ne;
obtenemos, obtenéis, obt**ie**nen

The 1st pers. sing. form is irregular. As a stem-changing verb, the **e** in the stem changes to **ie** when stressed.

---

obedecer / to obey
obede**zc**o, obedeces, obedece;
obedecemos, obedecéis, obedecen

An orthographical changing verb. This –**cer** verb changes **c** to **zc** only in the 1st pers. sing. of this tense.

---

ofrecer / to offer
ofre**zc**o, ofreces, ofrece;
otrecemos, ofrecéis, ofrecen

An orthographical changing verb. This –**cer** verb changes **c** to **zc** only in the 1st pers. sing. of this tense.

XV. Change the following verb forms using the new subject given in parentheses.

In this exercise you are practicing the following verbs: **negar, obedecer, obtener, ofrecer.**

Modelo: ¿Porqué me niega Ud.
ayuda? (Tú)
(Why are you refusing me help?)

Escriba: ¿Porqué me niegas
ayuda?
(Why are you refusing me help?)

1. Mi hermanita obedece a mi madre. **(Yo)** _____

2. Elisa obtiene buenas notas. **(Yo)** _____

3. Ana ofrece un regalo a María. **(Yo)** _____

4. Mi perro me obedece. **(Mis perros)** _____

5. Yo ofrezco ayuda. **(Nosotros)** _____

oír / to hear
oigo, oyes, oye;
oímos, oís, oyen

An irregular verb. Pres. part. is **oyendo.**

---

pedir / to ask for, to request
pido, pides, pide;
pedimos, pedís, piden

A stem-changing verb because **e** in the stem changes to **i** when stressed. Pres. part. is **pidiendo.**

---

oler / to smell
huelo, **hueles**, **huele**;
olemos, oléis, **huelen**

An orthographical and stem-changing verb because **o** in the stem changes to **ue** when stressed and *h* is added as noted. Pres. part. is regular: **oliendo.**

---

pensar / to think
pienso, piensas, piensa;
pensamos, pensáis, piensan

A stem-changing verb because **e** in the stem changes to **ie** when stressed.

XVI. Change the following verb forms using the new subject given in parentheses.
In this exercise you are practicing the following verbs: **oír, oler, pedir, pensar.**

Modelo: Nosotros oímos la música. (Yo)
(We hear the music.)

Escriba: Yo oigo la música.
(I hear the music.)

1. Nosotros no olemos nada. **(Yo)** _____

2. Roberto pide dinero. **(Nosotros)** _____

3. Alberto no piensa nunca. **(Ellos)** _____

4. ¿Qué me pides tú? **(Ud.)** _____

5. ¿Oye Ud. la música? **(Uds.)** _____

---

perder / to lose, to waste (time)
pierdo, pierdes, pierde
perdemos, perdéis, pierden

A stem-changing verb because **e** in the stem changes to **ie** when stressed.

---

poner / to put, to place
pongo, pones, pone;
ponemos, ponéis, ponen

Irregular in the 1st pers. sing. only of this tense.

---

poder / to be able, can
puedo, puedes, puede;
podemos, podéis, pueden

A stem-changing verb because **o** in the stem changes to **ue** when stressed. Pres. part. is **pudiendo.**

---

preferir / to prefer
prefiero, prefieres, prefiere;
preferimos, preferís, prefieren

A stem-changing verb because the second **e** in the stem changes to **ie** when stressed. Pres. part. is **prefiriendo.**

XVII. Change the following verb forms using the new subject given in parentheses. In this exercise you are practicing the following verbs: **perder, poder, poner, preferir.**

> **Modelo:** Mariana no pierde nada. (Yo)   **Escriba:** Yo no pierdo nada.
> (Mariana doesn't lose anything.)   (I don't lose anything.)

1. Usted pierde todo. **(Nosotros)** _____

2. Yo puedo ir al cine con Felipe. **(Sofía)** _____

3. Mi hermano pone las flores en la mesa. **(Yo)** _____

4. Isabel y Ana prefieren ir al centro. **(Pablo)** _____

5. Rosa no pierde un momento. **(Ellos)** _____

---

producir/ to produce
produ**zc**o, produces, produce;
producimos, producís, producen

This **–cir** verb changes **c** to **zc** only in the 1st pers. sing. of this tense.

---

querer/ to want, to wish
qu**ie**ro, qu**ie**res, qu**ie**re;
queremos, queréis, qu**ie**ren

A stem-changing verb because **e** in the stem changes to **ie** when stressed.

---

proteger/ to protect
prote**j**o, proteges, protege;
protegemos, protegéis, protegen

An orthographical changing verb because this **–ger** verb changes **g** to **j** in front of **o** or **a.**

---

recoger/ to pick, to pick up, to gather
reco**j**o, recoges, recoge;
recogemos, recogéis, recogen

An orthographical changing verb because this **–ger** verb changes **g** to **j** in front of **o** or **a.**

XVIII. Change the following verb forms using the new subject given in parentheses. In this exercise you are practicing the following verbs: **producir, proteger, querer, recoger.**

> **Modelo:** El señor López produce   **Escriba:** Yo produzco
> mucho trabajo. (Yo)   mucho trabajo.
> (Mr. López produces a lot of work.)   (I produce a lot of work.)

1. El perro protege la casa. **(Yo)** _____

2. Yo quiero pasar un año en España. **(Tú)** _____

3. Los hombres recogen las frutas. **(Yo)** _____

4. ¿Queremos comer ahora? **(Uds.)** _____

5. Yo protejo a los niños. **(La maestra)** _____

recomendar / to recommend, to advise, to commend
    recom**ie**ndo, recom**ie**ndas, recom**ie**nda;
    recomendamos, recomendáis,
      recom**ie**ndan

    A stem-changing verb because **e** in the stem changes to **ie** when stressed.

reír / to laugh
    río, **ríes**, **ríe**;
    reímos, **reís**, **ríen**

    The pres. part. is also irregular: **riendo.**

referir / to refer, to relate
    ref**ie**ro, ref**ie**res, ref**ie**re;
    referimos, referís, ref**ie**ren

    A stem-changing verb because the second **e** in the stem changes to **ie** when stressed. Pres. part. is **refiriendo.**

repetir / to repeat
    rep**i**to, rep**i**tes, rep**i**te;
    repetimos, repetís, rep**i**ten

    A stem-changing verb because the second **e** in the stem changes to **i** when stressed. Pres. part. is also irregular: **repitiendo.**

XIX. Change the following verb forms using the new subject given in parentheses. In this exercise you are practicing the following verbs: recomendar, referir, reír, repetir.

    Modelo: El camarero recomienda el arroz con pollo. (Yo) (The waiter recommends rice with chicken.)

    Escriba: Yo recomiendo el arroz con pollo. (I recommend rice with chicken.)

1. ¿Me recomienda Ud. un dentista? **(Tú)** _____

2. Nosotros te referimos la historia. **(Yo)** _____

3. La señora Sabelotodo ríe a carcajadas. **(Yo)** _____

4. Yo repito la pregunta. **(La profesora)** _____

5. Nosotros repetimos la canción. **(Uds.)** _____

resolver / to resolve, to solve (a problem)
    res**ue**lvo, res**ue**lves, res**ue**lve;
    resolvemos, resolvéis, res**ue**lven

    A stem-changing verb because **o** in the stem changes to **ue** when stressed.

salir / to go out, to leave
    salgo, sales, sale;
    salimos, salís, salen

    Irregular only in the 1st pers. sing. of this tense.

saber / to know, to know how
    sé, sabes, sabe;
    sabemos, sabéis, saben

    Irregular only in the 1st pers. sing. of this tense.

seguir / to follow, to pursue, to continue
    sigo, s**i**gues, s**i**gue;
    seguimos, seguís, s**i**guen

    An orthographical changing verb because **u** in the stem drops only in the 1st pers. sing. of this tense. Also, a stem-changing verb because **e** in the stem changes to **i** when stressed. Pres. part. is also irregular: **siguiendo.**

XX. Change the following verb forms using the new subject given in parentheses. In this exercise you are practicing the following verbs: **resolver, saber, salir, seguir.**

> **Modelo:** La profesora resuelve
> el problema. (Nosotros)
> (The professor is resolving
> the problem.)
>
> **Escriba:** Nosotros resolvemos
> el problema.
> (We are resolving the
> problem.)

1. Laura sabe el número de teléfono. **(Yo)** _____

2. ¿A qué hora sale el tren? **(Uds.)** _____

3. Nosotros salimos a las ocho. **(Yo)** _____

4. Yo sigo el mismo camino. **(Ester)** _____

5. Yo lo sé. **(Berta y Diego)** _____

---

sentarse / to sit down
   me s**ie**nto, te s**ie**ntas, se s**ie**nta;
   nos sentamos, os sentáis, se s**ie**ntan

   A stem-changing verb because **e** in the stem changes to **ie** when stressed.

---

ser / to be
   soy, eres, es;
   somos, sois, son

   Pres. part. is **siendo.**

---

sentir / to feel sorry, to regret, to feel, to experience, to sense
   s**ie**nto, s**ie**ntes, s**ie**nte;
   sentimos, sentís, s**ie**nten

   A stem-changing verb because **e** in the stem changes to **ie** when stressed. Pres. part. is also irregular: **sintiendo.**

---

servir / to serve
   s**i**rvo, s**i**rves, s**i**rve,
   servimos, servís, s**i**rven

   A stem-changing verb because **e** in the stem changes to **i** when stressed. Pres. part. is also irregular: **sirviendo.**

XXI. Change the following verb forms using the new subject given in parentheses. In this exercise you are practicing the following verbs: **sentarse, sentir, ser, servir.**

> **Modelo:** Usted se sienta aquí. (Yo)
> (You are sitting here.)
>
> **Escriba:** Yo me siento aquí.
> (I am sitting here.)

1. Uds. se sientan allá. **(Nosotros)** _____

2. Yo lo siento. **(Tú)** _____

3. Soy alumna. **(Roberta)** _____

4. Yo sirvo la comida. **(El camarero)** _____

5. El soldado sirve a la patria. **(Los soldados)** _____

---

sonar / to ring, to sound
s**ue**no, s**ue**nas, s**ue**na;
sonamos, sonáis, s**ue**nan

A stem-changing verb because **o** in the stem changes to **ue** when stressed.

---

sonreír / to smile
sonrío, sonríes, sonríe;
sonreímos, sonreís, sonríen

The pres. part. is also irregular: **sonriendo.**

---

soñar / to dream
s**ue**ño, s**ue**ñas, s**ue**ña;
soñamos, soñáis, s**ue**ñan

A stem-changing verb because **o** in the stem changes to **ue** when stressed.

---

sustituir / to substitute
sustitu**y**o, sustitu**y**es, sustitu**y**e;
sustituimos, sustituís, sustitu**y**en

This **–uir** verb requires the insertion of **y** in front of the regular present tense endings **o, es, e,** and **en.** Pres. part. is also irregular: **sustituyendo.**

XXII. **Change the following verb forms using the new subject given in parentheses. In this exercise you are practicing the following verbs: sonar, soñar, sonreír, sustituir.**

Modelo: Nosotros sonamos
la alarma. (Yo)
(We are sounding the alarm.)

Escriba: Yo sueno
la alarma.
(I am sounding the alarm.)

1. El teléfono suena. **(Los teléfonos)** _____

2. Los niños sueñan todas las noches. **(Yo)** _____

3. ¿Por qué sonríes? **(Ud.)** _____

4. Yo sustituyo una palabra por otra. **(María)** _____

5. Sueño con ir a Madrid. **(Tú)** _____

---

tener / to have, to hold
tengo, t**ie**nes, t**ie**ne;
tenemos, tenéis; t**ie**nen

An irregular form in the 1st pers. sing. of this tense. Also, **e** in the stem changes to **ie** when stressed.

---

traer / to bring
traigo, traes, trae;
traemos, traéis, traen

Irregular in the 1st pers. sing. only of this tense. Also, the pres. part. is irregular: **trayendo.**

---

traducir / to translate
tradu**zc**o, traduces, traduce;
traducimos, traducís, traducen

An orthographical changing verb because this **–cer** verb changes **c** to **zc** only in the 1st pers. sing. of this tense.

---

valer / to be worth, to be worthy
valgo, vales, vale;
valemos, valéis, valen

Irregular only in the 1st pers. sing. of this tense.

XXIII. **Change the following verb forms using the new subject given in parentheses. In this exercise you are practicing the following verbs: tener, traducir, traer, valer.**

Modelo: ¿Tiene Ud. coche? (Tú)   **Escriba:** ¿Tienes coche?
(Do you have a car?)   (Do you have a car?)

1. Usted tiene bastante dinero. **(Yo)** _____

2. La maestra traduce del inglés al español. **(Yo)** _____

3. Nosotros traemos el helado. **(Yo)** _____

4. ¿Cuánto vale esta casa? **(Estas casas)** _____

5. Mis amigos valen mucho. **(Yo)** _____

---

venir / to come
vengo, v**ie**nes, v**ie**ne;
venimos, venís, v**ie**nen

The pres. part. is also irregular: **viniendo.**

---

volar / to fly
v**ue**lo, v**ue**las, v**ue**la;
volamos, voláis, v**ue**lan

A stem-changing verb because **o** in the stem changes to **ue** when stressed.

---

ver / to see
veo, ves, ve;
vemos, veis, ven

---

volver / to return
v**ue**lvo, v**ue**lves, v**ue**lve;
volvemos, volvéis, v**ue**lven

A stem-changing verb because **o** in the stem changes to **ue** when stressed.

XXIV. **Change the following verb forms using the new subject given in parentheses. In this exercise you are practicing the following verbs: venir, ver, volar, volver.**

Modelo: Venimos a tu casa. (Yo)   **Escriba:** Vengo a tu casa.
(We are coming to your house.)   (I am coming to your house.)

1. Mis amigos vienen más tarde. **(Yo)** _____

2. ¿Qué ve Ud. en esta caja? **(Uds.)** _____

3. Nosotros no lo vemos nunca. **(Yo)** _____

4. El avión vuela. **(Los aviones)** _____

5. ¿A qué hora volvemos? **(Uds.)** _____

71

EJERCICIOS

I. Cambie el verbo del infinitivo al presente de indicativo. (Change the verb from the infinitive to the present indicative tense.)

The forms of the irregular verbs, stem-changing and orthographical changing verbs to be used in these exercises are found on the preceding pages in alphabetical order by infinitive so you can find them easily.

Modelo: estar   Yo _____ en la clase de español. (I _____ in Spanish class.)

Escriba: Yo estoy en la clase de español. (I am in Spanish class.)

1. volver: ¿A qué hora _____ Juana?

2. acordarse: Yo _____ de usted.

3. acostarse: Maria, ¿a qué hora te _____ todas las noches?

4. almorzar: Todas las mañanas yo _____ a las siete.

5. cerrar: Antes de comenzar la lección, el profesor _____ la puerta.

6. conocer: Yo _____ bien esta ciudad.

7. contar: Los alumnos _____ de uno a mil.

8. costar: ¿Cuánto _____ este libro?

9. dar: Todos los días yo _____ gracias a Dios.

10. decir: Siempre yo _____ la verdad. ¿Y Ud.?

II. Complete las oraciones a continuación. Escriba en cada oración el presente de indicativo de los verbos escritos abajo. (Complete the sentences below. In each sentence write the present indicative tense of the required verb from among the 15 verbs listed under the model. First, read each sentence for meaning. There is a clue in each sentence to help you figure out which verb to use. Among the 15 choices, there is only one verb that fits sensibly in each of the 15 statements.)

Modelo: dormir   Cada noche (yo) _____ ocho horas.
(Every night I _____ eight hours.)

Cada noche (yo) duermo ocho horas.
(Every night I sleep eight hours.)

dormir	**hacer**	**morir**	**perder**	**preferir**
empezar	**ir**	**oír**	**poder**	**querer**
estar	**jugar**	**pensar**	**poner**	**ser**

1. Yo duermo ocho horas cada noche. ¿Y Ud.? ¿Cuántas horas _____ usted cada noche?

2. ¿A qué hora _____ la clase de español?

3. Tú haces lo mejor posible y yo _____ lo mejor posible.

4. Ud. está aquí y yo _____ aquí también.

5. Tú vas al cine esta tarde y yo _____ al teatro.

6. La señora Sánchez es muy vieja. Está gravemente enferma y _____ .

7. Alberto juega al tenis y yo _____ al béisbol.

8. ¿Oye Ud. el ruido, señor? —Sí, yo _____ el ruido.

9. Algunas veces yo pierdo el tiempo. ¿Y Ud.? ¿Por qué _____ Ud. el tiempo?

10. Yo pienso en las vacaciones de Navidad. ¿En qué _____ Ud.?

11. ¿ _____ tú hacer esto?—Sí, yo _____ hacer eso.

12. ¿Qué _____ Ud. hacer esta tarde? ¿Ir al cine o ir a la biblioteca?

13. Cuando vuelvo a casa, siempre _____ mis libros sobre la mesa en la cocina.

14. ¿Quiere Ud. ir al cine conmigo? —Sí, yo _____ ir al cine con usted.

15. La señora Sánchez _____ muy vieja. Está gravemente enferma y muere.

III. **Conteste las siguientes preguntas en el afirmativo en el presente de indicativo con oraciones completas. En la oración (a) use la palabra Sí. En la oración (b) use la palabra también según los modelos.** (Answer the following questions in the affirmative in the present indicative tense in complete sentences. In sentence [a] use the word **Sí.** In sentence [b] use the word **también** [also], according to the models.)

Modelos: a. ¿Sabe Ud. la lección para hoy? (Do you know the lesson for today?)
   a. Sí, yo sé la lección para hoy. (Yes, I know the lesson for today.)

   b. ¿Y los otros alumnos? (And the other students?)
   b. Los otros alumnos saben la lección para hoy, también. (The other students know the lesson for today also.)

1. a. ¿Sabe Ud. qué hora es? _____

   b. ¿Y los otros alumnos? _____

2. a. ¿Sale Ud. de la escuela a las tres y media? _____

   b. ¿Y los profesores? _____

3. a. ¿Se sienta Ud. en esta silla? _____

   b. ¿Y Juana? _____

4. a. ¿Eres tú un buen alumno?_____

   b. ¿Y María? _____

5. a. ¿Sonríe Ud. de vez en cuando? _____

   b. ¿Y Pedro y Juana? _____

6. a. ¿Tiene Ud. dinero en el bolsillo? _____

   b. ¿Y el señor Rodríguez? _____

7. a. ¿Trae Ud. el libro de español a clase? _____

   b. ¿Y los otros alumnos? _____

8. a. ¿Viene Ud. a la fiesta esta noche? _____

   b. ¿Y nosotros? _____

9. a. ¿Ve Ud. el aeroplano en el cielo? _____

   b. ¿Y el niño? _____

10. a. ¿Vuela el pájaro en el cielo? _____

    b. ¿Y los otros pájaros? _____

IV. **En español hay muchas palabras que se escriben y se pronuncian idénticamente, pero un signo de acento es necesario para distinguir su significado.** (In Spanish there are many words that are written and pronounced identically, but an accent mark is needed to distinguish their meaning.)

Por ejemplo:

Yo sé / I know;   **se** *reflex. pron.* / oneself, himself, herself, yourself, yourselves, themselves

Yo sé que su amigo se llama José. / I know that your friend's name is José.

presente de indicativo

saber / to know

yo	sé	nosotros	sabemos
tú	sabes	vosotros	sabéis
Ud.		Uds.	
él	} sabe	ellos	} saben
ella		ellas	

Mnemonic Tip	Saber is to know something, to know a fact. Conocer is to know in the sense of to be acquainted with a person, a place, a thing.	
	Yo sé que tú conoces a José, mi mejor amigo. I know that you know José, my best friend.	

¿Cuántos ejemplos puede Ud. decir y escribir? (How many examples can you say and write?)
¿Puede Ud. dar un "mnemonic tip"? (Can you give a "mnemonic tip"?)

V. En español hay muchas palabras que se escriben y se pronuncian idénticamente, pero un signo de acento es necesario para distinguir su significado. (In Spanish there are many words that are written and pronounced identically, but an accent mark is needed to distinguish their meaning.)

Por ejemplo:

de *prep.* / of, from   **Dé al señor la taza grande de la cocina.** / Give to the gentleman the big cup from the kitchen.
dé *3rd person, singular (Ud.), Imperative* (Command) of **dar** / to give

dar / to give

presente de indicativo

yo	doy	nosotros	damos
tú	das	vosotros	dais
Ud.		Uds.	
él } da		ellos } dan	
ella		ellas	

Imperativo

(yo)	—	(nosotros)	demos
(tú)	da; no des	(vosotros)	dad; no deis
(Ud.)	**dé**	(Uds.)	den

¿Cuántos ejemplos puede Ud. decir y escribir? (How many examples can you say and write?)

The Present Participle (participio) and the Present Progressive Tense

Present participle: A present participle is a verb form that, in English, ends in *–ing*; for example, *singing, eating, receiving*. In Spanish, a present participle is regularly formed as follows:

drop the **ar** of an **–ar** ending verb, like **cantar**, and add **–ando: cantando** / singing
drop the **er** of an **–er** ending verb, like **comer**, and add **–iendo: comiendo** / eating
drop the **ir** of an **–ir** ending verb, like **recibir**, and add **–iendo: recibiendo** / receiving

In English, a gerund also ends in *-ing* but there is a distinct difference in use between a gerund and a present participle in English. In brief, it is this: In English, when a present participle is used as a noun it is called a gerund; for example: *Reading is good*. As a present participle in English: The boy fell asleep *while reading*.

In the first example (*Reading is good*), *reading* is a gerund because it is the subject of the verb *is*. In Spanish, however, we must not use the present participle form as a noun to serve as a subject; we must use the infinitive form of the verb in Spanish: **Leer es bueno.**

Common irregular present participles are as follows. You ought to know them so that you may be able to recognize them if they are on the next standardized test in Spanish that you take.

INFINITIVE

PRESENT PARTICIPLE

caer / to fall
cayendo / falling

conseguir / to attain, to achieve
consiguiendo / attaining, achieving

construir / to construct
construyendo / constructing

corregir / to correct
corrigiendo / correcting

creer / to believe
creyendo / believing

decir / to say, to tell
diciendo / saying, telling

despedirse / to say good-bye
despidiéndose / saying good-bye

destruir / to destroy
destruyendo / destroying

divertirse / to enjoy oneself
divirtiéndose / enjoying oneself

dormir / to sleep
durmiendo / sleeping

huir / to flee
huyendo / fleeing

ir / to go
yendo / going

leer / to read
leyendo / reading

75

mentir / to lie (tell a falsehood)	**mintiendo** / lying
morir / to die	**muriendo** / dying
oír / to hear	**oyendo** / hearing
pedir / to ask (for), to request	**pidiendo** / asking (for), requesting
poder / to be able	**pudiendo** / being able
reír / to laugh	**riendo** / laughing
repetir / to repeat	**repitiendo** / repeating
seguir / to follow	**siguiendo** / following
sentir / to feel	**sintiendo** / feeling
servir / to serve	**sirviendo** / serving
traer / to bring	**trayendo** / bringing
venir / to come	**viniendo** / coming
vestir / to dress	**vistiendo** / dressing

The present participle is needed to form the present progressive tense by using **estar** in the present indicative tense plus the present participle of the main verb you are using; *e.g.,* **Estoy hablando** (I am talking), *i.e.,* I am (in the act of) talking (right now). Review **estar** in Work Unit 1.

EJERCICIOS

I. Cambie el verbo del presente de indicativo al presente progresivo. (Change the verb from the present indicative to the present progressive.)

Modelo: Hablo. ⟶ Estoy hablando.

1. Trabajo. _____
2. Ando. _____
3. Bailo. _____
4. Busco. _____
5. Contesto. _____
6. Aprendo. _____
7. Bebo. _____
8. Como. _____
9. Leo. _____
10. Vendo. _____
11. Corro. _____
12. Abro. _____

13. Escribo. _____
14. Remito. _____
15. Subo. _____
16. Vivo. _____
17. Caigo. _____
18. Digo. _____
19. Duermo. _____
20. Voy. _____
21. Oigo. _____
22. Traigo. _____
23. Vengo. _____
24. Sirvo. _____

II. Cambie el verbo del presente progresivo al presente de indicativo. (Change the verb from the present progressive to the present indicative.)

Modelo: Estoy hablando. ——→ Hablo.

1. Estoy trabajando. _____

2. Estamos bailando. _____

3. Ud. está buscando. _____

4. Ella está aprendiendo. _____

5. Juana está trayendo. _____

6. Estoy sirviendo. _____

7. Estamos bebiendo. _____

8. Estoy andando. _____

9. Están comiendo. _____

10. Uds. están contestando. _____

11. Él está oyendo. _____

12. Pedro está diciendo. _____

13. Tú estás corriendo. _____

14. Estoy cayendo. _____

III. Dictado. Escriba las oraciones que su profesor de español va a leer. (Dictation. Write the sentences that your Spanish teacher is going to read.)

1. _____

2. _____

3. _____

IV. ¿Qué puede Ud. lanzar? (What can you throw?)

Escriba una lista de cosas que Ud. puede lanzar. (Write a list of things that you can throw.)

Por ejemplo:

Puedo lanzar una pelota / I can throw a ball.
Puedo lanzar una moneda / I can throw a coin.
       un lápiz / a pencil
       una pluma / a pen
       un libro /a book
       un cuaderno / a notebook
       un huevo / an egg
       un ladrillo / a brick

¿Cuántos ejemplos puede Ud. decir y escribir?

presente de indicativo

poder / to be able, can

yo	puedo	nosotros	podemos
tú	puedes	vosotros	podéis
Ud.		Uds.	
él	puede	ellos	pueden
ella		ellas	

V. ¿Qué puede Ud. mirar? (What can you look at?)

Escriba una lista de cosas que Ud. puede mirar. (Write a list of things that you can look at or watch.)

Por ejemplo:

Puedo mirar la televisión / I can look at (watch) television.
Puedo mirar el cielo / I can look at the sky.
        el pájaro en la jaula / the bird in the cage
        las estrellas / the stars
        la luna / the moon

¿Cuántos ejemplos puede Ud. decir y escribir? (How many examples can you say and write?)

VI. Activities. Proficiency in Speaking and Writing.

Today is Friday! T.G.I.F.! This is the day in Spanish class when students use their imagination and talents to do things while talking in Spanish. It's your turn. **¡Te toca a ti!**

A. **Situation:** You are supposed to say what you are doing and at the same time perform the action. You may use your own words and ideas or any of the following: **Estoy bailando** / I am dancing. Keep saying it while you do a short tap dance, or waltz around the room while saying **estoy bailando.** Then go to one of the windows in your classroom, open it, and say **estoy abriendo la ventana** / I am opening the window. Close the window while you are saying **estoy cerrando la ventana** / I am closing the window. You can keep opening and closing the window as many times as you wish but you must be sure to say in Spanish what you are doing at the same time.

Don't forget to use these: **Estoy cantando** / I am singing; **estoy buscando mi libro** / I'm looking for my book; **estoy comiendo** / I'm eating; **estoy bebiendo** / I'm drinking. You can perform these actions by using gestures and bodily movements as if you were a mime.

Use at least five of the actions in the present progressive that you practiced in this Work Unit. Later, practice what you said by writing the Spanish statements on these lines:

_____

_____

B. **Situation:** Tell us at least five things that you can throw. You may use your own words or any of the following that were used in this Work Unit: **Puedo lanzar una pelota** / I can throw a ball; **puedo lanzar un huevo** / I can throw an egg; **puedo lanzar un libro** / I can throw a book. How many more can you say and write?

_____

_____

C. **Situation:** Finally, you can tell your classmates at least five things that you can look at or watch. You may use your own words or any of the following that were used in this Work Unit: **Puedo mirar la televisión** / I can watch television; **puedo mirar el cielo** / I can look at the sky; **puedo mirar el pájaro amarillo en la jaula** / I can look at the yellow bird in the cage; **puedo mirar las estrellas** / I can look at the stars. How many more can you say and write?

_____

_____

_____

Indefinite and Negative Words Commonly Used

algo / something, anything (with **sin**, use **nada; sin nada** / without anything)

alguien / anybody, anyone, someone, somebody (with **sin, use nadie; sin nadie** / without anyone)

alguno, alguna, algunos, algunas / some, any

jamás / ever, never, not ever

nada / nothing (**sin nada** / without anything); after **sin, nada** is used instead of **algo; Ella no quiere nada** / She does not want anything.

nadie / nobody, no one, not anyone, not anybody (**sin nadie** / without anybody); after **sin, nadie** is used instead of **alguien**

ni / neither, nor

ni . . . ni / neither . . . nor

ni siquiera / not even

ninguno, ninguna / no one, none, not any, not anybody

nunca / never, not ever, ever

o / or

o . . . o / either . . . or

siempre / always

también / also, too

tampoco / neither; **ni yo tampoco** / nor I either

unos cuantos, unas cuantas / a few, some, several

EJERCICIOS

I. Una la palabra en español con su equivalente en inglés. (Match the word in Spanish with its equivalent in English.)

1. **algo** _____ always

2. **alguien** _____ not even

3. **alguno** _____ never

4. **jamás** _____ something

5. **nada** _____ nothing

6. **nadie** _____ someone

7. **ni** _____ some, any

8. **ni siquiera** _____ nobody, no one

9. **nunca** _____ neither, nor

10. **siempre** _____ ever

II. Traduzca. (Translate into Spanish.)

1. something _____

2. a few, some, several _____

3. ever _____

4. never _____

5. either . . . or _____

6. neither . . . nor _____

7. not even _____

8. no one, nobody _____

9. somebody, someone _____

10. without anything _____

III. Culture. Appreciating Spanish Art. Proficiency in Speaking and Writing.

Situation: Your Spanish teacher has handed out pictures to the students to look at and interpret the scenes. You were given the picture that is on the following page. It is a painting entitled **La Adoración de los Magos** / *The Adoration of the Magi* by the great Spanish artist MURILLO.

Look at the picture and, in three or four sentences, tell us what you see. You may use your own words and ideas or the following suggestions: **los tres Magos** / the three Magi; or, **los tres Reyes** / the three Kings; or, **los tres Sabios** / the three Wise Men; **ellos vienen a ver** / they come to see; **la madre tiene el nene en los brazos** / the mother is holding the baby in her arms; **los tres Magos traen regalos para el nene** / the three Magi are bringing gifts for the baby; **los tres Magos ofrecen regalos** / the three Magi are offering gifts; **uno de los tres reyes está de rodillas** / one of the three kings is on his knees; **todas las personas están contentas** / all the persons are happy. You may also want to use these words: **en esta pintura** / in this painting; **de Murillo** / of Murillo; **un gran artista español** / a great Spanish artist; **hay** / there is (there are); **algunas personas** / some persons. You may also want to use some adjectives to describe **la pintura**, for example: **es espléndida** / it is splendid; **magnífica** / magnificent; **soberbia** / superb.

You practiced the above suggested verbs in this Work Unit under the section about verbs irregular in the present indicative, including stem-changing and orthographical changing verbs. They are: **estar, ofrecer, ser, tener, traer, venir.** Are there other verbs in that section you can use in the present tense while talking about this picture?

Now, practice writing the three or four sentences you stated.

_____

_____

_____

_____

The Adoration of the Magi (ca. 1655–1660) by Bartolomé Esteban MURILLO (1617–1682)
Courtesy of The Toledo Museum of Art, Toledo, Ohio.

The Agony in the Garden (1590s) by EL GRECO (1541–1614)
Courtesy of The Toledo Museum of Art, Toledo, Ohio

IV. Culture. Appreciating Spanish Art. Proficiency in Speaking and Writing.

Situation: You are on a class field trip visiting The Toledo Museum of Art in Toledo, Ohio. You are admiring a painting by EL GRECO, called *The Agony in the Garden* / ***La Agonía en el Jardín.***

Look at the picture and say aloud a few words in Spanish. You may use your own words or the following: **la agonía** / the agony; **en el jardín** / in the garden; **en el museo** / in the museum; **yo veo** / I see; **una pintura** (or: **un cuadro**) **del gran artista español El Greco** / a painting by the great Spanish artist El Greco; **una obra de arte** / a work of art; **el hombre, los hombres** / the man, the men; **el cielo** / the sky; **la luna** / the moon; **las nubes** / the clouds; **el ángel, los ángeles** / the angel, angels; **las alas** / the wings; **las flores** / the flowers; **el árbol, los árboles** / the tree, trees; **la roca, las rocas** / the rock, rocks; **las manos** / the hands. A few adjectives: **maravilloso** / marvelous; **admirable** / admirable; **vivo, intenso** / poignant; **fascinante** / fascinating.

Now, practice writing the Spanish words you would use to describe or tell a story about this picture.

_____

_____

La señora Rodríguez levanta la mano para espantar las moscas.

Work Unit 4
Review of Level 1 Topics

Have you ever been at a public auction?
Let's see what happens to Señora Rodríguez.

¡Vete! ¡Vete!

La señora Rodríguez y su esposo salen de casa para ir a una subasta. A la señora Rodríguez le gustan mucho las ventas públicas. Quiere comprar una pequeña mesa redonda para el vestíbulo de la casa.

Los señores Rodríguez llegan y entran en la sala de ventas. Oyen la voz del subastador que está hablando a un grupo de personas. 5

El subastador: Señoras y señores, ¡Atención! ¡Por favor!
(*Los señores Rodríguez se sientan en la quinta fila cerca de la puerta.*)

El subastador: Tengo aquí, señoras y señores, un sillón muy hermoso. ¿Quién ofrece cincuenta pesetas?
(*El señor Rodríguez está hablando a su esposa en voz baja:—Todo es muy elegante aquí.* 10 *Muy elegante.*)
(*La señora Rodríguez responde en voz baja:—Sí, querido mío, pero a mí no me gustan todas estas moscas en esta sala. ¡Y el sillón es muy feo!*)

El subastador: ¡Muchas gracias, señor! ¡Tengo cincuenta pesetas por este sillón tan hermoso! ¿Quién ofrece sesenta pesetas? . . . Sesenta pesetas no es mucho 15 dinero por este sillón muy hermoso. ¿Quién ofrece sesenta pesetas?
(*La señora Rodríguez dice a su esposo en voz baja:—¡Las moscas en esta sala son terribles!*)

El subastador: ¡Muchas gracias, señora! ¡Muchas gracias! Tengo sesenta pesetas de la dama en la primera fila. ¿Quién ofrece setenta pesetas? 20
(*La señora Rodríguez pregunta a su esposo en voz baja:—Francisco, ¿quién es la dama en la primera fila que ofrece sesenta pesetas por el sillón monstruoso? ¡Está loca!*)

(*El señor Rodríguez responde:—Yo no sé, querida mía.*)

El subastador: ¡Muchas gracias, señora! ¡Muchas gracias! ¡Tengo una oferta de setenta pesetas! . . . ¡Muchas gracias, señor! Tengo una oferta de ochenta 25 pesetas. ¿Quién ofrece noventa pesetas? . . . ¡Muchas gracias, señora! Tengo una oferta de noventa pesetas de la dama allá en la tercera fila. ¿Quién ofrece cien pesetas? ¿Cien pesetas? ¿Cien pesetas? ¿Quién ofrece cien pesetas?
(*La señora Rodríguez levanta la mano para espantar las moscas—¡Oh! ¡Estas moscas!*) 30

El subastador: ¡Muchas gracias, señora! ¡Tengo cien pesetas de la dama en la quinta fila cerca de la puerta! ¡Tengo cien pesetas! ¿Quién ofrece más? ¡¿Nadie?! ¡Es la última oferta! Una vez, dos veces, tres veces. ¡Se terminó! ¡Vendido a la graciosa dama que está con su esposo en la quinta fila cerca de la puerta! Ud. puede pagar al cajero, por favor, señora. 35
(*Todo el mundo mira para ver quién es la señora. ¡Es la señora Rodríguez!*)
La señora Rodríguez: ¿Quién? ¿Yo?

KEY WORDS AND PHRASES

a *prep.* at, to

allá *adv.* over there

aquí *adv.* here

atención *n.f.* attention

baja *adv.* low; **en voz baja** in a low voice, in a whisper

cajero *n.m.* cashier

cerca (de) *adv.* near

cien *num.* one hundred

comprar *v.* to buy; see **comprar** in the regular verb tables

con *prep.* with

dama *n.f.* lady

de *prep.* from, of

decir *v.* to say, tell; see **decir** in the irregular verb tables

dice *3d pers., s., pres. indic. of* **decir**; he/she says

dinero *n.m.* money

en *prep.* in

entran *3d pers., pl., pres. indic. of* **entrar**

entrar *v.* to enter

espantar *v.* to chase away

esta *dem. adj., f.s.* this; **estas** these

está *3d pers., s., pres. indic. of* **estar**; **¡Ella está loca!** She's crazy!

está hablando *pres. prog.* is talking

este *dem. adj., m.s.* this

feo *adj., m.s.* ugly

fila *n.f.* row; **la quinta fila** the fifth row

graciosa *adj., f.s.* gracious

grupo *n.m.* group

gustar *v.* to be pleasing to; **A la señora Rodríguez le gustan las ventas públicas.** Mrs. Rodríguez likes public sales.

hablando *pres. part. of* **hablar**; talking, speaking; **está hablando** is talking

hablar *v.* to talk, speak; see **hablar** in the regular verb tables

hermoso *adj., m.s.* beautiful

irse *refl. v.* to go away

levanta *3d pers., s., pres. indic. of* **levantar**; **Ella levanta la mano.** She raises her hand.

levantar *v.* to raise

llegan *3d pers., pl., pres. indic. of* **llegar**

llegar *v.* to arrive

los señores Rodríguez Mr. and Mrs. Rodríguez

mano *n.f.* hand

más *adv.* more

mí *pron.* me; **A mí no me gustan todas estas moscas.** I don't like all these flies.

mío, mía *poss. pron.* mine; **querido mío (querida mía)** my dear, darling

mira *3d pers., s., pres. indic. of* **mirar**; **Todo el mundo mira.** Everybody looks.

mirar *v.* to look (at), watch

monstruoso *adj., m.s.* monstrous

mosca *n.f.* fly (insect)

nadie *pron.* nobody

no sé I don't know; see **saber** in the irregular verb tables

noventa *num.* ninety

ochenta *num.* eighty

oferta *n.f.* offer

ofrece *3d pers., s., pres. indic. of* **ofrecer**

ofrecer *v.* to offer; review orthographical changing verbs in Work Unit 3

oír *v.* to hear; see **oír** in the irregular verb tables

oyen *3d pers., pl., pres. indic. of* **oír**; they hear

pagar *v.* to pay

para *prep.* for, in order (to)

pequeña *adj., f.s.* small, little

peseta *n.f.* peseta (monetary unit of Spain)

poder *v.* can, be able; see **poder** in the irregular verb tables

por *prep.* for, by; **por favor** please

pregunta *3d pers., s., pres. indic. of* **preguntar**; he/she asks

preguntar *v.* to ask

primera *ordinal num., f.* first; **la primera fila** the first row; see Ordinal Numbers later in this Work Unit.

pública *adj., f.s.* public

puede *3d pers., s., pres. indic. of* **poder**; **Ud. puede pagar** You can pay.

que *rel. pron.* who

querer *v.* to want; see **querer** in the irregular verb tables

querido *adj. & past part. of* **querer**; **querido mío (querida mía)** my dear, darling

¿quién? *pron.* who

quiere *3d pers., s., pres. indic. of* **querer**; he/she wants

quinta *ordinal num., f.* fifth; **la quinta fila** the fifth row; see Ordinal Numbers later in this Work Unit.

redonda *adj., f.s.* round

responde *3d pers., s., pres. indic. of* **responder**; he/she answers

responder *v.* to answer, respond, reply

saber *v.* to know; see **saber** in the irregular verb tables

sala *n.f.* room; **la sala de ventas** salesroom

salen *3d pers., pl., pres. indic. of* **salir**; **salen de casa** they leave (go out of) the house

salir *v.* to leave, to go out; see **salir** in the irregular verb tables

sé *1st pers., s., pres. indic. of* **saber**; **yo no sé** I don't know

se sientan *3d pers., pl., pres. indic. of* **sentarse**; they sit

se terminó *3d pers., s., pret. of* **terminarse**; it's finished, ended, terminated

señoras y señores ladies and gentlemen

sentarse *refl. v.* to sit down; see **sentarse** in the irregular verb tables

sesenta *num.* sixty

setenta *num.* seventy

sillón *n.m.* armchair

son *3d pers., pl., pres. indic. of* **ser**; they are

su *poss. adj.* his, her, their

subasta *n.f.* auction sale

subastador *n.m.* auctioneer

tan *adv.* so; **tan hermoso** so beautiful

tener *v.* to have; see **tener** in the irregular verb tables

tengo *1st pers., s., pres. indic. of* **tener**; I have

tercera *ordinal num., f.* third; see Ordinal Numbers later in this Work Unit.

terminarse *refl. v.* to terminate, end, finish

terminó *3d pers., s., pret. of* **terminar**; it's finished, ended; see Tense No. 3 in the regular verb tables

terribles *adj., m.f., pl.* terrible, awful

todas *adj., f., pl.* all; **todas estas moscas** all these flies

todo *pron., m.s.* all, everything; **todo el mundo** everybody

última *adj., f.s.* last

vender *v.* to sell; see **vender** in the regular verb tables

vendido *adj. & past part. of* **vender**; sold

venta *n.f.* sale

ver *v.* to see; see **ver** in the irregular verb tables

vestíbulo *n.m.* vestibule, entrance hallway

¡Vete! *2d pers., s. (tú), imper. of* **irse**; Go away! Shoo! Scat!

vez *n.f.* time; **una vez** one time, once; **dos veces** two times, twice

voz *n.f.* voice; **en voz baja** in a low voice, in a whisper

yo no sé I don't know; see **saber** in the irregular verb tables

EJERCICIOS

I. Seleccione la respuesta correcta según la lectura de esta lección. (Select the correct answer according to the reading selection in this Work Unit.)

1. La señora Rodríguez y su esposo (a) llegan (b) pueden (c) se sientan (d) salen de casa para ir a una venta pública. _____

2. A la señora Rodríguez le gustan mucho (a) las pequeñas mesas redondas (b) los vestíbulos (c) los sillones (d) las ventas públicas. _____

3. Los señores Rodríguez oyen la voz (a) de la dama en la primera fila (b) de la dama en la tercera fila (c) del cajero (d) del subastador. _____

4. La señora Rodríguez piensa que el sillón es muy (a) fea (b) feo (c) hermoso (d) hermosa. _____

5. La dama en la tercera fila ofrece (a) sesenta (b) setenta (c) ochenta (d) noventa pesetas. _____

6. La dama que ofrece sesenta pesetas está en la (a) primera (b) segunda (c) tercera (d) quinta fila. _____

7. La señora Rodríguez levanta la mano para (a) ofrecer cien pesetas (b) responder

(c) contestar (d) espantar las moscas. _____

8. Los señores Rodríguez están sentados en la quinta fila cerca (a) de la ventana

(b) de la puerta (c) del sillón (d) de la pequeña mesa redonda. _____

9. La persona que está hablando a un grupo de personas es (a) la señora

Rodríguez (b) el señor Rodríguez (c) la dama en la primera fila (d) el subas-

tador. _____

10. La señora Rodríguez quiere comprar (a) un sillón (b) un vestíbulo (c) una silla

(d) una pequeña mesa redonda. _____

II. **Acróstico. Complete este acróstico en español.**
Acrostic. Complete this acrostic in Spanish. In the boxes, write the Spanish words for the English.

1. is **hablando**	5. nobody
2. to sit down	6. third, *m.s.*
3. door	7. attention
4. there	8. round, *m.s.*

1. E
2. S
3. P
4. A
5. N
6. T
7. A
8. R

III. **Escriba frases con el vocabulario a continuación. Consulte la lectura de esta lección.**
(Write sentences with the vocabulary below. Consult the reading selection in this Work Unit.)

1. el cajero _____

2. cien pesetas _____

3. espantar _____

4. está hablando _____

5. feo _____

6. loco _____

7. mosca _____

8. primer _____

9. tercer _____

10. todo el mundo _____

NOTE: For the use of **primer** in number 8 of this exercise and **tercer** in number 9, see Ordinal Numbers (first to tenth) later in this Work Unit. In front of a masc. sing. noun, **primero** changes to **primer,** as in **el primer muchacho** / the first boy. The same change occurs in **tercero,** as in **el tercer hombre** / the third man.

IV. Shopping. Proficiency in Speaking and Writing.

Situation: You are with a friend at an auction sale because you want to buy a small round table for your bedroom. In this dialogue you are speaking for yourself in the role of *Tú.* Select one of your friends to talk with you. Let's say her name is María. All the vocabulary in this dialogue is in the story and in Key Words and Phrases, as well as in previous Work Units. After the dialogue is completed, write what you said on the lines.

María: **¿Te gusta la pequeña mesa redonda que está allá?**

Tú: _____
(Tell her you like it a lot but you don't like the flies in this salesroom.)

María: **Sí. Las moscas en esta sala de ventas son terribles.**

Tú: _____
(Ask María who the lady is in the first row who is offering sixty pesetas for the monstrous armchair.)

_____

_____

María: **Yo no sé. ¡Está loca!**

Tú: _____
(Tell María you want to buy the little round table.)

María: **¿Tienes dinero?**

Tú: _____
(Tell her you have one hundred pesetas.)

María: **¡Es mucho! ¿Tú quieres ofrecer todo tu dinero?**

Tú: _____
(Tell her yes, all my money.)

María: **¡Tú estás loca!**
(María will use **loco** if you are a boy.)

ESTRUCTURAS DE LA LENGUA

NEGATION OF VERB FORMS

(a) To make a verb form negative, place **no** in front of the verb form:

Yo comprendo.	**Yo no comprendo.**	**Estoy leyendo.**	**¿Trabaja Ud.?**
I understand.	*I do not understand.*	***No estoy leyendo.***	***¿No trabaja Ud.?***

(b) To make an infinitive negative, place **no** in front of it:

No entrar.	**No fumar.**	**No estacionar.**	**Prefiero no escuchar.**
Do not enter.	*Do not smoke.*	*Do not park.*	*I prefer not to listen.*
	or	or	
	No smoking.	*No parking.*	

(c) To make a verb form negative when there is a direct object pronoun, place **no** in front of the direct object pronoun:

No lo creo.	**No lo sé.**	**No la conozco.**
I don't believe it.	*I don't know it.*	*I don't know her.*

(d) To make a verb form negative when there is an indirect object pronoun, place **no** in front of the indirect object pronoun:

No le hablo a él.	**Pablo no me habla.**	**Juan no le habla a ella.**
I don't talk to him.	*Paul does not talk to me.*	*John does not talk to her.*

(e) To make a verb form negative when the verb is reflexive, place **no** in front of the reflexive pronoun:

Tú no te lavas.	**No me siento aquí.**	**No me llamo Juan.**
You do not wash yourself.	*I am not sitting here.*	*My name is not John.*

(f) To make a verb form negative when the verb is in the imperative, place **no** in front of the verb form:

¡No hable Ud.!	**¡No me escriba (Ud.)!**	**¡No entres (tú)!**
Do not talk!	*Do not write to me!*	*Do not enter!*

(g) With some negations, particularly with the verb **tener**, or in an interrogative statement before an unmodified noun object, the indefinite article is not ordinarily used:

¿Tiene Ud. libro? —No, señor, no tengo libro.
Do you have a book? —No, sir, I do not have a book.

NUMBERS

Cardinal Numbers: Zero to One Hundred Million

0	cero		62	sesenta y dos, *etc.*
1	uno, una		**70**	**setenta**
2	dos		71	setenta y uno, setenta y una
3	tres		72	setenta y dos, *etc.*
4	cuatro		**80**	**ochenta**
5	cinco		81	ochenta y uno, ochenta y una
6	seis		82	ochenta y dos, *etc.*
7	siete		**90**	**noventa**
8	ocho		91	noventa y uno, noventa y una
9	nueve		92	noventa y dos, *etc.*
10	**diez**		**100**	**ciento (cien)**
11	once		101	ciento uno, ciento una
12	doce		102	ciento dos, *etc.*
13	trece		**200**	**doscientos, doscientas**
14	catorce		300	trescientos, trescientas
15	quince		400	cuatrocientos, cuatrocientas
16	**dieciséis**		500	quinientos, quinientas
17	**diecisiete**		600	seiscientos, seiscientas
18	**dieciocho**		700	setecientos, setecientas
19	**diecinueve**		800	ochocientos. ochocientas
20	**veinte**		900	novecientos, novecientas
21	**veintiuno**		**1,000**	**mil**
22	**veintidós**		2,000	dos mil
23	**veintitrés**		3,000	tres mil, *etc.*
24	**veinticuatro**		100,000	cien mil
25	**veinticinco**		200,000	doscientos mil, doscientas mil
26	**veintiséis**		300,000	trescientos mil, trescientas
27	**veintisiete**			mil, *etc.*
28	**veintiocho**		**1,000,000**	**un millón (de + noun)**
29	**veintinueve**		2,000,000	dos millones (de + noun)
30	**treinta**		3,000,000	tres millones (de + noun), *etc.*
31	treinta y uno, treinta y una		100,000,000	cien millones (de + noun)
32	treinta y dos, *etc.*			
40	**cuarenta**			
41	cuarenta y uno, cuarenta y una			Approximate numbers
42	cuarenta y dos, *etc.*			
50	**cincuenta**			**unos veinte libros** / about
51	cincuenta y uno, cincuenta y una			(some) twenty books
52	cincuenta y dos, *etc.*			**unas treinta personas** /
60	**sesenta**			about (some) thirty persons
61	sesenta y uno, sesenta y una			

Simple arithmetical expressions

dos **y** dos son cuatro	$2 + 2 = 4$
diez **menos** cinco son cinco	$10 - 5 = 5$
tres **por** cinco son quince	$3 \times 5 = 15$
diez **dividido por** dos son cinco	$10 \div 2 = 5$

Ordinal Numbers: First to Tenth

primero, primer, primera	first	1st
segundo, segunda	second	2nd
tercero, tercer, tercera	third	3rd
cuarto, cuarta	fourth	4th
quinto, quinta	fifth	5th
sexto, sexta	sixth	6th
séptimo, séptima	seventh	7th
octavo, octava	eighth	8th
noveno, novena	ninth	9th
décimo, décima	tenth	10th

NOTE that beyond 10th the cardinal numbers are used instead of the ordinal numbers, but when there is a noun involved, the cardinal number is placed after the noun: **el día 15** (**el día quince** / the fifteenth day).

NOTE also that in titles of monarchs, *etc.* the definite article is not used between the person's name and the number, but it is in English: **Alfonso XIII** (**Alfonso Trece** / Alfonso the Thirteenth).

AND NOTE that **noveno** (9th) changes to **nono** in such titles: **Luis IX** (**Luis Nono** / Louis the Ninth).

EJERCICIOS

I. **Escriba la palabra que corresponde a los números según el modelo.** (Write the Spanish words for each arithmetical expression according to the model.)

Modelo: $3 + 3 = 6$ Tres y tres son seis. (Three and three are six.)

1. $8 + 7 = 15$ _____

2. $15 - 7 = 8$ _____

3. $6 \times 8 = 48$ _____

4. $21 \div 7 = 3$ _____

II. **Dé la palabra en español. Escriba el nombre de los números a continuación.** (Give the word in Spanish for the following numbers.)

1. 0 _____

2. 4 _____

3. 6 _____

4. 7 _____

5. 15 _____

6. 16 _____

7. 20 _____

8. 22 _____

9. 30 _____

10. 32 _____

11. 40 _____

12. 50 _____

13. 60 _____

14. 70 _____

15. 80 _____

III. Traduzca al español. (Translate into Spanish.)

1. Do not talk! (Use **Ud.**) _____

2. Do not write to me! (Use **Ud.**) _____

3. Do not enter! (Use **Tú**) _____

4. I do not understand. _____

5. Don't you have a book? (Use **Ud.**) _____

6. I prefer not to listen. _____

7. They prefer not to work. _____

8. Mary doesn't talk to me. _____

9. Jane doesn't talk to her. _____

10. I don't know it. _____

IV. Dictado. Escriba las oraciones que su profesor de español va a leer.
(Dictation. Write the sentences that your Spanish teacher is going to read.)

1. _____

2. _____

3. _____

V. La palabra misteriosa. Usando el vocabulario dado más abajo, busque las palabras españolas en el árbol. Las palabras están escritas horizontalmente, verticalmente, y a la inversa. Raye las palabras encontradas. Ponga en orden las siete letras que quedan para hallar la palabra misteriosa.
(**The mystery word.** Using the vocabulary given below, look for the Spanish words in the tree. The words are written horizontally, vertically, and in reverse. Draw a line through the words you find. Put in correct order the seven letters that remain in order to find the mystery word.)

Feliz / Happy	**regalo** / gift	**nieve** / snow
Navidad / Christmas	**amor** / love	**luz** / light

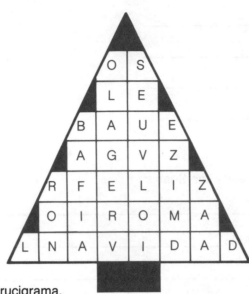

VI. Complete este crucigrama.

VI. Complete este crucigrama. (Complete this crossword.)

HORIZONTALES: 2. Una persona duerme sobre una _____ . 3. Sinónimo de **esposa.** 4. Forma del verbo **ser**, tercera persona, singular, en el presente de indicativo. 6. Gerundio de **hablar.** 7. Una persona se sienta en una _____ . 8. Forma del verbo **saber**, primera persona, singular, en el presente de indicativo. 9. Contrario de **hermoso.**

VERTICALES: 1. Contrario de **último.** 2. Sinónimo de **andar.** 5. Sinónimo de **esposo.**

KEY WORDS AND PHRASES

The following Spanish words with their English equivalents will help you understand what you are supposed to do in this crossword. The Spanish words you need to complete the crossword are not given in the following list—only the words in the statements above.

contrario *adj.* opposite, contrary
de *prep.* of
del (de + el > del) of the
dormir *v.* to sleep; see **dormir** in the irregular verb tables
duerme *3d pers., s., pres. indic. of* **dormir**; sleeps
en *prep.* in
forma *n.f.* form
gerundio *n.m.* gerund (equivalent to present participle in English)
horizontales *adj., m.f., pl.* horizontal

persona *n.f.* person
primera *ordinal num., f.s.* first
se sienta *3d pers., s., pres. indic. of* **sentarse**; sits
sentarse *refl. v.* to sit down (to sit oneself down)
sinónimo *n.m.* synonym (similar meaning)
sobre *prep.* on
tercera *ordinal num., f.s.* third
una *indef. art., f.s.* a, an, one
verbo *n.m.* verb
verticales *adj., m.f., pl.* vertical

VII. Culture. Appreciating Spanish Sculpture. Proficiency in Speaking and Writing.

Situation: You are on a field trip with your classmates. You are visiting a museum of photography where there is a large photograph of a statue of GOYA, another great Spanish artist. You have been asked to say a few words in Spanish about the photograph.

Look at the picture on the following page. It is a photograph entitled *Monumento a Goya*. The statue of Goya is in Madrid. Say aloud a few words in Spanish that come to your mind as you examine the photograph. You may use your own words or the following: **Goya, un gran artista español** / Goya, a great Spanish artist; **la estatua está en Madrid** / the statue is in Madrid; **impresionante** / impressive; **interesante** / interesting; **en un parque** / in a park; **el árbol, los árboles**; the tree, trees; **las hojas en los árboles** / the leaves on the trees; **gigante** / gigantic; **enorme** / enormous; **la piedra blanca** / white stone; **la escultura española** / Spanish sculpture; **majestuoso** / majestic.

Now, practice writing a list of Spanish words you would use in describing or telling a story about this picture.

_____

_____

_____

Madrid. Monumento a Goya.
Reprinted with permission of Oficina Nacional Española de Turismo, Paris.

VIII. Culture. Appreciating Spanish Art. Proficiency in Speaking and Writing.

Situation: You and a friend are at The National Gallery of Art in Washington, D.C. You are admiring a painting by GOYA. It is an impressive painting of *Doña Teresa Sureda* who is sitting majestically in a beautiful armchair.

Look at the picture on the following page. Say aloud a few words in Spanish that come to your mind while you appreciate looking at the picture. You may use your own words or, for starters, you may use the following:

La mujer está sentada en un sillón muy hermoso / the woman is sitting in a very beautiful armchair; **una silla de brazos** / an armchair; **una butaca** / an armchair; **tener** / to have; **ella tiene los ojos extraordinarios** / she has extraordinary eyes; **los rizos bonitos** / the pretty curls (ringlets); **en la frente** / on her forehead; **una expresión de dignidad, de orgullo** / an expression of dignity, of pride; **la nariz** / the nose; **la boca** / the mouth; **los brazos** / the arms; **elegante** / elegant; **los dedos** / the fingers; **las manos** / the hands; **una expresión pensativa en la cara** / a thoughtful expression on her face; **con aire noble, aristocrático** / with a noble, aristocratic air; **ella es muy hermosa** / she is very beautiful; **un vestido de seda** / a silk gown; **impresionante** / impressive; **majestuoso, magnífico, espléndido** / majestic, magnificent, splendid; **el arte español** / Spanish art; **Se llama Doña Teresa Sureda** / Her name is Doña Teresa Sureda.

How old do you think she is? **Yo pienso que ella tiene . . . años** / I think she is . . . years old.

To get you started, have you been provided with enough vocabulary to say a few words in Spanish?

A few verbs you may want to use are: **ver** / to see; **mirar** / to look (at); **tener** / to have; **ser** / to be; **estar** / to be; **pensar** / to think; **llamarse** / to be named. If you need any help with verb forms in the present indicative, review the previous Work Units or use the verb tables in the back pages.

Now, practice writing a few short, simple sentences in Spanish that you would use in a conversation with your friend about Goya's portrait / **el retrato** of this woman.

_____

_____

_____

_____

Doña Teresa Sureda by Francisco José de GOYA y Lucientes (1746–1828)
Courtesy of The National Gallery of Art, Washington, D.C.

Saint Martin and the Beggar *by EL GRECO (1541–1614)*
Courtesy of The National Gallery of Art, Washington, D.C.

¡Qué almuerzo!

In this scene, Clara and Francisco Rodríguez are with their friends María and José Sánchez. The Sánchez family lives in Puerto Rico but at present they are visiting their friends who now live in New York City. They are all with their children in Central Park to celebrate the 4th of July.

¡Viva el cuatro de julio!

Clara Rodríguez:	¡Vengan, todos, vengan! Vamos a sentarnos en la hierba ahora. Vamos a comenzar con los bocadillos de carne. Juana, ¿tienes los bocadillos?	
Juana:	¿Los bocadillos? ¿Qué bocadillos? No tengo los bocadillos. Tengo solamente los pasteles.	5
Clara Rodríguez:	¿No tienes los bocadillos de carne? Bueno, bueno . . . Pedro, tú tienes los bocadillos, de seguro.	
Pedro:	No, mamá, no los tengo. Tengo solamente los bizcochos.	
Clara Rodríguez:	Francisco, querido mío, tú tienes, seguramente, el rosbif, las chuletas de ternera, la carne de cerdo, el jamón, y el pollo.	10
Francisco Rodríguez:	No, querida mía, no los tengo. Tengo solamente tres cubos de helado.	
Clara Rodríguez:	María, tú tienes, seguramente, los bocadillos de carne, el rosbif, las chuletas de ternera, la carne de cerdo, el jamón, y el pollo.	
María Sánchez:	No, amiga mía. Tengo solamente bizcochos, pasteles, y postres.	15
Clara Rodríguez:	José, tú tienes, de seguro, las salchichas y los salchichones.	
José Sánchez:	No, amiga mía. Tengo solamente bizcochos, pasteles y postres. Tengo también una botella de agua mineral. El agua mineral es buena para la salud.	
Clara Rodríguez:	¡Qué almuerzo!	20
Los niños:	¡Qué fortuna! ¡Nosotros los niños preferimos los postres!	
Clara Rodríguez:	Pues, amigos míos, ¡vamos a comer los bizcochos, los pasteles, y el helado!	

KEY WORDS AND PHRASES

NOTE: The verbs in this vocabulary were used in previous Work Units. For a quick refresher of their forms, consult the regular verb tables and the irregular verb tables beginning on page 448.

abundante *adj.* abundant
agua *n.f.* **el agua** water; **las aguas; el agua mineral** mineral water
ahora *adv.* now
almuerzo *n.m.* lunch
amigo *n.m.*, **amiga** *n.f.*; **amigo mío, amiga mía** my friend; **amigos míos** my friends (This form is used when talking directly to a friend.)

bizcocho *n.m.* cookie, cake, sponge cake, biscuit
bocadillo *n.m.* snack, bite to eat, sandwich
botella *n.f.* bottle
bueno, buena *adj.*, *m., f., s.* good
carne *n.f.* meat
casa *n.f.* house; **en casa** at home
cerdo *n.m.* hog, pig; **la carne de cerdo** pork

chuleta *n.f.* chop; **las chuletas de ternera** veal chops

comedor *n.m.* dining room

comenzar *v.* to begin, start, commence

comer *v.* to eat

cubo *n.m.* bucket, pail

de *prep.* of, from; **de seguro** surely, for sure

deliciosos *adj., m. pl.* delicious

escena *n.f.* scene

especie *n.f.* species, kind, type

esta *dem. adj., f.s.* this; **en esta escena** in this scene

fortuna *n.f.* fortune, luck, chance; **¡Qué fortuna!** What luck!

hay there is, there are

helado *n.m.* ice cream

hierba *n.f.* grass

ir *v.* to go

jamón *n.m.* ham

los *def. art., m. pl.* **los pasteles** the pastries; **los** is also a *dir. obj. pron., m. pl.*, as in **los tengo** (I have them), **no los tengo** (I don't have them)

mamá *n.f.* mom

niños *n.m., pl.* children

nosotros los niños we kids

para *prep.* for

parque *n.m.* park

pastel *n.m.* pastry

persona *n.f.* person

pollo *n.m.* chicken

postre *n.m.* dessert

preferimos *1st pers., pl. (nosotros), pres. indic. of* **preferir**

preferir *v.* to prefer

pues *adv.* well, then

que *adj. & pron.* what, which; **¿Qué bocadillos?** What snacks? **¡Qué almuerzo!** What a lunch! **¡Qué fortuna!** What luck!

querido mío *m.s.,* **querida mía** *f.s.* my dear

rosbif *n.m.* roast beef

sabrosos *adj., m. pl.* tasty

salchicha *n.f.* sausage

salchichón *n.m.* thick, large sausage

salud *n.f.* health

seguramente *adv.* surely

seguro *adj.* sure; **de seguro** surely

sentarse *refl. v.* to sit (oneself) down

solamente *adv.* only

también *adv.* also, too

tener *v.* to have

tengo *1st pers., s. (yo), pres. indic. of* **tener**

ternera *n.f.* veal; **las chuletas de ternera** veal chops

tienes *2d pers., s. (tú), pres. indic. of* **tener**

todos *pron.* everybody

tomar *v.* to take; **van a tomar el almuerzo** they are going to have lunch

vamos *1st pers., pl. (nosotros), pres. indic. & imper. of* **ir**

¡Vamos a comenzar! Let's begin!

¡Vamos a comer! Let's eat!

¡Vamos a sentarnos! Let's sit down!

van *3d pers., pl. (ellos), pres. indic. of* **ir**; they are going

¡Vengan! *3d pers., pl. (Uds.), imper. of* **venir**; Come!

venir *v.* to come

¡Viva ...! Long live...!

vivir *v.* to live

EJERCICIOS

I. Seleccione la respuesta correcta según la lectura de esta lección. (Select the correct answer according to the reading selection in this Work Unit.)

1. Las ocho personas en esta escena van a tomar el almuerzo (a) en casa (b) en Puerto Rico (c) en la hierba (d) en el comedor _____

2. María y José Sánchez son (a) de Puerto Rico (b) de Nueva York (c) de España (d) de México _____

3. El rosbif y el jamón son (a) deliciosos (b) carnes (c) sabrosos (d) abundantes _____

4. Para el almuerzo hay solamente (a) carne (b) bocadillos (c) chuletas de ternera (d) pasteles y helado _____

5. Las ocho personas en esta escena van a comer (a) salchichas (b) salchichones (c) bocadillos (d) pasteles y helado _____

II. ¿Sí o No?

1. Francisco es el esposo de Clara Rodríguez. _____

2. María es la esposa de José Sánchez. _____

3. El Central Park es un parque en Puerto Rico. _____

4. El pastel es un postre. _____

5. El helado es una especie de carne. _____

III. Complete este crucigrama.(Complete this crossword.)

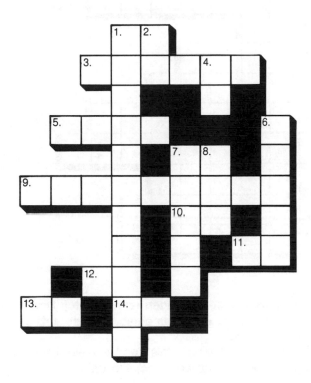

HORIZONTALES: **1.** Forma reflexiva del pronombre personal, tercera persona, s. y pl. **3.** Sustantivo del verbo *helar*. **5.** Líquido transparente. **7.** Adjetivo posesivo, segunda persona, singular. **9.** Nada más, únicamente. **10.** Contrario de *sí*. **11.** Complemento indirecto (indirect object pron.). **12.** Una preposición que se puede usar aquí en lugar de *sobre*. **13.** Complemento directo (direct object pron., f.s.). **14.** Forma reflexiva del pronombre personal, segunda persona, s.

VERTICALES: **1.** Sinónimo de *de seguro*. **2.** Artículo determinado, m.s. **4.** Preposición. **6.** Forma del verbo *tener,* pres. indic., tercera persona, s. **7.** Forma del verbo *tener*, pres. indic., primera persona, s. **8.** Número cardinal.

KEY WORDS AND PHRASES

The following Spanish words with their English equivalents will help you understand what you are supposed to do in this crossword. The Spanish words you need to complete the crossword are not given in the following list—only the words in the statements above. Other words not in this list were used in the crossword in Exercise VI, Work Unit 4. To refresh your memory, review that exercise and the vocabulary under it as well as the vocabulary beginning on page 86.

adjetivo *n.m.* adjective	**posesivo** *adj.* possessive
aquí *adv.* here	**preposición** *n.f.* preposition
artículo determinado definite article	**pronombre** *n.m.* pronoun
en lugar de in place of, instead of	**que se puede usar** that can be used
helar *v.* to freeze	**reflexiva** *adj., f.s.* reflexive
líquido *n.m.* liquid	**segunda** *adj., f.s.* second
nada más nothing more	**sustantivo** *n.m.* noun
número cardinal cardinal number (one, two, three, etc.)	**transparente** *adj.* transparent
	únicamente *adv.* only

IV. Acróstico. Complete las palabras en español.
   (**Acrostic.** Complete the words in Spanish.)

1. biscuit

2. eye

3. meat

4. to attack

5. surely

6. incredibie

7. language

8. lesson

9. eighty

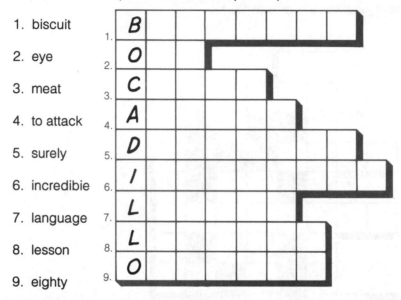

V. LETRA RELOJ. Cuatro palabras se esconden en este reloj: Una palabra de las doce a las tres, una palabra de las tres a las seis, una palabra de las seis a las nueve y, por fin, una palabra de las nueve a las doce.
   (**LETTER CLOCK.** Four words are hiding in this clock: one word from 12 to 3, one word from 3 to 6, one word from 6 to 9, and, finally, one word from 9 to 12.)

La misma letra es común a la palabra que sigue.

Este reloj no tiene agujas. ¡Es un reloj de palabras!

For an English translation of what to do in this exercise, review Exercise IV in Work Unit 1, page 19.

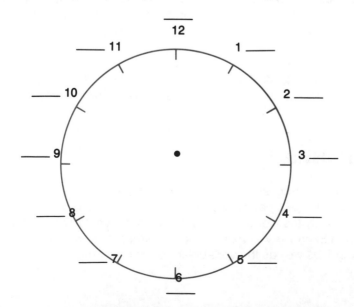

De las doce a las tres es un sinónimo del nombre **trabajo.**

De las tres a las seis es el antónimo de **nada.**

De las seis a las nueve es un animal, en el plural.

De las nueve a las doce es un sinónimo de **supremo.**

VI. Food and Drink. Proficiency in Speaking and Writing.

There is a new girl in your school from Puerto Rico. Her name is Lolita. She is in an advanced Spanish class because she speaks Spanish fluently. You want to get to know her so you can practice your Spanish!

A. Situation: Lolita plans to go on a picnic with you in the local park and she wants to know what you plan to bring. Tell her four kinds of foods you are bringing. You may use your own words or those used above when the Rodríguez family had their picnic with the Sánchez family. First, say them aloud, then practice writing them on these lines:

1. _____   3. _____

2. _____   4. _____

B. Situation: You are with Lolita at the meat section in a **supermercado** (supermarket). She wants to know what meats to plan for. Maybe ham, veal chops, pork, chicken?

1. _____   3. _____

2. _____   4. _____

C. Situation: Now you and Lolita are at the pastry and ice cream section in the supermarket. Tell her four things you prefer **(yo prefiero).**

1. _____   3. _____

2. _____   4. _____

D. Situation: Now for drinks **(las bebidas);** soft drink **(un refresco),** soda pop **(una gaseosa),** orange juice **(el jugo de naranja).** Tell Lolita four beverages you prefer.

1. _____   3. _____

2. _____   4. _____

E. Situation: Now that you and Lolita have decided on the meats, pastries, ice cream and drinks, you are wondering who is going to pay for everything. Choose Spanish verbs and other words you learned in these first four Work Units and use them in at least two sentences, for example: **Voy a pedir el dinero a mis padres** / I'm going to ask my parents for the money; **Tengo dinero en el tocador en mi dormitorio en casa** / I have money in the dresser in my room at home; **Vamos a trabajar el sábado para ganar dinero** / Let's work on Saturday to earn some money. If there are other verbs you prefer to use, review Work Units 1 to 4 and the tables of regular and irregular verbs.

1. _____

2. _____

ESTRUCTURAS DE LA LENGUA

TENSE NO. 1: PRESENTE DE INDICATIVO (PRESENT INDICATIVE)

This tense is used most of the time in Spanish and English. It indicates:

(a) An action or a state of being at the present time.

> EXAMPLES:
> **Hablo** español / *I speak* Spanish, or *I am speaking* Spanish, or *I do speak* Spanish.
> **Creo en** Dios / *I believe* in God.

(b) Habitual action.

> EXAMPLE:
> **Voy** a la biblioteca todos los días / *I go* to the library every day, or *I do go* to the library every day.

(c) A general truth, something that is permanently true.

> EXAMPLES:
> Seis menos dos **son** cuatro / Six minus two *are* four.
> El ejercicio **hace** maestro al novicio / Practice *makes* perfect.

(d) Vividness when talking or writing about past events.

> EXAMPLE:
> El asesino **se pone** pálido. **Tiene** miedo. **Sale** de la casa y **corre** a lo largo del río / The murderer *turns* pale. *He* is afraid. *He goes out* of the house and *runs* along the river.

(e) A near future.

> EXAMPLES:
> Mi hermano **llega** mañana / My brother *arrives* tomorrow.
> **¿Escuchamos** un disco ahora? / Shall we listen to a record now?

(f) An action or state of being that occurred in the past and *continues up to the present.* In Spanish this is an idiomatic use of the *Present tense* of a verb with **hace,** which is also in the *Present.*

> EXAMPLE:
> **Hace** tres horas que **miro** la televisión / *I have been watching* television for three hours.

(g) The meaning of *almost* or *nearly* when used with **por poco.**

> EXAMPLE:
> Por poco me **matan** / They almost *killed* me.

This tense is regularly formed as follows:

Drop the **–ar** ending of an infinitive, like **hablar,** and add the following endings: **o, as, a; amos, áis, an**
You then get: **hablo, hablas, habla;**
              hablamo, habláis, hablan

Drop the **–er** ending of an infinitive, like **beber,** and add the following endings: **o, es, e; emos, éis, en**
You then get: **bebo, bebes, bebe;**
              bebemos, bebéis, beben

Drop the **–ir** ending of an infinitive, like **recibir,** and add the following endings: **o, es, e; imos, ís, en**

You then get: **recibo, recibes, recibe;**

recibimos, recibís, reciben

NOTE: For verbs irregular in the present indicative, review Work Unit 3.

¿CUÁNTO TIEMPO HACE QUE + PRESENT TENSE . . . ?

(a) Use this formula when you want to ask *How long + the present perfect tense* in English:

¿Cuánto tiempo hace que Ud. estudia español? / How long have you been studying Spanish?

¿Cuánto tiempo hace que Ud. espera el autobús? / How long have you been waiting for the bus?

(b) When this formula is used, you generally expect the person to tell you how long a time it has been, *e g.,* one year, two months, a few minutes.

(c) This is used when the action began at some time in the past and continues up to the present moment. That is why you must use the present tense of the verb—the action of studying, waiting, *etc.* is still going on at the present.

HACE + LENGTH OF TIME + QUE + PRESENT TENSE

(a) This formula is the usual answer to the question above.

(b) Since the question is asked in terms of *how long*, the usual answer is in terms of time: a year, two years, a few days, months, minutes, *etc.*:

Hace dos años que estudio español / I have been studying Spanish for two years.

Hace veinte minutos que espero el autobús / I have been waiting for the bus for twenty minutes.

(c) The same formula is used if you want to ask *how many weeks, how many months, how many minutes,* etc.:

¿Cuántos años hace que Ud. estudia español? / How many years have you been studying Spanish?

¿Cuántas horas hace que Ud. mira la televisión? / How many hours have you been watching television?

¿DESDE CUÁNDO + PRESENT TENSE . . . ?

This is another way of asking *How long (since when) + the present perfect tense* in English, as given above.

¿Desde cuándo estudia Ud. español? / How long have you been studying Spanish?

PRESENT TENSE + DESDE HACE + LENGTH OF TIME

This formula is the usual answer to the previous question.

Estudio español desde hace dos años / I have been studying Spanish for two years.

ACABAR DE + INF.

The Spanish idiomatic expression **acabar de + inf.** is expressed in English as *to have just* + past participle.

In the present indicative:

> **María acaba de llegar** / Mary has just arrived.
> **Acabo de comer** / I have just eaten.
> **Acabamos de terminar la lección** / We have just finished the lesson.

NOTE: When you use **acabar** in the present tense, it indicates that the action of the main verb (+ inf.) has just occurred now in the present. In English, we express this by using *have just* + the past participle of the main verb: **Acabo de llegar** / I have just arrived.

COMMONLY USED IDIOMATIC EXPRESSIONS

> ### with **a**

a caballo on horseback
a eso de at about, around
a fines de around the end of
a mano by hand
a menudo often, frequently
a mi parecer in my opinion
a pie on foot
a principios de around the beginning of
a tiempo on time
a veces at times, sometimes
estar a punto de to be about to
> **Estoy a punto de salir.** / I am about to leave.
frente a in front of
junto a beside, next to
poco a poco little by little
ser aficionado a to be a fan of
> **Juana y Juan son aficionados a los deportes.** / Jane and John are sports fans.
uno a uno one by one

> ### with **a la**

a la derecha to (on, at) the right
a la española in the Spanish style
a la izquierda to (on, at) the left
a la semana weekly, per week
a la vez at the same time

> ### with **al**

al + *inf.* on, upon + *pres. part.*
> **Al entrar en la cocina, el muchacho comienza a comer.** / Upon entering into the kitchen, the boy begins to eat.
al aire libre in the open air, outdoors
al contrario on the contrary
al día current, up to date
al día siguiente on the following day, on the next day

al fin at last, finally
al lado de next to, beside
al menos at least
al mes monthly, per month
echar al correo to mail, post a letter

> ### with **con**

con frecuencia frequently
con los brazos abiertos with open arms
con mucho gusto with much pleasure, gladly
con permiso with your permission, excuse me
con rumbo a in the direction of
ser amable con to be kind to
> **Nosotros somos amables con nuestra profesora de español.** / We are kind to our Spanish teacher.

> ### with **cuanto, cuanta, cuantos, cuantas**

cuanto antes as soon as possible
¿Cuánto cuesta? How much does it cost? How much is it?
cuanto más ... tanto más ... the more ... the more. . .
> **Cuanto más estudio tanto más aprendo.** / The more I study the more I learn.
¿Cuántos años tienes tú (tiene Ud.)? / How old are you?
unas cuantas flores a few flowers
unos cuantos libros a few books

> ### with **dar**

dar a to face
> **El comedor da al jardín.** / The dining room faces the garden.
dar de beber a alguien to give something to drink to someone
dar de comer a alguien to give something to eat to someone
dar la mano a alguien to shake hands with someone
dar recuerdos a alguien to give one's regards (best wishes) to someone
dar un paseo to take a walk
dar un paseo en coche (en automóvil, en carro) to go for a drive
dar un paseo en bicicleta to go for a bicycle ride
dar una vuelta to go for a short walk, a stroll
dar voces to shout

> ### with **de**

acerca de about, concerning
billete de ida y vuelta a round-trip ticket
cerca de near, close to
de acuerdo in agreement, in accord
> **Estoy de acuerdo.** / I agree, I am in agreement.
de ayer en ocho días a week from yesterday
de buena gana willingly
de cuando en cuando from time to time
de día en día from day to day
de hoy en adelante from today on, from now on
de hoy en ocho días a week from today

de la mañana in the morning (Use this when a specific time is mentioned.)

   Tomo el desayuno a las ocho de la mañana. / I have breakfast at 8 o'clock in the morning.

de la noche in the evening (Use this when a specific time is mentioned.)

   Mi amigo llega a las nueve de la noche. / My friend is arriving at 9 o'clock in the evening.

de la tarde in the afternoon (Use this when a specific time is mentioned.)

   Voy a casa a las cuatro de la tarde. / I am going home at 4 o'clock in the afternoon.

de nada you're welcome

de noche by night, at night

de nuevo again

de prisa in a hurry

de rodillas kneeling, on one's knees

de vez en cuando from time to time

ir de compras to go shopping

no hay de qué you're welcome, don't mention it

un poco de a little of

EJERCICIOS

I. Escriba el número y la persona de los siguientes verbos que están en el presente de indicativo. (In Spanish write the number (singular or plural) and the person (primera persona, segunda persona, or tercera persona) of the following verbs that are in the present indicative tense.)

   Modelo: estudio   **Escriba:** singular, primera persona

1. hablo _____

2. voy _____

3. trabajamos _____

4. escriben _____

5. aprende _____

6. amo _____

7. andamos _____

8. vivimos _____

9. quepo _____

10. cierro _____

11. digo _____

12. sé _____

13. pongo _____

14. cuelgo _____

15. doy _____

16. cuesta _____

17. dais _____

18. soy _____

19. eres _____

20. son _____

II. Escriba el infinitivo de los siguientes verbos que están en el presente de indicativo.
(Write the infinitive of the following verbs that are in the present indicative.)

Modelo: voy   **Escriba:** ir

1. vamos _____
2. doy _____
3. acuerdo _____
4. almuerzo _____
5. cierran _____
6. quepo _____
7. cuezo _____
8. conozco _____
9. das _____
10. digo _____

11. duermen _____
12. estoy _____
13. sé _____
14. sabemos _____
15. hago _____
16. damos _____
17. muere _____
18. hacen _____
19. pienso _____
20. pueden _____

III. Escriba la forma femenina de los siguientes sustantivos. (Write the feminine equivalent of the following nouns; for example, husband/wife, woman/man, girl/boy, brother/sister.)

Modelo: esposo   **Escriba:** esposa

1. hombre _____
2. muchacho _____
3. hermano _____
4. tío _____
5. chico _____

6. padre _____
7. abuelo _____
8. dentista _____
9. profesor _____
10. amigo _____

IV. Escriba la forma femenina de los siguientes adjetivos. (Write the feminine form of the following adjectives.)

Modelo: hermoso   **Escriba:** hermosa

1. bello _____
2. feo _____
3. elegante _____
4. pequeño _____
5. pocos _____

6. viejos _____
7. interesantes _____
8. inglés _____
9. blanco _____
10. inteligente _____

111

V. Componga frases con el vocabulario de esta lección. (Write sentences using the vocabulary in this Work Unit.)

    Modelo: bocadillos (snacks)   **Escriba:** Juana, ¿tienes los bocadillos? (Jane, do you have the snacks?)

1. las salchichas _____

2. los bizcochos _____

3. el helado _____

4. fortuna _____

5. la carne _____

VI. Cambie el infinitivo del verbo al presente de indicativo. (Change the infinitive form of the verb to the present indicative tense.)

    Modelo: Yo no los *tener.*   **Escriba:** Yo no los tengo.

1. Yo no *saber* la lección. _____

2. Yo no *decir* la respuesta. _____

3. Nosotros *poder* escribir la lección. _____

4. ¿Qué *querer* Ud. hacer? _____

5. Yo *salir* de la escuela a las tres. _____

6. Estos libros *ser* excelentes. _____

7. María, ¿cuántos años *tener* tú? _____

8. Nosotros los estudiantes *ser* serios. _____

9. Yo *venir* a tu casa todos los días. Y María, ¿cuándo *venir* ella? _____

    _____

10. Yo *ver* la escuela. Y usted, ¿*ver* la casa? _____

VII. Responda en español en frases completas. (Answer in Spanish in complete sentences.)

    Modelo: ¿Adónde va Ud. esta tarde?   **Escriba:** Esta tarde voy a la playa.
    (Where are you going this   (This afternoon I am going to
    afternoon?)   the beach.)

1. ¿En qué cuarto de su casa mira Ud. la televisión? _____

    _____

2. ¿En qué mes del año comienzan las vacaciones de verano? _____

    _____

3. ¿En qué ciudad vive Ud.? _____

4. ¿Qué hace Ud. los sábados? _____

5. ¿Cuántos años tiene Ud.? ¿Y su madre? _____

VIII. Responda en español en frases completas. (Answer in Spanish in complete sentences.)

> **Modelo:** ¿Cuántos años hace que Ud. estudia español? (For how many years have you been studying Spanish?)
>
> **Escriba:** Hace dos años que estudio español. (I have been studying Spanish for two years.)

1. ¿Cuántos minutos hace que Ud. espera el autobús? _____

_____

2. ¿Cuánto tiempo hace que Ud. lee este libro? _____

_____

3. ¿Cuántas horas hace que Ud. mira la televisión? _____

_____

4. ¿Cuántos años hace que Ud. estudia español? _____

_____

5. ¿Desde cuándo estudia Ud. español? _____

_____

IX. Traduzca.

1. Mary has just arrived. _____

2. I have just eaten. _____

3. We have just finished the lesson. _____

4. I have just spoken. _____

5. I have just written a letter. _____

X. Varias palabras en una sola. Utilizando las letras en la palabra AFORTUNADAMENTE, ¿cuántas palabras puede used escribir? Escriba diez palabras, por lo menos.
(**Several words in one.** Using the letters in the word **AFORTUNADAMENTE,** how many words can you write? Write ten words, at least.)

> **AFORTUNADAMENTE**

1. _____   3. _____   5. _____   7. _____   9. _____

2. _____   4. _____   6. _____   8. _____   10. _____

XI. Humor. La adivinanza para hoy.
(**Humor.** The riddle for today.)

1. ¿Qué hay en el medio de Sevilla? (What is in the middle of Sevilla?)

Solución: _____   **113**

XII. Culture. Appreciation of Spanish Art. Proficiency in Speaking and Writing.

Situation: You and your classmates are on a field trip at The Toledo Museum of Art in Toledo, Ohio. You are admiring a painting by ZURBARÁN, a great Spanish artist, **un gran artista español.** It is a striking painting entitled *Return from Egypt.*

Look at the picture below. Say aloud a few words in Spanish that come to mind. You may use your own words or, just for starters, you may use the following:

El muchacho está sentado sobre un burro / The boy is sitting on a donkey; **una mujer tiene las manos sobre los hombros de una mujer que está llorando** / a woman has her hands on the shoulders of a woman who is weeping. A few nouns: **los hombres** / the men; **los hombros** / the shoulders; **las mujeres** / the women; **los muchachos** / the boys; **el niño** / the child; **la ropa** / the clothes, garments; **el sombrero** / the hat; **el cielo** / the sky; **el burro** / the donkey; **el gato** / the cat; **las barbas** / the beards; **el grupo de personas** / the group of persons. A few adjectives: **obscuro** / dark; **sentimental** / sentimental; **serio** / serious; **triste** / sad, sorrowful. A few verbs: **estar** / to be; **ser** / to be; **llorar** / to weep; **llevar** / to wear; **mirar** / to look at; **tener** / to have, to hold.

After you have said a few words in Spanish, write them in a list or use them in two or three sentences on these lines:

_____

_____

Return from Egypt by Francisco de ZURBARÁN
Courtesy of The Toledo Museum of Art, Toledo, Ohio

XIII. Educational Tour. Speaking and Writing Proficiencies.

Situation: You have just arrived in Madrid. You are on an educational tour with a group of students from your school. Your guide is **Señorita López** who is a student at the university. You have been asking her questions about Madrid. Now she has a few questions to ask you because she is impressed with your ability to speak some Spanish.

Participate in this dialogue. You are playing the role of **Tú.**

Señorita López: **Tú hablas español muy bien.**

Tú:

_____
(Thank her.)

Señorita López: **¿Cuántos años hace que tú estudias español?**

Tú:

_____
(Tell her you have been studying Spanish for two years.)

Señorita López: **¿Dónde vives?**

Tú:

_____
(Tell her in what city and country you live.)

Señorita López: **¿Qué asignaturas estudias en la escuela?**

Tú:

_____
(Tell her what subjects you are studying in school.)

Señorita López: **¿Te gusta mi país?**

Tú:

_____
(Tell her you like the country, the Spanish people, the culture, music, and art.)

Señorita López: **Gracias. Bueno. Ahora, vamos al Rastro. Es un mercado callejero de artículos baratos o de segunda mano.***

Tú:

_____
(Tell her, "Oh, the flea market!"

Señorita López: **Eso es. En español lo llamamos El Rastro.****

Tú:

_____
(Ask her what the word for "flea" is in Spanish: **¿Cómo se dice** _flea_ **en español?**)

Señorita López: **Se dice la pulga. Vamos. ¡Cuidado con las pulgas!*****

*un mercado callejero / street market; los artículos baratos / cheap articles; o / or; de segunda mano / secondhand.

**lo llamamos / we call it.

***¡Cuidado con las pulgas! / Watch out for the fleas!

XIV. Match the following commonly used Spanish idiomatic expressions with the English equivalents by writing the appropriate number on the line. They are in this Work Unit.

1. **a caballo**   ____ near

2. **a menudo**   ____ you're welcome

3. **poco a poco**   ____ to mail, post a letter

4. **a la derecha**   ____ from today on

5. **a la izquierda**   ____ often

6. **echar al correo**   ____ round-trip ticket

7. **con los brazos abiertos**   ____ kneeling, on one's knees

8. **dar la mano a alguien**   ____ from time to time

9. **un billete de ida y vuelta**   ____ on horseback

10. **cerca de**   ____ little by little

11. **de hoy en adelante**   ____ to go shopping

12. **ir de compras**   ____ to the right

13. **de vez en cuando**   ____ on the left

14. **de rodillas**   ____ with open arms

15. **de nada**   ____ to shake hands with someone

XV. Shopping. Speaking and Writing Proficiencies.

Situation: After your conversation with Señorita López, the other students in the group stay at the hotel for a snack. You and Señorita López go to El Rastro, the flea market. You are still playing the role of yourself, **Tú.** Refer to the commonly used idiomatic expressions in this Work Unit.

Señorita López: **¡Aquí estamos en El Rastro! ¿Quieres ir de compras?**

Tú: _____

(Tell her yes, you want to go shopping.)

Señorita López: **¿Qué piensas comprar? ¿Tienes bastante dinero?**

Tú: _____

(Tell her you have enough money and you want to buy **una almohada** / a pillow.)

Señorita López: **¡Una almohada! ¿Por qué?**

Tú: _____

(Tell her the pillow on your bed at the hotel is not good. Or, give another reason.)

Señorita López: **Bueno, si tú insistes.**

Tú: _____

(Say there are **(hay)** many inexpensive articles here. Then ask her where the pillows are.)

Señorita López: **Las almohadas están allá a la izquierda.**

Tú: _____

(Ask the saleslady **(la vendedora)** how much this pillow costs. Start with **Perdóneme, señora, con permiso** / Pardon me, madam, with your permission.)

La vendedora: **Esta almohada es muy bonita. No tiene muchas pulgas. Cuesta solamente diez centavos.***

Tú: _____

(Tell her you'll take it / **La tomo.**)

La vendedora: **¡Cuidado con las pulgas, señorita!**

Tú: _____

(Thank her and say good-bye. Say, "Have a nice day!"**)

*diez centavos / ten cents
**Pase un buen día.

The Return of the Prodigal Son by Bartolomé Esteban MURILLO (1617–1682)
Courtesy of The National Gallery of Art, Washington, D.C.

Appreciating Spanish Art. Speaking and Writing Proficiencies.

Look at the above photograph. The painting was done by MURILLO, a great Spanish artist / **un gran artista español.** Say aloud a few words in Spanish that come to mind as you look at the picture. You may use your own words or the following:

Este cuadro de Murillo es soberbio / This painting by Murillo is superb. Other adjectives: **excelente** / excellent; **espléndido** / splendid; **magnífico** / magnificent; **majestuoso** / majestic. A few nouns: **el padre** / the father; **el hombre viejo** / the old man; **el joven, los jóvenes** / the young man, young men; **la mujer, las mujeres** / the woman, women; **el muchacho, los muchachos** / the boy, boys; **el ternero** / the calf; **el perrito** / the little dog; **la ropa** / the clothes, clothing, garments; **los vestidos** / clothes, garments; **los pies** / feet; **los pies desnudos** / bare feet; **la barba** / beard. A few verbs: **ver** / to see; **yo veo** / I see; **hablar; el padre habla con su hijo; los dos jóvenes hablan; ser, estar; el joven está de rodillas** / the young man is kneeling. Other words: **con los brazos abiertos** / with open arms.

Now, practice writing the words you said or put a few together in two sentences:

1. _____

2. _____

Work Unit 6

Have you or any of your friends ever thought of leaving home? Of running away? Wait! Give it a second thought. Read what happens to Pablo in the following story, which is based on the parable of the prodigal son. There is something of value to be learned from Pablo's experience.

NOTE: An English translation is provided between the lines in this story to help you understand instantly the variety of verb tenses, vocabulary, and sentence structure that you might have forgotten since you first began to study Spanish.

Un padre y sus dos hijos

A Father and His Two Sons

Un padre tenía dos hijos que se llamaban Andrés y Pablo. Andrés tenía veinte años y
A father had two sons named Andrew and Paul. Andrew was twenty years old and

Pablo tenía dieciocho.
Paul was eighteen.

Un día, Pablo, el más joven, le dijo a su padre:
One day, Paul, the younger, said to his father:

—Padre, dame, por favor, la tierra de tu propiedad que me pertenece. Quiero partir para
"Father, give me, please, the land of your property that belongs to me. I want to leave

buscar mi libertad y para divertirme. Para hacer esto, necesito dinero. No me gusta vivir en   5
to find my freedom and to enjoy myself. To do this, I need money. I do not like living in

este pequeño pueblo porque no estoy contento aquí. Quiero ir a Nueva York donde hay
this small town because I am not happy here. I want to go to New York where there are

muchas diversiones y mucho que hacer.
many amusements and a lot to do."

El padre no sabía que hacer. Pensó en la petición de su hijo y después de algunos
The father did not know what to do. He thought of his son's request and, after a few

días, vendió la mitad de su tierra y le dio el dinero a su hijo. La otra mitad era la
days, he sold half of his land and gave the money to his son. The other half was the

herencia para Andrés, el hijo mayor, la cual recibiría a la muerte del padre.   10
inheritance for Andrew, the older son, which he would receive at the father's death.

Pablo tomó el dinero, que era una gran fortuna, y fue a Nueva York. En aquella ciudad
Paul took the money, which was a great fortune, and went to New York. In that city

se divertía todas las noches hasta la madrugada en las tabernas gastando mucho dinero.
he enjoyed himself every night until dawn in the taverns spending a lot of money.

Todos los días iba al cine, al teatro y a otros espectáculos divertidos con sus nuevos
Every day he went to the movies, the theater, and other entertaining attractions with his new

amigos. A las muchachas les daba regalos, dulces, y flores. Durante el día, dormía y
friends. To the girls he gave presents, candy, and flowers. During the day, he slept and

durante la noche se divertía. Estaba muy contento.
during the night he enjoyed himself. He was very happy.   15

Después de dos años, cuando Pablo había gastado toda la fortuna que su padre le
After two years, when Paul had spent the entire fortune that his father

había dado, no tenía nada que comer. Pidió dinero a sus amigos y a sus amigas pero
had given to him, he had nothing to eat. He asked his friends and girlfriends for money but

no le dieron nada, diciendo que no tenían bastante dinero.
they did not give him anything, saying that they did not have enough money.

Pablo fue a buscar trabajo para ganarse la vida, pero no halló nada.
Paul went to look for work to earn his living, but he found nothing.

Pablo se puso a pensar. Se dijo: No tengo más dinero. He gastado toda la
Paul began to think. He said to himself: I have no more money. I have spent the whole 20

fortuna que mi padre me dio como herencia. No tengo dinero para pagar la habitación
fortune that my father gave me as an inheritance. I don't have money to pay for the room

donde vivo. Tengo mucha hambre y no tengo nada que comer. Regresaré a la casa
where I live. I am very hungry and I have nothing to eat. I will return to the house

de mi padre porque él me ama.
of my father because he loves me.

Regresó a la casa de su padre. Pablo estaba sucio y los vestidos que llevaba también
He returned to his father's house. Paul was dirty and the clothes he wore were also

estaban sucios y rasgados. Cuando su padre lo vio llegar a la puerta de su casa,
dirty and torn. When his father saw him arriving at the door of his house, 25

lo reconoció inmediatamente, a pesar de su apariencia diferente. El padre corrió al encuentro
he recognized him immediately, in spite of his different appearance. The father ran to meet

de su hijo, lo recibió con abrazos y besos paternales.
his son, received him with paternal hugs and kisses.

De rodillas, Pablo le dijo a su padre:
On his knees, Paul said to his father:

—Padre mío, perdóname. He sido tonto, he hecho tantas cosas tontas, gasté
"My father, pardon me. I have been foolish, I have done so many foolish things. I spent

todo el dinero que tú me diste, no pude hallar trabajo para vivir, no tenía nada que comer. Mis
all the money that you gave me, I could not find any work to live, I had nothing to eat. My 30

amigos nuevos no me dieron ninguna ayuda. Padre, no merezco llamarme tu hijo.
new friends did not give me any help. Father, I don't deserve to call myself your son.

Perdóname, padre mío. ¿Puedes aceptarme en tu casa?
Forgive me, father. Can you accept me in your house?"

El padre respondió:
The father answered:

—Hijo mío, mi casa es tu casa. Todo lo que tengo es tuyo. Tú eres mi hijo. Por
"My son, my house is your house. Everything I have is yours. You are my son. Of

supuesto, te acepto. Entra en tu casa. Tú te habías perdido y yo te he encontrado.
course, I accept you. Come into your house. You had lost yourself and I have found you." 35

Entretanto, Andrés, el hijo mayor, regresó a casa por la noche después de haber
Meanwhile, Andrew, the older son, returned home in the evening after having

trabajado en los campos de su padre todo el día. Cuando vio a su hermano que había
worked in his father's fields all day long. When he saw his brother who had

regresado, se enojó al ver que el padre había recibido a su hermano depravado
returned, he got angry upon seeing that the father had received his corrupted brother

en la casa. Dijo a su padre:
in the house. He said to his father:

—Padre mío, ¿cómo puedes aceptar a tu hijo menor después de malgastar tu dinero y
"My father, how can you accept your younger son after spending your money and   40

después de perder dos años de su vida no haciendo más que divertirse? Este
after wasting two years of his life doing nothing more than having a good time? This

hermano ingrato no merece llamarse tu hijo y no merece
ungrateful brother doesn't deserve to call himself your son and doesn't deserve

llamarse mi hermano.
to call himself my brother."

El padre le contestó:
The father answered him:

—Hijo mío, tu hermano se había perdido. Estaba muerto y ahora vive. Pablo
"My son, your brother had lost himself. He was dead and now he lives. Paul   45

se ha encontrado y nosotros lo hemos encontrado también. Entra y vamos a comer los
has found himself and we have found him too. Come in and let's eat, the

tres juntos. Ahora estamos contentos, gracias a Dios.
three of us together. Now we are happy, thank God."

KEY WORDS AND PHRASES

abrazos *n.m.* hugs
al ver upon seeing
algunos *adj., m. pl.* some, a few
amar *v.* to love
apariencia *n.f.* appearance
aquella *dem. adj., f.s.* that
ayuda *n.f.* help
besos *n.m.* kisses
buscar *v.* to look for
campos *n.m.* fields
como *conj.* as
contento *adj.* happy, content
contestó *3d pers., s., pret. of* **contestar**; he replied
corrió *3d pers., s., pret. of* **correr**; he ran
cual *rel. pron.* **la cual** which
daba *3d pers., s., imperf. indic. of* **dar**; he gave, used to give
dame *2d pers., s. (tú), imper. of* **dar**; give + **me**; give me
depravado *adj.* depraved, corrupted
después *adv.* after
diciendo *pres. part. of* **decir**; saying
dieron *3d pers., pl., pret. of* **dar**; they gave
dijo *3d pers., s., pret. of* **decir**; he said
dio *3d pers., s., pret. of* **dar**; he gave
Dios God
diste *2d pers., s. (tú), pret. of* **dar**; you gave
diversiones *n.f., pl.* amusements
divertidos *adj., m. pl.* entertaining, enjoyable
divertirme *refl. v.* to have myself a good time
dormía *3d pers., s., imperf. indic. of* **dormir**; he slept, used to sleep
dulces *n.m., pl.* candies
encuentro *n.m.* encounter, meeting
entra *2d pers., s. (tú), imper. of* **entrar**; come in

entretanto *adv.* meanwhile
era *3d pers., s., imperf. indic. of* **ser**; was
espectáculo *n.m.* show
estaba *3d pers., s., imperf. indic. of* **estar**; he was
este *dem. adj., m.s.* this
esto *dem. pron., neuter* this
fortuna *n.f.* fortune
fue *3d pers., s., pret. of* **ir**; he went
ganarse *refl. v.* **la vida** to earn a living
gastado *past part. of* **gastar**; spent
gastando *pres. part. of* **gastar**; spending
gastar *v.* to spend (money)
gasté *1st pers., s., pret. of* **gastar**; I spent
gran, grande *adj.* great, big
gustar *v.* to be pleasing to, to like; **no me gusta vivir aquí** I don't like living here
había dado *3d pers., s., pluperf. indic. of* **dar**; he had given; **había gastado** he had spent; **había regresado** he had returned
habías perdido *2d pers., s., pluperf. indic. of* **perder**; you had lost
habitación *n.f.* room
haciendo *pres. part. of* **hacer**; doing
halló *3d pers., s., pret. of* **hallar**; he found
hasta *adv.* until
he encontrado *1st pers., s., pres. perf. of* **encontrar**; I have found; **he gastado** I have spent; **he hecho** I have done; **he sido** I have been
hemos encontrado *1st pers., pl., pres. perf. of* **encontrar**; we have found
herencia *n.f.* inheritance
iba *3d pers., s., imperf. indic. of* **ir**; he went, used to go

ingrato *adj.* ungrateful

joven *adj.* young; **el más joven** the younger

juntos *adj.* together

la cual *rel. pron.* which

le *indir. obj. pron.* to him; **le dijo** he said to him

libertad *n.f.* liberty, freedom

llegar *v.* to arrive

llevaba *3d pers., s., imperf. indic. of* **llevar**; he was wearing

lo *dir. obj. pron.* him

lo que *pron.* that; **todo lo que tengo** all that I have

madrugada *n.f.* dawn

malgastar *v.* to squander, spend foolishly

más *adv.* more; **el más joven** the younger

mayor *adj.* older

menor *adj.* younger; **tu hijo menor** your younger son

merecer *v.* to merit, deserve

merezco *1st pers., s., pres. indic. of* **merecer**; I deserve; **él no merece** he doesn't deserve

mitad *n.f.* half

mucho que hacer a lot to do

muerte *n.f.* death; **muerto** *adj.* dead

nada que comer nothing to eat

necesito *1st pers., s., pres. indic. of* **necesitar**; I need

ninguna *adj., f.s.* not any; **ninguna ayuda** no help, not any help

no me gusta vivir en este pueblo I don't like living in this town

otra *adj., f.s.* other

pagar *v.* to pay

partir *v.* to leave

pedir *v.* to ask for, request

pensó *3d pers., s., pret. of* **pensar; pensó en** he thought about

perder *v.* to lose, to waste; **perderse** *refl. v.* to lose oneself

perdido *past part. of* **perder**; lost; **tú te habías perdido** you had been lost

perdonar *v.* to pardon, to forgive

pertenece *3d pers., s., pres. indic. of* **pertenecer** to belong

pesar *v.* to weigh; **a pesar de** in spite of

petición *n.f.* request

pidió *3d pers., s., pret. of* **pedir**; he requested, asked for

poder *v.* to be able, can

poner *v.* to put; **ponerse a** to begin to

propiedad *n.f.* property

pude *1st pers., s., pret. of* **poder**; I could

pueblo *n.m.* town

puedes *2d pers, s., pres. indic. of* **poder**; you can

puso *3d pers. s., pret. of* **poner; se puso a** he began to

que *rel. pron.* who, which, that; **que hacer** what to do

rasgados *adj., m. pl.* torn

recibió *3d pers., s., pret. of* **recibir**; he received

recibiría *3d pers., s., cond. of* **recibir**; he would receive

reconoció *3d pers., s., pret. of* **reconocer**; he recognized

regresar *v.* to return; **yo regresaré** I will return; **él regresó** he returned

respondió *3d pers., s., pret. of* **responder**; he answered

sabía *3d pers., s., imperf. indic. of* **saber**; **no sabía que hacer** he did not know what to do

se dijo *3d pers., s., pret. of* **decirse**; he said to himself

se divertía *3d pers., s., imperf. indic. of* **divertirse**; he enjoyed himself

se enojó *3d pers., s., pret. of* **enojarse**; he got annoyed, angry

se ha encontrado *3d pers., s., pres. perf. of* **encontrarse**; he has found himself

se había perdido *3d pers., s., pluperf. indic. of* **perderse**; he had lost himself

se llamaban *3d pers., pl., imperf. indic. of* **llamarse**; were called

se puso *3d pers., s., pret. of* **ponerse; se puso a** he began to

su, sus *poss. adj.* his, her, your, their

sucio *adj.* dirty

supuesto *adj.* supposed; **por supuesto** of course

taberna *n.f.* tavern

tantas *adj.* so many

tenía *3d pers., s., imperf. indic. of* **tener**; had

tenía veinte años he was twenty years old

tierra *n.f.* land

todo *pron.* all; **todo lo que tengo** all that I have

tomó *3d pers., s., pret. of* **tomar**; he took

tonto *adj.* foolish

trabajado *past part. of* **trabajar; después de haber trabajado** after having worked

tu *poss. adj., fam.* your

tuyo *poss. pron.* yours

vendió *3d pers., s., pret. of* **vender**; he sold

vestidos *n.m.* clothes

vida *n.f.* life, living

vio *3d pers., s., pret. of* **ver**; he saw

vive *3d pers., s., pres. indic. of* **vivir**; he lives

EJERCICIOS

I. Seleccione la respuesta correcta conforme al significado de la lectura en esta lección.
(Select the correct answer that corresponds to the meaning of the reading selection in this Work Unit.)

1. ¿Cuántos hijos tenía el padre?
   (a) cinco (b) cuatro (c) tres (d) dos _____

2. ¿Cuántos años tenía Andrés?
   (a) diecisiete (b) dieciocho (c) diecinueve (d) veinte _____

3. ¿Cuántos años tenía Pablo?
   (a) diecisiete (b) dieciocho (c) diecinueve (d) veinte _____

4. Pablo quiere partir para
   (a) trabajar y ganar dinero (b) buscar su libertad y para divertirse (c) pedir dinero a sus amigos (d) dar regalos, dulces y flores a las muchachas _____

5. Después de haber gastado toda la fortuna, Pablo no tenía nada que
   (a) aceptar (b) amar (c) decir (d) comer _____

II. ¿Sí o No?

1. El padre vendió la mitad de su tierra y le dio el dinero a Pablo. _____

2. En Nueva York Pablo halló trabajo. _____

3. Pablo iba con frecuencia a la escuela. _____

4. Pablo quiere ir a Nueva York para divertirse. _____

5. Después de dos años, Pablo no tenía dinero para pagar la habitación donde vivía. _____

6. Al regresar a su casa, Pablo estaba sucio y los vestidos que llevaba también estaban sucios y rasgados. _____

7. Cuando el padre vio a Pablo llegar a la puerta de su casa, no lo reconoció. _____

8. Andrés estaba muy contento al ver a su hermano después de dos años. _____

9. Andrés cree que su hermano es ingrato. _____

10. El padre, Andrés y Pablo van a comer los tres juntos, y ahora están contentos. _____

III. Sopa de letras. Busque cuatro sinónimos del adjetivo contento. Los cuatro sinónimos pueden aparecer de derecha a izquierda, de izquierda a derecha, de abajo arriba y viceversa.
(**Alphabet soup.** In this puzzle, find four synonyms of the adjective **contento.** The four synonyms can appear from right to left, from left to right, from bottom to top, from top to bottom. **Tip:** Look up **contento** in the vocabulary beginning on page 481.)

G	A	C	S	E	X
C	O	N	A	N	O
I	Z	P	T	C	D
F	E	L	I	Z	A
K	L	Á	S	A	T
O	Q	C	F	N	N
R	I	I	E	T	A
J	M	D	C	O	C
N	P	O	H	P	N
D	E	L	O	X	E

IV. Putting It All Together. Speaking and Writing Proficiencies.

Situation: Today it is your turn **(te toca a ti)** to go to the front of the class and say a few sentences about the story, **Un padre y sus dos hijos.** Look at the five sentences below. The words are scrambled. Put them together in the right order and read them aloud to your teacher and classmates. For practice, write them on the lines.

1. hijos / dos / esta / en / historia / tiene / el padre.

   _____

2. años / veinte / tiene / el hijo mayor / Andrés.

   _____

3. años / dieciocho / tiene / el hijo menor / Pablo.

   _____

4. quiere / Pablo / partir / buscar / para / y / su libertad / divertirse.

   _____

5. vende / el padre / de su tierra / la mitad / y / el dinero / le da / a Pablo.

   _____

ESTRUCTURAS DE LA LENGUA

TENSE NO. 2: IMPERFECTO DE INDICATIVO (IMPERFECT INDICATIVE)

This is a past tense. Imperfect suggests incomplete. The imperfect tense expresses an action or a state of being that was continuous in the past and its completion is not indicated. This tense is used, therefore, to express:

(a)   An action that was going on in the past at the same time as another action.

EXAMPLE:

Mi hermano **leía** y mi padre **hablaba** / My brother *was reading* and my father *was talking*.

(b)   An action that was going on in the past when another action occurred.

EXAMPLE:

Mi hermana **cantaba** cuando yo entré / My sister *was singing* when I came in.

(c)   An action that a person did habitually in the past.

EXAMPLES:

Cuando **estábamos** en Nueva York, **íbamos** al cine todos los sábados / When *we were* in New York, *we went* to the movies every Saturday; When *we were* in New York, *we used to go* to the movies every Saturday.

Cuando **vivíamos** en California, **íbamos** a la playa todos los días / When *we used to live* in California *we would go* to the beach every day.

NOTE: In this last example, *we would go* looks like the conditional, but it is not. It is the imperfect tense in this sentence because habitual action in the past is expressed.

(d)   A description of a mental, emotional, or physical condition in the past.

EXAMPLES:

(mental condition) **Quería** ir al cine / I *wanted* to go to the movies.
　　　　Common verbs in this use are **creer, desear, pensar, poder, preferir, querer, saber, sentir.**
(emotional condition) **Estaba** contento de verle / I *was* happy to see him.
(physical condition) Mi madre **era** hermosa cuando **era** pequeña / My mother *was* beautiful when she *was* young.

(e)   The time of day in the past.

EXAMPLES:

¿Qué hora **era?** / What time *was* it?
Eran las tres / It *was* three o'clock.

(f)   An action or state of being that occurred in the past and *lasted for a certain length of time* prior to another past action. In English it is usually translated as a Pluperfect tense and is formed with *had been* plus the present participle of the verb you are using. It is like the special use of the **Presente de indicativo** except that the action or state of being no longer exists at present. This is an idiomatic use of the *imperfect tense* of a verb with **hacía**, which is also in the *imperfect*.

EXAMPLE:

Hacía tres horas que **miraba** la televisión cuando mi hermano entró / I *had been watching* television for three hours when my brother came in.

The Infanta María Teresa by Diego Rodríguez de Silva y VELÁZQUEZ
Courtesy, Museum of Fine Arts, Boston.

V. Appreciating Spanish Art. Speaking and Writing Proficiencies.

Situation: You and a friend are visiting The Museum of Fine Arts in Boston, Massachusetts. You are admiring a painting by VELÁZQUEZ, a great Spanish artist, **un gran artista español** (a great Spanish painter, **un gran pintor español**). It is a portrait **(un retrato)** entitled *La Infanta María Teresa.*

Look at the picture on the facing page. You and your friend are having a conversation about it. Your friend is playing the role of *Tu amigo (amiga)* and you are *Tú.*

Tu amigo (amiga):	**¿Te gusta este retrato?** (Do you like this portrait?)
Tú:	_____ (Tell your friend: Yes, of course, I like it very much. It is superb. Who is it?)
Tu amigo (amiga):	**Es la Infanta María Teresa. ¡Me parece que la Infanta es como una gran muñeca adorable!** (It's the Infanta María Teresa. It seems to me that the Infanta is like a large adorable doll!)
Tú:	_____ (Ask your friend: Do you like the hairdo / **el peinado**?)
Tu amigo (amiga):	**Es elegante. Mi profesora de español tiene el peinado de ese estilo.** (It is elegant. My Spanish teacher has a hairdo in that style.)
Tú:	_____ (Tell your friend: And her dress is glorious.)
Tu amigo (amiga):	**¡Qué ojos maravillosos! Y las manos son extraordinarias.**
Tú:	_____ (Tell your friend: I want to buy a dress like that one **(como ése)** for my mother for her birthday.)
Tu amigo (amiga):	**Es una buena idea. Ahora, ¿adónde vamos?**
Tú:	_____ (Tell your friend: I want to go to the hairstyling salon **(a la peluquería)** across the street **(al otro lado de la calle).**
Tu amigo (amiga):	**¿Por qué?**
Tú:	_____ (Say to your friend: Don't you know?)

Now do this dialogue again but this time switch roles. You may add your own ideas.

(g) An indirect quotation in the past.

> EXAMPLE:
> *Present*: Dice que **quiere** venir a mi casa / He says *he wants* to come to my house.
> *Past*:   Dijo que **quería** venir a mi casa / He said *he wanted* to come to my house.

This tense is regularly formed as follows:

Drop the **–ar** ending of an infinitive, like **hablar,** and add the following endings:
aba, abas, aba; ábamos, abais, aban

You then get: **hablaba, hablabas, hablaba;**
                    hablábamos, hablabais, hablaban

The usual equivalent in English is: I was talking OR I used to talk OR I talked; you were talking OR you used to talk OR you talked, *etc.*

Drop the **–er** ending of an infinitive, like **beber,** or the **–ir** ending of an infinitive, like **recibir,** and add the following endings: **ía, ías, ía; íamos, íais, ían**

You then get: **bebía, bebías, bebía;**
                    bebíamos, bebíais, bebían

                    recibía, recibías, recibía;
                    recibíamos, recibíais, recibían

The usual equivalent in English is: I was drinking OR I used to drink OR I drank; you were drinking OR you used to drink OR you drank, *etc*; I was receiving OR I used to receive OR I received; you were receiving OR you used to receive OR you received, *etc.*

Verbs irregular in the imperfect indicative

ir / to go   **iba, ibas, iba;** (I was going, I used to go, *etc.*)
                    íbamos, ibais, iban

ser / to be   **era, eras, era;** (I was, I used to be, *etc.*)
                    éramos, erais, eran

ver / to see   **veía, veías, veía;** (I was seeing, I used to see, *etc.*)
                    veíamos, veíais, veían

EJERCICIOS

I. **Cambie los verbos de las siguientes frases al imperfecto de indicativo.** (Change the verbs in the following sentences from the presente de indicativo to the imperfecto de indicativo. First, review the formation of this new tense above.)

Modelo: Mi hermana lee un buen libro. (My sister is reading a good book.)
Escriba: Mi hermana leía un buen libro. (My sister was reading a good book.)

1. José habla español. _____

2. Yo hablo español e inglés. _____

3. Nosotros trabajamos todos los días. _____

4. Tomo crema con el café. _____

5. Juanita bebe leche todas las mañanas. _____

6. Para el desayuno bebo café con leche. _____

7. Mis padres siempre reciben cartas en el correo. _____

8. Vivimos en esta casa. _____

9. Voy al cine los sábados. _____

10. ¿Qué hora es? _____

11. Son las tres. _____

12. Veo a mi amiga todas las noches. _____

13. Vemos muchas películas en español. _____

14. La casa es blanca. _____

II. Escriba las seis formas del verbo hablar en el imperfecto de indicativo.

_____

III. Escriba las seis formas del verbo beber en el imperfecto de indicativo.

_____

IV. Escriba las seis formas del verbo recibir en el imperfecto de indicativo.

_____

V. Escriba las seis formas del verbo ir en el imperfecto de indicativo.

_____

VI. Escriba las seis formas del verbo ser en el imperfecto de indicativo.

_____

VII. Escriba las seis formas del verbo ver en el imperfecto de indicativo.

_____

VIII. Escriba respuestas afirmativas según los modelos. (Write affirmative answers according to the models.)

    Modelos: a. ¿Cantaba Ud. ayer? (Were you singing yesterday?)
                a. Sí, yo cantaba ayer. (Yes, I was singing yesterday.)

                b. ¿Y los alumnos? (And the students?)
                b. Los alumnos cantaban ayer, también. (The students were singing yesterday also.)

A. **Verbos con la terminación –AR**

    1. a. ¿Bailaba Ud. todas las noches? _____

       b. ¿Y Juanita? _____

129

2. a. ¿Borraba la profesora las palabras en la pizarra? _____

_____

b. ¿Y los alumnos? _____

3. a. ¿Trabajaba Carlos en la clase de español? _____

_____

b. ¿Y Roberto y Juana? _____

4. a. ¿Tocabas tú el piano? _____

b. ¿Y las muchachas? _____

5. a. ¿Lloraba el niño? _____

b. ¿Y Uds.? _____

6. a. ¿Esperaba Elena el tren? _____

b. ¿Y tú? _____

B. **Verbos con la terminación –ER**

1. a. ¿Aprendía Ud. el francés? _____

b. ¿Y los otros alumnos? _____

2. a. ¿Bebían leche los niños? _____

b. ¿Y las mujeres? _____

3. a. ¿Comía la familia a las siete? _____

b. ¿Y María y José Sánchez? _____

4. a. ¿Leía Isabel el cuento? _____

b. ¿Y nosotros? _____

5. a. ¿Recibía Ud. regalos? _____

b. ¿Y las chicas? _____

C. **Verbos con la terminación –IR**

1. a. ¿Abría la profesora la ventana? _____

b. ¿Y Uds.? _____

2. a. ¿Recibía Juan buenas notas? _____

b. ¿Y Cristóbal? _____

3. a. ¿Escribías tú cartas a Roberto y a Adolfo? _____

   b. ¿Y tu hermano? _____

4. a. ¿Vivía Ud. aquí en esta casa? _____

   b. ¿Y María y Elena? _____

5. a. ¿Cubría Ud. la mesa? _____

   b. ¿Y Alicia y Claudia? _____

D. Verbos irregulares en el imperfecto de indicativo.

1. a. ¿Iba Ud. al centro con Juan? _____

   b. ¿Y Berta? _____

2. a. ¿Era verde la casa? _____

   b. ¿Y el garaje? _____

3. a. ¿Veías a Daniel por la tarde? _____

   b. ¿Y Ud. y Cristina? _____

IX. Componga preguntas en el imperfecto de indicativo empleando los siguientes verbos.
(Compose questions in the imperfecto de indicativo using the following verbs.)

1. hablar   ¿ _____

2. comer   ¿ _____

3. escribir   ¿ _____

4. ir   ¿ _____

5. ser   ¿ _____

The Present Participle and Past Progressive Tense

Review the present participle and the present progressive tense in Work Unit 3.

The past progressive tense is formed by using **estar** in the imperfect indicative plus the present participle of the main verb you are using; *e.g.,* **Estaba hablando** (*I was talking, i.e., I was* [in the act of] *talking* (then, at some point in the past).

The progressive forms (present and past) are generally used when you want to emphasize what you are saying or what you were saying; if you don't want to do that, then just use the simple present or the imperfect indicative, *e.g.,* say **Hablo,** rather than **Estoy hablando;** or **Hablaba,** rather than **Estaba hablando.**

In brief, the present progressive is used to describe with intensification what is happening or going on at present. The past progressive is used to describe with intensification what was happening, what was going on at some point in the past.

Instead of using **estar** to form these two progressive tenses, sometimes **ir** is used: **Va hablando** / He (she) keeps right on talking; **Iba hablando** / He (she) kept right on talking. Note that they do not have the exact meaning as **Está hablando** and **Estaba hablando.**

Estar / to be en el imperfecto de indicativo

Singular		Plural	
yo	**estaba**	nosotros (-as)	**estábamos**
tú	**estabas**	vosotros (-as)	**estabais**
Ud. (él, ella)	**estaba**	Uds. (ellos, ellas)	**estaban**

EJERCICIOS

I. Cambie el verbo del presente progresivo al pasado progresivo. (Change the verb from the present progressive to the past progressive. Review the formation explained above.)

Modelo: Estoy hablando. ——→ Estaba hablando.

1. Estoy cantando. _____

2. Estás trabajando. _____

3. Está aprendiendo. _____

4. Estamos leyendo. _____

5. Estáis riendo. _____

6. Están trayendo. _____

7. Estoy diciendo. _____

8. Estamos durmiendo. _____

9. Están oyendo. _____

10. Estás repitiendo. _____

II. Humor. La adivinanza para hoy.
   (**Humor.** The riddle for today.)

   ¿Qué tiene patas y brazos pero no tiene manos? (What has feet (**patas** / paws) and arms but does not have hands?)

   Respuesta: _____

Use of Acabar De in the Imperfecto de Indicativo

   The Spanish idiomatic expression **acabar de + inf.** is expressed in English as *to have just +* past participle. This is a very common expression that you surely will find on any standardized test in Spanish.

   In the imperfecto de indicativo:

   María acababa de llegar / Mary had just arrived.
   Acababa de comer / I had just eaten.
   Acabábamos de terminar la lección / We had just finished the lesson.

NOTE: When you use **acabar** in the imperfect indicative, it indicates that the action of the main verb (+ inf.) had occurred at some time in the past when another action occurred in the past. In English, we express this by using *had just* + the past participle of the main verb: **Acabábamos de entrar en la casa cuando el teléfono sonó** / We had just entered the house when the telephone rang.

When **acabar** is used in the imperfect indicative + the inf. of the main verb being expressed, the verb in the other clause is usually in the preterit tense. The preterit is tense no. 3 of the 7 simple tenses and it is introduced in the following lesson, Work Unit 7.

EJERCICIOS

I. Traduzca.(Translate into Spanish. Review the explanation above.)

1. Mary had just arrived. _____

2. I had just eaten. _____

3. We had just finished the lesson. _____

4. I had just left. _____

5. I had just written a letter. _____

II. Dictado. Escriba las frases que su profesor de español va a pronunciar.
   (**Dictation.** Write the sentences that your Spanish teacher is going to pronounce.)

1. _____

2. _____

3. _____

¿CUÁNTO TIEMPO HACÍA QUE + IMPERFECT TENSE . . . ?

   (a)   If the action of tho verb began in the past and ended in the past, use the imperfect tense.

   (b)   This formula is equivalent to the English: *How long + past perfect tense*:

      ¿Cuánto tiempo hacía que Ud. hablaba cuando entré en la sala de clase? / How long had you been talking when I entered into the classroom?

HACÍA + LENGTH OF TIME + QUE + IMPERFECT TENSE

   (a)   This formula is the usual answer to the question as stated above.

   (b)   The imperfect tense of the verb is used here because the action began in the past and ended in the past; it is not going on at the present moment.

      Hacía una hora que yo hablaba cuando Ud. entró en la sala de clase / I had been talking for one hour when you entered the classroom.

¿DESDE CUÁNDO + IMPERFECT TENSE . . . ?

      This is another way of asking the question stated above.

      ¿Desde cuándo hablaba Ud. cuando yo entré en la sala de clase? / How long had you been talking when I entered into the classroom?

IMPERFECT TENSE + DESDE HACÍA + LENGTH OF TIME

      This is another way of answering the question stated above.

      (Yo) hablaba desde hacía una hora cuando Ud. entró en la sala de clase / I had been talking for one hour when you entered into the classroom.

Hacer / to do, to make en el imperfecto de indicativo

Singular   Plural

yo   **hacía**   nosotros (-as)   **hacíamos**
tú   **hacías**   vosotros (-as)   **hacíais**
Ud. (él, ella) **hacía**   Uds. (ellos, ellas) **hacían**

EJERCICIOS

I. Traduzca al inglés. (Translate into English. First, review the explanation, examples, and translations above.)

1. ¿Cuánto tiempo hacía que Ud. hablaba cuando yo entré en la sala de clase? _____

_____

2. Hacía una hora que yo hablaba cuando Ud. entró en la sala de clase. _____

_____

3. ¿Desde cuándo hablaba Ud. cuando yo entré en la sala de clase? _____

_____

II. Responda en español en frases completas. (Answer in Spanish in complete sentences. First, review the explanation, examples, and translations above.)

Modelo: ¿Cuánto tiempo hacía que Ud. miraba la televisión cuando yo entré? (How long had you been watching television when I came in?)

Escriba: Hacía una hora que yo miraba la televisión cuando Ud. entró. (I had been watching television for one hour when you came in.)

1. ¿Cuánto tiempo hacía que Ud. hablaba con Elena cuando María entró? _____

_____

2. ¿Cuántos minutos hacía que Ud. esperaba el autobús cuando llegó? _____

_____

3. ¿Cuántos años hacía que Ud. vivía en Puerto Rico cuando Ud. partió para Nueva York? ____

_____

4. ¿Desde cuándo leía Ud. este libro cuando Ud. salió para ir al cine? _____

_____

III. Discriminación de los sonidos. Su profesor de español va a pronunciar una sola palabra, sea la de la letra A, sea la de la letra B. Escoja la palabra que su profesor pronuncia escribiendo la letra en la línea.
Sound discrimination. Your Spanish teacher is going to pronounce one word, either in letter A or letter B. Choose the word that your teacher pronounces by writing the letter on the line.

Modelo: A. pero
              B. perro _____B_____

He escrito la letra B en la línea porque mi profesor de español ha pronunciado la palabra de la letra B. (I have written the letter B on the line because my Spanish teacher has pronounced the word in letter B.)

1. A. lápiz

   B. lápices_____

2. A. donde

   B. ¿dónde?_____

3. A. huevo

   B. nuevo_____

4. A. cuando

   B. ¿cuándo?_____

5. A. hoja

   B. hogar_____

6. A. tras

   B. tres_____

IV. Uno por tres. Ponga en las casillas una palabra que, con la palabra ya inscrita, permitirá formar otra palabra. La tercera palabra—que será el resultado de la palabra ya inscrita y de la palabra que usted va a escribir—figura en la lectura de esta lección.
(**One times three.** Put in the boxes a word that, with the word already written, will form another word. The third word—which will be the result of the word already written plus the word you are going to write—is found in the reading selection in this Work Unit.)

Tip: The three missing new words are in the story at the beginning of this Work Unit. One is on line 4, another is on line 35, and another is on line 40.

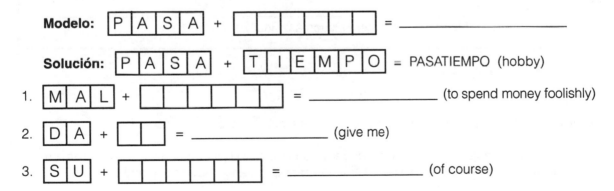

Modelo: | P | A | S | A | + | | | | | | | = _____

Solución: | P | A | S | A | + | T | I | E | M | P | O | = PASATIEMPO (hobby)

1. | M | A | L | + | | | | | | | = _____ (to spend money foolishly)

2. | D | A | + | | | = _____ (give me)

3. | S | U | + | | | | | | | = _____ (of course)

V. Providing / Obtaining Information. Speaking and Writing Proficiency.

Situation: You and some of your friends are waiting on the corner for the yellow school bus. One of your friends is Juana Rodríguez. She wants to obtain some information. Provide answers to her questions in this dialogue.

You are playing the role of **Tú.** You may provide the Spanish words for the suggested English words or you may use your own words and ideas.

Juana: **¡Hola! ¿Cómo estás?**

Tú: _____

(Greet her and tell her you are well.)

Juana: **Dime, ¿cuántos minutos hace que tú esperas el autobús?**
Tell me, how many minutes have you been waiting for the bus?

Tú: _____

(Say that you have been waiting for the bus for ten minutes.)

Juana: **¿Y ayer por la mañana? ¿Cuántos minutos hacía que tú esperabas el autobús cuando llegó?**
And yesterday morning? How minutes had you been waiting for the bus when it arrived?

Tú: _____

_____

(Tell her that yesterday morning you had been waiting for the bus twenty minutes when it arrived finally.)

Juana: **¡Mira, mira! ¡El autobús llega!**

Tú: _____

(Make an exclamation, such as, Finally!)

Adjectives

Definition: An adjective is a word that describes a noun or pronoun in some way.

Agreement: An adjective agrees in gender and number with the noun or pronoun it describes. **Gender** means masculine, feminine, or neuter. **Number** means singular or plural.

Descriptive adjectives

A descriptive adjective is a word that describes a noun or pronoun: **casa blanca, chicas bonitas, chicos altos;** Ella es **bonita.**

Limiting adjectives

A limiting adjective limits the number of the noun: **una casa, un libro, algunos muchachos, muchas veces, dos libros, pocos amigos.**

Gender

An adjective that ends in **o** in the masculine singular changes **o** to **a** to form the feminine: **rojo / roja, pequeño / pequeña**

An adjective that expresses a person's nationality, which ends in a consonant, requires the addition of **a** to form the feminine singular: **Juan es español / María es española; Pierre Cardin es francés / Simone Signoret es francesa; El señor Armstrong es inglés / La señora Smith es inglesa.** Note that the accent mark on **francés** and **inglés** drops in the feminine because the stress falls naturally on the vowel **e.**

An adjective that ends in **e** generally does not change to form the feminine: **un muchacho inteligente / una muchacha inteligente.**

An adjective that ends in a consonant generally does not change to form the feminine: **una pregunta difícil / un libro difícil; un chico feliz / una chica feliz**—except for an adjective of nationality and adjectives that end in **–án, –ón, –ín, –or (trabajador / trabajadora,** industrious).

Position

Normally, a descriptive adjective is placed after the noun it describes: **una casa amarilla; un libro interesante.**

Two descriptive adjectives, **bueno** and **malo,** are sometimes placed in front of the noun. When placed in front of a masculine singular noun, the **o** drops: **un buen amigo; un mal alumno.**

A limiting adjective is generally placed in front of the noun: **algunos estudiantes; mucho dinero; muchos libros; cada año; tres horas; pocos alumnos; varias cosas.**

In an interrogative sentence, the predicate adjective precedes the subject when it is a noun: **¿Es bonita María? ¿Es inteligente la profesora?**

Some adjectives have a different meaning depending on their position:

> **un nuevo sombrero** / a new (different, another) hat
> **un sombrero nuevo** / a new (brand new) hat
>
> **un gran hombre** / a great man
> **un hombre grande** / a large, big man
>
> **una gran mujer** / a great woman
> **una mujer grande** / a large, big woman
>
> **la pobre niña** / the poor girl (unfortunate, unlucky)
> **la niña pobre** / the poor girl (poor, not rich)

VI. Read the description of the persons in the following sentences, then answer the questions. Make sure that you change the adjectives, when required, to agree in gender (masculine or feminine) and number (singular or plural).

Modelo: Roberto es alto y simpático. ¿Y Rosa?
(Robert is tall and nice. And Rosa?)

Escriba: Rosa es alta y simpática.
(Rosa is tall and nice.)

1. David es inteligente. ¿Y Julia? _____

2. Juan es español. ¿Y María? _____

3. El señor Johnson es inglés. ¿Y la señora Smith? _____

4. Carlos es estudioso y diligente. ¿Y Carla? _____

5. Emilio es un muchacho feliz y trabajador. ¿Y Alicia? _____

_____

6. Pablo es ingrato y perezoso. ¿Y Dora? _____

7. Ahora Pablo está contento. ¿Y su padre y su hermano Andrés? _____

_____

8. Los tres hombres comen juntos. ¿Y las tres mujeres? _____

_____

9. Richard es francés. ¿Y Catherine? _____

10. Claudio es pequeño. ¿Y Claudia? _____

VII. Now, do the same thing in this exercise as you did in Exercise VI above. This time you are using adjectives to describe things.

1. El garaje es amarillo. ¿Y la casa? _____

2. El dormitorio es grande. ¿Y la sala? _____

3. El lápiz es rojo. ¿Y la tiza? _____

4. El cielo es azul. ¿Y los zapatos? _____

5. El pantalón es blanco. ¿Y la camisa? _____

As nouns

At times an adjective is used as a noun if it is preceded by an article or a demonstrative adjective: **el viejo** / the old man; **aquel viejo** / that old man; **la joven** / the young lady; **estos jóvenes** / these young men; **este ciego** / this blind man.

Shortened forms (apocopation of adjectives)

Certain masculine singular adjectives drop the final **o** when in front of a masculine singular noun:

alguno: algún día	**primero: el primer año**
bueno: un buen amigo	**tercero: el tercer mes**
malo: mal tiempo	**uno: un dólar**
ninguno: ningún libro	

NOTE that when **alguno** and **ninguno** are shortened, an accent mark is required on the **u.**

Santo shortens to **San** before a masculine singular saint: **San Francisco, San José;** but remains **Santo** in front of **Do–** or **To–: Santo Domingo, Santo Tomás.**

Grande shortens to **gran** when in front of any singular noun, whether masc. or fem.: **un gran hombre** / a great (famous) man; **una gran mujer** / a great (famous) woman.

Ciento shortens to **cien** when in front of any plural noun, whether masc. or fem.: **cien libros** / one (a) hundred books; **cien sillas** / one (a) hundred chairs.

Ciento shortens to **cien** when in front of a number greater than itself: **cien mil** / one hundred thousand; **cien millones** / one hundred million.

Ciento remains **ciento** when combined with any other number that is smaller than itself: **ciento tres dólares.**

NOTE that in English we say *one* hundred or *a* hundred, but in Spanish no word is used in front of **ciento** or **cien** to express *one* or *a*; it is merely **ciento** or **cien.** For an explanation of when to use **ciento** or **cien,** see above.

Cualquiera and **cualesquiera** lose the final **a** in front of a noun: **cualquier hombre, cualquier día,** but if after the noun, the final **a** remains: **un libro cualquiera.**

VIII. Choose the correct form of the adjective in parentheses and write it on the line.

> **Modelo:**   (cien, ciento, cientos) libros
>
> **Escriba:**   cien

1. (aquel, aquella) viejo   _____

2. (algún, alguno) día   _____

3. un (buen, bueno) amigo   _____

4. (mal, malo) tiempo   _____

5. (ningún, ninguno) libro   _____

6. un (gran, grande) hombre   _____

7. una (gran, grande) mujer   _____

8. (cien, cientas) sillas   _____

9. el (primer, primero) año   _____

10. el (tercero, tercer) mes   _____

11. (un, uno) dólar   _____

12. (San, Santo) Francisco   _____

13. (San, Santo) Domingo   _____

14. (cien, cientos) millones   _____

15. (cien, cientos) dólares   _____

16. (cien, ciento) mil   _____

Plural of adjectives

Like nouns, to form the plural of an adjective, add **s** if the adj. ends in a vowel: **blanco / blancos; blanca / blancas.**

If an adj. ends in a consonant, add **es** to form the plural: **español / españoles; difícil / difíciles.**

NOTE that the accent on **difícil** remains in the plural in order to keep the stress there: **difíciles.**

Some adjectives drop the accent mark in the plural because it is not needed to indicate the stress. The stress falls naturally on the same vowel in the plural: **cortés / corteses; alemán / alemanes.**

Some adjectives add the accent mark in the plural because the stress needs to be kept on the vowel that was stressed in the singular where no accent mark was needed. In the singular, the stress falls naturally on that vowel: **joven / jóvenes.**

An adjective that ends in **z** changes **z** to **c** and adds **es** to form the plural: **feliz / felices.** Here, there is no need to add an accent mark because the stress falls naturally on the vowel **i,** as it does in the singular.

If an adjective describes or modifies two or more nouns that are all masculine, naturally the masculine plural is used: **Roberto y Felipe están cansados.**

If an adjective describes or modifies two or more nouns that are all feminine, naturally the feminine plural is used: **Elena y Marta están cansadas.**

If an adjective describes or modifies two or more nouns of different genders, the masculine plural is used: **Pablo y Juanita están cansados; Marta, Elena, María, y Roberto están cansados.**

139

IX. Change the following adjectives from the singular to the plural.

Modelo: blanco

Escriba: blancos

1. blanca _____
2. español _____
3. cansada _____
4. cortés _____
5. alemán _____

6. joven _____
7. feliz _____
8. cansado _____
9. difícil _____
10. negro _____

X. Change the following adjectives from the plural to the singular.

Modelo: negros

Escriba: negro

1. difíciles _____
2. felices _____
3. alemanes _____
4. cansadas _____
5. amarillas _____

6. cansados _____
7. jóvenes _____
8. corteses _____
9. españoles _____
10. blancas _____

Comparatives and Superlatives

Comparatives

Of equality: **tan . . . como** (as . . . as)
   María es tan alta como Elena / Mary is as tall as Helen.

Of a lesser degree: **menos . . . que** (less . . . than)
   María es menos alta que Anita / Mary is less tall than Anita.

Of a higher degree: **más . . . que** (more . . . than)
   María es más alta que Isabel / Mary is taller than Elizabeth.

Superlatives

To express the superlative degree, use the comparative forms given above with the appropriate definite article:

With a proper noun: **Anita es la más alta** / Anita is the tallest.
   Roberto es el más alto / Robert is the tallest.
   Anita y Roberto son los más altos / Anita and Robert are the tallest.
   Marta y María son las más inteligentes / Martha and Mary are the most intelligent.

With a common noun: **La muchacha más alta de la clase es Anita**/ The tallest girl in the class is Anita.

El muchacho más alto de la clase es Roberto/ The tallest boy in the class is Robert.

NOTE that after a superlative in Spanish, *in* is expressed by **de**, not **en**.

When two or more superlative adjectives describe the same noun, **más** or **menos** is used only once in front of the first adjective: **Aquella mujer es la más pobre y vieja.**

Absolute superlative: adjectives ending in **–ísimo, –ísima, –ísimos, –ísimas**

To express an adjective in a very high degree, drop the final vowel (if there is one) and add the appropriate ending among the following, depending on the correct agreement: **–ísimo, –ísima, –ísimos, –ísimas: María está contentísima** / Mary is very (extremely) happy; **Los muchachos están contentísimos.** These forms may be used instead of **muy** + adj. **(muy contenta / muy contentos); una casa grandísima / una casa muy grande.**

Never use **muy** in front of **mucho**. Say: **muchísimo. Muchísimas gracias** / many thanks; thank you very, very much.

Irregular comparatives and superlatives

ADJECTIVE	COMPARATIVE	SUPERLATIVE
bueno (good)	**mejor** (better)	**el mejor** (best)
malo (bad)	**peor** (worse)	**el peor** (worst)
grande (large)	**más grande** (larger)	**el más grande** (largest)
	mayor (greater, older)	**el mayor** (greatest, oldest)
pequeño (small)	**más pequeño** (smaller)	**el más pequeño** (smallest)
	menor (smaller, younger)	**el menor** (smallest, youngest)

NOTE, of course, that you must be careful to make the correct agreement in gender and number.

NOTE also that in English, the superlative is sometimes expressed with the definite article *the* and sometimes it is not.

Más que (more than) or **menos que** (less than) becomes **más dé, menos de** + a number:

El Señor Gómez tiene más de cincuenta años.
Mi hermano tiene más de cien dólares.

BUT: **No tengo más que dos dólares**/ I have only two dollars.

In this example, the meaning is *only*, expressed by **no** in front of the verb; in this case, you must keep **que** to express *only*.

Tanto, tanta, tantos, tantas + noun + **como:** as much (as many) . . . as

Tengo tanto dinero como usted/ I have as much money as you.
Tengo tantos libros como usted/ I have as many books as you.
Tengo tanta paciencia como usted/ I have as much patience as you.
Tengo tantas plumas como usted/ I have as many pens as you.

XI. Traduzca al español. (Translate into Spanish.)

1. Mary is as tall as Helen. _____

2. Mrs. Robles is less tall than Mrs. Vega. _____

   _____

3. Anita is taller than Lisa. _____

4. Arturo is as tall as his father. _____

5. Gregorio is shorter than his brother. _____

6. Claudia is the tallest. _____

7. Alfonso is the shortest. _____

8. Claudia and Eduardo are the tallest. _____

9. Casandra and Ángela are the most intelligent. _____

10. The tallest girl in the class is Carmen. _____

11. The tallest boy in the class is Alano. _____

12. Your dog is the ugliest of all. _____

    _____

13. Mr. Gómez has more than a hundred dollars. _____

    _____

14. I have only two dollars. _____

15. Pablo has as much money as you. _____

16. Sonia has as many friends *(masc.)* as you. _____

17. The Spanish teacher *(masc. or fem.)* has as much patience as the English teacher. _____

    _____

18. Mrs. García has as many cats as Mrs. Santiago. _____

    _____

19. Pablo is the younger son. _____

20. Andrés is the older son. _____

Demonstrative Adjectives

A demonstrative adjective is used to point out someone or something. Like other adjectives, a demonstrative adjective agrees in gender and number with the noun it modifies. The demonstrative adjectives are:

ENGLISH MEANING	MASCULINE	FEMININE
this (here)	**este libro**	**esta pluma**
these (here)	**estos libros**	**estas plumas**
that (there)	**ese libro**	**esa pluma**
those (there)	**esos libros**	**esas plumas**
that (farther away or out of sight)	**aquel libro**	**aquella pluma**
those (farther away or out of sight)	**aquellos libros**	**aquellas plumas**

If there is more than one noun, a demonstrative adjective is ordinarily used in front of each noun: **este hombre y esta mujer** / this man and (this) woman.

The demonstrative adjectives are used to form the demonstrative pronouns.

XII. Traduzca al español. (Translate into Spanish.)

1. this book _____

2. this pen _____

3. these books _____

4. these pens _____

5. that book _____

6. that pen _____

7. that book (farther away) _____

8. those books _____

9. those pens _____

10. that pen (farther away) _____

11. those books (farther away) _____

12. those pens (farther away) _____

13. this man and woman _____

Possessive Adjectives

A possessive adjective is a word that shows possession and it agrees in gender and number with the noun, not with the possessor. A short form of a possessive adjective is placed in front of the noun. If there is more than one noun stated, a possessive adjective is needed in front of each noun: **mi madre y mi padre** / my mother and (my) father.

There are two forms for the possessive adjectives: the short form and the long form. **The short form is placed in front of the noun.** The short forms are:

ENGLISH MEANING	BEFORE A SINGULAR NOUN	BEFORE A PLURAL NOUN
1. my	**mi amigo, mi amiga**	**mis amigos, mis amigas**
2. your	**tu amigo, tu amiga**	**tus amigos, tus amigas**
3. your, his, her, its	**su amigo, su amiga**	**sus amigos, sus amigas**
1. our	**nuestro amigo** **nuestra amiga**	**nuestros amigos** **nuestras amigas**
2. your	**vuestro amigo** **vuestra amiga**	**vuestros amigos** **vuestras amigas**
3. your, their	**su amigo, su amiga**	**sus amigos, sus amigas**

In order to clarify the meanings of **su** or **sus,** when there might be ambiguity, do the following: Replace **su** or **sus** with the definite article + the noun and add **de Ud., de él, de ella, de Uds., de ellos, de ellas:**

su libro OR **el libro de Ud., el libro de él, el libro de ella; el libro de Uds., el libro de ellos, el libro de ellas**

sus libros OR **los libros de Ud., los libros de él, los libros de ella; los libros de Uds., los libros de ellos, los libros de ellas**

The long form is placed after the noun. The long forms are:

ENGLISH MEANING	AFTER A SINGULAR NOUN	AFTER A PLURAL NOUN
1. my; (of) mine	**mío, mía**	**míos, mías**
2. your; (of) yours	**tuyo, tuya**	**tuyos, tuyas**
3. your, his her, its; (of yours, of his, of hers, of its)	**suyo, suya**	**suyos, suyas**
1. our; (of) ours	**nuestro, nuestra**	**nuestros, nuestras**
2. your; (of) yours	**vuestro, vuestra**	**vuestros, vuestras**
3. your, their; (of yours, of theirs)	**suyo, suya**	**suyos, suyas**

EXAMPLES: **amigo mío** / my friend; **un amigo mío** / a friend of mine
The long forms are used primarily:

(a) In direct address, that is to say, when you are talking directly to someone or when writing a letter to someone:

¡Hola, amigo mío! ¿Qué tal? / Hello, my friend! How are things? **Queridos amigos míos** / My dear friends

(b) When you want to express *of mine, of yours, of his, of hers,* etc.

(c) With the verb **ser: Estos libros son míos** / These books are mine.

(d) In the expression: **¡Dios mío!** / My heavens! My God!

In order to clarify the meanings of **suyo, suya, suyos, suyas** (since they are third person singular or plural), do the same as for **su** and **sus: dos amigos suyos** can be clarified as **dos amigos de Ud., dos amigos de él, dos amigos de ella, dos amigos de Uds., dos amigos de ellos, dos amigos de ellas** / two friends of yours, of his, of hers, *etc.*

The long forms of the possessive adjectives are used to serve as possessive pronouns.

A possessive adjective is ordinarily not used when referring to an article of clothing being worn or to parts of the body, particularly when a reflexive verb is used: **Me lavo las manos antes de comer** / I wash my hands before eating.

XIII. Traduzca al español. (Translate into Spanish.)

1. my friend Pablo _____

2. my friend Anita _____

3. my friends Pablo and José _____

144   4. my friends Elena and Ana _____

5. your *(fam.)* friend Mary   _____

6. your *(fam.)* friends David and Roberto   _____

7. your *(polite)* friends Adolfo and Eva   _____

8. his friend Elisa   _____

9. his friends Bertha and Elena   _____

10. her friend Andrew   _____

11. her friend Mariana   _____

12. our friends *(masc.)*   _____

13. our friends *(fem.)*   _____

14. their friends Mr. and Mrs. Robles   _____

15. their friends Carlota and Carlos   _____

16. their friends Mary and Rosa   _____

17. Hi, my friend! How are things?   _____

18. My dear friends, how are you?   _____

19. These books are mine.   _____

20. My God!   _____

Two or More Descriptive Adjectives

Two or more descriptive adjectives of equal importance are placed after the noun. If there are two, they are joined by **y** (or **e**). If there are more than two, the last two are connected by **y** (or **e**):

un hombre alto y guapo / a tall, handsome man

una mujer alta, hermosa e inteligente / a tall, beautiful and intelligent woman

Cuanto más (menos) . . . tanto más (menos) / the more (the less) . . . the more (less)

A proportion or ratio is expressed by **cuanto más (menos) . . . tanto más (menos)** / the more (the less) . . . the more (less):

Cuanto más dinero tengo, tanto más necesito / The more money I have, the more I need.

Cuanto menos dinero tengo, tanto menos necesito / The less money I have the less I need.

Comparison Between Two Clauses

(a) Use **de lo que** to express *than* when comparing two clauses with different verbs if an adjective or adverb is the comparison:

Esta frase es más fácil de lo que Ud. cree / This sentence is easier than you think.

Paula trabaja mejor de lo que Ud. cree / Paula works better than you think.

(b) Use the appropriate form of **de lo que, de los que, de la que, de las que** when comparing two clauses with the same verbs if a noun is the comparison:

Tengo más dinero de lo que Ud. tiene / I have more money than you have.

María tiene más libros de los que Ud. tiene / Mary has more books than you have.

Roberto tiene más amigas de las que tiene Juan / Robert has more girlfriends than John has.

XIV. Traduza al español. (Translate into Spanish.)

1. My father is a tall, handsome man. _____

_____

2. My mother is a tall, beautiful, and intelligent woman. _____

_____

3. The more money I have, the more I need. _____

_____

4. The less money my brother has, the less he needs. _____

_____

5. This lesson is easier than you think. _____

_____

6. Paula works better than you think. _____

_____

7. have more money than you have. _____

_____

8. Gabriela has more boyfriends than Carlota has. _____

_____

9. Robert has more girlfriends than John has. _____

_____

10. Elena sings better than you think. _____

_____

EJERCICIOS

I. Traduzca al español. (Translate into Spanish.)

1. a white house _____

2. pretty girls _____

3. many times _____

4. two books _____

5. few friends _____

6. an intelligent girl _____

7. an intelligent boy _____

8. a difficult question _____

9. a difficult book _____

10. a happy girl _____

II. Escriba el femenino de los siguientes adjetivos. (Write the feminine form of the following adjectives.)

Modelos: blanco ⟶ blanca
rojos ⟶ rojas

1. amarillo _____

2. interesante _____

3. poco _____

4. muchos _____

5. varios _____

6. cada _____

7. algunos _____

8. inteligente _____

9. bonito _____

10. pobre _____

III. Traduzca al español. (Translate into Spanish.)

1. a new (different, another) hat _____

2. a new (brand new) hat _____

3. a great man _____

4. a large, big man _____

5. a great woman _____

6. a large, big woman _____

7. the poor girl (unfortunate, unlucky) _____

8. the poor girl (poor, not rich) _____

IV. Traduzca al español.

1. the old man _____

2. that old man _____

3. the young lady _____

4. the young man _____

5. these young men _____

6. this blind man _____

V. Traduzca al español.

1. some day _____

2. a good friend (*m.*) _____

3. bad weather _____

4. not any (not one) book _____

5. the first year _____

6. the third month _____

VI. Traduzca al español.

1. a great (famous) man _____

2. a great (famous) woman _____

3. one hundred books _____

4. one hundred chairs _____

5. one hundred thousand _____

6. one hundred million _____

VII. Cambie los siguientes adjetivos al plural. (Change the following adjectives to the plural).

Modelo: difícil ⟶ difíciles

1. español _____

2. cortés _____

3. alemán _____

4. joven _____

5. feliz _____

6. cansado _____

VIII. Traduzca al inglés. (Translate into English.)

1. María es tan alta como Elena. _____

2. Carlota es menos alta que Anita. _____

3. Ana es más alta que Isabel. _____

4. Anita es la más alta. _____

5. Roberto es el más alto. _____

6. Anita y Roberto son los más altos. _____

7. Marta y María son las más inteligentes. _____

8. La muchacha más alta de la clase es Anita. _____

   _____

9. El muchacho más alto de la clase es Roberto. _____

   _____

10. Aquella mujer es la más pobre y vieja. _____

   _____

IX. Escriba el superlativo absoluto de los siguientes adjetivos. (Write the absolute superlative of the following adjectives)

> **Modelos:** contento ———→ contentísimo
> grande ———→ grandísimo, grandísima

1. contentos _____

2. mucho _____

3. bueno _____

4. estudioso _____

5. hermosa _____

6. grande _____

X. Escriba la forma correcta del adjetivo demostrativo según el modelo a continuación. (Write the correct form of the demonstrative adjective according to the following models.)

> **Modelos:** libro ———→ este libro
> pluma   esta pluma
> chicos   estos chicos
> escuelas   estas escuelas

1. pluma _____

2. escuelas _____

3. lápiz _____

4. cuaderno _____

5. muchacha _____

6. hombre _____

7. mujer _____

8. lápices _____

9. libros _____

10. lección _____

XI. Escriba la forma correcta del adjetivo demostrativo según el modelo a continuación. (Write the correct form of the demonstrative adjective according to the following model.)

> **Modelos:** libro ———→ ese libro
> pluma   esa pluma
> chicos   esos chicos
> escuelas   esas escuelas

1. pluma _____

2. escuelas _____

3. lápiz _____

4. cuaderno _____

5. muchacha _____

6. hombre _____

7. mujer _____

8. lápices _____

9. libros _____

10. lección _____

XII. Escriba la forma correcta del adjetivo demostrativo según el modelo a continuación.
(Write the correct form of the demonstrative adjective according to the following models.)

Modelos: libro   ⟶ aquel libro
              pluma   aquella pluma
              chicos   aquellos chicos
              escuelas   aquellas escuelas

1. pluma _____

2. escuelas _____

3. lápiz _____

4. cuaderno _____

5. muchacha _____

6. hombre _____

7. mujer _____

8. lápices _____

9. libros _____

10. lección _____

XIII. Traduzca al español.

1. my friend *(m.)* _____

2. your friend *(f.) (2nd pers., s.)* _____

3. your book *(3rd pers., s.)* _____

4. my notebooks _____

5. your pencils *(2nd pers., s.)* _____

6. his car _____

7. her cars _____

8. our house _____

9. their tickets _____

10. your money *(2nd pers., pl.)* _____

XIV. Traduzca al español.

1. My dear friends (m.), how are you today? _____

2. Hello, my friend (f.)! How are things? _____

3. These books are mine. _____

4. My God! _____

5. Mrs. Rodríguez is a tall, beautiful, and intelligent woman. _____

   _____

6. Mr. Rodríguez is a tall, handsome man. _____

7. This sentence is easier than you think. _____

8. Mary has more books than you have. _____

9. Robert has more girlfriends than John has. _____

10. Isabel has more boyfriends than Mary has. _____

    _____

XV. Sopa de letras. Busque cuatro sinónimos del adjetivo *delicado.* Los cuatro sinónimos pueden aparecer de derecha a izquierda, de izquierda a derecha, de abajo arriba y viceversa.

(Alphabet soup. In this puzzle, find four synonyms of the adjective **delicado.** The four synonyms can appear from right to left, from left to right, from bottom to top, from top to bottom. **Tip:** Look up **delicado** in the vocabulary beginning on page 481.

O	Z	I	M	R	E	F	N	E
E	N	F	E	M	I	O	T	K
Z	Y	X	C	A	S	L	W	M
G	I	H	J	D	L	I	S	O
M	P	O	N	É	R	G	V	N
S	U	T	V	B	P	Á	R	J
F	D	E	T	I	E	R	N	O
D	G	E	C	L	B	F	Q	A

XVI. ¿Qué tiene Ud. en la mano? (What do you have in your hand?)

Respuesta: _____

XVII. ¿Cuántos alumnos hay en esta clase? (How many pupils are there in this class?)

Respuesta: _____

XVIII. Ponga las siguientes letras en orden para hallar adjetivos españoles. (Put the following letters in the right order to find Spanish adjectives.)

1. I O B T A N _____

2. R E D A N G _____

3. Q E Ñ U E P O _____

4. N E G I L T T I N E E _____

5. X R E A T Ñ A _____

XIX. Varias palabras en una sola. ¿Cuántas palabras españolas puede Ud. hallar en la palabra ADJETIVOS? Halle veinte y una palabras, por lo menos. Usted puede añadir signos de acento o tilde, si es necesario, para formar nuevas palabras. Por ejemplo: tío, adiós.
(Several words in one. How many Spanish words can you find in the word ADJETIVOS (ADJECTIVES)? Find 21 words at least. You may add accent marks or a tilde [~], if needed, to form new words. For example: tío (uncle), adiós (good-bye.)

$$\boxed{\text{A D J E T I V O S}}$$

1. _____   12. _____

2. _____   13. _____

3. _____   14. _____

4. _____   15. _____

5. _____   16. _____

6. _____   17. _____

7. _____   18. _____

8. _____   19. _____

9. _____   20. _____

10. _____   21. _____

11. _____

XX. Describa a una muchacha con tantos adjetivos como Ud. pueda decir y escribir.
(Describe a girl with as many adjectives as you can say and write.)

EJEMPLO:

Teresa es . . .

inteligente	**alta**
bonita	**americana**
bella	**española**
activa	**mexicana**

¿Cuántos adjetivos puede Ud. decir y escribir? (How many adjectives can you say and write? How many more can you add to these? Remember that your adjectives are describing a girl.)

XXI. En español hay muchas palabras que se escriben y se pronuncian idénticamente, pero tienen un significado diferente. Se distinguen por el acento ortográfico. (In Spanish there are many words that are written and pronounced identically, but have different meanings. They are distinguished by a written accent mark.)

Por ejemplo:

tu *poss. adj., fam., 2nd pers., sing.* / your
tú *subj. pron., 2nd pers., sing.* / you
¿Tú tienes tu libro? / You have your book?

¿Cuántos ejemplos puede Ud. decir y escribir? (How many examples can you say and write?)

Mnemonic Tip	Este, estos, esta, estas have the t's; Ese, esos, esa, esas DON'T.

¿Puede Ud. dar un "mnemonic tip"? (Can you give a "mnemonic tip"?)

The Annunciation by EL GRECO (1541–1614)

Courtesy of The Toledo Museum of Art, Toledo, Ohio

XXII. Culture. Appreciating Spanish Art. Proficiency in Speaking and Writing.

Situation: You and your classmates are on a field trip at The Toledo Museum of Art in Toledo, Ohio. You are having a conversation with a friend about the painting entitled *The Annunciation* by EL GRECO, **un gran artista español, un gran pintor español.**

Look at the picture facing this page. Your friend is playing the role of **Tu amigo (amiga)** and you are **Tú.**

Tu amigo (amiga): **¿Te gusta este cuadro, amigo mío (amiga mía)?**

Tú: _____

(Say you like it very much. Use the absolute superlative you learned in this lesson: **muchísimo.**)

Tu amigo (amiga): **Pienso que es majestuoso. ¿Qué dices tú?**

Tú: _____

(Tell your friend: I say—or I think—that the colors are marvelous and the style is original—or your own ideas.)

Tu amigo (amiga): **¿Qué ves en este cuadro?**

Tú: _____

_____

(Tell your friend you see a woman with her left hand on a page of an open book: **la mano izquierda / una página / un libro abierto.**)

Tu amigo (amiga): **¿Es todo? ¿Nada más?**

Tú: _____

(Say you also see a large angel with beautiful wings.)

Tu amigo (amiga): **¿Otra cosa?**

Tú: _____

_____

(Say: Of course. I also see a white bird, a dove **(una paloma),** beautiful flowers in a vase **(un jarrón).** The beautiful woman is looking at the angel.)

Tu amigo (amiga): **¿Quién es el pintor de este cuadro?**

Tú: _____

(Tell your friend it's El Greco, a great Spanish artist.)

XXIII. Helping Others. Speaking and Writing Proficiency.

Situation: You are the best student in your Spanish class. A classmate is having problems with comparative and superlative adjectives. You are together in your house with your Spanish books and some paper to write on.

Again, you are **Tú** and your friend is **Tu amigo (amiga).**

Tu amigo (amiga): **No comprendo los adjetivos comparativos y superlativos. Vamos a practicar, amigo mío (amiga mía).**

Tú: _____

_____

(Say: Good, let's practice. They are easier than you think.)

Tu amigo (amiga): **¿Son más fáciles de lo que yo pienso (yo creo)?**

Tú: _____

_____

(Say: Yes, there's no problem / **No hay problema.** Tell me **(Dime).** Mary is the prettiest girl in our Spanish class. Yes or No?)

Tu amigo (amiga): **No. Anita es la más bonita.**

Tú: _____

(Say: My father is as tall as your father. Yes or No?)

Tu amigo (amiga): **No. Tu padre no es tan alto como mi padre. Mi padre es más alto que tu padre.**

Tú: _____

(Say: Isabel is the most intelligent. Yes or No?)

Tu amigo (amiga): **No. Isabel no es la más inteligente. Tú eres el (la) mejor estudiante de la clase.**

Tú: _____

(Say: Me? / **Yo?** You think that I am the best student in the class? Thanks a lot!)

Tu amigo (amiga): **Sí, sí. Yo pienso que tú eres el (la) mejor estudiante. Yo sé todo. ¡Soy el señor (la señorita) Sabelotodo!**

TEST 1

PART ONE Speaking Proficiency

Directions: Read the three situations given below. Take a few minutes to organize your thoughts about the words you are going to speak. Select two of the three situations. Before you begin to speak, you may review the Oral and Written Proficiency exercises in this Work Unit.

1. **Situation:** In the family next door to where you live there are two teenagers, a brother and a sister. In two or three sentences, tell us their names and ages. Use adjectives to describe them; for example, tall, short, nice, friendly, interesting, intelligent, lazy, active, who is taller or shorter than whom, and other ideas of your own. Be sure to use adjectives you learned in this Work Unit as well as any others of your choice.

2. **Situation:** You are waiting for the yellow school bus on a corner with some friends. Roberto wants to know what you were doing last night when he telephoned you. Use at least three verbs in the *imperfecto de indicativo*; for example, an **ar** type verb **(hablar, cantar),** an **er** type **(beber, comer, leer),** and an **ir** type **(escribir, recibir).** You may want to say that you were talking with your brother (sister, mother, father, a friend), or you were singing in the bathroom, you were eating and drinking (mention what), or you were reading a book, or writing a letter. You may use these suggestions or words and ideas of your own. Either way, tell Roberto what you were doing, using the suggested verbs above in the *imperfecto de indicativo* tense. First, you may want to review that section in this Work Unit before your oral presentation.

3. **Situation:** Yesterday you saw a car accident. The police officer wants you to tell him what time it was, what the colors of the two cars were, and where you were going. You will need to use the verbs **ser** and **ir** in the *imperfecto de indicativo* tense. You may want to review them in this Work Unit before your oral presentation.

PART TWO Listening Proficiency

Directions: Your teacher will read aloud four short paragraphs. Each one will contain only a few sentences. You will hear each paragraph twice. Then you will hear one question based on each. You will hear the question only once. It is printed below. Choose the best suggested answer and check the letter of your choice.

Selection Number 1

1. ¿Cuántos años tenía Andrés?

    A. Tenía veinte años.

    B. Tenía veintiún años.

    C. Tenía dieciocho años.

    D. Tenía dieciséis años.

Selection Number 2

2. ¿Adónde iba Pablo todos los días?

    A. Iba a la escuela.

    B. Iba al cine y al teatro.

    C. Iba a ver a su padre.

    D. Iba a trabajar.

Selection Number 3

3. ¿Qué necesita Pablo?

    A. regalos, dulces, y flores

    B. vestidos sucios y rasgados

    C. nuevos amigos, nuevas amigas

    D. mucho dinero

Selection Number 4

4. ¿Quién es el hijo menor?

    A. los dos hijos

    B. el padre

    C. Andrés

    D. Pablo

PART THREE   Reading Proficiency

Directions: In the following passage there are five blank spaces numbered 1 through 5. Each blank space represents a missing verb form in the imperfect indicative tense. For each blank space, four possible completions are provided. Only one of them makes sense in the context of the passage.

First, read the passage in its entirety to determine its general meaning. Then read it a second time. For each blank space choose the completion that makes the best sense and write its letter in the space provided.

Pablo tomó el dinero, que _____ una gran fortuna, y fue a Nueva York. En aquella

    1. A. era
       B. hacía
       C. estaba
       D. iba

ciudad Pablo _____ todas las noches hasta la madrugada en las tabernas gastando

    2. A. estudiaba
       B. escribía
       C. leía
       D. se divertía

mucho dinero. Todos los días iba al cine, al teatro y a otros espectáculos divertidos con sus

nuevos amigos. A las muchachas les _____ regalos, dulces, y flores. Durante el

    3. A. daba
       B. hablaba
       C. cantaba
       D. estudiaba

día, _____ y durante la noche se divertía. Pablo _____ muy contento.

    4. A. hacía
       B. dormía
       C. recibía
       D. veía

    5. A. hablaba
       B. cantaba
       C. estaba
       D. era

PART FOUR   Writing Proficiency

Directions: Of the three situations in Part One (Speaking Proficiency) in this test, select two of them and write what you said on the lines below.

Situation 1 _____

_____

_____

_____

Situation 2 _____

_____

_____

_____

Situation 3 _____

_____

_____

_____

¡Oh, señor! ¡Su autógrafo, por favor! Aquí tiene Ud. mi programa y mi pluma.

Have you ever asked someone for an autograph? That's what Juana Rodríguez did while she was at the theater in Seville during intermission.

El autógrafo especial

Anoche, la familia Rodríguez fue al teatro. Vieron el drama *El Burlador de Sevilla,* una de las mejores comedias de Tirso de Molina. Salieron de la casa a las siete y media, y llegaron al teatro a las ocho. Entraron en el teatro y se sentaron en sus asientos a las ocho y cuarto. El espectáculo comenzó a las ocho y media.

Durante el entreacto, la señora Rodríguez fue a hablar con algunas damas. El señor   5
Rodríguez fue a tomar un café; Pedro, el hijo, fue a comprar chocolate y Juana, la hija, fue a beber jugo de naranja.

La señora Rodríguez habló con las damas y, después, regresó a su asiento. El señor Rodríguez tomó su café y regresó a su asiento también. Pedro comió su chocolate y regresó a su asiento. Juana bebió su jugo de naranja, pero antes de regresar a su asiento,   10
vio a un hombre y ella le dijo:

—¡Oh! ¡Señor! ¡Usted es el gran actor Juan Robles!
—Pero . . . , señorita . . . , respondió el señor.
—¡Oh! ¡Señor! ¡Su autógrafo, por favor! Aquí tiene mi programa y
mi pluma. Escriba su autógrafo on mi programa, por favor, dijo Juana.   15

—Pero . . . , pero . . . ,—dijo el señor.
—Usted es muy modesto—dijo Juana.
—Pero . . . , No soy modesto, señorita . . . Pero si Ud. insiste . . . Aquí tiene usted mi autógrafo—dijo el señor.
—Muchas gracias, señor. Muchas gracias—dijo Juana.   20

Juana regresó a su asiento.

La pieza se terminó, y todo el mundo salió del teatro.
Afuera, Juana anunció:
—¡Miren! ¡Miren mi programa! ¡Tengo el autógrafo de Juan Robles!
—¿Juan Robles? ¿De veras? ¡Increíble!—dijo la madre.   25

Juana dio el programa a su madre, y ésta leyó: "No soy Juan Robles. Me llamo José Blanco."

—¡No es posible! ¡Oh! ¡Yo hice una tontería!—exclamó Juana.
—No es una tontería. Tú tienes el autógrafo de José Blanco. Todo el mundo no tiene el autógrafo de José Blanco en su programa—, respondió Pedro.   30
—¿Quién es José Blanco?—preguntó el padre.
—Es una persona como tú y yo—, contestó la madre—. ¡Ahora tenemos un autógrafo especial!
Y rieron a carcajadas.

KEY WORDS AND PHRASES

afuera *adv.* outside

anoche *adv.* last night

anunció *3d pers., s., pret. of* **anunciar** to announce; you/he/she announced

aquí *adv.* here; **aquí tiene Ud.** here is, here are

asiento *n.m.* seat

autógrafo *n.m.* autograph

bebió *3d pers., s., pret. of* **beber** to drink; you/he/she/it drank

burlador *n.m.* jester, joker

comedia *n.f.* comedy

comenzó *3d pers., s., pret. of* **comenzar** to begin; it began

comió *3d pers., s., pret. of* **comer** to eat; you/he/she/it ate

como *conj.* as, like

contestó *3d pers., s., pret. of* **contestar** to answer; you/he/she answered

dijo *3d pers., s., pret. of* **decir** to say, tell; you/he/she said

dio *3d pers., s., pret. of* **dar** to give; you/he/she gave

entraron *3d pers., pl., pret. of* **entrar** to enter; they entered

entreacto *n.m.* intermission

escriba *3d pers., s., imper. of* **escribir** to write; write

especial *adj.* special

ésta *pron.* this one; the latter (she)

exclamó *3d pers., s., pret. of* **exclamar** to exclaim; you/he/she exclaimed

fue *3d pers., s., pret. of* **ir** to go; you/he/she/it went

habló *3d pers., s., pret. of* **hablar** to talk, speak; you/he/she talked

hice *1st pers., s., pret. of* **hacer** to do, make; I did

increíble *adj.* incredible, unbelievable

insiste *3d pers., s., pres. indic. of* **insistir** to insist; you/he/she insist(s)

jugo *n.m.* juice

leyó *3d pers., s., pret. of* **leer** to read; you/he/she read

llegaron *3d pers., pl., pret. of* **llegar** to arrive; they arrived

mejor, mejores *adj.* better, best

¡Miren! *3d pers., pl., (Uds.) imper. of* **mirar** to look (at); Look!

mundo *n.m.* world; **todo el mundo** everybody

naranja *n.f.* orange

pieza *n.f.* play (theater)

preguntó *3d pers., s., pret. of* **preguntar** to ask; you/he/she asked

programa *n.m.* program

regresar *v.* to return

regresó *3d pers., s., pret. of* **regresar**; you/he/she returned

respondió *3d pers., s., pret. of* **responder** to answer, reply; you/he/she replied

rieron *3d pers., pl., pret. of* **reír** to laugh; they laughed; **rieron a carcajadas** they burst out laughing

salieron *3d pers., pl., pret. of* **salir** to leave, go out; they left, went out

salió *3d pers., s., pret. of* **salir**; you/he/she left, went out

se sentaron *3d pers., pl., pret. of* **sentarse** to sit down; they sat down

se terminó *3d pers., s., pret. of* **terminarse** to end; it ended

Sevilla Seville (city in Spain)

su *poss. adj.* your, his, her, its, their

teatro *n.m.* theater; **al teatro** to the theater

tenemos *1st pers., pl., pres. indic. of* **tener**; we have

tiene *3d pers., s., pres. indic. of* **tener**; **aquí tiene Ud.** / here is, here are

tomó *3d pers., s., pret. of* **tomar**; you/he/she took

tontería *n.f.* foolish thing

veras *n.f., pl.* reality, truth; **de veras** really, truly

vieron *3d pers., pl., pret. of* **ver** to see; they saw

vio *3d pers., s., pret. of* **ver**; you/he/she saw

EJERCICIOS

I. Seleccione la respuesta correcta conforme al significado de la lectura en esta lección. (Choose the correct answer according to the meaning of the reading selection in this Work Unit.)

1. Anoche, la familia Rodríguez fue (a) al cine (b) al teatro (c) a la iglesia (d) a la biblioteca _____

2. Vieron el drama *El Burlador de Sevilla,* una de las mejores comedias de (a) Bartolomé Esteban Murillo (b) Francisco de Goya (c) El Greco (d) Tirso de Molina _____

3. Salieron de la casa a las siete y media y llegaron al teatro (a) a las ocho (b) a las ocho y cuarto (c) a las ocho y media (d) a las nueve _____

4. Entraron en el teatro y se sentaron en sus asientos (a) a las ocho (b) a las ocho y cuarto (c) a las ocho y media (d) a las nueve menos quince _____

5. Durante el entreacto, la señora Rodríguez fue a hablar con (a) Pedro (b) algunos señores (c) Juana (d) algunas damas _____

6. Durante el entreacto, el señor Rodríguez fue (a) a tomar un café (b) a hablar con algunos señores (c) a comprar chocolate (d) a beber jugo de naranja _____

7. Durante el entreacto, Pedro fue (a) a comprar chocolate (b) a beber jugo de naranja (c) a tomar un café (d) a hablar con las chicas bonitas _____

8. Durante el entreacto, Juana fue (a) a hablar con algunos muchachos (b) a comprar chocolate (c) a beber jugo de naranja (d) a hablar con algunas damas _____

9. Antes de regresar a su asiento, Juana vio a (a) una amiga (b) un amigo (c) unos amigos (d) un hombre _____

10. Juana recibió el autógrafo especial de (a) un gran actor (b) una persona común y corriente (c) Juan Robles (d) un amigo suyo _____

II. Seleccione la forma correcta del verbo en el pretérito. (Choose the correct form of the verb in the preterit tense.)

1. La señora Rodríguez _____ con algunas damas.
   (a) habla (b) está hablando (c) hablaba (d) habló _____

2. El señor Rodríguez _____ su café.
   (a) toma (b) está tomando (c) tomó (d) tomaba _____

3. La señora Rodríguez _____ a su asiento.
   (a) regresa (b) está regresando (c) regresaba (d) regresó _____

4. Pedro _____ su chocolate.
   (a) comió (b) come (c) comía (d) está comiendo _____

5. Juana _____ su jugo de naranja.
   (a) bebe (b) bebió (c) bebía (d) está bebiendo _____

III. Sopa de letras. Halle las palabras en español por las palabras en inglés. Las palabras pueden aparecer de derecha a izquierda, de izquierda a derecha, de abajo arriba y viceversa, y en diagonal.
(**Alphabet soup.** Find the Spanish words for the English words. The words can appear from right to left, from left to right, from bottom to top and top to bottom, and diagonally.)

1. stupid, foolish, dumb thing
2. everybody
3. really
4. play (theater)
5. better
6. orange (fruit)
7. to laugh
8. He took.
9. She drank.
10. He ate.

T	O	D	O	E	L	M	U	N	D	O
O	A	E	B	D	C	E	Ó	M	O	T
N	F	V	H	N	A	R	A	N	J	A
T	C	E	P	R	Q	A	E	V	A	U
E	O	R	O	J	E	M	X	Í	P	Z
R	M	A	C	B	E	D	G	H	R	O
Í	I	S	B	E	B	I	Ó	C	U	A
A	Ó	F	P	I	E	Z	A	T	E	O

IV. HUMOR. La adivinanza para hoy.
(**HUMOR:** The riddle for today.)

¿Qué hay en el medio de Sevilla? (What is in the middle of Sevilla?)

Solución: _____

V. ¿Cuál es la palabra más larga de la lengua española? (What is the longest word in the Spanish language?)

Respuesta: _____

VI. Varias palabras en una sola. Utilizando las letras en la palabra ARGENTINA, ¿cuántas palabras puede usted escribir? Escriba cinco palabras, por lo menos.
(**Several words in one.** Using the letters in the word ARGENTINA, how many words can you write? Write five words, at least. In Spanish, of course!)

ARGENTINA

1. _____   3. _____   5. _____

2. _____   4. _____

VII. **Discriminación de los sonidos. Su profesor de español va a pronunciar una sola palabra, sea la letra A, sea la letra B. Escoja la palabra que su profesor pronuncia y escriba la letra en la línea.**

(**Sound discrimination.** Your Spanish teacher is going to pronounce one word, either in letter A or letter B. Choose the word that your teacher pronounces and write the letter on the line.)

1. A. lama
   B. llama _____

2. A. hambre
   B. hombre _____

3. A. hallado
   B. helado _____

4. A. amo
   B. amó _____

VIII. **Providing/Obtaining Information. Speaking and Writing Proficiencies.**

Situation: You are on a school trip in Sevilla with your classmates and Mrs. Castillo, your Spanish teacher. Last night you returned very late to the hotel. Mrs. Castillo and your classmates were worried about you. You have been asked to explain where you were and what you did.

You are playing the role of **Usted** (sing. polite **You**). You may vary the dialogue by using your own words and ideas.

La profesora: **Anoche, Ud. regresó al hotel muy tarde. ¿Adónde fue Ud.?**

Usted: _____

(Say: I went to the theater.)

La profesora: **¿Al teatro? ¿Con quién?**
Usted: _____

(Say: Nobody / nadie. I went alone.)

La profesora: **Oh, Ud. fue al teatro solo (sola). ¿Qué pieza de teatro vio Ud.?**

Usted: _____

(Say: I saw a comedy, *El Burlador de Sevilla* by Tirso de Molina.)

La profesora: **¿Le gustó la comedia?**
Usted: _____

(Say: Yes, I liked the comedy. I enjoyed myself very much.)

La profesora: **¿Vio Ud. en el teatro a algunas personas que Ud. conoce?**

Usted: _____

(Say: Yes, I saw the Rodríguez family—the mother, father, Juana and Pedro. Their dog Coco was not with them / con ellos.)

La profesora: **Durante el entreacto, ¿qué comió y bebió?**
Usted: _____

_____

(Say: I ate chocolate with Pedro, I drank orange juice with Juana, and I talked with Señora Rodríguez and some ladies.)

La profesora: **¿Fue a tomar un café?**
Usted: _____

(Say: Yes. I went to have a coffee. Later, I returned to the hotel. It was midnight / Era medianoche.)

ESTRUCTURAS DE LA LENGUA

TENSE NO. 3: PRETÉRITO (PRETERIT)

This tense expresses an action that was completed at some time in the past.

EXAMPLES:

Mi padre **llegó** ayer / My father *arrived* yesterday; My father *did arrive* yesterday.

María **fue** a la iglesia esta mañana / Mary *went* to church this morning; Mary *did go* to church this morning.

¿Qué **pasó**? What *happened? What did happen?*

Tomé el desayuno a las siete / I *had* breakfast at seven o'clock. I *did have* breakfast at seven o'clock.

Salí de casa, **tomé** el autobús y **llegué** a la escuela a las ocho / I *left* the house, I *took* the bus and I *arrived* at school at eight o'clock.

In Spanish. some verbs that express a mental state have a different meaning when used in the preterit.

EXAMPLES:

La **conocí** la semana pasada en el baile / I *met* her last week at the dance. (**Conocer**, which means *to know* or *be acquainted with,* means *met,* that is, introduced to for the first time, in the preterit.)

Pude hacerlo / I *succeeded* in doing it. (**Poder**, which means *to be able,* means *succeeded* in the preterit.)

No pude hacerlo / I *failed* to do it. (**Poder**, when used in the negative in the preterit, means *failed* or *did not succeed.*)

Quise llamarlo / I *tried* to call you. (**Querer**, which means *to wish* or *want,* means *tried* in the preterit.)

No quise hacerlo / I *refused* to do it. (**Querer**, when used in the negative in the preterit, means *refused.*)

Supe la verdad / I *found out* the truth. (**Saber**, which means to *know,* means *found out* in the preterit.)

Tuve una carta de mi amigo Roberto / I *received* a letter from my friend Robert. (**Tener**, which means to *have,* means *received* in the preterit.)

This tense is regularly formed as follows:

Drop the **–ar** ending of an infinitive, like **hablar,** and add the following endings: **é, aste, ó; amos, asteis, aron**

You then get: **hablé, hablaste, habló;**
hablamos, hablasteis, hablaron

The usual equivalent in English is: I talked OR I did talk, you talked OR you did talk, *etc.* OR I spoke OR I did speak; you spoke OR you did speak, *etc.*

Drop the **–er** ending of an infinitive, like **beber,** or the **–ir** ending of an infinitive, like **recibir,** and add the following endings: **í, iste, ió; imos, isteis, ieron**

You then get: **bebí, bebiste, bebió;**
bebimos, bebisteis, bebieron

recibí recibiste, recibió;
recibimos, recibisteis, recibieron

The usual equivalent in English is: I drank OR I did drink; you drank OR you did drink, *etc.;* I received OR I did receive, *etc.*

Verbs Irregular in the Preterit, Including Stem-Changing Verbs and Orthographical Changing Verbs

NOTE that the first three forms up to the semicolon are the 1st, 2nd, and 3rd persons of the singular; the three verb forms under those are the 1st, 2nd, and 3rd persons of the plural. The subject pronouns are not given in order to emphasize the verb forms.

---

almorzar / to have lunch, to eat lunch
almorcé, almorzaste, almorzó;
almorzamos, almorzasteis, almorzaron

An orthographical changing verb because **z** changes to **c** in front of **é** in the 1st pers. sing. of this tense.

---

buscar / to look for, to search, to seek
busqué, buscaste, buscó;
buscamos, buscasteis, buscaron

An orthographical changing verb because **c** changes to **qu** in front of **é** in the 1st pers. sing. of this tense.

---

andar / to walk
**anduve, anduviste, anduvo;
anduvlmos, anduvisteis, anduvieron**

---

caer / to fall
**caí, caíste, cayó;
caímos, caísteis, cayeron**

An orthographical changing verb because **i** in **ió** of the 3rd pers. sing. ending changes to **y** and **i** in **ieron** of the 3rd pers. plural ending changes to **y.** The reason for this spelling change is the strong vowel **a** right in front of those two endings.

ALSO NOTE that **i** in **iste** changes to **í** in the 2nd pers. slng. and **I** in **Isteis** changes to **í** in the 2nd pers. plural because of the strong vowel **a** in front of those two endings. The same thing happens in **caímos.**

IX. **The following verb forms are in the preterit tense. Change them by using the new subject given in parentheses. Repeat the other words in the sentence. You may add additional words if you wish.**

   Refer to the boxed verbs above where you are given the verb forms in the preterit. In this exercise you are practicing the following verbs: almorzar, andar, buscar, caer.

Modelo: Juana almorzó a la una. (Yo)
         (Jane had lunch at one o'clock.)

Escriba: Yo almorcé a la una.
         (I had lunch at one o'clock.)

1. Ayer nosotros anduvimos a la escuela. **(Ellos)**   _____

2. Clara y Francisco Rodríguez buscaron un taxi. **(Yo)**   _____

3. El niño cayó. **(Los niños)**   _____

4. Las muchachas almorzaron a las dos. **(Yo)**   _____

5. ¿Anduvo Ud. al parque? **(Tú)**   _____   **167**

comenzar / to begin, to commence, to start
  comencé, comenzaste, comenzó;
  comenzamos, comenzasteis, comenzaron

An orthographical changing verb because **z** changes to **c** in front of **é** in the 1st pers. sing. of this tense.

dar / to give
  di, diste, dio;
  dimos, disteis, dieron

creer / to believe
  creí, creíste, creyó;
  creímos, creísteis, creyeron

An orthographical changing verb because **i** in **ió** of the 3rd pers. sing. ending changes to **y** and **i** in **ieron** of the 3rd pers. plural ending changes to **y.** Also note that **i** in **iste** changes to **í** in the 2nd pers. sing. and **i** in **isteis** changes to **í** in the 2nd pers. pl. because of the strong vowel **e** in front of those two endings. The same thing happens in **creímos.**

decir / to say, to tell
  dije, dijiste, dijo;
  dijimos, dijisteis, dijeron

X. **Do the same here as you did in Exercise IX. In this exercise you are practicing the preterit of the following verbs: comenzar, creer, dar, decir.**

  Modelo: La profesora comenzó a hablar en español. (Yo)
        (The teacher began to speak in Spanish.)

  Escriba: Yo comencé a hablar en español.
        (I began to speak in Spanish.)

1. Los estudios comenzaron ayer. **(La clase)**   _____

2. María creyó la historia. **(Yo)**   _____

3. Juana dio el programa a su madre. **(Pedro y Juana)**   _____

4. El señor dijo: Aquí tiene Ud. mi autógrafo. **(Yo)**   _____

5. ¿Qué dijeron ellos? **(Tú)**   _____

divertirse / to have a good time, to enjoy oneself
me divertí, te divertiste, **se divirtió;**
nos divertimos, os divertisteis,
se divirtieron

A stem-changing verb because **e** in the stem changes to **i** in the 3rd pers. sing. and pl. of this tense. Pres. part. is **divirtiéndose.**

elegir / to elect, to select, to choose
elegí, elegiste, **eligió;**
elegimos, elegisteis, **eligieron**

A stem-changing verb because **e** in the stem changes to **i** in the 3rd pers. sing. and pl. of this tense. Pres. part. is **eligiendo.**

dormir / to sleep
dormí, dormiste, **durmió;**
dormimos, dormisteis, **durmieron**

A stem-changing verb because **o** in the stem changes to **u** in the 3rd pers. sing. and pl. of this tense. Pres. part. is **durmiendo.**

empezar / to begin, to start
empecé, empezaste, empezó;
empezamos, empezasteis, empezaron

An orthographical changing verb because **z** changes to **c** in front of **é** in the 1st pers. sing. of this tense.

XI. **Do the same here as you did above. In this exercise you are practicing the preterit of the following verbs: divertirse, dormir, elegir, empezar.**

Modelo: Yo me divertí mucho en el teatro. (Ud.)
(I enjoyed myself very much at the theater.)

Escriba: Ud. se divirtió mucho en el teatro.
(You enjoyed yourself very much at the theater.)

1. Carlos durmió ocho horas. **(Yo)** _____

2. Yo elegí chocolate. **(Pablo)** _____

3. Roberto empezó a hablar español. **(Yo)** _____

4. Yo dormí toda la noche. **(Los niños)** _____

5. Tú empezaste el trabajo. **(Uds.)** _____

equivocarse / to be mistaken
me equivoqué, te equivocaste,
se equivocó; nos equivocamos,
os equivocasteis, se equivocaron

An orthographical changing verb because **c** changes to **qu** in front of **é** in the 1st pers. sing. of this tense.

explicar / to explain
expliqué, explicaste, explicó;
explicamos, explicasteis, explicaron

An orthographical changing verb because **c** changes to **qu** in front of **é** in the 1st pers. sing. of this tense.

estar / to be
estuve, estuviste, estuvo;
estuvimos, estuvisteis, estuvieron

hacer / to do, to make
hice, hiciste, hizo;
hicimos, hicisteis, hicieron

XII. Do the same here as you did above. In this exercise you are practicing the preterit of the following verbs: equivocarse, estar, explicar, hacer.

Modelo: Anoche, la familia Rodríguez estuvo en el teatro. (Yo)
(Last night, the Rodríguez family was at the theater.)

Escriba: Anoche, yo estuve en el teatro.
(Last night, I was at the theater.)

1. Perdóneme, Usted se equivocó. **(Yo)** _____

2. Anoche, estuvimos en el cine. **(Ellos)** _____

3. El profesor explicó el pretérito. **(Yo)** _____

4. Juana hizo una tontería. **(Tú)** _____

5. El verano pasado hicimos un viaje. **(Ellos)** _____

---

ir / to go
fui, fuiste, fue;
fuimos, fuisteis, fueron

NOTE that these forms are the same for **ser** in the preterit.

---

llegar / to arrive
llegué, llegaste, llegó;
llegamos, llegasteis, llegaron

An orthographical changing verb because **g** changes to **gu** in front of **é** in the 1st pers. sing. of this tense.

---

leer / to read
leí, **leíste, leyó;**
leímos, **leísteis, leyeron**

An orthographical changing verb because **i** in **ió** of the 3rd pers. sing. ending changes to **y** and **i** in **ieron** of the 3rd pers. plural ending changes to **y.** Also note that **i** in **iste** change to **í** in the 2nd pers. sing. and **i** in **isteis** changes to **í** in the 2nd pers. pl. because of the strong vowel **e** in front of those two endings. The same thing happens in **leímos.** Remember that the regular endings in the preterit of an **–er** and **–ir** verb are: **í, iste, ió; imos, isteis, ieron.**

---

morir / to die
morí, moriste, **murió;**
morimos, moristeis, **murieron**

A stem-changing verb because **o** in the stem changes to **u** in the 3rd pers. sing. and pl. of this tense. Pres. part. is **muriendo.**

XIII. Do the same here as you did above. In this exercise you are practicing the preterit of the following verbs: ir, leer, llegar, morir.

    Modelo: La familia Rodríguez fue al teatro.   (Yo)
               (The Rodríguez family went to the theater.)

    Escriba: Fui al teatro.
               (I went to the theater.)

1. Los alumnos leyeron la lectura. **(Yo)**   _____

2. Llegaron al cine a las siete. **(Yo)**   _____

3. Mariana Sánchez murió durante la noche. **(Ellos)**   _____

4. Tú leíste el libro. **(Inés)**   _____

5. El doctor llegó inmediatamente. **(Las cartas)**   _____

---

oír / to hear (sometimes can mean to *understand*)
  oí, oíste, oyó;
  oímos, oísteis, oyeron

An orthographical changing verb because **i** in **ió** of the 3rd pers. sing. ending and **i** in **ieron** of the 3rd pers. plural ending both change to **y.**

  ALSO NOTE that **iste** changes to **íste, imos** to **ímos,** and **isteis** to **ísteis** because of the strong vowel **o** in front of those endings. Remember that the regular endings in the preterit of an **–er** and **–ir** verb are: **í, iste, ió; imos, isteis, ieron.**

---

pedir / to ask for, to request
  pedí, pediste, **pidió;**
  pedimos, pedisteis, **pidieron**

A stem-changing verb because **e** in the stem changes to **i** in the 3rd pers. sing. and pl. of this tense. Pres. part. is **pidiendo.**

---

pagar / to pay
  pagué, pagaste, pagó;
  pagamos, pagasteis, pagaron

An orthographical changing verb because **g** changes to **gu** in front of **é** in the 1st pers. sing. of this tense.

---

pescar / to fish
  pesqué, pescaste, pescó;
  pescamos, pescasteis, pescaron

An orthographical changing verb because **c** changes to **qu** in front of **é** in the 1st pers. sing. of this tense.

XIV. **Do the same here as you did above. In this exercise you are practicing the preterit of the following verbs: oír, pagar, pedir, pescar.**

Modelo: Usted oyó la música. (Yo)
(You heard the music.)

Escriba: Yo oí la música.
(I heard the music.)

1. Usted pagó la cuenta. **(Yo)** _____

2. El hijo menor pidió dinero. **(Los chicos)** _____

3. Los dos amigos pescaron en este lago. **(Yo)** _____

4. Yo no oí nada. **(Las muchachas)** _____

5. Yo pedí papel. **(El alumno)** _____

poder / to be able, can **pude, pudiste, pudo;** **pudimos, pudisteis, pudieron**	**preferir** / to prefer preferí, preferiste, **prefirió;** preferimos, preferisteis, **prefirieron** A stem-changing verb because **e** in the stem changes to **i** in the 3rd pers. sing. and pl. of this tense. Pres. part. is **prefiriendo.**
poner / to put, to place **puse, pusiste, puso;** **pusimos, pusisteis, pusieron**	**querer** / to want, to wish **quise, quisiste, quiso;** **quisimos, quisisteis, quisieron**

XV. **Just a few more useful exercises. You will soon be an expert in commonly used Spanish verbs in the preterit tense. They are basic requirements for a solid foundation in Level 2.**
Are you referring to the boxed verb forms above for help?
Do the same here as you did above. In this exercise you are practicing the preterit of the following verbs: poder, poner, preferir, querer.

Modelo: María no pudo venir a la fiesta. (Yo)
(María was not able to come to the party.)

Escriba: Yo no pude venir a la fiesta.
(I was not able to come to the party.)

1. La profesora puso el libro en el escritorio. **(Yo)** _____

2. Yo preferí la camisa roja. **(Ud.)** _____

3. No quise hacerlo. **(Ellos)** _____

4. Los abuelos pusieron las flores en un jarrón. **(Nosotros)** _____

172 5. José prefirió jugo de manzana. **(Uds.)** _____

reír/ to laugh
reí, reíste, rió;
reímos, reísteis, rieron

Pres. part. is **riendo.**

saber/ to know, to know how
supe, supiste, supo;
supimos, supisteis, supieron

repetir/ to repeat
repetí, repetiste, **repitió;**
repetimos, repetisteis, **repitieron**

A stem-changing verb because **e** in the stem changes to **i** in the 3rd pers. sing. and pl. of this tense. Pres. part. is **repitiendo.**

sacar/ to take out
saqué, sacaste, sacó;
sacamos, sacasteis, sacaron

An orthographical changing verb because **c** changes to **qu** in front of **é** in the 1st pers. sing. of this tense.

XVI. In this exercise you are practicing the preterit of the following verbs: reír, repetir, saber, sacar.

Modelo: Todos rieron a carcajadas. (Yo)
(They all burst out laughing.)

Escriba: Yo reí a carcajadas.
(I burst out laughing.)

1. Juana rió. **(Nosotros)** _____

2. El alumno repitió la frase. **(Los alumnos)** _____

3. Supimos la verdad. **(Yo)** _____

4. Los turistas sacaron fotos. **(Yo)** _____

5. Yo repetí el número de teléfono. **(Tú)** _____

ser/ to be
fui, fuiste, fue;
fuimos, fuisteis, fueron

NOTE that these forms are the same for **ir** in the preterit.

sonreír/ to smile
sonreí, sonreíste, sonrió;
sonreímos, sonreísteis, sonrieron

Pres. part. is **sonriendo.**

servir/ to serve
serví, serviste, **sirvió;**
servimos, servisteis, **sirvieron**

A stem-changing verb because **e** in the stem changes to **i** in the 3rd pers. sing. and pl. of this tense. Pres. part. is **sirviendo.**

tener/ to have, to hold
tuve, tuviste, tuvo;
tuvimos, tuvisteis, tuvieron

XVII. **In this exercise you are practicing the preterit of the following verbs: ser, servir, son-reír, tener.**

Modelo: Murillo fue un gran artista español. (El Greco)
(Murillo was a great Spanish artist.)

Escriba: El Greco fue un gran artista español.
(El Greco was a great Spanish artist.)

1. La señora Rodríguez sirvió los pasteles. **(Yo)**   _____

2. Juana sonrió. **(Las muchachas)**   _____

3. Ayer yo tuve una carta de Pedro. **(Isabel)**   _____

4. Velázquez fue un gran pintor español. **(Goya)**   _____

5. Tecla tuvo regalos de sus amigos. **(Ellos)**   _____

---

tocar / to touch, to play (music or a musical instrument)
toqué, tocaste, tocó;
tocamos, tocasteis, tocaron

An orthographical changing verb because **c** changes to **qu** in front of **é** in the 1st pers. sing. of this tense.

---

venir / to come
vine, viniste, vino;
vinimos, vinisteis, vinieron

---

traer / to bring
traje, trajiste, trajo;
trajimos, trajisteis, trajeron

Pres. part. is **trayendo.**

---

ver / to see
vi, viste, vio;
vimos, visteis, vieron

XVIII. **In this exercise you are practicing the preterit of the following verbs: tocar, traer, venir, ver.**

Modelo: Inés tocó el piano en la fiesta. (Yo)
(Inés played the piano at the party.)

Escriba: Yo toqué el piano en la fiesta.
(I played the piano at the party.)

1. Los amigos trajeron regalos. **(Ud.)**   _____

2. Muchas personas vinieron a la tertulia. **(Pablo)**   _____

3. La familia Rodríguez vio una pieza de teatro. **(Yo)**   _____

4. Juana trajo el helado. **(Ellos)**   _____

5. ¿Qué vieron ellos? **(Tú)**   _____

EJERCICIOS

I. **Seleccione la forma correcta del verbo en el pretérito.**(Choose the correct form of the verb in the preterit tense.)

1. Antes de regresar a su asiento, Juana _____ a un hombre. (a) ve (b) está viendo (c) veía (d) vio _____

2. Cuando Juana vio al hombre, ella le _____ "Buenos días". (a) dice (b) está diciendo (c) decía (d) dijo _____

3. El hombre _____ su autógrafo en el programa que Juana tenía en la mano. (a) escribió (b) escribe (c) está escribiendo (d) escribía _____

4. Juana le _____ al hombre su programa y su pluma para escribir su autógrafo. (a) da (b) dio (c) está dando (d) daba _____

5. Cuando la pieza se terminó, todo el mundo _____ del teatro. (a) salió (b) sale (c) está saliendo (d) salía _____

6. Afuera, Juana (a) anuncia (b) anunció (c) está anunciando (d) anunciaba las noticias. _____

7. Juana dio el programa a su madre y ésta (a) lee (b) leyó (c) leía (d) está leyendo los anuncios. _____

8. Pedro _____ que todo el mundo no tiene el autógrafo de José Blanco. (a) dijo (b) dije (c) dice (d) está diciendo _____

9. Juana _____ una tontería. (a) hace (b) hizo (c) está haciendo (d) hacía _____

10. Juana _____ que hizo una tontería. (a) exclamó (b) exclama (c) exclamaba (d) está exclamando _____

II. **Cambie el verbo entre paréntesis al pretérito.** (Change the verb in parentheses to the preterit.)

   Modelo: Ayer, yo (ver) a mis amigos en el centro.   ____vi____

1. ¿Qué (ver) Ud. en la televisión ayer por la noche? _____

2. El año pasado Miguel (ir) a Puerto Rico. _____

3. Ayer, después de la comida, mi hermana (servir) el café. _____

4. Esta mañana una persona (tocar) a la puerta. _____

5. ¿Quién (traer) este pastel? _____

6. Ayer yo (tener) una carta de mi amigo Roberto que vive en España. _____

7. La semana pasada yo (conocer) a Juana en el baile. _____

8. Yo (poder) hacerlo. _____

9. Yo (querer) llamar a mi amiga Carlota. _____

10. Juana no (querer) ir a casa de Elena. _____

III. Escriba las seis formas de cada verbo en el pretérito. (Write the six forms of each verb in the preterit.)

Modelo: ser ___fui, fuiste, fue; fuimos, fuisteis, fueron___

1. ser _____

2. tener _____

3. traer _____

4. venir _____

5. preferir _____

6. querer _____

7. reír _____

8. saber _____

9. sacar _____

10. morir _____

IV. Seleccione el verbo en el imperfecto de indicativo o en el pretérito, según convenga. Estudie otra vez el imperfecto de indicativo en el Work Unit 6. (Choose the verb in the imperfect indicative tense or the preterit, according to which tense is required. Study again the imperfect indicative in Work Unit 6.)

Modelo: Mi hermano _____ un libro y mi padre hablaba cuando yo entré.
(a) leía (b) leyó ___a___

1. Mi hermana _____ cuando yo llamé. (a) cantó (b) cantaba _____

2. Cuando _____ en Nueva York, íbamos al cine todos los días. (a) estábamos (b) estuvimos _____

3. Mi padre _____ ayer. (a) llegaba (b) llegó _____

4. Cuando _____ en California, íbamos a la playa todos los días. (a) vivíamos (b) vivimos _____

5. Esta mañana María _____ a la iglesia. (a) iba (b) fue _____

6. Mi madre _____ hermosa cuando era pequeña. (a) era (b) fue _____

7. ¿Qué hora _____ cuando Ud. llegó? (a) era (b) fue _____

8. ¿Qué _____? (a) pasó (b) pasaba _____

9. ¿Qué hora era? _____ las tres. (a) Eran (b) Fueron _____

10. Hacía tres horas que yo _____ la televisión cuando mi madre llamó. (a) miré
    (b) miraba   _____

11. Salí de casa, _____ el autobús y llegué a la escuela a las ocho. (a) tomaba
    (b) tomé   _____

12. Esta mañana yo _____ el desayuno a las siete. (a) tomé (b) tomaba   _____

13. Juana _____ contentísima de ver a su amiga Carlota. (a) estuvo (b) estaba _____

V. Conteste las siguientes preguntas en el afirmativo con oraciones completas. En la oración (a) use la palabra **Sí**. En la oración (b) use la palabra **también** según los modelos.

(Answer the following questions in the affirmative in complete sentences. In sentence [a] use the word **Sí**. In sentence [b] use the word **también** [also], according to the models.)

Modelos: a. ¿Abrió Ud. la ventana?   a. Sí, (yo) abrí la ventana.
              (Did you open the window?)   (Yes, I opened the window.)

            b. ¿Y su madre?   b. Mi madre abrió la ventana, también.
              (And your mother?)   (My mother opened the window also).

1. a. ¿Escribió Ud. una carta? _____

    b. ¿Y Carlos? _____

2. a. ¿Oyó Ud. el ruido? _____

    b. ¿Y los alumnos? _____

3. a. ¿Oyeron la música los estudiantes? _____

    b. ¿Y usted? _____

4. a. ¿Pagó Ud. la cuenta? _____

    b. ¿Y Casandra y Claudio? _____

5. a. ¿Pidió Ud. dinero a su padre ayer? _____

    b. ¿Y su hermano? _____

6. a. ¿Pescaron los muchachos en este lago? _____

    b. ¿Y ustedes? _____

7. a. ¿Pudo Ud. abrir la ventana? _____

    b. ¿Y la profesora? _____

8. a. ¿Puso Ud. el dinero en el bolsillo? _____

    b. ¿Y el señor Rodríguez? _____

9. a. ¿Hizo Ud. muchas cosas ayer? _____

    b. ¿Y Daniel y David? _____

10. a. ¿Fue la señora Rodríguez al teatro el sábado pasado? _____

    b. ¿Y ustedes? _____

VI. Juego de palabras. Complete las palabras verticalmente en español por las palabras en inglés. Todas las palabras son formas de verbos en el pretérito.
(**Word Play.** Complete the words vertically in Spanish for the words in English. All the words are forms of the verbs in the **preterit tense.**)

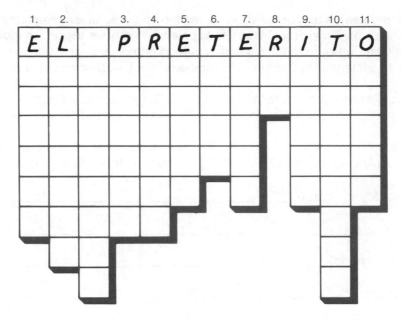

1. I studied.
2. They called.
3. We paid.
4. He repeated.
5. I began.
6. I brought.
7. He elected.
8. I laughed.
9. I invited.
10. I telephoned.
11. They dared.

VII. ¿Qué instrumento musical toca Ud? (What musical instrument do you play?)

Respuesta: _____

VIII. ¿Qué mira Ud? (What are you looking at?)

Respuesta: _____

IX. A veces, si Ud. pronuncia incorrectamente una palabra española, es posible que Ud. pronuncie otra palabra que existe en la lengua. Esto puede ser desconcertante.
(At times, if you pronounce a Spanish word incorrectly, it is possible that you are pronouncing another word that exists in the language. This can be confusing.)

EJEMPLO:

hablo / I speak, am speaking, do speak   (1st pers., sing., present indicative
          I talk, am talking, do talk   of **hablar**)

habló / He (She) spoke.   (3rd pers., sing., preterit of **hablar**)
          He (She) talked.

Mnemonic Tip	In hablo, the stress in on A. In habló, the stress in on O because there is an accent mark on O.

hablar / to speak, to talk

present indicative

yo **hablo**	nosotros hablamos
tú hablas	vosotros habláis

Ud. ⎫
él ⎬ habla
ella ⎭

Uds. ⎫
ellos ⎬ hablan
ellas ⎭

preterit

yo **hablé**	nosotros **hablamos**
tú **hablaste**	vosotros **hablasteis**

Ud. ⎫
él ⎬ **habló**
ella ⎭

Uds. ⎫
ellos ⎬ **hablaron**
ellas ⎭

¿Cuántos ejemplos puede Ud. decir y escribir? (How many examples can you say and write?)

Mnemonic Tip	The general rule for stress in pronouncing a Spanish word is:
	If a word in Spanish ends in a vowel, n, or s, stress (raise your voice) on the vowel in the syllable next to the last one:
	muCHAcha esTAban reGAlos
	If a word ends in a letter other than a vowel, n, or s, stress the last syllable:
	feLIZ abandoNAR reLOJ

X. LETRA RELOJ. Cuatro palabras se esconden en este reloj: una palabra de las doce a las tres, una palabra de las tres a las seis, una palabra de las seis a las nueve y, por fin, una palabra de las nueve a las doce.
(**WORD CLOCK.** Four words are hidden in this clock: one word from 12 to 3, one word from 3 to 6, one word from 6 to 9 and, finally, one word from 9 to 12.)

La misma letra es común a la palabra que sigue. (The same letter is common to the word that follows. In other words, the last letter of one word is the same as the first letter of the word that follows.)

Este reloj no tiene agujas. ¡Es un reloj de palabras! (This clock does not have any hands [needles]. It is a word clock!)

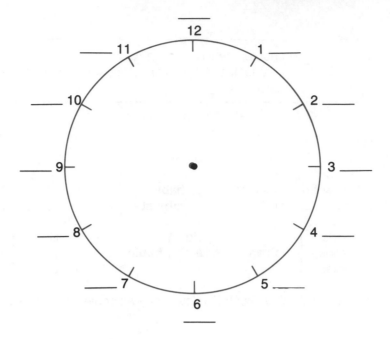

De las doce a las tres es un sinónimo de **años.**

De las tres a las seis es un sinónimo de **mujer.**

De las seis a las nueve es un sinónimo de **pájaros.**

De las nueve a las doce es la tercera persona, singular, presente de indicativo del verbo **salir.**
(Tip: If you get stuck in this word game, you can find a synonym for each of the three required words by looking them up in the vocabulary beginning on page 481.)

XI. Las palabras escondidas. En la rejilla, busque las palabras en español por las palabras en inglés de la lista que figuran a continuación.
(**Hidden Words.** In this grid, find the words in Spanish for the words in English on the list next to the grid.)

Las palabras están inscritas en todas las direcciones: de abajo arriba, de arriba abajo, de derecha a izquierda, de izquierda a derecha, y en diagonal.
(The words are written in all directions: from bottom to top, from top to bottom, from right to left, from left to right, and diagonally.)

La misma letra puede ser común a varias palabras. (The same letter can be common to several words.)

A	L	Á	M	P	A	R	A	A
B	D	C	E	U	I	O	E	U
A	M	P	L	E	L	A	M	A
V	N	E	H	R	V	E	S	L
P	U	C	E	T	R	E	O	F
L	O	P	C	A	M	A	S	O
C	M	E	A	S	A	N	E	M
A	M	C	S	A	S	A	C	B
A	R	T	U	P	I	T	I	R
A	I	E	O	U	L	N	P	A
L	F	A	M	B	L	E	Á	F
C	A	A	S	S	A	V	L	O

door
houses
car
pencils
beds
chair
window
table
lamp
carpet

XII. Expressing Personal Feelings. Proficiency in Speaking and Writing.

Situation: Your aunt Agatha (tu tía Ágata) was unable to be at your recent birthday party (tu fiesta de cumpleaños) because she was sick. You are visiting her in the hospital to express your feelings about her health and to thank her for the present she sent you.

In this dialogue with your aunt you are **Tú.** You may vary the dialogue by using your own words and ideas. After you have said your lines aloud, practice them on the lines.

Tu tía: **¡Qué sorpresa! ¡Tú viniste a verme! ¿Cómo estás? Dame un abrazo** (Give me a hug).

Tú: _____

_____

(Say: Me? / Yo? I am very well. I came to see you because I want to know how you are. I love you.)

Tu tía: **Mejor, mucho mejor, gracias a Dios. Pero prefiero estar en mi propia cama** (in my own bed) **en mi casa. Dime** (Tell me), **¿recibiste el regalito que te envié?**

Tú: _____

(Say: Yes, of course, I received the little gift and I want to say thank you very much. You are very nice.)

Tu tía: **¿Te gustó el regalito?**

Tú: _____

(Tell her you liked it a lot.)

Tu tía: **¿Y tu cumpleaños? ¿Cómo pasaste tu cumpleaños? ¡Dime todo!**

Tú: _____

_____

(Tell her who came to the party, what gifts they brought, what you all did at the party (ate, drank, sang, danced), and where you all went later.)

Tu tía: **Me parece que** (It seems to me that) **todo el mundo se divirtió. ¡Estoy muy contenta!**

Tú: _____

_____

(Tell her that you are happy too. Ask for a hug. Say: Now I have to leave because the Rodríguez family and their dog are coming to my house at four o'clock with presents for my birthday!)

XIII. Informal Note for Communication. Writing Proficiency.

Situation: Adolfo Hidalgo, an exchange student from Spain at your school, has returned home. Write him a note and tell him the following, or you may use your own words and ideas: Yesterday was your birthday / Ayer fue mi cumpleaños; many friends were at the party, you received many gifts, you ate, drank, sang, and danced, you played the piano and Carlos played the guitar; everybody had a good time.

Use the post card below to write your message. Begin the note with Querido amigo Adolfo / Dear friend Adolfo. End the note with Adiós. Then write your name. Don't forget to write the date in Spanish!

William T. Piper
Aviation Pioneer
USA Airmail

Señor Adolfo Hidalgo

Planta 1A - Goya 1

Avenida Los Manantiales

Torremolinos

Málaga

España   SPAIN

Air Mail

Correo Aéreo

ADVERBS

Definition: An adverb is a word that modifies a verb, an adjective, or another adverb.

Regular formation: An adverb is regularly formed by adding the ending **mente** to the fem. sing. form of an adj.:

lento, lenta / lentamente: slow / slowly; **rápido, rápida / rápidamente:** rapid / rapidly

If the form of the adj. is the same for the fem. sing. and masc. sing. (fácil, feliz), add **mente** to that form.

fácil (easy) / **fácilmente** (easily)
feliz (happy) / **felizmente** (happily)

NOTE that an accent mark on an adjective remains when changed to an adverb. And note that the Spanish ending **mente** is equivalent to the ending **-ly** in English.

An adverb remains invariable; that is to say, it does not agree in gender and number and therefore does not change in form.

There are many adverbs that do not end in **mente.** Some common ones are:

abajo / below	**bien** / well	**hoy** / today	**siempre** / always	**aquí** / here
arriba / above	**mal** / badly	**mañana** / tomorrow	**nunca** / never	**allí** / there

The adverbial ending **ísimo**

Never use **muy** in front of **mucho.** Say **muchísimo: Elena trabaja muchísimo** / Helen works a great deal; Helen works very, very much.

Regular comparison of adverbs

María corre tan rápidamente como Elena / Mary runs as rapidly as Helen.

María corre menos rápidamente que Anita / Mary runs less rapidly than Anita.

María corre más rápidamente que Isabel / Mary runs more rapidly than Elizabeth.

Irregular comparative adverbs

mucho, poco / much, little: **Roberto trabaja mucho; Felipe trabaja poco.**

bien, mal / well, badly: **Juan trabaja bien; Lucas trabaja mal.**

más, menos / more, less: **Carlota trabaja más que Casandra; Elena trabaja menos que Marta.**

mejor, peor / better, worse: **Paula trabaja mejor que Anita; Isabel trabaja peor que Elena.**

In the comparative and superlative

rápidamente	**más rápidamente**	**lo más rápidamente**
rapidly	more rapidly	most rapidly

Con, sin + noun

At times, an adverb can be formed by using the prep. **con** (with) or **sin** (without) + a noun.

con cuidado / carefully	**con dificultad** / with difficulty
sin cuidado / carelessly	**sin dificultad** / without difficulty

The adverb **recientemente** (recently) becomes **recién** before a past participle: **los recién llegados** / the ones recently arrived; the recently arrived (ones)

Interrogative adverbs

Some common interrogative adverbs are: **¿cómo?** / how? **¿cuándo?** / when? **¿por qué?** / why? **¿para qué?** / why? **¿dónde?** / where? **¿adónde?** / where to? (to where)?

Adverbs replaced by adjectives

An adverb may sometimes be replaced by an adjective whose agreement is with the subject, especially if the verb is one of motion:

Las muchachas van y vienen silenciosas / The girls come and go silently.

EJERCICIOS

I. Forme adverbios de los siguientes adjetivos. (Form adverbs from the following adjectives.)

    Modelo: lento ⟶ lentamente

1. rápido _____   4. absoluto _____

2. fácil _____   5. feliz _____

3. alegre _____   6. cierto _____

II. Escriba seis adverbios que no terminan en –mente. (Write six adverbs that do not end in –mente.)

1. _____   4. _____

2. _____   5. _____

3. _____   6. _____

III. Traduzca al español.

1. Cristina runs as rapidly as Helen. _____

2. Claudia runs less rapidly than Anita. _____

3. David runs more rapidly than Enrique. _____

4. Roberto works a lot; Felipe works a little. _____

5. Juana works well; Lucas works badly. _____

6. Carlota works more than Casandra. _____

7. Elena works less than Marta. _____

8. Paula works better than Dora. _____

9. Isabel works worse than Elisa. _____

10. Michael talks carelessly and he does not study well. _____

IV. Conteste las siguientes preguntas en el afirmativo con oraciones completas. En la oración (a) use la palabra Sí. En la oración (b) use la palabra también, según los modelos. (Answer the following questions in the affirmative in complete sentences. In sentence [a] use the word Sí. In sentence [b] use the word también [also], according to the models.)

    Modelos: a. ¿Trabaja Ud. con cuidado?   **Escriba:** a. Sí, trabajo con cuidado.
                b. ¿Y Emilia?   b. Emilia trabaja con cuidado, también.

1. a. ¿Estudia Ud. sin cuidado? _____

   b. ¿Y los otros alumnos? _____

2. a. ¿Lee Emilio con dificultad? _____

   b. ¿Y tú? _____

3. a. ¿Estudió Ud. la lección sin dificultad? _____

   b. ¿Y Uds.? _____

4. a. ¿Escribiste la carta con cuidado? _____

   b. ¿Y Edita? _____

5. a. ¿Corre María tan rápidamente como Elena? _____

   b. ¿Y ustedes? _____

6. a. ¿Habla Ricardo menos rápidamente que Ramón? _____

   b. ¿Y Rebeca y Tomás? _____

7. a. ¿Escribe Samuel más rápidamente que Sara? _____

   b. ¿Y ellos? _____

8. a. ¿Duerme Susana más que Teresa? _____

   b. ¿Y los niños? _____

9. a. ¿Van y vienen silenciosas Eva y María? _____

   b. ¿Y Roberto y Carlos? _____

10. a. ¿Trabaja Elena muchísimo? _____

   b. ¿Y todos los alumnos en la clase de español? _____

V. Varias palabras en una sola. Utilizando las letras en la palabra COLOMBIA, ¿cuántas palabras puede usted escribir? Escriba seis palabras, por lo menos.
(**Several words in one.** Using the letters in the word **COLOMBIA,** how many words can you write? Write at least six words.)

COLOMBIA

1. _____ 4. _____

2. _____ 5. _____

3. _____ 6. _____

VI. Jeroglífico. Rellene las casillas a continuación con las letras de la palabra que describe el dibujo.
(**Rebus.** A rebus is a verbal riddle solved by interpreting a series of pictures that represent syllables or words. Fill in the boxes below with the letters of the word that describes the drawing.)

Para hallar la solución de este jeroglífico, rellene las casillas del modo siguiente: en la casilla 1, escriba la primera letra de la persona en el primer dibujo; en la casilla 2, escriba la segunda letra de la persona en el segundo dibujo; en la casilla 3, escriba la tercera letra del objeto en el tercer dibujo; en la casilla 4, escriba la letra A.

(To find the solution to this rebus, fill in the four boxes next to the word Solución in the following way. In box 1, write the first letter of the Spanish word that describes the person in the first drawing (fat); in box 2, write the second letter of the Spanish word that describes the person in the second drawing (young); in box 3, write the third letter of the Spanish word for the object in the third drawing (jewel); in box 4, write the letter A.)

Después de haber rellenado las cuatro casillas de la solución de aquel modo, usted encontrará el nombre de un gran pintor español. (After having filled in the four boxes of the solution in that way, you will find the name of a great Spanish artist!)

✝ A

Solución: ☐ ☐ ☐ ☐

VII. Algunos alumnos confunden las palabras mujer y mejor. (Some students confuse the words mujer and mejor.)

la mujer / the woman
  mejor *adj., adv.* / better

Esta mujer trabaja mejor que ésa. / This woman works better than that one.

Mnemonic Tip	Mejor contains e after the first letter and so does *better.* ¿Qué palabras españolas confunde usted? ¿Puede Ud. dar un "mnemonic tip"?

Mnemonic Tip	Exception to the general rule of stress in pronouncing a Spanish word: If it is customary to stress a syllable other than the one next to the last syllable when the word ends in a vowel, *n,* or *s,* you must write an accent mark on the vowel in the syllable that is stressed to tell the reader to stress that syllable: pretérito.

VIII. **Convincing Someone about an Opinion. Proficiency in Speaking and Writing.**

Situation: You are having a discussion with Alano, a classmate. You are trying to convince him that in your opinion you are a better driver than he is. You think you drive carefully, easily, and without difficulty and he drives carelessly and with difficulty. He never obeys driving rules but you do.

You may use your own words and ideas or the following, all of which are in the section on adverbs and comparative adverbs on the preceding pages: **lentamente, rápidamente, tan rápidamente como, menos ... que, más ... que, con/sin cuidado, con/sin dificultad,** and others.

Verbs you probably need to use: **conducir, creer, decir, obedecer, pensar, poder, saber, ver.** You may want to review them in the present indicative tense in Work Unit 3. If you want to use a verb in the past tense, review the preterit in this Work Unit.

Tú: _____

(Tell Alano: I know that I drive a car better than you do.)

Alano: **Es tu opinión. Tú no tienes razón. Yo sé que yo conduzco un coche mejor que tú conduces.**

Tú: _____

(Say: You drive faster than I do. Everybody knows it / **todo el mundo lo sabe.**)

Alano: **¿Qué dices? Yo creo que conduzco bien. Tú conduces mal.**

Tú: _____

(Tell him: Yesterday you drove **(tú condujiste)** in the park as fast as an airplane in the sky.)

Alano: **Tú estás loco (loca). Nadie me vio.**

Tú: _____

(Say: Everybody saw you **(te vio).** You don't obey the driving rules / **las reglas de conducir.**)

Alano: **La semana pasada yo pasé por una luz roja, pero no es importante.**

Tú: _____

(Say: What did you say?)

Alano: **Yo dije que la semana pasada yo pasé por una luz roja.**

Tú: _____

(Say: To pass through a red light is very dangerous / **es muy peligroso.**)

Alano: **¡Tú eres imposible!**

Tú: _____

(Say: And you are foolish!)

COMMONLY USED IDIOMATIC EXPRESSIONS

with **decir**

Es decir . . . That is to say . . .
querer decir to mean; **¿Qué quiere Ud. decir?** What do you mean?

with **día**

al día current, up to date
algún día someday
de día en día day by day
día por día day by day
hoy día nowadays
por día by the day, per day
quince días two weeks
un día de éstos one of these days

with **en**

en casa at home; (Use **en casa** if you are in the house; use **a casa** with a verb of motion, if you are going home.) **Estoy en casa esta noche** / I am at home tonight; **Ahora voy a casa** / Now I'm going home.
en casa de at the house of; **Carla está en casa de Elena** / Carla is at Helen's house.
en caso de in case of
en coche by car
en efecto as a matter of fact, in fact
en este momento at this moment
en lugar de in place of, instead of
en medio de in the middle of
en ninguna parte nowhere
en seguida immediately
en todas partes everywhere
en vez de instead of

with **estar**

está bien all right, okay
estar a punto de + *inf.* to be about + *inf.*
  Estoy a punto de salir / I am about to go out.
estar de acuerdo to agree
estar de pie to be standing
estar de vuelta to be back
estar para + *inf.* to be about + *inf.*
  Estoy para comer / I am about to eat.

with **hacer**

hace poco a little while ago
hace un año a year ago
Hace un mes que partió la señora Robles Mrs. Robles left a month ago.
hace una hora an hour ago

hacer el papel de to play the role of
hacer un viaje to take a trip, to go on a trip
hacer una pregunta to ask a question
hacer una visita to pay a visit

EJERCICIOS

I. **Answer the following questions in complete sentences. In your answers use the cue words given in parentheses. Review the commonly used idiomatic expressions above.**

   Modelo: (día por día) ¿Aprendes mucho español?
   (day by day) (Are you learning much Spanish?)

   Escriba: Aprendo mucho español día por día.
   (I am learning a lot of Spanish day by day.)

   1. (algún día) ¿Cuándo vas a España? _____

   2. (en este momento) ¿Dónde estás? _____

   3. (en casa de) ¿Dónde está Carla? _____

   4. (en coche) ¿Cómo fue Ud. al teatro? _____

   5. (hace poco) ¿Cuándo regresó Ud. a casa? _____

   6. (hace un año) ¿Cuándo comenzó Ud. a estudiar español? _____

   _____

   7. (hace un mes) ¿Cuándo partió tu padre para México? _____

   _____

   8. (para hacer una visita) ¿Por qué vas a casa de tu tía? _____

   _____

   9. (hacer una pregunta) ¿Qué quieres? _____

   10. (en todas partes) ¿Dónde está nevando? / Where is it snowing? _____

   _____

II. **The verbs in the following sentences are in the preterit. In place of them, use the cue verb in parentheses. Rewrite the sentence using the new verb in the preterit.**

   Modelo: (regresar)   Los turistas almorzaron a las dos.
   (to return)   (The tourists had lunch at two o'clock.)

   Escriba: Los turistas regresaron a las dos.
   (The tourists returned at two o'clock.)

   1. (ir) Ayer nosotros anduvimos a la escuela. _____

2. (dar) ¿Qué dijeron ellos? _____

3. (leer) Isabel creyó la historia. _____

4. (dormir) Roberto bailó toda la noche. _____

5. (terminar) Tú empezaste el trabajo. _____

6. (andar) La semana pasada fuimos al cine. _____

7. (estar) Anoche comimos en casa. _____

8. (explicar) Yo escribí el pretérito en la pizarra. _____

9. (escribir) El profesor tomó el libro. _____

10. (hacer) Yo no oí nada. _____

III. Activities. Proficiency in Speaking and Writing.

A. Go to the front of the class and tell us what is happening in the picture at the beginning of this Work Unit. Say one sentence in Spanish, then ask another classmate to continue talking about the picture by adding another sentence. After the second student makes a statement in Spanish, he / she will ask another student to continue the story. Follow this procedure until the story has been told.

B. ¿Hizo Juana una tontería? ¿Qué piensas tú? ¿Estás de acuerdo con Juana o con Pedro?

C. ¿Pediste tú el autógrafo de una persona famosa? ¿Qué persona? ¿Dónde? ¿Cuándo? ¿Recibiste el autógrafo?

D. Now, for practice, write what you said in A, B, C above on these lines:

_____

_____

_____

_____

_____

_____

Niño espulgándose by Bartolomé Esteban MURILLO (1617–1682)
Reprinted with permission of La Réunion des Musées Nationaux, Paris.

IV. Culture. Appreciating Spanish Art. Proficiency in Speaking and Writing.

Situation: You are on a field trip with your classmates in a museum where you are admiring a painting by MURILLO. It is entitled *Niño espulgándose* (Child removing fleas from his body).

Look at the picture on the previous page. You and your friend are having a conversation about it. The painting illustrates the hardships of poor children. It is evident that the boy is poor. Observe the boy's torn clothes, no shoes, soiled feet, the sad expression on his face. What else do you see in the picture?

After the conversation, you may practice writing what you said on the lines. Feel free to vary the conversation with your own words and ideas. Review the uses of **ser** and **estar** in Work Unit 1.

Tu amigo (amiga):	**¿Qué piensas de este cuadro? ¿Te gusta?**
Tú:	_____
	(I think it is extraordinary. I like it.)

Tu amigo (amiga):	**¿Qué está haciendo el muchacho?**
Tú:	_____
	(Don't you see? He's picking fleas off his body. That's the name of the picture.)

Tu amigo (amiga):	**Veo que el muchacho está triste. Está pálido. Y tú, ¿Qué ves?**
Tú:	_____
	(I see that he is sad because he is poor. Yes, he is pale. He is wearing torn clothes / **lleva vestidos rasgados.**)

Tu amigo (amiga):	**Tiene los pies desnudos y sucios. No tiene zapatos.**
Tú:	_____
	(That's right / **Eso es.** He hasn't any shoes and his feet are bare and dirty. Poor boy! / **¡Pobre muchacho!**)

Tu amigo (amiga):	**Hay poco que comer, solamente dos manzanas y algunas gambas.**
Tú:	_____
	(Yes, yes. There is little to eat, only two apples and a few shrimps.)

Tu amigo (amiga):	**¡Qué realismo!** / What realism!

TEST 2

PART ONE   Speaking Proficiency

Directions: Read the three situations given below. Take a few minutes to organize your thoughts about the words you are going to speak. Select two of the three situations. Before you begin to speak, you may review the Speaking and Writing Proficiency exercises in this Work Unit.

1. **Situation:** Last night you and members of your family went to the theater. Tell us at what time you left the house, at what time you arrived at the theater, and at what time the show began. Did you all go to the theater in someone's car? A taxi? Was the play a drama? A comedy? A musical? Who wrote it? Did anything interesting happen during the intermission? Were any of your friends there? Tell us what you ate and drank during the intermission. Use at least five verbs in the preterit tense, for example, **ir, salir, llegar, comenzar, escribir, pasar** (to happen), **comer, beber, ser, estar.** Did you like the show? What did you do when you left the theater? You may add your own words and ideas.

2. **Situation:** This morning you arrived late to Spanish class. Your teacher and classmates were worried about you. They want you to tell them why you arrived late. Did you sleep late? Did you walk to school? Did you see a car accident? Did you have to explain to the police officer what you saw? Did one of the two cars go through a red light? You may use these suggestions or your own words and ideas. Either way, use the preterit tense to explain why you were late to class.

3. **Situation:** Yesterday was your birthday. Tell us who came to the party, what gifts they brought, what you all did at the party (ate, drank, sang, danced), where you went later, and what you did.

PART TWO   Listening Proficiency

Directions: Your teacher will read aloud four short paragraphs. Each one will contain only a few sentences. You will hear each paragraph twice. Then you will hear one question based on each. You will hear the question only once. It is printed below. Choose the best suggested answer and check the letter of your choice.

Selection Number 1

1. Durante el entreacto, ¿adónde fueron el señor Rodríguez, Pedro, y Juana?

   A. a hablar con algunas personas

   B. a comer y a beber

   C. a tomar sus asientos

   D. al teatro

Selection Number 2

2. Después de hablar con algunas damas, ¿qué hizo la señora Rodríguez?

   A. Tomó un café.

   B. Comió chocolate.

   C. Regresó a su asiento.

   D. Bebió jugo de naranja.

Selection Number 3

3. Antes de regresar a su asiento, ¿a quién vio Juana?

    A. Vio a un señor.

    B. Vio a una amiga.

    C. Vio la pieza.

    D. Vio el programa.

Selection Number 4

4. Después que terminó la función, ¿qué hicieron todas las personas?

    A. Regresaron a sus asientos.

    B. Salieron del teatro.

    C. Fueron al teatro.

    D. Hicieron una tontería.

PART THREE   Reading Proficiency

Directions: In the following passage there are five blank spaces numbered 1 through 5. Each blank space represents a missing verb form in the preterit tense. For each blank space, four possible completions are provided. Only one of them makes sense in the context of the passage.

First, read the passage in its entirety to determine its general meaning. Then read it a second time. For each blank space choose the completion that makes the best sense and write its letter in the space provided.

Ayer _____ mi cumpleaños. Muchos amigos _____ a mi casa para divertirse

    1. A. fui   2. A. salieron
       B. fue   B. trajeron
       C. dije   C. vinieron
       D. dijo   D. creyeron

en la fiesta. Ellos _____ muchos regalos. Yo _____ muchos libros, mucho

        3. A. trajeron   4. A. dije
           B. dijeron   B. dí
           C. almorzaron   C. dio
           D. fueron   D. recibí

dinero, y chocolates. Durante la fiesta todos mis amigos comieron, bebieron, bailaron, y

cantaron. Yo _____ el piano y uno de mis amigos tocó la guitarra. Nosotros nos

        5. A. tocó
           B. toqué
           C. compré
           D. quise

divertimos muchísimo.

PART FOUR   Writing Proficiency

Directions: Of the three situations in Part One (Speaking Proficiency) in this test, select two of them and write what you said on the lines below.

Situation 1 _____

_____

_____

_____

Situation 2 _____

_____

_____

_____

Situation 3 _____

_____

_____

_____

Los signos del Zodiaco.

Let's see what Pedro's horoscope reveals for today. What does yours say?

Zodiaco

Pedro está leyendo el periódico en la cocina. Lee la página que contiene el horóscopo.

I **Aries** (Aries)
21 marzo–20 abril

Ud. será rico (rica) en diez años.

II **Tauro** (Taurus)
21 abril–21 mayo

A la edad de noventa años, Ud. tendrá mucha paciencia.
Hoy Ud. recibirá una carta interesante.

5

III **Géminis** (Gemini)
22 mayo–21 junio

Una persona rica querrá casarse con usted en el porvenir. Tenga paciencia.

10

IV **Cáncer** (Cancer)
22 junio–23 julio

Hoy usted encontrará obstáculos peligrosos en su vida.

V **Leo** (Leo)
24 julio–23 agosto

15

Alguien que está enamorado de usted le dará muchos regalos para su cumpleaños. Escríbale una carta.

VI **Virgo** (Virgo)
24 agosto–23 septiembre

20

Alguien le regalará a usted un automóvil magnífico.

VII **Libra** (Libra)
24 septiembre–23 octubre

¡Qué fortuna! Ud. verá un gran cambio en su vida personal.

VIII **Escorpión** (Scorpio)
24 octubre–22 noviembre

25

Ud. hará un viaje a un país extranjero.

IX **Sagitario** (Sagittarius)
23 noviembre–21 diciembre

Hoy Ud. hablará con una mujer preciosa.

30

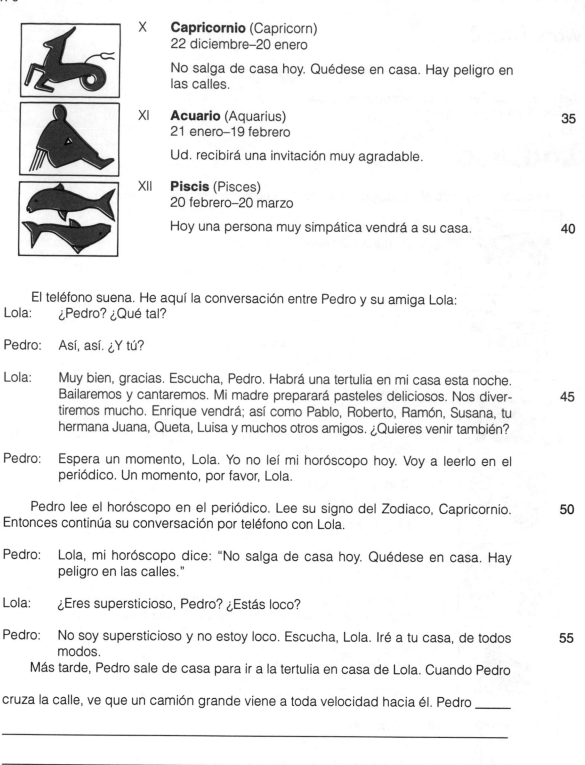

X **Capricornio** (Capricorn)
22 diciembre–20 enero

No salga de casa hoy. Quédese en casa. Hay peligro en las calles.

XI **Acuario** (Aquarius)   35
21 enero–19 febrero

Ud. recibirá una invitación muy agradable.

XII **Piscis** (Pisces)
20 febrero–20 marzo

Hoy una persona muy simpática vendrá a su casa.   40

El teléfono suena. He aquí la conversación entre Pedro y su amiga Lola:

Lola: ¿Pedro? ¿Qué tal?

Pedro: Así, así. ¿Y tú?

Lola: Muy bien, gracias. Escucha, Pedro. Habrá una tertulia en mi casa esta noche. Bailaremos y cantaremos. Mi madre preparará pasteles deliciosos. Nos diver-   45
tiremos mucho. Enrique vendrá; así como Pablo, Roberto, Ramón, Susana, tu hermana Juana, Queta, Luisa y muchos otros amigos. ¿Quieres venir también?

Pedro: Espera un momento, Lola. Yo no leí mi horóscopo hoy. Voy a leerlo en el periódico. Un momento, por favor, Lola.

Pedro lee el horóscopo en el periódico. Lee su signo del Zodiaco, Capricornio.   50
Entonces continúa su conversación por teléfono con Lola.

Pedro: Lola, mi horóscopo dice: "No salga de casa hoy. Quédese en casa. Hay peligro en las calles."

Lola: ¿Eres supersticioso, Pedro? ¿Estás loco?

Pedro: No soy supersticioso y no estoy loco. Escucha, Lola. Iré a tu casa, de todos   55
modos.
          Más tarde, Pedro sale de casa para ir a la tertulia en casa de Lola. Cuando Pedro

cruza la calle, ve que un camión grande viene a toda velocidad hacia él. Pedro _____

_____

_____

(NOTE TO THE STUDENT: WRITE YOUR OWN ENDING TO THIS STORY IN ONE OR TWO SENTENCES, IN SPANISH, OF COURSE!)

KEY WORDS AND PHRASES

agradable *adj.* pleasant

alguien *indef. pron.* someone, somebody

así *adv.* thus, like this; **así, así** so so; **así como** as well as

bailaremos *1st pers., pl., fut. of* **bailar**; we will dance

cambio *n.m.* change; **un gran cambio** a big change

camión *n.m.* truck

cantaremos *1st pers., pl., fut. of* **cantar**; we will sing

casarse (con alguien) *refl. v.* to get married (to someone), to marry (someone)

contiene *3d pers., s., pres. indic. of* **contener**; contains

continúa *3d pers., s., pres. indic. of* **continuar**; continues

cruza *3d pers., s., pres. indic. of* **cruzar**; crosses

divertirse *refl. v.* to have a good time

edad *n.f.* age

enamorado de in love with

encontrará *3d pers., s., fut. of* **encontrar**; will find, will meet

entonces *adv.* then

eres *2d pers., s. (tú), pres. indic. of* **ser**; you are

escriba *3d pers., s. (Ud.), imper. (command) of* **escribir**; write; **escriba + le > escríbale** write to him (to her)

escucha *2d pers., s., (tú), imper. (command) of* **escuchar**; listen; **escucha + me > escúchame** listen to me

espera *2d pers., s., (tú), imper. (command) of* **esperar**; wait (for); **espera + me > espérame** wait for me

está enamorado de is in love with

está leyendo *pres. prog. of* **leer;** is reading. Review the formation of present participles and present progressive tense in Work Unit 3.

extranjero *adj.* foreign

fortuna *n.f.* fortune, luck, chance; **¡Qué fortuna!** What luck!

hablará *3d pers., s., fut. of* **hablar**; will talk

habrá *3d pers., s., fut. of* **haber**; there will be

hacia *prep.* toward; **hacia él** toward him

hará *3d pers., s., fut. of* **hacer**; **Ud. hará un viaje** you will go on a trip

He aquí Here is

horóscopo *n.m.* horoscope

iré *1st pers., s., fut. of* **ir**; I will go

le *indir. obj. pron.* to you, to him, to her

lee *3d pers., s., pres. indic. of* **leer**; is reading

leer *v.* to read; **leer + lo > leerlo** to read it

leí *1st pers., s., pret. of* **leer**; **no leí** I did not read

leyendo *pres. part. of* **leer**; **está leyendo** is reading. Review the formation of present participles and present progressive tense in Work Unit 3.

lo *dir. obj. pron., m.s.* him, it

magnífico *adj.* magnificent

modo *n.m.* way; **de todos modos** anyway, anyhow

nos divertiremos *1st pers., pl., fut. of* **divertirse;** we will have a good time

obstáculo *n.m.* obstacle

paciencia *n.f.* patience

página *n.f.* page

país *n.m.* country

peligro *n.m.* danger; **peligroso** *adj.* dangerous

porvenir *n.m.* future

preciosa *adj., f.s.* lovely

preparará *3d pers., s. fut. of* **preparar**; will prepare

que *rel. pron.* who, which, that

¡Qué fortuna! What luck!

¿Qué tal? How are things?

quedarse *refl. v.* to remain, to stay

quédese *3d pers., s. (Ud.), imper. (command) of* **quedarse**; **Quédese en casa** Stay home.

querrá *3d pers., s., fut. of* **querer**; will want

Queta *n.f.* Harriet

recibirá *3d pers., s., fut. of* **recibir**; will receive

regalar *v.* to give a gift

regalará *3d pers., s., fut. of* **regalar**; will give as a gift

sale *3d pers., s., pres. indic. of* **salir**; leaves

salga *3d pers., s. (Ud.), imper. (command) of* **salir**; **no salga** don't go out

será *3d pers., s., fut. of* **ser**; will be

signo *n.m.* sign; **los signos del Zodiaco** the signs of the Zodiac

simpático, simpática *adj.* nice, likeable

su *poss. adj.* your, his, her, their

suena *3d pers., s., pres. indic. of* **sonar**; rings

tarde *adv.* late; **más tarde** later

tendrá *3d pers., s., fut. of* **tener**; will have

tenga *3d pers., s. (Ud.), imper. (command) of* **tener**; **¡Tenga paciencia!** Have patience!

tertulia *n.f.* evening party, social gathering

velocidad *n.f.* velocity; **a toda velocidad** at full speed

vendrá *3d pers., s., fut. of* **venir**; will come

verá *3d pers., s., fut. of* **ver**; you will see

vida *n.f.* life

voy a leerlo I am going to read it

Zodiaco *n.m.* Zodiac

EJERCICIOS

I. Seleccione la respuesta correcta conforme al significado de la lectura en esta lección. (Select the correct answer according to the meaning of the reading selection in this Work Unit.)

1. Pedro está leyendo el periódico en (a) el cuarto de baño (b) la sala (c) su dormitorio (d) la cocina _____

2. Pedro lee la página que contiene (a) las noticias internacionales (b) los deportes (c) las noticias de empleos (d) el horóscopo _____

3. La declaración que *Ud. será rico (rica) en diez años* se halla en el signo del Zodiaco (a) Tauro (b) Géminis (c) Aries (d) Libra _____

4. La persona que telefonea a Pedro es (a) Roberto (b) Ramón (c) Queta (d) Lola _____

5. Lola quiere invitar a Pedro a venir a su casa porque habrá (a) una discusión sobre temas políticos (b) una tertulia (c) una discusión sobre el horóscopo en el periódico (d) una conferencia _____

6. La persona que preparará pasteles deliciosos será (a) la madre de Pedro (b) la madre de Lola (c) Lola (d) Juana, la hermana de Pedro _____

7. En casa de Lola, todos bailarán y (a) estudiarán (b) llorarán (c) cantarán (d) dormirán _____

8. La declaración que *Ud. hará un viaje a un país extranjero* se halla en el signo del Zodiaco (a) Aries (b) Leo (c) Virgo (d) Escorpión _____

9. Al principio, Pedro no acepta la invitación de Lola porque el horóscopo dice que es necesario (a) hacer un viaje (b) leer el periódico (c) quedarse en casa a causa del peligro en las calles (d) preparar pasteles deliciosos _____

10. Más tarde, Pedro sale de casa para (a) ver un gran camión en la calle (b) comprar un periódico (c) leer su horóscopo en la biblioteca (d) ir a la tertulia en casa de Lola _____

II. ¿Sí o No?

1. Pedro está leyendo un libro en la cocina. _____

2. Pedro lee la página que contiene las noticias internacionales. _____

3. Pedro habla por teléfono con Lola. _____

4. Al principio, Lola piensa que Pedro es supersticioso. _____

5. Al fin, Pedro acepta la invitación de Lola. _____

III. Ordene las palabras hasta formar una oración con sentido. (Put the words in correct order to form a meaningful sentence. They are all in the story at the beginning of this Work Unit.)

1. leyendo / está / Pedro / la cocina / en / el periódico. _____

2. será / Ud. / años / en / diez / rico. _____

_____

3. hará / Ud. / viaje / un / a / país / un / extranjero. _____

_____

4. hablará / Ud. / una amiga / con / preciosa. _____

_____

5. recibirá / Ud. / carta / una / hoy / de / amigo / un / amable. _____

_____

IV. **Varias palabras en una sola. Utilizando las letras en la palabra VENEZUELA, ¿cuántas palabras puede usted escribir? Escriba ocho palabras, por lo menos.**
(**Several words in one.** Using the letters in the word **VENEZUELA,** how many words can you write? Write at least eight words.)

VENEZUELA

1. _____   5. _____

2. _____   6. _____

3. _____   7. _____

4. _____   8. _____

V. **Palabras en bloque. Junte las palabras en bloques de dos en dos para formar otras cuatro.**
(**Block words.** Join the words in blocks, two by two, to form four other words. Example: **con + tener > contener** / to contain)

| CON | POR | PARA | EN |
| QUE | TENER | DA | CERRAR |

Solución: 1. _____   3. _____

2. _____   4. _____

VI. Activities. Proficiency in Speaking and Writing.

A. Look at the signs of the Zodiac and the birth dates at the beginning of this Work Unit. Which is your sign? / **¿Cuál es tu signo?** Find it and read aloud what the horoscope reveals. Then write the statement on the chalkboard. You may take the book with you and use it. Or, write the statement on the lines below.

B. Your Spanish teacher has asked you to be the class astrologer (**el astrólogo, la astróloga**). With your book, go to the front of the class and select one class- mate. Ask your friend, by name, to get up (**¡Levántate, por favor!**) and to come with you (**Ven conmigo**). Ask your friend his / her date of birth (**¿Cuál es la fecha de tu nacimiento?**). Now, find your friend's **signo del Zodiaco.** Read it from the book where the horoscope is given. Or, make up another statement if you prefer. Write what you said on the lines below.

_____

_____

_____

_____

C. Now, switch roles with your friend.

VII. Write the missing Spanish words on the lines. They are in the story at the beginning of this Work Unit.

1. Pedro está _____ el periódico en la cocina.

2. Ud. _____ rico (rica) en diez años.

3. Alguien que está enamorado de usted le _____ muchos regalos.

4. Ud. _____ un gran cambio en su vida personal.

5. El teléfono _____ .

6. Esta noche _____ y _____ . Nosotros nos _____ mucho.

7. Yo no _____ mi horóscopo hoy. Voy a _____ en el periódico.

8. Pedro, ¿ _____ supersticioso?

9. No _____ supersticioso y no _____ loco, Lola.

10. Más tarde, Pedro _____ de casa para _____ a la tertulia en casa de Lola.

VIII. Preguntas personales / Personal questions. On the lines below, write your answers in complete sentences in Spanish.

1. ¿Lees el horóscopo en los periódicos?

2. ¿Cuál es la fecha de tu nacimiento?

3. ¿Cuál es tu signo del Zodiaco?

4. ¿Crees en los horóscopos?

5 ¿Eres una persona supersticiosa?

1. _____

2. _____

3. _____

4. _____

5. _____

IX. Leisure. Proficiency in Speaking and Writing.

Situation: Since you were selected as **el astrólogo** or **la astróloga** in your Spanish class, during Spanish Club you have been asked to foretell the future for five of your friends. This time use the subject pronoun **Ud.** instead of **tú** just for practice. You may use the following predictions or your own words and ideas. After you make a statement, write it on the line.

1. _____
   (Say: You will be rich in ten years.)

2. _____
   (Say: You will have much patience at the age of ninety.)

3. _____
   (Say: You will go on a trip to a foreign country.)

4. _____
   (Say: You will receive a very pleasant invitation.)

5. _____
   (Say: This evening a very nice person will come to your house.)

ESTRUCTURAS DE LA LENGUA

TENSE NO. 4: FUTURO (FUTURE)

In Spanish and English, the future tense is used to express an action or a state of being that will take place at some time in the future.

EXAMPLES:
   Lo haré/ *I shall do it; I will do it.*
   Iremos al campo la semana que viene/ *We shall go* to the country next week; *We will go* to the country next week.

Also, in Spanish the future tense is used to indicate:

(a) Conjecture regarding the present.

EXAMPLES:
> **¿Qué hora será?** / *I wonder* what time it is.
> **¿Quién será?** / Who *can that be? I wonder who that is.*

(b) Probability regarding the present.

EXAMPLES:
> **Serán las cinco** / *It is probably* five o'clock; *It must be* five o'clock.
> **Tendrá muchos amigos** / *He probably has* many friends; *He must have* many friends.
> **María estará enferma** / Mary *is probably* sick; Mary *must be* sick.

(c) An indirect quotation.

EXAMPLE: **María dice que vendrá mañana** / Mary says that she *will come* tomorrow.

Finally, remember that the future is never used in Spanish after **si** when **si** means *if*.

This tense is regularly formed as follows:
Add the following endings to the whole infinitive: **é, ás, á; emos, éis, án**

NOTE that these future endings happen to be related to the endings of **haber** in the present indicative: **he, has, ha; hemos, habéis, han.** ALSO NOTE the accent marks on the future endings, except for **emos.**

> You then get: **hablaré, hablarás, hablará;**
> **hablaremos, hablaréis, hablarán**
>
> **beberé, beberás, beberá;**
> **beberemos, beberéis, beberán**
>
> **recibiré, recibirás, recibirá;**
> **recibiremos, recibiréis, recibirán**

The usual equivalent in English is: I shall talk OR I will talk, you will talk, *etc.*; I shall drink OR I will drink, you will drink, *etc.*; I shall receive OR I will receive, you will receive, *etc.*

VERBS IRREGULAR IN THE FUTURE

caber / to fit, to be contained **cabré, cabrás, cabrá;** **cabremos, cabréis, cabrán** The **e** of the inf. ending drops.	**haber** / to have (as an auxiliary or helping verb) **habré, habrás, habrá;** **habremos, habréis, habrán** The **e** of the inf. ending drops.
decir / to say, to tell **diré, dirás, dirá;** **diremos, diréis, dirán** The **e** and **c** of the inf. drop.	**hacer** / to do, to make **haré, harás, hará;** **haremos, haréis, harán** The **c** and **e** of the inf. drop.

X. The following verb forms are in the future tense. Change them by using the new subject given in parentheses. Repeat the other words in the sentence. You may add additional words if you wish.

　　Refer to the boxed verbs above where you are given the verb forms in the future tense. In this exercise you are practicing the following irregular verbs: **caber, decir, haber, hacer.**

　　Modelo: ¿Cabrá esta cosa en la caja? (Estas cosas) (Will this thing fit in the box?)

　　Escriba: ¿Cabrán estas cosas en la caja? (Will these things fit in the box?)

1. Nosotros diremos la verdad. **(Yo)** _____

2. Mañana habrá una fiesta en la escuela. **(muchas fiestas)** _____

3. La semana que viene Miguel hará un viaje. **(Yo)** _____

4. ¿Qué diré yo a tus padres? **(Tú)** _____

5. ¿Cuándo haremos el trabajo? **(Uds.)** _____

---

poder / to be able, can
podré, podrás, podrá;
podremos, podréis, podrán

The **e** of the inf. ending drops.

---

querer / to want, to wish
querré, querrás, querrá;
querremos, querréis, querrán

The **e** of the inf. ending drops and you are left with two **r**'s.

---

poner / to put, to place
pondré, pondrás, pondrá;
pondremos, pondréis, pondrán

The **e** of the inf. ending drops and **d** is added.

---

saber / to know, to know how
sabré, sabrás, sabrá;
sabremos, sabréis, sabrán

The **e** of the inf. ending drops.

XI. The following verb forms are in the future tense. Change them by using the new subject given in parentheses. Repeat the other words in the sentence. You may add additional words if you wish.

　　Refer to the boxed verbs above where you are given the verb forms in the future tense. In this exercise you are practicing the following irregular verbs: **poder, poner, querer, saber.**

　　Modelo: ¿Podrás venir a mi casa mañana? (Uds.)
　　　　　　　　(Will you be able to come to my house tomorrow?)

　　Escriba: ¿Podrán Uds. venir a mi casa mañana?
　　　　　　　　(Will you be able to come to my house tomorrow?)

1. ¿Pondrás las flores en la mesa? **(Uds.)** _____

2. Mañana querré tener mucho dinero para ir de compras. **(Nosotros)** _____

_____

3. ¿Sabrá Ud. la respuesta mañana? **(Tú)** _____

205

4. Nosotros podremos salir en dos horas. **(Vosotros)** _____

5. Yo pondré el café en la cocina. **(Ella)** _____

---

salir / to go out, to leave
   saldré, saldrás, saldrá;
   saldremos, saldréis, saldrán

The **i** of the inf. ending drops and **d** is added.

---

valer / to be worth, to be worthy
   valdré, valdrás, valdrá;
   valdremos, valdréis, valdrán

The **e** of the inf. ending drops and **d** is added.

---

tener / to have, to hold
   tendré, tendrás, tendrá;
   tendremos, tendréis, tendrán

The **e** of the inf. ending drops and **d** is added.

---

venir / to come
   vendré, vendrás, vendrá;
   vendremos, vendréis, vendrán

The **i** of the inf. ending drops and **d** is added.

XII. The following verb forms are in the future tense. Change them by using the new subject given in parentheses. Repeat the other words in the sentence. You may add additional words if you wish.

    Refer to the boxed verbs above where you are given the verb forms in the future tense. In this exercise you are practicing the following irregular verbs: salir, tener, valer, venir.

Modelo: ¿A qué hora saldrás? (Nosotros) (At what time will you go out?)

Escriba: ¿A qué hora saldremos? (At what time will we go out?)

1. ¿Tendrá Ud. trabajo la semana que viene? **(Yo)** _____

2. Esta casa valdrá mucho en veinte años. **(Estas casas)** _____

3. ¿A qué hora vendrás a verme? **(Uds.)** _____

4. Nosotros vendremos a verte a la una. **(Yo)** _____

5. El tren saldrá a las dos. **(Yo)** _____

EJERCICIOS

I. Seleccione la forma correcta del verbo en el futuro. (Select the correct form of the verb in the future.)

1. La semana que viene _____ al campo.
   (a) vamos (b) fuimos (c) íbamos (d) iremos   _____

2. ¿Cuándo _____ Ud. un viaje a España?
   (a) hace (b) hacía (c) hizo (d) hará   _____

3. Marta dice que _____ mañana.
   (a) viene (b) venía (c) vendrá (d) vino   _____

4. ¿Cuándo lo hará Ud.? Lo _____ en algunos días.
   (a) hago (b) hice (c) estoy haciendo (d) haré   _____

5. Pedro, ¿ _____ (tú) la lección para mañana?
   (a) sabes (b) sabrás (c) sabías (d) supiste   _____

II. **Escriba las seis formas de cada verbo en el futuro.** (Write the six forms of each verb in the future.)

   Modelo: caber   cabré, cabrás, cabrá; cabremos, cabréis, cabrán

   1. decir _____

   2. haber _____

   3. hacer _____

   4. poder _____

   5. poner _____

   6. querer _____

   7. saber _____

   8. salir _____

   9. tener _____

   10. valer _____

   11. venir _____

   12. hablar _____

   13. aprender _____

   14. vivir _____

III. **Conteste las siguientes preguntas en el afirmativo con oraciones completas. En la oración (a) use la palabra Sí. En la oración (b) use la palabra también según los modelos.**
   (Answer the following questions in the affirmative in complete sentences. In sentence [a] use the word **Sí.** In sentence [b] use the word **también** [also], according to the models.)

   Modelos: a. ¿Cantará Ud. en el baile   a. Sí, cantaré en el baile
                      esta noche?   esta noche.
                      (Will you sing at the dance   (Yes, I will sing at the dance tonight.)
                      tonight?)

               b. ¿Y las otras personas?   b. Las otras personas, también,
                      (And the other people?)   cantarán en el baile esta noche.
                                                            (The other people, also, will sing at the
                                                            dance tonight.)

1. a. ¿Hablarán los alumnos a la profesora de español? _____

   _____

   b. ¿Y tú? _____

2. a. ¿Aprenderás la lección de español para mañana? _____

   _____

   b. ¿Y Esteban? _____

3. a. ¿Escribirán Uds. las cartas a sus amigos? _____

   _____

   b. ¿Y Edmundo y Emilio? _____

4. a. ¿Escucharéis (vosotros) la música esta noche? _____

   b. ¿Y Elisa y Ud.? _____

5. a. ¿Beberás la leche? _____

   b. ¿Y Arturo? _____

IV. Conteste las siguientes preguntas en el negativo con oraciones completas. En la oración (a) use la palabra No. En la oración (b) use la palabra tampoco según los modelos.
(Answer the following questions in the negative in complete sentences. In sentence [a] use the word **No**. In sentence [b] use the word **tampoco** [either], according to the models.)

Modelos: a. ¿Vendrá Ud. a mi casa esta tarde?
(Will you come to my house this afternoon?)

    a. No. No vendré a su casa esta tarde.
(No, I will not come to your house this afternoon.)

    b. ¿Y Uds.? (And you?)

    b. No. No vendremos a su casa esta tarde tampoco.
(No. We will not come to your house this afternoon either.)

1. a. ¿Saldrá Ud. de casa esta noche? _____

   _____

   b. ¿Y sus padres? _____

   _____

2. a. ¿Dirás mentiras? _____

   b. ¿Y tu hermanito? _____

3. a. ¿Harán sus amigos un viaje a Francia? _____

   b. ¿Y Ud. y Enrique? _____

4. a. ¿Irán los señores Rodríguez al restaurante? _____

   b. ¿Y los señores Sánchez? _____

5. a. ¿Cabrán estas cosas en la caja? _____

   b. ¿Y este vaso? _____

V. Ordene las palabras en las cajas para formar una oración con sentido.

Modelo:

los señores Rodríguez	al restaurante	irán

Escriba: Los señores Rodríguez irán al restaurante.

1.

las cartas	Uds.	sus amigos	a	escribirán

_____

2.

mi padre	hoy	me dará	dinero	mucho

_____

3.

mi madre	saldrá	no	hoy	de casa

_____

VI. En español hay muchas palabras que se escriben y se pronuncian idénticamente, pero un signo de acento es necessario para distinguir su significado. (In Spanish there are many words that are written and pronounced identically, but an accent mark is necessary to distinguish their meaning.)

Por ejemplo:
   si *conj.* / if   Sí. Si Pablo viene, le hablaré.
   sí *adv.* / yes   Yes. If Paul comes, I will talk to him.

   ¿Cuántos ejemplos puede Ud. decir y escribir?

VII. Helping Others. Proficiency in Speaking and Writing.

Situation: Today you are serving as an interpreter. A conference of school principals is being held in your school. One of the visitors is Señor Carlos Gómez who is principal of a school in Spain. Your school principal does not speak Spanish and the visitor speaks very little English.

In this dialogue the three of you are in the office of your school principal, Mr. Johnson. Your role is **Usted.** Don't forget to use the Usted form when talking to Señor Gómez. It's polite and you don't know him well enough to use tú. After Señor Gómez makes a statement, tell Mr. Johnson in English what he is saying. Note that you are using Spanish verbs in the future tense. You may vary and extend the dialogue with your own words and ideas.

Mr. Johnson:	Ask him if he will be able to have lunch with us in the school cafeteria.
Usted:	Señor, ¿ _____ _____ ?
Señor Gómez:	**Sí, podré almorzar con ustedes en la cafetería de la escuela. Con mucho gusto.**
Mr. Johnson:	That's good. Ask him if he will eat meat or fish.
Usted:	Señor, ¿ _____ ?
Señor Gómez:	**Yo comeré carne, por favor. No me gusta el pescado.**
Mr. Johnson:	Now ask him if he will speak in Spanish to the students in the auditorium at two o'clock.
Usted:	Señor, ¿ _____ _____ ?
Señor Gómez:	**Sí, sí, por supuesto. Hablaré en español a los estudiantes en el auditorio a las dos. Con mucho gusto.**
Mr. Johnson:	Ask him at what time he will have to leave to go to the airport.
Usted:	Señor, ¿ _____ _____ ?
Señor Gómez:	**Tendré que partir a las tres para ir al aeropuerto.**
Mr. Johnson:	Please thank him for his visit and tell him to have a nice day.
Usted:	_____

VIII. Discussing Plans for the Future. Proficiency in Speaking and Writing.

Situation: You are discussing plans for next summer's vacation with a friend. You are acting your part, **Tú.** A classmate can act Juana's part. After you and your friend complete the dialogue, you may write what you said on the lines for practice. You may vary and extend the dialogue with your own words and ideas. Use as many verbs in the future tense as possible.

Juana:	**Dime** (Tell me), **¿Qué harás el verano que viene? ¿Adónde irás?**
Tú:	_____
	_____
	(Say: I will take a trip next summer. I will go to Mexico with my family.)
Juana:	**¡Qué buena idea! ¡Y yo, también, iré a México con mi familia!**
Tú:	_____
	(Say: Don't tell me! / **(¡No me digas!)**. What a surprise! When will you leave?)
Juana:	**Partiremos el primero de julio.**
Tú:	_____
	_____
	(Say: My family and I will leave on July first, too. Will you visit the famous beaches in Mexico?)
Juana:	**Naturalmente. Iremos a Acapulco. Es un centro turístico, tú sabes. Visitaremos las famosas playas. Me gustan mucho los acapulqueños.**
Tú:	_____
	_____
	(Say: We will go to Acapulco, too! I know that it's a tourist center. We will visit the famous beaches. I like the inhabitants of Acapulco, too!)
Juana:	**¿Podremos partir juntos, tu familia y la mía?**
Tú:	_____
	(Say: What a good idea! I will talk to my parents and I will tell you their decision in a few days.)
Juana:	**Yo, también, hablaré a mis padres y yo te diré su decisión en algunos días.**
Tú:	_____
	(Say: Good! Okay / **(De acuerdo)**. See you tomorrow!)
Juana:	**¡Bueno! De acuerdo. ¡Hasta mañana!**

REFLEXIVE VERBS

REFLEXIVE PRONOUNS

EXAMPLES

Singular
1. **me** / myself
2. **te** / yourself
3. **se** / yourself, himself,
   herself, itself

Me lavo / I wash myself.
Te lavas / You wash yourself.
Ud. se lava / You wash yourself.
Pablo se lava / Paul washes himself, *etc.*

Plural
1. **nos** / ourselves
2. **os** / yourselves
3. **se** / yourselves, themselves

Nosotros (–as) nos lavamos.
Vosotros (–as) os laváis.
Uds. se lavan / You wash yourselves;
Ellos (Ellas) se lavan / They wash themselves.

A reflexive verb contains a reflexive pronoun, and the action of the verb falls on the subject and its reflexive pronoun either directly or indirectly. For that reason the reflexive pronoun must agree with the subject: **yo me . . . , tú te . . . , Ud. se . . . , él se . . . , ella se . . . , nosotros nos . . . , vosotros os . . . , Uds. se . . . , ellos se . . . , ellas se . . . .**

A reflexive pronoun is ordinarily placed in front of the verb form, as you can see in the examples.

To make these sentences negative, place **no** in front of the reflexive pronoun: **Yo no me lavo, Tú no te lavas, Ud. no se lava,** *etc.*

NOTE that **me, te, nos, os** are not only reflexive pronouns but they are also direct object pronouns and indirect object pronouns.

A reflexive verb in Spanish is not always reflexive in English, for example:

Spanish	English
levantarse	to get up
sentarse	to sit down

There are some reflexive verbs in Spanish that are also reflexive in English, for example:

Spanish	English
bañarse	to bathe oneself
lavarse	to wash oneself

The following reflexive pronouns are also used as reciprocal pronouns, meaning "each other" or "to each other": **se, nos, os.** Examples:

Ayer por la noche, María y yo nos vimos en el cine / Yesterday evening, Mary and I saw each other at the movies.
Roberto y Teresa se escriben todos los días / Robert and Teresa write to each other every day.

If the meaning of these three reflexive pronouns (**se, nos, os**) is not clear when they are used in a reciprocal meaning, any of the following may be added accordingly to express the idea of "each other" or "to each other": **uno a otro, una a otra, unos a otros,** *etc.*

Some important common reflexive verbs

abstenerse   to abstain
aburrirse   to be bored, to grow tired, to grow weary
acercarse (qu)   (a + obj.)   to approach, to draw near
acordarse (ue)   (de + obj.)   to remember
acostarse (ue)   to go to bed, to lie down
adelantarse a   to go forward, to go ahead, to move **ahead**, to take the lead
afeitarse   to shave oneself

alegrarse (de)   to be glad, to rejoice
apresurarse   to hasten, to hurry, to rush
asustarse   to be frightened, to be scared
bañarse   to bathe oneself, to take a bath
burlarse de   to make fun of, to poke fun at, to ridicule
callarse   to be silent, to keep quiet
cansarse   to become tired, to become weary, to get tired
casarse con   to get married, to marry
cuidarse   to take care of oneself
dedicarse (qu)   to devote oneself
desayunar (se)   to breakfast, to have breakfast (may be reflexive or not)
despedirse (i)   to take leave of, to say good-bye to
despertarse (ie)   to wake (oneself) up
desvestirse (i)   to undress oneself, to get undressed
detenerse   to stop (oneself)
disculparse   to apologize, to excuse (oneself)
divertirse (ie, i)   to have a good time, to enjoy oneself
ducharse   to take a shower, to shower oneself
enfadarse   to become angry
enfermarse   to get sick, to fall sick, to become ill
enojarse   to become angry, to get angry, to get cross
equivocarse (qu)   to be mistaken
hacerse   to become
informarse   to inform oneself, to find out
interesarse en   to be interested (in)
irse   to go away
lavarse   to wash oneself
levantarse   to get up, to rise
limpiarse   to clean oneself
llamarse   to be called, to be named
marcharse   to go away, to leave
mirarse   to look at oneself, to look at each other **(uno a otro; unos a otros)**
mojarse   to get wet, to wet oneself
ocultarse   to hide oneself
pararse   to stop (oneself)
parecerse (zc)   to resemble each other, to look alike
pasearse   to take a walk, to parade
peinarse   to comb one's hair
pintarse   to make up (one's face)
ponerse   to put (clothing), to become, to set (of sun)
preocuparse   to be concerned, to worry, to be worried
prepararse   to be prepared, to get ready, to prepare oneself
protegerse (j)   to protect oneself
quedarse   to remain, to stay
quitarse   to take off (clothing), to remove oneself, to withdraw
reírse   to laugh
secarse (qu)   to dry oneself
sentarse (ie)   to sit down
sentirse (ie, i)   to feel (well, ill)
vestirse (i)   to dress oneself, to get dressed

EJERCICIOS

I. Escriba las seis formas del verbo lavarse en el presente de indicativo.

_____

II. Escriba las seis formas del verbo bañarse en el presente de indicativo.

_____

III. Escriba las seis formas del verbo lavarse en el futuro.

_____

IV. Escriba las seis formas del verbo bañarse en el futuro.

_____

V. Traduzca al español. (Translate into Spanish. Study again the explanations, uses, and examples of reflexive verbs above.)

1. Yesterday evening, Mary and I saw each other at the movies.

_____

2. Robert and Teresa write to each other every day.

_____

3. I wash myself every morning before leaving for school.

_____

4. Do you wash yourself every evening before going to bed?

_____

5. Robert does not wash himself every day.

_____

VI. Conteste las preguntas siguientes en el afirmativo con oraciones completas. En la oración (a) use la palabra Sí. En la oración (b) use la palabra también según los modelos.
(Answer the following questions in the affirmative in complete sentences. In sentence [a], use the word **Sí**. In sentence [b], use the word **también** [also], according to the models.)

Modelos: a. ¿Se lava Ud. todos los días?
   (Do you wash yourself every day?)

a. Sí, me lavo todos los días.
   (Yes, I wash myself every day.)

b. ¿Y María y José?
   (And Mary and Joseph?)

b. María y José se lavan, también, todos los días.
   (Mary and Joseph wash themselves every day also.)

1. a. ¿Se lavan Uds. todas las noches? _____

   _____

   b. ¿Y tú? _____

   _____

2. a. ¿Se baña Ud. todas las mañanas? _____

   _____

   b. ¿Y los otros miembros de su familia? _____

   _____

3. a. ¿Te lavarás antes de comer? _____

   _____

   b. ¿Y sus amigos? _____

   _____

4. a. ¿Se acuerda Ud. de que hoy es mi aniversario? _____

   _____

   b. ¿Y Carolina y Carlota? _____

   _____

5. a. ¿Se acostará Ud. a las diez? _____

   _____

   b. ¿Y ustedes? _____

   _____

VII. Conteste las siguientes preguntas. Son preguntas personales. (Answer the following questions. They are personal questions.)

Modelo: ¿A qué hora se acuesta Ud. todas las noches?
Escriba: Todas las noches me acuesto a las once.

1. ¿A qué hora se levanta Ud. todas las mañanas? _____

   _____

2. ¿A qué hora se levantará Ud. mañana? _____

   _____

3. ¿A qué hora se acostó Ud. anoche? _____

   _____

215

4. ¿Se afeita su padre todas las mañanas? _____

_____

5. ¿Se alegra Ud. cuando recibe buenas notas? _____

_____

6. ¿Se alegró Ud. ayer cuando recibió buenas notas en español? _____

_____

7. ¿Se bañó su hermanito ayer por la noche? _____

_____

8. ¿Se burla Ud. de un alumno cuando no sabe la lección? _____

_____

9. ¿A qué hora se despierta Ud. por la mañana? _____

_____

10. ¿A qué hora se despertó Ud. esta mañana? _____

_____

11. ¿A qué hora se despertará Ud. mañana? _____

_____

12. ¿Se divertirán sus amigos en el baile esta noche? _____

_____

13. ¿Se quedará Ud. en casa hoy? _____

_____

14. ¿Se secarán los niños después de bañarse? _____

_____

15. ¿Y usted? ¿Se secará Ud. después de bañarse? _____

_____

VIII. Dictado. Escriba las oraciones que su profesor de español va a leer.
(Dictation. Write the sentences that your Spanish teacher is going to read.)

1. _____

2. _____

3. _____

IX. **Talking about a Future Career. Proficiency in Speaking and Writing.**

Situation: It's Career Week in your school. The Guidance Department has arranged for guest speakers in various professions to give presentations in the school auditorium. One of them is Señora Fuentes who is an interpreter at the **Naciones Unidas** / United Nations. Your Spanish teacher has invited her to talk to the students at a Spanish Club party.

You are playing the role of **Usted.** After you and Señora Fuentes complete your conversation, you may write what you said on the lines for practice. Later, you may vary and extend the dialogue with your own words and ideas. At that time, ask a classmate to play the role of Señora Fuentes.

Tip: Review the important commonly used reflexive verbs listed above with their English translations. Use a few of them in this dialogue.

Señora Fuentes:	**Bueno. ¿En qué profesión, en qué carrera se interesa usted? ¿Qué quiere ser?**
Usted:	_____ (Tell her you are interested in the United Nations. You want to become an interpreter or translator.)
Señora Fuentes:	**¡Ah! Ud. se interesa en las Naciones Unidas. Ud. quiere hacerse intérprete o traductor (traductora). ¡Como yo!**
Usted:	_____ (Say: That's it! / **¡Eso es!** Like you! I will devote myself to the profession.)
Señora Fuentes:	**Ud. dice que se dedicará a la profesión. ¡Es admirable! Dígame** (Tell me), **¿habla Ud. mucho en la clase de español?**
Usted:	_____ (Of course! / **(¡Claro que sí!)**. All the time. I can't shut up!)
Señora Fuentes:	**¿Todo el tiempo? ¿Usted no puede callarse? ¡Es fantástico! Ud. habla muy bien español. Dígame, ¿cuántos años hace que Ud. estudia español?**
Usted:	_____ (Tell her: I've been studying Spanish for two years.)
Señora Fuentes:	**¡Solamente dos años! ¡Qué talento! No se preocupe** / Don't worry. **Creo que en algunos años Ud. será intérprete o traductor (traductora) en las Naciones Unidas. Estoy segura de eso. Yo soy intérprete.**
Usted:	_____ (Tell her: I'm not going to worry. I know that I will be an interpreter or translator at the United Nations some day. I'm sure of that. Thank her and ask if she wants a cup of coffee.)

PRONOUNS

Definition: A pronoun is a word that takes the place of a noun; for example, in English there are these common pronouns: I, you, he, she, it, we, they, me, him, her, us, them—to mention a few.

Pronouns are divided into certain types: personal, prepositional, relative, interrogative, demonstrative, possessive, indefinite, and negative.

A personal pronoun is used as the subject of a verb, direct or indirect object of a verb or verb form, as a reflexive pronoun object, and as object of a preposition.

Correct use of pronouns in Spanish is not easy—nor in English, for that matter. For example, in English, you can often hear people using pronouns incorrectly: "between you and *I*" ought to be stated as "between you and *me*"; "if you have any questions, see *myself*" ought to be stated as "if you have any questions, see *me*"; "Who did you see?" ought to be stated as "*Whom* did you see?" And there are many more incorrect uses of pronouns in English.

Personal Pronouns

SUBJECT PRONOUNS　　　　　　　　　　　　EXAMPLES

Singular
1. **yo** / I　　　　　　　　　　　　　　　**Yo** hablo.
2. **tú** / you (*familiar*)　　　　　　　　　**Tú** hablas.
3. **usted** / you (*polite*)　　　　　　　　**Usted** habla.
　él / he, it　　　　　　　　　　　　　**Él** habla.
　ella / she, it　　　　　　　　　　　　**Ella** habla.

Plural
1. **nosotros (nosotras)** / we　　　　　　**Nosotros** hablamos.
2. **vosotros (vosotras)** / you (*fam.*)　　**Vosotros** habláis.
3. **ustedes** / you (*polite*)　　　　　　　**Ustedes** hablan.
　ellos / they　　　　　　　　　　　　**Ellos** hablan.
　ellas / they　　　　　　　　　　　　**Ellas** hablan.

As you can see in the examples given here, a subject pronoun is ordinarily placed in front of the main verb.

In Spanish, subject pronouns are not used at all times. The ending of the verb tells you if the subject is 1st, 2nd, or 3rd person in the singular or plural. Of course, in the 3rd person sing. and pl. there is more than one possible subject with the same ending on the verb form. In that case, if there is any doubt as to what the subject is, it is mentioned for the sake of clarity. At other times, subject pronouns in Spanish are used when you want to be emphatic, to make a contrast between this person and that person, or out of simple courtesy. You must be certain to know the endings of the verb forms in all the tenses (see the entry **Verb Tables** in the Index) in the three persons of the singular and of the plural so that you can figure out the subject if it is not clearly stated. In addition to pronouns as subjects, nouns are also used as subjects. Any noun— whether common **(el hombre, la mujer, el cielo, la silla,** *etc.*) or proper (**María, Juan y Elena, los Estado Unidos,** *etc.*) are always 3rd person, either singular or plural.

Generally speaking, in some Latin American countries **ustedes** (3rd pers., pl.) is used in place of **vosotros** or **vosotras** (2nd pers., pl.)

DIRECT OBJECT PRONOUNS　　　　　　　　EXAMPLES

Singular
1. **me** / me　　　　　　　　　　　　　**María me ha visto** / Mary has seen me.
2. **te** / you (*fam.*)　　　　　　　　　　**María te había visto** / Mary had seen you.
3. **lo, la** / you　　　　　　　　　　　　**María lo (la) ve** / Mary sees you.
　lo / him: **lo** / him, it　　　　　　　　**María lo (lo) ve** / Mary sees him (it).
　la / her, it　　　　　　　　　　　　**María la ve** / Mary sees her (it).

Plural

1. **nos** / us	**María nos había visto** / Mary had seen us.
2. **os** / you (*fam.*)	**María os ha visto** / Mary has seen you.
3. **los, las** / you	**María los (las) ve** / Mary sees you.
los / them	**María los ve** / Mary sees them.
las / them	**María las ve** / Mary sees them.

In Latin American countries, **lo** is generally used instead of **le** to mean *him.* You can tell from the context of what is written or said if **lo** means *him* or *it* (masc.).

NOTE that in the 3rd pers., plural, the direct objects **los** (masc.) and **las** (fem.) refer to people and things.

ALSO NOTE that in the 3rd pers. singular, the direct object pronoun **lo** is masc. and **la** is fem. and both mean *you.* You can tell from the context of what is written or said if **lo** means *you* (masc. sing.) or if it means *him.*

Here is a summing up of the various meanings of the direct object pronouns **lo, la, los, las:**

lo: him, it, you (*masc.*)
la: her, you (*fem.*), it (*fem.*)
los: you (*masc. pl.*), them (*people or things, masc., pl.*)
las: you (*fem. pl.*), them (*people or things, fem., pl.*)

As you can see in the examples given, a direct object pronoun ordinarily is placed in front of the main verb.

There is also the neuter **lo** direct object pronoun. It does not refer to any particular noun that is f. or m.; that is why it has no gender and is called *neuter.* It usually refers to an idea or a statement:

¿Está Ud. enfermo? / Are you sick? **Sí, lo estoy** / Yes, I am.
¿Son amígos? / Are they friends? **Sí, lo son** / Yes, they are.

Of course, your reply could be **Sí, estoy enfermo** and **Sí, son amigos.** But because your verb is a form of **estar** or **ser,** you do not have to repeat what was mentioned; neuter **lo** takes its place as a direct object pronoun. This neuter **lo** direct object pronoun is also used with other verbs, *e.g.,* **pedir, preguntar,** and **parecer:**

María parece contenta / Mary seems happy. **Sí, lo parece** / Yes, she does (Yes, she does seem *so*).

To make the above object pronouns negative, place **no** in front of the direct object pronouns: **María no me ve,** *etc.* To make the other examples negative place **no** in front of the verb.

INDIRECT OBJECT PRONOUNS	EXAMPLES
Singular	
1. **me** / to me	**Pablo me ha hablado** / Paul has talked to me.
2. **te** / to you (*fam.*)	**Pablo te habla** / Paul talks to you.
3. **le** / to you, to him, to her, to it	**Pablo le habla** / Paul talks to you (to him, to her, to it).
Plural	
1. **nos** / to us	**Pablo nos ha hablado** / Paul has talked to us.
2. **os** / to you (*fam.*)	**Pablo os habla** / Paul talks to you.
3. **les** / to you, to them	**Pablo les habla** / Paul talks to you (to them).

To make these sentences negative, place **no** in front of the indirect object pronouns: **Pablo no me habla** / Paul does not talk to me.

NOTE that **me, te, nos, os** are direct object pronouns and indirect object pronouns.

NOTE that **le** as an indirect object pronoun has more than one meaning. If there is any doubt as to the meaning, merely add after the verb any of the following accordingly to clarify the meaning: **a Ud., a él, a ella: Pablo le habla a usted** / Paul is talking to you.

NOTE that **les** has more than one meaning. If there is any doubt as to the meaning, merely add after the verb any of the following, accordingly: **a Uds., a ellos, a ellas: Pablo no les habla a ellos** / Paul is not talking to them.

As you can see in the examples given, an indirect object pronoun ordinarily is placed in front of the main verb.

An indirect object pronoun is needed when you use a verb that indicates a person is being deprived of something, *e.g.,* to steal something *from* someone, to take something *off* or from someone, to buy something from someone, and actions of this sort. The reason why an indirect object pronoun is needed is that you are dealing with the preposition **a + noun** or **pronoun** and it must be accounted for. Examples:

Los ladrones le robaron todo el dinero a él / The robbers stole all the money from him.
La madre le quitó al niño el sombrero / The mother took off the child's hat.
Les compré mi automóvil a ellos / I bought my car from them.

The indirect object pronouns are used with the verb **gustar** and with the following verbs: **bastar, faltar** or **hacer falta, sobrar, quedarle (a uno), tocarle (a uno), placer, parecer.**

EXAMPLES:
A Ricardo le gusta el helado / Richard likes ice cream (*i.e.,* Ice cream is pleasing to him, to Richard.)
A Juan le bastan cien dólares / One hundred dollars are enough for John.
A los muchachos les faltan cinco dólares / The boys need five dollars (*i.e.,* Five dollars are lacking to them, to the boys). OR: **A la mujer le hacen falta cinco dólares** / The woman needs five dollars (*i.e.,* Five dollars are lacking to her, to the woman).

To put it simply, the indirect object pronoun is needed in the examples given above because some kind of action is being done *to* someone.

EJERCICIOS

I. Cambie las siguientes frases usando el pronombre que convenga por el complemento directo, según los modelos.

(Change the following sentences using the appropriate direct object pronoun in place of the direct object noun, according to the models. Review the direct object pronouns above where there are explanations and examples of sentences in Spanish with English translations.)

In the first model sentence that follows, **Elena** is the direct object noun. In place of it, the direct object pronoun **la** (*her*) is used and it is placed in front of the verb **vio.** The appropriate direct object pronoun is **la** because it is *fem. sing.,* referring to **Elena.** In other words, **Mary saw Helen** is changed to **Mary saw her.**

In the second model sentence, **el libro** is the direct object noun. In place of it, the direct object pronoun **lo** (*it*) is used and it is placed in front of the verb **leyó.** The appropriate direct object pronoun in this sentence is **lo** because it is *masc. sing.,* referring to **el libro.** In other words, **Pepe read the book** is changed to **Pepe read it.**

Modelos: María vio a Elena. (Mary saw Helen.)
Pepe leyó el libro. (Pepe read the book.)

Escriba: María la vio. (Mary saw her.)
Pepe lo leyó. (Pepe read it.)

1. José vio a Margarita. _____

2. Pablo verá a Paula mañana. _____

3. Los alumnos miraban la pizarra. _____

4. La profesora leía la página. _____

5. El profesor escribió la oración. _____

6. La alumna leyó el libro. _____

7. Juana comió el pastel. _____

8. Esteban bebió la leche. _____

9. El vendedor vendió las bicicletas. _____

10. La señora Rodríguez compró los zapatos. _____

11. El presidente anunció las noticias. _____

12. Los profesores corrigieron los temas. _____

13. Los alumnos vieron a los profesores. _____

14. La profesora abrió las ventanas. _____

15. Los alumnos cerraron los libros. _____

II. Cambie las siguientes frases usando el pronombre que convenga por el complemento indirecto, según los modelos.
(Change the following sentences using the appropriate indirect object pronoun in place of the indirect object noun, according to the models. Review the indirect object pronouns above where there are explanations and examples of sentences in Spanish with English translations.)

In the first model sentence that follows, **Florencia** is the indirect object noun. In place of it, the indirect object pronoun **le** (*to her*) is used and it is placed in front of the verb **habla.** In other words, **Ricardo talks to Florencia** is changed to **Ricardo talks to her.**

In the second model sentence, **a su padre** (*to his father*) is the indirect object noun. In place of it, the indirect object pronoun **le** (*to him*) is used and it is placed in front of the verb **dice.** In other words, **Miguel does not tell the truth to his father** is changed to **Miguel does not tell the truth to him.** The direct object noun is **la verdad** (*the truth*), but you are not asked to replace it with a direct object pronoun. In this exercise, you are practicing the use of indirect object pronouns (*to her, to him, to them*).

Modelos: Ricardo habla con Florencia. (Richard talks *to Florence.*)
Miguel no dice la verdad a su padre. (Michael does not tell the truth *to his father.*)

Escriba: Ricardo le habla. (Richard talks *to her.*)
Miguel no le dice la verdad. (Michael does not tell the truth *to him.*)

1. Mañana Pablo hablará a la profesora. _____

2. Pedro dirá la verdad a su madre. _____

3. María dará los chocolates a sus amigas. _____

4. Los señores Rodríguez dieron un regalo a Juana y a Pedro. _____

_____

5. La profesora de español dará buenas notas a los alumnos. _____

_____

III. Conteste las siguientes preguntas en el afirmativo según el modelo.
(Answer the following questions in the affirmative according to the model. In this exercise you are practicing the use of indirect object pronouns in your answers. Remember that indirect and direct object pronouns normally go in front of the verb.)

Modelo: ¿Me dará Ud. mi libro? (Will you give my book *to me*?
or: Will you give *me* my book?)

Escriba: Sí, le daré su libro. (Yes, I will give your book *to you.*
or: Yes, I will give *you* your book.)

1. ¿Me dirá Ud. la verdad? _____

2. ¿Os habla Pablo a vosotros? _____

3. ¿Le dio María a usted el dinero? _____

4. ¿Les habla Alicia a ustedes? _____

5. ¿Les dio Ricardo a ellos el chocolate? _____

6. ¿A Ricardo le gusta el helado? _____

7. ¿A Juan le bastan cien dólares? _____

8. ¿A los muchachos les faltan cinco dólares? _____

_____

9. ¿A la mujer le hacen falta diez pesetas? _____

_____

10. ¿Le robaron los ladrones todo el dinero a él? _____

_____

IV. Look who's talking to whom! Proficiency in Speaking and Writing.

Situation: You have been on the phone for about an hour. Your brother wants to call someone and he is pestering you by asking you one question after the next. You interrupt your telephone conversation every few seconds to answer his questions. You are acting the role of **Tú.**

After you have finished answering his questions, you may practice writing what you said on the lines. You may add your own words and ideas to expand this dialogue. Ask a classmate to play the role of your brother / **tu hermano.** Or, if you prefer, **tu hermana** / your sister.

Tu hermano: **Quiero telefonear a mi amigo.**

Tú: _____
(Say: Don't you see I'm talking to someone?)

Tu hermano: **Sí, yo veo que tú hablas con alguien. ¿Con quién hablas? ¿Tú hablas con Lola?**

Tú: _____
(No. I'm not talking to Lola.)

Tu hermano: **¿Tú no hablas con Lola?**

Tú: _____
(I'm not talking to her this minute. I talked to her yesterday.)

Tu hermano: **¿Tú hablas con María y con Juana?**

Tú: _____
(I'm not talking to them now. I talked to them this morning.)

Tu hermano: **¿Con quién hablas?**

Tú: _____
(I'm talking *to you.* Go away! Shoo! Scat! / **¡Vete!**)*

*The expression **¡Vete!** is the title of the story in Work Unit 4. Do you remember it?

V. Who gives the coin to whom? Proficiency in Speaking and Writing.

Situation: You are at Gabriela's birthday party. You are standing in a circle with your friends playing a game with a coin / **una moneda**. The coin is being circulated from one person to another.

The players take turns saying: Who gives the coin to whom? / **¿Quién da la moneda a quién?** I give the coin to José / **Yo le doy la moneda a José.** I give the coin to him / **Yo le doy la moneda a él.** José gives the coin to me / **José me da la moneda a mí.** All the indirect object pronouns are summed up below. In this game you will use as many of them as you can. Your role is to provide the Spanish on the blank lines!

SINGULAR INDIRECT OBJECT PRONOUNS

José	**me**	da la moneda (a mí).	José gives the coin *to me.*
	te	(a ti).	*to you* (fam.sing.).
	le	(a él).	*to him.*
	le	(a ella)	*to her.*
	le	(a Ud.).	*to you* (polite sing.).

PLURAL INDIRECT OBJECT PRONOUNS

José	**nos**	da la moneda (a nosotros).	José gives the coin *to us.*
	os	(a vosotros).	*to you* (fam. pl.).
	les	(a ellos).	*to them* (masc.).
	les	(a ellas).	*to them* (fem.).
	les	(a Uds.).	*to you* (polite pl.).

Cristina: **¿Quién da la moneda a quién?**

Clemente: _____

(I give the coin to her, to Dolores / **Yo le doy la moneda a ella, a Dolores.**)

Dolores: **Clemente me dio la moneda a mí /** Clemente gave me the coin. **Ahora yo te doy la moneda a ti /** Now I give the coin to you.

Daniel: _____

(Dolores gave me the coin. Now I give the coin to Rosa.)

Rosa: **Daniel me dio la moneda a mí. Ahora yo les doy la moneda a ellos, a David y a Julia.**

David y Julia: _____

(Rosa gave us the coin. Now we give the coin to her, to Ana.)

Ana: _____

(David and Julia gave the coin to me. Now I give the coin to our Spanish teacher.)

La maestra (El maestro):   **Ana me dio la moneda a mí. ¡La guardaré! /** I will keep it! **¡Muchas gracias, Ana!**

VI. Giving Something to Someone. Proficiency in Speaking and Writing.

Situation: You just came from a stationery shop / **una papelería.** You bought four rubber erasers / **una goma de borrar** or **un borrador.**

Now you are giving them to four persons in your Spanish class. Tell us what you plan to say. Then write your statements on the lines for practice. For starters, try this:

Te doy un borrador a ti, María, porque tú eres mi amiga.

(I am giving an eraser to you, Mary, because you are my friend.)

1. I am giving an eraser to you, Alberto, because you are my friend.

   _____

2. I am giving an eraser to him, to Alfredo, because he is my friend.

   _____

3. I am giving an eraser to her, to Carolina, because she is my friend.

   _____

4. I am giving an eraser to you *(polite sing.* **Ud.***)*, Señora López, because you are an excellent Spanish teacher.

   _____

VII. Who knows whom? Proficiency in Speaking and Writing.

Situation: You and your brother Darío are at a friend's birthday party. Darío does not know everybody at the party. You and he are mingling in the group as statements are made about who knows whom. You are acting the role of **Tú.** You may vary and extend the dialogue with your own words and ideas. We are going to use direct object pronouns *referring to persons*. But first, let's sum them up.

SINGULAR DIRECT OBJECT PRONOUNS

María	**me**	conoce (a mí).	Mary knows	*me.*
	te	(a ti).		*you* (familiar sing.).
	lo	(a él).		*him.*
	la	(a ella).		*her.*
	lo	(a Ud.).		*you* (formal, masc. sing.).
	la	(a Ud.).		*you* (formal, fem. sing.).

PLURAL DIRECT OBJECT PRONOUNS

María	**nos**	conoce (a nosotros).	Mary knows	*us.*
	os	(a vosotros).		*you* (familiar pl.).
	los	(a ellos).		*them* (masc. or masc. + fem.).
	las	(a ellas).		*them* (fem.).
	los	(a Uds.)		*you* (formal, masc. pl.).
	las	(a Uds.).		*you* (formal, fem. pl.).

Tú: _____
(Elena, do you know my brother Darío? / **Elena, ¿conoces a mi hermano Darío?**)

Elena: **No. Yo no lo conozco. ¡Hola, Darío!**

Darío: **¡Hola, Elena! ¡Ahora, tú me conoces y yo te conozco!**

Tú: _____
(Lolita, do you know my brother Darío?)

Lolita: **Sí. Yo lo conozco. Y él me conoce. Conozco a todos los muchachos. ¡Yo los conozco bien!**

Tú: _____
(Darío, do you know my friends Sara and Susana?)

Darío: **No. No las conozco. ¡Hola, Sara y Susana!**

Sara y Susana: **¡Hola, Darío! ¡Ahora nosotras te conocemos y tú nos conoces!**

Darío: **¡Qué alegría! Ahora yo lo conozco a él, yo la conozco a ella, yo los conozco a ellos, yo las conozco a ellas. ¡Todos me conocen y todos nos conocen!**

VIII. **Who brought what? Proficiency in Speaking and Writing.**

Situation: You are having a picnic in a park with your friends. You and your friends want to know who brought what.

In the dialogue below we are going to use direct object pronouns *referring to things*. You are acting the role of **Tú.** You may vary and extend the dialogue with your own words and ideas. But first, let's sum up the direct object pronouns referring to things.

SINGULAR DIRECT OBJECT PRONOUNS REFERRING TO THINGS

Yo traje el pan.
(I brought the bread.)

Yo lo traje. (I brought **it.**)

María trajo la ensalada.
(Mary brought the salad.)

María la trajo. (Mary brought **it.**)

PLURAL DIRECT OBJECT PRONOUNS REFERRING TO THINGS

Susana trajo los salchichones.
(Susana brought the sausages.)

Susana los trajo. (Susana brought **them.**)

Roberto trajo las papas fritas.
(Roberto brought the fried potatoes.)

Roberto las trajo. (Robert brought **them.**)

Anita: **¿Quién trajo el pan?**

Tú: _____
(I brought it.)

Roberto: **¿Quién trajo la ensalada?**

Tú: _____
(María brought it.)

Pablo: **¿Quién trajo los salchichones?**

Tú: _____
(Susana brought them.)

Luisa: **¿Quién trajo las papas fritas?**

Tú: _____
(Roberto brought them.)

PROPER NAMES OF BOYS AND GIRLS IN SPANISH AND ENGLISH

GIRLS		BOYS	
SPANISH	ENGLISH	SPANISH	ENGLISH
Adela	Adele	**Abrahán**	Abraham
Ágata	Agatha	**Adán**	Adam
Alejandra	Alexandra	**Adolfo**	Adolph
Alejandrlna	Alexandrina	**Alano**	Alan, Allen
Alicia	Alice	**Alberto**	Albert
Amada	Amy	**Alejandro**	Alexander
Amelia	Amelie	**Alfonso**	Alphonso
Ana	Anne, Anna, Hannah	**Alfredo**	Alfred
Bárbara	Barbara	**Aluino**	Alwin
Beatriz	Beatrice	**Andrés**	Andrew
Berta	Bertha	**Antonio**	Anthony
Brígida	Bridget	**Arturo**	Arthur
Carlota	Charlotte	**Atanasio**	Athanasios
Carolina	Caroline	**Bartolomé**	Bartholomew
Casandra	Cassandra	**Basilio**	Basil
Catarina	Catherine	**Beltrán**	Bertram
Clara	Clare, Clara	**Bernardo**	Bernard
Claudia	Claudia	**Carlos**	Charles
Constanza	Constance	**Claudio**	Claude
Cristina	Christine	**Clemente**	Clement
Dolores	Dolores	**Constantino**	Constantine
Dora	Dora, Doris	**Cristián**	Christian
Dorotea	Dorothy	**Cristóbal**	Christopher
Edita	Edith	**Daniel**	Daniel
Elena	Ellen, Helen	**Darío**	Darius
Elisa	Eliza	**David**	David
Ema	Emma	**Diego**	James
Emilia	Emily	**Dionisio**	Dennis
Engracia	Grace	**Domingo**	Dominic
Enriqueta	Harriet, Henrietta	**Edmundo**	Edmund
Ester	Esther	**Eduardo**	Edward
Eugenia	Eugenia	**Eliseo**	Ellis, Elisha
Eva	Eve	**Emilio**	Emil
Florencia	Florence	**Enrique**	Henry
Francisca	Frances	**Ernesto**	Ernest
Gabriela	Gabrielle	**Esteban**	Stephen, Steven
Genoveva	Genevieve	**Eugenio**	Eugene
Gerarda	Geraldine	**Federico**	Frederick
Gertrudis	Gertrude	**Francisco**	Francis
Hilda	Hilda	**Geofredo**	Geoffrey
Inés	Agnez, Inez	**Gerardo**	Gerald, Gerard
Irene	Irene	**Gilberto**	Gilbert
Isabel	Elizabeth	**Gregorio**	Gregory
Josefa	Josephine	**Gualtero**	Walter
Juana	Jane	**Guillermo**	William
Judit	Judith	**Herberto**	Herbert
Julia	Julia, Juliet	**Hugo**	Hugh
Lola	Lola, Dolores	**Hunfredo**	Humphrey
Lolita	Lolita, Dolores	**Isidoro**	Isidor
Lucía	Lucy	**Jacobo**	Jacob
Luisa	Louise, Louisa	**Jaime**	James
Manola	Emma	**Javier**	Xavier
Manuela	Emma	**Jerónimo**	Jerome

PROPER NAMES OF BOYS AND GIRLS IN SPANISH AND ENGLISH

GIRLS		BOYS	
SPANISH	ENGLISH	SPANISH	ENGLISH
Margarita	Margaret, Margery	**Jesús**	Jesus
María	Mary	**Jonatán**	Jonathan
Mariana	Marian	**Jorge**	George
Marta	Martha	**José**	Joseph
Matilde	Mathilda	**Juan**	John
Paula	Paula	**Julián**	Julian
Paulina	Pauline	**Julio**	Julius
Queta	Harriet, Henrietta	**Justino**	Justin
Rebeca	Rebecca	**León**	Leo, Leon
Rosa	Rose	**Leonardo**	Leonard
Rosalía	Rosalie	**Lorenzo**	Lawrence
Sara	Sarah	**Luis**	Louis, Lewis
Sofía	Sophia, Sophie	**Manuel**	Manuel, Emmanuel
Susana	Susan, Suzanne	**Marcelo**	Marcel
Teodora	Theodora	**Marcos**	Mark
Teresa	Theresa	**Mateo**	Matthew

PERSONAL A

1. The preposition **a** is used in front of a noun direct object if it is a person.

Por ejemplo:

> **Yo conozco a María.** / I know Mary.
> **Veo a los niños.** / I see the children.
> **Isabel vio a sus amigos.** / Isabel saw her friends.
>
> **Lolita mira al muchacho.** / Lolita is looking at the boy.
> **Pedro escucha al profesor (a la profesora).** / Pedro is listening to the teacher.

2. The personal **a** is *not* used in front of a noun direct object if it is a thing.

Por ejemplo:

> **Lolita mira el árbol.** / Lolita is looking at the tree.
> **Pedro escucha la música.** / Pedro is listening to the music.

3. The personal **a** is also used in front of a direct object that is an indefinite pronoun and it refers to a person.

Por ejemplo:

> **No conozco a nadie aquí.** / I don't know anybody here.
> **¿Ve Ud. a alguien?** / Do you see anybody?

4. The personal **a** is *not* used with the verb **tener** even if the direct object is a person.

Por ejemplo:

> **Tengo un hermano y una hermana.** / I have a brother and a sister.
>
> **Clara y Francisco Rodríguez tienen una hija y un hijo.** / Clara and Francisco Rodríguez have one daughter and one son.

EJERCICIOS

I. Translate the following sentences into Spanish. Refer to the uses of the Personal a as needed.

1. I know Mary.

   _____

2. I see the children.

   _____

3. Isabel saw her friends.

   _____

4. Lolita is looking at the boy.

   _____

5. Pedro is listening to the teacher.

   _____

6. Lolita is looking at the tree.

   _____

7. Pedro is listening to the music.

   _____

8. I don't know anybody here.

   _____

9. Do you (Ud.) see anybody?

   _____

10. I have a brother and a sister.

    _____

II. Helping Others. Proficiency in Speaking and Writing.

Situation: Your friend Bob is taking a course in Spanish Level 1. He does not understand the uses of the **Personal a.** You are studying Spanish Level 2, so he wants you to help him with his homework.

Below, in Column A, there are incomplete sentences that Bob wrote. He wants you to complete them in Column B. On the lines, write the complete sentences using the Spanish **Personal a** where it is required. After you have finished, go back to sentence number 1 and read aloud the complete Spanish sentence. Then explain to him why the **Personal a** was used or why it was not used. In your completed sentence include the words in parentheses in Column A.

Column A	Column B
1. **(Isabel)** ¿Conoces tú . . . ?	1. _____
2. **(los niños)** ¿Ves tú . . . ?	2. _____
3. **(la casa)** ¿Ves tú . . . ?	3. _____
4. **(los muchachos)** Lolita mira . . .	4. _____
5. **(alguien)** ¿Vio Ud. . . . ?	5. _____
6. **(nadie)** No conozco . . . aquí.	6. _____
7. **(dos hermanas)** Tengo . . .	7. _____
8. **(el cielo)** Miro . . .	8. _____
9. **(la profesora)** Luis escucha . . .	9. _____
10. **(la música)** Escuchamos . . .	10. _____

Still Life by Juan VAN DER HAMEN Y LEÓN (1596–1631)
Courtesy of The National Gallery of Art, Washington, D.C.

III. Spanish Art. Proficiency in Speaking and Writing.

Situation: You are on a field trip with your Spanish teacher and classmates at The National Gallery of Art in Washington, D.C. You are admiring the *Still Life* painting by Juan VAN DER HAMEN Y LEÓN.

Look at the picture above and say aloud Spanish words that come to mind. Then write them on the lines below or use them in one or two sentences. You may use your own words and ideas or the following suggestions.

Some verbs: **Yo veo** / I see; **Yo aprecio** / I appreciate; **Es** / It is; **Son** / they are; **Hay** / there is, there are.

Some nouns: **el cuadro** / the picture; **el artista** / the artist; **la naturaleza muerta** / still life; **las frutas** / the fruits; **los higos** / the figs; **una cesta** / a basket; **un jarrón** / a vase; **el plato es de plata** / the plate is made of silver; **las aceitunas** / the olives.

Some adjectives: **interesante** / interesting; **estupendo** / stupendous, wonderful; **artístico** / artistic; **impresionante** / impressive.

_____

_____

_____

_____

231

COMMONLY USED IDIOMATIC EXPRESSIONS

with **hasta**

hasta ahora until now
hasta entonces until then
hasta la vista see you later
hasta luego see you later
hasta mañana until tomorrow

with **lo**

a lo lejos in the distance
a lo menos at least
¡Lo bueno que es! How good it is!
¡Lo bien que está escrito! How well it is written!
lo más pronto posible as soon as possible
Lo primero que debo decir . . . The first thing I must say . . .
por lo contrario on the contrary
por lo menos at least
¡Ya lo creo! I should certainly think so!

with **mañana**

ayer por la mañana yesterday morning
de la mañana in the morning (Use this when a specific time is mentioned):
> **Voy a tomar el tren a las seis de la mañana.** I'm going to take the train at six o'clock in the morning.

mañana por la mañana tomorrow morning
mañana por la noche tomorrow night, tomorrow evening
mañana por la tarde tomorrow afternoon
pasado mañana the day after tomorrow
por la mañana in the morning (Use this when no exact time is mentioned):
> **El Señor Blanco llegó por la mañana.** Mr. Blanco arrived in the morning.

por la mañana temprano early in the morning

with **mismo**

ahora mismo right now
al mismo tiempo at the same time
allá mismo right there
aquí mismo right here
el mismo de siempre the same old thing
eso mismo that very thing
hoy mismo this very day
lo mismo the same, the same thing

with **no**

Creo que no. I don't think so. I think not.
No es verdad. It isn't so. It isn't true. **¿No es verdad?** Isn't that so?
No hay de qué. You're welcome.
No hay problema. No problem.
No hay remedio. There's no way. It can't be helped.
No importa. It doesn't matter.

No tengo más que dos dólares. I have only two dollars.
todavía no not yet
ya no no longer

---

with **para**

estar para + inf. to be about to, to be at the point of;
    El tren está para salir. The train is about to leave.
para mí for my part
para ser in spite of being; **Para ser tan viejo, él es muy ágil.** In spite of being so old, he is very
    agile.
para siempre forever
un vaso para agua a water glass; **una taza para café** a coffee cup

---

with **poco**

a poco in a short while, presently
dentro de poco in a short while, in a little while
en pocos días in a few days
poco a poco little by little
poco antes shortly before
poco después shortly after
un poco de a little (of); **Deme un poco de azúcar, por favor.** Give me a little sugar, please.

EJERCICIOS

I. **Answer the following questions in complete sentences. In your answers use the cue
words given in parentheses. Review the commonly used idiomatic expressions above.**

    Modelo: lo más pronto posible   ¿Cuándo irá Ud. de compras?
            (as soon as possible)   (When will you go shopping?)

    Escriba: Iré de compras lo más pronto posible.
            (I will go shopping as soon as possible.)

1. **(por lo menos)** ¿Cuánto dinero necesitará Ud.? _____

_____

2. **(ayer por la mañana)** ¿Cuándo regresó Ud. de vacaciones? _____

_____

3. **(de la mañana)** ¿A qué hora tomará Ud. el tren? _____

_____

4. **(mañana por la mañana)** ¿Cuándo vendrás a mi casa? _____

_____

5. **(mañana por la noche)** ¿Cuándo le darás los regalos a Lisa? _____

_____

6. **(mañana por la tarde)** ¿Cuándo partirán Uds. de vacaciones? _____

_____

7. **(al mismo tiempo)** ¿Cuándo llegaron Juan y Juana a tu casa? _____

_____

8. **(¡Ya lo creo!)** ¿Es importante estudiar? _____

9. **(No hay problema.)** ¿Tienes un problema? _____

10. **(dentro de poco)** ¿A qué hora llegaremos a Madrid? _____

_____

II. Helping Others. Proficiency in Speaking and Writing.

Situation: Your friend Sonya, who is in your Spanish class, wants you to help her with her homework. She needs to write five simple sentences. Help her select five of the commonly used idiomatic expressions from the above section. Use one in a complete sentence in Spanish. After that is done, read the sentences aloud with her, then explain to her how easy it was!

1. _____

2. _____

3. _____

4. _____

5. _____

TEST 3

PART ONE Speaking Proficiency

Directions: Read the five situations given below. Take a few minutes to organize your thoughts about the words you are going to speak. Select three of the five situations. Before you begin to speak, you may review the Oral and Written Proficiency exercises that you did in this Work Unit.

1. **Situation:** You have been selected as **el astrólogo** or **la astróloga** in your Spanish class. During Spanish Club you have been asked to foretell the future for five of your friends. In each of the five predictions you make, use the subject pronoun **Ud.** and verbs in the future tense.

2. **Situation:** You are discussing plans for next summer's vacation with a friend. Make five statements about what you will do next summer. Use the future tense of the verbs in your statements.

3. **Situation:** It's Career Week in your school. Your adviser in the Guidance Department, Señora Santiago, has asked you to tell her the kind of career you are interested in. In at least five sentences, using verbs in the future, tell her about your career plans.

4. **Situation:** You have been on the phone for about an hour. Your brother or sister wants to call someone and he / she is pestering you by asking you one question after the next about whom you are talking to. You interrupt your telephone conversation every few seconds to answer his / her questions.

    Using indirect object pronouns, make at least three statements saying that you are not talking to Lola, or to María and Juana, or somebody else's name; for example: **Yo no le hablo a Lola, Yo no les hablo a María y a Juana.** In your last statement, tell your brother (or sister): Go away! You may add your own words or ideas.

5. **Situation:** You and your brother Darío are at a friend's birthday party. Darío does not know everybody at the party. You and he are mingling in the group as statements are made about who knows whom.

    Using direct object pronouns, make at least five statements about who knows whom; for example: **Elena, ¿conoces a mi hermano Darío? Yo no lo conozco, María me conoce, José nos conoce, Tú no la conoces, ¿Las conoces a Sara y a Susana?**

PART TWO Listening Proficiency

Directions: Your teacher will read aloud four short paragraphs. Each one will contain only a few sentences. You will hear each paragraph twice. Then you will hear one question based on each. You will hear the question only once. It is printed below. Choose the best suggested answer based on what you heard and check the letter of your choice.

Selection Number 1

1. ¿Qué está leyendo Pedro?

    A. un libro

    B. una carta de Pablo

    C. en la cocina

    D. el horóscopo en el periódico

Selection Number 2

2. ¿Qué haremos en la fiesta esta noche?

    A. Prepararemos pasteles deliciosos.

    B. Bailaremos y cantaremos.

C. Tendremos una fiesta.

D. Estudiaremos.

Selection Number 3

3. ¿Adónde irá Pedro?

  A. a su casa

  B. a casa de Lola

  C. Pedro está loco.

  D. Pedro no es supersticioso.

Selection Number 4

4. Cuando Pedro cruza la calle, ¿qué ve?

  A. para ir a la fiesta en casa de Lola

  B. un gran camión

  C. a toda velocidad

  D. hacia él

PART THREE   Reading Proficiency

Directions: In the following passage there are five blank spaces numbered 1 through 5. Each blank space represents a missing verb form in the future tense. For each blank space, four possible completions are provided. Only one of them makes sense in the context of the passage.

First, read the passage in its entirety to determine its general meaning. Then read it a second time. For each blank space choose the completion that makes the best sense and write its letter in the space provided.

Escucha, Pedro. Esta noche _____ una tertulia en mi casa. Bailaremos y

  1. A. habrá
     B. hablaremos
     C. estarán
     D. regalará

cantaremos. Mi madre _____ pasteles deliciosos. Nosotros nos _____

  2. A. prepararán   3. A. divertiremos
     B. preparará   B. saldremos
     C. cantará   C. estaremos
     D. vendrá   D. tendremos

mucho. Enrique _____; así como Pablo, Ramón, Susana, tu hermana Juana, Queta,

  4. A. habrá
     B. valdrá
     C. vendrá
     D. pondrá

y muchos otros amigos. ¿_____?

  5. A. venderás
     B. vendrás
     C. sabrás
     D. aprenderás

PART FOUR   Writing Proficiency

Directions: Of the five situations in Part One (Speaking Proficiency) in this test, select three of them and write what you said on the lines below.

Situation 1 _____

_____

_____

Situation 2 _____

_____

_____

Situation 3 _____

_____

_____

Situation 4 _____

_____

_____

Situation 5 _____

_____

_____

El pelo está corto y se mueve con gracia en el viento. Este corte es revuelto. Es el modelo A. The hair is short and moves gracefully in the wind. This cut is windblown. It is model A.

Este corte es serio y sencillo Es la moderación elegante. Es el modelo C. This cut is serious and simple. It is elegant moderation. It is model C.

En este modelo, el pelo, ya sea seco o mojado, se repone con los dedos. Este corte es realmente revuelto. Es el modelo B. In this model the hair, whether dry or moist, can be put back in place with the fingers. This cut is really wild. It is model B.

Este corte sencillo y serio es clásico. Es el modelo D. This simple and serious cut is classic. It is model D.

Work Unit 9

Have you ever wanted to change the style of your hair for some special reason? Let's see what happens to Juana and Pedro.

En la peluquería para señoras y señores

Hoy, Juana se va a la peluquería. Le gustaría tener un corte de pelo porque esta noche se va al baile con Carlos, uno de sus amigos. Tiene cita en la peluquería a las cuatro y media de la tarde.

Pedro está con Juana. Le gustaria también tener un nuevo corte de pelo ya que va al mismo baile con Lolita, una de sus amigas. 5

Aquí están entrando en la peluqueria.

Juana:	Buenas tardes.
Pedro:	Buenas tardes.
El Peluquero:	Buenas tardes, Juana. Buenas tardes, Pedro. Ustedes han llegado a las cuatro en punto. Juana, siéntese aquí. Una de mis peluqueras, que se 10 llama Nina, va a encargarse de usted. Pedro, siéntese allí. Voy a encargarme de usted.
Juana:	De acuerdo, gracias.
Pedro:	De acuerdo, gracias.
El Peluquero:	Bueno, Pedro, voy a empezar con un champú, como siempre, ¿no? 15
Pedro:	Sí, eso es. Empiece con un champú, como siempre, por favor.
El Peluquero:	Bueno, Juana, voy a empezar con un champú, como siempre, ¿no?
Juana:	Sí, eso es. Empiece con un champú, como siempre, por favor.
El Peluquero:	¿Le gustaría más un corte de pelo revuelto o serio?
Juana:	Me parece que prefiero un corte de pelo revuelto . . . no . . . no revuelto . . . 20 Hágame un corte de pelo serio y sencillo . . . no . . . No estoy segura. No puedo elegir entre un corte de pelo revuelto y un corte serio y sencillo. ¿Qué opina usted?
El Peluquero:	Voy a enseñarle dos cortes de pelo revueltos para darle una idea.
	¿Le gusta este corte? 25

El pelo está corto y se mueve con gracia en el viento. Este corte es revuelto. Es el modelo A.

¿O le gusta más éste?

En este modelo, el pelo, ya sea seco o mojado, se repone con los dedos.

Este corte es realmente revuelto. Es el modelo B.   30

Juana: Oh, yo no sé. Me gustan estos dos cortes revueltos. Me parece que pre-
                  fiero el modelo A . . . No . . . Me gusta más el modelo B. Oh, yo no sé.
                  Enséñeme un corte serio y sencillo.

La Peluquera: De acuerdo. Voy a enseñarle dos cortes de pelo serios y sencillos.

                  ¿Le gusta éste?   35

Este corte es serio y sencillo. Es la moderación elegante. Es el modelo C.

¿O tal vez éste?

Este corte sencillo y serio es clásico. Es el modelo D.

Juana: Bueno, he tomado una decisión. Hágame un corte serio y sencillo tal
                  como en el modelo C. Me comportaré bien esta noche después del baile   40
                  con Carlos.

La Peluquera: Muy bien. Ahora empiezo.

El Peluquero: Y usted, Pedro ¿qué tipo de corte le gustaría? Le voy a enseñar dos.
                  ¿Cuál le gusta más? Éste es el modelo A.

¿Le gusta éste?

Este corte es corto, bonito y fácil de cepillar. Es el modelo A.

¿O más bien éste?

De perfil, el pelo está pegado hacia atrás. Le cortaré un mechón desordenado que caerá sobre la frente. Esto le dará un toque natural. Es el   50
modelo B.

¿O tal vez preferiría usted un corte realmente revuelto? ¿Como éste? Es
un verdadero revoltijo. Es el modelo C.

Entonces, Pedro, ¿usted ha elegido?

Pedro: Sí, he elegido. Hágame un corte tal como en el modelo B. Éste es muy   55
                serio. No me gusta en absoluto el corte revuelto del modelo C.

Una hora después, Juana y Pedro se marchan de la peluquería y los dos están muy
felices y contentos con sus nuevos cortes de pelo. Ahora están listos para el baile de esta
noche. Juana se comportará bien y Pedro también porque tienen cortes de pelo serios y
sencillos.   60
        ¿Y usted? Si usted es una joven, ¿qué tipo de corte le gusta? ¿El modelo A, B, C o D?
Si usted es un joven, ¿le gusta más el modelo A o B? ¿O tal vez el C?
        Tome una decisión pronto. El peluquero está esperando.

KEY WORDS AND PHRASES

absoluto *adj.* absolute; **No me gusta en absoluto.** I don't like it at all.

acuerdo *n.m.* agreement; **de acuerdo** okay

atrás *adv.* back, backward; **hacia atrás** toward the back

cabellos *n.m., pl.* hair; **con los cabellos al cepillo** with the hair in a brush cut

champú *n.m.* shampoo

cita *n.f.* appointment, date

clásico *adj.* classic

como *conj.* as, like; **como siempre** as always; **¿Como éste?** Like this one?

comportarse *refl. v.* to behave oneself; **Me comportaré bien** I will behave myself.

contentos *adj., m. pl.* pleased, content

cortar *v.* to cut

cortaré *1st pers., s., fut. of* **cortar**; **Le cortaré . . .** I will cut (on your hair) . . .

corte *n.m.* cut; **un corte de pelo** a haircut

corto *adj.* short

¿cuál? *pron.* which, which one; **¿Cuál le gusta más?** Which one do you like better?

dar *v.* to give; **para darle una idea** in order to give (to) you an idea

de acuerdo okay

dedo *n.m.* finger

deslumbrante *adj.* dazzling

desordenado *adj.* wild, unruly, disarranged

después (de) *adv.* after

elegir *v.* to choose, to select; **elegido** *past part. of* **elegir**; chosen

empiece *3d pers., s., imper. (command) of* **empezar**; begin

empiezo *1st pers., s., pres. indic. of* **empezar**; I begin

encargarse (de) *refl. v.* to take charge (of)

encima *adv.* above; **por encima** at the top

enseñar *v.* to show; **Le voy a enseñar dos** I am going to show (to) you two; **enseñar + le > enseñarle** to show (to) you; **Voy a enseñarle** I am going to show you.

enseñe *3d pers., s., imper. (command) of* **enseñar**; **Enseñe + me > Enséñeme** Show me.

entonces *adv.* then

eso *neuter dem. adj.* that; **eso es** that's it, that's right

esperando *pres. part. of* **esperar**; waiting; **está esperando** is waiting

esta *dem. adj., f.s.* this; **esta noche** this evening, tonight

están entrando *3d pers., pl., pres. prog. of* **entrar**; they are entering, going (into)

este *dem. adj., m.s.* this

éste *dem. pro. m.s.* this one; **¿Le gusta éste?** Do you like this one?

esto *neuter dem. adj.* this; **Esto dará . . .** This will give . . .

feliz *adj., m.s.,* **felices** *m. pl.* happy

frente *n.f.* forehead, brow

gracia *n.f.* grace; **con gracia** gracefully

gusta *3d pers., s., pres. indic. of* **gustar**; **Me gusta más . . .** I like it more . . .

gustan *3d pers., pl., pres. indic. of* **gustar**; **Me gustan estos dos cortes revueltos** I like these two windblown cuts.

gustar *v.* to be pleasing to; **¿Le gusta este corte?** Do you like this cut?

gustaría *3d pers., s., cond. of* **gustar**; **A Juana le gustaría . . .** Juana would like . . .; **A Pedro le gustaría también . . .** Pedro would also like . . .; **¿Le gustaría más . . .** Would you like better (prefer) . . . ?

¿Ha elegido Ud.? *3d pers., s., pres. perf. of* **elegir**; Have you chosen?

hacia *prep.* toward; **hacia atrás** toward the back

haga *3d pers., s., imper. (command) of* **hacer**; make, do; **Haga + me > Hágame un corte de pelo** Do me (give me) a haircut.

han llegado *3d pers., pl., pres. perf. of* **llegar**; you have arrived

he elegido *1st pers., s., pres. perf. of* **elegir**; I have chosen

he tomado *1st pers., s., pres. perf. of* **tomar**; I have taken

irse *refl. v.* to leave, to be on one's way

joven *adj.* young; **una joven** a young woman; **un joven** a young man

Le voy a enseñar dos I am going to show you two.

marcharse *refl. v.* to leave

más *adv.* more; **¿O más bien, éste?** Or rather, this one? **¿Le gusta más . . . ?** Do you like better . . . ?

Me comportaré bien I will behave myself well.

Me parece que . . . It seems to me that . . .

mechón *n.m.* mesh, tuft of hair

mismo *adj.* same

mojado *adj.* moist, wet

moverse *refl. v.* to move

mueve (se) *3d pers., s., pres. indic. of* **moverse**; it moves

neto *adj.* neat, distinct

nota *n.f.* note; **una nota de natural** a natural look

nuevo *adj.* new

o *conj.* or

opinar *v.* to think, judge, opine; **¿Qué opina Ud.?** / What do you think?

parecer *v.* to seem, appear; **Me parece que . . .** It seems to me that . . .

pegado *adj., past part. of* **pegar**; **el pelo está pegado hacia atrás** the hair is slick toward the back

pegar *v.* to stick, glue, paste

pelo *n.m.* hair
peluquera *n.f.* hairdresser (woman)
peluquería *n.f.* hairdressing salon; **para señoras y señores** for women and men
peluquero *n.m.* hairdresser (man)
perfil *n.m.* profile; **de perfil** side view
poner *v.* to put; **ponerse** to put itself; **reponerse** to put itself back in place
preferiría *3d pers., s., cond. of* **preferir**; would prefer
prefiero *1st pers., s., pres. indic. of* **preferir**; I prefer
puedo *1st pers., s., pres. indic. of* **poder**; I can
punto *n.m.* period, dot; **a las cuatro en punto** at four o'clock on the dot
recaer *v.* to fall over
reponerse *refl. v.* to put itself back in place
revoltijo *n.m.* twisted mess
revuelto *adj.* windblown, wild
se mueve *3d pers., s., pres. indic. of* **moverse**; it moves
se repone *3d pers., s., pres. indic. of* **reponerse**; can be put back in place
se va *3d pers., s., pres. indic. of* **irse**; is leaving, is on her way
sea *3d pers., s., pres. sub. of* **ser**; be
seco *adj.* dry

seguro, segura *adj.* sure
sencillo *adj.* simple
serio *adj.* serious
siempre *adv.* always; **como siempre** as always
siéntese *3d pers., s., imper. (command) of* **sentarse**; sit down
suave *adj.* suave, soft, smooth
tal *adj.* such; **tal como** such as, like; **tal vez** *adv.* perhaps
tipo *n.m.* type
tomado *past part. of* **tomar**. **He tomado una decisión** I have made a decision.
tome *3d pers., s., imper. (command) of* **tomar**. **Tome una decisión** Make a decision.
verdadero *adj.* real
viento *n.m.* wind
Voy a empezar I am going to begin.
Voy a encargarme de usted I will take care of you.
Voy a enseñarle dos cortes de pelo serios y sencillos I am going to show you two serious and simple haircuts.
ya ... ya *conj.* whether ... or
ya que *conj.* inasmuch as, since
ya sea seco o mojado whether it is dry or moist

EJERCICIOS

I. Conteste las siguientes preguntas con frases completas. (Answer the following questions in complete sentences.)

1. ¿Adónde va Juana hoy? _____

_____

2. ¿Por qué ella quiere tener un corte de pelo deslumbrante? _____

_____ _____

3. ¿A qué hora Juana tiene cita en la peluquería? _____

_____

4. ¿Quién va a la peluquería con Juana? _____

_____

5. ¿Por qué Pedro quiere tener un nuevo corte? _____

_____

6. ¿Cuántos modelos de cortes enseña la peluquera a Juana? _____

_____

7. ¿Juana ha elegido un corte serio y sencillo? ¿O un corte revuelto? _____

_____

8. ¿Cuántos modelos de cortes enseña el peluquero a Pedro? _____

_____

9. ¿Pedro ha elegido un corte serio y sencillo? ¿O un corte revuelto? _____

_____

10. ¿Y ustedes? ¿Cuál de estos modelos les gusta más? ¿Por qué? _____

_____

II. **Discriminación de los sonidos. Su profesor de español va a pronunciar una sola palabra, sea la de la letra A, sea la de la letra B. Puntee A o B para indicar que su profesor de español ha pronunciado la palabra de la letra A o la palabra de la letra B.**
(**Sound discrimination.** Your Spanish teacher is going to pronounce one word, either in letter A or letter B. Check A or B to indicate that your Spanish teacher has pronounced the word in letter A or B.)

Modelo: ◼ A. hoy
☐ B. hay

He punteado la letra A porque creo que mi profesor de español ha pronunciado la palabra de la letra A. (I have checked letter A because I think that my Spanish teacher has pronounced the word in letter A.)

1. ☐ A. gustará   3. ☐ A. cuatro
   ☐ B. gustaría   ☐ B. cuarto

2. ☐ A. amigos   4. ☐ A. pero
   ☐ B. amigas   ☐ B. perro

III. **Uno por tres. Ponga en las casillas una palabra que—con la palabra ya inscrita—permitirá formar otra palabra. La tercera palabra (que será el resultado de la palabra ya inscrita y de la palabra que usted va a escribir) figura en la lectura de esta lección.**
(**One times three.** Put in the boxes a word that, with the word already written, will form another word. The third word—which will be the result of the word already written plus the word you are going to write—is found in the reading selection in this Work Unit.)

Modelo: | R | E | P | R | E | S | E | N | T | A | + | | | | = _____

Solución: representados | D | O | S | = representados
(represented)

1. | P | O | R | + | | | | = _____ (because)

2. | H | A | G | A | + | | | = _____ (Do me, Make me, Give me)

3. | D | E | + | | | | = _____ (fingers)

IV. Las palabras escondidas. En la rejilla, busque las palabras en español por las palabras en inglés en la lista a continuación. Cuando las haya encontrado, ráyelas. Las palabras escondidas están en la lectura de esta lección.
(**Hidden Words.** In the grid, find the words in Spanish for the words in English on the list next to the grid. When you have found them, draw a line through them. The hidden words are in the reading selection in this Work Unit.)

En la rejilla, las palabras están escritas en todas las direcciones: de abajo arriba, de arriba abajo, de derecha a izquierda, de izquierda a derecha, y en diagonal. Anote que la misma letra puede ser común a varias palabras. (In the grid, the words are written in all directions: from bottom to top, from top to bottom, from right to left, from left to right, and diagonally. Note that the same letter can be common to several words.)

hair
hairstylist, *fem.*
dance, *n.*
haircut
fingers
afternoon
appointment
okay
shampoo
always

O	D	R	E	U	C	A	E	D	A
D	E	A	C	E	O	R	D	T	S
C	C	H	P	O	R	O	I	D	I
A	H	E	E	L	T	C	I	E	E
B	A	I	L	E	E	E	O	D	M
P	M	L	U	P	D	D	L	O	P
S	P	I	Q	M	E	P	R	S	R
A	U	H	U	O	P	R	A	A	E
B	A	I	E	L	E	D	E	D	T
A	C	U	R	D	L	O	C	I	T
P	L	E	A	O	O	C	O	R	E

V. Sopa de letras. Busque cinco sinónimos del sustantivo *gusto*. Los cinco sinónimos pueden aparecer de derecha a izquierda, de izquierda a derecha, de abajo arriba y viceversa, y en diagonal.
(**Alphabet soup.** Find five synonyms of the noun **gusto**. The five synonyms can appear from right to left, from left to right, from bottom to top and vice versa, and diagonally. Tip: Look up **gusto** in the vocabulary in the Appendix.)

G	G	T	S	O	L	R
S	C	E	D	M	E	A
A	P	Q	R	C	T	S
T	A	L	A	G	I	R
I	O	L	I	B	Ú	J
S	P	L	A	E	R	U
F	S	S	A	T	I	S
A	L	E	G	R	Í	A
C	L	I	E	N	T	I
C	A	M	O	P	I	R
I	N	A	L	E	S	O
Ó	M	U	N	O	E	F
N	A	T	U	V	I	U
L	O	V	E	M	E	E

VI. Making a Decision. Proficiency in Speaking and Writing.

Situation: You are in a hairdressing salon. You are looking at four hair styles, models A, B, C, and D. They are on the page facing the beginning of the story in this Work Unit. You are discussing with the hairdresser the four models and are trying to make a decision.

In this dialogue, you are acting the role of **Usted.** When you talk to **la peluquera** (hairdresser), use **Usted** for courtesy. As in previous Work Units, all the vocabulary you need to know to do this dialogue is in this Work Unit as well as in previous units. Your knowledge of Spanish has been cumulative since Work Unit 1. You may vary and extend the dialogue with your own words and ideas. After it is completed, switch roles with a classmate.

La peluquera:	**Entonces, ¿qué modelo le gusta más?**
Usted:	_____ (Say: I don't know. What do you think?)
La peluquera:	**Voy a enseñarle dos cortes de pelo revueltos para darle una idea.**
Usted:	_____ (Say: I don't like this cut in model A.)
La peluquera:	**¿Le gustaría más un corte de pelo revuelto o serio?**
Usted:	_____ (Say: I would like a wild windblown haircut.)
La peluquera:	**En este modelo, el pelo, ya sea seco o mojado, se repone con los dedos. Este corte es realmente revuelto. Es el modelo B.**
Usted:	_____ (Say: Okay. I have made a decision. Give me a serious and simple cut, like in model C.)
La peluquera:	**De acuerdo. Voy a hacerle un corte serio y sencillo tal como en el modelo C.**
Usted:	_____ (Ask: When are you going to begin?)
La peluquera:	**Ahora empiezo.** _____

VII. Planning Ahead. Proficiency in Speaking and Writing.

Situation: You have been invited to a wedding. Make three statements about what you are planning ahead in preparation for the occasion. You may use your own words and ideas or the following:

1. **Me gustaría tener un corte de pelo diferente** / I would like to have a different haircut.

2. **Tengo que telefonear a la peluquera** / I have to telephone the hairdresser.

3. **Voy a tener cita con la peluquera** / I am going to have an appointment with the hairdresser.

After you make these three statements, or your own, write what you said on the lines below.

1. _____

2. _____

3. _____

VIII. Write the Spanish for the following sentences. They are all in the story in this Work Unit.

1. The hair is short. _____

2. The hair moves gracefully in the wind. It is model A. _____

_____

3. This cut is windblown. _____

4. This cut is really wild. It is model B. _____

5. This cut is simple. It is model C. _____

6. This cut is classic. It is model D. _____

IX. Increase your vocabulary. Match the following vocabulary that was used in the story in this Work Unit. On the line write the number of the Spanish words that match the English words.

1. Siéntese aquí.   _____ That's it, that's right.

2. No estoy segura.   _____ haircut

3. un corte de pelo   _____ Sit there.

4. la peluquería   _____ hairdresser

5. la cita   _____ Okay

6. Me gustaría   _____ I am not sure.

7. Siéntese allí.   _____ hairdressing salon

8. De acuerdo.   _____ Sit here.

9. Eso es.   _____ appointment

10. la peluquera   _____ I would like

X. Activities. Proficiency in Speaking and Writing.

A. Read again the story about Juana and Pedro at the hairdressing salon. Begin to retell the story in a few words in Spanish. After you make one or two statements, ask a classmate to continue. The second classmate will ask a third classmate to continue. Follow this procedure until the story has been retold. After the summary is finished, you may write what was said on the lines below.

B. Pretend you are on the telephone telling a friend of yours that you are going to a dance on Saturday and you need to have a haircut. Give a couple of details about the kind of haircut you have in mind. Also, say a few things about the occasion, with whom you are going to the dance, and other ideas. Begin with **¡Hola!** and mention your friend's name. Then say who you are. After you finish talking, write what you said on the lines below.

_____

_____

_____

_____

_____

_____

XI. Write affirmative answers in complete sentences. In answer (a) use Sí. In answer (b) use también.

Modelos: a. Hoy, ¿se va Juana a la
peluquería?
(Today, is Juana going off to
the hairdressing salon.?)

a. Sí. Hoy, Juana se va a la
peluquería.
(Yes. Today, Juana is going off to the
to the hairdressing salon.)

b. ¿Y nosotros?
(And are we?)

b. Nosotros nos vamos a la
peluquería, también.
(We are going off to the hairdressing
salon also.)

1. a. ¿Le gustaría a Juana un champú? _____

b. ¿Y a usted? _____

2. a. ¿Preferiría usted un corte realmente revuelto? _____

b. ¿Y sus amigos? _____

3. a. ¿Te gustaría este tipo de corte? _____

b. ¿Y a Juana? _____

4. a. ¿Ha tomado usted una decisión? _____

b. ¿Y Juana? _____

5. a. ¿Están muy felices Juana y Pedro? _____

b. ¿Y tú? _____

XII. Write the missing Spanish word on the line. Refer to the story at the beginning of this Work Unit, if needed.

Hoy, Juana se va a la peluquería. _____ gustaría tener un corte de pelo porque
                                        (1)

_____ noche se va al baile con Carlos, uno de _____ amigos. Tiene
        (2)   (3)

_____ en la peluquería a las cuatro y media de la tarde. Pedro _____ con ella.
      (4)   (5)

A Pedro le gustaría también tener un nuevo corte de pelo.

ESTRUCTURAS DE LA LENGUA
TENSE NO. 5: POTENCIAL SIMPLE (CONDITIONAL)

The conditional is used in Spanish and in English to express:

(a) An action that you *would do* if something else were possible.

EXAMPLE:
Iría a España si tuviera dinero / *I would go* to Spain if I had money.

(b) A conditional desire. This is a conditional of courtesy.

EXAMPLE:
Me gustaría tomar una limonada / *I would like (I should like)* to have a lemonade . . .
(if you are willing to let me have it).

(c) An indirect quotation.

EXAMPLES:
María *dijo* que vendría mañana / Mary *said* that she *would come* tomorrow.
María *decía* que vendría mañana / Mary *was saying* that she *would come* tomorrow.
María *había dicho* que vendría mañana / Mary *had said* that she *would come* tomorrow.

(d) Conjecture regarding the past.

EXAMPLE:
¿Quién sería? / *I wonder who that was.*

(e) Probability regarding the past.

EXAMPLE:
Serían las cinco cuando salieron / *It was probably* five o'clock when they went out.

This tense is regularly formed as follows:
Add the following endings to the whole infinitive: **ía, ías, ía; íamos, íais, ían**

NOTE that these conditional endings are the same endings of the imperfect indicative for **–er** and **–ir** verbs.

You then get: **hablaría, hablarías, hablaría;
hablaríamos, hablaríais, hablarían**

**bebería, beberías, bebería;
beberíamos, beberíais, beberían**

**recibiría, recibirías, recibiría;
recibiríamos, recibiríais, recibirían**

The usual translation in English is: I would talk, you would talk, *etc.*; I would drink, you would drink, *etc.*; I would receive, you would receive, *etc.*

Verbs Irregular in the Conditional

---

caber/ to fit, to be contained
**cabría, cabrías, cabría;
cabríamos, cabríais, cabrían**

The **e** of the inf. ending drops.

---

haber/ to have (as an auxiliary or helping verb)
**habría, habrías, habría;
habríamos, habríais, habrían**

The **e** of the inf. ending drops.

---

decir/ to say, to tell
**diría, dirías, diría;
diríamos, diríais, dirían**

The **e** and **c** of the inf. drop.

---

hacer/ to do, to make
**haría, harías, haría;
haríamos, haríais, harían**

The **c** and **e** of the inf. drop.

XIII. The following verb forms are in the conditional. Change them by using the new subject given in parentheses. Repeat the other words in the sentence. You may add additional words if you wish.

Refer to the boxed verbs above where you are given the irregular verb forms in this new tense. Review above where the formation of regular verbs in this tense is explained with examples. Also, review the English translation of the conditional that is given above between the three regular verbs and these irregular verbs. In this exercise you are practicing the following irregular verbs: **caber, decir, haber, hacer.**

Modelo: ¿Cabrían estas cosas en la caja?   (Esta cosa)
(Would these things fit in the box?)

Escriba: ¿Cabría esta cosa en la caja?
(Would this thing fit in the box?)

1. ¿Diría usted la verdad? **(Yo)** _____

2. ¿Habría dos bailes? **(un baile)** _____

3. ¿Harías (tú) un viaje? **(Ud.)** _____

4. ¿Harían ellos el trabajo? **(Nosotros)** _____

5. ¿Dirían ustedes la historia? **(Tú)** _____

---

poder/ to be able, can
**podría, podrías, podría;
podríamos, podríais, podrían**

The **e** of the inf. ending drops.

---

querer/ to want, to wish
**querría, querrías, querría;
querríamos, querríais, querrían**

The **e** of the inf. ending drops and you are left with two **r's**.

---

poner/ to put, to place
**pondría, pondrías, pondría;
pondríamos, pondríais, pondrían**

The **e** of the inf. ending drops and **d** is added.

---

saber/ to know, to know how
**sabría, sabrías, sabría;
sabríamos, sabríais, sabrían**

The **e** of the inf. ending drops.

251

XIV. **The following verb forms are in the conditional. Change them by using the new subject given in parentheses. Repeat the other words in the sentence. You may add additional words if you wish.**

Refer to the instructions in the previous exercise. In this exercise you are practicing the following irregular verbs: poder, poner, querer, saber.

Modelo: ¿Podrías venir a mi casa? (Ellos)
(Would you be able to come to my house?)

Escriba: ¿Podrían ellos venir a mi casa?
(Would they be able to come to my house?)

1. ¿Pondría Ud. estas cosas en la caja, por favor? **(Tú)** _____

2. Yo querría un corte de pelo clásico. **(Nosotros)** _____

3. ¿Sabría Ud. qué hacer? **(Ellas)** _____

4. ¿Qué pondrías en la sopa? **(Ud.)** _____

5. ¿Podría Ud. hacer esto para mí? **(Ana)** _____

---

salir / to go out, to leave
saldría, saldrías, saldría;
saldríamos, saldríais, saldrían

The **i** of the inf. ending drops and **d** is added.

---

valer / to be worth, to be worthy
valdría, valdrías, valdría;
valdríamos, valdríais, valdrían

The **e** of the inf. ending drops and **d** is added.

---

tener / to have, to hold
tendría, tendrías, tendría;
tendríamos, tendríais, tendrían

The **e** of the inf. ending drops and **d** is added.

---

venir / to come
vendría, vendrías, vendría;
vendríamos, vendríais, vendrían

The **i** of the inf. ending drops and **d** is added.

XV. **The following verb forms are in the conditional. Change them by using the new subject given in parentheses. Repeat the other words in the sentence. You may add additional words if you wish.**

Refer to the instructions in Exercise XIII. In this exercise you are practicing the following irregular verbs: salir, tener, valer, venir.

Modelo: ¿Saldrías de la casa sin dinero? (Uds.)
(Would you go out of the house without any money?)

Escriba: ¿Saldrían Uds. de la casa sin dinero?
(Would you go out of the house without any money?)

1. ¿Tendría Ud. paciencia? **(ellos)** _____

2. ¿Cuánto valdría esta casa en un año? **(estas casas)** _____

3. ¿A qué hora vendrías a verme? **(Uds.)** _____

4. ¿Saldrían ustedes de la casa sin decir nada? **(Tú)** _____

5. ¿Vendrían ustedes a verme en México? **(Ud.)** _____

EJERCICIOS

I. Traduzca al español. (Translate into Spanish. Tip: To do your best, review Tense No. 5, the conditional (el potencial simple on page 250.)

1. I would go to Spain if I had money. _____

_____

2. I would like to have a lemonade. _____

_____

3. Mary said that she would come tomorrow. _____

_____

4. Mary was saying that she would come tomorrow. _____

_____

5. Mary had said that she would come tomorrow. _____

_____

6. I wonder who that was. _____

_____

7. It was probably five o'clock when they went out. _____

_____

8. I would like to have a haircut. _____

_____

9. Would you like a simple haircut or a "wild, crazy" **(revuelto)** haircut? _____

_____

10. It would be a great honor for me. _____

_____

NOTE: To do your best in the following exercises, review the regular formation of verb forms in the conditional **(el potencial simple)** and the commonly used irregular verbs on pages 251 and 252. This tense is basic for a solid foundation in Spanish Level 2.

II. Escriba las seis formas del verbo hablar en el potencial. (Write the six forms of the verb hablar in the conditional.)

_____

III. Escriba las seis formas del verbo beber en el potencial. (Write the six forms of the verb beber in the conditional.)

_____

IV. Escriba las seis formas del verbo recibir en el potencial. (Write the six forms of the verb **recibir** in the conditional.)

_____

V. Escriba las seis formas de cada verbo en el potencial. (Write the six forms of each verb in the conditional.)

Modelo: caber   cabría, cabrías, cabría; cabríamos, cabríais, cabrían

1. decir _____

2. haber _____

3. hacer _____

4. poder _____

5. poner _____

6. querer _____

7. saber _____

8. salir _____

9. tener _____

10. valer _____

11. venir _____

12. trabajar _____

13. aprender _____

VI. Cambie el verbo al potencial. (The verbs in the following sentences are in the future tense. Change them to the **conditional.**)

Modelo: ¿Le hablará Ud. a José?
(_Will you talk_ to him, to José?)

Escriba: ¿Le hablaría Ud. a José?
(_Would you talk_ to him, to José?)

1. ¿Beberás (tú) la leche? _____

2. ¿Recibirán los niños los juguetes? _____

3. ¿Trabajarán Uds. esta noche? _____

4. ¿Cabrá el vaso en esta caja? _____

5. ¿Dirá el alumno la verdad? _____

6. ¿Hará Ud. un viaje al Canadá? _____

254

7. ¿Irá Ud. a Inglaterra? _____

8. ¿Podrás venir a mi casa? _____

9. ¿Sabrán los estudiantes la lección?_____

10. ¿Saldremos a las nueve? _____

VII. Daydreaming. Proficiency in Speaking and Writing.

Situation: You are daydreaming about what *you would do* if you won the six million dollar lottery. For example, you would go on a shopping spree, you would buy a limousine and a boat, a castle in Spain, a ranch in Mexico. You would give a lot of money to the poor, you would travel all over the world. These are a few suggestions.

Use your own words and ideas or the following, making sure that you use at least three verbs in the conditional tense *(I would...)*.

Yo iría de compras. Compraría una limosina y un barco. Compraría un castillo en España. Daría mucho dinero a los pobres. Compraría un rancho (una hacienda) en México. Viajaría por todo el mundo.

After you have made three statements, write them on the lines for practice.

1. _____

2 _____

3. _____

VIII. Physical Characteristics. Proficiency in Speaking and Writing.

Situation: It's your turn in Spanish class to say a few words about a person's physical characteristics. Look at the picture on the next page. Tell us what the boy is doing. Why is he smiling? Does he have beautiful white teeth? Is his hair black or blond? Does he have small or big ears? Does he have dark or blue eyes? Let's say his name is Pepe. How old do you think he is? Ten? Twelve?

Use your own words and ideas or the following suggestions: **El muchacho en esta fotografía es Pepe. Está sonriendo** or **Sonríe (sonreír** / to smile) **porque está feliz (contento). Tiene los dientes bellos y blancos. Tiene el pelo negro. No es rubio** / He is not blond. **Tiene las orejas pequeñas** / small (**grandes** / big). **Tiene los ojos oscuros** / He has dark brown eyes. **No son azules** / They are not blue. **Pienso que tiene diez años. O, tal vez, doce años. Es simpático.**

After you make at least three statements about Pepe's physical characteristics, you may write them on the lines for practice.

1. _____

2. _____

3. _____

Reprinted with permission of The Mexican Government Tourism Office, New York, N.Y.

INTRODUCTION TO SIMPLE LETTER WRITING

The Date

Examples of acceptable forms are as follows.

4 de diciembre de 1996   **Diciembre 4, 1996**
el 4 de diciembre de 1996   **Diciembre 4 de 1996**

Note that the month is not usually capitalized. However, it is capitalized when it is the first word of the date statement. In Spanish newspapers, magazines, and business letters, you will find the month sometimes capitalized, sometimes not.

Abbreviations of titles in front of the name of the person to whom the letter is addressed.

      Sr. for señor   **Sra.** for señora   **Srta.** for señorita   **Dr.** for Doctor

Salutations

Examples of acceptable salutations are as follows.

Estimado señor:	**Estimable señor:**
Estimado señor Blanco:	**Estimable señor García:**
Estimada señora:	**Estimable señora:**
Estimada señora Sánchez:	**Estimable señora Rodríguez:**
Distinguido señor:	**Distinguida señora:**
Señores:	**Muy estimados señores:**
Muy estimables señores:	**Muy señores nuestros:**
Estimados señores:	**Muy estimado señor López:**

Phrases commonly used

Acuso recibo de . . . I acknowledge receipt of . . .
Sírvanse (Sírvase) enviarme . . . Please send me . . .
Estoy interesado en . . . I am interested in . . .
En espera de . . . Hoping for . . . Waiting for . . .
Tengo el gusto de informar . . . I have the pleasure of informing . . .
Me es grato informar . . . I am happy to inform . . .
Doy a usted las gracias por . . . I thank you for . . .
Mucho apreciaría . . . I would very much appreciate . . .

En contestación a . . . In reply to . . .
Con referencia a . . . With reference to . . .
Gracias por . . . Thank you for . . .

Closing line

Examples of acceptable complimentary closing statements are as follows.

Atentamente,   **Cordialmente,**
Muy atentamente,   **Sinceramente,**

EJERCICIOS

I. Traduzca esta carta al español. (Translate this letter into Spanish. Make use of the Spanish vocabulary and standard sentences given above. Consult the vocabulary beginning on page 481 for other words you would like to use.)

January 1, 1996

Mr. Juan López, Director
Compañía Bicicletas Para Todos
Avenida Mucho Macho 123
San Juan, Puerto Rico

Dear Mr. López:

Please send me some pictures of all the bicycles that you sell. I would very much appreciate a prompt reply.

Thank you for your kindness.

(Here, write a complimentary closing)

(Here, write your name
and address.)

You may vary the letter with your own words and ideas or use the following: **el primero de enero de 1996; Estimado señor; Sírvase enviarme algunas fotos (fotografías) de todas las bicicletas que usted vende. Mucho apreciaría una pronta contestación (una respuesta lo más pronto posible). Doy a usted las gracias por su bondad. Cordialmente.**

_____

_____

_____

_____

_____

_____

_____

_____

_____

_____

_____

II. Write a letter in Spanish to a friend. It must contain at least five sentences. In Work Unit 8, you will find a list of names of boys and girls in Spanish with English equivalents. Tell the boy or girl that (1) your birthday is next Saturday, (2) you would like him or her to come to your party at your house, (3) everyone will have a lot of fun, (4) many friends will be there, and (5) you would like to know if he or she can come. Don't forget to write the date on your letter, a salutation, a complimentary closing, and write your name, in Spanish, of course!

You may use your own words and ideas or the following: **Querido amigo Juan, Querida amiga Juana. Mi cumpleaños es el sábado próximo (el sábado que viene). Me gustaría que vinieras a una fiesta en mi casa. Todo el mundo se divertirá muchísimo. Muchos amigos estarán allí. Me gustaría saber si tú puedes venir. Abrazos /** Hugs. **Tu amigo (amiga).**

_____

_____

_____

_____

_____

_____

_____

_____

III. Write another letter in Spanish. Write about anything. This is free composition. Be sure to write at least five sentences. Remember that a sentence must contain a verb form. Suggested topics: a movie you saw or you are going to see, a party you went to or will go to, how you spent last weekened or how you will spend this coming weekend, a vacation you took or plan to take, something about yourself or about your best friend.

You may use your own words and ideas. For starters, you may want to consider using the following: **El sábado pasado** / last Saturday; **yo vi** / I saw; **una película** / a film, movie; **voy a ver** / I am going to see; **una fiesta** / a party; **fui** / I went; **iré** / I will go; **el fin de semana** / the weekend; **pasar dos días** / to spend two days; **este fin de semana** / this weekend; **fui de vacaciones** / I went on vacation; **pienso ir de vacaciones** / I intend to go on vacation; **mi mejor amigo (amiga) es...** / my best friend is...; **tiene el pelo muy largo** / he/she has long hair; **es simpático (simpática).**

_____

_____

_____

_____

_____

_____

_____

_____

PRONOUNS (Continuation from Work Unit 8)

Prepositional Pronouns

Pronouns that are used as objects of prepositions are called prepositional pronouns or disjunctive pronouns. They are as follows:

Singular

1. **para mí** / for me, for myself

2. **para ti** / for you, for yourself

3. **para usted (Ud.)** / for you
   para él / for him, for it
   para ella / for her, for it

Plural

1. **para nosotros (nosotras)** / for us, for ourselves

2. **para vosotros (vosotras)** / for you, for yourselves

3. **para ustedes (Uds.)** / for you
   para ellos / for them
   para ellas / for them

Also note the following:

3. **para sí** / for yourself, for himself, for herself, for itself

3. **para sí** / for yourselves, for themselves

NOTE the following exceptions with the prepositions **con, entre,** and **menos:**

conmigo / with me
contigo / with you (*fam.*)
consigo / with yourself, with yourselves, with himself, with herself, with themselves
entre tú y yo / between you and me
menos yo / except me

EJERCICIOS

I. **Family Life. Proficiency in Speaking and Writing.**

Situation: The members of the Rojas family are gathered around their Christmas tree. Mom and Dad are distributing the gifts.

You have more than one role to act out here. You may provide the Spanish on the blank lines. When this dialogue is completed, switch roles with other classmates. You may vary and extend the dialogue with your own words and ideas. Here is some useful vocabulary: **el árbol de Navidad** / Christmas tree; **los regalos de Navidad** / Christmas presents; **traer** / to bring; **trajo** / he brought; **éste** / this one; **éstos** / these; **ése** / that one; **ésos** / those; **eso es** / that's right; **no hay nada** / there is nothing; **la abuela** / grandmother; **no te preocupes** / don't worry; **está bien** / okay; **también** / also; **querido mío** / darling; **¿qué regalo?** / which present?

Nina: ¿Qué regalo de Navidad es para mí, mamá?

La madre: Éste es para ti, Nina.

María: _____
(And for me? Which Christmas present is for me?)

El padre: Ése es para ti, María.

José: _____
(Which present did **San Nicolás** bring for me? This one?)

La madre:	**San Nicolás trajo ése para ti, José. Éste es para Roberto.**
Roberto:	_____ (That one is for me. It's not for him.)
El padre:	**Eso es. Ése es para ti, Roberto. No es para él.**
La abuela:	_____ (There's nothing for me? There are gifts for everybody except me.)
La madre:	**¡No te preocupes! San Nicolás trajo éste para ti.**
La abuela:	**Y estos regalos aquí, ¿para quiénes son éstos? ¿Para mí, también?**
El padre:	_____ (These gifts here are for us!)
La madre:	**No, querido mío. No son para nosotros. Son para ellas, para Nina y para María. Y ésos son para ellos, para José y para Roberto.**
El padre:	_____ (Okay. They are not for us. They are for them, for Nina and for María. And those are for them, for José and for Roberto.)
La madre:	**Entre tú y yo, querido mío, ¡San Nicolás no nos trajo nada!**
Todos:	**¡Felices Navidades! ¡Felices Pascuas! /** Merry Christmas! Merry Christmas!

II. Socializing. Proficiency in Speaking and Writing.

Situation: You and a friend are talking about going to the circus that is in town. You are wondering whom to ask to go with you. Let's say your friend's name is Alicia. You are playing the role of Alberto.

Refer to the above prepositional pronouns as needed.

You may vary and extend this dialogue by using your own words and ideas.

Later, you may switch roles with your friend. Some vocabulary you may want to use: **¿Quieres ir?** / Do you want to go? **al circo** / to the circus; **Ricardo querrá venir** / Ricardo will want to come; **Carlota puede venir** / Carlota can come; **es latoso** / he's boring.

Alberto:	_____ (Say: Hi, Alicia! Do you want to go to the circus with me?
Alicia:	**¡Qué buena idea! Me gustaría mucho ir al circo contigo.**
Alberto:	_____ (Carlota can come with us, too.)
Alicia:	**¿Carlota? No quiero ir al circo con ella. Ricardo querrá venir con nosotros. Estoy segura.**
Alberto:	_____ (Ricardo? Between you and me, I don't want to go to the circus with him. He's boring.)

Position of Object Pronouns

You surely must review pronouns and their positions. You can expect to find them in short sentences and in reading passages on any standardized test in Spanish because they are used very commonly in the Spanish language. In the reading passages, you will have to recognize their meaning according to their position with regard to a verb form. In sentences, sometimes short or long, you will probably have to choose the correct pronoun to fit in the blank space.

In Work Unit 8, I reviewed for you single object pronouns and their position. In this section, there is a summary review of the position of a single object pronoun and a review of double object pronouns and their position with regard to a verb or verb form. By double object pronouns is meant one direct object pronoun and one indirect object pronoun. Which one comes first and where do you put them?

Position of a Single Object Pronoun: A Summary

Review the normal position of a single object pronoun as given above in the examples when dealing with a simple tense or a compound tense.

Attach the single object pronoun to an infinitive. **Juan quiere escribirlo** / John wants to write it.

OR

If the main verb is **poder, querer, saber, ir a,** you may place the object pronoun in front of the main verb:

Juan lo quiere escribir / John wants to write it; **¿Puedo levantarme?** or **¿Me puedo levantar?** / May I get up?

Attach the single object pronoun to a present participle: **Juan está escribiéndolo** / John is writing it.

NOTE that when you attach an object pronoun to a present participle, you must add an accent mark on the vowel that was stressed in the present participle before the object pronoun was attached. The accent mark is needed to keep the stress where it originally was.

OR

If the main verb is a progressive form with **estar** or another auxiliary, you may place the object pronoun in front of the main verb:

Juan lo está escribiendo / John is writing it.

When you are dealing with a verb form in the affirmative imperative (command), you must attach the single object pronoun to the verb form and add an accent mark on the vowel that was stressed in the verb form before the single object pronoun was added. The accent mark is needed to keep the stress where it originally was:

¡Hábleme Ud., por favor! / Talk to me, please!

When you are dealing with a verb form in the negative imperative (command), you must place the object pronoun in front of the verb form, where it normally goes:

¡No me hable Ud., por favor! / Do not talk to me, please!

REVIEW OF THE FORMATION OF VERB FORMS IN THE IMPERATIVE / COMMAND

A. We form the imperative of verbs ending in **ar, er,** or **ir** by dropping the ending **o** of the first person singular, present indicative tense.

For **ar** verbs, add **e** for Ud., **en** for Uds., **emos** for nosotros.

For **er** and **ir** verbs, add **a** for Ud., **an** for Uds., **amos** for nosotros.

You may mention or omit **Ud.** or **Uds.** in a command, but **nosotros** is not stated.

EXAMPLES:

hablar / to talk, to speak **Yo hablo** / I talk.	**¡Hable Ud.!** (Talk!)	**¡Hablen Uds.!** (Talk!)	**¡Hablemos!** (Let's talk!)
beber / to drink **Yo bebo** / I drink.	**¡Beba Ud.!** (Drink!)	**¡Beban Uds.!** (Drink!)	**¡Bebamos!** (Let's drink!)
escribir / to write **Yo escribo** / I write.	**¡Escriba Ud.!** (Write!)	**¡Escriban Uds.!** (Write!)	**¡Escribamos!** (Let's write!)

B. Here are some examples of verbs irregular in the first person singular, present indicative; however, they end in **o** and the formation of the imperative is regular as above.

decir / to say, to tell **Yo digo** / I say	**¡Diga Ud.!** (Say!)	**¡Digan Uds.!** (Say!)	**¡Digamos!** (Let's say!)
hacer / to do, to make **Yo hago** / I do, I make.	**¡Haga Ud.!** (Do!)	**¡Hagan Uds.!** (Do!)	**¡Hagamos!** (Let's do!)
oír / to hear **Yo oigo** / I hear.	**¡Oiga Ud.!** (Hear!)	**¡Oigan Uds.!** (Hear!)	**¡Oigamos!** (Let's hear!)
poner / to put, to place **Yo pongo** / I put.	**¡Ponga Ud.!** (Put!)	**¡Pongan Uds.!** (Put!)	**¡Pongamos!** (Let's put!)
traer / to bring **Yo traigo** / I bring.	**¡Traiga Ud.!** (Bring!)	**¡Traigan Uds.!** (Bring!)	**¡Traigamos!** (Let's bring!)

EJERCICIOS

I. Translate into Spanish. Review the above section on position of object pronouns according to your needs.

1. John wants to write the letter. He wants to write it. _____

   _____

2. May I get up, please? _____

3. Mary is writing the sentence on the chalkboard. Mary is writing it. _____

   _____

4. Talk to me, Mrs. López, please! _____

5. Do not talk to me! _____

II. Your adviser in the Guidance Department at your school is giving you some advice so you can learn more Spanish and get better grades. Write the Ud. command form for the infinitive in parentheses as your adviser would say it to you.

Modelo: (Estudiar) todos los días. (to study) (every day)

Escriba: ¡Estudie (Ud.) todos los días! (Study every day!)

1. **(hablar)** en español en la clase. _____

2. **(escribir)** las lecciones todos los días. _____

3. **(hacer)** los ejercicios. _____

4. **(traer)** el libro consigo. _____

5. **(escuchar)** al profesor (a la profesora). _____

III. Change the infinitive in parentheses to the affirmative command (imperative) in the Ud. form. Add the direct or indirect object pronoun given in parentheses. Add the required accent mark on the vowel of the verb form where the stress was before you added the object pronoun.

Modelo: (hablar / me) (to talk) (to me)

Escriba: ¡Hábleme! (Talk to me!)

1. **(escribir / las)** _____

2. **(hacer / los)** _____

3. **(traer / lo)** _____

4. **(decir / le)** _____

5. **(poner / lo)** _____

6. **(llamar / me)** _____

7. **(invitar / los)** _____

IV. Change the following affirmative command sentences in the Ud. form to the negative command. The direct or indirect object pronoun will now go back in front of the verb. Note that the accent mark in the affirmative form will now drop in the negative form.

Modelo: ¡Escríbalas Ud. ahora! (Write them now!)

Escriba: ¡No las escriba Ud. ahora! (Don't write them now!)

1. ¡Hágalos Ud. ahora! _____

2. ¡Tráigalo Ud. consigo! _____

3. ¡Dígale Ud. la verdad! _____

4. ¡Dígame Ud. todo! _____

5. ¡Póngalo Ud. aquí! _____

6. ¡Llámeme Ud. esta noche! _____

7. ¡Invítelos Ud. para mañana! _____

V. Look at Exercise IV that you just wrote. Now change the verb from the Ud. affirmative command (3d person singular) to the Uds. form. All you have to do is add the letter n to the verb form to make it 3d person plural Uds.

Modelo: ¡Escríbalas Ud.! / Write them!

Write it in the **Uds.** form: **¡Escríbanlas Uds.!** / Write them!

Then write it in the **Uds.** negative form: **¡No las escriban Uds.!**

	AFFIRMATIVE **UDS.** FORM	NEGATIVE **UDS.** FORM
1. ¡Hágalos Ud.!	_____	_____
2. ¡Tráigalo Ud.!	_____	_____
3. ¡Dígale Ud.!	_____	_____
4. ¡Dígame Ud.!	_____	_____
5. ¡Póngalo Ud.!	_____	_____
6. ¡Llámeme Ud.!	_____	_____

VI. Your Spanish teacher has asked all the students in the class to talk more in Spanish, to write more, and to do more activities. Now the students are saying, "Let's talk more in Spanish!" and "Let's write more in Spanish!"

Change the infinitive form in parentheses to the 1st person plural **nosotros** form in the affirmative imperative (command). Do not mention **nosotros** in a command statement. It is understood because of the imperative ending on the verb form, which is **emos** for **ar** verbs and **amos** for **er** and **ir** verbs. Study again the above Review, according to your needs.

Modelo: (hablar) más en español. (to talk) (more in Spanish)

Escriba: ¡Hablemos más en español! (Let's talk more in Spanish!)

1. **(escribir)** más en español. _____

2. **(hablar)** más en español. _____

3. **(hacer)** más en español. _____

4. **(decir)** más en español. _____

VII. In this exercise do the same as you did in Exercise VI above. This time, add the direct or indirect object pronoun given in parentheses. Don't forget to add the required accent mark on the vowel of the verb form where the stress was before you added the object pronoun. The accent mark is needed because you are adding another syllable to the verb form.

Modelo: (decir / lo) en español. (to say / it) (in Spanish)

Escriba: ¡Digámoslo en español! (Let's say it in Spanish!)

1. **(escribir / las)** en español. _____

2. **(hacer / los)** en español. _____

3. **(pronunciar / lo)** en español. _____

4. **(leer / la)** en español. _____

5. **(aprender / las)** en español. _____

VIII. **Change the following affirmative command sentences in the nosotros form to the negative command. The direct or indirect object pronoun will now go back in front of the verb. Note that the accent mark in the affirmative form will now drop in the negative form.**

   Modelo: ¡Digámoslo! (Let's say it!)

   Escriba: ¡No lo digamos! (Let's not say it!)

1. ¡Escribámoslas! _____

2. ¡Hagámoslo! _____

3. ¡Traigámoslos! _____

IX. **Volunteering. Proficiency in Speaking and Writing.**

Situation: Your Spanish teacher is asking for a volunteer to go to the chalkboard and write one sentence in Spanish using one object pronoun. You are playing the role of **Tú.**

You may vary and extend this dialogue with your own words and ideas.

La maestra (El maestro):	**¿Quién quiere escribir una frase con un pronombre de complemento en la pizarra hoy?**
Ramón:	**¡Yo! Yo quiero escribirla en la pizarra.**
Tú:	_____ (Me! Me! I want to write it on the board. Ramón wrote it on the board yesterday.)
La maestra (El maestro):	**Está bien. Tú puedes pasar a la pizarra y escribirla.**
Tú:	_____ (May I get up?)
La maestra (El maestro):	**Claro que sí. Tú puedes levantarte. ¿Qué vas a escribir?**
Tú:	_____ (I'm going to write: "Let's write it in Spanish!")

Position of Double Object Pronouns: A Summary

An indirect object pronoun is always placed in front of a direct object pronoun. They are never separated from each other.

WITH A VERB IN A SIMPLE TENSE OR IN A COMPOUND TENSE IN THE AFFIRMATIVE OR NEGATIVE:

The indirect object pronoun is placed in front of the direct object pronoun and both are placed in front of the verb form:

Juan me lo da / John is giving it to me.
Juan te la daba / John was giving it to you.
Juan nos los dio / John gave them to us.
Juan os las dará / John will give them to you.

María no me lo ha dado / Mary has not given it to me.
María no te la había dado / Mary had not given it to you.
María no nos los habrá dado / Mary will not have given them to us.
María no os las habría dado / Mary would not have given them to you.

WITH A VERB IN A SIMPLE TENSE OR IN A COMPOUND TENSE IN THE INTERROGATIVE:

The indirect object pronoun still remains in front of the direct object pronoun and both still remain in front of the verb form. The subject (whether a noun or pronoun) is placed after the verb form:

¿Nos la dio Juan? / Did John give it to us?
¿Te lo ha dado Juan? / Has John given it to you?

EJERCICIOS

I. **Match the following by writing on the line the number of the Spanish sentence that matches the English. Refer to the above as needed.**

1. **Juan me lo da.** _____ John will give them to you.

2. **Juan te la daba.** _____ John gave them to us.

3. **Juan nos los dio.** _____ John gives it to me.

4. **Juan os las dará.** _____ John gave it to us.

5. **Juan nos la dio.** _____ John was giving it to you.

II. **Traduzca al español.**

1. John is giving it *(fem., s.)* to me. _____

2. Mary was giving it *(masc., s.)* to you *(fam.).* _____

3. Robert gave them *(masc., pl.)* to us. _____

4. Ricardo will give them *(fem., pl.)* to you *(2d pers., pl.,* **os***)* _____

   _____

5. Did John give it *(fem., s.)* to us? _____

WITH A VERB IN THE AFFIRMATIVE IMPERATIVE (COMMAND):

The object pronouns are still in the same order (indirect object + direct object) but they are attached to the verb form and an accent mark is added on the vowel that was stressed in the verb form before the two object pronouns were added. The accent mark is needed to keep the stress where it originally was:

¡Dígamelo Ud., por favor! / Tell it to me, please!

WITH A VERB IN THE NEGATIVE IMPERATIVE (COMMAND):

The position of **no** and the two object pronouns is still the same as usual, in front of the verb form:

¡No me lo diga Ud., por favor! / Don't tell it to me, please!

When dealing with an infinitive, attach both object pronouns (indirect, direct) to the infinitive:

Juan quiere dármelo / John wants to give it to me.
Juan no quiere dármelo / John does not want to give it to me.

OR

If the main verb is **poder, querer, saber, ir a,** you may place the two object pronouns in front of the main verb:

Juan me lo quiere dar / John wants to give it to me.
Juan no me lo quiere dar / John does not want to give it to me.

When dealing with a present participle, attach both object pronouns (indirect, direct) to the present participle:

Juan está escribiéndomelo / John is writing it to me.
Juan no está escribiéndomelo / John is not writing it to me.

OR

If the main verb is a progressive form with **estar** or another auxiliary, you may place the two object pronouns (indirect, direct) in front of the main verb:

Juan me lo está escribiendo / John is writing it to me.
Juan no me lo está escribiendo / John is not writing it to me.
Juana me lo estaba escribiendo / Jane was writing it to me.

EJERCICIOS

I. Translate into English.

1. ¡Dígamelo Ud., por favor. _____

2. No me lo digan Uds. _____

3. Juan quiere dármelo. _____

4. Anita quiere escribírmelo. _____

5. Roberta no quiere decírmelo. _____

6. Juan me lo quiere dar. _____

7. José no me lo quiere decir. _____

8. Emilio está escribiéndomelo. _____

9. Berta no está diciéndonoslo. _____

10. Claudia nos lo está escribiendo. _____

II. **The words in the following sentences are scrambled. Put them in the right order to get a meaningful statement. Attach the direct and indirect object pronoun to the verb when required. The statements are all in the imperative.**

1. lo / me / diga / Ud.! _____

2. me / lo / no / digan / Uds.! _____

3. Juan / me / lo / dar / quiere. _____

4. escribir / lo / me / quiere / Anita. _____

5. Emilio / escribiendo / me / lo / está. _____

When an indirect object pronoun and a direct object pronoun are both 3rd person, either singular or plural or both singular or both plural, the indirect object pronoun (**le** or **les**) changes to **se** because it cannot stand as **le** or **les** in front of a direct object pronoun beginning with the letter "**l**." Review the direct object pronouns, 3rd person sing. and plural. Also, review the indirect object pronouns, 3rd person sing. and plural.

Juan se lo da / John is giving it to you (to him, to her, to it, to you *plural*, to them).

¡Dígaselo Ud.! / Tell it to him!
¡No se lo diga Ud.! / Don't tell it to him!

Juan quiere dárselo.
Juan se lo quiere dar. }John wants to give it to her.

Juan está escribiéndoselo.
Juan se lo está escribiendo. }John is writing it to them.

Since the form **se** can have more than one meaning (to him, to her, to them, *etc.*), in addition to the fact that it looks exactly like the reflexive pronoun **se,** any doubt as to its meaning can be clarified merely by adding any of the following accordingly: **a Ud., a él, a ella, a Uds., a ellos, a ellas.**

If you are dealing with a reflexive pronoun, it is normally placed in front of an object pronoun:

Yo me lo puse / I put it on (me, on myself).

EJERCICIOS

I. Translate into Spanish. When you write the statement, clarify the meaning of the indirect object pronoun se. If by se you mean *to you (sing. or pl.), to him, to her, to them*, add any of the following accordingly: a Ud., a Uds., a él, a ella, a ellos, a ellas.

1. John is giving it to you **(a Ud.)**. _____

2. Tell it to him **(a él)**! _____

3. Don't tell it to him **(a él)**! _____

4. Arturo wants to write it to her **(a ella)**. _____

5. John is writing it to them **(a ellos)**. _____

II. The words in the following sentences are scrambled. Put them in the right order to get a meaningful statement.

1. Juan / lo / se / da / a ella. _____

2. lo / se / diga / Ud. / a él. _____

3. se / lo / no / Ud. / diga / a ellos. _____

4. dárselo / Juan / quiere / a Ud. _____

5. lo / me / puse / yo. _____

Demonstrative Pronouns

Demonstrative pronouns are formed from the demonstrative adjectives. To form a demonstrative pronoun write an accent mark on the stressed vowel of a demonstrative adjective.

A demonstrative pronoun is used to take the place of a noun. It agrees in gender and number with the noun it replaces. The demonstrative pronouns are:

MASCULINE	FEMININE	NEUTER	ENGLISH MEANING
éste	ésta	esto	this one (here)
éstos	éstas		these (here)
ése	ésa	eso	that one (there)
ésos	ésas		those (there)
aquél	aquélla	aquello	that one (farther away or
aquéllos	aquéllas		those out of sight)

EXAMPLES:
  Me gustan este cuadro y ése / I like this picture and that one.
  Me gustan estos guantes y aquéllos / I like these gloves and those.
  Esta falda y ésa son bonitas / This skirt and that one are pretty.
  Estas camisas y aquéllas son hermosas / These shirts and those are beautiful.

NOTE that the neuter forms do not have an accent mark. They are not used when you are referring to a particular noun. They are used when referring to an idea, a statement, a situation, a clause, a phrase. Never use the neuter pronouns to refer to a person. Examples:

  ¿Qué es esto? / What is this?
  ¿Qué es eso? / What is that?
  ¿Qué es aquello? / What is that (way over there)?

  Eso es fácil de hacer / That is easy to do.
  Es fácil hacer eso / It is easy to do that.
  Eso es / That's right.

  Juan no estudia, y esto me inquieta / John does not study and this worries me.

I. Shopping. Proficiency in Speaking and Writing.

Situation: You and a friend are shopping for gloves, skirts, shirts, and other items of clothing. In this dialogue, you are acting out the role of Casandra and your friend's name is Bárbara. The saleslady is **la vendedora.**

Refer to the demonstrative pronouns above, as needed. You may vary and extend this dialogue with your own words and ideas. Later, the three of you can exchange roles for practice.

La vendedora:	**Buenas tardes. ¿En qué puedo servirles a ustedes?** (In what (way) can I be of service to you?)
Bárbara:	**Me gustaría comprar guantes.**
La vendedora:	**Dígame, señorita. ¿Para usted? ¿O para otra persona?**
Bárbara:	**No son para mí. Son para mi madre. Voy a dárselos a ella el Día de las Madres** (Mother's Day). **Me gustan éstos y aquéllos. Casandra, ¿qué opinas?** (What do you think?).
Casandra:	_____ (I don't like these. And I don't like those. Why are you going to give gloves to her? A new skirt would be better.)
Bárbara:	**De acuerdo. Señora** (madam), **muéstrenos** (show us) **las faldas.**
La vendedora:	**Con mucho gusto. Voy a mostrárselas a Uds.** (I'm going to show them to you (pl.). **Nuestras faldas son muy bonitas. ¿Les gustan a Uds. éstas?** (Are these pleasing to you (pl.)? Do you like these?)
Casandra:	_____ (I like those and those over there. What do you think, Bárbara?)
Bárbara:	**No me gustan en absoluto. ¿Qué es esto?**
La vendedora:	**Es una camisa para hombres.**
Casandra:	_____ (And what is that?)
La vendedora:	**Yo no sé.**
Bárbara:	**Casandra, ¿quieres ir a tomar un café?**
Casandra:	_____ (Good idea! Thank you very much, madam. Have a nice day!)
La vendedora:	**¡No hay problema!**

II. Write the Spanish word on the line for the English under it.

1. ¿Qué es _____?
   (this)

2. ¿Qué es _____?
   (that)

3. ¿Qué es _____?
   (that / *way over there*)

4. _____ es fácil de hacer.
   (That)

5. Es fácil hacer _____.
   (that)

6. _____ es.
   (That)

7. Juan no estudia, y _____
   (this)
   me inquieta.

NOTE also that the English term *the latter* is expressed in Spanish as **éste, ésta, éstos,** or **éstas;** and *the former* is expressed in Spanish as **aquél, aquélla, aquéllos, aquéllas**—depending on the gender and number of the noun referred to.

AND NOTE that in English the order is generally "the former . . . the latter"—in other words, "the one that was mentioned first . . . the one that was mentioned last." In Spanish, however, the stated order is the opposite: "the latter . . . the former"—in other words, "the one that was just mentioned last . . . the one that was mentioned first:"

Roberto y Antonio son inteligentes; éste (meaning Antonio) **es alto y aquél es pequeño** / Robert and Anthony are intelligent; the former (meaning Roberto) is short and the latter is tall.

The pronouns **el de, la de, los de, las de; el que, la que, los que, las que**
These pronouns are used in place of nouns.

EXAMPLES:

mi hermano y el *(hermano)* de mi amigo / my brother and my friend's (the one of my friend *or* that of my friend)

mi hermana y la *(hermana)* de mi amigo / my sister and my friend's (the one of my friend *or* that of my friend)

mis hermanos y los *(hermanos)* del muchacho / my brothers and the boy's (the ones of the boy *or* those of the boy)

mis hermanas y las *(hermanas)* de la muchacha / my sisters and the girl's (the ones of the girl *or* those of the girl)

El *(muchacho)* que baila con María es mi hermano / The one who (The boy who) is dancing with Mary is my brother.

La *(muchacha)* que baila con Roberto es mi hermana / The one who (The girl who) is dancing with Robert is my sister.

Los *(muchachos)* que bailan son mis amigos / The ones who (The boys who) are dancing are my friends.

Las *(muchachas)* que bailan son mis amigas / The ones who (The girls who) are dancing are my friends.

EJERCICIOS

I. Who's Who? Proficiency in Speaking and Writing.

A. Situation: You are at a Valentine's Day dance in the school gymnasium. You are having a soda with a friend at the refreshment table while talking about who's who among the people who are dancing. In this dialogue, you are acting out the role of Carlos and your friend's name is Claudia.

Refer to the pronouns above, according to your needs. You may vary and extend this dialogue with your own words and ideas. Later, you may exchange roles with Claudia.

Claudia:	**Dime** (Tell me), **Carlos, el que está bailando con tu hermana, ¿quién es?**
Carlos:	_____
	(The one who is dancing with my sister is Sara's brother.)
Claudia:	**¿El que está bailando con tu hermana es el hermano de Sara? ¿Quién es Sara?**
Carlos:	_____
	(Sara is Alicia's sister. The one who is dancing with Alberto is Sara.)
Claudia:	**Y nosotros, ¿vamos a bailar?**
Carlos:	_____
	(Of course! Let's dance!)

B. Situation: At this Valentine's Day dance there is a guest entertainer from New York City who is going to dance the **Jarabe Tapatío,** a popular Mexican folk dance. Her name is Rosa López. Look at the picture on the next page and say a few words in Spanish about Rosa's costume **(el traje).** You may use your own words and ideas or the following: **Esta bailadora es Rosa López** / This dancer is Rosa López; **está bailando el Jarabe Tapatío, un baile folklórico que es muy popular** / she is dancing the Jarabe Tapatío, a folkloric dance that is very popular; **está sonriendo** / she is smiling; **su traje es muy bonito** / her costume is very pretty.

After you have made at least three statements, write them on the lines for practice.

1. _____

2. _____

3. _____

Reprinted with permission of The Mexican Government Tourism Office, New York, N.Y.

II. Complete este crucigrama.

HORIZONTALES: **1.** Demonstrative pronoun, f., s. **2.** Personal pronoun as subject, 1st pers., s. **5.** Indirect object pronoun, 3d pers., pl. **6.** Reflexive pronoun, 3d pers., s. and pl. **7.** Possessive adjective, 2d person, s. **8.** Direct and indirect object pronoun, 1st pers., s. **10.** Direct object pronoun, 3d pers., s., m.

VERTICALES: **3.** Personal pronoun as subject, 3d pers., s. **4.** Direct object pronoun, 3d pers., s., f. **5.** Indirect object pronoun, 3d pers., s. **9.** Personal pronoun as subject, 3d pers., s., m.

III. Traduzca al español.

1. This book is for me. _____

2. This pencil is for you (*2nd pers., s.*) _____

3. These notebooks are for us. _____

4. These chocolates are for you (*3rd pers., s.*) _____

5. Those letters (over there) are for them (*m.*) _____

_____

6. John is going to the movies with me. _____

_____

7. Can I go to the movies with you? (*2nd pers., s.*) _____

_____

8. There is a problem between you and me. _____

_____

9. Everyone is going to the theater except me. _____

_____

10. Robert took away the cake with him (himself). _____

_____

IV. **Traduzca al español las palabras inglesas. Escriba la oración enteramente en español, según el modelo.** (Translate the English words into Spanish. Write the sentence entirely in Spanish, according to the model.)

Modelo: Juan quiere escribir (it, *m.*) (John wants to write.)

Escriba: Juan quiere escribirlo. (John wants to write it.)

1. Daniel querría comprar (it, *f.*) _____

2. Dora desea leer (them, *m.*). _____

3. Ernesto está escribiendo (them, *f.*) _____

4. Juan (it, *m.*) está leyendo. _____

5. Pablo está leyendo (it, *m.*) _____

6. Hable (me) Ud., por favor. _____

7. Juan (it, *m.*, to me) da. _____

8. Roberto (it, *f.*, to you, *2nd pers., s.*) daba. _____

9. Diego (them, *m.*, to us) dio ayer. _____

10. Carolina (them, *f.*, to you, *2nd pers., pl.*) dará. _____

V. **Conteste las siguientes preguntas afirmativamente, según el modelo.** (Answer the following questions affirmatively, according to the model.)

Modelo: ¿Nos la dio Juan? (Did John give it to us?)

Escriba: Sí, Juan nos la dio. (Yes, John gave it to us.)

1. ¿Te lo dio Juan? _____

2. ¿Estás escribiéndola? _____

3. ¿Está Ud. leyéndolo? _____

VI. Reemplace los complementos directos por los pronombres que correspondan.
(Replace the direct object nouns with the corresponding direct object pronouns, according to the model.)

Modelo: ¿Está Ud. escribiendo la carta? (Are you writing the letter?)

Escriba: ¿Está Ud. escribiéndola? (Are you writing it?)

1. ¿Está Ud. leyendo los libros? _____

2. ¿Quiere Ud. comer el pastel? _____

3. ¡Dígame la verdad, por favor! _____

4. ¡No me diga la verdad! _____

5. Juan quiere darme el dinero. _____

6. Esteban hizo la lección. _____

7. El señor Rodríguez bebió el vino. _____

8. Pedro comió las salchichas. _____

9. Las muchachas compraron las bicicletas. _____

10. La vendedora vendió todos los chocolates. _____

VII. Reemplace los complementos indirectos por los pronombres que correspondan.
(Replace the indirect object nouns with the corresponding indirect object pronouns, according to the model.)

Modelo: Juana está hablando a Francisca. (Juana is talking to Francisca.)

Escriba: Juana está hablándole. (Juana is talking to her.)

1. Rafael no dijo la verdad a su padre. _____

2. Eugenia dio los pasteles a sus amigos. _____

3. Los alumnos dieron un regalo a la profesora de español. _____

4. Los estudiantes escribieron una carta al profesor de español. _____

5. Ester envió un paquete a sus padres. _____

VIII. Reemplace los complementos indirectos y directos por los pronombres que correspondan.
(Replace the indirect and direct object nouns with the corresponding direct and indirect object pronouns, according to the model.)

Modelo: Juan da el libro al profesor. (John gives the book to the teacher.)

Escriba: Juan se lo da. (John gives it to him.)

1. ¡Diga la verdad al padre! _____

2. ¡No diga una mentira a la madre! _____

3. Cristóbal quiere dar el regalo a Clara. _____

4. Juan está escribiendo una carta a sus amigos. _____

5. María está dando el chocolate al niño. _____

IX. Reemplace los adjetivos demostrativos y los nombres por los pronombres demostrativos que convengan, según el modelo. (Replace the demonstrative adjective and the nouns with the appropriate demonstrative pronouns, according to the model.)

   Modelo: Me gusta este libro. (I like this book.)

   Escriba: Me gusta éste. (I like this one.)

1. Me gusta este cuaderno. _____

2. Estoy leyendo esta carta. _____

3. Estamos comiendo estos pasteles. _____

4. María escribió estas oraciones. _____

5. Querría comprar ese vaso. _____

6. Pedro comprará esa corbata. _____

7. El vendedor va a mostrarnos esos zapatos. _____

_____

8. La vendedora quiere mostrarme esas faldas. _____

_____

9. Mi hermanito quiere comprar aquel juguete. _____

_____

10. Mi padre va a comprar aquella bicicleta. _____

_____

X. Traduzca al español.

1. What is this? _____

2. What is that? _____

3. What is that (way over there)? _____

4. That is easy to do. _____

5. It is easy to do that. _____

6. That's right. _____

7. John does not study and this worries me. _____

_____

8. Robert and Anthony are intelligent; the former is short and the latter is tall.

_____

9. I like this picture and that one. _____

_____

10. I like these gloves and those. _____

_____

XI. Una las expresiones en inglés con su traducción en español. (Match the expressions in English with their translation in Spanish.)

_____ my brother and my friend's   1. mis hermanas y las de la muchacha

_____ my sister and my friend's   2. mis hermanos y los del muchacho

_____ my brothers and the boy's   3. mi hermana y la de mi amigo

_____ my sisters and the girl's   4. mi hermano y el de mi amigo

XII. Una las oraciones en inglés con su traducción en español.

_____ The one who (The boy who) is dancing with Mary is my brother.
     1. Las (muchachas) que bailan son mis amigas.

_____ The one who (The girl who) is dancing with Robert is my sister.
     2. Los (muchachos) que bailan son mis amigos.

_____ The ones who (The boys who) are dancing are my friends.
     3. El (muchacho) que baila con María es mi hermano.

_____ The ones who (The girls who) are dancing are my friends.
     4. La (muchacha) que baila con Roberto es mi hermana.

XIII. Spanish Art. Proficiency in Speaking and Writing.

Situation: You and your classmates are on a field trip at The National Gallery of Art in Washington, D.C. It's your turn **(Le toca a usted)** to say a few words in Spanish about the painting entitled *Santa Lucía* by Francisco de ZURBARÁN.

Look at the picture on the following page. You may use your own words and ideas or the following: **La mujer en este cuadro es muy bella** / The woman in this painting is very beautiful; **Lleva flores en el cabello** / She is wearing flowers in her hair; **labios bonitos** / pretty lips; **un collar de joyas** / a necklace of jewels; **un vestido elegante** / an elegant dress; **en la mano derecha** / in her right hand; **un plato de metal** / a plate made of metal; **veo dos ojos en el plato** / I see two eyes in the plate; **en la mano izquierda** / in her left hand; **las palmas** / palms; **una obra de arte** / a work of art; **impresionante realismo** / impressive realism; **como una fotografía** / like a photograph.

After you have jotted down a few words in Spanish that you plan to use, say them aloud, then use them in at least three sentences, for practice, on these lines:

1. _____

2. _____

3. _____

S.LVCIA.

Santa Lucía by Francisco de ZURBARÁN (1598–1664)

Courtesy of The National Gallery of Art, Washington, D.C.

TEST 4

PART ONE   Speaking Proficiency

Directions: Read the five situations given below. Take a few minutes to organize your thoughts about the words you are going to speak. Select three of the five situations. Before you begin to speak, it would be a good idea to review the Oral and Written Proficiency exercises that you practiced in this Work Unit.

1. **Situation:** You are in a hairdressing salon. You are looking at four hair styles, models A, B, C, and D. They are on the page facing the beginning of the story in this Work Unit. You are discussing with the hairdresser the four models and are trying to make a decision about what kind of haircut you want. Make at least five statements about the hair styles; for example, if you like this cut or that one, which one you prefer, the windblown style or the simple one, other words and ideas of your own, and make a decision.

2. **Situation:** You have been invited to a wedding. Make at least three statements about what you would do in preparation for the occasion. The verbs you use must be in the conditional tense.

3. **Situation:** You are daydreaming about what you would do if you won the six million dollar lottery. Make at least three statements using verbs in the conditional tense; for example, you would buy a limousine and a boat, or a castle in Spain, you would give a lot of money to the poor, you would buy a ranch in Mexico, you would travel all over the world, and other words and ideas of your own.

4. **Situation:** You and the members of your family are gathered around the Christmas tree for the distribution of gifts. Make at least four statements using prepositional pronouns; for example, **para mí, para ti, para él, para ella, para ellas, para ellos.** Also, use **traer** (to bring) in the preterit tense **(¿Qué trajo San Nicolás?)** and demonstrative adjectives and demonstrative pronouns, such as, **este regalo** (this present), **éste** (this one), **ese regalo** (that present), **ése** (that one), and other words or ideas of your own.

5. **Situation:** You and a friend are talking about going to the circus that is in town. You are wondering whom to ask to go with both of you. Use prepositional pronouns with **con;** for example, with me, with him, with her, and verbs in the present tense, future, and conditional. Make at least three statements.

PART TWO   Listening Proficiency

Directions: Your teacher will read aloud four short paragraphs. Each one will contain only a few sentences. You will hear each paragraph twice. Then you will hear one question based on each. You will hear the question only once. It is printed below. Choose the best suggested answer based on what you heard and check the letter of your choice.

Selection Number 1

1. A Juana, ¿qué le gustaría?

   A. una cita

   B. ir al baile

   C. una peluquería

   D. un corte de pelo

Selection Number 2

2. ¿De dónde se marchan las dos personas?

  A. de sus nuevos cortes de pelo

  B. muy contentos y felices

  C. de la peluquería

  D. para el baile de esta noche

Selection Number 3

3. ¿Qué le da Pedro Rodríguez al Señor Santiago?

  A. algunas fotos

  B. las gracias

  C. su bicicleta

  D. una contestación

Selection Number 4

4. ¿Quién está bailando con mi hermana?

  A. la hermana de Sara

  B. mi hermano

  C. el hermano de Sara

  D. la hermana de Alicia

PART THREE Reading Proficiency

Directions: In the following passage there are five blank spaces numbered 1 through 5. Each blank space represents a missing word. For each blank space, four possible completions are provided. Only one of them is grammatically correct and makes sense in the context of the passage.

  First, read the passage in its entirety to determine its general meaning. Then read it a second time. For each blank space choose the completion that makes the best sense and is grammatically correct. Write its letter in the space provided.

Ahora voy a distribuir los regalos de Navidad. _____ regalo no es

  1. A. Esto
     B. Este
     C. Esta
     D. Estos

para _____. Es para _____ y _____ son para los niños.

 2. A. me   3. A. ti   4. A. éstos
   B. mi   B. tu   B. éstas
   C. mí   C. tú   C. éste
   D. yo   D. yo   D. ésta

Entre tú y yo, querido mío, ¡San Nicolás no nos _____ nada este año!

  5. A. trajo
     B. traje
     C. traerías
     D. traeríamos

PART FOUR   Writing Proficiency

Directions: Of the five situations in Part One (Speaking Proficiency) in this test, select three of them and write what you said on the lines below.

Situation 1 _____

_____

_____

Situation 2 _____

_____

_____

Situation 3 _____

_____

_____

Situation 4 _____

_____

_____

Situation 5 _____

_____

_____

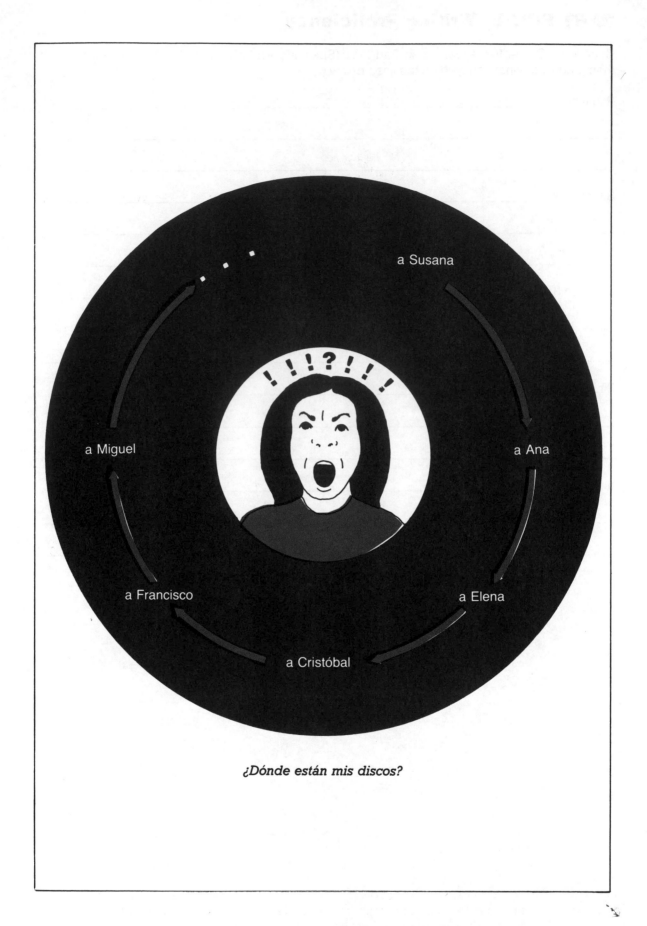

¿Dónde están mis discos?

¿Los discos? ¿Qué discos? No los tengo, Juana. Se los dí a Ana. Pídeselos a ella.

Work Unit 10

Round and round the records go and where do they end up? ¿Quién sabe?

A la redonda

Juana prestó sus discos a su amiga Susana en septiembre. Hoy es el primero de diciembre. Juana quiere recobrar sus discos para escucharlos durante los días festivos de Navidad. Ella va a ver a su amiga Susana y le dice:

Juana:	Susana, yo te presté mis discos en el mes de septiembre, y hoy es el primero de diciembre. Quiero escucharlos durante los días festivos de Navidad. ¿Quieres devolvérmelos, por favor?	5
Susana:	No los tengo, Juana. Se los dí a Ana.* Puedes ir a verla. Pídeselos a ella.	

(Juana va a ver a Ana.)

Juana:	Ana, yo le presté mis discos a Susana y ella me dijo que tú los tienes ahora. Le dí mis discos a ella en el mes de septiembre.	10
Ana:	No los tengo, Juana. Se los presté a Elena. Puedes ir a verla. Se los dí a ella. Pídeselos a ella.	

(Juana va a ver a Elena.)

Juana:	Elena, ¿tienes mis discos? Los tienes, yo lo sé. Se los presté a Susana. Susana se los dio a Ana, y Ana me dijo que tú los tienes ahora.	15
Elena:	¡Oh! ¡Los discos! ¿Qué discos? ¿Los discos de Victoria de Los Ángeles? ¿de Plácido Domingo? ¿de Lily Pons? ¿de Judy Garland? ¿de Barry Manilow?	
Juana:	¡Sí! ¡Sí! ¡Eso es!	
Elena:	No. No los tengo. Se los dí a Cristóbal. Puedes ir a verlo. Se los dí a él. Pídeselos a él.	20

(Juana va a ver a Cristóbal.)

Juana:	Cristóbal, yo presté mis discos a Susana en septiembre, y hoy es el primero de diciembre. Susana me dijo que se los dio a Ana. Ana me dijo que se los dio a Elena. Elena me dijo que tú los tienes. Devuélvemelos, por favor.	
Cristóbal:	¡Oh! Los discos. Se los dí a Francisco, y Francisco se los dio a Miguel, y Miguel se los dio a . . .	25

*NOTE: **Se los dí a Ana** / *I gave them to Anna*. When the dir. obj. pronouns **lo, la, los, las**—all in the 3rd pers., s. or pl. —are preceded by the indir. obj. pronouns **le** or **les,** both in the 3rd pers., s. or pl. also, **le** or **les** changes to **se.** Review Work Unit 9.

KEY WORDS AND PHRASES

a la redonda round and round, roundabout
devolver v. to return (something); **devolver + me + los = devolvérmelos** to return them to me
devuelva 3d pers., s., pres. sub. of **devolver**; **que se los devuelva** that she return them to her

devuelve 2d pers., s. (tú), imper. (command) of **devolver**; **devuelve + me + los = devuélvemelos, por favor** return them to me, please.
dí 1st pers., s., pret. of **dar**; I gave
dijo 3d pers., s., pret. of **decir**; **ella me dijo** she said to me

283

dio *3d pers., s., pret. of* **dar**; he / she gave
disco *n. m.* record
durante *prep.* during
escuchar *v.* to listen (to); **escuchar + los =
escucharlos** to listen to them
ésta *dem. pron., f. s.* this one; the latter
festivos *adj., m., pl.* festive; **los días festivos**
holidays
la *dir. obj. pron., f., 3d pers., s.* her
le *indir. obj. pron., 3d pers., s.* to you, to him,
to her
lo *dir. obj. pron., m., 3d pers., s.* him
pedir *v.* to ask for, to request
pide *3d pers., s., pres. indic. of* **pedir**; asks,
requests; **pide** *is also 2d pers., s. (tú),
imper. (command) of* **pedir**; ask *(tú)*; **Pide
+ se + los = Pídeselos** Ask her for them.

prestar *v.* to lend
preste *3d pers., s., pres. sub. of* **prestar**;
que se los preste that she lend them
to her
presté *1st pers., s., pret. of* **prestar**; I lent
prestó *3d pers., s., pret. of* **prestar**; **Juana
prestó** Juana lent
puedes *2d pers., s. (tú), pres. indic. of* **poder**;
puedes ir a verla you can go see her.
recobrar *v.* to retrieve, get back, recover
Se los dí a Ana I gave them to Anna.
Se los presté a Elena I lent them to Helen.
su, sus *poss. adj., s., pl.* her, his, your, their
te *indir. obj. pron., 2d pers., s. (tú)* to you
ver + la = verla to see her
ver + lo = verlo to see him

EJERCICIOS

I. Seleccione la respuesta correcta conforme al significado de la lectura en esta lección.
(Select the correct answer according to the meaning of the reading selection in this
Work Unit.)

1. La persona que prestó los discos a Ana es   (a) Juana   (b) Susana   (c) Elena
   (d) Cristóbal   _____

2. Juana prestó sus discos en   (a) la primavera   (b) el invierno   (c) el otoño
   (d) el verano   _____

3. Juana pide a Susana que ésta se los   (a) escuche   (b) preste   (c) devuelva
   (d) tenga   _____

4. Susana dio los discos a   (a) Miguel   (b) Cristóbal   (c) Elena   (d) Ana   _____

5. Elena dice a Juana que ésta puede ir a ver a   (a) Francisco   (b) Miguel
   (c) Cristóbal   (d) Ramón   _____

II. Acróstico. Complete este acróstico en español.
   (**Acrostic.** Complete this acrostic in Spanish.)

1. to return something to someone or to
   some place

2. Imperf. indic. of **ir,** 1st & 3rd pers., s.

3. ind. obj. pron. in front of **lo, la, los** or
   las

4. box

5. Pres. indic. of **oír,** 1st pers., s.

6. I gave them (*m.*) to her.

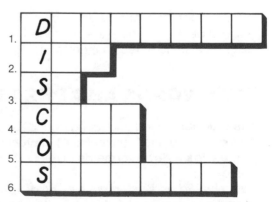

III. Ordene las palabras para hallar una oración significativa. (Put the words in correct order to find a meaningful sentence.)

Modelo: Juana / discos / sus / prestó / Susana / a / amiga / su

Escriba: Juana prestó sus discos a su amiga Susana.
(Jane lent her records to her friend Susan.)

1. quiere / Juana / discos / sus / recobrar

   _____

2. ver / a / va / Juana / Ana / a

   _____

3. verlo / ir / puedes / a

   _____

4. los / se / a / presté / Cristóbal

   _____

5. dijo / me / Susana / que / dio / los / se / a / Ana

   _____

IV. Use las siguientes palabras en oraciones completas y luego traduzca las oraciones al inglés. Consulte el diálogo de esta lección. (Use the following words in complete sentences and then translate the sentences into English. Consult the dialogue in this Work Unit.)

1. se los: _____

   Traducción al inglés: _____

2. presté: _____

   Traducción al inglés: _____

3. escucharlos: _____

   Traducción al inglés: _____

4. va a ver: _____

   Traducción al inglés: _____

5. dí: _____

   Traducción al inglés: _____

ESTRUCTURAS DE LA LENGUA

TENSE NO. 6: PRESENTE DE SUBJUNTIVO (PRESENT SUBJUNCTIVE)

The subjunctive mood is used in Spanish much more than in English. In Spanish the present subjunctive is used:

(a) To express a command in the **usted** or **ustedes** form, either in the affirmative or negative.

EXAMPLES:
Siéntese Ud. / *Sit down.*
No se siente Ud. / *Don't sit down.*
Cierren Uds. la puerta / *Close the door.*
No cierren Uds. la puerta / *Don't close the door.*
Dígame Ud. la verdad / *Tell me the truth.*

NOTE: Review the imperative (command) in Work Unit 9.

I. (a) Match the Spanish statements in the imperative with the English translations.

1. **Dígame Ud. la verdad.**   _____ Close the door.

2. **Cierren Uds. la puerta.**   _____ Don't sit down.

3. **Siéntese Ud.**   _____ Tell me the truth.

4. **No cierren Uds. la puerta.**   _____ Sit down.

5. **No se siente Ud.**   _____ Don't close the door.

(b) To express a negative command in the familiar form **(tú).**

EXAMPLES:
No te sientes / *Don't sit down.*
No entres / *Don't come in.*
No duermas / *Don't sleep.*
No lo hagas / *Don't do it.*

I. (b) Match the Spanish statements in the negative imperative with the English translations.

1. **No te sientes.**   _____ Don't do it.

2. **No lo hagas.**   _____ Don't sit down.

3. **No entres.**   _____ Don't sleep.

4. **No duermas.**   _____ Don't come in.

(c) To express a negative command in the second person plural **(vosotros).**

EXAMPLES:
No os sentéis / *Don't sit down.*
No entréis / *Don't come in.*
No durmáis / *Don't sleep.*
No lo hagáis / *Don't do it.*

I. (c) Translate the following negative commands into Spanish using the second person familiar plural form of vosotros.

1. Don't sit down. _____

2. Don't do it. _____

3. Don't come in. _____

4. Don't sleep. _____

    (d) To express a command in the first person plural, either in the affirmative or negative **(nosotros).**

EXAMPLES:
    Sentémonos / *Let's sit down.*
    No entremos / *Let's not go in.*

I. (d) Translate the following commands into Spanish in the nosotros form. Review Work Unit 9 according to your needs.

1. Let's sit down here. _____

2. Let's not go in. _____

3. Let's talk in Spanish. _____

4. Let's drink the milk. _____

5. Let's write some letters. _____

6. Let's do it now. _____

7. Let's put the table here. _____

8. Let's bring some presents. _____

9. Let's hear the music. _____

10. Let's tell the truth. _____

    (e) After a verb that expresses some kind of wish, insistence, preference, suggestion, or request.

EXAMPLES:
    1. *Quiero* que María lo **haga** / I want Mary to do it.

NOTE: In this example, English uses the infinitive form, *to do.* In Spanish, however, a new clause is needed introduced by *que* because there is a new subject, María. The present subjunctive of *hacer* is used (**haga**) because the main verb is *Quiero*, which indicates a wish. If there were no change in subject, Spanish would use the infinitive form as we do in English, for example, **Quiero hacerlo** / *I want to do it.*
    2. *Insisto* en que María lo **haga** / I insist that Mary *do* it.
    3. *Prefiero* que María lo **haga** / I prefer that Mary *do* it.
    4. *Pido* que María lo **haga** / I ask that Mary *do* it.
NOTE: In examples 2, 3, and 4 here, English also uses the subjunctive form *do.* Not so in example no. 1, however.

287

I. (e) Preferring and Insisting. Proficiency in Speaking and Writing.

Situation: You and your friend Juan are trying to convince each other about adopting a course of action. Your role is **Tú.**

You may vary and extend this dialogue with your own words and ideas, using as many verbs in the present subjunctive as you can.

Juan: **¿Quién va a hacer el trabajo para nosotros?**

Tú: _____
(I want María to do it.)

Juan: **Pero yo prefiero que José lo haga.**

Tú: _____
(And I'm telling you that I want María to do it.)

Juan: **¿Por qué insistes?**

Tú: _____
(I am insisting because María knows how to do the work.)

Juan: **¿Y José no sabe hacerlo?**

Tú: _____
(José doesn't know anything.)

Juan: **¿Tú dices que José no sabe nada?**

Tú: _____
(That's right. José doesn't know how to do the work.)

Juan: **Pide a Elena que escriba los ejercicios para nosotros.**

Tú: _____
(Good idea! I'm going to ask Elena to write the exercises for us.)

(f) After a verb that expresses doubt, fear, joy, hope, sorrow, or some other emotion. Notice in the following examples, however, that the subjunctive is not used in English.

EXAMPLES:
Dudo que María lo **haga** / I doubt that Mary is *doing* it: I doubt that Mary *will do* it.
No creo que María **venga** / I don't believe (I doubt) that Mary *is coming*; I don't believe (I doubt) that Mary *will come*.
Temo que María **esté** enferma / I fear that Mary *is* ill.
Me alegro de que **venga** María / I'm glad that Mary is *coming*; I'm glad that Mary *will come*.
Espero que María no **esté** enferma / I hope that Mary *is* not ill.

I. (f) Expressing Personal Feelings. Proficiency in Speaking and Writing.

Situation: You and your sister Ofelia have been waiting for Julia at your house for lunch. It's very late, she hasn't arrived, and you are worried that she may be sick.

Your role is **Tú.** You may vary and extend this dialogue with your own words and ideas. Later, after you have written on the lines what you said, you may exchange roles for more practice in speaking and writing.

Ofelia: **Es muy tarde. ¿Dónde está Julia?**

Tú: _____

(You're asking me where Julia is? I don't know. I doubt that she is coming.)

Ofelia: **¿Por qué dices eso?**

Tú: _____

(Why do I say that? Because I'm afraid she's ill.)

Ofelia: **(Tú) tienes razón** (You are right). **No creo que venga. Es muy tarde. ¿Qué hacemos ahora? Yo sé. ¡Comamos y bebamos!**

Tú: _____

(You're right! I don't believe she's coming. Let's eat and drink!)

(While you and Ofelia are having lunch, the phone rings. It's Julia.)

Julia: **¡Hola! Julia aquí. Escucha, Ofelia. Llamo de la peluquería. Llegaré a tu casa en algunos minutos. ¡Hasta pronto!**

Tú: _____

(What did Julia say?)

Ofelia: **¿Qué dijo Julia? Vendrá en algunos minutos.**

Tú: _____

(Where is she? Where did she call from? Is she sick?)

Ofelia: **Está en la peluquería. Llamó de la peluquería. No está enferma. Vendrá pronto.**

Tú: _____

(I'm glad that Julia is coming. I'm glad she's not sick.)

(g) After certain impersonal expressions that show necessity, doubt, regret, importance, urgency, or possibility. Notice, however, that the subjunctive is not used in English in all of the following examples.

EXAMPLES:

Es necesario que María lo **haga** / It is necessary for Mary to do it; It is necessary that Mary *do* it.

No es cierto que María **venga** / It is doubtful (not certain) that Mary is *coming*; It is doubtful (not certain) that Mary *will come.*

Es lástima que María no **venga** / It's too bad (a pity) that Mary *isn't coming.*

Es importante que María **venga** / It is important for Mary to come. It is important that Mary *come*.

Es preciso que María **venga** / It is necessary for Mary to come; It is necessary that Mary *come*.

Es urgente que María **venga** / It is urgent for Mary to come; It is urgent that Mary *come*.

I. (g) Necessity and Urgency. Proficiency in Speaking and Writing.

Situation: You and members of your family are confronted with an emergency because Grandma **(la abuelita)** is sick in bed. It's necessary to call the doctor, it's not certain that he will come soon, it's a pity that Grandma is sick.

Your role, again, is **Tú.** You may vary and extend this dialogue with your own words and ideas. Later, after you have written on the lines what you said, you may exchange roles for more practice in speaking and writing.

La madre:	**Mi madre está enferma. Es necesario que llamemos pronto al doctor Sánchez.**
Tú:	_____

(You're right, Mom. It is urgent that we call Dr. Sánchez.)

El padre:	**No es seguro que venga el doctor a esta hora. Son las dos de la mañana.**
Tú:	_____

(You're right, Dad. It isn't certain that the doctor will come at this hour. At two in the morning! It's too bad that Grandma is sick.)

El hermano:	**Sí. Es lástima que la abuelita esté enferma. Es preciso que yo llame al doctor por teléfono. Voy a llamarlo.**

(The brother picks up the phone and calls the doctor. Dr. Sánchez speaks.)

El doctor:	**Habla el doctor Sánchez . . . Escucho . . . ¿Tu abuelita? . . . Sí, voy inmediatamente . . . ¡Hasta pronto!**
La madre:	**¿Qué dijo el doctor? ¿Vendrá o no?**
El hermano:	**Vendrá inmediatamente.**
Tú:	_____
	_____

(I'm very glad that the doctor is coming. Grandma will be better now. Dr. Sánchez is a good doctor. He's a good man, too.)

(h) After certain conjunctions of time, such as **antes (de) que, cuando, en cuanto, después (de) que, hasta que, mientras**, and the like. The subjunctive form of the verb is used when introduced by any of these time conjunctions if the time referred to is either indefinite or is expected to take place in the future. However, if the action was completed in the past, the indicative mood is used.

EXAMPLES:

Le hablaré a María cuando **venga** / I shall talk to Mary when she *comes*.

Vámonos antes (de) que **llueva** / Let's go before *it rains*.

En cuanto la **vea** yo, le hablaré / As soon as *I see* her, I shall talk to her.
Me quedo aquí hasta que **vuelva** / I'm staying here until *he returns*.

NOTE: In the above examples, the subjunctive is not used in English.

I. (h) Patience, Patience. Proficiency in Speaking and Writing.

Situation: You and Sofía have been waiting and waiting for Rosa to arrive so the three of you can go to the Cine 10. You are both getting impatient.

Sofía: **Hace una hora que esperamos a Rosa. ¡Qué muchacha!**

Tú: _____

(Let's have patience, Sofía. I think she will come.)

Sofía: **¿Tengamos paciencia? Yo no tengo paciencia. Le hablaré a Rosa cuando venga.**

Tú: _____

(Me, too **[Yo, también]**. I will talk to Rosa when she comes.)

Sofía: **En cuanto yo la vea, le hablaré francamente** (frankly).

Tú: _____

(Me, too. As soon as I see her, I will talk to her frankly.)

Sofía: **Quedémonos** (Let's stay) **aquí hasta que llegue.**

Tú: _____

(You can stay **[Tú puedes quedarte]** here until she arrives. I'm leaving **[Yo me voy]** before it rains.)

II. Read the following newspaper announcement and answer the question under it.

¡Ponga

su anuncio

en este periódico!

Llámenos

al 1-800-por-amor

o

Llene y envíenos este cupón.

Nombre _____

Dirección _____

Ciudad _____ Estado _____ Zona postal _____

Teléfono ( ) _____.

Escriba su anuncio aquí. _____

_____

_____

Envíenos este cupón a: **El Mundo Hoy,** 59 Hudson Avenue, Albany, New York, 12206.

Who would be interested in this newspaper advertisement?
  A. Sports fans.
  B. People who love to read newspapers.
  C. Someone who wants to place an advertisement.
  D. Anyone who wants to give an opinion about **El Mundo Hoy.**

(i) After certain conjunctions that express a condition, negation, purpose, such as **a menos que, con tal que, para que, a fin de que, sin que, en caso (de) que**, and the like. Notice, however, that the subjunctive is not used in English in the following examples.

EXAMPLES:

Démelo con tal que **sea** bueno / Give it to me provided that *it is* good
Me voy a menos que **venga** / I am leaving unless *he comes.*

(j) After certain adverbs, such as **acaso, quizá,** and **tal vez.**

EXAMPLE:

Acaso **venga** mañana / Perhaps *he will come* tomorrow; Perhaps *he is* coming tomorrow.

(k) After **aunque** if the action has not yet occurred.

EXAMPLE:

Aunque María **venga** esta noche, no me quedo / Although Mary *may come* tonight, I'm not staying; Although Mary *is coming tonight*, I'm not staying.

(l) In an adjectival clause if the antecedent is something or someone that is indefinite, negative, vague, or nonexistent.

EXAMPLES:

Busco un libro que **sea** interesante / I'm looking for a book that *is* interesting.

NOTE: In this example, *que* (which is the relative pronoun) refers to *un libro* (which is the antecedent). Since *un libro* is indefinite, the verb in the following clause must be in the subjunctive **(sea).** Notice, however, that the subjunctive is not used in English.

¿Hay alguien aquí que **hable** francés? / Is there anyone here who *speaks* French?

NOTE: In this example, *que* (which is the relative pronoun) refers to *alguien* (which is the antecedent). Since *alguien* is indefinite and somewhat vague—we do not know who this anyone might be—the verb in the following clause must be in the subjunctive **(hable).** Notice, however, that the subjunctive is not used in English.

No hay nadie que **pueda** hacerlo / There is no one who *can* do it.

NOTE: In this example, *que* (which is the relative pronoun) refers to *nadie* (which is the antecedent). Since *nadie* is nonexistent, the verb in the following clause must be in the subjunctive **(pueda).** Notice, however, that the subjunctive is not used in English.

(m) After **por más que** or **por mucho que.**

EXAMPLES:

Por más que hable usted, no quiero escuchar / *No matter how much you talk,* I don't want to listen.
Por mucho que se alegre, no me importa / *No matter how glad he is*, I don't care.

(n) After the expression **ojalá (que)**, which expresses a great desire. This interjection means *would to God!* or *may God grant!* . . . It is derived from the Arabic, **ya Allah!** / (Oh, God !)

EXAMPLE:

¡Ojalá que vengan mañana! / *Would to God that they come* tomorrow! *May God grant that they come* tomorrow! *How I wish that they would come* tomorrow! *If only they would come* tomorrow!

Finally, remember that the present subjunctive is never used in Spanish after *si* when *si* means *if*.

III. Dining Out. Proficiency in Speaking and Writing.

Situation: You and Mariana are looking for a good Spanish restaurant to have lunch. You are looking at the menu on the window and you decide to go in. You talk to the waiter **(el camarero)**.

Refer to the above section from (i) to (n) for examples using the subjunctive. You may vary and extend this dialogue with your own words and ideas. Later, after you have written on the lines what you said, you may play the roles of Mariana and the waiter for more practice in speaking and writing.

Mariana: **¿Te gusta este restaurante? Los precios son buenos. ¿Vamos a entrar?**

Tú: _____

(You're right. The prices are good but I don't know if it's a good restaurant. Let's go in.)

Mariana: **De acuerdo. ¡Entremos!** (Let's go in).

Camarero: **Buenos días. ¿En qué puedo servirles?**

Tú: _____

(We are looking for a restaurant that is good. Is this a good restaurant?)

Camarero: **¿Uds. buscan un restaurante que sea bueno? Éste es el mejor restaurante de este barrio comercial** (in this shopping district). **¡Entren y siéntense!**

Tú: _____

(Good. Let's go in and let's sit down) **(sentémonos.)**

Mariana: **Para empezar, tráiganos dos sopas de verduras** (vegetable soups). **Dígame, ¿hay alguien aquí que hable francés?**

Camarero: **Lo siento** (I'm sorry). **No hay nadie aquí que hable francés. Voy a traerles a ustedes las dos sopas de verduras.**

Tú: _____

(Give us the soups provided that they are good.)

(You have been waiting ten minutes for the waiter to return.)

Tú: _____

(Where is that waiter? I'm leaving unless he comes now. That makes me furious!) **(¡Eso me vuelve furioso, furiosa!)**

Mariana: **¡Ojalá que venga pronto! Me muero de hambre** (I'm dying of hunger). **¡Acaso vuelva mañana!**

(The waiter is back with the two soups.)

Tú: _____

(Waiter, there are flies in the soups! Let's leave, Mariana!)

The present subjunctive of regular verbs and many irregular verbs is normally formed as follows:

Go to the present indicative, 1st pers. sing., of the verb you have in mind, drop the ending **o**, and

> for an **–ar** ending type, add: **e, es, e; emos, éis, en**

> for an **–er** or **–ir** ending type, add: **a, as, a; amos, áis, an**

As you can see, the characteristic vowel in the present subjunctive endings for an **–ar** type verb is **e** in the six persons.

As you can see, the characteristic vowel in the present subjunctive endings for an **–er** or **–ir** type verb is **a** in the six persons.

> You then get, for example: **hable, hables, hable;**
> **hablemos, habléis, hablen**
>
> **beba, bebas, beba;**
> **bebamos, bebáis, beban**
>
> **reciba, recibas, reciba;**
> **recibamos, recibáis, reciban**

The usual equivalent in English is: (that I) talk OR (that I) may talk, (that you) talk OR (that you) may talk, (that he / she) talk OR (that he / she) may talk, *etc.*; (that I) drink OR (that I) may drink, (that you) drink OR (that you) may drink, (that he / she) drink OR (that he / she) may drink, *etc.*; (that I) receive OR (that I) may receive, (that you) receive OR (that you) may receive, (that he / she) receive, *etc.*

Verbs Irregular in the Present Subjunctive Commonly Used

The following verbs are irregular because if you go to the present indicative, 1st pers. sing. of these verbs, you will find a form that you cannot work with according to the process of forming the present subjunctive normally, as explained above.

dar / to give **dé, des, dé;** **demos, deis, den**	**ir** / to go **vaya, vayas, vaya;** **vayamos, vayáis, vayan**
estar / to be **esté, estés, esté;** **estemos, estéis, estén**	**saber** / to know, to know how **sepa, sepas, sepa;** **sepamos, sepáis, sepan**
haber / to have (as an auxiliary or helping verb) **haya, hayas, haya;** **hayamos, hayáis, hayan**	**ser** / to be **sea, seas, sea;** **seamos, seáis, sean**

EJERCICIOS

I. The irregular verb forms in the following sentences are in the present subjunctive. Change them by using the new subject given in parentheses. Repeat the other words in the sentence. You may add additional words if you wish.

Refer to the boxed verbs above where you are given commonly used irregular verb forms in this new tense. In this exercise you are practicing the following irregular verbs in the present subjunctive: **dar, estar, haber, ir, saber, ser.**

Modelo: Quiero que Ud. dé dinero a los pobres. (Uds.)
(I want you to give money to the poor people.)

Escriba: Quiero que Uds. den dinero a los pobres.
(I want you *(pl.)* to give money to the poor people.)

1. Quiero que Uds. den dinero a ese hombre pobre. **(Ud.)** _____

2. Dudo que María esté en casa. **(María y José)** _____

3. ¡Me alegro de que mi amigo haya *(has)* llegado! **(mis amigos)** _____

4. Es urgente que tú vayas al hospital **(nosotros)** _____

5. Es importante que tú sepas el subjuntivo. **(Ud.)** _____

6. Busco un libro que sea interesante. **(dos libros)** _____

II. Do the same here as you did above in Exercise I. In this exercise you are practicing verbs that are formed regularly in the present subjunctive.

1. Es importante que tú hables español en la clase. **(Uds.)** _____

2. Prefiero que tú bebas la leche ahora mismo. **(vosotros)** _____

3. No es cierto que Paula reciba la carta hoy. **(nosotros)** _____

4. Es lástima que el niño no pueda comer. **(los niños)** _____

5. Es urgente que yo llame al doctor. **(nosotros)** _____

Other Verbs Irregular in the Present Subjunctive

Stem-changing verbs in the present indicative have the same stem changes in the present subjunctive, generally speaking. If you go to the present indicative, 1st pers. sing. of those verbs, you will find the stem change there. Drop the ending **o** and add the appropriate endings of the present subjunctive. For example, to form the present subjunctive of **pensar**, go to the 1st pers. sing. of the present indicative and there you will find **pienso.** Drop the ending **o** and add: **e, es, e; emos, éis, en.** The verbs irregular in the present indicative, including stem-changing and orthographical changing verbs, are given to you alphabetically.

Orthographical changing verbs (those that change in spelling), which end in **car, gar,** and **zar** in the infinitive form, have the same spelling changes in the present subjunctive as they do in the 1st pers. sing. of the preterit. Just drop the accent mark on **é** and you have the form of the present subjunctive, generally speaking.

EXAMPLES:

Preterit, 1st pers. sing.	Present subjunctive
abracé (abra**zar**)	**abrace, abraces, abrace;** **abracemos, abracéis, abracen**
busqué (bus**car**)	**busque, busques, busque;** **busquemos, busquéis, busquen**
pagué (pa**gar**)	**pague, pagues, pague;** **paguemos, paguéis, paguen**

However, there are some verbs of the type that end in **car, gar,** and **zar** which are stem-changing when stressed and the process described above will not work for them. For example:

Take **almorzar.** If you go to the preterit, 1st pers. sing., you will find **almorcé.** If you drop the accent mark on **é,** you are left with **almorce,** which is not the correct form in the present subjunctive. The **o** in the stem is stressed and it changes to **ue;** the forms in the present subjunctive for this verb contain the stem change, which is found in the present indicative. The forms of **almorzar** in the present subjunctive, therefore, are: **almuerce, almuerces, almuerce; almorcemos, almorcéis, almuercen.**

Finally, remember that there is really no easy perfect system of arriving at verb forms no matter what process is used because there is usually some exception—even if only one exception. The best thing for you to do is to be sure you know the regular forms in all the tenses and the irregular forms that are commonly used. All those that you need to know and to recognize are given to you in these sections on Spanish verbs.

EJERCICIOS

I. **Traduzca las palabras inglesas al español y escriba las oraciones enteramente en español.** (Translate the English words into Spanish and write the sentences entirely in Spanish.)

1. *Sit down* **(Ud.),** *please.* _____

2. *Don't sit down* **(Ud.)** _____

3. *Close* **(Uds.)** las ventanas. _____

4. *Don't close* **(Ud.)** la puerta. _____

5. *Tell me* **(Ud.)** la verdad. _____

II. **Dé la forma negativa de las siguientes oraciones.** (Give the negative form of the following sentences. They are in the imperative [command].)

Modelo: ¡Levántate! (Get up!)   **Escriba:** ¡No te levantes! (Don't get up!)

1. ¡Lávate! _____

2. ¡Siéntate! _____

3. ¡Entra! _____

4. ¡Duerme! _____

5. ¡Hazlo! _____

6. ¡Acuéstate! _____

III. Dé la forma negativa de las siguientes oraciones. (Give the negative form of the following sentences. They are in the imperative [command].)

    Modelo: ¡Levántese! (Get up!)   **Escriba:** ¡No se levante! (Don't get up!)

1. ¡Lávese! _____

2. ¡Levántese! _____

3. ¡Duerma! _____

4. ¡Siéntese! _____

5. ¡Entre! _____

6. ¡Hágalo! _____

IV. Dé la forma afirmativa de las siguientes oraciones. (Give the affirmative form of the following sentences. They are in the imperative [command].)

    Modelo: ¡No os sentéis!   **Escriba:** ¡Sentaos!

1. ¡No entréis! _____

2. ¡No durmáis! _____

3. ¡No lo hagáis! _____

4. ¡No os levantéis! _____

5. ¡No os lavéis! _____

6. ¡No os acostéis! _____

V. Traduzca al inglés.

1. Sentémonos _____

2. Lavémonos _____

3. Levantémonos _____

4. Acostémonos _____

5. Divirtámonos _____

6. Vámonos _____

VI. Cambie el verbo entre paréntesis al presente de subjuntivo. (Change the verb in parentheses to the present subjunctive.)

    Modelo: Quiero que María lo (hacer).   **Escriba:** Quiero que María lo haga.

1. Quiero que José lo **(hacer)**. _____

2. Insisto en que Gabriela la **(escribir)**. _____

3. Prefiero que Juan me **(amar)**. _____

4. Deseo que mis amigos me **(amar)**. _____

5. Pido que Pedro me **(responder)**. _____

6. Dudo que Miguel me **(olvidar)**. _____

7. No creo que María **(venir)**. _____

8. Temo que Arturo **(estar)** enfermo. _____

9. Me alegro de que **(trabajar)** María. _____

10. Espero que Edmundo no **(estar)** enfermo. _____

11. Es necesario que usted **(estudiar)**. _____

12. No es cierto que Pablo **(llegar)**. _____

13. Es lástima que ustedes no **(poder)** leer. _____

14. Es importante que tú **(leer)**. _____

15. Es preciso que nosotros **(partir)**. _____

VII. Escriba las seis formas de los siguientes verbos en el presente de subjuntivo, según el modelo. (Write the six forms of the following verbs in the present subjunctive, according to the model. Refer to the above section on how to form the present subjunctive of regular **ar, er,** and **ir** verbs.)

Modelo: hablar   **Escriba:** hable, hables, hable; hablemos, habléis, hablen

1. trabajar: _____

2. beber: _____

3. recibir: _____

VIII. Escriba las seis formas de los siguientes verbos en el presente de subjuntivo. (Do the same here. Some are irregular, some are formed regularly.)

1. dar: _____

2. estar: _____

3. haber: _____

4. ir: _____

5. saber: _____

6. decir: _____

7. pensar: _____

8. buscar: _____

9. pagar: _____

10. almorzar: _____

Subjunctive — A Summary of When to Use it with Examples

The subjunctive is not a tense; it is a mood or mode. Usually, when we speak in Spanish or English, we use the indicative mood. We use the subjunctive mood in Spanish for certain reasons. The following are the principal reasons.

AFTER CERTAIN CONJUNCTIONS

When the following conjunctions introduce a new clause, the verb in that new clause is in the subjunctive mood:

a fin de que / so that, in order that
a menos que / unless
a no ser que / unless
antes que *or* **antes de que** / before
como si / as if
con tal que *or* **con tal de que** / provided that
en caso que *or* **en caso de que** / in case, in case that, supposing that
para que / in order that, so that
sin que / without

EXAMPLES:

Se lo explico a ustedes a fin de que puedan comprenderlo / I am explaining it to you so that (in order that) you may be able to understand it.

Saldré a las tres y media a menos que esté lloviendo / I will go out at three thirty unless it is raining.

EJERCICIOS

I. Increase your vocabulary. Match the following conjunctions.

1. **a fin de que**   _____ in case that

2. **a menos que**   _____ so that, in order that

3. **antes que**   _____ as if

4. **como si**   _____ before

5. **con tal que**   _____ unless

6. **en caso que**   _____ provided that

II. Write the questions that were asked for the following answers.

Modelo: The answer is: The question was:

Se lo explico a Ud.   ¿Por qué me lo explica Ud.?
a fin de que pueda   (Why are you explaining it to me?)
comprenderlo.

(I am explaining it to you
so that you may be able
to understand it.)

1. The answer is: **Se lo explico a ustedes a fin de que puedan comprenderlo.**

The question was: _____

2. The answer is: **Saldré a las tres y media a menos que esté lloviendo.**

The question was: _____

When the following conjunctions introduce a new clause, the verb in that new clause is sometimes in the indicative mood, sometimes in the subjunctive mood. Use the subjunctive mood if what is being expressed indicates some sort of anxious anticipation, doubt, indefiniteness, vagueness, or uncertainty. If these are not implied and if the action was completed in the past, use the indicative mood:

a pesar de que / in spite of the fact that
así que / as soon as, after
aunque / although, even if, even though
cuando / when
de manera que / so that, so as
de modo que / so that, in such a way that
después que or **después de que** / after
en cuanto / as soon as
hasta que / until
luego que / as soon as, after
mientras / while, as long as
siempre que / whenever, provided that
tan pronto como / as soon as

EXAMPLES:

Le daré el dinero a Roberto cuando me lo pida / I shall give the money to Robert when he asks me for it. (**Pida** is in the subjunctive mood because some doubt or uncertainty is suggested and Robert may not ask for it.)

BUT: **Se lo dí a Roberto cuando me lo pidió** / I gave it to Robert when he asked me for it. (No subjunctive of **pedir** here because he actually did ask me for it.)

Esperaré hasta que llegue el autobús / I shall wait until the bus arrives (**Llegue** is in the subjunctive mood here because some doubt or uncertainty is suggested and the bus may never arrive.)

BUT: **Esperé hasta que llegó el autobús** / I waited until the bus arrived. (No subjunctive of **llegar** here because the bus actually did arrive.)

Trabajaré hasta que Ud. venga / I shall work until you come (**Venga** is used here because some doubt or uncertainty is suggested and **Ud.** may never come.)

BUT: **Trabajé hasta que Ud. vino** / I worked until you came. (No subjunctive of **venir** here because **Ud.** actually did come.)

EJERCICIOS

I. Increase your vocabulary. Match the following conjunctions.

1. **a pesar de que** _____ while

2. **aunque** _____ in spite of the fact that

3. **cuando** _____ as soon as

4. **de modo que** _____ although

5. **después que** _____ until

6. **hasta que** _____ in such a way that

7. **luego que** _____ when

8. **mientras** _____ after

301

II. Write the present subjunctive form of the verb in parentheses.

Modelo: Yo le hablaré a Anita cuando yo la (ver).
(I will talk to Anita when I *[to see]* her.)

Escriba: Yo le hablaré a Anita cuando yo la vea.
(I will talk to Anita when I see her.)

1. Yo le daré el dinero a Roberto cuando me lo **(pedir)**. _____

   _____

2. Yo esperaré hasta que **(llegar)** el autobús. _____

   _____

3. Trabajaré hasta que Ud. **(venir)**. _____

III. Sports. Proficiency in Speaking and Writing.

Situation: Look at the picture below of the two scuba divers **(los dos buceadores).**
Let's imagine what they are saying to each other. You are playing the role of **El hombre.** The two persons are using the polite **usted** form with each other.

You may vary and extend this dialogue with your own words and ideas. Later, after you have written on the lines what you said, you may exchange roles with your partner and use the **tú** form if you wish for more practice in speaking and writing.

El hombre: _____
(Are you having a good time? / **¿Se divierte Ud. ?**)

La mujer: **Sí, me divierto mucho. Dígame, ¿Cuánto tiempo vamos a quedarnos** (are we going to stay) **en el agua?**

El hombre: _____
(We are going to stay in the water until a shark **(un tiburón)** arrives!

La mujer: **¡Ojalá que no veamos un tiburón!**

El hombre: _____
(We can get out now if you want.)

La mujer: **Buena idea. ¡Salgamos pronto!**

Reprinted with permission of The Mexican Government Tourism Office, New York, N.Y.

AFTER CERTAIN ADVERBS

acaso
quizá *or* **quizás** ⎫ perhaps, maybe
tal vez ⎭

Tal vez hayan perdido / Perhaps they have lost. (Subjunctive is used here because some degree of uncertainty or pessimism is implied.)

Tal vez han ganado / Perhaps they have won. (No subjunctive is used here because some degree of certainty or optimism is implied.)

Por + adj. or **adv. + que** / however, no matter how

Por (más) interesante que sea, no quiero ver esa película / No matter how interesting it may be, I do not want to see that film.

Por bien que juegue Roberto, no quiero jugar con él / However well (No matter how well) Robert plays, I do not want to play with him.

EJERCICIOS

I. Rewrite the entire sentence using the present subjunctive form of the verb in parentheses.

1. Tal vez ellos **(haber)** perdido. _____

2. Por más interesante que **(ser),** no quiero ver esa película. _____

   _____

3. Por bien que **(jugar)** Roberto, no quiero jugar con él. _____

   _____

AFTER CERTAIN INDEFINITE EXPRESSIONS

cualquier, cualquiera, cualesquier, cualesquiera / whatever, whichever, any (the final **a** drops in **cualquiera** and **cualesquiera** when the word is in front of a noun)
cuandoquiera / whenever
dondequiera / wherever; **adondequiera** / to wherever
quienquiera, quienesquiera / whoever

EXAMPLES:
No abriré la puerta, quienquiera que sea / I will not open the door, whoever it may be.
Dondequiera que Ud. esté, escríbame / Wherever you may be, write to me.
Adondequiera que Ud. vaya, dígamelo / Wherever you may go, tell me.

AFTER AN INDEFINITE OR NEGATIVE ANTECEDENT

For a definition of *antecedent*, see the section Definitions of Basic Grammatical Terms with Examples beginning on page 431. Remember to use the Index for references to explanations and examples located in different parts of this book.

The reason the subjunctive is needed after an indefinite or negative antecedent is that the person or thing desired may possibly not exist; or, if it does exist, you may never find it.

303

EXAMPLES:

Busco un libro que sea interesante / I am looking for a book that is interesting.

BUT: **Tengo un libro que es interesante** / I have a book that is interesting.

¿Conoce Ud. a alguien que tenga paciencia? / Do you know someone who has patience?

BUT: **Conozco a alguien que tiene paciencia** / I know someone who has patience.

No encuentro a nadie que sepa la respuesta / I do not find anyone who knows the answer.

BUT: **Encontré a alguien que sabe la respuesta** / I found someone who knows the answer.

No puedo encontrar a nadie que pueda prestarme dinero / I can t meet (find) anyone who can lend me money.

BUT: **Conozco a alguien que puede prestarme dinero** / I know somebody who can lend me money.

AND: **Encontré a alguien que puede prestarme dinero** / I met (found) someone who can lend me money.

AFTER ¡QUE . . . !

In order to express indirectly a wish, an order, a command in the 3rd person singular or plural, you may use the exclamatory **¡Que . . . !** alone to introduce the subjunctive clause. The words generally understood to be omitted are: **Quiero que** . . . or **Deje que** . . ., which mean **I want . . .** or **Let. . .**

EXAMPLES:

¡Que lo haga Jorge! / Let George do it! (In other words, the complete statement would be: **¡Deje que lo haga Jorge!** *or* **¡Quiero que lo haga Jorge!** / I want George to do it!)

¡Que entre! / Let him enter! *or* I want him to enter! **(¡Quiero que entre!)**

AFTER ¡OJALÁ QUE . . . !

The exclamatory expression **Ojalá** is of Arabic origin meaning "Oh, God!" Examples:

¡Ojalá que vengan! / If only they would come! (Would that they come! Oh, God, let them come!)

¡Ojalá que lleguen! / If only they would arrive! (Would that they arrive! Oh, God, let them arrive!)

EJERCICIOS

I. Increase your vocabulary. Match the following indefinite expressions.

1. **quienquiera, quienesquiera**   _____ to wherever

2. **cualquier, cualquiera**   _____ wherever

3. **dondequiera**   _____ whoever

4. **adondequiera**   _____ whenever

5. **cuandoquiera**   _____ whatever, whichever

II. Rewrite the entire sentence using the present subjunctive form of the verb in parentheses.

1. No abriré la puerta, quienquiera que **(ser).** _____

2. Dondequiera que Ud. **(estar),** escríbame. _____

3. Adondequiera que Ud. **(ir),** dígamelo. _____

4. Busco un restaurante que **(ser)** bueno. _____

5. ¿Conoce Ud. a alguien que **(tener)** paciencia? _____

6. No puedo encontrar a nadie que **(saber)** la respuesta. _____

7. No encuentro a nadie que **(poder)** prestarme dinero. _____

8. ¡Que lo **(hacer)** Jorge! _____

9. Quiero que lo **(hacer)** ellos. _____

10. ¡Ojalá que **(llegar)** San Nicolás con regalos para mí! _____

AFTER CERTAIN IMPERSONAL EXPRESSIONS

Generally speaking, the following impersonal expressions require the subjunctive form of the verb in the clause that follows.

Basta que . . . / It is enough that . . . ; It is sufficient that . . .
Conviene que . . . / It is fitting that   ; It is proper that . . .
Importa que . . . / It is important that . . .
Más vale que . . . / It is better that . . .
Es aconsejable que . . . / It is advisable that . . .
Es bueno que . . . / It is good that . . .
Es importante que . . . / It is important that . . .
Es imposible que . . . / It is impossible that . . .
Es lástima que . . . / It is a pity that . . .
Es malo que . . . / It is bad that . . .
Es mejor que . . . / It is better that . . .
Es menester que . . . / It is necessary that . . .
Es necesario que . . . / It is necessary that . . .
Es posible que . . . / It is possible that . . .
Es preciso que . . . / It is necessary that . . .
Es probable que . . . / It is probable that . . .
Es raro que . . . / It is rare that . . .
Es urgente que . . . / It is urgent that . . .

EXAMPLES:

Basta que sepan la verdad / It is sufficient that they know the truth.

Conviene que venga ahora mismo / It is proper that she come right now.

Es aconsejable que salga inmediatamente / It is advisable that she leave immediately.

Es probable que María regrese a las tres / It is probable that Mary will return at three o'clock.

Es necesario que Ud. escriba la composición / It is necessary that you write the composition *or* It is necessary for you to write the composition.

EJERCICIOS

I. **Increase your vocabulary. Match the following impersonal expressions.**

1. **Basta que . . .**   _____ It is urgent that . . .

2. **Más vale que . . .**   _____ It is a pity that . . .

3. **Es bueno que . . .**   _____ It is advisable that . . .

4. **Es importante que . . .**   _____ It is bad that . . .

5. **Es lástima que . . .**   _____ It is enough that . . .

6. **Es preciso que . . .**   _____ It is good that . . .

7. **Es raro que . . .**   _____ It is better that . . .

8. **Es urgente que . . .**   _____ It is important that . . .

9. **Es malo que . . .**   _____ It is rare that . . .

10. **Es aconsejable que . . .**   _____ It is necessary that . . .

II. **Write the present subjunctive form of the verb given in parentheses. It is not necessary to rewrite the entire sentence. Refer to the above sections or use the verb tables in the back pages of this book for the correct forms, according to your needs.**

1. Basta que nosotros **(saber)** la verdad.   _____

2. Es aconsejable que los alumnos **(salir)** ahora mismo.   _____

3. Es probable que Juana **(regresar)** a la una.   _____

4. Es importante que Uds. **(hablar)** en español.   _____

5. Es bueno que los niños **(beber)** leche.   _____

6. Es malo que ellos **(acostarse)** tarde todas las noches.   _____

7. Es urgente que tú **(escribir)** a tu abuelita.   _____

AFTER VERBS OR EXPRESSIONS THAT INDICATE DENIAL, DOUBT OR LACK OF BELIEF, AND UNCERTAINTY

dudar que . . . / to doubt that . . .
negar que . . . / to deny that . . .
no creer que . . . / not to believe that . . .
Es dudoso que . . . / It is doubtful that . . .
Es incierto que . . . / It is uncertain that . . .
Hay duda que . . . / There is doubt that . . .
No es cierto que . . . / It is not certain that . . .
No estar seguro que . . . / Not to be sure that . . .
No suponer que . . . / Not to suppose that . . .

EXAMPLES:
    Dudo que mis amigos vengan a verme / I doubt that my friends are coming (will come) to see me.
    No creo que sea urgente / I do not believe that it is urgent.
    Es dudoso que Pablo lo haga / It is doubtful that Paul will do it.

EJERCICIOS

I. Increase your vocabulary. Match the following.

1. **negar que . . .**　　　　　　　　　　＿＿＿＿＿ it is doubtful that . . .

2. **no creer que**　　　　　　　　　　＿＿＿＿＿ not to be sure that . . .

3. **no es cierto que . . .**　　　　　　　　＿＿＿＿＿ it is uncertain that . . .

4. **no estar seguro que . . .**　　　　　＿＿＿＿＿ to doubt that . . .

5. **no suponer que . . .**　　　　　　　＿＿＿＿＿ to deny that . . .

6. **dudar que . . .**　　　　　　　　　　＿＿＿＿＿ there is doubt that . . .

7. **hay duda que . . .**　　　　　　　　＿＿＿＿＿ not to suppose that . . .

8. **es dudoso que . . .**　　　　　　　　＿＿＿＿＿ it is not certain that . . .

9. **es incierto que . . .**　　　　　　　＿＿＿＿＿ not to believe that . . .

II. Read the following advertisement and answer the question under it.

Es menester que

usted sepa español.

Hay clases indiv. y de grupo

para jóvenes y adultos.

¡LLÁMEME!

Alberto López

 **123-4567**

Ahora mismo

What does Alberto López want?

A. to learn English because he is a Spanish-speaking person
B. people to call him for lessons in Spanish
C. private or group lessons
D. to learn Spanish

AFTER VERBS OR EXPRESSIONS THAT INDICATE AN EMOTION OF JOY, GLADNESS, HAPPINESS, SORROW, REGRET, FEAR, SURPRISE

estar contento que . . . / to be happy that . . ., to be pleased that . . .
estar feliz que . . . / to be happy that . . .
estar triste que . . . / to be sad that . . .
alegrarse (de) que . . . / to be glad that . . .
sentir que . . . / to regret that . . ., to feel sorry that . . .
sorprenderse (de) que . . . / to be surprised that . . .
temer que . . . / to fear that . . .
tener miedo (de) que . . . / to be afraid that . . .

EXAMPLES:

Estoy muy contento que mis amigos vengan a verme / I am very pleased that my friends are coming (will come) to see me.

Me alegro de que ellos hayan venido / I am glad that they have come.

Siento mucho que su madre esté enferma / I am very sorry that your mother is ill.

EJERCICIOS

I. Increase your vocabulary. Match the following.

1. **estar contento (feliz) que . . .**   _____ to be afraid that . . .

2. **estar triste que . . .**   _____ to regret, to feel sorry that . . .

3. **alegrarse de que . . .**   _____ to be surprised that . . .

4. **sentir que . . .**   _____ to be happy, pleased that . . .

5. **sorprenderse de que . . .**   _____ to fear that . . .

6. **temer que . . .**   _____ to be sad that . . .

7. **tener miedo de que . . .**   _____ to be glad that . . .

II. Expressing Personal Feelings. Proficiency in Speaking and Writing.

Situation: You and your sister Helen are expressing personal feelings about who is coming and who is not coming to your birthday party.

Your role is **Tú.** You may vary and extend this dialogue with your own words and ideas. Later, after you have written on the lines what you said, you may exchange roles with your sister for more practice in speaking and writing.

Elena: **Estoy muy contenta que Rebeca venga a tu fiesta de cumpleaños.**

Tú: _____
(Me, too. I'm glad that she's coming.)

Elena: **Pero estoy triste que León no pueda estar con nosotros.**

Tú: _____
(True. I feel sorry that he can't be with us. Do you know that he went to Guadalajara?)

Elena:	**Sí. Yo lo sé. Su abuelo está enfermo.**
Tú:	_____
	(Don't worry **(No te preocupes).** It is certain that his grandfather will be better.)

AFTER CERTAIN VERBS THAT IMPLY A WISH OR DESIRE THAT SOMETHING BE DONE, INCLUDING A COMMAND, ORDER, PREFERENCE, ADVICE, PERMISSION, REQUEST, PLEA, INSISTENCE, SUGGESTION

aconsejar / to advise
consentir / to consent
decir / to tell (someone to do something)
dejar / to allow, to let
desear / to want, to wish
esperar / to hope
exigir / to demand, to require
hacer / to make (someone do something or that something be done)
insistir (en) / to insist (on, upon)
mandar / to order, to command
pedir / to ask, to request
permitir / to allow, to permit
preferir / to prefer
prohibir / to forbid, to prohibit
querer / to want, to wish (someone to do something or that something be done)
recomendar / to recommend
rogar / to beg, to request
sugerir / to suggest
suplicar / to beg, to plead, to make a plea

EXAMPLES:

Les aconsejo a ellos que hagan el trabajo / I advise them to do the work.

Les digo a ellos que escriban los ejercicios / I am telling them to write the exercises.

Mi madre quiere que yo vaya a la escuela ahora / My mother wants me to go to school now.

BUT: **Yo quiero ir a la escuela ahora** / I want to go to school now

NOTE: In this example, there is no change in subject; therefore, the infinitive **ir** is used. But in the previous example there is a new subject **(yo)** in the dependent clause and **ir** is in the subjunctive because the verb **querer** is used in the main clause.

El capitán me manda que yo entre / The captain orders me to come in.

OR: **El capitán me manda entrar** / The captain orders me to come in.
(NOTE that **mandar** can take a new clause in the subjunctive or it can take an infinitive.)

El maestro me permite que yo salga / The teacher permits me to leave.

OR: **La maestra me permite salir** / The teacher permits me to leave.
(NOTE that **permitir** can take a new clause in the subjunctive or it can take an infinitive. You can do the same with the verbs **dejar, hacer, mandar,** and **prohibir.**)

Mi profesor exige que yo escriba los ejercicios / My professor demands that I write the exercises.

Espero que mi perrito vuelva pronto / I hope that my little dog returns soon.

Le ruego a usted que me devuelva mi libro / I beg you to return my book to me.

IN SUM, NOTE THAT:

(a) The subjunctive form of the verb in the dependent clause is used because what precedes is either a certain conjunction, a certain adverb, the expression **por + adj. or adv. + que**, a certain indefinite expression, an indefinite or negative antecedent, a superlative, an indirect wish or command or order introduced by **¡Que . . . !** (which is short for **"Quiero que . . ."** or **"Deje que . . ."**), **¡Ojalá que . . . !** or a certain impersonal expression, or a certain verb.

(b) When you are dealing with two different subjects, you need two clauses: the main clause (also known as independent clause) and the dependent clause, which contains the new subject. When there is no change in subject, there is no need for a second clause.

(c) Generally speaking, only the verbs **dejar, hacer, mandar, permitir, prohibir** can be followed by just the infinitive or a new clause with its verb in the subjunctive.

(d) In English, it is possible not to use a second clause even when the subject changes and to use an infinitive, but this is not so in Spanish—except for what is noted.

EXAMPLE:

I want you to leave / **Quiero que Ud. salga.**

EJERCICIOS

I. Escriba seis conjunciones en español que exigen el subjuntivo. (Write six conjunctions in Spanish that require the subjunctive. Refer to the above sections, according to your needs.)

1. _____   4. _____

2. _____   5. _____

3. _____   6. _____

II. Cambie el verbo en infinitivo al presente de subjuntivo. (Change the verb from the infinitive form in parentheses to the present subjunctive.)

Modelo: Saldré a las tres y media a menos que (estar) lloviendo.

Escriba: Saldré a las tres y media a menos que esté lloviendo.
(I will leave at 3:30 unless it is raining.)

1. Se lo explico a ustedes a fin de que **(poder)** comprenderlo. _____

_____

2. Partiré a la una a menos que **(estar)** nevando. _____

_____

3. Le daré el dinero a Roberto cuando me lo **(pedir).** _____

_____

4. Esperaré hasta que **(llegar)** el autobús. _____

_____

Trabajaré hasta que Ud. **(venir).** _____

III. Escriba el verbo entre paréntesis en el presente de subjuntivo. (Write the verb in parentheses in the present subjunctive.)

1. Tal vez ellos **(haber)** perdido. _____

2. Por más interesante que **(ser),** no quiero ver esa película. _____

3. No abriré la puerta, quienquiera que **(ser)**. _____

4. Adondequiera que Ud. **(ir),** dígamelo. _____

5. Busco un libro que **(ser)** interesante. _____

6. No encuentro a nadie que **(saber)** la respuesta. _____

7. Quiero que Juan lo **(hacer)**. _____

8. ¡Que lo **(hacer)** Jorge! _____

9. ¡Ojalá que ellos **(venir)**! _____

10. ¡Ojalá que Juan **(llegar)**! _____

IV. Escriba seis expresiones impersonales en español que exigen el subjuntivo. (Write six impersonal expressions in Spanish that require the subjunctive; for example: Es necesario que . . ., Es importante que . . ., Basta que . . . . Refer to the above sections, according to your needs.)

1. _____   4. _____

2. _____   5. _____

3. _____   6. _____

V. Complete las oraciones a continuación, usando en cada una el presente de subjuntivo de los verbos en la siguiente lista. Cada verbo debe usarse solamente una vez.

(Complete the six sentences below. In each one use the present subjunctive of the six verbs in the following list. Each verb must be used only once.)

hacer	venir
ser	ir
estar	escribir

1. Dudo que mis amigos _____ a verme.

2. No creo que _____ urgente.

3. Es dudoso que Pablo lo _____ .

4. Siento mucho que su madre _____ enferma.

5. Les digo a ellos que _____ los ejercicios.

6. Mi madre quiere que yo _____ a la escuela ahora.

311

VI. Cambie el verbo entre paréntesis a la forma correcta. No es necesario escribir toda la oración. (Change the verb in parentheses to the correct form. It is not necessary to write the whole sentence. One of them will remain in the infinitive form. Follow the models.)

Modelos: Mi profesor exige que yo (escribir) los ejercicios. _____escriba_____

Yo quiero (ir) al cine ahora. _____ir_____

Mi madre quiere que yo (ir) al cine ahora. _____vaya_____

1. El capitán me manda que yo **(entrar)**. _____

2. El profesor me permite que yo **(salir)**. _____

3. Espero que mi perrito **(volver)** pronto. _____

4. Le ruego a usted que me **(devolver)** mis discos. _____

5. Quiero **(salir)** ahora. _____

6. Quiero que Ud. **(salir)** ahora. _____

Possessive Pronouns

Definition: A possessive pronoun is a word that takes the place of a noun to show possession, as in English: *mine, yours,* etc., instead of saying *my mother, your car,* etc.

We form a possessive pronoun by using the appropriate definite article **(el, la, los, las)** + the long form of the possessive adjective. As you realize by now, a pronoun must agree in gender and number with the noun it replaces. It does not agree with the possessor.

The possessive pronouns are:

ENGLISH MEANING	SINGULAR FORM	PLURAL FORM
	(agreement In gender and number with the noun it replaces)	(agreement in gender and number wlth the noun it replaces)
1. mine	**el mío, la mía**	**los míos, las mías**
2. yours (*fam. sing.*)	**el tuyo, la tuya**	**los tuyos, las tuyas**
3. yours, hls, hers, its	**el suyo, la suya**	**los suyos, las suyas**
1. ours	**el nuestro, la nuestra**	**los nuestros, las nuestras**
2. yours (*fam. pl.*)	**el vuestro, la vuestra**	**los vuestros, las vuestras**
3. yours, theirs	**el suyo, la suya**	**los suyos, las suyas**

EXAMPLES:

Mi hermano es más alto que el suyo / My brother is taller than yours (his, hers, theirs).
Su hermana es más alta que la mía / Your sister is taller than mine.
Mi casa es más grande que la suya / My house is larger than yours (his, hers, theirs).

In order to clarify the meanings of **el suyo, la suya, los suyos, la suyas** (since they can mean *yours, his, hers, its, theirs*), do the following: drop the **suyo** form, keep the appropriate definite article **(el, la, los, las),** and add, appropriately, any of the following: **de Ud., de él, de ella, de Uds., de ellos, de ellas:**

mi libro y el de Ud., mi casa y la de él, mis amigos y los de ella, mis amigas y las de Uds., mis libros y los de ellos, mis cuadernos y los de ellas / my book and yours, my house and his, my friends and hers, my friends and yours, *etc.*)

¿De quién es . . . ? ¿De quiénes es . . . ? ¿De quién son . . . ? ¿De quiénes son . . . ?
Whose is . . . ? Whose are . . . ?

Whose, when asking a question (usually at the beginning of a sentence), is expressed by any of the above. If you believe that the possessor is singular, use **¿De quién es . . . ?** If you think that the possessor is plural, use **¿De quiénes es . . . ?** And if the noun you have in mind **(whose . . .)** is plural, use the third person plural form of **ser:**

¿De quién es esta casa? / Whose is this house? **Es de mi tío** / It is my uncle's.
¿De quiénes es esta casa? / Whose is this house? **Es de mis amigos** / It is my friends'.
¿De quién son estos guantes? / Whose are these gloves? **Son de Juan** / They are John's.
¿De quiénes son estos niños? / Whose are these children? **Son de los Señores Pardo** / They are Mr. and Mrs. Pardo's.

NOTE that the verb **ser** is used in these expressions showing possession.

ALSO NOTE that if a possessive pronoun is used with the verb **ser,** the definite article is dropped:

¿De quién es este lápiz? / Whose is this pencil? **Es mío** / It is mine.
¿De quién son estas camisas? / Whose are these shirts? **Son suyas** / They are theirs (yours, his, hers). OR, to clarify **suyas**, say: **Son de Ud., Son de él, Son de ella,** *etc.* / They are yours, They are his, They are hers, *etc.*

Relative Pronouns

Definition: A pronoun is a word that takes the place of a noun. A relative pronoun is a pronoun that refers (relates) to an **antecedent.** An antecedent is something that comes before something; it can be a word, a phrase, a clause that is replaced by a pronoun or some other substitute.
Example: *Is it Mary who did that?* In this sentence, *who* is the relative pronoun and *Mary* is the antecedent. Another example, a longer one: *It seems to me that you are right, which is what I had thought right along.* The relative pronoun in this example is *which* and the antecedent of it is the clause, *that you are right.*

In Spanish, a relative pronoun can refer to an antecedent that is a person or a thing, or an idea. A relative pronoun can be subject or object of a verb, or object of a preposition.

COMMON RELATIVE PRONOUNS

que / who, that, whom, which. This is the most common relative pronoun.

As subject referring to a person: La muchacha **que** habla con Juan es mi hermana / The girl **who** is talking with John is my sister.

Here, the relative pronoun **que** is subject of the verb **habla** and it refers to **la muchacha,** which is the subject of the verb **es.**

As subject referring to a thing: El libro **que** está en la mesa es mío / The book **which (that)** is on the table is mine.

Here, the relative pronoun **que** is subject of the verb **está** and it refers to **el libro,** which is the subject of **es.**

As direct object of a verb referring to a person: El señor Molina es el profesor **que** admiro / Mr. Molina is the professor **whom** I admire.

Here, the relative pronoun **que** is object of the verb form **admiro.** It refers to **el profesor.**

As direct object of a verb referring to a thing: La composición **que** Ud. lee es mía / The composition **(that, which)** you are reading is mine.

Here, the relative pronoun **que** is object of the verb form **lee.** It refers to **la composición,** which is the subject of **es.** The subject of **lee** is **Ud.**

NOTE here, in the English translation of this example, that we do not always have to use a relative pronoun in English. In Spanish, it must be stated.

As object of a preposition referring only to a thing: La cama **en que** duermo es grande / The bed **in which** I sleep is large.

Here, the relative pronoun **que** is object of the preposition **en.** It refers to **la cama.** Other prepositions used commonly with **que** are **a, con, de.**

As object of a preposition, **que** refers to a thing only—not to a person. Use **quien** or **quienes** as object of a preposition referring to persons.

quien / who (after a preposition, whom)

As subject of a verb referring only to persons: Yo sé **quien** lo hizo / I know **who** did it.

Here, **quien** is the subject of **hizo.** It does not refer to a specific antecedent. Here, **quien** includes its antecedent.

When used as a subject, **quien** (or **quienes,** if plural) can also mean *he who, she who, the one who, the ones who, those who.* In place of **quien** or **quienes** in this sense, you can also use **el que, la que, los que, las que:**

Quien escucha oye / Who listens hears; He who listens hears; She who listens hears; The one who listens hears.

OR: **El que escucha** oye / He who listens hears; **La que escucha** oye / She who listens hears; The one who listens hears.

Quienes escuchan oyen / Who listen hear; Those who listen hear; The ones who listen hear.

OR: **Los que escuchan** oyen; **Las que escuchan** oyen / Those who listen hear; The ones who listen hear.

As subject of a verb, the relative pronoun **quien** may be used instead of **que** referring only to persons when it is the subject of a non-restrictive dependent clause set off by commas; La señora Gómez, **quien** (or **que**) es profesora, conoce a mi madre / Mrs. Gómez, who is a teacher, knows my mother.

As direct object of a verb referring only to persons, the relative pronoun **quien** or **quienes** may be used with the personal **a (a quien, a quienes)** instead of **que:** La muchacha **que** (*or* **a quien**) Ud. vio al baile es mi hermana / The girl **whom** you saw at the dance is my sister.

As object of a preposition referring only to persons: ¿Conoces a la chica **con quien** tomé el almuerzo? / Do you know the girl **with whom** I had lunch? ¿Conoces a los chicos **con quienes** María tomó el almuerzo? / Do you know the boys **with whom** Mary had lunch? ¿Conoce Ud. a los hombres **de quienes** hablo? / Do you know the men **of whom (about whom)** I am talking?

el cual, la cual, los cuales, las cuales / who, that, whom, which, the one which, the ones which, the one who, the ones who.

These relative pronouns may be used in place of **que.** This can be especially needed when it is desired to clarify the gender and number of **que:** La madre de José, **la cual** es muy inteligente, es dentista / Joseph's mother, **who** is very intelligent, is a dentist.

These substitute relative pronouns may also refer to things: El libro, **el cual** está sobre la mesa, es mío / The book, **which (the one which)** is on the table, is mine.

These relative pronouns may also be used as substitutes for **el que, la que, los que, las que** when used as the subject of a non-restrictive dependent clause set off by commas: La señora Gómez, **la cual** (or **la que,** or **quien,** or **que**) es profesora, conoce a mi madre / Mrs. Gómez, **who** is a teacher, knows my mother.

These relative pronouns, as well as **el que, la que, los que, las que**, are used as objects of prepositions except with **a, con, de, en**—in which case the relative pronoun **que** is preferred with things. These relative pronouns **(el cual, la cual, los cuales, las cuales** and **el que, la que, los que, las que)** are commonly used with the following prepositions: **para, por, sin,**

     delante de, cerca de, and **sobre:** En este cuarto, hay una gran ventana **por la cual** se ve el sol por la mañana / In this room, there is a large window **through which** you (one, anyone) can see the sun in the morning.

These compound relative pronouns (**el cual, el que**, *etc.*) refer to persons as well as things and can be used as subject of a verb or direct object of a verb when used in a non-restrictive dependent clause separated from its antecedent and set off with commas.

    lo cual / which; **lo que** / what, that which

        These are neuter compound relative pronouns. They do not refer to an antecedent of any gender or number. That is why they are called *neuter.*

    Lo cual or **lo que** are used to refer to a statement, a clause, an idea: Mi hijo Juan estudia sus lecciones todos los días, **lo cual** es bueno / My son John studies his lessons every day, **which** is good. Mi hija recibió buenas notas, **lo que** me gustó / My daughter received good marks, **which** pleased me.

    Lo que is also used to express *what* in the sense of *that which:* Comprendo **lo que** Ud. dice / I understand **what (that which)** you say. **Lo que** Ud. dice es verdad / **What (That which)** you say is true.

    cuanto = todo lo que / all that

    As a relative pronoun, **cuanto** may be used in place of **todo lo que: Todo lo que** Ud. dice es verdad: OR: **Cuanto** Ud. dice es verdad / **All that (All that which)** you say is true.

    cuyo, cuya, cuyos, cuyas / whose

    This word (and its forms as given) refers to persons and things. Strictly speaking, **cuyo**, *etc.* is not regarded as a relative pronoun but rather as a relative possessive adjective. It agrees in gender and number with what is possessed (whose . . .), not with the possessor. Its position is directly in front of the noun it modifies. Examples:

    El señor García, **cuyos hijos** son inteligentes, es profesor / Mr. García, **whose children** are intelligent, is a professor.

    La muchacha, **cuyo padre** es profesor, es inteligente / The girl, **whose father** is a professor, is intelligent.

    El muchacho, **cuya madre** es profesora, es inteligente / The boy, **whose mother** is a professor, is intelligent.

    The forms of **cuyo** cannot be used as an interrogative when you ask: Whose is . . . ? You must use **de quién: ¿De quién es este libro?**

    When referring to parts of the body, use **a quien** instead of **cuyo:** La niña, **a quien** la madre lavó las manos, es bonita / The child, **whose** hands the mother washed, is pretty.

EJERCICIOS

I. Obtaining and Providing Information. Proficiency in Speaking and Writing.

Situation: Your friend Teresa is visiting you in your house. She is always asking questions. Provide answers for her.

Your role is **Tú.** You may vary and extend this dialogue with your own words and ideas. Later, after you have written on the lines what you said, you may exchange roles with Teresa for more practice in speaking and writing. If you need to refresh your memory in the use of pronouns, refer to the above section where there are many examples in Spanish and English.

Teresa: **Dime, en esta foto, ¿quién es la mujer que está sonriendo?**

Tú: _____
(In this photo, the woman who is smiling is my aunt Sofía.)

Teresa: **Y estos dos bolígrafos** (ball-point pens) **en el escritorio** (desk) **¿de quiénes son?**

Tú: _____
(This one is mine and that one is my brother's.)

Teresa: **Y en esa foto, ¿de quién es esa casa?**

Tú: _____
(In that photo, that house is my uncle's.)

Teresa: **Y estos guantes en la cama, ¿de quién son?**

Tú: _____
(These gloves on the bed are John's.)

Teresa: **¿Tú duermes en esta cama?**

Tú: _____

_____
(No. I don't sleep in this bed. The bed in which I sleep is big. It's that one over there near the window. Do you have other questions?)

Teresa: **No. No tengo otras preguntas.**

Tú: _____

_____
(Now it's my turn. I have some questions and you can give me some answers. Let's go into the kitchen. We can have some ice cream.)

II. Llene los blancos con los pronombres posesivos, en español, naturalmente. (Write the possessive pronouns on the lines. The first one [mine] was done for you to get you started. Refer to the possessive pronouns in the above section, according to your needs.)

ENGLISH MEANING ↓	SINGULAR FORM (agreement in gender and number with the noun it replaces)	PLURAL FORM (agreement in gender and number with the noun it replaces)
Singular		
1. mine	**el mío, la mía**	**los míos, las mías**
2. yours (*fam. sing.*)	_____	_____
3. yours, his, hers, its	_____	_____
Plural		
1. ours	_____	_____
2. yours (*fam. pl.*)	_____	_____
3. yours, theirs	_____	_____

III. Traduzca al español.

1. My brother is taller than yours. _____

2. Your sister is taller than mine. _____

3. My house is larger than theirs. _____

4. Whose is this house? It is my uncle's. _____

5. Whose is this car? It is my parents'. _____

6. Whose are these gloves? They are John's. _____

7. Whose are these children? They are Mr. and Mrs. Pardo's. _____

_____

8. Whose is this pencil? It's mine. _____

9. Whose are these shirts? They're theirs. _____

10. Whose is this skirt? It's Jane's. _____

IV. Obtaining and Providing Information. Proficiency in Speaking and Writing.

Situation: You just went into the kitchen with your friend Teresa to continue talking while having some ice cream. In the previous conversation you told her that it's your turn to ask questions. Again, according to your needs, refer to the above section where there are many examples of possessive pronouns and relative pronouns in Spanish and English sentences.

Tú: _____

(Now it's my turn. I have some questions and you can give me some answers.)

Teresa: **Está bien. Ahora te toca a ti. Escucho. ¡Espero que tus preguntas no sean difíciles!**

Tú: _____

(My questions are not difficult. They are easy. Tell me, Teresa, is your brother taller than mine?)

Teresa: **No hay duda que mi hermano es más alto que el tuyo.**

Tú: _____

(And your sister? Is she as tall as mine?)

Teresa: **Mi hermana no es tan alta como la tuya.**

Tú: _____

(In our school, which teacher do you admire?)

Teresa: **En nuestra escuela el Señor Smith es el profesor que admiro. ¿Y tú? ¿Cuál de nuestros profesores admiras?**

Tú: _____

_____

_____

(In our school Señora López is the teacher that I admire. She always talks in Spanish with us. Tell me, do you know the boy with whom I had lunch in the cafeteria yesterday?)

Teresa: **Claro que sí. Su nombre es José Robles. Es el muchacho cuya madre es dentista.**

Tú: _____

(What you are saying is true. Now I know that you know my friends. Do you want to have a soda with the ice cream?)

V. Llene los blancos con quien o que. (Complete the sentences with either **quien** or **que**.)

1. La muchacha _____ habla con Juan es mi hermana.

2. _____ escucha oye.

3. El libro _____ está en la mesa es mío.

4. El muchacho _____ Ud. vio en el baile es mi hermano.

5. El señor Molina es el profesor _____ admiro.

VI. **Llene los blancos con el cual, la cual, los cuales, o las cuales.** (Complete the sentences with either **el cual, la cual, los cuales,** or **las cuales.**)

1. La madre de José, _____ es muy inteligente, es dentista.

2. El padre de Juana, _____ es médico, está enfermo hoy.

3. En este cuarto, hay dos ventanas por _____ se ve el sol por la mañana.

4. Aquellos hombres, cerca de _____ está mi padre son mis tíos.

VII. **Llene los blancos con cuyo, cuya, cuyos, o cuyas.** (Complete the sentences with either **cuyo, cuya, cuyos,** or **cuyas.**)

1. El señor García, _____ hijos son inteligentes, es profesor.

2. La muchacha, _____ padre es profesor, es inteligente.

3. El muchacho, _____ madre es profesora, es inteligente también.

4. El señor Villanueva, _____ hijas son bonitas, es muy rico.

VIII. **En español hay muchas palabras que se escriben y se pronuncian idénticamente. pero un signo de acento es necesario para distinguir su significado.** (In Spanish there are many words that are written and pronounced identically, but an accent mark is necessary to distinguish their meaning.)

Ejemplo:
   mi *poss, adj., 1st pers., sing.* / my
   mí *obj. of a prep.* / me

¡Es mi caramelo! ¡Es para mí! / It's my caramel! It's for me!

---

   este *dem. adj., masc., sing.* / this
   éste *dem. pron., masc., sing.* / this one

Este té es para ti y éste es para él. / This tea is for you and this one is for him.

Mnemonic Tip	The accent mark on **éste** is a signal for *this one.*

---

   estos *dem. adj., masc., pl.* / these
   éstos *dem. pron., masc., pl.* / these (*not* these ones)

Estos caramelos son para mí y éstos son para ti. / These caramels are for me and these are for you.

Mnemonic Tip	The accent mark on **éstos** is a signal for *these*, a demonstrative pronoun.

IX. **En español hay muchas palabras que se escriben y se pronuncian idénticamente, pero un signo de acento es necesario para distinguir su significado.** (In Spanish there are many words that are written and pronounced identically, but an accent mark is necessary to distinguish their meaning.)

EJEMPLO:

> **esta** *dem. adj., fem., sing.* / this
> **ésta** *dem. pron., fem., sing.* / this one

Esta bicicleta es para ti y ésta es para mí. / This bicycle is for you and this one is for me.

Mnemonic Tip	The accent mark on **ésta** is a signal for *this one*.

> **ese** *dem. adj., masc., sing.* / that
> **ése** *dem. pron., masc., sing.* / that one

Ese anzuelo es para él y ése es para ella. / That fish hook is for him and that one is for her.

Mnemonic Tip	The accent mark on **ése** is a signal for *that one*.

Mnemonic Tip	The letter *t* on **éste** (this) drops off and falls to the wayside on its way to **ese anzuelo** (that fish hook).

Mnemonic Tip	*This* and *these* have the *t*'s and *that* and *those* don't: **este libro, estos libros** (this book, these books) **ese libro, esos libros** (that book, those books) **esta carta, estas cartas** (this letter, these letters) **esa carta, esas cartas** (that letter, those letters)

X. Complete este crucigrama. (Complete this crossword.)

VERTICALES

1. Personal pron. as subject, 1st pers., sing.
2. Personal pron. as subject. 3rd pers., sing.
3. Indirect obj. pron., 3rd pers., pl.
5. Direct obj. pron., 3rd pers., sing., fem.
6. Personal pron., as object of a prep., 3rd pers., sing., masc.
7. Subject pron., 2nd pers., sing.

HORIZONTALES

3. Direct obj. pron., 3rd pers., sing., masc.
4. Reflexive pron., 3rd pers.,sing. & pl.
6. Demonstrative pron., fem., sing.
8. Direct & indirect obj. pron., 1st pers., sing.

XI. Culture. Appreciating Spanish Art. Proficiency in Speaking and Writing.

Situation: You are on a field trip with your Spanish teacher and classmates, visiting the Museum and Library of The Hispanic Society of America in New York City. You are admiring a painting entitled *The Duchess of Alba* by GOYA.

It's your turn to say a few words in Spanish about the painting. Look at the picture on the following page. You may use your own words and ideas or the following.

A few verbs you may want to use: **ver** / to see; **mirar** / to look at; **admirar** / to admire; **ser** / to be; **estar** / to be; **está escrito** / is written; **llevar** / to wear; **señalar con el dedo** / to point at.

A few nouns: **la mujer** / the woman; **la cara** / the face; **la expresión** / the expression; **los ojos** / the eyes; **las cejas** / the eyebrows; **el vestido** / the dress; **los anillos** / rings; **los dedos** / fingers; **el suelo** / the floor, ground; **la firma de Goya** / Goya's signature; **los zapatos** / the shoes; **el pie** / the foot; **el paisaje** / landscape.

A few adjectives: **elegante** / elegant; **impresionante** / impressive; **majestuoso** / majestic; **magnífico** / magnificent; **espléndido** / splendid; **noble** / noble.

After you have jotted down a few words in Spanish that you plan to use, say them aloud, then use them in at least five short sentences for practice on the following lines. Remember that each sentence must contain at least one verb. Did you notice that the woman is pointing at the ground? What is she pointing at on the ground? You may want to say: **La mujer señala con el dedo la firma de Goya que está escrita en el suelo cerca del pie derecho** / The woman is pointing at Goya's signature that is written on the ground near her right foot. **Veo, también, el año 1797 que está escrito cerca de la firma** / I see, also, the year 1797, which is written near the signature.

1. _____

2. _____

3. _____

4. _____

5. _____

The Duchess of Alba by Francisco José de GOYA y Lucientes (1746–1828)

Courtesy of The Hispanic Society of America (Museum and Library), New York, N.Y.

TEST 5

PART ONE   Speaking Proficiency

Directions: Read the five situations given below. Take a few minutes to organize your thoughts about the words you are going to speak. You may want to jot them down on a card as key words to use in your statements. Select three of the five situations. Before you begin to speak, it would be a good idea to review the Speaking and Writing Proficiency exercises that you did in this Work Unit.

1. **Situation:** You are trying to convince your friend Juan to adopt a course of action by preferring and insisting that someone in particular do the work you have in mind. For example, you want María to do the work but Juan prefers that José do it. You insist that María do it because she knows how and José doesn't know anything. Make at least three statements. You will have to use the present subjunctive of the verbs because your remarks will begin with I want . . ., I prefer . . ., I insist . . . ; for example, **Yo quiero que María haga el trabajo.**

2. **Situation:** You and your sister Ofelia have been waiting for Julia at your house for lunch. It's very late, she hasn't arrived, and you are worried that she may be sick. In this situation you are expressing your personal feelings about the matter. Make at least three statements. You will have to use the present subjunctive of verbs after verbs, such as, I doubt that . . ., I'm afraid that . . ., as in: I doubt that she is coming, I'm afraid that she is sick.

3. **Situation:** You and members of your family are confronted with an emergency because Grandma is sick in bed. It's necessary to call the doctor, it's not certain that he will come soon, it's a pity that Grandma is sick. You will have to use the present subjunctive after impersonal statements, such as: **Es necesario que . . ., Es urgente que . . ., No es cierto que . . . .**

4. **Situation:** You and Mariana are looking for a good Spanish restaurant in which to have lunch. You look at the menu on the window and you decide to go in. The waiter is standing by the door. Tell him that you and your friend are looking for a good restaurant. Ask him if this is a good restaurant. He persuades you to come in. Begin to order by telling the waiter to bring you two soups. Also tell him to give you the soups, provided that they are good. In this situation you will practice the present subjunctive in your statements because the imperative (command) form will be used when you tell the waiter to bring you this, to give you that. When you see that there are flies in the soups, tell the waiter about it and end the scene by telling your friend, "Mariana, let's get out of here now!"

5. **Situation:** You are looking at a picture of two scuba divers, a man and a woman, up to their waists in water. One of them is afraid that a shark might arrive. Imagine a conversation that takes place between these two people.

PART TWO   Listening Proficiency

Directions: Your teacher will read aloud four short paragraphs. Each one will contain only a few sentences. You will hear each paragraph twice. Then you will hear one question based on each. You will hear the question only once. It is printed below. Choose the best suggested answer based on what you heard and check the letter of your choice.

Selection Number 1

1. ¿Quién prestó los discos?

   A. en el mes de septiembre

   B. Juana

   C. el primero de diciembre

   D. Susana

Selection Number 2

2. ¿Qué dice Ana a Juana?

    A. que Juana puede ir a ver a Elena

    B. que se los dio los discos a Juana

    C. que se los prestó a Ana

    D. que tiene los discos

Selection Number 3

3. ¿Cuándo prestó Juana sus discos?

    A. en la primavera

    B. en el invierno

    C. en el otoño

    D. en el verano

Selection Number 4

4. ¿Qué busca Juana?

    A. su amiga Ana

    B. su amiga Elena

    C. un favor

    D. sus discos

PART THREE   Reading Proficiency

Directions: In the following passage there are five blank spaces numbered 1 through 5. Each blank space represents a missing verb form. For each blank space, four possible completions are provided. Only one of them is grammatically correct and makes sense in the context of the passage.

First, read the passage in its entirety to determine its general meaning. Then read it a second time. For each blank space choose the completion that makes the best sense and is grammatically correct. Write its letter in the space provided.

Mi abuela está enferma. Es necesario que nosotros _____ pronto al doctor

    1. A. llamamos
        B. llamemos
        C. llamar
        D. laman

Sánchez. No es seguro que _____ el doctor a esta hora. Son las dos de la mañana.

    2. A. viene
        B. vendrá
        C. vendría
        D. venga

Es lástima que mi abuelita _____ enferma. Es preciso que yo _____

    3. A. está   4. A. llamo
        B. es   B. llama
        C. esté   C. llame
        D. fue   D. llamar

al doctor por teléfono. ¡Ojalá que _____ llegar inmediatamente!

5. A. puede
   B. podrá
   C. podría
   D. pueda

PART FOUR   Writing Proficiency

Directions: Of the five situations in Part One (Speaking Proficiency) in this test, select three of them and write what you said on the lines below. For each situation, write at least three statements in Spanish, each containing at least one verb.

Situation 1 _____

_____

_____

Situation 2 _____

_____

_____

Situation 3 _____

_____

_____

Situation 4 _____

_____

_____

Situation 5 _____

_____

_____

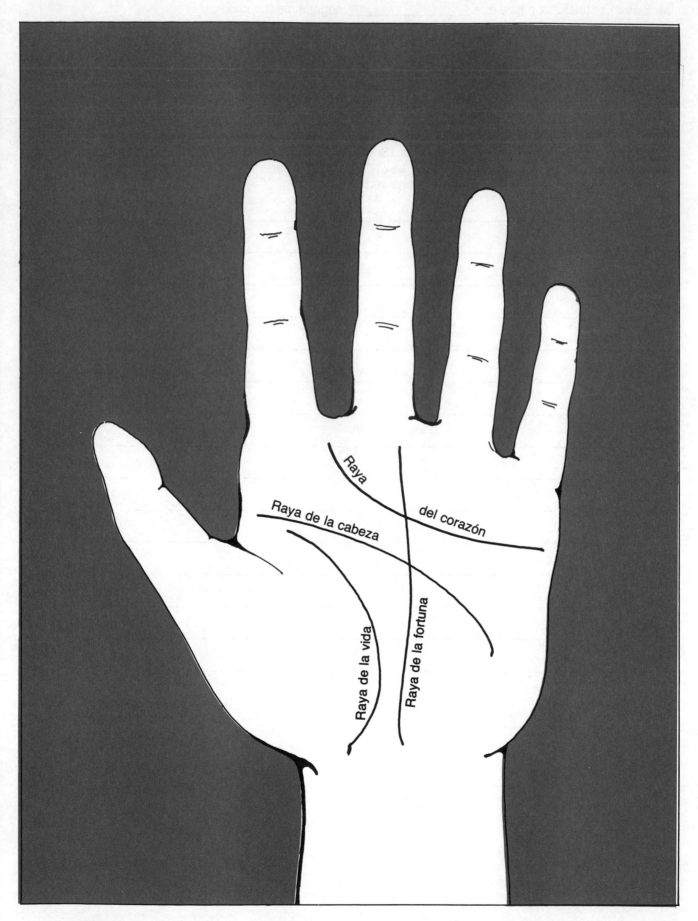

Los secretos de su mano

Work Unit 11

Some people like to have their palms read. It
can be fun—believe it or not.

Los secretos de su mano

Clara y Francisco Rodríguez fueron a la feria el sábado pasado. Allá, se divirtieron mucho. Vieron varias exposiciones, compraron muchas cosas, comieron mucho. También, entraron en la tienda de una quiromántica para que ella les leyera las rayas de las manos.

—¡Mira! ¡Francisco! ¡Una quiromántica!—exclamó Clara.

—¿Dónde?—le preguntó Francisco a Clara.   5

—Aquí, delante de nosotros. ¿No ves el anuncio?

> La señora Sabelotodo,
> quiromántica,
> revela los secretos de su mano.

—Francisco, yo quisiera entrar para saber el porvenir. ¿Quieres entrar conmigo?—preguntó su esposa.

—Sí, sí, estoy dispuesto. Pero, tú sabes bien que no creeré nada—dijo su esposo. Entraron en la tienda de la quiromántica.   10

—¿Podemos entrar, señora?—preguntó Clara.

—Sí, sí. ¡Entren! ¡Entren!—contestó la señora Sabelotodo.

—Me gustaría mucho que usted leyera las rayas de mi mano. Y las de mi marido también—dijo Clara.

—¡Bueno!—dijo la quiromántica—. Siéntese, señora, por favor. Y deme la mano,   15
señora.

La señora Sabelotodo mira fijamente la mano de Clara y comienza a leer las rayas.

—¡Ah! Veo en la raya de la fortuna que usted va a hacer un viaje a Australia con un hombre—, exclama la señora Sabelotodo.

—¡No me diga! ¡Es extraño! Mi marido y yo comenzamos a hacer preparaciones para   20
un viaje a Australia.

—Ahora—, dice la señora Sabelotodo, estoy mirando la raya del corazón. Veo que usted está enamorada de un hombre.

—¡No me diga! ¡Es extraño! Ud. tiene razón. ¡Estoy enamorada de mi marido!

—Ahora, señor, siéntese y deme la mano—, dice la señora Sabelotodo.   25
El señor Rodríguez se sienta y le da la mano a la quiromántica.

—¡Ah! Veo en la raya de la fortuna que usted va a hacer un viaje a Australia con una mujer—, exclama la señora Sabelotodo.

—¡No me diga! ¡Es extraño! Mi esposa y yo comenzamos a hacer preparaciones para   30
un viaje a Australia.

—Ahora—, dice la señora Sabelotodo, estoy mirando la raya del corazón. Veo que usted está enamorado de una mujer.

—¡No me diga! ¡Es extraño! Ud. tiene razón. ¡Estoy enamorado de mi esposa! La mano revela todo, ¿no es verdad?

—Sí, señor, las rayas de la mano revelan los secretos de su vida. Cuesta cien pesetas   35
por las revelaciones.
Francisco da las cien pesetas a la señora Sabelotodo.
Afuera, Clara dice a Francisco:

—La señora Sabelotodo lo sabe todo, ¿no es verdad?

—Sí. La señora Sabelotodo lo sabe todo, pero yo no aprendí nada.   40

—Ni yo tampoco. Ya sabemos que vamos a hacer un viaje a Australia, y que estamos enamorados. ¿Verdad?

—¡Verdad! responde Francisco.

KEY WORDS AND PHRASES

NOTE: Use the verb tables of regular and irregular verbs beginning on page 448.

afuera *adv.* outside

allá *adv.* there

anuncio *n.m.* advertisement, notice, announcement

aprendí *1st pers., s., pret. of* **aprender**; I learned

comienza *3d pers., s., pres. indic. of* **comenzar**; she begins

comieron *3d pers., pl., pret. of* **comer**; they ate

contestó *3d pers., s., pret. of* **contestar**; he / she answered

corazón *n.m.* heart

creeré *1st pers., s., fut. of* **creer**; I will believe

cuesta *3d pers., s., pres. indic. of* **costar**; it costs

dé *3d pers.,s., (Ud.), imper. of* **dar**; give; **dé + me = deme**; **Deme la mano** Give me your hand.

delante *adv.* in front

diga *3d pers., s., imper. (pres.sub.) of* **decir**; **¡No me diga!** Don't tell me!

dijo *3d pers., s., pret. of* **decir**; he / she said

dispuesto *adj.* ready, prepared

enamorado, enamorada *adj.* in love

entraron *3d pers., pl., pret. of* **entrar**; they entered, went in

¡Entren! *3d pers., pl., imper. (command) of* **entrar**; Come in!

estoy mirando *1st pers., s., pres. prog. of* **mirar**; I am looking at

exposición *n.f.* exhibit, exposition

extraño *adj.* strange, odd

feria *n.f.* fair, bazaar

fijamente *adv.* staringly, fixedly; **mira fijamente** she stares at

fortuna *n.f.* fortune, luck

fueron *3d pers., pl., pret. of* **ir**; they went

gustaría *3d pers., s., cond. of* **gustar**; **Me gustaría mucho** I would like very much

las de *pron., fem., pl.* those of, the ones of

leyera *3d pers., s., imperf. sub. of* **leer**; **para que ella leyera** so that she might read

mira *3d pers., s., pres. indic. of* **mirar**; she looks (at); **¡Mira!** Look!

para que *conj.* in order that; **para que ella leyera** so that she might read

¿Podemos entrar? May we come in?

porvenir *n.m.* future

preguntó *3d pers., s., pret. of* **preguntar**; asked

quiromántica *n.f.* palm reader

quisiera *1st & 3d pers., sing., imperf. sub. of* **querer**; I would like

raya *n.f.* line; **las rayas de las manos** the lines on (the palms of) their hands

revela *3d pers., s., pres. indic. of* **revelar**; reveals; **las revelaciones** revelations

secreto *n.m.* secret

señor *n.m.* sir, Mr.; **Señora Sabelotodo** Mrs. Know-It-All

siéntese *3d pers., s., (Ud.), imper. of* **sentarse**; sit down

también *adv.* also

tampoco *adv.* neither, not either; **ni yo tampoco** me neither

tienda *n.f.* tent; shop, store

tiene *3d pers., s., pres. indic. of* **tener** to have; **Ud. tiene razón** You are right.

todo *pron.* all

varios, varias *adj.* several

verdad *n.f.* truth; **¿No es verdad?** Isn't it true? Isn't it so?

ves *2d pers., s., (tú), pres. indic. of* **ver**; you see

vida *n.f.* life

vieron *3d pers., pl., pret. of* **ver**; they saw

ya *adv.* already

EJERCICIOS

I. Seleccione la respuesta correcta conforme al significado de la lectura en esta lección.
(Select the correct answer according to the meaning of the reading selection in this Work Unit.)

1. Clara y Francisco Rodríguez fueron a _____ el sábado pasado.
   (a) México (b) Australia (c) Inglaterra (d) la feria   _____

2. Delante de ellos, Clara y Francisco Rodríguez vieron
   (a) un anuncio (b) a una quiromántica (c) el porvenir (d) muchos secretos   _____

3. A Clara le gustaría mucho saber
   (a) si Francisco está dispuesto (b) el porvenir (c) cuando van a comer
   (d) cuando van a regresar a casa   _____

4. La quiromántica comienza a leer
   (a) el anuncio (b) un gran libro (c) las rayas de la mano (d) una carta   _____

5. La quiromántica ve en la raya de la fortuna de Clara que va a hacer un viaje
   (a) al Canadá (b) a Australia (c) a Puerto Rico (d) a los Estados Unidos   _____

6. Cuando la quiromántica examina la raya del corazón de la señora Rodríguez, ve
   que ésta (a) va a hacer un viaje (b) tiene dolor de cabeza (c) comienza a hacer
   preparaciones para un viaje (d) está enamorada de un hombre   _____

7. La señora Sabelotodo dice a Francisco que él está
   (a) enfermo (b) dispuesto (c) loco (d) enamorado   _____

8. Francisco está enamorado de
   (a) la quiromántica (b) Australia (c) su esposa (d) la señora Sabelotodo   _____

9. El señor Rodríguez paga _____ pesetas por las revelaciones.
   (a) diez (b) veinte (c) treinta (d) cien   _____

10. Cuando Clara y Francisco están afuera, dicen que
    (a) va a llover (b) van a regresar a casa (c) hace un tiempo magnífico
    (d) no aprendieron nada   _____

II. ¿Sí o No?

1. En la feria, Clara y Francisco se divirtieron mucho.   _____

2. Clara y Francisco entraron en la tienda de la quiromántica para saber el porvenir.   _____

3. Francisco no quiere entrar en la tienda de la quiromántica.   _____

4. Francisco creerá todo lo que dirá la quiromántica.   _____

5. Clara y Francisco están enamorados.   _____

III. Activities. Speaking Proficiency.

A. Review the story at the beginning of this Work Unit, then give a summary of it. You may begin, then let classmates continue by making at least one statement until the story has been summarized in their own words. You may want to start by saying: **Clara y Francisco Rodríguez fueron a la feria el sábado pasado** / Clara and Francisco Rodríguez went to the fair last Saturday.

B. After the story has been retold by you and your classmates, ask each other questions based on what happened in the story. Each classmate will ask one question and another student will answer. You may want to begin with: **¿Adónde fueron Clara y Francisco Rodríguez el sábado pasado?** / Where did Clara and Francisco Rodríguez go last Saturday?

IV. Singing and Dancing. Proficiency in Speaking and Writing.

Situation: At the fair where Clara and Francisco Rodríguez had their palms read, there was singing and dancing.

Look at the picture below and tell us what musical instruments the two men are playing, which of the two is singing, and other words and ideas of your own. Also, imagine that there are people dancing nearby. Are there many persons dancing? Are they having a good time? Does the guitarist sing well while he is strumming the guitar? Is he playing well? Words you will want to use: **tocar (tañer) la guitarra** / to play (strum) the guitar; **el, la guitarrista** / guitarist; **tocar el violín** / to play the violin; **el, la violinista** / violinist; **cantar** / to sing; **bailar** / to dance; **hay muchas personas que bailan** / there are many persons who are dancing; **hay músicos** / there are musicians.

After you have completed your oral presentation, write what you said on the lines below. Make at least three statements.

_____

_____

_____

ESTRUCTURAS DE LA LENGUA

TENSE NO. 7 IMPERFECTO DE SUBJUNTIVO (IMPERFECT SUBJUNCTIVE)

This past tense is used for the same reasons as the **presente de subjuntivo**—that is, after certain verbs, conjunctions, impersonal expressions, etc., which were explained and illustrated in Work Unit 10. The main difference between these two tenses is the time of the action.

If the verb in the main clause is in the present indicative or future or present perfect indicative or imperative, *the present subjunctive* or the *present perfect subjunctive* is used in the dependent clause—provided, of course, that there is some element that requires the use of the subjunctive.

However, if the verb in the main clause is in the imperfect indicative, preterit, conditional, or pluperfect indicative, the *imperfect subjunctive* (this tense) or *pluperfect subjunctive* is ordinarily used in the dependent clause—provided, of course, that there is some element that requires the use of the subjunctive.

EXAMPLES:

Insistí en que María lo **hiciera** / I insisted that Mary *do* it.

Se lo *explicaba* a María **para que lo comprendiera** / I was explaining it to Mary *so that she might understand it.*

NOTE that the *imperfect subjunctive* is used after **como si** to express a condition contrary to fact.

EXAMPLE:

Me habla como si **fuera** un niño / He speaks to me as if *I were* a child.

NOTE: In this last example, the subjunctive is used in English also for the same reason.

Finally, note that **quisiera** (the imperfect subjunctive or **querer**) can be used to express in a very polite way, *I should like:* **Quisiera hablar ahora** / I should like to speak now.

The imperfect subjunctive is regularly formed as follows:

For all verbs, drop the **ron** ending of the 3rd pers. pl. of the preterit and add the following endings:

ra, ras, ra;	OR	**se, ses, se;**
ramos, rais, ran		**semos, seis, sen**

The only accent mark on the forms of the imperfect subjunctive is on the 1st pers. pl. form **(nosotros)** and it is placed on the vowel that is right in front of the ending **ramos** or **semos**.

EXAMPLES:

Preterit 3rd pers. plural	Imperfect subjunctive
bebieron (beber)	**bebiera, bebieras, bebiera; bebiéramos, bebierais, bebieran**
	OR
	bebiese, bebieses, bebiese; bebiésemos, bebieseis, bebiesen
creyeron (creer)	**creyera, creyeras, creyera; creyéramos, creyerais, creyeran**
	OR
	creyese, creyeses, creyese; creyésemos, creyeseis, creyesen

dieron (dar)	**diera, dieras, diera;** **diéramos, dierais, dieran** OR **diese, dieses, diese;** **diésemos, dieseis, diesen**
dijeron (decir)	**dijera, dijeras, dijera;** **dijéramos, dijerais, dijeran** OR **dijese, dijeses, dijese;** **dijésemos, dijeseis, dijesen**
durmieron (dormir)	**durmiera, durmieras, durmiera;** **durmiéramos, durmierais, durmieran** OR **durmiese, durmieses, durmiese;** **durmiésemos, durmieseis, durmiesen**
hubieron (haber)	**hubiera, hubieras, hubiera;** **hubiéramos, hubieras, hubieran** OR **hubiese, hubieses, hubiese;** **hubiésemos, hubieseis, hubiesen**
hablaron (hablar)	**hablara, hablaras, hablara;** **habláramos, hablarais, hablaran** OR **hablase, hablases, hablase;** **hablásemos, hablaseis, hablasen**
hicieron (hacer)	**hiciera, hicieras, hiciera;** **hiciéramos, hicierais, hicieran** OR **hiciese, hicieses, hiciese;** **hiciésemos, hicieseis, hiciesen**
fueron (ir)	**fuera, fueras, fuera;** **fuéramos, fuerais, fueran** OR **fuese, fueses, fuese;** **fuésemos, fueseis, fuesen**
leyeron (leer)	**leyera, leyeras, leyera;** **leyéramos, leyerais, leyeran** OR **leyese, leyeses, leyese;** **leyésemos, leyeseis, leyesen**

recibieron (recibir)	**recibiera, recibieras, recibiera;** **recibiéramos, recibierais, recibieran** OR **recibiese, recibieses, recibiese;** **recibiésemos, recibieseis, recibiesen**
fueron (ser)	**fuera, fueras, fuera;** **fuéramos, fuerais, fueran** OR **fuese, fueses, fuese;** **fuésemos, fueseis, fuesen**
tuvieron (tener)	**tuviera, tuvieras, tuviera;** **tuviéramos, tuvierais, tuvieran** OR **tuviese, tuvieses, tuviese;** **tuviésemos, tuvieseis, tuviesen**

Using the first three examples given above **(beber, creer, dar),** the usual English equivalents are as follows:

(that I) might drink, (that you) might drink, (that he / she) might drink, *etc.*
(that I) might believe, (that you) might believe, (that he / she) might believe, *etc.*
(that I) might give, (that you) might give, (that he / she) might give, *etc.*

EJERCICIOS

I. **Alphabet soup. Find the imperfect subjunctive forms of the four verbs given below. They are all in the first and third persons singular. Review the above section on the formation of the imperfect subjunctive.**

dar   decir   leer   querer

D	I	E	R	A	L	A	E	I
I	A	E	A	R	E	J	I	D
D	J	I	E	R	Y	D	I	O
L	Y	E	R	A	E	N	A	M
P	R	E	T	Y	R	A	J	Y
D	I	J	E	P	A	L	C	O
Q	U	I	S	I	E	R	A	L

II. **Cambie el verbo en infinitivo al imperfecto de subjuntivo.** (Change the verb from the infinitive form to the imperfect subjunctive.)

Modelo: Clara entró en la tienda de la quiromántica para que ésta *leer* las rayas de su mano.

Escriba: leyera

1. Yo insistí en que María lo *hacer*. _____

2. Se lo explicaba a María para que lo *comprender*. _____

3. Ud. me habla como si *ser* un niño. _____

4. La madre pidió a la niña que *beber* la leche. _____

5. El señor Rodríguez exigió que Pedro *estudiar* sus lecciones. _____

6. Dudé que José lo *aprender*. _____

7. Me alegraba de que *venir* Elena. _____

8. Temí que el alumno no *decir* la verdad. _____

9. La profesora no creía que Roberto *contestar* correctamente. _____

10. Cristóbal esperaba que Adela *telefonear*. _____

III. **Acróstico. Complete enteramente en español los doce verbos expresados abajo en el imperfecto de subjuntivo, primera y tercera personas, en el singular.**
(**Acrostic.** In the boxes, complete entirely in Spanish the twelve verbs listed below in the imperfect subjunctive, first and third persons singular. Review the above section on the formation of this new tense.)

1. querer	4. reír	7. aprender	10. invitar
2. usar	5. olvidar	8. nacer	11. caer
3. insistir	6. matar	9. tener	12. abrir

1. Q
2. U
3. I
4. R
5. O
6. M
7. A
8. N
9. T
10. I
11. C
12. A

EXCLAMATORY ¡Qué . . . !

In English, when we exclaim *What a class! What a student!* we use the indefinite article *a* or *an.* In Spanish, however, we do not use the indefinite article:

¡Qué clase! ¡Qué alumno! ¡Qué alumna! ¡Qué idea!

If an adjective is used to describe the noun, we generally use **más** in front of the adjective, or **tan**, in order to intensify the exclamation:

¡Qué chica tan bonita! / What a pretty girl!
¡Qué libro más interesante! / What an interesting book!

When we use **¡Qué!** + an adjective, the meaning in English is *How . . . !*

¡Qué difícil es! / How difficult it is!

¿Para qué . . . ? and ¿Por qué . . . ?

Both of these interrogatives mean *why* but they are not used interchangeably. If by *why* you mean *for what reason,* use **¿por qué . . . ?** If by *why* you mean *for what purpose* (*what for?*) use **¿para qué . . . ?**

Juanita, ¿Por qué lloras? / Jeanie, why [for what reason] are you crying?
Mamá, ¿para qué tenemos uñas? / Mom, why [what for, for what purpose] do we have fingernails?
¿Para qué sirven los anteojos? / What [why, what for, for what purpose] are eyeglasses used for?

EJERCICIOS

I. Escriba cuatro frases empleando ¡Qué . . . ! (Write four sentences using **¡Qué . . . !** Refer to the above section for examples, as needed.)

1. ¡Qué _____ !   3. ¡Qué _____ !

2. ¡Qué _____ !   4. ¡Qué _____ !

II. Escriba dos oraciones empleando ¿Por qué . . . y dos oraciones empleando ¿Para qué . . . (Write two sentences using **¿Por qué . . .** and two sentences using **¿Para qué . . .**)

1. ¿Por qué _____ ?   3. ¿Para qué _____ ?

2. ¿Por qué _____ ?   4. ¿Para qué _____ ?

III. Conteste las siguientes preguntas con oraciones completas. (Answer the following questions in complete sentences.)

1. ¿Por qué lloras? _____

2. ¿Para qué sirven los anteojos? _____

_____

3. ¿Por qué llora el niño? _____

GUSTAR

(a) Essentially, the verb **gustar** means *to be pleasing to* . . .

(b) In English, we say, for example, *I like ice cream.* In Spanish, we say **Me gusta el helado;** that is to say, "Ice cream is pleasing to me" [To me ice cream is pleasing].

(c) In English, the thing that you like is the direct object. In Spanish, the thing that you like is the subject. Also, in Spanish, the person who likes the thing is the indirect object: to me, to you, *etc.*: **A Roberto le gusta el helado** / Robert likes ice cream; in other words, "To Robert, ice cream is pleasing to him."

(d) In Spanish, therefore, the verb **gustar** is used in the third person, either in the singular or plural, when you talk about something that you like—something that is pleasing to you. Therefore, the verb form must agree with the subject; if the thing liked is singular, the verb is third person singular; if the thing liked is plural, the verb **gustar** is third person plural: **Me gusta el café** / I like coffee; **Me gustan el café y la leche** / I like coffee and milk ["Coffee and milk are pleasing to me."]

(e) When you mention the person or the persons who like something, you must use the preposition **a** in front of the person; you must also use the indirect object pronoun of the noun which is the person:

A los muchachos y a las muchachas les gusta jugar / Boys and girls like to play; that is to say, "To play is pleasing to them, to boys and girls."

(f) Review the indirect object pronouns. They are: **me, te, le; nos, os, les.**

(g) Other examples:

Me gusta leer / I like to read.
Te gusta leer / You *(familiar)* like to read.
A Felipe le gusta el helado / Philip likes ice cream.
Al chico le gusta la leche / The boy likes milk.
A Carlota le gusta bailar / Charlotte likes to dance.
A las chicas les gustó el libro / The girls liked the book.
Nos gustó el cuento / We liked the story.
¿Le gusta a Ud. el español? / Do you like Spanish?
A Pedro y a Ana les gustó la película / Peter and Anna liked the film.
A mi amigo le gustaron los chocolates / My friend liked the chocolates; that is to say, the chocolates were pleasing [pleased] to him (to my friend).
A la Señora Rodríguez le gustan las subastas / Mrs. Rodríguez likes auction sales.

EJERCICIOS

I. Traduzca las siguientes oraciones. (Translate the following sentences into English.)

1. Me gusta el helado. _____

2. A Roberto le gusta el chocolate. _____

3. A Miguel le gusta la cereza. _____

4. Me gustan el café y la leche. _____

5. A los muchachos y a las muchachas les gusta jugar. _____

6. ¿Le gusta a usted leer? _____

336   7. Sí, me gusta leer. _____

8. ¿Te gusta comer? _____

9. ¿Le gusta a Ud. el español? _____

10. A Pedro y a Ana les gustó la película. _____

II. Conteste las siguientes preguntas afirmativamente con oraciones completas. En la oración (a) use la palabra Sí. En la oración (b) use la palabra tambíen, según los modelos.
(Answer the following questions affirmatively in complete sentences. In sentence (a) use the word **Sí.** In sentence (b) use the word **tambíen** (also), according to the models.)

   Modelos: a. ¿Le gusta a Ud. el helado? (Do you like ice cream?)
               b. ¿Y a los chicos? (And the boys?)

   Escriba: a. Sí. Me gusta el helado. (Yes, I like ice cream.)
             b. Sí. A los chicos, tambíen, les gusta el helado. (Yes. The boys also like ice cream.)

   1. a. ¿Le gusta a Ud. el español? _____

       b. ¿Y a los otros alumnos? _____

   2. a. ¿Te gusta leer? _____

       b. ¿Y a tu hermano? _____

   3. a. ¿A Carlota le gustan los pasteles y el helado? _____

   _____

       b. ¿Y a usted? _____

III. Varias palabras en una sola. Utilizando las letras en PUERTO RICO, ¿cuántas palabras puede usted escribir? Escriba cinco palabras, por lo menos. (Several words in one. Using the letters in **PUERTO RICO,** how many words can you write? Write five words, at least. Do you see **te** and **tu** in **PUERTO?** And **ir** in **RICO?**)

> **PUERTO RICO**

1. _____   2. _____   3. _____

    4. _____   5. _____

IV. Algunos alumnos confunden las palabras jueves y huevos. (Some students confuse the words jueves and huevos.)

jueves _n.m._ / Thursday
huevos _n.m., pl._ / eggs

Me gusta comer huevos los jueves. / I like to eat eggs on Thursdays.

Mnemonic Tip	**Jueves** is the day before **viernes; j** precedes **v** in the alphabet; **jueves** and **viernes** both end in **es.** **Huevos,** therefore, is the word that means eggs. Pronounce the j in **jueves** as the English *h* in *hello* but do not pronounce the *h* in **huevo** or **huevos.**

¿Qué palabras españolas confunde usted? ¿Puede Ud. dar un "mnemonic tip"? (What Spanish words do you confuse? Can you give a "mnemonic tip" so you can make a distinction to remember which means what?)

V. **En español hay muchas palabras que se escriben y se pronuncian idénticamente, pero un signo de acento es necesario para distinguir su significado.** (In Spanish there are many words that are written and pronounced identically, but an accent mark is needed to distinguish their meaning.)

   EJEMPLO:

   te *reflexive pronoun, 2nd person, singular* / yourself
   also direct & indirect object pronoun, 2nd person, singular / you, to you

   té *n.m.* / tea

   ¿Te gusta el té? / Do you like tea?

   ¿Cuántas palabras españolas puede Ud. decir y escribir? (How many Spanish words can you say and write?)

VI. **Practique el uso del verbo gustar en el condicional, por ejemplo: Me gustaría una taza de café / I would like a cup of coffee.** (Practice the use of the verb **gustar** in the conditional tense.)

EJEMPLO:

Me gustaría tener
(I would like to have)
{
mantequilla / butter
pan / bread
pimienta / pepper
chile con carne / chili with meat
sal / salt
una servilleta / a napkin
una rosa / a rose
una casita / a little house
una muñeca / a doll
un tenedor / a fork
}

¿Cuántos nombres puede Ud. añadir? (How many nouns can you add?)

Mnemonic Tip	**Una moneda** is a coin. **El dinero** is money. You need **dinero** to buy yourself a dinner.

VII. Humor. La adivinanza para hoy.

   (**Humor.** The riddle for today.)

Vuelo como un pájaro. ¿Qué soy? (I fly like a bird. What am I?)

Respuesta: _____

VIII. Expressing Love on Mother's Day. Proficiency in Speaking and Writing.

   Situation: Next Sunday is Mother's Day. Below, write your own card and give it to your mother or to some friend or relative who has been like a mother to you. Before you start, take a few minutes to gather your thoughts, jot down a few words in Spanish that you will use, then say them aloud.

   You may use your own words and ideas or the following: **a mi madre, con carlño** / to my mother, with love; **feliz Día de las Madres** / happy Mother's Day; **muchas alegrías siempre** / many joys always; **te quiero, Madre** / I love you, Mother; **deseo que (tú) tengas un feliz Día de las Madres** / I want you to have a happy Mother's Day; **en nuestra casa yo aprendí lo que es el amor** / in our house I learned what love is.

IX. Activities. Proficiency in Speaking and Writing.

A. Next Sunday is Mother's Day. You and your friend Carmen are talking about gifts you are planning to give to your mothers. Tell her four things you are considering, then write them on the lines.

1. _____   3. _____

2. _____   4. _____

B. You are on vacation in Mexico. You are very hungry this morning. Tell the hotel waiter six things that you would like to eat and drink for breakfast. Then write them on the lines.

1. _____   4. _____

2. _____   5. _____

3. _____   6. _____

C. Now you are having dinner in the hotel dining room. You are looking at the menu. Tell the waiter four vegetables you would like to have, then write them on the lines.

1. _____   3. _____

2. _____   4. _____

X. Proficiency in Writing.

Situation: It's your turn to go to the chalkboard in your Spanish class and write the forms only in the first person singular **(yo)** of the following verb tenses that you have practiced since Work Unit 1. The first verb, **hablar**, was done for you to get you started. Review the previous Work Units where they are all given or consult the Index and the Verb Tables in the back pages of this book, as needed.

	PRESENT INDICATIVE	PRESENT PROGRESSIVE	IMPERFECT INDICATIVE
hablar	yo hablo	yo estoy hablando	yo hablaba
aprender	_____	_____	_____
escribir	_____	_____	_____
decir	_____	_____	_____
hacer	_____	_____	_____

	PAST PROGRESSIVE	PRETERIT	FUTURE
hablar	yo estaba hablando	yo hablé	yo hablaré
aprender	_____	_____	_____
escribir	_____	_____	_____
decir	_____	_____	_____
hacer	_____	_____	_____

	POTENCIAL (CONDITIONAL)	PRESENT SUBJUNCTIVE	IMPERFECT SUBJUNCTIVE
hablar	yo hablaría	que yo hable	que yo hablara / hablase
aprender	_____	_____	_____
escribir	_____	_____	_____
decir	_____	_____	_____
hacer	_____	_____	_____

SEQUENCE OF TENSES WHEN THE SUBJUNCTIVE IS REQUIRED: A SUMMARY

When the verb in the main clause is in the:	The verb in the following clause (the dependent clause) most likely will be in the:
1. Present Indicative or Future or Present Perfect Indicative or Imperative (Command)	1. Present Subjunctive or Present Perfect Subjunctive
2. Conditional or a past tense (Imperfect Indicative or Preterit or Pluperfect Indicative)	2. Imperfect Subjunctive or Pluperfect Subjunctive

EXAMPLES:

Deseo que Ana cante / I want Anna to sing.

Le diré a Ana que baile / I will tell Anna to dance.

Le he dicho a Ana que cante y baile / I have said to Anna to sing and dance.

Dígale a Ana que cante y baile / Tell Anna to sing and dance.

Dudo que mi madre tome el tren / I doubt that my mother is taking (or will take) the train.

Dudo que mi madre haya tomado el tren / I doubt that my mother has taken the train.

Le gustaría al profesor que los alumnos hicieran los ejercicios / The professor would like the pupils to do the exercises.

Sentía que su madre estuviera enferma / I felt sorry that your mother was ill.

Dudé que mi madre hubiera tomado el tren / I doubted that my mother had taken the train.

SI CLAUSE: A SUMMARY OF CONTRARY-TO-FACT CONDITIONS

When the verb in the **Si** clause is:	The verb in the main or result clause is:
1. Present Indicative	1. Future

EXAMPLE:

Si tengo bastante tiempo, vendré a verle / If I have enough time, I will come to see you.

Note that the present subjunctive form of a verb is never used in a clause beginning with the conjunction *si*.

2. Imperfect Subjunctive (**–se** form or **–ra** form)	2. Conditional or Imperfect Subjunctive (**–ra** form)

EXAMPLE:
>   **Si yo tuviese** (or **tuviera**) **bastante tiempo, vendría a verle** / If I had enough
>   time, I would come to see you.
>
> OR: **Si yo tuviese** (or **tuviera**) **bastante tiempo, viniera a verle** / If I had enough
>   time I would come to see you.

3. Pluperfect Subjunctive
   (**–se** form or **–ra** form)

2. Conditional Perfect or Pluperfect
   Subjunctive (**–ra** form)

EXAMPLE:
>   **Si yo hubiese tenido** (or **hubiera tenido**) **bastante tiempo, habría venido a
>   verle** / If I had had enough time, I would have come to see you.
>
> OR: **Si yo hubiese tenido** (or **hubiera tenido**) **bastante tiempo, hubiera venido a
>   verle** / If I had had enough time. I would have come to see you.

XI. Read the following newspaper advertisement and answer the question under it.

COLOQUE

SU AVISO

CLASIFICADO

EN ESTE PERIÓDICO.

LLAME AL

1-800-123-4567

Who would be interested in this announcement?

A. Someone who needs advice by calling a 1-800 number.
B. Someone looking for a person named Al classified as missing.
C. Someone who wants to subscribe to a newspaper.
D. Someone interested in placing an announcement.

XII. Read the Spanish words in the advertisement on the following page about glass containers and answer the following question.

Why do the four well-informed consumers in this advertisement prefer containers made of glass rather than other kinds of containers for food products?

A. Glass is less expensive than other materials.
B. Glass is easy to manufacture.
C. Glass is more elegant than tin, paper, or plastic.
D. Glass is hygienic, it does not contaminate the food product in it, it preserves the contents better, and it lasts longer.

El consumidor tiene la palabra:

"Digan lo que quieran, el envase de vidrio para mí es el más cómodo. Puedo volverlo a cerrar y guardar tranquila lo que haya sobrado."

"Sólo el envase de vidrio no estropea el sabor de lo que contiene, por tiempo que pase. Sólo el vidrio no sabe absolutamente a nada."

"Para mí la principal ventaja del envase de vidrio es que se ve lo que se compra. Por eso, lo mejor siempre va envasado en vidrio. Clarísimo, ¿no?."

"Lo principal en un envase tiene que ser la higiene. Y en eso no conozco ningún tipo de envase, por nuevo que sea, que se pueda comparar al vidrio."

El consumidor bien informado ya prefiere envases de vidrio.

El vidrio es natural, higiénico, y no contamina ni altera los alimentos. Conserva mejor, más tiempo.

VIDRIO ES SALUD

Centro del Envase de Vidrio
Claudio Coello, 126, 2.º, Escalera-A, Madrid-6

TEST 6

PART ONE   Speaking Proficiency

Directions: Read the five situations given below. Take a few minutes to organize your thoughts about the words you are going to speak. Select three of the five situations. Before you begin to speak, you may review the Speaking and Writing Proficiency exercises that you practiced in this Work Unit.

1. **Situation:** Review the story at the beginning of this Work Unit, then give a summary of it. When you practiced this oral proficiency exercise in this Work Unit, other classmates added a statement in Spanish until the story was summarized. Here is your chance to give the entire summary yourself! Do you remember what your classmates said? You may want to start by saying: **Clara y Francisco Rodríguez fueron a la feria el sábado pasado.**

2. **Situation:** At the fair where Clara and Francisco Rodríguez had their palms read, there was singing and dancing. Using your own words and ideas, or the following suggestions, tell us a few things about the entertainment; for example, imagine that there are people dancing nearby. Are there many people dancing? Are they having a good time? Does the guitarist sing well while he is plucking on the guitar? Is he playing well? Is the violinst playing well? Did you sing and dance with them? Make at least three statements.

3. **Situation:** Next Sunday is Mother's Day. Make up your own card and give it to your mother or to some friend or relative who has been like a mother to you. Before you start, take a few minutes to gather your thoughts, jot down a few words in Spanish that you will use, then say them aloud. Make at least three statements.

4. **Situation:** Next Sunday is Mother's Day. You and your friend Carmen are talking about gifts you are planning to give to your mothers. Tell her four things you are considering. You may use your own words and ideas or the following, just for starters: **Pienso dar flores a mi madre. Quisiera darle una caja de chocolates.** Make at least three statements.

5. **Situation:** You are on vacation in Mexico. You are very hungry this morning. Tell the hotel waiter to bring you six things you would like to eat and drink for breakfast. Make at least three statements.

PART TWO   Listening Proficiency

Directions: Your teacher will read aloud four short paragraphs. Each one will contain only a few sentences. You will hear each paragraph twice. Then you will hear one question based on each. You will hear the question only once. It is printed below. Choose the best suggested answer based on what you heard and check the letter of your choice.

Selection Number 1

1. ¿Qué hicieron Clara y Francisco Rodríguez en la feria?

    A. Fueron a la feria el sábado pasado.

    B. Vieron varias exposiciones.

    C. Vendieron varias exposiciones.

    D. Nada comieron.

Selection Number 2

2. ¿Por qué entraron en la tienda de una quiromántica?

    A. para comprar muchas cosas

    B. para comer mucho

    C. porque Francisco entró con ella

    D. para que ella les leyera las rayas de la mano

Selection Number 3

3. ¿Quién está enamorada de su esposo?

    A. La Señora Sabelotodo

    B. Francisco

    C. Clara

    D. Francisco y la Señora Sabelotodo

Selection Number 4

4. ¿Qué comienza a hacer la Señora Sabelotodo?

    A. a hacer preparaciones para ir a Australia

    B. a leer las rayas de la mano de Clara

    C. a mirar fijamente la mano de Francisco

    D. a hacer un viaje

PART THREE   Reading Proficiency

Directions: In the following passage there are five blank spaces numbered 1 through 5. Each blank space represents a missing verb form or some other word. For each blank space, four possible completions are provided. Only one of them is grammatically correct and makes sense in the context of the passage.

First, read the passage in its entirety to determine its general meaning. Then read it a second time. For each blank space choose the completion that makes the best sense and is grammatically correct. Write its letter in the space provided.

Rosa López es una alumna _____ en mi clase de arte en la escuela. Es española.

    1. A. extranjero
         B. extranjera
         C. extranjeros
         D. extranjeras

Rosa acaba de _____ de su país natal, la República Argentina. Va a _____

    2. A. llegado   3. A. se queda
         B. llegando   B. quedarse
         C. llegó   C. quedando
         D. llegar   D. quedándola

aquí solamente un año. Yo _____ muy feliz. En mi escuela, Washington High

    4. A. soy
         B. estoy
         C. está
         D. iré

School, hay una _____ piscina pero en la escuela de Rosa en su país no hay piscina.

    5. A. gran
         B. grande
         C. grandes
         D. ninguna

PART FOUR   Writing Proficiency

Directions: Of the five situations in Part One (Speaking Proficiency) in this test, select three of them and write what you said on the lines below.

Situation 1 _____

_____

_____

Situation 2 _____

_____

_____

Situation 3 _____

_____

_____

Situation 4 _____

_____

_____

Situation 5 _____

_____

_____

¡Adiós, señor! ¡Hasta mañana, señor!

Work Unit 12

Have you ever received a note from a boy or girl in a class at school? In this scene, Pedro is reading a note that Lolita just passed to him.

Lolita

Pedro está en clase de matemáticas. Está leyendo una nota escondida en las páginas de su libro. He aquí la nota:

Pedro, querido mío,

 Detesto esta asignatura y detesto al profesor. Es un mal profesor de matemáticas. Es un hombre monstruoso.   5

 Te quiero, te amo, te adoro.

Lolita

El maestro de matemáticas dice a Pedro:

—Tú no has hecho la lección, tú no has escuchado nada esta mañana en la clase, tú no has aprendido nada hoy, tú no has escrito nada. No tienes nada en la   10 cabeza. ¿Qué tienes escondido en las páginas de tu libro?

—Nada, señor, nada.

—Sí, sí, tienes algo que estás leyendo. Es una nota, un billete como ayer y como anteayer. ¡Dámela!

Pedro se pone rojo. Mira hacia Lolita, su novia bonita, y ella le pide cariñosa-   15 mente con sus ojos azules, que Pedro no revele el amor secreto entre los dos, y que no entregue la nota al profesor.

En este momento, toca el timbre. La lección de matemáticas ha terminado. Todos los alumnos salen de la sala de clase inmediatamente y Pedro, también, con la nota escondida en las páginas de su libro.   20

Cuando Pedro está cerca de la puerta para salir, exclama:

—¡Adiós, señor! ¡Hasta mañana, señor! ¡A buen fin no hay mal principio!

En el pasillo, Lolita dice a Pedro:

—Querido mío, ¡eres magnífico!

—Lolita, te amo. ¿Qué haces esta noche? ¿Vamos al cine?   25

KEY WORDS AND PHRASES

¡A buen fin no hay mal principio! All's well that ends well!

adorar *v.* to adore

algo *indef. pron.* something

amar *v.* to love; **te amo** I love you.

amor *n.m.* love

anteayer *adv.* day before yesterday

aprendido *past part. of* **aprender; tú no has aprendido nada** you have learned nothing (you haven't learned anything).

asignatura *n.f.* subject, course

ayer *adv.* yesterday

azul, azules *adj.* blue; **con sus ojos azules** with her blue eyes

billete *n.m.* note

cariñosamente *adv.* tenderly, lovingly

cerca *adv.* near, close by; **cerca de la puerta** near the door

como *conj.* as, like

da *2d pers., s. (tú), imper. (command) of* **dar**; give

¡Dámela! Give it to me! **(da + me + la = dámela)**

detesto *1st pers., s., pres. indic. of* **detestar**; I detest

entregue *3d pers., s., pres. sub. of* **entregar** to hand over; **que Pedro no entregue la nota al profesor** that Peter not hand over the note to the teacher

eres *2d pers., s. (tú), pres. indic. of* **ser**; you are

escondido, escondida *adj.* hidden; **esconder** to hide

escrito *irreg. past part. of* **escribir; tú no has escrito nada** you have written nothing (you haven't written anything).

escuchado *past part. of* **escuchar; tú no has escuchado nada** you have listened to nothing (you haven't listened to anything).

esta *dem. adj., f.s.* this; **esta noche** this evening, tonight

fin *n.m.* end

haces *2d pers., s. (tú), pres. indic. of* **hacer; ¿Qué haces esta noche?** What are you doing tonight?

hacia *prep.* to, toward, in the direction of

has *2d pers., s. (tú), pres. indic. of* **haber**; you have

¡Hasta mañana! See you tomorrow!

he aquí ... here is ...

hecho *irreg. past part. of* **hacer**; done, made; **tú no has hecho la lección** you have not done the lesson.

le *indir. obj. pron., s.* to him, to you **(a Ud.)**

les *indir. obj. pron., pl.* to them, to you **(a Uds.)**

leyendo *pres. part. of* **leer;** reading; **tú estás leyendo** you are reading

maestro *n.m.* teacher

mal, malo *adj., m.* bad

mira *3d pers., s., pres. indic. of* **mirar**; he looks

monstruoso *adj.* monstrous

nada *indef. pron.* nothing

nota *n.f.* note

novia *n.f.* sweetheart

página *n.f.* page

pasillo *n.m.* hallway, corridor

pedir *v.* to ask (for), to request

pide *3d pers., s., pres. indic. of* **pedir**; she asks

poner *v.* to put; **ponerse** to become; **Pedro se pone rojo** Pedro blushes (his face gets red).

por *prep.* by, for

principio *n.m.* beginning

querer *v.* to want, wish, desire; like, love

querido mío my darling

quiero *1st pers., s., pres. indic. of* **querer**

revele *3d pers., s., pres. sub. of* **revelar** to reveal; **que Pedro no revele** that Pedro not reveal

salen *3d pers., pl., pres. indic. of* **salir**; they leave; **todos los alumnos salen de la sala de clase** all the students leave the classroom.

te *dir. obj. pron., 2d pers., s.* you; **te amo** I love you.

terminado *past part. of* **terminar;** ended; **la lección ha terminado** the lesson has ended.

tienes *2d pers., s. (tú), pres. indic. of* **tener**; you have

toca *3d pers., s., pres. indic. of* **tocar** to touch, knock, ring; **toca el timbre** the bell rings.

¿Vamos al cine? Shall we go to the movies?

EJERCICIOS

I. Seleccione la respuesta correcta conforme al significado de la lectura en esta lección. (Select the correct answer according to the meaning of the reading selection in this Work Unit.)

1. Pedro y Lolita están (a) en casa (b) en la biblioteca (c) en la hierba (d) en la escuela _____

2. Pedro está (a) estudiando su libro de matemáticas (b) escribiendo la lección (c) escuchando (d) enamorado de Lolita _____

3. Lolita está (a) enferma (b) estudiando (c) escribiendo (d) enamorada de Pedro _____

4. Lolita ha escrito (a) la lección de matemáticas (b) en la pizarra (c) una nota (d) una carta al maestro de matemáticas _____

5. En la nota Lolita dice que (a) a ella le gusta mucho la asignatura (b) el maestro de matemáticas es simpático (c) el maestro de matemáticas es un hombre monstruoso (d) quiere al profesor _____

II. ¿Sí o No?

1. Lolita piensa que Pedro es magnífico. _____

2. Pedro quiere a Lolita. _____

3. Lolita quiere a Pedro. _____

4. El maestro de matemáticas es muy amable. _____

5. El maestro de esta asignatura es un hombre monstruoso. _____

III. Sopa de letras. La palabra misteriosa (the mystery word). En esta sopa de letras, busque las palabras expresadas abajo. Las palabras pueden aparecer de derecha a izquierda, de izquierda a derecha, de abajo arriba y viceversa, y en diagonal. La palabra que queda es la palabra misteriosa y contiene cuatro letras.

(**Alphabet Soup.** In this alphabet soup, look for the words given below in two columns. The words can appear from right to left, from left to right, from bottom to top and vice versa, and diagonally. The word that remains unmarked in the grid is the mystery word and it contains four letters.)

A	D	O	R	A	R	B
M	A	F	H	L	L	U
A	Z	I	A	G	E	E
R	U	N	Y	O	S	N
E	L	L	A	S	O	Y
P	O	R	A	M	O	R
A	Y	E	R	M	A	L

adorar   fin
algo   hay
amar   soy
ayer   mal
azul   buen
por   les
ella

La palabra misteriosa es: _____

IV. Activities. Proficiency in Speaking and Writing.

A. You are on the phone telling a classmate what your impressions are of the new teacher in your mathematics class.

You may use your own words and ideas and/or any of the following: **Me gusta** or **No me gusta esta asignatura** / I like or I don't like this course; **el profesor/la profesora no ha explicado nada claramente** / the teacher has not explained anything clearly; or, **el profesor/la profesora ha explicado todo claramente** / the teacher has explained everything clearly.

There is a lot of static on the telephone and your listener is not sure of what you are saying. Write a note containing three statements about your impressions. Practice writing your note on the lines below.

La fecha / the date _____

Querido amigo (Querida amiga) _____,

_____

_____

_____

Tu amigo (amiga),

_____

B. A friend of yours is home in bed with a very bad cold. Write a get-well note expressing your feelings and best wishes. Use your own words and ideas and / or any of the following: **sentir** / to feel sorry; **Siento mucho que tú estés enfermo (enferma); ¿Cómo te sientes hoy?** / How do you feel today? **Tu madre me ha dicho que tú ...** / Your mother has said to me that you ...

_____

_____

_____

ESTRUCTURAS DE LA LENGUA

TENSE NO. 8: PERFECTO DE INDICATIVO (PRESENT PERFECT INDICATIVE)

This is the first of the seven compound tenses. This tense expresses an action that took place at no definite time in the past. It is also called past indefinite. It is a compound tense because it is formed with the present indicative of **haber** (the auxiliary or helping verb) plus the past participle of the verb you have in mind. Note the translation into English in the examples that follow.

(Yo) **he hablado** / *I have spoken.*
(Tú) no **has venido** a verme / *You have not come* to see me.
Elena **ha ganado** el premio / Helen *has won* the prize.

Es preciso saber las seis formas del verbo **haber** en el presente de indicativo para formar el perfecto de indicativo. (It is necessary to know the six forms of **haber** in the present indicative in order to form the present perfect indicative tense.)

SINGULAR	PLURAL
1. **he**	1. **hemos**
2. **has**	2. **habéis**
3. **ha**	3. **han**

PAST PARTICIPLE

A past participle is a verb form which, in English, usually ends in *-ed:* for example, *worked, talked, arrived*, as in *I have worked, I have talked, I have arrived.* There are many irregular past participles in English; for example *gone, sung*, as in *She has gone, We have sung.* In Spanish, a past participle is regularly formed as follows:

drop the **ar** of an **–ar** ending verb, like **trabajar**, and add **–ado: trabajado** / worked
drop the **er** of an **–er** ending verb, like **comer**, and add **–ido: comido** / eaten
drop the **ir** of an **–ir** ending verb, like **recibir**, and add **–ido: recibido** / received

Common Irregular Past Participles Are as Follows

Infinitive

Past Participle

abrir / to open — **abierto** / opened
caer / to fall — **caído** / fallen
creer / to believe — **creído** / believed
cubrir / to cover — **cubierto** / covered
decir / to say, to tell — **dicho** / said, told
descubrir / to discover — **descubierto** / discovered
deshacer / to undo — **deshecho** / undone
dovolver / to return (something) — **devuelto** / returned (something)
escribir / to write — **escrito** / written
hacer / to do, to make — **hecho** / done, made
imponer / to impose — **impuesto** / imposed
imprimir / to print — **impreso** / printed
ir / to go — **ido** / gone
leer / to read — **leído** / read
morir / to die — **muerto** / died
oír / to hear — **oído** / heard
poner / to put — **puesto** / put
rehacer / to redo, to remake — **rehecho** / redone, remade
reír / to laugh — **reído** / laughed
resolver / to resolve, to solve — **resuelto** / resolved, solved
romper / to break — **roto** / broken
traer / to bring — **traído** / brought
ver / to see — **visto** / seen
volver / to return — **vuelto** / returned

Uses of the Past Participle

To form the compound tenses:

As in English, the past participle is needed to form the compound tenses in Spanish, of which there are seven.

THE COMPOUND TENSES / LOS TIEMPOS COMPUESTOS

NAME OF TENSE IN SPANISH / ENGLISH	EXAMPLE (1ST PERS., SING.)
Perfecto de Indicativo / Present Perfect Indicative	**he hablado**
Pluscuamperfecto de Indicativo / Pluperfect Indicative	**había hablado**
Pretérito Anterior / Preterit Perfect	**hube hablado**
Futuro Perfecto / Future Perfect	**habré hablado**
Potencial Compuesto / Conditional Perfect	**habría hablado**
Perfecto de Subjuntivo / Present Perfect Subjunctive	**haya hablado**
Pluscuamperfecto de Subjuntivo / Pluperfect Subjunctive	**hubiera hablado** *or* **hubiese hablado**

To form the perfect infinitive: **haber hablado** / to have spoken

To form the perfect participle: **habiendo hablado** / having spoken

To serve as an adjective, which must agree in gender and number with the noun it modifies:
El señor Molina es muy respetado de todos los alumnos / Mr. Molina is very respected by all the students; **La señora González es muy conocida** / Mrs. González is very well known.

To express the result of an action with **estar** and sometimes with **quedar** or **quedarse: La puerta está abierta** / The door is open; **Las cartas están escritas** / The letters are written; **Los niños se quedaron asustados** / The children remained frightened.

To express the passive voice with **ser: La ventana fue abierta por el ladrón** / The window was opened by the robber.

EJERCICIOS

I. **Escriba el participio pasado (past participle) de los siguientes verbos.** (Write the past participle of the following verbs. Review above the formation of a past participle for regular **ar, er,** and **ir** verbs and the commonly used irregular past participles.)

1. trabajar _____

2. hablar _____

3. comer _____

4. aprender _____

5. recibir _____

6. vivir _____

7. abrir _____

8. caer _____

9. creer _____

10. cubrir _____

11. decir _____

12. escribir _____

13. hacer _____

14. ir _____

15. leer _____

16. morir _____

17. oír _____

18. poner _____

19. reír _____

20. resolver _____

II. **Escriba el gerundio (present participle) y el participio pasado (past participle) de los siguientes verbos según el modelo.** (Write the present participle and the past participle of the following verbs, according to the model. Review the formation of present participles in Work Unit 3.)

Modelo: descubrir ⟶ descubriendo descubierto

	gerundio	**participio pasado**
1. hacer	_____	_____
2. escribir	_____	_____
3. volver	_____	_____
4. devolver	_____	_____
5. poner	_____	_____
6. traer	_____	_____
7. abrir	_____	_____

8. ir _____ _____

9. romper _____ _____

10. traer _____ _____

11. ver _____ _____

12. decir _____ _____

13. hablar _____ _____

14. aprender _____ _____

15. vivir _____ _____

III. Escriba el infinitivo compuesto (perfect infinitive) de los siguientes infinitivos simples, según el modelo. (Write the perfect infinitive of the following simple infinitives, according to the model. Review the formation of the perfect infinitive on page 353.)

Modelo: hablar   **Escriba:** haber hablado

1. trabajar _____   4. comer _____

2. recibir _____   5. hacer _____

3. decir _____   6. escribir _____

IV. Escriba el gerundio compuesto (perfect participle) de los siguientes infinitivos simples, según el modelo. (Write the perfect participle of the following simple infinitives, according to the model. Review the formation of the perfect participle on page 353.)

Modelo: hablar   **Escriba:** habiendo hablado

1. amar _____   6. ir _____

2. escribir _____   7. decir _____

3. tener _____   8. romper _____

4. estudiar _____   9. ver _____

5. recibir _____   10. poner _____

V. Escriba las seis formas del verbo haber en el presente de indicativo. Es preciso saber estas formas para formar el perfecto de indicativo. (Write the six forms of the verb **haber** in the present indicative tense [three forms in the singular and three forms in the plural]. You must know these verb forms so you can form the present perfect indicative tense; for example, **he hablado** / I have spoken.)

SINGULAR   PLURAL

1. **Yo** _____ **hablado.**   1. **Nosotros (Nosotras)** _____ **hablado.**
2. **Tú** _____ **hablado.**   2. **Vosotros (Vosotras)** _____ **hablado.**
3. **Ud.**   3. **Uds.**
   él } _____ **hablado.**   **ellos** } _____ **hablado.**
   ella   **ellas**

355

VI. Traduzca al español.

1. I have spoken. _____

2. You **(tú)** have learned. _____

3. You **(Ud.)** have eaten. _____

4. He has come. _____

5. She has received. _____

6. Helen has left. _____

7. We have believed. _____

8. You **(vosotros)** have heard. _____

9. You **(Uds.)** have laughed. _____

10. They **(ellos)** have seen. _____

VII. Conteste las siguientes preguntas afirmativamente con oraciones completas. En la oración (a) use la palabra Sí. En la oración (b) use la palabra también, según los modelos.(Answer the following questions positively with complete sentences. In sentence (a) use the word **yes.** In sentence (b) use the word **also,** according to the models.)

Modelos: a. ¿Ha escrito Ud. la carta? (Have you written the letter?)
b. ¿Y Pablo? (And Pablo?)

Escriba: a. Sí, yo he escrito la carta. (Yes, I have written the letter.)
b. Sí, Pablo ha escrito, también, la carta. (Yes, Pablo has also written the letter.)

1. a. ¿Han comido los chicos? _____

b. ¿Y María? _____

2. a. ¿Ha abierto la profesora la ventana? _____

b. ¿Y usted? _____

3. a. ¿Han leído los alumnos la lección? _____

b. ¿Y Juana? _____

4. a. ¿Ha puesto María el vaso en la mesa? _____

_____

b. ¿Y nosotros? _____

5. a. ¿Ha devuelto Ud. el libro a la biblioteca? _____

_____

b. ¿Y su hermano? _____

6. a. ¿Han estudiado Uds. los problemas de matemáticas? _____

   _____

   b. ¿Y Carlos? _____

7. a. ¿Ha muerto el pobre viejo? _____

   _____

   b. ¿Y su esposa? _____

8. a. ¿Han bebido los niños la leche? _____

   _____

   b. ¿Y tú? _____

9. a. ¿Ha hablado el hombre monstruoso? _____

   _____

   b. ¿Y Pedro y Lolita? _____

10. a. ¿Ha escrito Lolita una nota? _____

   _____

   b. ¿Y las otras alumnas? _____

VIII. Acróstico. Complete cada palabra en español, escribiendo el participio (past participle) de los siguientes infinitivos simples.
(**Acrostic.** Complete each word in Spanish, writing the past participle of the following simple infinitives.)

1. escribir
2. nacer
3. abrir
4. morir
5. oír
6. reír
7. aprender
8. decir
9. obtener

1. **E**
2. **N**
3. **A**
4. **M**
5. **O**
6. **R**
7. **A**
8. **D**
9. **O**

IX. En español hay muchas palabras que se escriben y se pronuncian idénticamente, pero tienen distinto significado. (In Spanish there are many words that are written and pronounced identically, but an accent mark is necessary to distinguish their meaning.)

EJEMPLO:

pescado *past participle of* **pescar** / to fish
pescado *n.m.* / fish (caught for eating)
¡Mire este pescado! He pescado toda la mañana. / Look at this fish! I have fished all morning.

pescar / to fish
perfecto de indicativo

yo he pescado	nosotros hemos pescado
tú has pescado	vosotros habéis pescado
Ud.	Uds.
él } ha pescado	ellos } han pescado
ella	ellas

Mnemonic Tip	**El pez (los peces)** is the word for fish in the water; **el pescado** is the word for fish caught, taken out of the water intended for eating.

Una adivinanza / a riddle   Tengo ojos pero no tengo párpados. Vivo en el agua. ¿Quién soy?

X. En español hay muchas palabras que se escriben y se pronuncian idénticamente, pero tienen distinto significado. (In Spanish there are many words that are written and pronounced identically, but an accent mark is necessary to distinguish their meaning.)

EJEMPLO:

cuidado *n.m.* / care, concern
cuidado *past part.* of **cuidar** / to care for, take care of, look after
He cuidado la ropa con gran cuidado. / I have taken care of the clothes with great care.

perfecto de indicativo
cuidar / to care for

yo	he cuidado	nosotros	hemos cuidado
tú	has cuidado	vosotros	habéis cuidado
Ud.		Uds.	
él	} ha cuidado	ellos	} han cuidado
ella		ellas	

¿Tiene Ud. otros ejemplos?

XI. What have you done so far today? Proficiency in Speaking and Writing.

Situation: Your friend Roberto did not go to school yesterday and today because he is not feeling well. He has called you at home to find out what you have done so far in Spanish class.

You are playing the role of **Tú.** You may vary and extend this conversation with your own words and ideas. The English under the lines are suggestions of what you may be willing to say and write just to get you started with some enthusiasm. In this exercise you are practicing the present perfect tense, which is new in this Work Unit.

Roberto: **¿Qué has hecho en la clase de español hasta ahora?**
(What have you done in Spanish class until now?)

Tú: _____
(Tell him: I have talked a lot in Spanish.)

Roberto: **¿Y los otros alumnos, también?**

Tú: _____
(Some students have talked in Spanish and some have said nothing.)

Roberto: **¿Han escrito los alumnos en español en la pizarra?**

Tú: _____

_____
(María has written many times on the board and we have written in our notebooks.)

Roberto: **¿Quién ha ganado el premio hoy en la clase de español?**

Tú: _____
(I have won the prize today in Spanish class!)

Roberto: **¡Felicitaciones!** (Congratulations!) **¿Qué te ha dado la maestra?**

Tú: _____

_____
(She has given me a book of Spanish art. Robert, tell me, who has come to see you at home?)

Roberto:	**Nadie ha venido a verme.**
Tú:	_____
	(I will come to see you tonight. I will bring some ice cream with me.)
Roberto:	**¡Qué buena idea! ¡Hasta luego!**
Tú:	_____
	(See you later!)

XII. Physical Characteristics. Proficiency in Speaking and Writing.

Situation: It's your turn in Spanish class to say a few words about a person's physical characteristics.

Look at the picture below. It is a snapshot of Lolita and Pedro taken on their honeymoon in Acapulco, Mexico, ten years after they were graduated from high school. Do you remember how devoted they were to each other when they were classmates? Pedro protected her from embarrassment when he did not reveal the note she had written to him. Read again the story at the beginning of this work unit to refresh your memory.

Use your own words and ideas and/or any of the following suggestions: **pasar la luna de miel en Acapulco, centro turístico en México** / to spend the honeymoon in Acapulco, a tourist center in Mexico; **Lolita y Pedro están sonriendo** / Lolita and Pedro are smiling; **Están felices** / They are happy **¡Lolita es tan linda!** / Lolita is so pretty! **¡Y Pedro es tan guapo!** / And Pedro is so handsome! **Ella tiene el pelo negro y él tiene el pelo rubio** / She has black hair and he has blond hair; **Lolita lleva flores en el cabello y Pedro lleva anteojos** / Lolita is wearing flowers in her hair and Pedro is wearing eyeglasses; **Me parece que están divirtiéndose** / It seems to me that they are having a good time.

After you make at least three statements about Lolita and Pedro, you may write them on the lines for practice.

1. _____

2. _____

3. _____

Reprinted with permission of The Mexican Government Tourism Office, New York, N.Y.

XIII. The verbs in the following statements are in the preterit tense. Change them to the present perfect and rewrite the entire sentence.

Refer to page 352 where this new tense is introduced and explained with examples in Spanish and English. This time the verbs in the preterit are not identified by infinitive. Do you recognize the irregular ones? If not, review them in Work Unit 7. Also, look up the preterit in the regular and irregular verb tables beginning on page 448.

Modelo: Isabel *habló* mucho en la clase de español.
Isabel spoke a lot in Spanish class.

Escriba: Isabel *ha hablado* mucho en la clase de español.
Isabel has spoken a lot in Spanish class.

1. El camarero llegó. _____

2. María tomó el autobús. _____

3. Yo llegué a la escuela. _____

4. El niño bebió la leche. _____

5. Carmen recibió un regalo. _____

6. Yo almorcé en casa. _____

7. Ustedes anduvieron al cine. _____

8. Tú buscaste un taxi. _____

9. La maestra abrió la puerta. _____

10. La muchacha cayó. _____

11. Nosotros creímos la historia. _____

12. Ana cubrió la mesa. _____

13. Juana hizo una tontería. _____

14. Lolita dio algo a Pedro. _____

15. Ellos dijeron la verdad. _____

16. Usted estuvo enfermo. _____

XIV. Activities. Proficiency in Speaking and Writing.

A. Write a note containing at least three sentences and leave it on the kitchen table so members of your family know what you have done and where you have gone. After you write it, read it aloud to see how it sounds to you.

You may use your own words and ideas and/or any of the following, just to get you started: **Yo he hecho mis lecciones** / I have done my lessons; **He leído el periódico** / I have read the newspaper; **He bebido un vaso de leche** / I have drunk a glass of milk; **He escrito una carta a Miguel en México** / I have written a letter to Miguel in Mexico; **He ido a la oficina de correos** / I have gone to the post office; **Madre, ¡no te preocupes!** / Mother, don't worry!

1. _____

2. _____

3. _____

B. You are on a tourist bus in Madrid. The person sitting next to you has asked you where you have been and what you have done.

Using your own words and ideas and/or any of the following, tell the person that you have visited the Prado Museum / **He visitado el Museo del Prado**; you have seen the paintings of El Greco, Murillo, and Goya / **He visto los cuadros de El Greco, de Murillo, y de Goya**; you have eaten in good Spanish restaurants / **He comido en buenos restaurantes españoles**; and you have spent a lot of money / **He gastado mucho dinero.**

After you have made at least five statements using verbs in the preterit or present perfect indicative tense (the new tense in this Work Unit), write your statements on the following lines for practice.

1. _____

2. _____

3. _____

4. _____

5. _____

XV. Expressing Love on Father's Day. Proficiency in Speaking and Writing.

Situation: Next Sunday is Father's Day. Write your own card (next page) and give it to your father or to some friend or relative who has been like a father to you. Before you start, take a few minutes to gather your thoughts, jot down a few words in Spanish that you will use, then say them aloud to see how they sound to you.

You may use your own words and ideas, of course, and/or the following: **a mi padre, con cariño** / to my father, with love; **feliz Día de los Padres** / happy Father's Day; **muchas alegrías siempre** / many joys always; **te quiero, Padre** / I love you, Father; **deseo que (tú) tengas un feliz Día de los Padres** / I want you to have a happy Father's Day; **en nuestra casa yo aprendí lo que es el amor** / in our house I learned what love is.

HABER, HABER DE + INF., AND TENER

The verb **haber** (to have) is used as an auxiliary verb (or helping verb) in order to form the seven compound tenses, which are as follows:

Compound Tenses	Example (in the 1st person sing.)
Present Perfect (or Perfect) Indicative	**he hablado** (I have spoken)
Pluperfect (or Past Perfect) Indicative	**había hablado** (I had spoken)
Preterit Perfect (or Past Anterior)	**hube hablado** (I had spoken)
Future Perfect (or Future Anterior)	**habré hablado** (I will have spoken)
Conditional Perfect	**habría hablado** (I would have spoken)
Present Perfect (or Past) Subjunctive	**haya hablado** (I may have spoken)
Pluperfect (or Past Perfect) Subjunctive	**hubiera hablado** or **hubiese hablado** (I might have spoken)

The verb **haber** is also used to form the perfect (or past) infinitive: **haber hablado** (to have spoken). As you can see, this is formed by using the infinitive form of **haber** + the past participle of the main verb.

The verb **haber** is also used to form the perfect participle: **habiendo hablado** (having spoken). As you can see, this is formed by using the present participle of **haber** + the past participle of the main verb.

The verb **haber + de + inf.** is equivalent to the English use of "to be supposed to . . ." or "to be to . . ."

EXAMPLES:

> **María ha de traer un pastel, yo he de traer el helado, y mis amigos han de traer sus discos** / Mary is supposed to bring a pie, I am supposed to bring the ice cream, and my friends are to bring their records.

The verb **tener** is used to mean *to have* in the sense of *to possess* or *to hold:* **Tengo un perro y un gato** / I have a dog and a cat; **Tengo un lápiz en la mano** / I have (am holding) a pencil in my hand.

In the preterit tense, **tener** can mean *received:* **Ayer mi padre tuvo un choque** / Yesterday my father received a shock.

XVI. Making Preparations. Proficiency in Speaking and Writing.

Situation: You have already created your own Father's Day card. Now you and your sister Elena are making preparations for a party. In this dialogue you are talking about who is supposed to do what.

You are playing the role of **Tú.** You may vary and extend this conversation by adding your own words and ideas. The English under the lines are suggestions of what you may be willing to say and write just to get you started. In this exercise you are practicing the use of **haber de +** infinitive, which is presented above.

Elena:　　**Tenemos que hacer** (We have to make) **preparativos para una fiesta el Día de los Padres.**

Tú:　　　　_____
　　　　　　(I know it, Elena. We have to talk about gifts, too.)

Elena:　　**Yo he de preparar los pasteles.**
　　　　　　(I am supposed to prepare the pastries.)

Tú:　　　　_____
　　　　　　(And I am supposed to buy a necktie for Dad.)

Elena:　　**Yo sé que papá no quiere recibir una corbata. Prefiere tirantes** (suspenders).

Tú:　　　　_____
　　　　　　(Okay. I will buy suspenders for him.)

Elena:　　**Dime, ¿quién ha de traer el helado?**

Tú:　　　　_____
　　　　　　(Our Aunt Ágata is supposed to bring the ice cream.)

Elena:　　**¿Y nuestros primos** (cousins)**? ¿Qué han de traer?**

Tú:　　　　_____
　　　　　　(Our cousins are supposed to bring their records. We are going to sing and dance.)

Elena:　　**¿Y mamá? ¿Qué va a preparar?**

Tú:　　　　_____
　　　　　　(I can't tell you. It's a secret!)

HAY AND HAY QUE + INF.

The word **hay** is not a verb. You might regard it as an impersonal irregular form of **haber.** Actually, the word is composed of **ha** + the archaic **y,** meaning *there.* It is generally regarded as an adverbial expression because it points out that something or someone "is there." Its English equivalent is *There is . . .* or *There are . . . ,* for example:

Hay muchos libros en la mesa / There are many books on the table; **Hay una mosca en la sopa** / There is a fly in the soup; **Hay veinte alumnos en esta clase** / There are twenty students in this class.

Hay que + inf. is an impersonal expression that denotes an obligation and it is commonly translated into English as: *One must . . .* or *It is necessary to . . .*

EXAMPLES:

Hay que estudiar para aprender/ It is necessary to study in order to learn.
Hay que comer para vivir/ One must eat in order to live.

EJERCICIOS

I. Componga dos oraciones empleando haber + de + inf.(Write two sentences using **haber + de + inf.**)

1. _____

2. _____

II. Componga dos oraciones empleando hay.(Write two sentences using **hay.**)

1. _____

2. _____

III. Componga dos oraciones empleando hay que + inf.(Write two sentences using **hay que + inf.**)

1. _____

2. _____

IV. Componga dos oraciones empleando tener en el presente de indicativo y en el pretérito.(Write two sentences using **tener;** one in the present indicative and one in the preterit.)

1. _____

2. _____

V. Traduzca al inglés los siguientes verbos que están en el perfecto de indicativo. (Translate the following statements into English. The verbs are in the present perfect tense.)

Modelo: María ha trabajado.   **Escriba:** Mary has worked.

1. Yo he hablado. _____

2. Tú has aprendido. _____

3. Ud. ha escrito. _____

4. Él ha recibido. _____

5. Ella ha puesto. _____

6. Juan ha dicho. _____

7. Nosotros hemos viajado. _____

8. Vosotros habéis hecho. _____

9. Uds. han visto. _____

10. Ellos han ido. _____

11. Ellas han cubierto. _____

12. Juan y Juana han vuelto. _____

365

VI. **Dictado. Escriba las oraciones que su profesor de español va a leer.**
(**Dictation.** Write the sentences that your Spanish teacher is going to read.)

1. _____

2. _____

3. _____

VII. **¿Qué estás haciendo? ¿Dónde estás?** (What are you doing? Where are you?)

Respuesta: _____

VIII. **Culture. Appreciation of Spanish Literature. Reading Proficiency.**

Situation: Your neighbor, Mrs. Johnson, found the following short passage of Spanish literature in a book she was reading. She knows some Spanish vocabulary but she does not recognize Spanish verb forms. She doesn't know what they mean. She needs your help. As you know, the most important word in a sentence is the verb.

Directions: Read the literary passage below. All the verb forms in the paragraph have been presented in this book since Work Unit 1. Identify the verb forms with their subjects printed in **bold face type** by giving:

(a) the infinitive of the verb form
(b) the name of the tense
(c) the person and number of the verb form

Example: **son**   You write: (a) ser
(b) present indicative
(c) 3d person plural

Sancho salió, diciendo:
        (1)   (2)

—**Señor don Quijote, puede** entrar, que al punto que **yo llegué**, **se dieron todos** por
                        (3)   (4)   (5)

vencidos. **Baje, baje,** que **todos son** amigos y **hemos echado** pelillos a la mar, y nos
                (6)   (7)   (8)

están aguardando con una muy gentil **olla** de vaca, tocino, carnero, nabos y berzas, que
        (9)

está diciendo: "¡**Cóme**me, **cóme**me!"
    (10)   (11)

Selection from *Don Quijote de la Mancha*,
by Miguel de Cervantes

KEY WORDS AND PHRASES

aguardar *v.* to wait for, expect
al punto que at the moment when, just when
bajar *v.* to come down, get down
berza *n.f.* cabbage
carnero *n.m.* mutton
come *2d pers., s. (tú), imper. of* **comer**; **come
+ me = ¡Cómeme!** Eat me!
darse *refl. v.* to give oneself up, surrender;
  darse por vencidos to surrender as
  conquered
echar *v.* to throw
gentil *adj.* nice, pleasant
mar *n.m.* sea
nabos *n.m., pl.* turnips
olla *n.f.* pot, kettle
pelillos *n.m.* trifles; **echar pelillos al mar** to
  bury the hatchet (to throw trifles, disagree-
  ments into the sea)

poder *v.* to be able, can
que *conj.* because [short for **porque**];
  que al punto que because just when
que *rel. pron.* which, that; **que está
  diciendo** which [the pot of food]
  is saying
que todos son because they are all
salir *v.* to go out, to come out
se dieron todos por vencidos they all
  gave up, considering themselves beaten,
  conquered
tocino *n.m.* bacon
todos *pron.* all [all the men]
vaca *n.f.* beef
vencidos *adj.* conquered

Now you are ready to identify the following verb forms according to the example given above. They are numbered from **(1)** to **(11).** The numbers match the numbers under the verb forms in the above passage. Did you enjoy reading this short, humorous literary selection from *Don Quijote de la Mancha* by Cervantes?

(1) salió
  (a) _____
  (b) _____
  (c) _____

(2) diciendo
  (a) _____
  (b) _____
  (c) _____

(3) puede
  (a) _____
  (b) _____
  (c) _____

(4) llegué
  (a) _____
  (b) _____
  (c) _____

(5) se dieron
  (a) _____
  (b) _____
  (c) _____

(6) baje
  (a) _____
  (b) _____
  (c) _____

(7) son
  (a) _____
  (b) _____
  (c) _____

(8) hemos echado
  (a) _____
  (b) _____
  (c) _____

(9) están aguardando
  (a) _____
  (b) _____
  (c) _____

(10) está diciendo
  (a) _____
  (b) _____
  (c) _____

(11) come
  (a) _____
  (b) _____
  (c) _____

IX. Activities. Proficiency in Speaking.

A. Review the story at the beginning of this Work Unit, then give a summary of it. You may begin, then let classmates continue by making at least one statement until the story has been summarized in their own words. You may want to start by saying: **Pedro está en clase de matemáticas. Está leyendo una nota escondida en las páginas de su libro. Lolita escribió la nota.**

B. After the story has been retold by you and your classmates, ask each other questions based on what happened in the story. Each classmate will ask one question and another student will answer. You may want to begin with: **¿Dónde está Pedro? ¿Qué está leyendo?**

TEST 7

PART ONE   Speaking Proficiency

Directions: Read the five situations given below. Take a few minutes to organize your thoughts about the words you are going to speak. Select three of the five situations. Before you begin to speak, you may review the Speaking and Writing Proficiency exercises that you practiced in this Work Unit.

1. **Situation:** You are on the phone telling a classmate what your impressions are of the substitute teacher while your Spanish teacher is on sick leave. Make at least three statements. When using verbs, try to make use of the present perfect tense (new in this Work Unit) as well as the present tense. You may want to consider saying the following: The new Spanish teacher has not explained anything clearly; there are students who talk in English; there are students who go out of the classroom without permission and they do not return to class.

2. **Situation:** Your classmate Carlota is in the hospital because of an illness that will require surgery. There is a telephone at her bedside within her reach. Call her up and make at least three statements. You may want to use the following suggestions: **Siento mucho que tú estés enferma en el hospital; ¿Cómo te sientes hoy? Voy a verte esta tarde; Tu madre me ha dicho que tú ...**

3. **Situation:** Your friend Roberto did not go to school yesterday and today for personal reasons. He has called you at home to find out what you have done so far in Spanish class. When using verbs, try to make use of the present perfect tense (new in this Work Unit) as well as the present tense; for example, I have talked a lot in Spanish / **He hablado mucho en español;** I have written in Spanish on the chalkboard / **He escrito en español en la pizarra.**

4. **Situation:** It's your turn in Spanish class to say a few words about a person's physical characteristics. Take another look at the snapshot of Lolita and Pedro taken on their honeymoon in Acapulco, Mexico. It is in Exercise XII in this unit. In at least three statements, tell us something about their physical characteristics.

5. **Situation:** You are on a tourist bus in Madrid. The person sitting next to you has asked you where you have been and what you have done. Make at least three statements in Spanish.

PART TWO   Listening Proficiency

Directions: Your teacher will read aloud four short paragraphs. Each one will contain only a few sentences. You will hear each paragraph twice. Then you will hear one question based on each. You will hear the question only once. It is printed below. Choose the best suggested answer based on what you heard and check the letter of your choice.

Selection Number 1

1. ¿Qué hace Pedro?

    A. Está en la clase de matemáticas.

    B. La nota es de Lolita.

    C. La nota está escondida en las páginas de su libro.

    D. Lee una nota.

Selection Number 2

2. ¿Qué ha hecho Pedro en la clase de matemáticas esta mañana?

    A. Ha escuchado.

    B. Ha escrito.

C. Ha hablado.

D. Nada.

Selection Number 3

3. ¿De qué color son los ojos de Lolita?

    A. bonitos

    B. azules

    C. rojos

    D. su novia

Selection Number 4

4. ¿Cuándo terminó la lección?

    A. cuando tocó el timbre

    B. cuando Pedro se puso rojo

    C. cuando los alumnos entraron en la sala de clase

    D. la lección de matemáticas

PART THREE   Reading Proficiency

Directions: In the following passage there are five blank spaces numbered 1 through 5. Each blank space represents a missing verb form or some other word. For each blank space, four possible completions are provided. Only one of them is grammatically correct and makes sense in the context of the passage.

First, read the passage in its entirety to determine its general meaning. Then read it a second time. For each blank space choose the completion that makes the best sense and is grammatically correct. Write its letter in the space provided.

El maestro dice a Pedro:

—Tú no has _____ la lección. Tú no has _____ nada esta mañana en la

    1. A. hacer   2. A. escuchar

       B. hace   B. escucha

       C. haces   C. escuchas

       D. hecho   D. escuchado

clase. Tú no _____ nada en el cuaderno. Pedro se _____ rojo. Mira hacia

    3. A. he escrito   4. A. pone

       B. ha escrito   B. pones

       C. has escrito   C. pongo

       D. escribiendo   D. puede

Lolita, su novia bonita, y ella _____ pide cariñosamente con sus ojos azules, que Pedro

    5. A. lo

       B. la

       C. le

       D. les

no revele el amor secreto entre los dos, y que no entregue la nota al profesor.

PART FOUR   Writing Proficiency

Directions: Of the five situations in Part One (Speaking Proficiency) in this test, select three of them and write what you said on the lines below.

Situation 1 _____

_____

_____

Situation 2 _____

_____

_____

Situation 3 _____

_____

_____

Situation 4 _____

_____

_____

Situation 5 _____

_____

_____

Cuando el gato va a sus devociones, bailan los ratones.

El apetito se abre al comer.

Veinte proverbios (refranes)

When you are speaking Spanish at a party or any kind of social gathering, you may find it appropriate to say a proverb or two. Spanish-speaking persons like to use proverbs to make a point in certain situations. Here are a few useful proverbs. The word **refrán** (**refranes** in the plural) is another word for **proverbio.**

A Dios rogando y con el mazo dando / Put your faith in God and keep your powder dry. OR: Praise the Lord and pass the ammunition.

El apetito se abre al comer / The more you have, the more you want; *ie.,* Appetite comes while eating.

Cuando el gato va a sus devociones, bailan los ratones / When the cat is away, the mice will play.

Dicho y hecho / No sooner said than done.

Dime con quien andas y te diré quien eres / Tell me who your friends are and I will tell you who you are.

La práctica hace maestro al novicio / Practice makes perfect.

El que mucho abarca poco aprieta / Do not bite off more than you can chew.

El que no se aventura no cruza la mar / Nothing ventured, nothing gained.

El tiempo da buen consejo / Time will tell.

Más vale pájaro en mano que ciento volando / A bird in the hand is worth two in the bush.

Más vale tarde que nunca / Better late than never.

Mientras hay vida hay esperanza / Where there is life there is hope.

Mucho ruido y pocas nueces / Much ado about nothing.

Perro que ladra no muerde / A barking dog does not bite.

Piedra movediza, el moho no la cobija / A rolling stone gathers no moss.

Quien canta su mal espanta / When you sing you drive away your grief.

Quien siembra vientos recoge tempestades / If you sow the wind, you will reap the whirlwind.

Si a Roma fueres, haz como vieres / When in Rome do as the Romans do. [Note that it is not uncommon to use the future subjunctive in proverbs, as in *fueres* (*ir* or *ser*) and *vieres* (*ver*).]

Tal madre, tal hija / Like mother, like daughter.

Tal padre, tal hijo / Like father, like son.

KEY WORDS AND PHRASES

abarcar *v.* to grasp all, take in all
abrirse *refl. v.* to open itself up
andar *v.* to walk
apretar *v.* to hold on to, hold tight; **aprieta** *3d pers., s., pres. indic.*
aventurarse *refl. v.* to venture, risk
cobijar *v.* to cover up
comer *v.* to eat; **al comer** while eating

como *conj.* as
consejo *n.m.* advice, counsel
cruzar *v.* to cross
da *3d pers., s., pres. indic. of* **dar**; gives
dando *pres. part. of* **dar**; giving; **con el mazo dando** hammering away with a mallet
devociones *n.f., pl.* devotions (prayers)

di *2d pers., s., imper. (command) of* **decir**; tell; **di + me = dime** / tell me
dicho *past part. of* **decir**; said
Dios God
diré *1st pers., s., fut. of* **decir**; **te diré** I will tell you
el que *pron.* the one who, the person who, he who
eres *2d pers., s., pres. indic. of* **ser**; you are
espantar *v.* to chase away, drive away, scare away
haz *2d pers., s., imper. (command) of* **hacer**; do
hecho *past part. of* **hacer**; done
ladrar *v.* to bark
maestro *n.m.* master
mal *n.m.* misfortune, grief
mar *n.m.f.* sea
mazo *n.m.* mallet, heavy wooden hammer
moho *n.m.* moss

morder *v.* to bite
movediza *adj., f.* rolling
muerde *3d pers., s., pres. indic. of* **morder**; bites
novicio *n.m.* novice, beginner
nuez, nueces *n.f., s., pl.* walnut, walnuts
piedra *n.f.* stone
poco *adv.* little, not much; **pocas** *adj., f.* few
quien *pron.* who, whom
ratón *n.m.* mouse; **los ratones** mice
rogar *v.* to pray, beg; **rogando** *pres. part.*; praying
ruido *n.m.* noise
se abre *3d pers., s., pres. indic. of* **abrirse**; opens up
sembrar *v.* to sow, to seed; **siembra** *3d pers., s., pres. indic.*
tal *adj.* such
valer *v.* to be worth; **vale** *3d pers., s., pres. indic.*

EJERCICIOS

I. Escriba en español los siguientes refranes.

1. When the cat is away, the mice will play. _____

    _____

2. Tell me who your friends are and I will tell you who you are. _____

    _____

3. Practice makes perfect. _____

    _____

4. Time will tell. _____

5. A bird in the hand is worth two in the bush. _____

    _____

6. Better late than never. _____

7. A barking dog does not bite. _____

8. Much ado about nothing. _____

9. When in Rome do as the Romans do. _____

10. Like father, like son. _____

II. Llene los blancos con la palabra correcta según los refranes de esta lección.(Complete the sentences with the missing words according to the Spanish proverbs you studied above.)

1. A Dios _____ y con el mazo dando.

2. Cuando el _____ va a sus devociones, _____ los ratones.

3. El tiempo da _____ consejo.

4. Perro _____ ladra no _____ .

5. Si a Roma _____ , haz como _____ .

6. Más vale _____ que _____ .

7. Quien _____ su mal _____ .

8. La práctica hace maestro _____ novicio.

9. Dicho y _____ .

10. Tal padre, tal _____ .

III. Una los refranes en inglés con los equivalentes en español.(Increase your vocabulary power. Match the English proverbs with the Spanish.)

1. Better late than never.   _____ Mucho ruido y pocas nueces.

2. Time will tell.   _____ Perro que ladra no muerde.

3. No sooner said than done.   _____ Más vale tarde que nunca.

4. Much ado about nothing.   _____ El tiempo da buen consejo.

5. A barking dog does not bite.   _____ Dicho y hecho.

6. The more you have, the more you want.   _____ El apetito se abre al comer.

IV. Culture. Spanish Proverbs. Proficiency in Speaking and Writing.

Situation: The fun activity today in class is to see who can complete a Spanish proverb that a student begins. The one who completes the most wins a prize **(ganar el premio).** You are playing the role of **Tú.** After this game is completed, you may write the Spanish words on the lines. Later, switch roles with the other players.

La maestra (El maestro): **Bueno. Ahora, ¿quién quiere comenzar un proverbio español? ¿Quién quiere completarlo?**

Tú: _____
(Me! Me! I want to begin a Spanish proverb. Juan can can complete it.)

La maestra (El maestro): **Está bien. Puedes comenzar.**

Tú: _____
(Better late...)

La maestra (El maestro): **¡Excelente! Juan, completa el refrán, por favor.**

375

Juan:	**No me acuerdo.** (I don't remember.)
La maestra (El maestro):	**Anita, completa el refrán, por favor.**
Anita:	**No me acuerdo.**
José:	**¡Yo sé! ... es ... que nunca. ¡Más vale tarde que nunca!**
La maestra (El maestro):	**¡Bravo, José!**
Tú:	_____ (Now it's my turn.)
La maestra (El maestro):	**Bueno. Puedes comenzar.**
Tú:	**Dime con quien andas y ...**
Carmen:	**¡Yo sé! ... es ... te diré quien eres. ¡Dime con quien andas y te diré quien eres!**
La maestra (El maestro):	**¡Excelente!**
Tú:	_____ (Who has won the prize, señora/señor?)
La maestra (El maestro):	**Nadie. Vamos a continuar mañana con los otros estudiantes.**

V. Culture. Spanish Proverbs. Proficiency in Speaking and Writing.

Say a proverb in Spanish that would make a point in the following situations. Then write it on the line.

A. Situation: You just arrived twenty minutes late to Spanish class for a test. What might the teacher say to you?

_____

B. Situation: It's time for Pepe to practice his violin lessons but he's not in the mood. What might his mother say to him?

_____

C. Situation: Anita tells her father that she doesn't feel like having dinner because she doesn't have an appetite just now. What might her father say to her?

_____

D. Situation: The Spanish teacher tells the class that he has to leave the room for about ten minutes to make an important phone call in the main office. What might one of the students say when he is out of the room?

_____

E. Situation: Señorita Aquino is not sure if she ought to marry José Robles who has proposed to her. She needs some advice and time to think about it. What would her best girlfriend say to her?

_____

VI. Culture. Spanish Proverbs. Proficiency in Writing.

Situation: Now it's your turn. Review Exercise V. Write two situations in English and the Spanish proverbs that would apply to them.

1. Situation: _____

_____

Spanish proverb: _____

2. Situation: _____

_____

Spanish proverb: _____

VII. Reading Proficiency.

Read the following newspaper announcement and answer the questions under it.

1. Qué personas se interesan en este aviso?

    A. Personas de habla inglesa
    B. Personas de habla española
    C. Cuotas semanales
    D. Cursos conversacionales

2. On what days of the week are classes held?

    A. Saturdays only
    B. Sundays only
    C. Mondays only
    D. Saturdays and Sundays

3. What kind of classes are being advertised?

    A. Conversational English
    B. Conversational Spanish
    C. Reading skills
    D. Writing skills

VIII. Proficiency in Reading and Writing.

Read the following newspaper announcement and answer the questions under it.

Reprinted with permission of *EL DIARIO/LA PRENSA*, New York, N.Y.

1. As examples, what kinds of articles does this store accept?

    A. Household furniture
    B. Rare books
    C. Clocks, watches, and fur coats
    D. Rare caged birds

2. In this advertisement, find the Spanish words for *pawned articles* and write them on the line.

_____

3. Find the Spanish words for *Bring us your (pl.)* and write them on the line.

_____

4. Find the Spanish expression for *instantly* and write it on the line.

_____

5. Find the Spanish words for *at good prices* and write them on the line.

_____

ESTRUCTURAS DE LA LENGUA

TENSE NO. 9: PLUSCUAMPERFECTO DE INDICATIVO (PLUPERFECT OR PAST PERFECT INDICATIVE)

This is the second of the compound tenses. In Spanish and English, this past tense is used to express an action that happened in the past *before* another past action. Since it is used in relation to another past action, the other past action is ordinarily expressed in the preterit. However, it is not always necessary to have the other past action expressed, as in example no. 2 below.

In English, this tense is formed with the past tense of *to have* (had) plus the past participle of the verb you have in mind. In Spanish, this tense is formed with the imperfect indicative of **haber** plus the past participle of the verb you have in mind. Note the translation into English in the examples that follow.

1. Cuando **llegué** a casa, mi hermano **había salido** / When I *arrived* home, my brother *had gone out*.

NOTE: *First*, my brother went out; *then*, I arrived home. Both actions happened in the past. The action that occurred in the past *before* the other past action is in the pluperfect, and in this example it is *my brother had gone out* (**mi hermano había salido**).

NOTE ALSO that **llegué** (*I arrived*) is in the preterit because it is an action that happened in the past and it was completed.

2. Juan lo **había perdido** en la calle / John *had lost* it in the street.

NOTE: In this example, the pluperfect indicative is used even though no other past action is expressed. It is assumed that John *had lost* something **before** some other past action.

Es preciso saber las seis formas del verbo **haber** en el imperfecto de indicativo para formar el pluscuamperfecto de indicativo. (It is necessary to know the six forms of the verb **haber** in the imperfect indicative in order to form the pluperfect indicative tense. They are as follows. Say them aloud at least three times.)

SINGULAR	PLURAL
1. **había**	1. **habíamos**
2. **habías**	2. **habíais**
3. **había**	3. **habían**

I. Providing Information. Proficiency in Speaking and Writing.

Situation: You telephoned your friend Clara but she was not at home. You recorded a message on her telephone answering machine / **el teléfono con contestador y grabador automáticos.**

You provided her with the information she *had requested* earlier in the day.

First, say the Spanish words aloud, then write them on the lines. You may vary and extend the message using your own words and ideas. Use *tú* because you are talking to your friend.

Hi, Clara! ... Your friend María is speaking ... This morning you talked to me about

_____

my brother Juan ... I don't know where he is ... When I arrived home, my brother had

_____

gone out ... My mother and father had gone out, too ... When you telephoned, I had

_____

gone to the movies ... Call me soon! **(¡Llámame pronto!)** *I will tell you more!*

_____

INFINITIVES

Definition:

In English, an infinitive is identified as a verb with the preposition *to* in front of it: *to talk, to eat, to live.* In Spanish, an infinitive is identified by its ending: those that end in **–ar, –er, –ir,** for example, **hablar** (to talk, to speak), **comer** (to eat), **vivir** (to live).

Negation: To make an infinitive negative, place **no** in front of it: **No entrar** / Do not enter; **No fumar** / Do not smoke or No smoking; **No estacionar** / Do not park or No Parking.

As a verbal noun: In Spanish, an infinitive may be used as a noun. This means that an infinitive may be used as a subject, a direct object, a predicate noun, or object of a preposition. A verbal noun is a verb used as a noun.

EXAMPLES:

● **As a subject: Ser o no ser es la cuestión** / To be or not to be is the question. In this sentence, the subject is **ser** and **no ser.**

● **El estudiar es bueno** or **Estudiar es bueno** / Studying (to study) is good. Here, when the infinitive is a subject and it begins the sentence, you may use the definite article **el** in front of the infinitive or you may omit it.

But if the sentence does not begin with the infinitive, do not (as a general rule) use the definite article **el** in front of it: **Es bueno estudiar** / It is good to study.

● **As a direct object: No deseo comer** / I do not want to eat. Here the infinitive **comer** is used as a noun and it functions as the direct object of the verb **deseo.**

● **As a predicate noun: Ver es creer** / Seeing is believing (To see is to believe). Here, the infinitive **ver** is used as a noun and it functions as the subject. The infinitive **creer** is used as a noun and it functions as the predicate noun because the verb is of a form of **ser**, which takes a predicate noun or predicate adjective.

Do you know what these grammatical terms mean? A predicate noun is a noun that has the same referent as the subject; in other words, the predicate noun and the subject are pretty much the same thing; for example, in English: He is a father. A predicate adjective is an adjective that is attributive to the subject; in other words, the predicate adjective describes the subject in some way; for example, in English: She is pretty; She is tall. A predicate adjective is also known as an attribute complement because, as an adjective, it is attributive to the subject and it complements (describes) it in some way.

One last comment: In English, we can use an infinitive as a verbal noun, as in the above examples. In English, we can also use a gerund as a noun. A gerund in English looks like a present participle (ends in –ing, like *seeing, believing*) and it is used as a noun. But in Spanish, we do not use gerunds as nouns; we use only infinitives as nouns, as in the above examples. The Spanish word **gerundio** is normally translated into English as *gerund*. In a word, when we use a gerund as a noun in English its equivalent use is the infinitive in Spanish: Seeing is believing / **Ver es creer.**

As object of a preposition: después de llegar / after arriving. Here, the infinitive (verbal noun) **llegar** is object of the preposition **de.** In English, the word *arriving* in this example is a present participle, not a gerund. In English, present participles and gerunds both end in *-ing* but there is a distinct difference in their use. The point here is that in Spanish, only an infinitive can be used as a verbal noun, not a present participle and not a gerund in the English sense of these two terms.

In Spanish, an infinitive is ordinarily used after such verbs as, **dejar, hacer, mandar,** and **permitir** with no preposition needed: **Luis dejó caer sus libros** / Louis dropped his books; **Mi madre me hizo leerlo** / My mother made me read it; **Mi padre me mandó comerlo** / My father ordered me to eat it; **Mi profesor me permitió hacerlo** / My teacher permitted me to do it. Note that when **dejar** is followed by the preposition **de** it means *to stop* or *to cease*: **Luis dejó de trabajar** / Louis stopped working.

The verb **pensar** is directly followed by an infinitive with no preposition required in front of the infinitive when its meaning is *to intend:* **Pienso ir a Chile** / I intend to go to Chile.

Ordinarily, the infinitive form of a verb is used right after a preposition: **Antes de estudiar, Rita telefoneó a su amiga Beatriz** / Before studying, Rita telephoned her friend Beatrice; **El alumno salió de la sala de clase sin decir nada** / The pupil left the classroom without saying anything. Here, note **de estudiar** and **sin decir.**

The infinitive form of a verb is ordinarily used after certain verbs of perception, such as **ver** and **oír: Las vi salir** / I saw them go out; **Las oí cantar** / I heard them singing.

After **al,** a verb is used in the infinitive form: **Al entrar en la escuela, Dorotea fue a su clase de español** / Upon entering the school, Dorothy went to her Spanish class.

The perfect infinitive (also known as the past infinitive) is formed by using **haber** in its infinitive form + the past participle of the main verb: **haber hablado** (to have spoken), **haber comido** (to have eaten), **haber escrito** (to have written).

EJERCICIOS

I. Writing Proficiency. Write the Spanish words on the lines for the English words under them.

1. _____ es la cuestión.
   (To be or not to be)

2. _____ es bueno.
   (Studying)

3. _____ estudiar.
   (It is good)

4. _____ es _____.
   (Seeing)   (believing)

5. _____ salir.
   (I don't want)

6. _____ fumar.
   (It is not good)

II. Increase your vocabulary power. Match the following.

1. **antes de llegar**

2. **después de llegar**

3. **dejar caer**

4. **dejar de**

5. **sin decir nada**

6. **al llegar**

7. **haber llegado**

8. **pensar llegar**

9. **Las vi salir.**

10. **Las oí cantar.**

_____ to intend to arrive

_____ I heard them singing.

_____ to stop, to cease

_____ before arriving

_____ to have arrived

_____ without saying anything

_____ after arriving

_____ I saw them go out.

_____ to drop

_____ upon arriving

III. Pictures. Proficiency in Speaking and Writing.

Situation: It's your turn to talk about what you see in a picture. Choose one of the two drawings at the beginning of this Work Unit.

Make at least two statements, then write them on the lines below.

1. _____

2. _____

IV. Proficiency in Reading and Writing.

Read the following newspaper announcement and answer the questions under it.

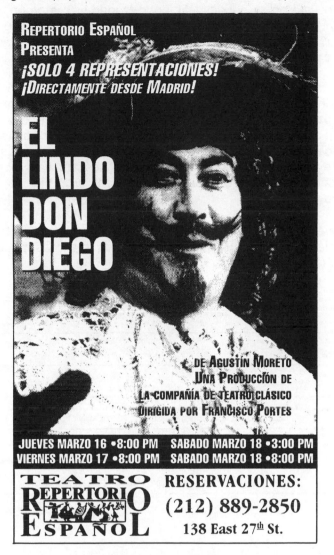

REPERTORIO ESPAÑOL
PRESENTA
¡SOLO 4 REPRESENTACIONES!
¡DIRECTAMENTE DESDE MADRID!

EL LINDO DON DIEGO

DE AGUSTÍN MORETO
UNA PRODUCCIÓN DE
LA COMPAÑÍA DE TEATRO CLÁSICO
DIRIGIDA POR FRANCISCO PORTES

JUEVES MARZO 16 •8:00 PM   SABADO MARZO 18 •3:00 PM
VIERNES MARZO 17 •8:00 PM   SABADO MARZO 18 •8:00 PM

TEATRO REPERTORIO ESPAÑOL

RESERVACIONES:
(212) 889-2850
138 East 27th St.

Reprinted with permission of *EL DIARIO/LA PRENSA,* New York, N.Y.

1. In this advertisement, find the Spanish words for *directly from Madrid* and write them on the line.

   _____

2. What is the title of this play?

   _____

3. What is the name of the author of this play?

   _____

4. What is the name of the theater company producing this play?

   _____

5. How many shows will be given? _____

6. What is the name of the theater where this play will be shown?

   _____

V. Culture. Appreciation of Spanish Art. Proficiency in Speaking and Writing.

Situation: You are on an educational trip in Madrid with a group of students and your Spanish teacher. You are in a museum admiring the painting *Paseo a orillas del mar* (*Stroll along the seashore*) by SOROLLA, another great Spanish artist / **otro gran pintor español.**

It's your turn to say a few words in Spanish about the painting. Look at the picture on the following page. You may use your own words and ideas and / or the following: **dar un paseo** / to take a stroll, a walk; **a orillas del mar** / along the seashore; **la arena** / the sand; **dos damas hermosas** / two beautiful ladies; **llevar** / to wear, to carry; **zapatos blancos** / white shoes; **zapatos negros** / black shoes; **los vestidos blancos** / the white dresses; **sombreros bellos** / beautiful hats; **el parasol blanco** / white parasol; **la brisa** / breeze; **elegante** / elegant; **hay** / there is, there are; **veo** / I see; **admiro** / I admire.

After you have jotted down a few words in Spanish that you plan to use, say them aloud, organize your thoughts, then use the words in at least three sentences for practice on the lines below.

1. _____

   _____

2. _____

   _____

3. _____

   _____

Paseo a orillas del mar (Stroll along the seashore) by Joaquín SOROLLA y Bastida (1863–1923)
Reprinted with permission of Oficina Nacional Española de Turismo, Paris.

EJERCICIOS

I. **Escriba las seis formas de haber en el imperfecto de indicativo. Es preciso saber estas formas para formar el pluscuamperfecto de indicativo.** (Write the six forms of **haber** in the imperfect indicative tense. It is necessary to know these forms in order to form the pluperfect indicative tense. Review them above under the section **Estructuras de la lengua.**)

Singular

1. _____

2. _____

3. _____

Plural

1. _____

2. _____

3. _____

II. **Cambie los siguientes verbos al pluscuamperfecto de indicativo.** (Change the following verbs to the pluperfect indicative tense.)

Modelo: Los chicos han comido. (The boys have eaten.)

Escriba: Los chicos habían comido. (The boys had eaten.)

1. El alumno ha leído la página. _____

2. Los alumnos han escrito en la pizarra. _____

   _____

3. La profesora abrió la ventana. _____

4. María puso el vaso en la mesa. _____

5. Ud. devolvió el libro a la biblioteca. _____

   _____

6. Uds. estudiaron la lección. _____

7. El pobre viejo murió. _____

8. Juana dice siempre la verdad. _____

9. Lolita escribió una nota. _____

10. Clara y Francisco hacen un viaje a Australia. _____

    _____

III. **Conteste las siguientes preguntas en el afirmativo con oraciones completas. En la oración (a) use la palabra Sí. En la oración (b) use la palabra también,** según los modelos.

Modelos: a. ¿Había recibido Ud. una carta? (Had you received a letter?)
b. ¿Y el señor Vargas? (And Mr. Vargas?)

Escriba: a. Sí. Yo había recibido una carta. (Yes. I had received a letter.)
b. El señor Vargas había recibido una carta también. (Mr. Vargas had also received a letter.)

1. a. ¿Habían pedido los alumnos el libro a la profesora? _____

_____

   b. ¿Y Ud.? _____

2. a. ¿Habíamos visto esa película? _____

_____

   b. ¿Y ellos? _____

3. a. ¿Había hecho Ud. un viaje a Inglaterra? _____

_____

   b. ¿Y Uds.? _____

4. a. ¿Habían escrito los estudiantes las lecciones? _____

_____

   b. ¿Y vosotros? _____

5. a. ¿Había abierto el profesor la puerta? _____

   b. ¿Y nosotros? _____

IV. Ordene las palabras para hallar una oración significativa. (Put the words in the correct order to find a meaningful sentence.)

Modelo:

visto	habíamos	la película	nosotros

Escriba: Nosotros habíamos visto la película. (We had seen the film.)

1.

recibido	había	una carta	Ud.

_____

2.

puesto	habían	de flores	el vaso	la mesa	en

_____

3.

padre	mi	vuelto	había	a medianoche

_____

4.

yo llegué	cuando	a casa	hermano	mi	salido	había

_____

V. Traduzca.

1. When I arrived home, my brother had gone out. _____

   _____

2. John had lost it in the street. _____

3. To be or not to be is the question. _____

4. Studying (to study) is good. _____

5. It is good to study. _____

6. I do not want to eat. _____

7. Seeing is believing. _____

8. Tell me who your friends are and I will tell you who you are. _____

   _____

9. The more you have, the more you want (*i.e.,* Appetite comes while eating.) _____

   _____

10. After arriving home, Mr. Rodríguez went to the bathroom and washed himself. _____

   _____

VI. Traduzca al inglés.

1. Luis dejó caer sus libros. _____

2. Mi padre me mandó comerlo. _____

3. Mi profesor me permitió hacerlo. _____

4. Luis dejó de trabajar. _____

5. Pienso ir a Inglaterra. _____

6. Antes de estudiar, Rita telefoneó a su amiga Beatriz. _____

   _____

7. El alumno salió de la sala de clase sin decir nada. _____

   _____

8. Las vi salir. _____

9. Las oí cantar. _____

10. Al entrar en la escuela, Dorotea fue a su clase de español. _____

VII. Traduzca al inglés los siguientes verbos que están en el pluscuamperfecto de indicativo. (Translate the Spanish sentences into English. The verbs are all in the pluperfect indicative tense.)

Modelo: María había hablado.   **Escriba:** Mary had spoken.

1. Yo había trabajado doce horas. _____

2. Tú habías cerrado la puerta. _____

3. Ud. había terminado la lección. _____

4. El había aprendido el poema. _____

5. Ella había vivido ochenta años. _____

6. José había escrito una carta a sus amigos. _____

_____

7. Nosotros habíamos hecho el trabajo. _____

8. Vosotros habíais puesto los libros en la mesa. _____

9. Uds. habían dicho la verdad. _____

10. Ellos habían muerto. _____

11. Ellas habían abierto las ventanas _____

12. María y José habían leído cartas de sus amigos en España. _____

_____

VIII. Discriminación de los sonidos. Su profesor de español va a pronunciar una sola palabra, sea la letra A, sea la letra B. Escoja la palabra que su profesor pronuncia escribiendo la letra en la línea.
(**Sound discrimination.** Your Spanish teacher is going to pronounce one word, either in letter A or letter B. Choose the word that your teacher pronounces, writing the letter on the line.)

Modelo: A. lama
        B. llama   ___B___

He escrito la letra B en la línea porque mi profesor de español ha pronunciado la palabra de la letra B.

1. A. bosque
   B. busque _____

2. A. hambre
   B. hombre _____

3. A. cuando
   B. ¿cuándo? _____

4. A. hacía
   B. hacia _____

5. A. como
   B. coma _____

6. A. ya
   B. yo _____

IX. **Varias palabras en una sola. Utilizando las letras en la palabra MEXICO ¿cuántas palabras puede usted escrlbir? Escriba tres palabras, por lo menos.**
(**Several words in one.** Using the letters in the word **MEXICO,** how many words can you write? Write three words, at least.)

$$\boxed{\text{MEXICO}}$$

1. _____   2. _____   3. _____

X. **¿Cuántos infinitivos y palabras puede Ud. añadir a al?** (How many infinitives and words can you add to al? Follow the examples.)

Al entrar en la escuela, . . . Upon entering the school, . . .
Al salir de la biblioteca, . . . Upon leaving the library, . . .
Al llegar al cine, . . . Upon arriving at the movies, . . .
Al partir de Nueva York, . . . Upon leaving New York, . . .

Escriba diez, por lo menos.

1. _____   6. _____

2. _____   7. _____

3. _____   8. _____

4. _____   9. _____

5. _____   10. _____

Mnemonic Tip	If you confuse the English meaning of **verano** and **invierno,** remember this:
	IN VIERNO W IN TER

CAMPO, PAÍS, PATRIA, NACIÓN

The first three nouns (**el campo, el país, la patria**) all mean *country*. However, note the following:

(a) **campo** means *country* in the sense of countryside, where you find farmlands, as opposite to life in a city: **en el campo** / in the country; **Vamos a pasar el fin de semana en el campo** / We are going to spend the weekend in the country; **Voy al campo este verano** / I am going to the country this summer.

(b) **país** means *country* in the meaning of a *nation:* **¿En qué país nació Ud.?** / In what country were you born?

(c) **patria** means *country* in the sense of *native land:* **El soldado defendió a su patria** / The soldier defended his country.

(d) **nación** means *country* in the sense of *nation:* **Las Naciones Unidas** / the United Nations; **La Sociedad de las Naciones** / The League of Nations.

CONOCER AND SABER

These two verbs mean *to know* but they are used in a distinct sense:

(a) Generally speaking, **conocer** means to know in the sense of *being acquainted* with a person, a place, or a thing: **¿Conoce Ud. a María?** / Do you know Mary? **¿Conoce Ud. bien los Estados Unidos?** / Do you know the United States well? **¿Conoce Ud. este libro?** / Do you know (Are you acquainted with) this book?

In the preterit tense, **conocer** means *met* in the sense of *first met, first became acquainted with someone*: **¿Conoce Ud. a Elena?** / Do you know Helen? / **Sí, (yo) la conocí anoche en casa de un amigo mío** / Yes, I met her [for the first time] last night at the home of one of my friends.

(b) Generally speaking, **saber** means to know a fact, to know something thoroughly: **¿Sabe Ud. qué hora es?** / Do you know what time it is? **¿Sabe Ud. la lección?** / Do you know the lesson?

When you use **saber + inf.**, it means *to know how*: **¿Sabe Ud. nadar?** / Do you know how to swim? **Sí, (yo) sé nadar** / Yes, I know how to swim.

In the preterit tense, **saber** means *found out;* **¿Lo sabe Ud.?** / Do you know it? **Sí, lo supe ayer** / Yes, I found it out yesterday.

Mnemonic Tip	If you're not sure about the difference in use between **conocer** and **saber**, remember that **conocer** means to know in the sense of to be acquainted with. Associate the letter c in **conocer** and **acquainted**.

If you have to, memorize this:

—¿Conoces a Carlos?
—Sí, lo conozco.
—¿Sabes qué es un sabichoso? (a know-it-all)
—Sí, lo sé.

DEBER, DEBER DE, AND TENER QUE

Generally speaking, use **deber** when you want to express a moral obligation, something you ought to do but you may or may not do it: **Debo estudiar esta noche pero estoy cansado y no me siento bien** / I ought to study tonight but I am tired and I do not feel well.

Generally speaking, **deber de + inf.** is used to express a supposition, something that is probable: **La señora Gómez debe de estar enferma porque sale de casa raramente** / Mrs. Gomez must be sick (is probably sick) because she goes out of the house rarely.

Generally speaking, use **tener que** when you want to say that you have to do something: **No puedo salir esta noche porque tengo que estudiar** / I cannot go out tonight because I have to study.

EJERCICIOS

I. Componga oraciones usando las siguientes palabras. (Write sentences using the following words.)

1. campo: _____

2. país: _____

3. patria: _____

4. nación: _____

II. Traduzca al español.

1. Do you know Mary? _____

2. I know Michael very well. _____

3. Do you know the United States well? _____

4. Do you know this book? _____

5. I know this book. It's a very good book. _____

_____

6. Do you know Christopher? Yes, I met him last night at the home of one of my friends. _____

_____

7. Do you know what time it is? _____

8. Do you know the lesson for today? _____

_____

9. Do you know how to swim? _____

10. Yes, I know how to swim. _____

11. Do you know it? Yes, I found it out yesterday. _____

_____

12. I ought to study tonight but I am tired and I do not feel well. _____

_____

13. Mrs. Gómez must be sick because she goes out of the house rarely. _____

_____

14. I cannot go out tonight because I have to study. _____

III. Componga oraciones empleando las siguientes palabras en español. (Write sentences using the following words in Spanish.)

1. deber: _____

_____

2. deber de + inf.: _____

_____

3. tener que: _____

_____

4. conocer: _____

_____

5. saber: _____

_____

IV. Varias palabras en una sola. Utilizando las letras en la palabra AGRADABLE, ¿cuántas palabras puede usted escribir? Escriba diez palabras, por lo menos.
(**Several words in one.** Using the letters in the word **AGRADABLE,** how many words can you write? Write ten words, at least.)

> **AGRADABLE**

1. _____   3. _____   5. _____   7. _____   9. _____

2. _____   4. _____   6. _____   8. _____   10. _____

V. LETRA RELOJ. Cuatro palabras se esconden en este reloj: una palabra de las doce a las tres, una palabra de las tres a las seis, una palabra de las seis a las nueve y, por fin, una palabra de las nueve a las doce.
(**LETTER CLOCK.** Four words are hiding in this clock: one word form 12 to 3, one word from 3 to 6, one word from 6 to 9, and, finally, one word from 9 to 12.)

La misma letra es común a la palabra que sigue.

Este reloj no tiene agujas. ¡Es un reloj de palabras!

De las doce a las tres es el número entre diez y doce.

De las tres a las seis es la forma masculina, singular, de **esta**.

De las seis a las nueve es el pronombre demostrativo, neutro.

De las nueve a las doce es la forma masculina, singular, de **otra**.

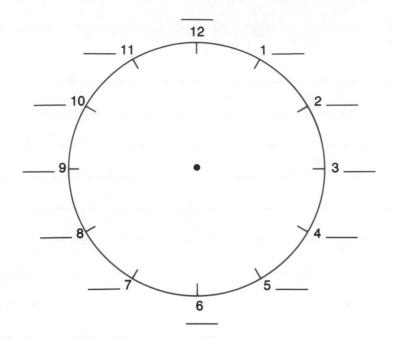

VI. Dictado. Escriba las oraciones que su profesor de español va a leer.
(**Dictation.** Write the sentences that your Spanish teacher is going to read.)

1. _____

2. _____

3. _____

VII. ¿Qué está haciendo Ud.? ¿Dónde está Ud.? ¿En un parque?

Respuesta: _____

_____

VIII. En este diálogo Juanita y usted hablan de los exámenes de junio y de las vacaciones de verano.

Complete el diálogo.

Juanita: ¿Estás bien preparado para tus exámenes?

Usted: _____

Juanita: Mañana tengo un examen más y luego empiezan las vacaciones.

Usted: _____

Juanita: En julio hacemos un viaje a Puerto Rico.

Usted: _____

Juanita: El verano pasado lo pasamos en las montañas.

Usted: _____

Juanita: Voy a mandarte una tarjeta postal desde San Juan si me das tu dirección.

Usted: _____

IX. Escoja la palabra apropiada para completar los siguientes proverbios (refranes). (Choose the appropriate word to complete the following proverbs.)

1. Mucho ruido y pocas _____ .
   - A. casas
   - B. peras
   - C. calles
   - D. nueces

2. El tiempo da buen _____ .
   - A. tiempo
   - B. hora
   - C. consejo
   - D. conejo

3. Si a Roma fueres, _____ como vieres.
   - A. hace
   - B. haga
   - C. haces
   - D. haz

4. Más vale pájaro en mano que _____ volando.
   - A. cien
   - B. ciento
   - C. cientos
   - D. un cien

5. Dime con quien andas y te diré quien _____ .
   - A. es
   - B. esta
   - C. eres
   - D. fueres

X. ¿Qué palabras españolas tienen las siguientes letras? (What Spanish words contain the following letters?)

Modelo: CHE   noche, coche, chiste

1. MJR _____   4. AGA _____

2. CSA _____   5. TPO _____

3. PTL _____   6. AHR _____

Mnemonic Tip	If you confuse the meaning of **vieja** (old, *fem., sing.*) and **viaje** (trip), remember this statement: **Esta mujer vieja hace un viaje por autobús** / This old woman is taking a trip by bus.

XI. Word Game. Proficiency in Speaking and Writing.

Situation: Charlene, the president of the Spanish Club, has a new word game to play. She is asking students to give Spanish words that contain certain letters. Your role is **Tú.** Later, you may expand this game by using other combinations of letters so other students can join in.

Charlene:	**¿Qué palabras contienen las letras MJR? ¿Quién sabe?**
Alberto:	**Yo sé. Mejor y mujer.**
Charlene:	**¡Bravo! ¿Qué palabras contienen las letras CSA?**
Tú:	_____
	(I know! Thing and house.)
Charlene:	**¡Bravo! ¿Y las letras PTL?**
Casandra:	**Pantalón y postal.**
Charlene:	**¡Bravo! ¿Y las letras AHR?**
Tú:	_____
	(I know! Hour, now, to do.)
Charlene:	**¡Estupendo!**

XII. Culture. El Museo del Prado, Madrid. Proficiency in Speaking and Writing.

Situation: On your educational trip in Madrid, you are visiting the Prado Museum.

On the following page, look at the top picture of a portion of the interior of the museum. Do you see the two women and one man listening to the guide with his arm held out? Let's imagine what they are saying. You may use your own words and ideas or the words under the lines. Before you write the statements in Spanish, say the words aloud.

El guía:	_____
	(Do you want to see the paintings of El Greco over there?)
El señor:	_____
	(Yes, sir, with much pleasure. I would like to see them.)
La primera señora:	_____
	(I would like to see the marvelous paintings by Goya, too.)
La segunda señora:	_____
	(My favorite Spanish artist is Murillo. In what room are his paintings? I want to see them, too.)

Madrid. Interior del Museo del Prado.
Courtesy of Oficina Nacional Española de Turismo, Paris.

Museo del Prado, Madrid (Fachada principal)
Courtesy of Spanish National Tourist Office, New York, N.Y.

TEST 8

PART ONE   Speaking Proficiency

Directions: Read the four situations given below. Take a few minutes to organize your thoughts about the words you are going to say. Select three of the four situations. Before you begin to speak, you may review the Speaking and Writing Proficiency exercises that you practiced in this Work Unit.

1. Say a proverb in Spanish that would make a point in the following situations.

   A. Situation: You just arrived twenty minutes late to Spanish class for a test. What might the teacher say to you?

   B. Situation: It's time for Pepe to practice his violin lessons but he's not in the mood. What might his mother say to him?

   C. Situation: Anita tells her father that she doesn't feel like having dinner because she doesn't have an appetite just now. What might her father say to her?

   D. Situation: The Spanish teacher tells the class that he has to leave the room for about ten minutes to make an important phone call in the main office. What might one of the students say when he is out of the room?

   E. Situation: Señorita Aquino is not sure if she ought to marry José Robles who has proposed to her. She needs some advice and time to think about it. What would her best girlfriend say to her?

2. **Situation:** It is your turn to state two different Spanish proverbs that would apply to two different situations that you make up.

3. **Situation:** You are on an educational trip in Madrid with a group of students and your Spanish teacher. You are in a museum admiring the painting *Paseo a orillas del mar* (*Stroll along the seashore*) by Sorolla, a great Spanish artist. Look at the picture again in this Work Unit and say at least three sentences about it.

4. **Situation:** Look at the picture again of the interior of the Prado Museum in this Work Unit. Do you see the two women and one man listening to the guide with his arm held out? Imagine a conversation that is taking place. Make at least four statements; in other words, one statement in Spanish for each of the four persons.

PART TWO Listening Proficiency

Directions: Your teacher will read aloud four short paragraphs. Each one will contain only a few sentences. You will hear each paragraph twice. Then you will hear one question based on each. You will hear the question only once. It is printed below. Choose the best suggested answer based on what you heard and check the letter of your choice.

Selection Number 1

1. ¿Adónde va Pedro después del examen?

   A. a casa

   B. al cine

   C. a estudiar

   D. a la playa

Selection Number 2

2. ¿Adónde piensa ir Lisa?

   A. a México

   B. a Nueva York

   C. a hacer un viaje

   D. a un estado de los Estados Unidos

Selection Number 3

3. ¿Cuánto tiempo va a pasar Lisa con María?

   A. la semana que viene

   B. dos semanas

   C. cuatro semanas

   D. la semana próxima

Selection Number 4

4. ¿Por qué desea Carlos quedarse en Madrid dos semanas más?

   A. porque tiene mucho dinero

   B. porque no tiene más dinero

   C. porque desea escribir cartas

   D. porque le gusta Madrid

PART THREE   Reading Proficiency

Directions: In the following passage there are five blank spaces numbered 1 through 5. Each blank space represents a missing verb form or some other word. For each blank space, four possible completions are provided. Only one of them is grammatically correct and makes sense in the context of the passage.

First, read the passage in its entirety to determine its general meaning. Then read it a second time. For each blank space choose the completion that makes the best sense and is grammatically correct. Write its letter in the space provided.

La semana pasada mi primo David nos _____ . David _____ veinte años.

1. A. visita	2. A. tenía
B. visitará	B. tiene
C. visitaría	C. tengo
D. visitó	D. tuve

Siempre yo _____ divierto muchísimo durante sus visitas. Ayer por la mañana nosotros

3. A. me
   B. te
   C. se
   D. nos

_____ al museo. _____ salir del museo, empezó a llover.

4. A. fuimos	5. A. Al
B. estamos	B. De
C. iremos	C. A
D. vamos	D. En

PART FOUR Writing Proficiency

Directions: Of the four situations in Part One (Speaking Proficiency) in this test, select three of them and write what you said on the lines below.

Situation 1 _____

_____

_____

Situation 2 _____

_____

_____

Situation 3 _____

_____

_____

Situation 4 _____

_____

_____

A Pedro le gustan los deportes. Su deporte favorito es el fútbol.

Work Unit 14

Are you as eager as Pedro to play in a soccer game?

¡Sorpresa! ¡Sorpresa!

A Pedro le gustan los deportes. Su deporte favorito es el fútbol. Siempre quiere que su cuerpo esté en buena forma porque es guardameta del equipo de fútbol de su escuela. Quiere estar siempre dispuesto para jugar bien. Siempre cuida su salud; por ejemplo, Pedro come solamente alimentos que son buenos para la salud. Cuando juega al fútbol, evita el helado, las patatas fritas y los pasteles. Es un buen muchacho y buen futbolista. 5

Pedro se acuesta temprano todas las noches, se despierta temprano, se levanta con el sol, se lava cuidadosamente, se viste pronto y toma un buen desayuno todas las mañanas.

Pedro anuncia a sus padres:

—Hoy es el gran partido de fútbol. Tendrá lugar después de clase.

Pedro dice a Juana: 10

—Juanita, tú vas a jugar en el equipo con los muchachos y las muchachas también, ¿no es verdad?

—Sí—, contesta Juana—. A las muchachas nos gustan los deportes también. Estaré en el estadio esta tarde para jugar con los muchachos y mis amigas.

Pedro se apresuró para llegar temprano al gran campo de la escuela. Corrió un 15 kilómetro en la pista antes de entrar en la escuela.

Para Pedro, el fútbol es todo. Se acuerda de los buenos consejos de su entrenador de fútbol:

¡Guárdate de la red! ¡Guárdate de la red! ¡El gol! ¡El gol!

Pedro juega extremadamente bien. Es un muchacho admirable. Nos gusta mucho. Es 20 todo un hombre. Es un buen estudiante, buen jugador, futbolista excelente. Los compañeros de Pedro lo quieren.

Después de la última clase, Pedro fue al gimnasio. Se preparó para el gran partido de fútbol. Se puso su traje de gimnasio, hizo ejercicios para estar en buena forma antes de comenzar el partido. 25

Pedro hizo ejercicios por tres horas. ¡Ahora está listo para el gran partido!

Pedro corre a toda velocidad al estadio. Cuando llega al estadio, ve que todo el mundo parte.

—¡Pedro! ¿Por qué llegas tarde?—pregunta el entrenador.

Pedro no contesta. Está estupefacto. 30

—¿Por qué llegas tarde?—repite el entrenador.

—¿Tarde? ¿Tarde?—pregunta Pedro con sorpresa.

—El partido ha terminado—, dice el entrenador.

—¡El partido ha terminado!—exclama Pedro.

—Sí, sí. ¡Terminado! ¡Se acabó! ¡Hemos ganado! ¡Sorpresa! ¡Sorpresa! 35

KEY WORDS AND PHRASES

alimentos *n.m.* foods

antes (de) *adv.* before; **antes de comenzar** before beginning

campo *n.m.* field

compañeros *n.m.* friends, companions

consejo *n.m.* advice

corre *3d pers., s., pres. indic. of* **correr**; he runs

corrió *3d pers., s., pret. of* **correr**; he ran

cuerpo *n.m.* body

cuidadosamente *adv.* carefully

cuidar *v.* to take care of

deporte *n.m.* sport

desayuno *n.m.* breakfast; **tomar el desayuno** to have (take) breakfast

después (de) *adv.* after

dice *3d pers., s., pres. indic. of* **decir**; he says

dispuesto *adj.* ready

403

entrenador *n.m.* trainer, coach
equipo *n.m.* team
esta *dem. adj., f.s.* this
estadio *n.m.* stadium
estaré *1st pers., s., fut. of* **estar**; I will be
esté *3d pers., s., pres. sub. of* **estar**; be
estupefacto *adj.* stupefied, stunned
evitar *v.* to avoid
extremadamente *adv.* extremely
forma *n.f.* form, shape
fue *3d pers., s., pret. of* **ir**; he went
fútbol *n.m.* soccer; **el fútbol americano** football
futbolista *n.m.f.* soccer player
ganado *past part. of* **ganar; hemos ganado** we have won
gimnasio *n.m.* gym, gymnasium
gol *n.m.* goal
guardameta *n.m.* goalie, goalkeeper
¡Guárdate de la red! Guard the net! Watch out for the net!
ha terminado *3d pers., s., pres. perf. of* **terminar**; it has ended, terminated
hemos ganado *1st pers., pl., pres. perf. of* **ganar**; we have won
hizo *3d pers., s., pret. of* **hacer**; he did
jugador, jugadora *n.m.f.* player
kilómetro *n.m.* kilometer (1 kilometer = about 0.62 mile)
listo *adj.* ready
lo quieren they love him
lugar *n.m.* place; **tener lugar** to take place
¿no es verdad? isn't that so? aren't you?
Nos gusta mucho We like him a lot.
ofrecer *v.* to offer
padres *n.m.* parents
parte *3d pers., s., pres. indic. of* **partir**; is leaving
partido *n.m.* game, match; **el gran partido** the big game
pasteles *n.m.* pastries

pista *n.f.* track
predilecto *adj.* favorite
red *n.f.* net
repetir *v.* to repeat
salud *n.f.* health
se acabó *3d pers., s., pret. of* **acabarse**; to be over, finished
se acuerda *3d pers., s., pres. indic. of* **acordarse**; to remember, recall
se acuesta *3d pers., s., pres. indic. of* **acostarse**; to go to bed
se apresuró *3d pers., s., pret. of* **apresurarse**; to hurry
se despierta *3d pers., s., pres. indic. of* **despertarse**; to wake up
se lava *3d pers., s., pres. indic. of* **lavarse**; to wash oneself
se levanta *3d pers., s., pres. indic. of* **levantarse**; to get up
se preparó *3d pers., s., pret. of* **prepararse**; to prepare oneself
se puso *3d pers., s., pret. of* **ponerse**; to put on (oneself)
se viste *3d pers., s., pres. indic. of* **vestirse**; to get dressed
sorpresa *n.f.* surprise
tarde *n.f.* afternoon; *adv.* late
tendrá *3d pers., s., fut. of* **tener**; **tener lugar** to take place
terminado *past part. of* **terminar**; **ha terminado** has ended
todas *adj., f. pl.* all; **todas las noches** every night; **todas las mañanas** every morning
todo *pron.* all, everything; **todo el mundo** everybody
traje *n.m.* suit, outfit
última *adj.* last
ve *3d pers., s., pres. inc. of* **ver**; he sees
velocidad *n.f.* velocity, speed; **a toda velocidad** at full speed

---

EJERCICIOS

I. Conteste las siguientes preguntas conforme a la lectura de esta lección. (Answer the following questions according to the reading selection in this Work Unit.)

1. ¿Cuál es el deporte favorito de Pedro? _____

_____

2. ¿Por qué quiere Pedro estar siempre en buena forma? _____

_____

3. ¿Qué alimentos come Pedro? _____

_____

4. ¿Qué alimentos evita él? _____

_____

5. ¿Se levanta Pedro temprano o tarde? _____

_____

6. ¿Va a jugar Juanita en el equipo? _____

_____

7. ¿Cómo se lava Pedro? _____

_____

8. ¿Cuándo tendrá lugar el gran partido de fútbol? _____

_____

9. ¿Por qué llegó tarde Pedro al gran partido de fútbol? _____

_____

10. Cuando Pedro llegó tarde al estadio, ¿quién le dice a él que el partido ha terminado? _____

_____

II. Conteste las siguientes preguntas. Son preguntas personales. (Answer the following questions. They are personal questions.)

1. ¿Le gustan a usted los deportes? _____

_____

2. ¿Cuál es su deporte favorito? _____

_____

3. ¿Se acuesta usted temprano o tarde? _____

_____

4. Por lo general, ¿a qué hora se levanta usted todas las mañanas? _____

_____

5. Y, por lo general, ¿a qué hora se acuesta usted todas las noches? _____

_____

6. Por lo general, ¿se apresura Ud. por la mañana? _____

_____

7. ¿Se lava Ud. todas las mañanas con cuidado o sin cuidado? _____

_____

8. Por lo general, ¿qué toma Ud. en el desayuno todas las mañanas? _____

_____

9. ¿Se viste Ud. pronto o lentamente? _____

_____

10. ¿Prefiere Ud. helado o pastel? _____

_____

III. ¿Sí o No?

1. El deporte predilecto de Pedro es el tenis.   _____

2. Pedro es guardameta de su equipo de fútbol.   _____

3. A Juanita le gustan los deportes también.   _____

4. Pedro se despierta tarde.   _____

5. Pedro se viste pronto.   _____

6. Pedro se lava con cuidado.   _____

7. Pedro desea estar en buena forma.   _____

8. El gran partido de fútbol tendrá lugar por la mañana antes de las clases. _____

9. Pedro es todo un hombre.   _____

10. Pedro está listo para el gran partido después de hacer ejercicios por tres horas. _____

IV. Acróstico. Traduzca al español horizontalmente las palabras inglesas expresadas abajo.
(**Acrostic.** Write the Spanish words horizontally for the English words listed below.)

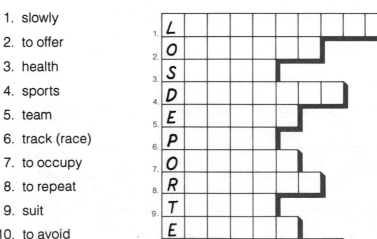

1. slowly
2. to offer
3. health
4. sports
5. team
6. track (race)
7. to occupy
8. to repeat
9. suit
10. to avoid
11. surprise

LOS ANGELES-84

Un gran espectáculo alrededor del deporte

En Los Angeles todo el mundo vive pendiente de la Olimpiada, pero al margen de la competición, los miles de turistas llegados de todas partes dan el toque de color al gran acontecimiento. El vaivén de la gente, los souvenirs, las anécdotas de todo tipo unido a la presencia casi constante de los famosos de Hollywood entre el público son ya casi tan importantes como los propios récords y medallas.

LOS ANGELES. Diana Domken

TODAS las previsiones catastrofistas que anunciaban unos Juegos Olímpicos cargados de problemas, ahogados por la polución, congestionados por el tráfico de las autopistas, atemorizados por la masiva seguridad y el acecho del terrorismo, han caído por su propio peso. Ni siquiera el boicot soviético y de los países del este se está notando en algo más que no sean las frías cifras de los récords y mejores tiempos. Las calles y autopistas de Los Angeles, están más vacías que nunca. Ni los más viejos del lugar recuerdan la facilidad con que se circula. El terrorismo no ha hecho su aparición, y la polución, la temible nube amarilla que se concentra en los días más calurosos del verano, se mantiene bajo control.

Al contrario, las competiciones están llenas de bote en bote. A pesar de las distancias y los extravagantes horarios impuestos por la cadena de televisión que transmite los Juegos (incluso a las ocho de la mañana, en deportes como el Hockey sobre Hierba o el Balonmano, que en Estados Unidos son totalmente desconocidos), la demanda de entradas es extraordinaria.

Claro que, entre el público, están, muy a menudo, las grandes atracciones. El día de la espectacular ceremonia de inauguración en el viejo Coliseo de Los Angeles, que ya había sido la sede de los Juegos de 1932, justo en el punto opuesto del lugar donde se hallaban las autoridades, se encontraban sentadas Brooke Shields, Linda Evans y John Forsythe.

Reprinted with permission of LECTURAS (Ediciones HYMSA), Barcelona

---

V. Providing Information. Proficiency in Speaking and Writing.

Situation: Last Saturday you and a few friends saw an exciting high school soccer game. Your friend Pablo wasn't able to be there. He wants you to tell him about the game.

For starters, look at the picture of a scene at a soccer game at the beginning of this Work Unit. Provide Pablo with the information he wants. You may use your own words and ideas and/or any of the following: **un partido de fútbol** / a soccer game; **el balón de fútbol** / the soccer ball; **la portería (la meta)** / the goal; **la red** / the net; **el saque de meta** / goal kick; **cocear** / to kick; **correr** / to run; **llevar** / to wear; **la camiseta** / shirt (jersey); **el pantalón corto de deporte** / sport shorts; **las medias** / socks; **el guardameta (el portero)** / goalie, goalkeeper; **mi deporte predilecto es el fútbol** / my favorite sport is soccer; **me gustan los deportes** / I like sports; **mi equipo favorito ganó** / my favorite team won.

After you have jotted down a few words in Spanish that you plan to use, say them aloud, organize your thoughts, then use the words in at least three sentences for practice on the lines below.

1. _____

2. _____

3. _____

VI. Activities. Proficiency in Speaking.

A. Review the story at the beginning of this Work Unit, then give a summary of it. You may begin, then let classmates continue by making at least one statement until the story has been summarized in their own words. You may use your own words or you may want to start by saying: **A Pedro le gustan los deportes. Su deporte favorito es el fútbol. Pedro es guardameta del equipo de fútbol de su escuela.**

B. After the story has been retold by you and your classmates, ask each other questions based on what happened in the story. Each classmate will ask one question and another student will answer. During the question and answer period, you may want to begin with: **¿Cuál es el deporte favorito de Pedro?**

VII. Expressing Personal Feelings. Proficiency in Speaking and Writing.

Situation: You are on the phone expressing your personal feelings to Carlota about the soccer game you saw yesterday.

You may use your own words and ideas and/or any of the following: **Me gustó mucho el partido de fútbol de ayer** / I liked yesterday's soccer game very much; **mi equipo favorito ganó** / my favorite team won; **en mi opinión, Pedro es el mejor futbolista de la escuela** / in my opinion, Pedro is the best soccer player in the school.

You have to hang up now because the sports news is on television. In at least three statements, write a note to Carlota about your impressions. Practice writing on the lines below.

La fecha / the date _____

Querida amiga Carlota,

_____

_____

_____

Tu amigo (amiga),

_____

VIII. Shopping. Proficiency in Speaking and Writing.

Situation: The course in keyboarding Juana Rodríguez is taking in school has inspired her to get a weekend job and save money to buy a computer for personal use at home. Here she is in a store looking at computers.

You are playing Juana's role. Ask a classmate to be the salesperson / **el vendedor, la vendedora**. You may vary and extend this conversation with your own words and ideas. Later, switch roles. Useful words: **la computadora** / computer; **las computadoras personales** / personal computers; **las impresoras** / printers; **las impresoras laser** / laser printers; **los descuentos** / discounts; **eso es** / that's right; **sólo estoy mirando** / I'm only looking; **cuesta demasiado** / it costs too much; **¿hay ... ?** / is there ..., are there ...? **¿En qué puedo servirle?** / How may I help you? **Tengo que trabajar** / I have to work; **ahorrar dinero** / to save money; **Volveré** / I will return; **Pase muy buenos días** / Have a very nice day.

Vendedor: **Buenos días. ¿En qué puedo servirle?**

Juana: _____
                   (I want to buy a computer.)

Vendedor: **¿Desea usted una computadora personal?**

Juana: _____
                   (That's right. But I'm only looking.)

Vendedor: **Esta computadora es mejor que ésa.**

Juana: _____
                   (But it costs too much. Are there discounts?)

Vendedor: **¡Claro! Ofrecemos descuentos.**

Juana: _____
                   (Show me the printers, please. How much do they cost?)

Vendedor: **Aquí están las impresoras. Hay varios precios.**

Juana: _____

                   _____
                   (I have to work and save money. I will return in three years! Thank you and good-bye!)

Vendedor: **Adiós, señorita. ¡Pase muy buenos días!**

IX. **Reading Proficiency.**

Read the following newspaper advertisement and answer the questions under it.

Reprinted with permission of *EL DIARIO/LA PRENSA,* New York, N.Y.

1. For whom is this newspaper advertisement intended?
   A. owners of bakery stores
   B. owners of butcher shops
   C. owners of clothing stores
   D. owners of grocery stores

2. What is the purpose of the advertisement?
   A. to offer a bonus
   B. to stimulate home deliveries
   C. to ask for an opinion in a survey
   D. to stimulate the sales of the newspaper in certain stores

ESTRUCTURAS DE LA LENGUA

TENSE NO. 10: PRETÉRITO ANTERIOR (PAST ANTERIOR OR PRETERIT PERFECT)

This is the third of the compound tenses. This past tense is compound because it is formed with the preterit of **haber** plus the past participle of the verb you are using. It is translated into English like the pluperfect indicative explained above. This tense is not used much in spoken Spanish. Ordinarily, the pluperfect indicative is used in spoken Spanish (and sometimes even the simple preterit) in place of the past anterior.

This tense is ordinarily used in formal writing, such as history and literature. It is normally used after certain conjunctions of time, *e.g.*, **después que, cuando, apenas, luego que, en cuanto.**

You must become familiar with this tense because you will have to recognize its meaning in reading comprehension selections. Remember that it is translated into English the same as the pluperfect indicative. It is used in literature and formal writings, rarely in informal conversation.

EXAMPLE:

Después que **hubo hablado**, salió / After *he had spoken*, he left.

Es preciso saber las seis formas del verbo **haber** en el pretérito para formar el pretérito perfecto (pretérito anterior).

	Singular	Plural
1.	**hube**	**hubimos**
2.	**hubiste**	**hubisteis**
3.	**hubo**	**hubieron**

PASSIVE VOICE AND USES OF SE

Passive voice means that the action of the verb falls on the subject; in other words, the subject receives the action: **La ventana fue abierta por el ladrón** / The window was opened by the robber. NOTE that **abierta** (really a form of the past participle **abrir** / **abierto**) is used as an adjective and it must agree in gender and number with the subject that it describes.

Active voice means that the subject performs the action and the subject is always stated: **El ladrón abrió la ventana** / The robber opened the window.

To form the true passive, use **ser** + the past participle of the verb you have in mind; the past participle then serves as an adjective and it must agree in gender and number with the subject that it describes. In the true passive, the agent (the doer) is always expressed with the preposition **por** in front of it. The formula for the true passive construction is: subject + tense of **ser** + past participle + **por** + the agent (the doer): **Estas composiciones fueron escritas por Juan** / These compositions were written by John.

The reflexive pronoun **se** may be used to substitute for the true passive voice construction. When you use the **se** construction, the subject is a thing (not a person) and the doer (agent) is not stated: **Aquí se habla español** / Spanish is spoken here; **Aquí se hablan español e inglés** / Spanish and English are spoken here; **Se venden libros en esta tienda** / Books are sold in this store.

There are a few standard idiomatic expressions that are commonly used with the pronoun **se.** These expressions are not truly passive, the pronoun **se** is not truly a reflexive pronoun, and the verb form is in the 3rd person singular only. In this construction, there is no subject expressed; the subject is contained in the use of **se** + the 3rd person singular of the verb at all times and the common translations into English are: it is . . . , people . . . , they . . . , one . . . :

EXAMPLES:

Se cree que . . . / It is believed that . . . , people believe that . . . , they believe that . . . , one believes that . . .

Se cree que este criminal es culpable / It is believed that this criminal is guilty.

Se dice que . . . / It is said that . . ., people say that . . ., they say that . . ., one says that . . .

Se dice que va a nevar esta noche / They say that it's going to snow tonight.

¿Cómo se dice en español *ice cream?* / How do you say *ice cream* in Spanish?

Se sabe que . . . / It is known that . . ., people know that . . ., they know that . . .

Se sabe que María va a casarse con Juan / People know that Mary is going to marry John.

The **se** reflexive pronoun construction is avoided if the subject is a person because there can be ambiguity in meaning. For example, how would you translate into English the following: **Se da un regalo.** Which of the following two meanings is intended? She (he) is being given a present, *or* She (he) is giving a present to himself (to herself). In correct Spanish you would have to say: **Le da (a María, a Juan,** *etc.***) un regalo** / He (she) is giving a present to Mary (to John, *etc.*) Avoid using the **se** construction in the passive when the subject is a person; change your sentence around and state it in the active voice to make the meaning clear. Otherwise, the pronoun **se** seems to go with the verb, as if the verb itself is reflexive, which gives an entirely different meaning. Another example: **Se miró** would mean *He (she) looked at himself (herself),* not *He (she) was looked at!* If you mean to say *He (she) looked at him (at her),* say: **La miró** or, if in the plural, say: **La miraron** / They looked at her.

Mnemonic Tip	**Se venden libros en una librería** / Books are sold in a bookstore. Associate **libros** with **librería.** The ending **ría** is used to denote the store where something is sold; e.g., **una panadería** (where **pan** is sold), **una lechería** (where **leche** is sold), **una librería** (where books are sold). **Una biblioteca** is a library.

EJERCICIOS

I. **Escriba las seis formas de haber en el pretérito. Es preciso saber estas formas para formar el pretérito perfecto (pretérito anterior).** (Write the six forms of **haber** in the preterit. It is necessary to know these forms in order to form the preterit perfect [preterit anterior].)

Singular   Plural

1. _____   1. _____

2. _____   2. _____

3. _____   3. _____

II. **Cambie los siguientes verbos que están en el pluscuamperfecto de indicativo al pretérito perfecto (pretérito anterior), y traduzca este cambio al inglés.** (Change the following verbs that are in the pluperfect indicative tense to the preterit perfect tense and translate the change into English. The preterit perfect tense is the new tense introduced and explained above. The translation into English is the same for both tenses.)

Modelo: María había hablado.   **Escriba:** (a) María hubo hablado.
              (Mary had spoken.)   (b) Mary had spoken.

1. Yo había trabajado toda la noche. (a) _____

(b) _____

2. Tú habías hablado incesantemente. (a) _____

(b) _____

3. Ud. había abierto todas las ventanas. (a) _____

(b) _____

4. Él había caído en la calle. (a) _____

(b) _____

5. Ella había creído la verdad. (a) _____

(b) _____

6. Roberto había cubierto su bicicleta. (a) _____

(b) _____

7. Nosotros habíamos dicho la verdad. (a) _____

(b) _____

8. Vosotros habíais descubierto la mentira. (a) _____

(b) _____

9. Uds. habían escrito las lecciones. (a) _____

(b) _____

10. Ellos habían roto la silla. (a) _____

(b) _____

III. Reading Proficiency.

Read the following newspaper announcement and answer the question under it.

**Soy
vendedora de ropa.
Busco empleo.
Llámeme.
123-4567**

1. What is the advertiser looking for?
   A. a job
   B. used clothing
   C. articles made of rope
   D. old vending machines for resale

IV. Traduzca al español.

1. The window was opened by the robber. _____

_____

2. The robber opened the window. _____

_____

3. These compositions were written by John. _____

_____

4. John wrote these compositions. _____

_____

5. Spanish is spoken here. _____

_____

6. Spanish and English are spoken here. _____

_____

7. Books are sold in this store. _____

_____

8. It is believed that this criminal is guilty. _____

_____

9. They say that it's going to snow tonight. _____

_____

10. How do you say *ice cream* in Spanish? _____

_____

V. Traduzca al inglés.

1. Se venden zapatos en una zapatería. _____

_____

2. Se venden pasteles en una pastelería. _____

_____

3. Se venden libros en una librería. _____

_____

4. Se vende pan en una panadería. _____

_____

5. Se venden medicamentos en una farmacia. _____

_____

VI. Conteste las siguientes preguntas en español con oraciones completas. (Answer the following questions in Spanish in complete sentences.)

Modelo: ¿Dónde se venden zapatos? (Where are shoes sold?)

Ecriba: Se venden zapatos en una zapatería. (Shoes are sold in a shoe store.)

1. ¿Dónde se venden pasteles? _____

_____

2. ¿Cómo se dice *ice cream* en español? _____

_____

3. ¿Dónde se vende pan? _____

_____

Carl Lewis ya tiene su primera medalla de oro

Printed with permission of YA (periódico), Madrid.

VII. **Sports. Speaking Proficiency.**

Situation: In Spanish class the students are reading Spanish newspapers and magazines. You have volunteered to say a few words in Spanish about the pictures on page 415 and the Spanish sentence above them.

You may use your own words and ideas and/or the following: **ya tiene** / now has; **su** / his; **primera** / first; **la medalla de oro** / gold medal; **el corredor** / runner; **el sprinter** / sprinter; **el corredor de fondo** / long-distance runner; **la pista** / track; **la pista de carreras** / running track; **el ganador** / winner. Verbs: **tener** / to have; **correr** / to run; **ser** / to be; **ver** / to see.

After organizing your thoughts and words, say at least three short sentences in Spanish. All you need is a subject and a verb and you have a sentence.

DEJAR, SALIR, AND SALIR DE

These verbs mean *to leave*, but notice the difference in use:

Use **dejar** when you leave someone or when you leave something behind you: **El alumno dejó sus libros en la sala de clase** / The pupil left his books in the classroom.

Dejar also means *to let* or *to allow* or *to let go*: **¡Déjelo!** / Let it! (Leave it!)

Use **salir de** when you mean *to leave* in the sense of *to go out of* (a place): **El alumno salió de la sala de clase** / The pupil left the classroom; **¿Dónde está su madre? Mi madre salió** / Where is your mother? My mother went out.

Dejar De + Inf. and Dejar Caer

Use **dejar de + inf.** when you mean *to stop* or *to fail to*: **Los alumnos dejaron de hablar cuando la profesora entró en la sala de clase** / The students stopped talking when the teacher came into the classroom.

¡No deje Ud. de llamarme! / Don't fail to call me!

Dejar caer means *to drop*: **Luis dejó caer sus libros** / Louis dropped his books.

Ir, Irse

Use **ir** when you simply mean *to go*: **Voy al cine** / I am going to the movies.

Use **irse** when you mean *to leave* in the sense of *to go away*: **Mis padres se fueron al campo para visitar a mis abuelos** / My parents left for (went away to) the country to visit my grandparents.

EJERCICIOS

I. Conteste las siguientes preguntas con oraciones completas. (Answer the following questions in complete sentences.)

Modelo: ¿Quién dejó estos libros en la mesa? (Who left these books on the table?)

Escriba: Pedro dejó estos libros en la mesa. (Pedro left these books on the table.)

1. ¿Quién dejó sus libros en la sala de clase? _____

   _____

2. ¿Quién salió del cuarto? _____

3. ¿Dónde está su madre? ¿Salió? _____

4. ¿Quién dejó de hablar cuando la profesora entró en la sala de clase? _____

   _____

5. ¿Quién dejó caer sus libros? _____

6. ¿Adónde va Ud. esta tarde? _____

7. ¿Adónde se fueron sus padres? _____

8. ¿Por qué se fueron sus padres al campo? _____

9. ¿Quién abrió la ventana? _____

10. ¿Quién rompió esta silla? _____

II. Sopa de letras. En esta sopa de letras, busque los verbos ver, abrir, escribir en el pretérito perfecto.

(**Alphabet soup.** In this alphabet soup, look for the verbs **ver, abrir, escribir** in the preterit perfect tense, the new tense introduced and explained in this Work Unit. You are looking for **hube visto** (I had seen), which is printed across from left to right; **hube abierto** (I had opened), which is printed vertically but backwards; **hubo escrito** (you/he/she had written), which is printed vertically. As you look for them, pronounce each one aloud. When you find them, draw a line around each verb form. Tip: They cross each other.)

B	U	H	O	H	B	U	T	O
H	B	U	A	G	I	R	O	T
H	U	B	E	V	I	S	T	O
R	I	O	E	S	C	I	R	T
H	U	E	B	I	M	O	E	S
O	R	S	E	I	B	U	I	H
E	S	C	R	I	O	T	B	U
V	I	R	T	O	A	B	A	E
H	A	I	B	A	B	I	E	R
I	S	T	O	V	H	U	B	E
R	O	O	T	R	O	T	U	I
R	C	S	E	E	B	U	H	O

III. **Discriminación de los sonidos. Su profesor de español va a pronunciar una sola pa-labra, sea la letra A, sea la letra B. Escoja la palabra que su profesor pronuncia y escri-ba la letra en la línea.**

Modelo: A. lama
B. llama   <u> A </u>

He escrito la letra A en la línea porque mi profesor de español ha pronunciado la palabra de la letra A.

1. A. fuego
   B. luego _____

2. A. llana
   B. lana _____

3. A. amó
   B. amo _____

4. A. digo
   B. dijo _____

5. A. aun
   B. aún _____

6. A. cesta
   B. sexta _____

IV. **Dining Out. Speaking Proficiency.**

Situation: You are in a Spanish restaurant having dinner. The waiter made a mis-take and brought you tea instead of coffee. What would you say to him?

You may use your own words and ideas and/or the following: **equivocarse** / to be mistaken, to make a mistake; **usted se equivocó** / you made a mistake; **traer** / to bring; **usted me trajo** / you brought me; **el té** / tea; **el café** / coffee; **en lugar de** / instead of.

V. **Varias palabras en una sola. Utilizando las letras en la palabra CHILE, ¿cuántas palabras puede usted escribir? Escriba dos palabras, por lo menos.**

CHILE

1. _____   2. _____

VI. **Las palabras escondidas. En la rejilla, busque las palabras en español por las palabras en inglés. Cuando las haya encontrado, ráyelas.**
(Hidden Words. In the grid, look for the words in Spanish for the words in English. When you have found them, draw a line through them. They are printed vertically and horizontally. Tip: Two of the words are printed backwards. Some cross each other.)

M	A	D	O	M	A	D	R	E	I
H	E	R	A	H	E	R	D	A	P
B	U	E	H	I	J	O	T	Í	O
H	I	J	E	J	A	E	O	I	U
P	A	D	R	A	B	U	E	L	A
H	E	R	M	A	N	A	T	Í	A·
P	A	D	A	E	R	B	U	E	L
E	H	M	N	O	L	E	U	B	A
T	O	I	O	I	T	A	O	T	O

mother	grandmother	son	uncle	brother
father	grandfather	daughter	aunt	sister

VII. Dictado. Escriba las oraciones que su profesor de español va a leer.

1. _____

2. _____

3. _____

VIII. ¿Qué tiempo hace?

Respuesta: _____

IX. ¿Qué están haciendo Uds.?

Respuesta: _____

X. ¿Qué está haciendo usted?

Respuesta: _____

XI. Seleccione la respuesta correcta para completar cada oración.

1. Ayer no nos visitó (1) alguien (2) nadie (3) algunos (4) ningunos _____

2. El Año Nuevo empieza el . . . de enero. (1) un (2) una (3) primero (4) primer _____

3. Antes de . . . las noticias, el joven estaba bastante nervioso. (1) oyera (2) oír (3) oiga (4) oyendo _____

4. María es . . . guapa como las otras chicas. (1) tan (2) tanto (3) más (4) menos _____

5. Me pidió que lo . . . a clase. (1) traer (2) traeré (3) traje (4) trajera _____   **419**

XII. En este diálogo, usted trabaja en una librería. Usted es librero. Un señor entra en la librería para comprarle un libro a su primo. Usted le recomienda varios libros. El señor escoge un libro de historia. (In this dialogue, you work in a bookstore. You are a bookseller. A gentleman enters the bookstore to buy a book for his cousin. You recommend several books to him. The gentleman choose a history book.)

Complete el diálogo.

Usted: Buenos días, señor. ¿Qué clase de libro busca?

El cliente: _____

Usted: Muchos clientes prefieren libros de arte.

El cliente: _____

Usted: Tenemos un magnífico libro sobre los toros.

El cliente: _____

Usted: ¿A su primo le gusta la música?

El cliente: _____

Usted: Aquí tiene usted un nuevo libro sobre nuestra Guerra Civil.

El cliente: _____

XIII. Lea el siguiente párrafo dos veces, por lo menos. Entonces, escoja la palabra más apropiada para completar la frase. (Read the following paragraph at least twice. Then, choose the word that is most appropriate to complete the sentence.)

    A Pedro le gustan los deportes. Su deporte favorito es el fútbol. Siempre quiere que su _____ esté en buena forma porque es

1. A. cuerda
   B. cuerpo
   C. cuenta
   D. cuesta

guardameta del _____ de fútbol de su escuela. Quiere _____

2. A. equipaje   3. A. estar
   B. equipo   B. ser
   C. tema   C. tener
   D. tempestad   D. haber

siempre dispuesto para jugar bien. Siempre cuida su salud; por ejemplo, Pedro

_____ solamente alimentos que son buenos para la salud. Cuando _____

4. A. come   5. A. jugo
   B. bebe   B. juega
   C. compra   C. juego
   D. vende   D. jugar

al fútbol, evita el helado, las patatas fritas y los pasteles.

TEST 9

PART ONE   Speaking Proficiency

Directions: Read the five situations given below. Take a few minutes to organize your thoughts about the words you are going to say. Select three of the five situations. Before you begin to speak, you may review the Speaking and Writing Proficiency exercises that you practiced in this Work Unit. You may want to speak in brief sentences. Remember that all you need is a subject and a verb and you have a sentence. You may fill in the sentence with other words.

1. **Situation:** Last Saturday you and a few friends saw an exciting high school soccer game. Your friend Pablo wasn't able to be there. He wants you to tell him about the game. Make at least three statements.

2. **Situation:** Review the story at the beginning of this Work Unit, then give a summary of it in a few sentences.

3. **Situation:** You are on the phone expressing your personal feelings to Carlota about the soccer game you saw yesterday. Make at least three statements.

4. **Situation:** You have become interested in computers and laser printers. You are in a store looking at the different models and prices. Make at least three statements that you would say to the salesperson.

5. **Situation:** In class the students are reading Spanish newspapers and magazines. You have volunteered to say a few words in Spanish about the two pictures in this Work Unit showing Carl Lewis, who has won his first gold medal.

PART TWO   Listening Proficiency

Directions: Your teacher will read aloud four short paragraphs. Each one will contain only a few sentences. You will hear each paragraph twice. Then you will hear one question based on each. You will hear the question only once. It is printed below. Choose the best suggested answer based on what you heard and check the letter of your choice.

Selection Number 1

1. ¿Cómo se lava Pedro?

    A. con cuidado

    B. con el sol

    C. temprano

    D. tarde

Selection Number 2

2. ¿Cuándo tendrá lugar el gran partido?

    A. antes de la clase

    B. durante la clase

    C. después de la clase

    D. el sábado

Selection Number 3

3. ¿Dónde estará Juana esta tarde?

    A. en la escuela

    B. en el estadio

    C. con sus padres

    D. con su madre

Selection Number 4

4. ¿Qué hizo Pedro para estar en buena forma?

    A. ejercicios

    B. su traje de gimnasio

    C. antes de comenzar

    D. el gran partido de fútbol

PART THREE   Reading Proficiency

Directions: In the following passage there are five blank spaces numbered 1 through 5. Each blank space represents a missing verb form or some other word. For each blank space, four possible completions are provided. Only one of them is grammatically correct and makes sense in the context of the passage.

First, read the passage in its entirety to determine its general meaning. Then read it a second time. For each blank space choose the completion that makes the best sense and is grammatically correct. Write its letter in the space provided.

Pedro _____ extremadamente bien. Es un muchacho admirable. Es todo un

    1. A. juego
       B. juega
       C. jugar
       D. jugaré

hombre. Es un _____ estudiante, buen jugador, futbolista excelente. Los compañeros

    2. A. bien
       B. bueno
       C. buen
       D. malo

de Pedro _____ quieren. Después de la última clase ayer, Pedro _____ al

    3. A. la
       B. lo
       C. las
       D. los

    4. A. fui
       B. fue
       C. irá
       D. iré

gimnasio. Se preparó para el gran partido de fútbol. Se _____ su traje de gimnasio

    5. A. puse
       B. puso
       C. pongo
       D. ponemos

y, después, hizo ejercicios.

PART FOUR   Writing Proficiency

Directions: Of the five situations in Part One (Speaking Proficiency) in this test, select three of them and write what you said on the lines below.

Situation 1 _____

_____

_____

Situation 2 _____

_____

_____

Situation 3 _____

_____

_____

Situation 4 _____

_____

_____

Situation 5 _____

_____

_____

Appendix

PRONUNCIATION GUIDE

PURE VOWEL SOUNDS

	Pronounced as in the	
	Spanish word	English word
a	**la**	father
e	**le**	let
i	**ti**	see
o	**yo**	cold
u	**tu**	too

OTHER SOUNDS

h	**justo**	
	general }	help
	gigante	

The letter *h* in a Spanish word is not pronounced.

| y | **yo** } | yes |
| | **llave** | |

DIPHTHONGS (2 vowels together)

ai	**baile** }	eye
ay	**hay**	
au	**aula**	cow
ei	**reino** }	they
ey	**ley**	
eu	**Europa**	wayward
ya	**enviar** }	yard
	ya	
ye	**tiene** }	yes
	yendo	
yo	**iodo** }	yore
	yodo	
yu	**viuda** }	you
	yugo	
oi	**oigo** }	toy
oy	**estoy**	
wa	**cuando**	want
we	**bueno**	way
wi	**suizo**	week
wo	**cuota**	woke
y (when alone)	**y**	city

CONSONANT SOUNDS

	Pronounced as in the	
	Spanish word	English word
b	**bien** }	boy
	va	
d	**dar**	this
f	**falda**	fan
g	**gato**	
	goma }	gap
	gusto	
k	**casa**	
	culpa	
	que }	cap
	quito	
l	**la**	lard
m	**me**	may
n	**no**	no
ñ	**niño**	canyon
p	**papá**	papa
r	**pero**	April
rr	**perro**	burr, gr-r-r
s	**sopa**	
	cero	
	cita }	soft
	zumo	
t	**tu**	sit
ch	**mucho**	church

TRIPHTHONGS (3 vowels together)

yai	**enviáis**	yipe
yau	**miau**	meow
yei	**enviéis**	yea
wai	**guaina** }	wise
	Uruguay	
wau	**guau**	wow
wei	**continuéis** }	wait
	buey	

NOTE: The pronunciation guide above contains Spanish and English words as examples to illustrate sounds that approximate those in acceptable standard speech in both languages. Sometimes there are variations; for example, the pronunciation of the Spanish consonant **d** changes from soft **d**, as in the sound of **th** in the English words "**th**is fa**th**er," to hard **d**, as in the English word **d**id. At other times, it is almost silent when the tip of the tongue barely touches the upper teeth. The pronunciation also depends on the position of **d** in the word or in a phrase. It also depends on the speaker in any of the many Spanish-speaking countries in the world as well as in some regions of the United States. Here is another example of differences in the pronunciation of Spanish letters: In most Latin American countries, the letter **c** in front of **e** or **i** is pronounced **s** as in the English words *cent* / **centavo**, *city* / **ciudad.** However, it is pronounced **th** as in the English word *think* in northern and central Spain. The same is done for the letter **z.***

The following is a general rule concerning which syllable in a Spanish word is emphasized or stressed.

If a Spanish word ends in a vowel, the letter **n** or **s**, emphasize the syllable right in front of the last syllable of the word. A syllable contains a vowel.

mu / CHA / ch**o**	re / SU / me**n**	mu / CHA / cha**s**
(boy)	(summary)	(girls)

If a Spanish word ends in a letter other than a vowel, **n** or **s**, emphasize that last syllable:

com / pren / **DER**	re / a / li / **DAD**	es / pa / **ÑOL**
(to understand)	(reality)	(Spanish)

A written accent mark (´) is placed over the vowel that must be stressed when the pronunciation does not follow the above rule. The accent mark tells the reader which vowel to stress:

LA / piz	**JO** / ve / nes	pre / **TE** / ri / to
(lápiz / pencil)	(jóvenes / young)	(pretérito / preterit tense)

The accent mark is also used to distinguish the meaning of two words pronounced identically. Examples:

si / if, **sí** / yes   **el** / the, **él** / he   **de** / of, **dé** / give (imperative of **dar**, Ud. form)

The accent mark is also used on the stressed vowel of some words when used in questions. Examples:

¿cómo? / how?   **¿dónde?** / where?   **¿cuándo?** / when?   **¿quién?** / who?

FIVE COMMONLY USED SPANISH VERBS CONJUGATED IN ALL 14 TENSES

Here are some commonly used irregular verbs conjugated fully in all the tenses and moods. If any verbs *not* given here are of interest to you, consult *501 Spanish Verbs Fully Conjugated in All the Tenses in a New Easy-to-Learn Format,* Fourth Edition, which contains them all, also published by Barron's.

In the format of the verbs that follow, the subject pronouns have been omitted in order to emphasize the verb forms. The subject pronouns are, as you know:

Subject Pronouns

singular	*plural*
yo	**nosotros (nosotras)**
tú	**vosotros (vosotras)**
Ud. (él, ella)	**Uds. (ellos, ellas)**

---

*If you want to improve your pronunciation of Spanish, I would recommend Barron's *Pronounce It Perfectly in Spanish.* It comes with two 90-minute cassettes. You can listen to authentic Spanish pronunciation and imitate the sounds during the pauses.

estar / to be
Gerundio **estando**   Part. pas. **estado**

The Seven Simple Tenses		The Seven Compound Tenses	
Singular	Plural	Singular	Plural
1 presente de indicativo		**8 perfecto de indicativo**	
estoy	estamos	he estado	hemos estado
estás	estáis	has estado	habéis estado
está	están	ha estado	han estado
2 imperfecto de indicativo		**9 pluscuamperfecto de indicativo**	
estaba	estábamos	había estado	habíamos estado
estabas	estabais	habías estado	habíais estado
estaba	estaban	había estado	habían estado
3 pretérito		**10 pretérito anterior**	
estuve	estuvimos	hube estado	hubimos estado
estuviste	estuvisteis	hubiste estado	hubisteis estado
estuvo	estuvieron	hubo estado	hubieron estado
4 futuro		**11 futuro perfecto**	
estaré	estaremos	habré estado	habremos estado
estarás	estaréis	habrás estado	habréis estado
estará	estarán	habrá estado	habrán estado
5 potencial simple		**12 potencial compuesto**	
estaría	estaríamos	habría estado	habríamos estado
estarías	estaríais	habrías estado	habríais estado
estaría	estarían	habría estado	habrían estado
6 presente de subjuntivo		**13 perfecto de subjuntivo**	
esté	estemos	haya estado	hayamos estado
estés	estéis	hayas estado	hayáis estado
esté	estén	haya estado	hayan estado
7 imperfecto de subjuntivo		**14 pluscuamperfecto de subjuntivo**	
estuviera	estuviéramos	hubiera estado	hubiéramos estado
estuvieras	estuvierais	hubieras estado	hubierais estado
estuviera	estuvieran	hubiera estado	hubieran estado
OR		OR	
estuviese	estuviésemos	hubiese estado	hubiésemos estado
estuvieses	estuvieseis	hubieses estado	hubieseis estado
estuviese	estuviesen	hubiese estado	hubiesen estado

imperativo

—	estemos
está; no estés	estad; no estéis
esté	estén

Common idiomatic expressions using this verb

—**¿Cómo está Ud.?**
—**Estoy muy bien, gracias. ¿Y usted?**
—**Estoy enfermo hoy.**

estar para + inf.   to be about + inf.
   Estoy para salir.   I am about to go out.
estar por   to be in favor of

haber / to have (as an auxiliary verb to form compound tenses)
Gerundio **habiendo**   Part. pas. **habido**

The Seven Simple Tenses		The Seven Compound Tenses	
Singular	Plural	Singular	Plural
1 presente de indicativo		**8 perfecto de indicativo**	
he	hemos	he habido	hemos habido
has	habéis	has habido	habéis habido
ha	han	ha habido	han habido
2 imperfecto de indicativo		**9 pluscuamperfecto de indicativo**	
había	habíamos	había habido	habíamos habido
habías	habíais	habías habido	habíais habido
había	habían	había habido	habían habido
3 pretérito		**10 pretérito anterior**	
hube	hubimos	hube habido	hubimos habido
hubiste	hubisteis	hubiste habido	hubisteis habido
hubo	hubieron	hubo habido	hubieron habido
4 futuro		**11 futuro perfecto**	
habré	habremos	habré habido	habremos habido
habrás	habréis	habrás habido	habréis habido
habrá	habrán	habrá habido	habrán habido
5 potencial simple		**12 potencial compuesto**	
habría	habríamos	habría habido	habríamos habido
habrías	habríais	habrías habido	habríais habido
habría	habrían	habría habido	habrían habido
6 presente de subjuntivo		**13 perfecto de subjuntivo**	
haya	hayamos	haya habido	hayamos habido
hayas	hayáis	hayas habido	hayáis habido
haya	hayan	haya habido	hayan habido
7 imperfecto de subjuntivo		**14 pluscuamperfecto de subjuntivo**	
hubiera	hubiéramos	hubiera habido	hubiéramos habido
hubieras	hubierais	hubieras habido	hubierais habido
hubiera	hubieran	hubiera habido	hubieran habido
OR		OR	
hubiese	hubiésemos	hubiese habido	hubiésemos habido
hubieses	hubieseis	hubieses habido	hubieseis habido
hubiese	hubiesen	hubiese habido	hubiesen habido

imperativo

—	hayamos
hé; no hayas	habed; no hayáis
haya	hayan

Words and expressions related to this verb

el haber   credit (in bookkeeping)
los haberes   assets, possessions, property
habérselas con alguien   to have a showdown with someone
hay ...   there is ..., there are ...
No hay de qué.   You're welcome.
He aquí la verdad.   Here is the truth.

hacer / to do, to make
Gerundio **haciendo**   Part. pas. **hecho**

The Seven Simple Tenses		The Seven Compound Tenses	
Singular	Plural	Singular	Plural

1   presente de indicativo

Singular	Plural
hago	hacemos
haces	hacéis
hace	hacen

8   perfecto de indicativo

Singular	Plural
he hecho	hemos hecho
has hecho	habéis hecho
ha hecho	han hecho

2   imperfecto de indicativo

Singular	Plural
hacía	hacíamos
hacías	hacíais
hacía	hacían

9   pluscuamperfecto de indicativo

Singular	Plural
había hecho	habíamos hecho
habías hecho	habíais hecho
había hecho	habían hecho

3   pretérito

Singular	Plural
hice	hicimos
hiciste	hicisteis
hizo	hicieron

10   pretérito anterior

Singular	Plural
hube hecho	hubimos hecho
hubiste hecho	hubisteis hecho
hubo hecho	hubieron hecho

4   futuro

Singular	Plural
haré	haremos
harás	haréis
hará	harán

11   futuro perfecto

Singular	Plural
habré hecho	habremos hecho
habrás hecho	habréis hecho
habrá hecho	habrán hecho

5   potencial simple

Singular	Plural
haría	haríamos
harías	haríais
haría	harían

12   potencial compuesto

Singular	Plural
habría hecho	habríamos hecho
habrías hecho	habríais hecho
habría hecho	habrían hecho

6   presente de subjuntivo

Singular	Plural
haga	hagamos
hagas	hagáis
haga	hagan

13   perfecto de subjuntivo

Singular	Plural
haya hecho	hayamos hecho
hayas hecho	hayáis hecho
haya hecho	hayan hecho

7   imperfecto de subjuntivo

Singular	Plural
hiciera	hiciéramos
hicieras	hicierais
hiciera	hicieran
OR	
hiciese	hiciésemos
hicieses	hicieseis
hiciese	hiciesen

14   pluscuamperfecto de subjuntivo

Singular	Plural
hubiera hecho	hubiéramos hecho
hubieras hecho	hubierais hecho
hubiera hecho	hubieran hecho
OR	
hubiese hecho	hubiésemos hecho
hubieses hecho	hubieseis hecho
hubiese hecho	hubiesen hecho

imperativo

—	hagamos
haz; no hagas	haced; no hagáis
haga	hagan

Common idiomatic expressions using this verb

Dicho y hecho.   No sooner said than done.
La práctica hace maestro al novicio.   Practice makes perfect.
Si a Roma fueres, haz como vieres.   When in Rome do as the Romans do. Note that it is not uncommon to use the future subjunctive in proverbs, as in *fueres* (**ir** or **ser**) and *vieres* (**ver**).

ir / to go
Gerundio **yendo**   Part. pas. **ido**

The Seven Simple Tenses		The Seven Compound Tenses	
Singular	Plural	Singular	Plural
1 presente de indicativo		8 perfecto de indicativo	
voy	**vamos**	**he ido**	**hemos ido**
vas	**vais**	**has ido**	**habéis ido**
va	**van**	**ha ido**	**han ido**
2 imperfecto de indicativo		9 pluscuamperfecto de indicativo	
iba	**íbamos**	**había ido**	**habíamos ido**
ibas	**ibais**	**habías ido**	**habíais ido**
iba	**iban**	**había ido**	**habían ido**
3 pretérito		10 pretérito anterior	
fui	**fuimos**	**hube ido**	**hubimos ido**
fuiste	**fuisteis**	**hubiste ido**	**hubisteis ido**
fue	**fueron**	**hubo ido**	**hubieron ido**
4 futuro		11 futuro perfecto	
iré	**iremos**	**habré ido**	**habremos ido**
irás	**iréis**	**habrás ido**	**habréis ido**
irá	**irán**	**habrá ido**	**habrán ido**
5 potencial simple		12 potencial compuesto	
iría	**iríamos**	**habría ido**	**habríamos ido**
irías	**iríais**	**habrías ido**	**habríais ido**
iría	**irían**	**habría ido**	**habrían ido**
6 presente de subjuntivo		13 perfecto de subjuntivo	
vaya	**vayamos**	**haya ido**	**hayamos ido**
vayas	**vayáis**	**hayas ido**	**hayáis ido**
vaya	**vayan**	**haya ido**	**hayan ido**
7 imperfecto de subjuntivo		14 pluscuamperfecto de subjuntivo	
fuera	**fuéramos**	**hubiera ido**	**hubiéramos ido**
fueras	**fuerais**	**hubieras ido**	**hubierais ido**
fuera	**fueran**	**hubiera ido**	**hubieran ido**
OR		OR	
fuese	**fuésemos**	**hubiese ido**	**hubiésemos ido**
fueses	**fueseis**	**hubieses ido**	**hubieseis ido**
fuese	**fuesen**	**hubiese ido**	**hubiesen ido**

imperativo

—	**vamos (no vayamos)**
ve; no vayas	**id; no vayáis**
vaya	**vayan**

Common idiomatic expressions using this verb

ir de compras   to go shopping
ir de brazo   to walk arm in arm
¿Cómo le va?   How goes it? How are you?
Cuando el gato va a sus devociones, bailan los ratones.   When the cat is away, the mice will play.

ir a caballo   to ride horseback
un billete de ida y vuelta   return ticket
¡Qué va!   Nonsense!

ser / to be
Gerundio **siendo**   Part. pas. **sido**

The Seven Simple Tenses		The Seven Compound Tenses	
Singular	Plural	Singular	Plural
1 presente de indicativo		8 perfecto de indicativo	
soy	somos	he sido	hemos sido
eres	sois	has sido	habéis sido
es	son	ha sido	han sido
2 imperfecto de indicativo		9 pluscuamperfecto de indicativo	
era	éramos	había sido	habíamos sido
eras	erais	habías sido	habíais sido
era	eran	había sido	habían sido
3 pretérito		10 pretérito anterior	
fui	fuimos	hube sido	hubimos sido
fuiste	fuisteis	hubiste sido	hubisteis sido
fue	fueron	hubo sido	hubieron sido
4 futuro		11 futuro perfecto	
seré	seremos	habré sido	habremos sido
serás	seréis	habrás sido	habréis sido
será	serán	habrá sido	habrán sido
5 potencial simple		12 potencial compuesto	
sería	seríamos	habría sido	habríamos sido
serías	seríais	habrías sido	habríais sido
sería	serían	habría sido	habrían sido
6 presente de subjuntivo		13 perfecto de subjuntivo	
sea	seamos	haya sido	hayamos sido
seas	seáis	hayas sido	hayáis sido
sea	sean	haya sido	hayan sido
7 imperfecto de subjuntivo		14 pluscuamperfecto de subjuntivo	
fuera	fuéramos	hubiera sido	hubiéramos sido
fueras	fuerais	hubieras sido	hubierais sido
fuera	fueran	hubiera sido	hubieran sido
OR		OR	
fuese	fuésemos	hubiese sido	hubiésemos sido
fueses	fueseis	hubieses sido	hubieseis sido
fuese	fuesen	hubiese sido	hubiesen sido

imperativo

—	seamos
sé; no seas	sed; no seáis
sea	sean

Common idiomatic expressions using this verb

Dime con quien andas y te diré quien eres.   Tell me who your friends are and I will tell you
   who you are.
es decir   that is, that is to say; **Si yo fuera usted. . .**   If I were you. . .
¿Qué hora es?   What time is it?   **Es la una.**   It is one o'clock.   **Son las dos.**   It is
   two o'clock.

DEFINITIONS OF BASIC GRAMMATICAL TERMS WITH EXAMPLES

Active Voice

When we speak or write in the active voice, the subject of the verb performs the action of the verb. The action falls on the direct object if there is one.

Example:
The robber opened the window / **El ladrón abrió la ventana.**

The subject is *the robber*. The verb is *opened*. The direct object is *the window*.
See also passive voice. Compare the above sentence with the example in the passive voice.

Adjective

An adjective is a word that modifies a noun or a pronoun. In grammar, to modify a word means to describe, limit, expand, or make the meaning particular.

Examples:
a beautiful garden / **un jardín hermoso**; she is pretty / **ella es bonita.** The adjective *beautiful* / **hermoso** modifies the noun *garden* / **jardín.** The adjective *pretty* / **bonita** modifies the pronoun *she* / **ella.**

In Spanish there are different kinds of adjectives. *See also* comparative adjective, demonstrative adjective, descriptive adjective, interrogative adjective, limiting adjective, possessive adjective, superlative adjective.
Review Work Unit 6.

Adverb

An adverb is a word that modifies a verb, an adjective, or another adverb. An adverb says something about how, when, where, to what extent, or in what way.

Examples:
Mary runs swiftly / **María corre rápidamente.** The adverb *swiftly* / **rápidamente** modifies the verb *runs* / **corre.** The adverb shows *how* she runs.

John is very handsome / **Juan es muy guapo.** The adverb *very* / **muy** modifies the adjective *handsome* / **guapo.** The adverb shows *how handsome* he is.

The boy is talking very fast now / **El muchacho habla muy rápidamente ahora.** The adverb *very* / **muy** modifies the adverb *fast* / **rápidamente.** The adverb shows *to what extent* he is talking *fast*. The adverb *now* / **ahora** tells us *wh*

The post office is there / **La oficina de correos está allá.** The adverb *there* / **allá** modifies the verb *is* / **está.** It tells us *where* the post office is.

Mary writes meticulously / **María escribe meticulosamente.** The adverb m*eticulously* / **meticulosamente** modifies the verb *writes* / **escribe.** It tells us *in what way* she writes.

Review Work Unit 7.

Affirmative Statement, Negative Statement

A statement in the affirmative is the opposite of a statement in the negative. To negate an affirmative statement is to make it negative.

Example in the affirmative: I like ice cream / **Me gusta el helado.**

Example in the negative: I do not like ice cream / **No me gusta el helado.**

Review negation of verb forms in Work Unit 4.

Agreement of Adjective with Noun

Agreement is made on the adjective with the noun it modifies in gender (masculine or feminine) and number (singular or plural).

Examples:

a white house / **una casa blanca.** The adjective **blanca** is feminine singular because the noun **una casa** is feminine singular.

many white houses / **muchas casas blancas.** The adjectives **muchas** and **blancas** are feminine plural because the noun **casas** is feminine plural.

Review the different kinds of adjectives in Work Unit 6.

Agreement of Verb with its Subject

A verb agrees in person (1st, 2d, or 3d) and in number (singular or plural) with its subject.

Examples:

Paul tells the truth / **Pablo dice la verdad.** The verb **dice** (of **decir**) is 3d person singular because the subject *Pablo* / *Paul* is 3d person singular.

Where are the tourists going? / **¿Adónde van los turistas?** The verb **van** (of **ir**) is 3d person plural because the subject *los turistas* / *the tourists* is 3d person plural.

For subject pronouns in the singular and plural, review Work Unit 2.

Antecedent

An antecedent is a word to which a relative pronoun refers. It comes *before* the pronoun.

Examples:

The girl who is laughing loudly is my sister / **La muchacha que está riendo a carcajadas es mi hermana.** The antecedent is *girl* / *la muchacha*. The relative pronoun *who* / *que* refers to the girl.

The car that I bought is very expensive / **El carro que yo compré es muy costoso.**

The antecedent is *car* / **el carro.** The relative pronoun *that* / *que* refers to the car.
Review **comprar** in the regular verb tables and **reír** in the irregular verb tables.
Note that **está riendo** is the present progressive of **reír.** Review Work Units 1, 3, and 9. Also review present participles in Work Unit 3.
Review antecedent in the section on relative pronouns in Work Unit 10. *See also* relative pronoun.

Auxiliary Verb

An auxiliary verb is a helping verb. In English grammar it is *to have*. In Spanish grammar it is **haber** / *to have*. An auxiliary verb is used to help form the compound tenses.

Example in the present perfect tense:
I *have* eaten / **(Yo) he comido.**

Review the six forms of **haber** in the present indicative tense in Work Unit 12. You need to know them to form the present perfect tense, which is also in Work Unit 12.
Review the formation of past participles in the same Work Unit. You need to know them to form the seven compound tenses. Also, review the forms of **haber** in the irregular verb tables and on page 427 where all the forms are given. You need to know them to form the seven compound tenses.

Cardinal Number

A cardinal number is a number that expresses an amount, such as *one, two, three,* and so on.
Review Work Unit 4. *See also* ordinal number.

Clause

A clause is a group of words that contains a subject and a predicate. A predicate may contain more than one word. A conjugated verb form is revealed in the predicate.

Example:
Mrs. Gómez lives in a large apartment / **La señora Gómez vive en un gran apartamento.** The subject is *Mrs. Gómez* / **la señora Gómez**. The predicate is *lives in a large apartment* / **vive en un gran apartamento.** The verb is *lives* / **vive.**

Review **vivir** in the regular verb tables.
See also dependent clause, independent clause, predicate.

Comparative Adjective

When making a comparison between two persons or things, an adjective is used to express the degree of comparison in the following ways.

Examples:
Of the same degree of comparison:
Helen is *as tall as* Mary / **Elena es *tan alta como* María.**

Of a lesser degree of comparison:
Jane is *less intelligent than* Eva / **Juana es *menos inteligente que* Eva.**

Of a higher degree of comparison:
This apple is *more delicious than* that one / **Esta manzana es *más deliciosa que* ésa.**

Review Work Unit 6. *See also* superlative adjective.

Comparative Adverb

An adverb is compared in the same way as an adjective is compared. *See* comparative adjective above.

Examples:
Of the same degree of comparison:
Mr. Robles speaks *as well as* Mr. Vega / **El señor Robles habla *tan bien como* el señor Vega.**

Of a lesser degree of comparison:
Alice studies *less diligently than* her sister / **Alicia estudia *menos diligentemente que* su hermana.**

Of a higher degree of comparison:
Albert works *more slowly than* his brother / **Alberto trabaja *más lentamente que* su hermano.**

Review Work Unit 7. *See also* superlative adverb.

Complex Sentence

A complex sentence contains one independent clause and one or more dependent clauses.

Examples:
One independent clause and one dependent clause:
Joseph works but his brother doesn't / **José trabaja pero su hermano no trabaja.**

The independent clause is *Joseph works.* It makes sense when it stands alone because it expresses a complete thought. The dependent clause is *but his brother doesn't.* The dependent clause, which is introduced by the conjunction *but* / **pero,** does not make complete sense when it stands alone because it *depends* on the thought expressed in the independent clause.

One independent clause and two dependent clauses:
Anna is a good student because she studies but her sister never studies / **Ana es una buena alumna porque estudia pero su hermana nunca estudia.**

433

The independent clause is *Anna is a good student.* It makes sense when it stands alone because it expresses a complete thought. The first dependent clause is *because she studies.* This dependent clause, which is introduced by the conjunction *because / **porque***, does not make complete sense when it stands alone because it *depends* on the thought expressed in the independent clause. The second dependent clause is *but her sister never studies.* That dependent clause, which is introduced by the conjunction *but / **pero,*** does not make complete sense either when it stands alone because it *depends* on the thought expressed in the independent clause.

See also dependent clause, independent clause.

Compound Sentence

A compound sentence contains two or more independent clauses.

Example:
Mrs. Fuentes went to the supermarket, she bought a few things, and then she went home / **La señora Fuentes fue al supermercado, compró algunas cosas, y entonces fue a casa.**

This compound sentence contains three independent clauses. They are independent because they make sense when they stand alone.

Review the explanation, uses, and examples of the **pretérito** (Tense No. 3) in Work Unit 7. Review **comprar** in the regular verb tables and **ir** in the irregular verb tables.

See also independent clause.

Conditional Present Tense

In Spanish grammar, the conditional **(el potencial simple)** is considered a mood. This tense is defined with examples in Work Unit 9.

Conjugation

The conjugation of a verb is the fixed order of all its forms showing their inflections (changes) in the three persons of the singular and plural in a particular tense.

See also number and person (1st, 2d, 3d).

For examples, see the conjugation of regular and irregular verbs in the verb tables. Also, see pages 426–430 for the complete conjugation in all the tenses of the following five commonly used verbs: **estar, haber, hacer, ir,** and **ser.**

Conjunction

A conjunction is a word that connects words or groups of words.

Examples:

and / **y**, or / **o**, but / **pero,** because / **porque**

Charles *and* Charlotte / **Carlos y Carlota**

You can stay home *or* you can come with me / **(Tú) puedes quedarte en casa o venir conmigo.**

Note that **y** (and) changes to **e** if the word right after **y** begins with **i** or **hi.**

Examples:
María es bonita e inteligente / Mary is pretty and intelligent.

Fernando e Isabel / Fernando and Isabel

padre e hijo / father and son; **madre e hija** / mother and daughter

However, if **y** is followed by a word that begins with **hie**, keep **y: flores y hierba** / flowers and grass.

Contrary to Fact

This term refers to an "if" clause. *See* if **(si)** clause.

Declarative Sentence

A declarative sentence makes a statement.

Example:
> I have finished the work / **(Yo) he terminado el trabajo.**

Review the **perfecto de indicativo** / present perfect indicative (Tense No. 8) and the formation of past participles in Work Unit 12.

Definite Article

The definite article in Spanish has four forms and they all mean *the*. They are: **el, la, los, las.** Review Work Unit 1.

Examples:
> **el libro** / the book,   **la casa** / the house,   **los libros** / the books,   **las casas** / the houses. The definite articles **la, los, las** are also used as direct object pronouns.

See direct object pronoun.

Demonstrative Adjective

A demonstrative adjective is an adjective that points out. It is placed in front of a noun.

Examples:
> this book / **este libro;**   these books / **estos libros;**   this cup / **esta taza;**   these flowers / **estas flores.**

Revlew Work Unit 6.

Demonstrative Pronoun

A demonstrative pronoun is a pronoun that points out. It takes the place of a noun. It agrees in gender and number with the noun it replaces.

Examples:
> I have two oranges; do you prefer *this one* or *that one?* / **Tengo dos naranjas; ¿prefiere usted *ésta* o ésa?**

> I prefer *those* [over there] / **Prefiero *aquéllas.***

Review Work Unlt 9. For demonstrative pronouns that are neuter, *see* neuter.

Dependent Clause

A dependent clause is a group of words that contains a subject and a predicate. It does not express a complete thought when it stands alone. It is called *dependent* because it depends on the independent clause for a complete meaning. Subordinate clause is another term for dependent clause.

Example:
> Edward is absent today because he is sick / **Eduardo está ausente hoy porque está enfermo.** The independent clause is *Edward is absent today.* The dependent clause is *because he is sick.*

See also clause, independent clause.

Descriptive Adjective

A descriptive adjective is an adjective that describes a person, place, or thing.

Examples:

a pretty girl / **una muchacha bonita**;   a big house / **una casa grande;** an expensive car / **un carro costoso.**

Review Work Unit 6. *See also* adjective.

Direct Object Noun

A direct object noun receives the action of the verb *directly.* That is why it is called a direct object, as opposed to an indirect object. A direct object noun is normally placed *after* the verb.

Example:

I am writing a letter / **Escribo una carta.** The direct object is the noun *letter* / **una carta.**

Review Work Units 8 and 9. *See also* direct object pronoun.

Direct Object Pronoun

A direct object pronoun receives the action of the verb *directly.* It takes the place of a direct object noun. In Spanish a pronoun that is a direct object of a verb is ordinarily placed *in front of* the verb.

Example:

I am writing it [the letter] / **La escribo.**

Review the direct object pronouns, their uses and positions with examples in Work Units 8, 9, and 10.

However, in the *affirmative imperative*, a direct object pronoun is placed *after* the verb and is joined to it, resulting in one word.

Example:

Write it [the letter] now! / **¡Escríbala [Ud.] ahora!**

Review the imperative in Work Units 3, 4, 9, and 10.

Note that an accent mark is added on the vowel **i [í]** in order to keep the emphasis on that vowel as it was in **escriba** before the direct object pronoun **la** was added to the verb form. Review the simple rule about stressed vowel sounds in Spanish and when accent marks are needed in the Pronunciation Guide.

See also imperative.

Disjunctive Pronoun

A disjunctive pronoun is a pronoun that is stressed; in other words, emphasis is placed on it. It is usually object of a preposition. Prepositional pronoun is another term for disjunctive pronoun.

Examples:

for me / **para mí;** for you *(fam.)* / **para ti; con usted** / with you; **con él** / with him; **con ella** / with her

Note the following exceptions with **con:**

conmigo / with me; **contigo** / with you *(fam.)*; **consigo** / with yourself (yourselves, himself, herself, themselves).

Review the prepositional pronouns in Work Unit 9.

Ending of a Verb

In Spanish grammar the ending of a verb form changes according to the person and number of the subject and the tense of the verb.

Example:

To form the present indicative tense of a regular **–ar** type verb like **hablar**, drop **ar** of the infinitive and add the following endings: **–o, –as, –a** for the 1st, 2d, and 3d persons of the singular;–**amos**, –**áis**, **-an** for the 1st, 2d, and 3d persons of the plural. You then get: **hablo, hablas, habla; hablamos, habláis, hablan**

Review Work Unit 2. *See also* stem of a verb.

Feminine

In Spanish grammar the gender of a noun, pronoun, or adjective is feminine or masculine, not male or female.

Examples:

	Masculine			*Feminine*	
noun	*pronoun*	*adjective*	*noun*	*pronoun*	*adjective*
el hombre	**él**	**guapo**	**la mujer**	**ella**	**hermosa**
the man	*he*	*handsome*	*the woman*	*she*	*beautiful*

See also gender.

Future Tense

This tense is defined with examples in Work Unit 8.

Gender

Gender means masculine or feminine.

Examples:
> *Masculine*: the boy / **el muchacho;** the book / **el libro**
> *Feminine*: the girl / **la muchacha;** the house / **la casa**

Gerund

In English grammar, a gerund is a word formed from a verb. It ends in *ing*. Actually, it is the present participle of a verb. However, it is not used as a verb. It is used as a noun.

Example:
> Seeing is believing / **Ver es creer** *[to see is to believe].* It is sometimes stated as **Ver y creer** *[to see and to believe].*

However, in Spanish grammar, the infinitive form of the verb is used, as in the above example, when the verb is used as a noun.

The Spanish gerund is also a word formed from a verb. It is the present participle of a verb. The Spanish gerund **[el gerundio]** regularly ends in **ando** for **ar** type verbs (of the 1st conjugation)**,** in **iendo** for **er** type verbs (of the 2d conjugation), and **iendo** for **ir** type verbs (of the 3d conjugation). There are also irregular present participles that end in **yendo.**

Examples of a Spanish gerund:
> **hablando** / talking   **comiendo** / eating   **viviendo** / living

Review the gerund in Work Unit 13. Review the present participles and their uses in in Work Units 3 and 6. *See also* present participle.

If (si) Clause

Another term for an "if" clause is contrary to fact, as in English, if I were king..., if I were rich... .

Example:
> **Si yo tuviera bastante dinero, iría a España** / If I had enough money, I would go to Spain.

Review the imperfect subjunctive (Tense No. 7) of **tener (tuviera)** and the summary of contrary-to-fact conditions in a **si** (if) clause in Work Unit 11.

437

You may also want to review the conditional (Tense No. 5) in Work Unit 9 for the regular formation of **ir** in that tense (**iría** / I would go).

See also clause.

Imperative

The imperative is a mood, not a tense. It is used to express a command. In Spanish it is used in the 2d person of the singular **(tú)**, the 3d person of the singular **(usted)**, the 1st person of the plural **(nosotros, nosotras)**, the 2d person of the plural **(vosotros, vosotras)**, and in the 3d person of the plural **(ustedes)**.

Review the uses of the imperative (command) in Work Units 4, 9, and 10, and in the verb tables.

Imperfect Indicative Tense

This tense is defined with examples in Work Unit 6.

Imperfect Subjunctive Tense

This tense is defined with examples in Work Unit 11.

Indefinite Article

In English the indefinite articles are *a, an*, as in *a book, an apple*. They are indefinite because they do not refer to any definite or particular noun.

In Spanish there are two indefinite articles in the singular: one in the masculine form **(un)** and one in the feminine form **(una)**.

Examples:
> Masculine singular: **un libro** / *a book*
> Feminine singular: **una manzana** / *an apple*

In the plural they change to **unos** and **unas.**

Examples:
> **unos libros** / some books; **unas manzanas** / some apples

Review them in Work Unit 1.

Indefinite Pronoun

An indefinite pronoun is a pronoun that does not refer to any definite or particular noun.

Examples:
> something / **algo;** someone, somebody / **alguien**

Independent Clause

An independent clause is a group of words that contains a subject and a predicate. It expresses a complete thought when it stands alone.

Example:
> The cat is sleeping on the bed / **El gato está durmiendo sobre la cama.**

See also clause, dependent clause, predicate.

Indicative Mood

The indicative mood is used in sentences that make a statement or ask a question. The indicative mood is used most of the time when we speak or write in English or Spanish.

Examples:
> I am going to the movies now / **Voy al cine ahora.**
> Where are you going? / **¿Adónde vas?**

Indirect Object Noun

An indirect object noun receives the action of the verb *indirectly.*

Example:

I am writing a letter to Christine *or* I am writing Christine a letter / **Estoy escribiendo una carta a Cristina.** The verb is *am writing / **estoy escribiendo.*** The direct object noun is *a letter / **una carta.*** The indirect object noun is *Cristina* / Christine.

See also indirect object pronoun.

Indirect Object Pronoun

An indirect object pronoun takes the place of an indirect object noun. It receives the action of the verb *indirectly.*

Example:

I am writing a letter to her *or* I am writing her a letter / **Le escribo una carta a ella.** The indirect object pronoun is *(to) her /* **le.** It is clarified by adding **a ella.**

Review the indirect object pronouns, their uses and positions with examples in Work Units 8, 9, and 10.
See also indirect object noun.

Infinitive

An infinitive is a verb form. In English, it is normally stated with the preposition *to,* as in *to talk, to drink, to receive.* In Spanish, the infinitive form of a verb consists of three major types: those of the 1st conjugation that end in **–ar,** the 2d conjugation that end in **–er,** and the 3d conjugation that end in **–ir.**

In Spanish grammar, the infinitive **(el infinitivo)** is considered a mood.

Examples:

hablar / *to talk, to speak*   **beber** / *to drink*   **recibir** / *to receive*

Review infinitives in Work Unit 13.

Interjection

An interjection is a word that expresses emotion, a feeling of joy, of sadness, an exclamation of surprise, and other exclamations consisting of one or two words.

Examples:

Ah! / **¡Ah!**   Ouch! / **¡Ay!**   Darn it! / **¡Caramba!**   My God! / **¡Dios mío!**

Interrogative Adjective

In Spanish, an interrogative adjective is an adjective that is used in a question. As an adjective, it is placed in front of a noun.

Examples:

What book do you want? / **¿Qué libro desea usted?**
What time is it? / **¿Qué hora es?**

Review adjectives in Work Unit 6.

Interrogative Adverb

In Spanish, an interrogative adverb is an adverb that introduces a question. As an adverb, it modifies the verb.

Examples:

How are you? / **¿*Cómo* está usted?**

How much does this book cost? / *¿Cuánto* **cuesta este libro?**
When will you arrive? / *¿Cuándo* **llegará usted?**

Review adverbs in Work Unit 7.

Interrogative Pronoun

An interrogative pronoun is a pronoun that asks a question. There are interrogative pronouns that refer to persons and those that refer to things.

Examples:
Who is it? / *¿Quién* **es?**
What are you saying? / *¿Qué* **dice usted?**

Review the different kinds of pronouns in Work Units 2, 8, 9, and 10.

Interrogative Sentence

An interrogative sentence asks a question.

Example:
What are you doing? / **¿Qué hace usted?**

Review interrogative sentence word order in Work Unit 2.

Intransitive Verb

An intransitive verb is a verb that does not take a direct object.

Example:
The professor is talking / **El profesor habla.**

An intransitive verb takes an indirect object.

Example:
The professor is talking to us / **El profesor nos habla.**

See also direct object pronoun, indirect object pronoun, transitive verb.

Irregular Verb

An irregular verb is a verb that does not follow a fixed pattern in its conjugation in the various verb tenses.

Examples of basic irregular verbs in Spanish:
estar / to be   **hacer** / to do, to make   **ir** / to go   **ser** / to be

For examples, see the irregular verb tables.
See also conjugation, regular verb.

Limiting Adjective

A limiting adjective is an adjective that limits a quantity.

Example:
three lemons / **tres limones**   a few candies / **algunos dulces**

Review them in Work Unit 6.

Main Clause

Main clause is another term for independent clause. *See* independent clause.

440

Masculine

In Spanish grammar the gender of a noun, pronoun, or adjective is masculine or feminine, not male or female.

See also feminine, gender.

Mood of Verbs

Some grammarians use the term *the mode* instead of *the mood* of a verb. Either term means *the manner or way* a verb is expressed. In English and Spanish grammar a verb expresses an action or state of being in a particular mood.

In Spanish grammar, there are five moods **(modos)**: the infinitive **(el infinitivo)**, the indicative **(el indicativo)**, the imperative **(el imperativo)**, the conditional **(el potencial)**, and the subjunctive **(el subjuntivo)**.

In English grammar, there are three moods: the indicative mood, the subjunctive mood, and the imperative mood.

Most of the time, in English and Spanish, we speak and write in the indicative mood.

Negative Statement, Affirmative Statement

See affirmative statement, negative statement.

Neuter

A word that is neuter is neither masculine nor feminine. Common neuter demonstrative pronouns in Spanish are **esto** / *this*, **eso** / *that*, **aquello** / *that* (farther away). Review them in Work Unit 9.

Examples:

What's this? / **¿Qué es esto?** What's that? / **¿Qué es eso?**

For demonstrative pronouns that are not neuter, *see* demonstrative pronoun.

There is also the neuter pronoun **lo.** It usually refers to an idea or statement. It is not normally translated into English but often the translation is *so*.

Examples:

¿Estás enferma, María? / Are you sick, Mary? **Sí, lo estoy** / Yes, I am.
No lo creo / I don't think so.
Lo parece / It seems so.

Review the neuter direct object *pronoun* **lo** in Work Unit 8 and the neuter *article* **lo** with examples in Spanish and English in Work Unit 1.

Noun

A noun is a word that names a person, animal, place, thing, condition or state, or quality.

Examples:

the man / **el hombre,** the woman / **la mujer,** the horse / **el caballo,** the house / **la casa,** the pencil / **el lápiz,** happiness / **la felicidad,** excellence / **la excelencia**

In Spanish the noun **el nombre** is the word for name and noun. Another word for noun in Spanish is **el sustantivo** / *substantive*.

Review nouns in Work Units 1 and 6.

Number

In English and Spanish grammar, number means singular or plural.

Examples:

Masc. sing.: the boy / **el muchacho**   the pencil / **el lápiz**   the eye / **el ojo**
Masc. pl.: the boys / **los muchachos**   the pencils / **los lápices**   the eyes / **los ojos**

| Fem. sing.: the girl / **la muchacha** | the house / **la casa** | the cow / **la vaca** |
| Fem. pl.: the girls / **las muchachas** | the houses / **las casas** | the cows / **las vacas** |

Ordinal Number

An ordinal number is a number that expresses position in a series, such as *first, second, third*, and so on. In English and Spanish grammar we talk about 1st person, 2d person, 3d person singular or plural regarding subjects and verbs.

See also cardinal number and person (1st, 2d, 3d).

Orthographical Changes in Verb Forms

An orthographical change in a verb form is a change in spelling.

Example:

The verb **conocer** / *to know, to be acquainted with* changes in spelling in the 1st person singular of the present indicative. The letter **z** is inserted in front of the second **c**. When formed regularly, the ending **er** of the infinitive drops and **o** is added for the 1st person singular form of the present indicative. That would result in **conoco,** a peculiar sound to the Spanish ear for a verb form of **conocer.** The letter **z** is added to keep the sound of **s** as it is in the infinitive **conocer.** Therefore, the spelling changes and the form is **yo conozco.** In the other forms of **conocer** in the present indicative **z** is not inserted because they retain the sound of **s.**

There are many verb forms in Spanish that contain orthographical changes.

Review orthographical changing verbs in Work Units 3, 7, 10, and in the irregular verb tables.

Passive Voice

When we speak or write in the active voice and change to the passive voice, the direct object becomes the subject, the subject becomes the object of a preposition, and the verb becomes *to be* plus the past participle of the active verb. The past participle functions as an adjective.

Example:
The window was opened by the robber / **La ventana fue abierta por el ladrón.**

The subject is *la ventana.* The verb is *fue.* The word *abierta* is a feminine adjective agreeing with *la ventana*. Actually, it is the past participle of **abrir** / *to open* but here it serves as an adjective. The object of the preposition *by* / *por* is *the robber* / **el ladrón.**

See also active voice. Compare the above sentence with the example in the active voice. Review passive voice in Work Unit 14.

Past Anterior Tense

This tense is also called the preterit perfect. *See* preterit perfect tense.

Past Participle

A past participle is derived from a verb. It is used to form the compound tenses. Its auxiliary verb in English is *to have*. In Spanish, the auxiliary verb is **haber** / *to have.* It is part of the verb tense.

Examples:

INFINITIVE	PRESENT PERFECT INDICATIVE
hablar / to speak, to talk	I have *spoken* / **he** *hablado*
comer / to eat	I have *eaten* / **he** *comido*
recibir / to receive	I have *received* / **he** *recibido*

Review Work Unit 12 for the regular formation of a past participle and a list of common irregular past participles. You need to know them to form the seven compound tenses. The present perfect tense, which is commonly used, is one of them.

442   *See also* auxiliary verb.

Past Perfect Tense

This tense is also called the pluperfect indicative tense. *See* pluperfect indicative tense.

Person (1st, 2d, 3d)

Verb forms in a particular tense are learned systematically according to person (1st, 2d, 3d) and number (singular, plural).

Example, showing the present indicative tense of the verb **ir** / to go:

	Singular		*Plural*
1st person:	**(yo) voy**	1st person:	**(nosotros, nosotras) vamos**
2d person:	**(tú) vas**	2d person:	**(vosotros, vosotras) vais**
3d person:	**(Ud., él, ella) va**	3d person:	**(Uds., ellos, ellas) van**

Personal Pronoun

A personal pronoun is a pronoun that refers to a person.
Review the subject pronouns in Work Unit 2.
For examples of other types of pronouns, *see also* demonstrative pronoun, direct object pronoun, disjunctive pronoun, indefinite pronoun, indirect object pronoun, interrogative pronoun, possessive pronoun, reflexive pronoun, relative pronoun.

Pluperfect Indicative Tense

This tense is defined with examples in Work Unit 13. It is also called the past perfect tense.

Plural

Plural means more than one. *See also* person (1st, 2d, 3d) and singular.

Possessive Adjective

A possessive adjective is an adjective that is placed in front of a noun to show possession.

Examples:
 my book / **mi libro**   my friends / **mis amigos**   our school / **nuestra escuela**

Review possessive adjectives in Work Unit 6.

Possessive Pronoun

A possessive pronoun is a pronoun that shows possession. It takes the place of a possessive adjective with the noun. Its form agrees in gender (masculine or feminine) and number (singular or plural) with what it is replacing.

Examples in English: mine, yours, his, hers, its, ours, theirs
Examples in Spanish:

Possessive Adjective	*Possessive Pronoun*
my book / **mi libro**	*mine* / **el mío**
my house / **mi casa**	*mine* / **la mía**
my shoes / **mis zapatos**	*mine* / **los míos**

For all the forms of possessive pronouns with examples in Spanish and English review Work Unit 10.

Predicate

The predicate is that part of the sentence that tells us something about the subject. The main word of the predicate is the verb.

Example:

Today the tourists are going to the Prado Museum / **Hoy los turistas van al Museo del Prado.** The subject is *the tourists* / *los turistas.* The predicate is *are going to the Prado Museum* / *van al Museo del Prado.* The verb is *are going* / *van.*

Preposition

A preposition is a word that establishes a rapport between words.

Examples: with, without, to, at, between
with her / *con* **ella**
between you and me / *entre* **tú y yo**
without money / *sin* **dinero**
to Spain / *a* **España**

Review prepositions and their uses in Work Units 5, 7, 8, and 9.

Prepositional Pronoun

A prepositional pronoun is a pronoun that is the object of a preposition. The term disjunctive pronoun is also used.

For examples, *see* disjunctive pronoun. Review them in Work Unit 9.

Present Indicative Tense

This tense is defined with examples in Work Unit 5.

Present Participle

A present participle is derived from a verb form. In English a present participle ends in *ing.* In Spanish a present participle is called **un gerundio.**

Examples:
cantando / singing   **comiendo** / eating   **yendo** / going

Review Work Units 3 and 6 for regular and irregular present participles and their uses. *See also* gerund.

Present Perfect Indicative Tense

This tense is defined with examples in Work Unit 12.

Present Subjunctive Tense

This tense is defined with examples in Work Unit 10.

Preterit Tense

This tense is defined with examples in Work Unit 7.

Preterit Perfect Tense

This tense is also called the past anterior. It is defined with examples in Work Unit 14.

Pronoun

A pronoun is a word that takes the place of a noun.

Examples:
el hombre / *él* la mujer / *ella*
(the man / *he*)   (the woman / *she*)

Review Work Units 2, 8, 9, and 10 for the different kinds of pronouns and their uses.

Reflexive Pronoun and Reflexive Verb

In English a reflexive pronoun is a personal pronoun that contains *self* or *selves*. In Spanish and English a reflexive pronoun is used with a verb that is called reflexive because the action of the verb falls on the reflexive pronoun.

In Spanish there is a required set of reflexive pronouns for a reflexive verb.

Examples:

lavarse
(to wash oneself)

(Yo) me lavo.
(I wash myself.)

afeitarse
(to shave oneself)

Pablo se ha afeitado.
(Paul has shaved himself.)

Review Work Unit 8 to become familiar with many reflexive verbs and their reflexive pronouns in the three persons of the singular and plural.

Regular Verb

A regular verb is a verb that is conjugated in the various tenses according to a fixed pattern. For examples, see the regular verb tables. *See also* conjugation, irregular verb.

Relative Pronoun

A relative pronoun is a pronoun that refers to its antecedent.

Example:

The girl who is talking with John is my sister / **La muchacha que está hablando con Juan es mi hermana.** The antecedent is *girl* / *la muchacha.* The relative pronoun *who* / *que* refers to the girl.

Review the relative pronouns in Work Unit 10. *See also* antecedent.

Sentence

A sentence is a group of words that contains a subject and a predicate. The verb is contained in the predicate. A sentence expresses a complete thought.

Example:

The train leaves at two o'clock in the afternoon / **El tren sale a las dos de la tarde.** The subject is *train* / **el tren.** The predicate is *leaves at two o'clock in the afternoon* / **sale a las dos de la tarde.** The verb is *leaves* / **sale.**

See also complex sentence, compound sentence, simple sentence.

Simple Sentence

A simple sentence is a sentence that contains one subject and one predicate. The verb is the core of the predicate. The verb is the most important word in a sentence because it tells us what the subject is doing.

Example:

Mary is eating an apple from her garden / **María está comiendo una manzana de su jardín.** The subject is *Mary* / **María.** The predicate is *is eating an apple from her garden* / **está comiendo una manzana de su jardín.** The verb is *is eating* / **está comiendo.** The direct object is *an apple* / **una manzana.** *From her garden* / **de su jardín** is an adverbial phrase. It tells you from where the apple came.

See also complex sentence, compound sentence.

Singular

Singular means one. *See also* plural.

Stem of a Verb

The stem of a verb is what is left after we drop the infinitive form ending. The required endings of a regular verb in a particular verb tense are added to the stem.

Examples:

INFINITIVE	ENDING OF INFINITIVE	STEM
hablar / to talk	**ar**	**habl**
comer / to eat	**er**	**com**
escribir / to write	**ir**	**escrib**

See also ending of a verb.

Stem-changing Verb

In Spanish there are many verb forms that change in the stem.

Example:

The verb **dormir** / *to sleep* changes the vowel **o** in the stem to **ue** when the stress (emphasis, accent) falls on that **o;** for example, **(yo) duermo.** When the stress does not fall on that **o,** it does not change; for example, **(nosotros) dormimos.** Here, the stress is on the vowel **i.**

Review stem-changing verbs in Work Units 3, 7, 10, and in the irregular verb tables.

Subject

A subject is that part of a sentence that is related to its verb. The verb says something about the subject.

Example:

Clara and Isabel are beautiful / **Clara e Isabel son hermosas.** The subject of this sentence is **Clara e Isabel.** To know when to use **e** instead of **y** for *and*, review the entry *conjunction* in this list.

Subjunctive Mood

The subjunctive mood is the mood of a verb that is used in specific cases, *e.g.,* after certain verbs expressing a wish, doubt, emotion, fear, joy, uncertainty, an indefinite expression, an indefinite antecedent, certain conjunctions, and others. The subjunctive mood is used more frequently in Spanish than in English.

Review Work Units 10 and 11 for the uses of the subjunctive mood with examples in Spanish and English.

See also mood of verbs.

Subordinate Clause

Subordinate clause is another term for dependent clause. *See* dependent clause.

Superlative Adjective

A superlative adjective is an adjective that expresses the highest degree when making a comparison of more than two persons or things.

Examples:

ADJECTIVE	COMPARATIVE	SUPERLATIVE
bueno / good	**mejor** / better	**el mejor** / best
alto / tall	**más alto** / taller	**el más alto** / tallest

Review Work Units 6 and 7. *See also* comparative adjective.

Superlative Adverb

A superlative adverb is an adverb that expresses the highest degree when making a comparison of more than two persons or things.

Example:

ADVERB	COMPARATIVE	SUPERLATIVE
lentamente /	**más lentamente** /	**lo más lentamente** /
slowly	more slowly	most slowly

Review Work Units 6 and 7. *See also* comparative adverb.

Tense of Verb

In English and Spanish grammar, tense means time. The tense of the verb indicates the time of the action or state of being. The three major segments of time are past, present, and future. In Spanish there are fourteen major verb tenses, of which seven are simple tenses and seven are compound.

For the names of the seven simple tenses and the seven compound tenses in Spanish and English, see the verb tables.

Transitive Verb

A transitive verb is a verb that takes a direct object.

Example:

I am closing the window / **Cierro la ventana.** The subject is *I* / *(Yo).* The verb is *am closing* / *cierro.* The direct object is *the window* / *la ventana.*

See also intransitive verb.

Verb

A verb is a word that expresses action or a state of being.

Examples:

Action: **Los pájaros están volando** / The birds are flying. The verb is *están volando* / *are flying.*

State of being: **La señora López está contenta** / Mrs. López is happy. The verb is *está* / *is.*

SPANISH REGULAR VERB TABLES

FORMATION OF THE SEVEN SIMPLE TENSES
NUMBERS 1 TO 7 FOR REGULAR VERBS

For an in-depth and extensive presentation of Spanish verb tenses and their uses, consult Barron's *501 Spanish Verbs Fully Conjugated in All the Tenses.*

In Spanish there are fourteen major verb tenses. There are seven simple tenses identified below as Tense Numbers 1–7. A simple tense contains one verb form. There are seven compound tenses identified as Tense Numbers 8–14. A compound tense contains one verb form and a past participle. There is also the imperative, which is not a tense but a mood.

There are three major types of regular verbs. In the infinitive form, they end in either **–ar, –er,** or **–ir.** For example, **hablar, beber, recibir.**

Tense No. 1 Presente de Indicativo (Present Indicative)

In the verb forms that follow on these pages, the subject pronouns are not stated.
As you know, they are:

Singular:	**yo, tú, Ud. (él, ella)**
Plural:	**nosotros (nosotras), vosotros (vosotras), Uds. (ellos, ellas)**

For **–ar** type verbs, drop **ar** from the infinitive form. What is left is called the stem. Then add the following endings to the stem:

Singular:	**o, as, a**
Plural:	**amos, áis, an**

hablar to talk, to speak

Singular:	**hablo, hablas, habla**
Plural:	**hablamos, habláis, hablan**

For **–er** type verbs, drop **er** from the infinitive form. What is left is called the stem. Then add the following endings to the stem:

Singular:	**o, es, e**
Plural:	**emos, éis, en**

beber to drink

Singular:	**bebo, bebes, bebe**
Plural:	**bebemos, bebéis, beben**

For **–ir** type verbs, drop **ir** from the infinitive form. What is left is called the stem. Then add the following endings to the stem:

Singular:	**o, es, e**
Plural:	**imos, ís, en**

recibir to receive

Singular:	**recibo, recibes, recibe**
Plural:	**recibimos, recibís, reciben**

Refer to the above patterns of formation for the following regular **–ar, –er, –ir** verbs in the present indicative tense.

Note that at times some verb forms contain spelling changes in the stem. They are called orthographical changing verbs. Review Work Units 3, 7, and 10.

abrir to open

Singular:	**abro, abres, abre**
Plural:	**abrimos, abrís, abren**

acabar to finish, to end, to complete

Singular:	**acabo, acabas, acaba**
Plural:	**acabamos, acabáis, acaban**

aceptar to accept

Singular:	**acepto, aceptas, acepta**
Plural:	**aceptamos, aceptáis, aceptan**

admitir to admit, to grant, to permit

Singular:	**admito, admites, admite**
Plural:	**admitimos, admitís, admiten**

afeitarse to shave oneself

Singular:	**me afeito, te afeitas, se afeita**
Plural:	**nos afeitamos, os afeitáis, se afeitan**

This is a reflexive verb because it contains the reflexive pronouns **me, te, se, nos, os, se**, as you can see. Review Work Units 8 and 14.

amar to love

Singular:	**amo, amas, ama**
Plural:	**amamos, amáis, aman**

aprender to learn

Singular:	**aprendo, aprendes, aprende**
Plural:	**aprendemos, aprendéis, aprenden**

ayudar to help, to aid, to assist

Singular:	**ayudo, ayudas, ayuda**
Plural:	**ayudamos, ayudáis, ayudan**

bailar to dance

Singular:	**bailo, bailas, baila**
Plural:	**bailamos, bailáis, bailan**

bajar to go down, to come down, to descend

Singular:	**bajo, bajas, baja**
Plural:	**bajamos, bajáis, bajan**

bañarse to bathe oneself, to take a bath

Singular:	**me baño, te bañas, se baña**
Plural:	**nos bañamos, os bañáis, se bañan**

This is a reflexive verb because it contains the reflexive pronouns **me, te, se, nos, os, se**, as you can see. Review Work Units 8 and 14.

cantar to sing

Singular:	**canto, cantas, canta**
Plural:	**cantamos, cantáis, cantan**

casarse to get married

Singular:	**me caso, te casas, se casa**
Plural:	**nos casamos, os casáis, se casan**

Review the reflexive verbs and their pronouns in work Units 8 and 14.

cenar to dine, to have supper

Singular:	**ceno, cenas, cena**
Plural:	**cenamos, cenáis, cenan**

comer to eat

Singular:	**como, comes, come**
Plural:	**comemos, coméis, comen**

comprar to buy, to purchase

Singular:	**compro, compras, compra**
Plural:	**compramos, compráis, compran**

comprender to understand

Singular:	**comprendo, comprendes, comprende**
Plural:	**comprendemos, comprendéis, comprenden**

correr to run, to race, to flow

Singular:	**corro, corres, corre**
Plural:	**corremos, corréis, corren**

cubrir to cover

Singular:	**cubro, cubres, cubre**
Plural:	**cubrimos, cubrís, cubren**

deber to owe, must, ought

Singular:	**debo, debes, debe**
Plural:	**debemos, debéis, deben**

decidir to decide

Singular:	**decido, decides, decide**
Plural:	**decidimos, decidís, deciden**

desear to desire

Singular:	**deseo, deseas, desea**
Plural:	**deseamos, deseáis, desean**

escribir to write

Singular:	**escribo, escribes, escribe**
Plural:	**escribimos, escribís, escriben**

estudiar to study

Singular:	**estudio, estudias, estudia**
Plural:	**estudiamos, estudiáis, estudian**

insistir to insist

Singular:	**insisto, insistes, insiste**
Plural:	**insistimos, insistís, insisten**

llamarse to be named, to be called

Singular:	**me llamo, te llamas, se llama**
Plural:	**nos llamamos, os llamáis, se llaman**

Review the reflexive verbs and their pronouns in Work Units 8 and 14.

partir to leave, to depart, to divide, to split
| | Singular: | **parto, partes, parte** |
| | Plural: | **partimos, partís, parten** |

permitir to permit, to allow
| | Singular: | **permito, permites, permite** |
| | Plural: | **permitimos, permitís, permiten** |

prohibir to prohibit, to forbid
| | Singular: | **prohibo, prohibes, prohibe** |
| | Plural: | **prohibimos, prohibís, prohiben** |

subir to go up, to get on (a train, bus)
| | Singular: | **subo, subes, sube** |
| | Plural: | **subimos, subís, suben** |

sufrir to suffer, to endure
| | Singular: | **sufro, sufres, sufre** |
| | Plural: | **sufrimos, sufrís, sufren** |

temer to fear, to dread
| | Singular: | **temo, temes, teme** |
| | Plural: | **tememos, teméis, temen** |

tomar to take, to have (something to eat or drink)
| | Singular: | **tomo, tomas, toma** |
| | Plural: | **tomamos, tomáis, toman** |

trabajar to work
| | Singular: | **trabajo, trabajas, trabaja** |
| | Plural: | **trabajamos, trabajáis, trabajan** |

unir to unite, to join
| | Singular: | **uno, unes, une** |
| | Plural: | **unimos, unís, unen** |

vender to sell
| | Singular: | **vendo, vendes, vende** |
| | Plural: | **vendemos, vendéis, venden** |

viajar to travel
| | Singular: | **viajo, viajas, viaja** |
| | Plural: | **viajamos, viajáis, viajan** |

vivir to live
| | Singular: | **vivo, vives, vive** |
| | Plural: | **vivimos, vivís, viven** |

For the uses of the present indicative tense with English translations, review work Unit 5.

There is also the ***progressive present tense***, when you say, *e.g.,* **estoy hablando**/I am talking, **Elena está estudiando**/Helen is studying. For the formation and use of that tense, review Work Units 1, 3, and 9.

Tense No. 2   Imperfecto de Indicativo (Imperfect Indicative)

For **–ar** type verbs, drop **ar** from the infinitive form. What is left is called the stem. Then add the following endings to the stem:

Singular:	**aba, abas, aba**
Plural:	**ábamos, abais, aban**

hablar to talk, to speak

Singular:	**hablaba, hablabas, hablaba**
Plural:	**hablábamos, hablabais, hablaban**

For **–er** and **–ir** verbs, drop **er** or **ir** from the infinitive form and add these endings:

Singular:	**ía, ías, ía**
Plural:	**íamos, íais, ían**

beber to drink

		recibir to receive
Singular:	**bebía, bebías, bebía**	**recibía, recibías, recibía**
Plural:	**bebíamos, bebíais, bebían**	**recibíamos, recibíais, recibían**

cantar to sing

Singular:	**cantaba, cantabas, cantaba**
Plural:	**cantábamos, cantabais, cantaban**

comer to eat

Singular:	**comía, comías, comía**
Plural:	**comíamos, comíais, comían**

escribir to write

Singular:	**escribía, escribías, escribía**
Plural:	**escribíamos, escribíais, escribían**

For the uses of the imperfect indicative tense with English translations, review Work Unit 6.

There is also the ***progressive past tense***, when you say, *e.g,* **(yo) estaba durmiendo**/ I was sleeping, **José estaba comiendo**/Joseph was eating. For the formation and use of that tense, review Work Units 1, 6, and 9.

Tense No. 3   Pretérito (Preterit)

For **–ar** type verbs, drop **ar** and add these endings:

	Singular:	**é, aste, ó**
	Plural:	**amos, asteis, aron**

---

hablar   to talk, to speak

	Singular:	**hablé, hablaste, habló**
	Plural:	**hablamos, hablasteis, hablaron**

For **–er** and **–ir** verbs, drop **er** or **ir** and add these endings:

	Singular:	**í, iste, ió**
	Plural:	**imos, isteis, ieron**

---

beber   to drink

recibir   to receive

	Singular:	**bebí, bebiste, bebió**	**recibí, recibiste, recibió**
	Plural:	**bebimos, bebisteis, bebieron**	**recibimos, recibisteis, recibieron**

---

cantar   to sing

	Singular:	**canté, cantaste, cantó**
	Plural:	**cantamos, cantasteis, cantaron**

---

comer   to eat

	Singular:	**comí, comiste, comió**
	Plural:	**comimos, comisteis, comieron**

---

escribir   to write

	Singular:	**escribí, escribiste, escribió**
	Plural:	**escribimos, escribisteis, escribieron**

For the uses of the preterit tense with English translations, review Work Unit 7.

Tense No. 4   Futuro (Future)

For **–ar, –er, –ir** verbs, add the following endings to the whole infinitive:

Singular:	**é, ás, á**
Plural:	**emos, éis, án**

Note the accent marks on the future endings except for **emos.**

---

hablar to talk, to speak

Singular:	**hablaré, hablarás, hablará**
Plural:	**hablaremos, hablaréis, hablarán**

---

beber to drink

recibir to receive

Singular:	**beberé, beberás, beberá**	**recibiré, recibirás, recibirá**
Plural:	**beberemos, beberéis, beberán**	**recibiremos, recibiréis, recibirán**

---

aceptar to accept

Singular:	**aceptaré, aceptarás, aceptará**
Plural:	**aceptaremos, aceptaréis, aceptarán**

---

aprender to learn

Singular:	**aprenderé, aprenderás, aprenderá**
Plural:	**aprenderemos, aprenderéis, aprenderán**

---

subir to go up, to get on (a train, bus)

Singular:	**subiré, subirás, subirá**
Plual:	**subiremos, subiréis, subirán**

For the uses of the future tense with English translations, review Work Unit 8.

Tense No. 5   Potencial Simple (Conditional)

For **–ar, –er, –ir** verbs, add the following endings to the whole infinitive:

Singular:	**ía, ías, ía**
Plural:	**íamos, íais, ían**

Note that these endings are the same for the imperfect indicative (Tense No. 2) for **–er** and **–ir** verbs, added to the stem of the infinitive, but for the conditional they are added to the whole infinitive.

---

hablar to talk, to speak

Singular:	**hablaría, hablarías, hablaría**
Plural:	**hablaríamos, hablaríais, hablarían**

---

beber to drink · **vivir** to live

Singular:	**bebería, beberías, bebería**	**viviría, vivirías, viviría**
Plural:	**beberíamos, beberíais, beberían**	**viviríamos, viviríais, vivirían**

---

bailar to dance

Singular:	**bailaría, bailarías, bailaría**
Plural:	**bailaríamos, bailaríais, bailarían**

---

comer to eat

Singular:	**comería, comerías, comería**
Plural:	**comeríamos, comeríais, comerían**

---

partir to leave

Singular:	**partiría, partirías, partiría**
Plural:	**partiríamos, partiríais, partirían**

For the uses of the conditional with English translations, review Work Unit 9.

Tense No. 6   Presente de Subjuntivo (Present Subjunctive)

To form this tense regularly, go to the present indicative (Tense No. 1), 1st person singular of the verb you have in mind to use, drop the ending **o** and...

for **–ar** verbs, add
these endings:

Singular: **e, es, e**
Plural: **emos, éis, en**

for **–er** and **–ir** verbs, add
these endings:

Singular: **a, as, a**
Plural: **amos, áis, an**

As you can see, the characteristic vowel in the present subjunctive endings for **–ar** verbs is **e** in the six persons.

---

hablar to talk, to speak

Singular: **hable, hables, hable**
Plural: **hablemos, habléis, hablen**

The characteristic vowel in the present subjunctive endings for **–er** and **–ir** verbs is **a** in the six persons. To know when to use the subjunctive, review Work Units 10 and 11.

---

beber to drink

Singular: **beba, bebas, beba**
Plural: **bebamos, bebáis, beban**

vivir to live

viva, vivas, viva
vivamos, viváis, vivan

---

cenar to dine, to have supper

Singular: **que yo cene, que tú cenes, que Ud. (él, ella) cene**
Plural: **que nosotros cenemos, que vosotros cenéis,**
que Uds. (ellos, ellas) cenen

---

deber to owe, must, ought

Singular: **que yo deba, que tú debas, que Ud. (él, ella) deba**
Plural: **que nosotros debamos, que vosotros debáis, que Uds.**
(ellos, ellas) deban

---

subir to go up, to get on (a train, bus)

Singular: **que yo suba, que tú subas, que Ud. (él, ella) suba**
Plural: **que nosotros subamos, que vosotros subáis, que Uds.**
(ellos, ellas) suban

For the uses of the present subjunctive with English translations, review Work Unit 10.

Tense No. 7   Imperfecto de Subjuntivo (Imperfect Subjunctive)

For all verbs, drop the **ron** ending of the 3d person plural of the preterit tense (No. 3) and add these endings:

		or	
Singular:	**ra, ras, ra**	or	**se, ses, se**
Plural:	**ramos, rais, ran**		**semos, seis, sen**

---

hablar to talk, to speak

Singular:	**hablara, hablaras, hablara**	or	**hablase, hablases, hablase**
Plural:	**habláramos, hablarais, hablaran**		**hablásemos, hablaseis, hablasen**

---

beber to drink

Singular:	**bebiera, bebieras, bebiera**	or	**bebiese, bebieses, bebiese**
Plural:	**bebiéramos, bebierais, bebieran**		**bebiésemos, bebieseis, bebiesen**

---

vivir to live

Singular:	**viviera, vivieras, viviera**	or	**viviese, vivieses, viviese**
Plural:	**viviéramos, vivierais, vivieran**		**viviésemos, vivieseis, viviesen**

---

amar to love

Singular:	**amara, amaras, amara**	or	**amase, amases, amase**
Plural:	**amáramos, amarais, amaran**		**amásemos, amaseis, amasen**

---

comer to eat

Singular:	**comiera, comieras, comiera**	or	**comiese, comieses, comiese**
Plural:	**comiéramos, comierais, comieran**		**comiésemos, comieseis, comiesen**

---

subir to go up, to get on (a train, bus)

Singular:	**subiera, subieras, subiera**	or	**subiese, subieses, subiese**
Plural:	**subiéramos, subierais, subieran**		**subiésemos, subieseis, subiesen**

Note that the only accent mark on the forms of the imperfect subjunctive is on the 1st person plural form and it is placed on the vowel that is *right in front* of the ending **ramos** or **semos**.

For the uses of the imperfect subjunctive with English translations, review Work Unit 11.

FORMATION OF THE SEVEN COMPOUND TENSES NUMBERS 8 TO 14 FOR REGULAR VERBS

Tense No. 8   Perfecto de Indicativo (Present Perfect Indicative)

This commonly used compound past tense is based on Tense No. 1 of **haber**. In other words, you form this tense by using the auxiliary verb **haber** in the present indicative plus the past participle of the verb you have in mind to use.

To be able to form the seven compound tenses in Spanish, you must know the seven simple tenses of **haber**. For the complete conjugation of **haber** in the seven simple tenses, see the appendix.

To learn how to form a past participle regularly and to learn the common irregular past participles, review Work Unit 12.

For the uses of this tense with English translations, review Work Unit 12.

---

abrir to open

Singular:	**he abierto, has abierto, ha abierto**
Plural:	**hemos abierto, habéis abierto, han abierto**

---

aceptar to accept

Singular:	**he aceptado, has aceptado, ha aceptado**
Plural:	**hemos aceptado, habéis aceptado, han aceptado**

---

acostarse to go to bed, to lie down

Singular:	**me he acostado, te has acostado, se ha acostado**
Plural:	**nos hemos acostado, os habéis acostado, se han acostado**

---

aprender to learn

Singular:	**he aprendido, has aprendido, ha aprendido**
Plural:	**hemos aprendido, habéis aprendido, han aprendido**

---

escribir to write

Singular:	**he escrito, has escrito, ha escrito**
Plural:	**hemos escrito, habéis escrito, han escrito**

Tense No. 9 Pluscuamperfecto de Indicativo (Pluperfect Ind.)

This tense is based on Tense No. 2 of **haber**. In other words, you form this tense by using the auxiliary verb **haber** in the imperfect indicative plus the past participle of the verb you have in mind to use.

To be able to form the seven compound tenses in Spanish, you must know the seven simple tenses of **haber**. For the complete conjugation of **haber** in the seven simple tenses, see the appendix.

To learn how to form a past participle regularly and to learn the common irregular past participles, review Work Unit 12.

For the uses of this tense with English translations, review Work Unit 13.

---

abrir to open

Singular:	**había abierto, habías abierto, había abierto**
Plural:	**habíamos abierto, habíais abierto, habían abierto**

---

aceptar to accept

Singular:	**había aceptado, habías aceptado, había aceptado**
Plural:	**habíamos aceptado, habíais aceptado, habían aceptado**

---

acostarse to go to bed, to lie down

Singular:	**me había acostado, te habías acostado, se había acostado**
Plural:	**nos habíamos acostado, os habíais acostado, se habían acostado**

---

aprender to learn

Singular:	**había aprendido, habías aprendido, había aprendido**
Plural:	**habíamos aprendido, habíais aprendido, habían aprendido**

---

bailar to dance

Singular:	**había bailado, habías bailado, había bailado**
Plural:	**habíamos bailado, habíais bailado, habían bailado**

---

dar to give

Singular:	**había dado, habías dado, había dado**
Plural:	**habíamos dado, habíais dado, habían dado**

---

escribir to write

Singular:	**había escrito, habías escrito, había escrito**
Plural:	**habíamos escrito, habíais escrito, habían escrito**

---

ir to go

Singular:	**había ido, habías ido, había ido**
Plural:	**habíamos ido, habíais ido, habían ido**

---

lavarse to wash oneself

Singular:	**me había lavado, te habías lavado, se había lavado**
Plural:	**nos habíamos lavado, os habíais lavado, se habían lavado**

---

salir to go out

Singular:	**había salido, habías salido, había salido**
Plural:	**habíamos salido, habíais salido, habían salido**

Tense No. 10   Pretérito Anterior (Preterit Perfect)

This tense is based on Tense No. 3 of **haber**. In other words, you form this tense by using the auxiliary verb **haber** in the preterit tense plus the past participle of the verb you have in mind to use.

To be able to form the seven compound tenses in Spanish, you must know the seven simple tenses of **haber**. For the complete conjugation of **haber** in the seven simple tenses, see the appendix.

To learn how to form a past participle regularly and to learn the common irregular past participles, review Work Unit 12.

For the uses of this tense with English translations, review Work Unit 14.

---

decir to say, to tell

Singular:	**hube dicho, hubiste dicho, hubo dicho**
Plural:	**hubimos dicho, hubisteis dicho, hubieron dicho**

---

estar to be

Singular:	**hube estado, hubiste estado, hubo estado**
Plural:	**hubimos estado, hubisteis estado, hubieron estado**

For the complete conjugation of **estar** in all 14 tenses plus the imperative, see the appendix.

---

hablar to talk, to speak

Singular:	**hube hablado, hubiste hablado, hubo hablado**
Plural:	**hubimos hablado, hubisteis hablado, hubieron hablado**

---

hacer to do, to make

Singular:	**hube hecho, hubiste hecho, hubo hecho**
Plural:	**hubimos hecho, hubisteis hecho, hubieron hecho**

For the complete conjugation of **hacer** in all 14 tenses plus the imperative, see the appendix.

---

ir to go

Singular:	**hube ido, hubiste ido, hubo ido**
Plural:	**hubimos ido, hubisteis ido, hubieron ido**

For the complete conjugation of **ir** in all 14 tenses plus the imperative, see the appendix.

---

salir to go out

Singular:	**hube salido, hubiste salido, hubo salido**
Plural:	**hubimos salido, hubisteis salido, hubieron salido**

---

ser to be

Singular:	**hube sido, hubiste sido, hubo sido**
Plural:	**hubimos sido, hubisteis sido, hubieron sido**

For the complete conjugation of **ser** in all 14 tenses plus the imperative, see the appendix.

Tense No. 11 Futuro Perfecto (Future Perfect)

This tense is based on Tense No. 4 of **haber**. In other words, you form this tense by using the auxiliary verb **haber** in the future tense plus the past participle of the verb you have in mind to use.

To be able to form the seven compound tenses in Spanish, you must know the seven simple tenses of **haber.** For the complete conjugation of **haber** in the seven simple tenses, see the appendix.

To learn how to form a past participle regularly and to learn the common irregular past participles, review Work Unit 12.

This compound tense is not normally presented in a course of study in Spanish Level 2. It is in these verb tables for the enrichment of your knowledge.

---

acostarse to go to bed, to lie down

Singular: **me habré acostado, te habrás acostado, se habrá acostado**
Plural: **nos habremos acostado, os habréis acostado, se habrán acostado**

---

leer to read

Singular: **habré leído, habrás leído, habrá leído**
Plural: **habremos leído, habréis leído, habrán leído**

---

levantarse to get up

Singular: **me habré levantado, te habrás levantado, se habrá levantado**
Plural: **nos habremos levantado, os habréis levantado, se habrán levantado**

---

llegar to arrive

Singular: **habré llegado, habrás llegado, habrá llegado**
Plural: **habremos llegado, habréis llegado, habrán llegado**

---

morir to die

Singular: **habré muerto, habrás muerto, habrá muerto**
Plural: **habremos muerto, habréis muerto, habrán muerto**

---

oír to hear

Singular: **habré oído, habrás oído, habrá oído**
Plural: **habremos oído, habréis oído, habrán oído**

---

poner to put

Singular: **habré puesto, habrás puesto, habrá puesto**
Plural: **habremos puesto, habréis puesto, habrán puesto**

---

terminar to finish

Singular: **habré terminado, habrás terminado, habrá terminado**
Plural: **habremos terminado, habréis terminado, habrán terminado**

---

ver to see

Singular: **habré visto, habrás visto, habrá visto**
Plural: **habremos visto, habréis visto, habrán visto**

---

volver to return

Singular: **habré vuelto, habrás vuelto, habrá vuelto**
Plural: **habremos vuelto, habréis vuelto, habrán vuelto**

Tense No. 12   Potencial Compuesto (Conditional Perfect)

This tense is based on Tense No. 5 of **haber**. In other words, you form this tense by using the auxiliary verb **haber** in the conditional plus the past participle of the verb you have in mind to use.

To be able to form the seven compound tenses in Spanish, you must know the seven simple tenses of **haber**. For the complete conjugation of **haber** in the seven simple tenses, see the appendix.

To learn how to form a past participle regularly and to learn the common irregular past participles, review Work Unit 12.

This compound tense is not normally presented in a course of study in Spanish Level 2. It is in these verb tables for the enrichment of your knowledge.

---

andar to walk

Singular:	**habría andado, habrías andado, habría andado**
Plural:	**habríamos andado, habríais andado, habrían andado**

---

comer to eat

Singular:	**habría comido, habrías comido, habría comido**
Plural:	**habríamos comido, habríais comido, habrían comido**

---

creer to believe

Singular:	**habría creído, habrías creído, habría creído**
Plural:	**habríamos creído, habríais creído, habrían creído**

---

dormir to sleep

Singular:	**habría dormido, habrías dormido, habría dormido**
Plural:	**habríamos dormido, habríais dormido, habrían dormido**

---

ir to go

Singular:	**habría ido, habrías ido, habría ido**
Plural:	**habríamos ido, habríais ido, habrían ido**

---

pensar to think

Singular:	**habría pensado, habrías pensado, habría pensado**
Plural:	**habríamos pensado, habríais pensado, habrían pensado**

---

reír to laugh

Singular:	**habría reído, habrías reído, habría reído**
Plural:	**habríamos reído, habríais reído, habrían reído**

---

romper to break

Singular:	**habría roto, habrías roto, habría roto**
Plural:	**habríamos roto, habríais roto, habrían roto**

---

sentir to feel sorry, to regret, to feel

Singular:	**habría sentido, habrías sentido, habría sentido**
Plural:	**habríamos sentido, habríais sentido, habrían sentido**

---

ser to be

Singular:	**habría sido, habrías sido, habría sido**
Plural:	**habríamos sido, habríais sido, habrían sido**

Tense No. 13   Perfecto de Subjuntivo (Present Perfect Sub.)

This tense is based on Tense No. 6 of **haber**. In other words, you form this tense by using the auxiliary verb **haber** in the present subjunctive plus the past participle of the verb you have in mind to use.

To be able to form the seven compound tenses in Spanish, you must know the seven simple tenses of **haber**. For the complete conjugation of **haber** in the seven simple tenses, see the appendix.

To learn how to form a past participle regularly and to learn the common irregular past participles, review Work Unit 12.

This compound tense is not normally presented in a course of study in Spanish Level 2. It is in these verb tables for the enrichment of your knowledge.

---

abrir to open

Singular:	**haya abierto, hayas abierto, haya abierto**
Plural:	**hayamos abierto, hayáis abierto, hayan abierto**

---

contestar to answer, to reply

Singular:	**haya contestado, hayas contestado, haya contestado**
Plural:	**hayamos contestado, hayáis contestado, hayan contestado**

---

cubrir to cover

Singular:	**haya cubierto, hayas cubierto, haya cubierto**
Plural:	**hayamos cubierto, hayáis cubierto, hayan cubierto**

---

dar to give

Singular:	**haya dado, hayas dado, haya dado**
Plural:	**hayamos dado, hayáis dado, hayan dado**

---

decir to say, to tell

Singular:	**haya dicho, hayas dicho, haya dicho**
Plural:	**hayamos dicho, hayáis dicho, hayan dicho**

---

estar to be

Singular:	**haya estado, hayas estado, haya estado**
Plural:	**hayamos estado, hayáis estado, hayan estado**

For the complete conjugation of **estar** in all 14 tenses plus the imperative, see the appendix.

---

pedir to ask for, to request

Singular:	**haya pedido, hayas pedido, haya pedido**
Plural:	**hayamos pedido, hayáis pedido, hayan pedido**

---

servir to serve

Singular:	**haya servido, hayas servido, haya servido**
Plural:	**hayamos servido, hayáis servido, hayan servido**

---

telefonear to telephone

Singular:	**haya telefoneado, hayas telefoneado, haya telefoneado**
Plural:	**hayamos telefoneado, hayáis telefoneado, hayan telefoneado**

---

vestirse to dress oneself, to get dressed

Singular:	**me haya vestido, te hayas vestido, se haya vestido**
Plural:	**nos hayamos vestido, os hayáis vestido, se hayan vestido**

Tense No. 14   Pluscuamperfecto de Subjuntivo (Pluperfect Sub.)

This tense is based on Tense No. 7 of **haber**. In other words, you form this tense by using the auxiliary verb **haber** in the imperfect subjunctive plus the past participle of the verb you have in mind to use.

To be able to form the seven compound tenses in Spanish, you must know the seven simple tenses of **haber**. For the complete conjugation of **haber** in the seven simple tenses, see the appendix.

To learn how to form a past participle regularly and to learn the common irregular past participles, review Work Unit 12.

This compound tense is not normally presented in a course of study in Spanish Level 2. It is in these verb tables for the enrichment of your knowledge.

---

dar to give

Singular:	**hubiera dado, hubieras dado, hubiera dado**
Plural:	**hubiéramos dado, hubierais dado, hubieran dado**
or:	**hubiese dado, hubieses dado, hubiese dado**
	hubiésemos dado, hubieseis dado, hubiesen dado

---

decir to say, to tell

Singular:	**hubiera dicho, hubieras dicho, hubiera dicho**
Plural:	**hubiéramos dicho, hubierais dicho, hubieran dicho**
or:	**hubiese dicho, hubieses dicho, hubiese dicho**
	hubiésemos dicho, hubieseis dicho, hubiesen dicho

---

ir to go

Singular:	**hubiera ido, hubieras ido, hubiera ido**
Plural:	**hubiéramos ido, hubierais ido, hubieran ido**
or:	**hubiese ido, hubieses ido, hubiese ido**
	hubiésemos ido, hubieseis ido, hubiesen ido

---

oír to hear

Singular:	**hubiera oído, hubieras oído, hubiera oído**
Plural:	**hubiéramos oído, hubierais oído, hubieran oído**
or:	**hubiese oído, hubieses oído, hubiese oído**
	hubiésemos oído, hubieseis oído, hubiesen oído

---

saber to know, to know how

Singular:	**hubiera sabido, hubieras sabido, hubiera sabido**
Plural:	**hubiéramos sabido, hubierais sabido, hubieran sabido**
or:	**hubiese sabido, hubieses sabido, hubiese sabido**
	hubiésemos sabido, hubieseis sabido, hubiesen sabido

---

tomar to take

Singular:	**hubiera tomado, hubieras tomado, hubiera tomado**
Plural:	**hubiéramos tomado, hubierais tomado, hubieran tomado**
or:	**hubiese tomado, hubieses tomado, hubiese tomado**
	hubiésemos tomado, hubieseis tomado, hubiesen tomado

SPANISH IRREGULAR VERB TABLES

Note that the verb tables in this section also contain some commonly used verbs that change in spelling. They are called orthographic changing verbs. Review Work Units 3, 7, and 10.

The names of the seven simple tenses for the seven tense numbers are given below. In the tables that follow, the tense number is used instead of the tense name. Refer to this list when you have to.

Tense Number
1. *Presente de Indicativo* (Present Indicative)
2. *Imperfecto de Indicativo* (Imperfect Indicative)
3. *Pretérito* (Preterit)
4. *Futuro* (Future)
5. *Potencial Simple* (Conditional)
6. *Presente de Subjuntivo* (Present Subjunctive)
7. *Imperfecto de Subjuntivo* (Imperfect Subjunctive)

The Imperative (Command) mood is used when telling someone to do or not to do something, *e.g.,* get up, don't get up; go, don't go. For the uses of the Imperative mood, review Work Units 4, 9, and 10. The forms of the Imperative given in the tables below are in the following order:

> 2d pers. s. **(tú)**, 3d pers. s. **(Ud.)**
> 1st pers. pl. **(nosotros)**, 2d pers. pl. **(vosotros)**, 3d pers. pl. **(Uds.)**

For the formation of the *gerundio* (present participle) and for irregular present participles, review Work Unit 3.

For the formation of the past participle and for irregular past participles, review Work Unit 12. See the appendix for the complete forms of the commonly used irregular verbs **estar, haber, hacer, ir,** and **ser.**

In the following tables, the first line is the 1st, 2d, 3d persons of the singular. The second line is the 1st, 2d, 3d persons of the plural.

Verb forms that are irregular in certain tenses, including those with spelling changes (orthographic), are given only in those tenses. They are printed in boldface type. All the forms in the Imperative are printed in boldface type.

---

almorzar to lunch *gerundio* **almorzando** *past part.* **almorzado**

1 **almuerzo, almuerzas, almuerza**
   almorzamos, almorzáis, **almuerzan**

3 **almorcé**, almorzaste, almorzó
   almorzamos, almorzasteis, almorzaron

6 **almuerce, almuerces, almuerce**
   almorcemos, almorcéis, almuercen

Imperativo: **almuerza (no almuerces), almuerce**
            almorcemos, almorzad (no almorcéis), almuercen
Note: **zar** verbs change **z** to **c** before **e.** The stem vowel **o** changes to **ue** because it is stressed.

---

andar to walk   *gerundio* **andando**   *past part.* **andado**

3   **anduve, anduviste, anduvo
anduvimos, anduvisteis, anduvieron**

7   **anduviera, anduvieras, anduviera
anduviéramos, anduvierais, anduvieran**

or: **anduviese, anduvieses, anduviese
anduviésemos, anduvieseis, anduviesen**

Imperativo: **anda (no andes), ande
andemos, andad (no andéis), anden**

---

buscar to look for, to seek   *gerundio* **buscando**   *past part.* **buscado**

3   **busqué,** buscaste, buscó
buscamos, buscasteis, buscaron

6   **busque, busques, busque
busquemos, busquéis, busquen**

Imperativo: **busca (no busques), busque
busquemos, buscad (no busquéis), busquen**
Note: **car** verbs change **c** to **qu** before **e.**

---

caber to be contained, to fit into   *gerundio* **cabiendo**   *past part.* **cabido**

1   **quepo,** cabes, cabe
cabemos, cabéis, caben

3   **cupe, cupiste, cupo
cupimos, cupisteis, cupieron**

4   **cabré, cabrás, cabrá
cabremos, cabréis, cabrán**

5   **cabría, cabrías, cabría
cabríamos, cabríais, cabrían**

6   **quepa, quepas, quepa
quepamos, quepáis, quepan**

7   **cupiera, cupieras, cupiera
cupiéramos, cupierais, cupieran**

or: **cupiese, cupieses, cupiese
cupiésemos, cupieseis, cupiesen**

Imperativo: **cabe (no quepas), quepa
quepamos, cabed (no quepáis), quepan**

466

---

caer to fall   *gerundio* **cayendo**   *past part.* **caído**

1   **caigo,** caes, cae
     caemos, caéis, caen

3   caí, caíste, **cayó**
     caímos, caísteis, **cayeron**

6   **caiga, caigas, caiga**
     caigamos, caigáis, caigan

7   **cayera, cayeras, cayera**
     cayéramos, cayerais, cayeran

or: **cayese, cayeses, cayese**
     cayésemos, cayeseis, cayesen

Imperativo: **cae (no caigas), caiga**
             caigamos, caed (no caigáis), caigan

---

coger to catch   *gerundio* **cogiendo**   *past part.* **cogido**

1   **cojo,** coges, coge
     cogemos, cogéis, cogen

6   **coja, cojas, coja**
     cojamos, cojáis, cojan

Imperativo: **coge (no cojas), coja**
             cojamos, coged (no cojáis), cojan
Note: **ger** verbs change **g** to **j** before **a** and **o.**

---

conducir to conduct, to drive   *gerundio* **conduciendo**   *past part.* **conducido**

1   **conduzco,** conduces, conduce
     conducimos, conducís, conducen

3   **conduje, condujiste, condujo**
     condujimos, condujisteis, condujeron

6   **conduzca, conduzcas, conduzca**
     conduzcamos, conduzcáis, conduzcan

7   **condujera, condujeras, condujera**
     condujéramos, condujerais, condujeran

or: **condujese, condujeses, condujese**
     condujésemos, condujeseis, condujesen

Imperativo: **conduce (no conduzcas), conduzca**
             conduzcamos, conducid (no conduzcáis), conduzcan
Note: **ducir** verbs, like **traducir** (to translate), have the same irregular forms
       as **conducir.**

---

conocer to know, to be acquainted with   *gerundio* **conociendo**   *past part.* **conocido**

1   **conozco,** conoces, conoce
     conocemos, conocéis, conocen

6   **conozca, conozcas, conozca**
     conozcamos, conozcáis, conozcan

Imperativo: **conoce (no conozcas), conozca**
             conozcamos, conoced (no conozcáis), conozcan
Note: When preceded by a vowel, **cer** verbs insert **z** before **c** if **c** is followed by **a** or **o.**

---

contar to count, to relate   *gerundio* **contando**   *past part.* **contado**

1   **cuento, cuentas, cuenta**
     contamos, contáis, **cuentan**

6   **cuente, cuentes, cuente**
     contemos, contéis, **cuenten**

Imperativo: **cuenta (no cuentes), cuente**
               contemos, contad (no contéis), cuenten
Note: The stem vowel **o** changes to **ue** because it is stressed.

---

creer to believe   *gerundio* **creyendo**   *past part.* **creído**

3   creí, creíste, **creyó**
     creímos, creísteis, **creyeron**

7   **creyera, creyeras, creyera**
     creyéramos, creyerais, creyeran

or: **creyese, creyeses, creyese**
     creyésemos, creyeseis, creyesen

Note: When between vowels, unstressed **i** changes to **y.**

---

dar to give   *gerundio* **dando**   *past part.* **dado**

1   **doy,** das, da
     damos, dais, dan

3   **dí, diste, dio**
     dimos, disteis, dieron

6   **dé,** des, **dé,**
     demos, deis, den

7   **diera, dieras, diera**
     diéramos, dierais, dieran

or: **diese, dieses, diese**
     diésemos, dieseis, diesen

Imperativo: **da (no des), dé**
               demos, dad (no deis), den

---

decir to say, to tell   *gerundio* **diciendo**   *past part.* **dicho**

1   **digo, dices, dice**
     decimos, decís, **dicen**

3   **dije, dijiste, dijo**
     dijimos, dijisteis, dijeron

4   **diré, dirás, dirá**
     diremos, diréis, dirán

5   **diría, dirías, diría**
     diríamos, diríais, dirían

6   **diga, digas, diga**
     digamos, digáis, digan

7   **dijera, dijeras, dijera**
     dijéramos, dijerais, dijeran

or: **dijese, dijeses, dijese**
     dijésemos, dijeseis, dijesen

Imperativo: **di (no digas), diga**
               digamos, decid (no digáis), digan

delinquir to be guilty, to offend   *gerundio* **delinquiendo**   *past part.* **delinquido**

1   **delinco,** delinques, delinque
       delinquimos, delinquís, delinquen

6   **delinca, delincas, delinca
       delincamos, delincáis, delincan**

Imperativo: **delinque (no delincas), delinca
              delincamos, delinquid (no delincáis), delincan**
Note: **quir** verbs change **qu** to **c** before **a** and **o**.

---

dirigir to direct   *gerundio* **dirigiendo**   *past part.* **dirigido**

1   **dirijo,** diriges, dirige
       dirigimos, dirigís, dirigen

6   **dirija, dirijas, dirija
       dirijamos, dirijáis, dirijan**

Imperativo: **dirige (no dirijas), dirija
              dirijamos, dirigid (no dirijáis), dirijan**
Note: **gir** verbs change **g** to **j** before **a** and **o**.

---

distinguir to distinguish   *gerundio* **distinguiendo**   *past part.* **distinguido**

1   **distingo,** distingues, distingue
       distinguimos, distinguís, distinguen

6   **distinga, distingas, distinga
       distingamos, distingáis, distingan**

Imperativo: **distingue (no distingas), distinga
              distingamos, distinguid (no distingáis), distingan**
Note: **guir** verbs drop **u** before **o** and **a**.

---

dormir to sleep   *gerundio* **durmiendo**   *past part.* **dormido**

1   **duermo, duermes, duerme**
       dormimos, dormís, **duermen**

3   dormí, dormiste, **durmió**
       dormimos, dormisteis, **durmieron**

6   **duerma, duermas, duerma
       durmamos, durmáis, duerman**

7   **durmiera, durmieras, durmiera
       durmiéramos, durmierais, durmieran**

or: **durmiese, durmieses, durmiese
       durmiésemos, durmieseis, durmiesen**

Imperativo: **duerme (no duermas), duerma
              durmamos, dormid (no durmáis), duerman**
Note: The stem vowel **o** changes to **ue** because it is stressed. When the stem vowel **o** is not
        stressed, it changes to **u** if the syllable that follows contains stressed **a, ie,** or **ió.**

enviar to send	*gerundio* **enviando**	*past part.* **enviado**

1 **envío, envías, envía**
enviamos, enviáis, **envían**

6 **envíe, envíes, envíe**
enviemos, enviéis, **envíen**

Imperativo: **envía (no envíes), envíe**
enviemos, enviad (no enviéis), envíen

---

errar to err, to wander, to roam	*gerundio* **errando**	*past part.* **errado**

1 **yerro, yerras, yerra**
erramos, erráis, **yerran**

6 **yerre, yerres, yerre**
erremos, erréis, **yerren**

Imperativo: **yerra (no yerres), yerre**
erremos, errad (no erréis), yerren

---

estar to be	*gerundio* **estando**	*past part.* **estado**

1 **estoy, estás, está**
estamos, estáis, **están**

3 **estuve, estuviste, estuvo**
estuvimos, estuvisteis, estuvieron

6 **esté, estés, esté**
estemos, estéis, **estén**

7 **estuviera, estuvieras, estuviera**
estuviéramos, estuvierais, estuvieran

or: **estuviese, estuvieses, estuviese**
estuviésemos, estuvieseis, estuviesen

Imperativo: **está (no estés), esté**
estemos, estad (no estéis), estén

---

haber to have	*gerundio* **habiendo**	*past part.* **habido**

(as an auxiliary verb
to form the compound tenses)

1 **he, has, ha**
hemos, habéis, **han**

3 **hube, hubiste, hubo**
hubimos, hubisteis, hubieron

4 **habré, habrás, habrá**
habremos, habréis, habrán

5 **habría, habrías, habría**
habríamos, habríais, habrían

6 **haya, hayas, haya**
hayamos, hayáis, hayan

7 **hubiera, hubieras, hubiera,**
hubiéramos, hubierais, hubieran

or: **hubiese, hubieses, hubiese,**
hubiésemos, hubieseis, hubiesen

Imperativo: **hé (no hayas), haya**
hayamos, habed (no hayáis), hayan

hacer to do, to make   *gerundio* **haciendo**   *past part.* **hecho**

1   **hago,** haces, hace
     hacemos, hacéis, hacen

3   **hice, hiciste, hizo**
     hicimos, hicisteis, hicieron

4   **haré, harás, hará**
     haremos, haréis, harán

5   **haría, harías, haría**
     haríamos, haríais, harían

6   **haga, hagas, haga**
     hagamos, hagáis, hagan

7   **hiciera, hicieras, hiciera**
     hiciéramos, hicierais, hicieran

or: **hiciese, hicieses, hiciese**
     hiciésemos, hicieseis, hiciesen

Imperativo: **haz (no hagas), haga**
             hagamos, haced (no hagáis), hagan

---

huir to flee, to run away   *gerundio* **huyendo**   *past part.* **huido**

1   **huyo, huyes, huye**
     huimos, huís, **huyen**

3   huí, huiste, **huyó**
     huimos, huisteis, **huyeron**

6   **huya, huyas, huya**
     huyamos, huyáis, huyan

7   **huyera, huyeras, huyera**
     huyéramos, huyerais, huyeran

or: **huyese, huyeses, huyese**
     huyésemos, huyeseis, huyesen

Imperativo: **huye (no huyas), huya**
             huyamos, huid (no huyáis), huyan

Note: In Spanish novels, newspapers, and magazines the trend is to drop the accent mark on **í** in
       the past participle **huido** and others that end in **uido.**

---

ir to go   *gerundio* **yendo**   *past part.* **ido**

1 **voy, vas, va**
       vamos, vais, van

2 **iba, ibas, iba**
       íbamos, ibais, iban

3 **fui, fuiste, fue**
       fuimos, fuisteis, fueron

6 **vaya, vayas, vaya**
       vayamos, vayáis, vayan

7 **fuera, fueras, fuera**
       fuéramos, fuerais, fueran

or: **fuese, fueses, fuese**
       fuésemos, fueseis, fuesen

Imperativo: **ve (no vayas), vaya**
             vamos (no vayamos), id (no vayáis), vayan

---

jugar to play   *gerundio* **jugando**   *past part.* **jugado**

1 **juego, juegas, juega**
       jugamos, jugáis, **juegan**

3 **jugué,** jugaste, jugó
       jugamos, jugasteis, jugaron

6 **juegue, juegues, juegue**
       juguemos, juguéis, **jueguen**

Imperativo: **juega (no juegues), juegue**
             juguemos, jugad (no juguéis), jueguen
Note: Compare the irregular forms of this verb with those of **contar** above and **llegar** below.

---

llegar to arrive   *gerundio* **llegando**   *past part.* **llegado**

3 **llegué,** llegaste, llegó
       llegamos, llegasteis, llegaron

6 **llegue, llegues, llegue**
       lleguemos, lleguéis, lleguen

Imperativo: **llega (no llegues), llegue**
             lleguemos, llegad (no lleguéis), lleguen
Note: **gar** verbs change **g** to **gu** before **e**.

---

mostrar to show   *gerundio* **mostrando**   *past part.* **mostrado**

1   **muestro, muestras, muestra**
     mostramos, mostráis, **muestran**

6   **muestre, muestres, muestre**
     mostremos, mostréis, **muestren**

Imperativo: **muestra (no muestres), muestre**
             mostremos, mostrad (no mostréis), muestren
Note: The stem vowel **o** changes to **ue** because it is stressed.

---

oír to hear   *gerundio* **oyendo**   *past part.* **oído**

1   **oigo, oyes, oye**
     oímos, oís, **oyen**

3   oí, oíste, **oyó**
     oímos, oísteis, **oyeron**

6   **oiga, oigas, oiga**
     oigamos, oigáis, oigan

7   **oyera, oyeras, oyera**
     oyéramos, oyerais, oyeran

or: **oyese, oyeses, oyese**
     oyésemos, oyeseis, oyesen

Imperativo: **oye (no oigas), oiga**
             oigamos, oíd (no oigáis), oigan

---

oler to smell, to scent   *gerundio* **oliendo**   *past part.* **olido**

1   **huelo, hueles, huele**
     olemos, oléis, **huelen**

6   **huela, huelas, huela**
     olamos, oláis, **huelan**

Imperativo: **huele (no huelas), huela**
             olamos, oled (no oláis), huelan

---

pedir to ask for, to request   *gerundio* **pidiendo**   *past part.* **pedido**

1   **pido, pides, pide**
     pedimos, pedís, **piden**

3   pedí, pediste, **pidió**
     pedimos, pedisteis, **pidieron**

6   **pida, pidas, pida**
     pidamos, pidáis, pidan

7   **pidiera, pidieras, pidiera**
     pidiéramos, pidierais, pidieran

or: **pidiese, pidieses, pidiese**
     pidiésemos, pidieseis, pidiesen

Imperativo: **pide (no pidas), pida**
             pidamos, pedid (no pidáis), pidan
Note: The stem vowel **e** changes to **i** because it is stressed. When the stem vowel **e** is not
       stressed, it changes to **i** if the syllable that follows contains stressed **a, ie,** or **ió.**

pensar to think　　　　　　*gerundio* **pensando**　　　　　*past part.* **pensado**

1　**pienso, piensas, piensa**
　　pensamos, penséis, **piensan**

6　**piense, pienses, piense**
　　pensemos, penséis, **piensen**

Imperativo: **piensa (no pienses), piense
　　　　　　pensemos, pensad (no penséis), piensen**
Note: The stem vowel **e** changes to **ie** because it is stressed.

---

poder to be able, can　　　　*gerundio* **pudiendo**　　　　*past part.* **podido**

1　**puedo, puedes, puede**
　　podemos, podéis, **pueden**

3　**pude, pudiste, pudo
　　pudimos, pudisteis, pudieron**

4　**podré, podrás, podrá
　　podremos, podréis, podrán**

5　**podría, podrías, podría
　　podríamos, podríais, podrían**

6　**pueda, puedas, pueda**
　　podamos, podáis, **puedan**

7　**pudiera, pudieras, pudiera
　　pudiéramos, pudierais, pudieran**

or:　**pudiese, pudieses, pudiese
　　pudiésemos, pudieseis, pudiesen**

Imperativo: **puede (no puedas), pueda
　　　　　　podamos, poded (no podáis), puedan**

---

poner to put, to place　　　　*gerundio* **poniendo**　　　　*past part.* **puesto**

1　**pongo,** pones, pone
　　ponemos, ponéis, ponen

3　**puse, pusiste, puso
　　pusimos, pusisteis, pusieron**

4　**pondré, pondrás, pondrá
　　pondremos, pondréis, pondrán**

5　**pondría, pondrías, pondría
　　pondríamos, pondríais, pondrían**

6　**ponga, pongas, ponga
　　pongamos, pongáis, pongan**

7　**pusiera, pusieras, pusiera
　　pusiéramos, pusierais, pusieran**

or:　**pusiese, pusieses, pusiese
　　pusiésemos, pusieseis, pusiesen**

Imperativo: **pon (no pongas), ponga
　　　　　　pongamos, poned (no pongáis), pongan**

474

preferir to prefer | *gerundio* **prefiriendo** | *past part.* **preferido**

1 **prefiero, prefieres, prefiere**
preferimos, preferís, **prefieren**

3 preferí, preferiste, **prefirió**
preferimos, preferisteis, **prefirieron**

6 **prefiera, prefieras, prefiera**
prefiramos, prefiráis, prefieran

7 **prefiriera, prefirieras, prefiriera**
prefiriéramos, prefirierais, prefirieran

or: **prefiriese, prefirieses, prefiriese**
prefiriésemos, prefirieseis, prefiriesen

Imperativo: **prefiere (no prefieras), prefiera**
prefiramos, preferid (no prefiráis), prefieran
Note: The stem vowel **e** changes to **ie** because it is stressed. When the stem vowel **e** is not stressed, it changes to **i** if the syllable that follows contains stressed **a, ie,** or **ió.**

---

querer to want, to wish, to like | *gerundio* **queriendo** | *past part.* **querido**

1 **quiero, quieres, quiere**
queremos, queréis, **quieren**

3 **quise, quisiste, quiso**
quisimos, quisisteis, quisieron

4 **querré, querrás, querrá**
querremos, querréis, querrán

5 **querría, querrías, querría**
querríamos, querríais, querrían

6 **quiera, quieras, quiera**
queramos, queráis, **quieran**

7 **quisiera, quisieras, quisiera**
quisléramos, quisierais, quisieran

or: **quisiese, quisieses, quisiese**
quisiésemos, quisieseis, quisiesen

Imperativo: **quiere (no quieras), quiera**
queramos, quered (no queráis), quieran

---

reír to laugh | *gerundio* **riendo** | *past part.* **reído**

1 **río, ríes, ríe**
reímos, reís, **ríen**

3 reí, reíste, **rió**
reímos, reísteis, **rleron**

6 **ría, rías, ría**
riamos, riáis, rían

7 **riera, rieras, riera**
riéramos, rierais, rieran

or: **riese, rieses, riese**
riésemos, rieseis, riesen

Imperativo: **ríe (no rías), ría**
riamos, reíd (no riáis), rían

saber to know, to know how   *gerundio* **sabiendo**   *past part.* **sabido**

1 **sé,** sabes, sabe
   sabemos, sabéis, saben

3 **supe, supiste, supo**
   supimos, supisteis, supieron

4 **sabré, sabrás, sabrá**
   sabremos, sabréis, sabrán

5 **sabría, sabrías, sabría**
   sabríamos, sabríais, sabrían

6 **sepa, sepas, sepa**
   sepamos, sepáis, sepan

7 **supiera, supieras, supiera**
   supiéramos, supierais, supieran

or: **supiese, supieses, supiese**
     supiésemos, supieseis, supiesen

Imperativo: **sabe (no sepas), sepa**
             sepamos, sabed (no sepáis), sepan

Note: The form **(yo) sé** (I know), 1st pers., s., pres. ind. (tense no. 1), is the same as the 2d pers., s., imperative of the verb **ser**, which is given below. There can be no doubt as to the meaning of **sé** when used in a sentence. Note also that the accent mark on **sé** is used to distinguish it from the Spanish reflexive pronoun **se** (himself, herself, yourself, oneself, itself, yourselves, themselves). The pronunciation of **sé** and **se** is the same. See **se** among the reflexive pronouns in Work Unit 8. Also, see Work Units 9 and 10 where **lo, la, le** or **les** change to **se.**

---

salir to go out, to leave   *gerundio* **saliendo**   *past part.* **salido**

1 **salgo,** sales, sale
   salimos, salís, salen

4 **saldré, saldrás, saldrá**
   saldremos, saldréis, saldrán

5 **saldría, saldrías, saldría**
   saldríamos, saldríais, saldrían

6 **salga, salgas, salga**
   salgamos, salgáis, salgan

Imperativo: **sal (no salgas), salga**
             salgamos, salid (no salgáis), salgan

---

sentarse to sit down   *gerundio* **sentándose**   *past part.* **sentado**

1 **me siento, te sientas, se sienta**
   nos sentamos, os sentáis, **se sientan**

6 **me siente, te sientes, se siente**
   nos sentemos, os sentéis, **se sienten**

Imperativo: **siéntate (no te sientes), siéntese (no se siente)**
             sentémonos (no nos sentemos), sentaos (no os sentéis), siéntense (no se sienten)

Note: The stem vowel **e** changes to **ie** because it is stressed.

---

sentir   to feel sorry, to feel   *gerundio* **sintiendo**   *past part.* **sentido**

1   **siento, sientes, siente**
        sentimos, sentís, **sienten**

3   sentí, sentiste, **sintió**
        sentimos, sentisteis, **sintieron**

6   **sienta, sientas, sienta**
        sintamos, sintáis, sientan

7   **sintiera, sintieras, sintiera**
        sintiéramos, sintierais, sintieran

or: **sintiese, sintieses, sintiese**
      sintiésemos, sintieseis, sintiesen

Imperativo: **siente (no sientas), sienta**
             sintamos, sentid (no sintáis), sientan

Note: The stem vowel **e** changes to **ie** because it is stressed. When the stem vowel **e** is not stressed, it changes to **i** if the syllable that follows contains stressed **a, ie,** or **ió.**

---

sentirse   to feel (well, ill)   *gerundio* **sintiéndose**   *past part.* **sentido**

1   **me siento, te sientes, se siente**
        nos sentimos, os sentís, **se sienten**

3   me sentí, te sentiste, **se sintió**
        nos sentimos, os sentisteis, **se sintieron**

6   **me sienta, te sientas, se sienta**
        nos sintamos, os sintáis, se sientan

7   **me sintiera, te sintieras, se sintiera**
        nos sintiéramos, os sintierais, se sintieran

or: **me sintiese, te sintieses, se sintiese**
      nos sintiésemos, os sintieseis, se sintiesen

Imperativo: **siéntete (no te sientas), siéntase**
             sintámonos, sentíos (no os sintáis), siéntanse

Note: The stem vowel **e** changes to **ie** because it is stressed. When the stem vowel **e** is not stressed, it changes to **i** if the syllable that follows contains stressed **a, ie,** or **ió.**

ser to be	*gerundio* **siendo**		*past part.* **sido**

1   **soy, eres, es**
       somos, sois, son

2   **era, eras, era**
       éramos, erais, eran

3   **fui, fuiste, fue**
       fuimos, fuisteis, fueron

6   **sea, seas, sea**
       seamos, seáis, sean

7   **fuera, fueras, fuera**
       fuéramos, fuerais, fueran

or: **fuese, fueses, fuese**
       fuésemos, fueseis, fuesen

Imperativo: **sé (no seas), sea**
           seamos, sed (no seáis), sean

Note: The form **sé** (be), 2d pers., s., imperative is the same as the 1st pers., s. **(yo) sé** (I know),
       pres. ind. (tense no. 1) of the verb **saber**, which is given above. See the note under **saber.**

---

servir to serve	*gerundio* **sirviendo**		*past part.* **servido**

1   **sirvo, sirves, sirve**
       servimos, servís, **sirven**

3   serví, serviste, **sirvió**
       servimos, servisteis, **sirvieron**

6   **sirva, sirvas, sirva**
       sirvamos, sirváis, sirvan

7   **sirviera, sirvieras, sirviera**
       sirviéramos, sirvierais, sirvieran

or: **sirviese, sirvieses, sirviese**
       sirviésemos, sirvieseis, sirviesen

Imperativo: **sirve (no sirvas), sirva**
           sirvamos, servid (no sirváis), sirvan

Note: The stem vowel **e** changes to **i** because it is stressed. When the stem vowel **e** is not
       stressed, it changes to **i** if the syllable that follows contains stressed **a, ie,** or **ió.**

tener to have, to hold   *gerundio* **teniendo**   *past part.* **tenido**

1   **tengo, tienes, tiene**
     tenemos, tenéis, **tienen**

3   **tuve, tuviste, tuvo**
     tuvimos, tuvisteis, tuvieron

4   **tendré, tendrás, tendrá**
     tendremos, tendréis, tendrán

5   **tendría, tendrías, tendría**
     tendríamos, tendríais, tendrían

6   **tenga, tengas, tenga**
     tengamos, tengáis, tengan

7   **tuviera, tuvieras, tuviera**
     tuviéramos, tuvierais, tuvieran

or: **tuviese, tuvieses, tuviese**
     tuviésemos, tuvieseis, tuviesen

Imperativo: **ten (no tengas), tenga**
             tengamos, tened (no tengáis), tengan

---

traer to bring   *gerundio* **trayendo**   *past part.* **traído**

1   **traigo,** traes, trae
     traemos, traéis, traen

3   **traje, trajiste, trajo**
     trajimos, trajisteis, trajeron

6   **traiga, traigas, traiga**
     traigamos, traigáis, traigan

7   **trajera, trajeras, trajera**
     trajéramos, trajerais, trajeran

or: **trajese, trajeses, trajese**
     trajésemos, trajeseis, trajesen

Imperativo: **trae (no traigas), traiga**
             traigamos, traed (no traigáis), traigan

---

valer to be worth   *gerundio* **valiendo**   *past part.* **valido**

1   **valgo,** vales, vale
     valemos, valéis, vale

4   **valdré, valdrás, valdrá**
     valdremos, valdréis, valdrán

5   **valdría, valdrías, valdría**
     valdríamos, valdríais, valdrían

6   **valga, valgas, valga**
     valgamos, valgáis, valgan

Imperativo: **val** *or* **vale (no valgas), valga**
             valgamos, valed (no valgáis), valgan

venir to come   *gerundio* **viniendo**   *past part.* **venido**

1   **vengo, vienes, viene**
     venimos, venís, **vienen**

3   **vine, viniste, vino**
     vinimos, vinisteis, vinieron

4   **vendré, vendrás, vendrá**
     vendremos, vendréis, vendrán

5   **vendría, vendrías, vendría**
     vendríamos, vendríais, vendrían

6   **venga, vengas, venga**
     vengamos, vengáis, vengan

7   **viniera, vinieras, viniera**
     viniéramos, vinierais, vinieran

or: **viniese, vinieses, viniese**
     viniésemos, vinieseis, viniesen

Imperativo: **ven (no vengas), venga**
             vengamos, venid (no vengáis), vengan

---

ver to see   *gerundio* **viendo**   *past part.* **visto**

1   **veo,** ves, ve
     vemos, veis, ven

2   **veía, veías, veía**
     veíamos, veíais, veían

6   **vea, veas, vea**
     veamos, veáis, vean

Imperativo: **ve (no veas), vea**
             veamos, ved (no veáis), vean

Vocabulary
Spanish and English Words
in One Alphabetical Listing

This list of vocabulary contains words and expressions in Spanish and English in one alphabetical order because I think it is convenient if you look in one place instead of two for an entry. One listing prevents you from looking inadvertently in a Spanish listing for an English word or in an English listing for a Spanish word. Also, cognates and near-cognates in both languages are reduced to a single entry. All Spanish words are printed in bold face.

The preposition *to* in an English infinitive is omitted, e.g., *to eat* is listed under *eat*.

Vowels placed in parentheses after an infinitive in the following list, *e.g.,* **(ue), (ie, i)** mean that the vowel in the stem of the verb form changes when stressed. These are called stem-changing verbs. For example, the entry **pensar (ie)** means that the vowel **e** in the stem changes to **ie** when stressed, as in **pienso.** See the entry *stem-changing verbs* in the index. Also, consult the index for Work Units where stem-changing verbs and verbs that change in spelling (orthographical changing verbs) are presented. Consonants placed in parentheses after an infinitive, *e.g.,* **(z), (j)** mean that the verb form changes in spelling; e.g., **conocer (z) > yo conozco; elegir (i, j) > yo elijo.**

For a list of names of boys and girls in Spanish with English equivalents, see Work Unit 8.

Consult the conjugation tables of regular verbs beginning on p. 448 and the tables of irregular verbs beginning on p. 465.

If you do not understand the meaning of an abbreviation, look it up in the list of abbreviations in the beginning pages of this book. Entries in this vocabulary pertain to words used in this book. For any not listed here, consult a standard Spanish-English/English-Spanish dictionary.

THE SPANISH ALPHABET AND THE NEW SYSTEM OF ALPHABETIZING

The Association of Spanish Language Academies met in Madrid for its 10th Annual Congress on April 27, 1994 and voted to eliminate **CH** and **LL** as separate letters of the Spanish alphabet. The move was taken to simplify dictionaries, to make Spanish more compatible with English, and to aid translation and computer standardization.

Words beginning with **CH** will be listed alphabetically under the letter **C.** Words beginning with **LL** will be listed alphabetically under the letter **L.** The two separate letters historically have had separate headings in dictionaries and alphabetized word lists. Spanish words that contain the letter **ñ** are now alphabetized accordingly with words that do not contain the tilde over the **n.** For example, the Spanish system of alphabetizing used to place the word **andar** before **añadir** because the **ñ** would fall in after all words containing **n.** According to the new system, **añadir** is placed before **andar** because alphabetizing is now done letter by letter. The same applies to words containing **rr.**

In the following vocabulary list, we have made use of the new system of alphabetizing Spanish words with English words, not only to make Spanish more compatible with English and to facilitate computer standardization, but also to make it easy for you to find Spanish words and English words in one alphabetical listing. All Spanish words are given in boldface (dark) print. *NOTE*: the WU notation means Work Unit.

VOCABULARY

A

a *prep.* at, to, in; **a cargo de** in care of; **¡A ver!/** Let's see! Also used as personal **a** (see WU 8) in front of a dir.obj.n. referring to a person, *e.g.,* **Conozco a María.** I know Mary. See **a** in the index.

a, an *indef.art.* **un, una**; see WU 1.

abierto *past part. of* **abrir**; see *past part.* in WU 12.

able (to be able), can *v.* **poder (ue, u)**; see verb tables.

about (on) *prep.* **sobre**; about (on) art **sobre el arte**

above *adv.* **arriba, sobre**

abrazos *n.m.* hugs; **dar un abrazo** to hug

abrir *v.* to open; see verb tables.

absent *adj.* **ausente**

absolutamente *adv.* absolutely; **No me gustan en absoluto.** I don't like them at all.

abuela *n.f.* grandmother; **el abuelo** grandfather

abundante *adj.* abundant

acabar *v.* to finish, to end, to complete; see **acabar** in the verb tables and index.

accept *v.* **aceptar**; see verb tables.

accompany *v.* **acompañar**

ache *v.* **doler (ue)**; *n.* **el dolor**; I have a headache. **Tengo dolor de cabeza;** My feet ache. **Me duelen los pies.**

acordarse (ue) *refl.v.* to remember; **No me acuerdo.** I don't remember; see this verb in WU 3.

acostarse (ue) *refl.v.* to go to bed; **Me acuesto temprano.** I go to bed early; see this verb in WU 3.

acuerdo *n.m.* agreement; **de acuerdo** okay

address *n.* **la dirección**

¡Adelante! Come in!

adjetivo *n.m.* adjective

admirar *v.* to admire

admitir *v.* to admit

¿adónde? *adv.* to where? where to?

adore *v.* **adorar**

adventure *n.* **la aventura**

advice *n.* **el consejo**

afeitarse *refl. v.* to shave oneself; see verb tables.

affectionately *adv.* **cariñosamente**

after *adv.* **después (de)**; after having dinner **después de cenar**

afternoon *n.* **la tarde**; in the afternoon **por la tarde**; good afternoon **buenas tardes**

afuera *adv.* outside

again *adv.* **otra vez, de nuevo**

against *prep.* **contra**

age *n.* **la edad**

agradable *adj.* pleasant

Agreed! (Okay) **¡De acuerdo! ¡Está bien!**

agreement *n.m.* **el acuerdo**

agua *n.f.* **el agua** water; **las aguas; el agua mineral** mineral water

ahora *adv.* now

aid *n.* **la ayuda**; *v.* **ayudar**

air *n.* **el aire**; in the open air **al aire libre**

airplane *n.* **el avión, el aeroplano**

airport *n.* **el aeropuerto**

al (a + el > al) to the, at the; **al teatro** to the theater; **al cine** to the movies; **al mismo tiempo** at the same time; **al día siguiente** on the following day; **al entrar** upon entering; **al llegar** upon arriving; **al ver** upon seeing. See **al** in the index.

alarma *n.f.* alarm

alas *n.f. pl.* wings; but in the sing. **el ala**

alegre *adj.* happy, joyful

alemán, alemanes *n., adj.* German

alegremente *adv.* happily, joyfully

alegría *n.f.* joy, happiness

algo *pron.* something; see **algo** in the index.

alguien *indef. pron.* someone, somebody; see **alguien** in the index.

algún, alguno, alguna, algunos, algunas *adj.* some, any, a few; see WU 3 and 6.

all *pron.* **todo**; *adj.* all the boys **todos los muchachos**; all the girls **todas las muchachas**; all day **todo el día**; all my money **todo mi dinero**; all right, okay **bueno, está bien**

allá, allí *adv.* there

allow *v.* **dejar, permitir**

almorcé *1st pers. sing., pret. of* **almorzar**; I had lunch

almorzar (ue, c) *v.* to lunch, to have lunch; **Yo almuerzo.** I have lunch. **Yo almorcé.** I had lunch; **el almuerzo** lunch; see **almorzar** in WU 3.

alone *adj.* **solo, sola**

already *adv.* **ya**

also *adv.* **también**

always *adv.* **siempre**; as always **como siempre**

amable *adj.* kind, gentle, amiable

amar *v.* to love; *n.* **el amor**; see verb tables.

amigo *n.m.,* **amiga** *n.f.* friend

among *prep.* **entre**

amuse oneself, have fun *v.* **divertirse (ie, i)**; **Yo me divierto.** I have fun; Everybody had fun. **Todo el mundo se divirtió.**

amusement, amusements *n.* **la diversión, las diversiones**

amusing *adj.* **divertido**

añadir *v.* to add

and *conj.* **y** or **e**; see **y** and **e** in the index.

andar *v.* to walk

ángel *n.m.* angel; **los ángeles** angels

anniversary *n.* **al aniversario**

announce *v.* **anunciar**

año *n.m.* year (synonym: **edad**)

anoche *adv.* last night

another *adj.* **otro, otra**; another book **otro libro**; another house **otra casa**

answer *v.* **responder, contestar**; *n.* **la respuesta, la contestación**

antes *adv.* before; **antes de cerrar** before closing

anunciar *v.* to announce

any, a few, some *adj.* **algún, alguno, alguna, algunos, algunas**; see WU 3 and 6.

apartment *n.* **el apartamento**

appear *v.* **aparecer (zc); yo aparezco**; see **aparecer** in WU 3.

appearance *n.* **la apariencia**

appetite *n.* **el apetito**

apple *n.* **la manzana**

appointment *n.* **la cita**

appreciate *v.* **apreciar**

aprender *v.* to learn; see verb tables.

aquel, aquella, aquellos, aquellas *dem.adj.* that, those; see WU 6.

aquél, aquélla, aquéllos, aquéllas *dem.pron.* that one, those; see WU 9.

aquí *adv.* here; **aquí tiene Ud. ...** here is... here are ...

arm *n.* **el brazo**

armchair *n.* **el sillón**

arrive *v.* **llegar (gu); Yo llegué tarde.** I arrived late.

arroz *n.m.* rice

art *n.* **el arte**

artículo determinado *n.m.* definite article

artista *n.m.f.* artist

as *conj.* **como**

as ... as **tan ... como**; see WU 6.

as always **como siempre**

as many (as much) **tanto, tanta, tantos, tantas**; see WU 6 .

as much ... as **tanto ... como**; see WU 6.

así *adv.* so, (in) this way; **así, así** so, so; **así como** as well as

asiento *n.m.* seat

ask *v.* **preguntar**; to ask for, to request **pedir (i); Yo pido dinero a mi padre.** I ask my father for money.

assist *v.* **ayudar**

at *prep.* **a, en**; at the, to the **al, a la, a los, a las**; at once **en seguida**; At what time? **¿A qué hora?** See **a** in the index.

atención *n.f.* attention; to pay attention **prestar atención**

atrás *adv.* back, backward; **hacia atrás** toward the back

attend *v.* **asistir (a)**

auction sale *n.* **la subasta**

auctioneer *n.* **el subastador**

auditorium *n.* **el auditorio**

aunt *n.* **la tía**

Australia *n.f.* **la Australia**

autógrafo *n.m.* autograph

automobile *n.* **el automóvil**

ave *n.f.* bird (synonym: **el pájaro**)

aventura *n.f.* adventure

avenue *n.* **la avenida**

aviso *n.m.* classified advertisement

avoid *v.* **evitar**

ayuda *n.f.* help, aid

ayudar *v.* to help; see verb tables.

B

baby *n.* **el nene**

babysitter *n.* **la niñera, el niñero**

bad *adj.* **mal, malo, mala**; see WU 6.

bailar *v.* to dance

baile *n.m.* dance

baja *adv.* low; **en voz baja** in a low voice, in a whisper

bajar *v.* to come down

baker *n.* **el panadero**

bakery *n.* **la panadería**

ball *n.* **la pelota**; large ball **el balón**

ball point pen *n.* **el bolígrafo**

baño *n.m.* bath

barber shop *n.* **la barbería**

baseball *n.* **el béisbol**; to play baseball **jugar al béisbol**

basket *n.* **la cesta**

bath *n.* **el baño**; bathroom **el cuarto de baño**

bathe oneself *refl.v.* **bañarse**; I bathe every day. **Me baño todos los días.** See verb tables.

be *v.* **ser, estar**; see verb tables on p. 448.

be, feel cold (persons) *v.* **tener frío**; to be afraid **tener miedo**; to be hungry **tener hambre**; to be warm (persons) **tener calor**

be able *v.* **poder (ue, u)**; see verb tables.

be in love with **estar enamorado de**

be pleasing to *v.* **gustar a**; see WU 2 and 11.

be worth *v.* **valer**

beach *n.* **la playa**

beautiful *adj.* **bello, bella; hermoso, hermosa**

beber *v.* to drink; see verb tables.

bebida *n.f.* drink, beverage

because *conj.* **porque**; because of, on account of **a causa de**

become *v.* **ponerse**

bed *n.* **la cama**; bedroom **el dormitorio**

before *adv.* **antes (de)**; before closing **antes de cerrar**

begin *v.* **comenzar (ie, c); empezar (ie, c); Yo comienzo, yo empiezo** I begin; **Yo comencé, yo empecé** I began.

beginning *n.* **el principio**; at the beginning **al principio**

behave oneself *v.* **comportarse**

believe *v.* **creer (y); Ud. creyó.** You believed.

bell *n.* **el timbre**

bello, bella, bellos, bellas *adj.* beautiful

belong (to) *v.* **pertenecer (z); yo pertenezco**

below *adv.* **debajo (de), abajo**

beso *n.m.* kiss; **dar un beso a** to give a kiss to, to kiss; **a besos** with kisses

better, best *adj.* **mejor, mejores**

between *prep.* **entre**

beverage *n.* **la bebida**

bicycle *n.* **la bicicleta**

bien *adv.* well

big *adj.* **gran, grande**; see index.

biology *n.* **la biología**

bird *n.* **el pájaro**

birthday *n.* **el cumpleaños**

biscuit *n.* **el bizcocho**

bit of... **un poco de...**

bite *v.* **morder (ue); Este perro muerde.** This dog bites; bite, snack to eat **el bocadillo**

bizcocho *n.m.* cookie, cake, sponge cake, biscuit

black *adj.* **negro, negra, negros, negras**

blanco, blanca, blancos, blancas *adj.* white

blanket *n.* **la manta de cama**

blond *adj.* **rubio, rubia**

blouse *n.* **la blusa**

blue *adj.* **azul**; blue eyes **los ojos azules**

blush *v.* **ponerse rojo (roja); He blushed. Él se puso rojo.**

boat *n.* **el barco, el bote, el buque**

boca *n.f.* mouth

bocadillo *n.m.* snack, bite to eat, sandwich

bodeguero *n.m.* grocer; **la bodeguera**

body *n.* **el cuerpo**

bolígrafo *n.m.* ballpoint pen

book *n.* **el libro**; book shop **la librería**

bored *adj.* **aburrido, aburrida**

born, to be *v.* **nacer (z)**

botella *n.f.* bottle

both *adj.* **ambos**; (the two) **los dos, las dos**

bother *v.* **molestar**

bottle *n.* **la botella**

box *n.* **la caja**

boy *n.* **el chico, el muchacho**

bread *n.* **el pan**

break *v.* **romper**; *past part.* **roto**; see *past part.* in WU 12; to break one's arm **romperse el brazo**

breakfast *n.* **el desayuno**; to have breakfast **tomar el desayuno**

breeze *n.* **la brisa**

bring *v.* **traer (j); Yo traje el helado.** I brought the ice cream; Bring me ..., please; **Tráigame ..., por favor**; see **traer** in the verb tables.

brisa *n.f.* breeze

broom *n.* **la escoba**

brother *n.* **el hermano**; little brother **el hermanito**

brown *adj.* **pardo, parda**

brunette *adj.* **moreno, morena**

brush *v.* **cepillar**; *n.* **el cepillo**

bucket *n.* **el cubo**

buen, bueno, buena, buenos, buenas *adj.* good; see WU 6.

buenas tardes good afternoon

building *n.* **el edificio**

burlador *n.m.* jester, joker

burst out laughing **reír a carcajadas**

bus *n.* **el autobús; los autobuses**

buscando *pres.part. of* **buscar**

buscar (qu) *v.* to look for, to search; **Yo busqué un taxi.** I looked for a taxi.

but *conj.* **pero**

butcher *n.* **el carnicero**; butcher shop **la carnicería**

butter *n.* **la mantequilla**

buy *v.* **comprar**; see verb tables.

by *prep.* **por**; by no means **de ninguna manera**

C

caballo *n.m.* horse

cabbage *n.* **la col**

cabello *n.m.* hair

caber *v.* to fit; see **caber** in WU 3.

cabeza *n.f.* head; **tener dolor de cabeza** to have a headache; see **tener** in the index.

cacerola *n.f.* casserole

cada *adj.* each; **cada muchacho** each boy; **cada muchacha** each girl

caer *v.* to fall; see **caer** in WU 3 and verb tables.

café *n.m.* coffee, coffee shop

caja *n.f.* box; teller's, cashier's window

cajero, cajera *n.m.f.* cashier

cake *n.* **el bizcocho**

calidad *n.f.* quality

call *v.* **llamar**

calle *n.f.* street

cama *n.f.* bed

cambio *n.m.* change

caminar *v.* to walk

camión *n.m.* truck

camp *n.* **el campamento**; summer camp **el campamento de verano**

campo *n.m.* field, country. See **campo** in the index.

campocomidas *n.f.* country meals

can (be able) *v.* **poder (ue, u); Yo puedo.** I can; **Yo pude.** I was able to, I could; see verb tables.

can (tin can) *n.* **la lata**

can opener *n.* **el (los) abrelatas**

Canada *n.* **el Canadá**

candies *n.* **los dulces**

cantar *v.* to sing

car *n.* **el carro, el coche**

¡Caramba! *interj.* Darn it!

carbonated soda *n.* **la gaseosa**

card *n.* **la tarjeta**

cardinal number *n.* **el número cardinal**

carefully *adv.* **con cuidado, cuidadosamente**

carne *n.f.* meat

carrot *n.* **la zanahoria**

carry *v.* **llevar**

carta *n.f.* letter (that you write). See letter writing and notes in the index.

casa *n.f.* house; **en casa** at home

casados *adj.* married

casarse con alguien *refl.v.* to get married to someone

cashier *n.* **el cajero, la cajera**; cashier's desk, window **la caja**

casita *n.f.* little house

cat *n.* **el gato;** little cat **el gatito**

celebrar *v.* to celebrate

celebration *n.* **la fiesta**

cellar *n.* **el sótano**

cena *n.f.* dinner

cenar *v.* to dine, to have dinner

centavo *n.m.* cent

centro *n.m.* center; **Voy al centro.** I'm going downtown.

cerca (de) *adv.* near

cerdo *n.m.* hog, pig; **la carne de cerdo** pork

cerrar (ie) *v.* to close; **Yo cierro.** I close; see **cerrar** in WU 3.

chair *n.* **la silla**

chalk *n.* **la tiza;** chalkboard **la pizarra**

champú *n.m.* shampoo

change *v.* **cambiar;** *n.* **el cambio; un gran cambio** a big change; **la moneda** coin

character *n.* **el personaje**

charlar *v.* to chat

charming *adj.* **gracioso, graciosa**

chase away *v.* **espantar**

cheap *adj.* **barato**

cheese *n.* **el queso**

check (that you pay, *e.g.,* in a restaurant) **la cuenta**

chemistry *n.* **la química**

cherry *n.* **la cereza**

chest (body) *n.* **el pecho**

chest of drawers *n.* **el tocador**

chica *n.f.* girl

chicken *n.* **el pollo**

chico *n.m.* boy

child *n.* **el niño, la niña;** children **los niños**

chocolate *n.* chocolate

choose *v.* **elegir (i, j), escoger (j); Yo elijo, yo escojo.** I choose, I select.

chop *n.* **la chuleta;** veal chops **las chuletas de ternera**

Christmas *n.* **la Navidad;** Merry Christmas **Feliz Navidad, Felices Navidades**

chuleta *n.f.* chop; **las chuletas de ternera** veal chops

church *n.* **la iglesia**

cien, ciento *num.* one hundred; see index; see also WU 4.

cinco *num.* five

cincuenta *num.* fifty; see WU 4.

cinema *n.* **el cine**

cita *n.f.* appointment, date

city *n.* **la ciudad**

¡Claro! *excl.* Of course!

clásico *adj.* classic

classified advertisement *n.* **el aviso**

classroom *n.* **la sala de clases**

close *v.* **cerrar;** see WU 3; to close the door **cerrar la puerta;** close by **cerca de**

clothes closet *n.* **el guardarropa**

clothes *n.* **los vestidos, la ropa;** clothing store **la tienda de ropa**

clothes washing machine *n.* **la lavadora**

cocer (ue, z) *v.* to cook; see **cocer** in WU 3.

cocina *n.f.* kitchen

coffee *n.* **el café,** coffee shop **el café**

coger (j) *v.* to catch; **Cojo la pelota.** I catch the ball; see **coger** in WU 3.

coin *n.* **la moneda, una pieza**

cold *n.* **el frío;** to be cold (persons) **tener frío;** to be cold weather **hacer frío**

colgar (ue) *v.* to hang; hang up the phone; **Yo cuelgo;** see **colgar** in WU 3.

come *v.* **venir (ie);** Everybody is coming to the party. **Todo el mundo viene a la fiesta;** see **venir** in the verb tables.

come down *v.* **bajar**

Come in! **¡Entra!** *2d pers.,s. (tú);* **¡Entre!** *3d pers.,s. (Ud.);* **¡Adelante!**

comedia *n.f.* comedy

comedor *n.m.* dining room

comenzar (ie, c) *v.* to begin, to start, to commence; **Ahora comienzo.** Now I begin; see **comenzar** in WU 3 and 7.

comer *v.* to eat

comiendo *pres.part. of* **comer;** see *pres.part.* in WU 3

como *conj.* as, like; **como siempre** as always

companion *n.* **el compañero, la compañera**

complete *v.* **acabar, completar**

comportarse *refl.v.* to behave oneself

comprar *v.* to buy, to purchase

comprender *v.* to understand

computadora *n.f.* computer

con *prep.* with; **conmigo** with me; see **con, conmigo, contigo, consigo** in the index.

concert *n.* **el concierto**

conocer (z) *v.* to know, be acquainted with; **Yo conozco a María.** I know Mary; see **conocer** in the verb tables and index.

contain *v.* **contener**

contento, contenta *adj.* happy, content (synonyms: **encantado, feliz, plácido, satisfecho**)

contest *n.* **el concurso, la competencia, la competición**

contestación *n.f.* answer

contestar *v.* to answer

continue *v.* **continuar**

cook *v.* **cocinar, cocer (ue);** see **cocer** in WU 3; *n.* **el cocinero, la cocinera**

cookie *n.* **el bizcocho, la galleta, la galletita**

cool *adj.* **fresco, fresca;** to be cool weather **hacer fresco**

cordero *n.m.* lamb

correr *v.* to run; see verb tables.

correct *v.* **corregir (i, j);** I am correcting the homework. **Corrijo la tarea;** *adj.* **correcto**

cortar *v.* to cut

corte *n.m.* cut

cortés, corteses *adj.* courteous, polite

corto *adj.* short

485

cost *v.* **costar (ue)**; How much does it cost? **¿Cuánto cuesta?**

count *v.* **contar (ue)**; **yo cuento**

country *n.* **el país**; countryside **el campo**; see **campo** in the index.

course (of study) *n.* **la asignatura**

cousin *n.* **el primo, la prima**

cover *v.* **cubrir**; see verb tables.

crazy *adj.* **loco, loca**

cream *n.* **la crema**

creer (y) *v.* to believe; see verb tables.

creyeron *3d pers.,pl. pret. of* **creer**

cross *v.* **cruzar (c)**; **Yo crucé el lago.** I crossed the lake.

crossword puzzle *n.* **el crucigrama**

cry (weep) *v.* **llorar**

cuadro *n.m.* picture, painting; frame

cual *rel.pron.* **la cual** which; *pron.* **¿cuál?** which? **¿Cuál es su deporte favorito?** What (which) is your favorite sport? See **cual** in the index.

cualquier, cualquiera *adj.* whichever, whatever

cuarto *n.m.* room; **el cuarto de baño** bathroom

cuatro *num.* four; see numbers in WU 4.

cubo *n.m.* bucket, pail

cubrir *v.* to cover

cup *n.* **la taza**; a cup of coffee **una taza de café**; a cup of tea **una taza de té**

curiosidad *n.f.* curiosity

customer *n.* **el, la cliente**

cut *v.* **cortar**; *n.* **el corte**

cuyo, cuya, cuyos, cuyas *rel.pron.* whose; see these words in WU 10.

D

daba *1st & 3d pers.,s., imperf.indic. of* **dar**; see **dar** in the verb tables and index.

dad *n.* **el papá**

dado *past part. of* **dar**; given; see *past part.* in WU 12.

dama *n.f.* lady

dame *2d pers.,s. (tú), imper. of* **dar**; **da + me = dame**; give me

dance *v.* **bailar**; *n.* **el baile**

danger *n.* **el peligro**; dangerous **peligroso, peligrosa**

dar *v.* to give; **dar un paseo** to take a walk; see **dar** in the verb tables and index.

darling **querido mío, querida mía**

Darn it! *interj.* **¡Caramba!**

date (appointment) *n.* **la cita; la fecha** (on calendar)

daughter *n.* **la hija**; sons and daughters **los hijos**

dawn *n.* **la madrugada**

day *n.* **el día**; good day, hello **buenos días**; Have a nice day! **¡Pase muy buenos días!** day before yesterday **anteayer**; see **día** in index.

dazzling *adj.* **deslumbrante**

de *prep.* of, from; **¿De quién es?** Whose is it? See WU 10 and **de** in the index.

dé *3d pers.,s., imper. (command) (Ud.) of* **dar**; give

dear *adj.* **querido, querida**

debajo (de) *adv.* under, underneath

deber *v.* to owe, must, ought; see **deber** in the index.

decidir *v.* to decide

decir (i) *v.* to say, to tell; **Yo digo.** I say; see **decir** in verb tables and index.

dedo *n.m.* finger

definite article *n.* **el artículo determinado**

dejar *v.* to let, permit, allow, leave; see **dejar** in index.

del (de + el > del) of the, from the; see **de + el** in index.

delicado *adj.* delicate; weak, sickly (synonyms: **débil, tierno, frágil, enfermizo**)

delicioso *adj.* delicious

dentist *n.* **el, la dentista**

department store *n.m.* **el almacén; los almacenes**

desayunar *v.* to breakfast, to have breakfast

desayuno *n.m.* breakfast

desde *prep.* since, from; see **desde** in the index.

deserve *v.* **merecer (z); yo merezco**

desfile *n.m.* parade

desk *n.* **el escritorio**

después (de) *adv.* after; **después de cenar** after having dinner

dessert *n.* **el postre**

dí *1st pers.,s., pret. of* **dar**; I gave

día *n.m.* day; **buenos días** good day; see **día** in the index.

dice *3d pers. s., pres.indic. of* **decir**; see verb tables.

dicho *past part. of* **decir**; see *past part.* in WU 12.

diciendo *pres.part. of* **decir**; saying; see *pres.part.* in WU 3.

dictation *n.* **el dictado**

die *v.* **morir (ue, u)**; see verb tables.

dieron *3d pers.,pl., pret. of* **dar**; they gave; see **dar** in verb tables.

difficult *adj.* **difícil**

dijo *3d pers.,s., pret. of* **decir**; he/she/you said

diligent *adj.* **diligente**

dine *v.* **cenar**

dinero *n.m.* money

dining car (train) *n.* **el coche-comedor**

dining room *n.* **el comedor**

dinner *n.* **la cena, la comida**; to have dinner **cenar, tomar la cena**

dio *3d pers.,s., pret. of* **dar**; he/she/you gave

¡Dios mío! *excl.* My God!

dirty *adj.* **sucio**

disk (computer) *n.* **el diskette**

diste *2 d pers.,s. (tú), pret. of* **dar**; you gave

diversión, diversiones *n.f., s.,pl.* amusement, amusements

divertido *adj.* entertaining, enjoyable

divertirse (ie, i) *refl.v.* to have a good time, to enjoy oneself; **Me divierto mucho.** I'm having a very good time; **Elena se divirtió.** Ellen had a good time.

do *v.* **hacer**; see **hacer** in the index and verb tables, p. 448.

Do you want...? **¿Quieres (tú)...? ¿Quiere (Ud.)...?** See **querer** in the verb tables.

doctor *n.* **el doctor, el médico**

dog *n.* **el perro**

doler (ue) *v.* to ache, to pain; **Me duele la cabeza.** I have a headache.

doll *n.* **la muñeca**

dolor *n.m.* ache, pain

done *past part.* **hecho**, past part. of **hacer**; see *past part.* in WU 12.

Don't tell me! **¡No me digas (tú)! ¡No me diga (Ud.)!**

Don't worry! **¡No te preocupes (tú)! ¡No se preocupe (Ud.)!**

¿dónde? *adv.* where?

door *n.* **la puerta**

dormir (ue, u) *v.* to sleep; **Yo duermo bien.** I sleep well; **Ud. durmió.** You slept.

dormitorio *n.m.* bedroom

dot *n.* **el punto**

downtown *n.m.* **el centro**; to go downtown **ir al centro**

dresser (chest of drawers) *n.* **el tocador**

drink *v.* **beber**; *n.* **la bebida**

dry *adj.* **seco**

dulces *n.m.,pl.* candies

durante *prep.* during

durar *v.* to last

durmiendo *pres.part. of* **dormir**; sleeping

duró *3d pers.,s., pret. of* **durar**

E

e *conj.* and; see **e** and **y** in the index.

each *adj.* **cada**; each boy **cada muchacho**; each girl **cada muchacha**

early *adv.* **temprano**

earn *v.* **ganar**

earth *n.* **la tierra**

Easter *n.* **La Pascua Florida**; Happy Easter **Felices Pascuas**

easy *adj.* **fácil, fáciles**

eat *v.* **comer**

ecstatic *adj.* **extático**

edad *n.f.* age

egg *n.* **el huevo**

eight *num.* **ocho**; see numbers in WU 4.

ejemplo *n.m.* example; **por ejemplo** for example

el cual, el de, el mío, el que, el suyo, el tuyo See these words in the index.

elegante *adj.* elegant

elegir (i, j) *v.* to choose, to select, to elect; **Yo elijo.** I choose.

embrace, hug *v.* **abrazar (c)**; **Yo abracé.** I embraced, hugged; *n.* **el abrazo** hug

empecé *1st pers.,s., pret. of* **empezar**

empezar (ie, c) *v.* to begin; **Yo empiezo.** I begin. **Yo empecé.** I began.

empleo *n.m.* employment, job

empty *adj.* **vacío**

en *prep.* in, on; see **en** in the index.

enamorado de in love with

encargarse (ue) *v.* to take charge

encima *adv.* above; **por encima** at the top

encontrar (ue) *v.* to meet; to find; **Encuentro a mis amigos.** I'm meeting my friends.

encuentro *n.m.* encounter, meeting; *1st pers.,s., pres.indic. of* **encontrar**

end *n.* **el fin**; *v.* **acabar, terminar**; see **acabar** in the index.

England *n.* **la Inglaterra**

enjoy *v.* **gozar (c)**

enjoyable *adj.* **divertido**

enough *adj.,adv.* **bastante**

enseñar *v.* to show; to teach

enter *v.* **entrar**

entertaining *adj.* **divertido**

entonces *adv.* then

¡Entra! *2d pers.,s. (tú), imper. of* **entrar**; Come in!

entrance hallway *n.* **el vestíbulo**

entrar *v.* to enter

entre *prep.* between, among; see **entre tú y yo** in WU 9.

entreacto *n.m.* intermission

entretanto *adv.* meanwhile

envelope *n.* **el sobre**

era *1st & 3d pers.,s., imperf. indic. of* **ser**; was; see **ser** in the verb tables, p. 448

erase *v.* **borrar**; eraser **el borrador**; rubber eraser **la goma de borrar**

eres *2d pers.,s. (tú), pres.indic. of* **ser**; you are

es *3d pers.,s., pres.indic. of* **ser**; is

escena *n.f.* scene

escoger (j) *v.* to choose, to select; **Yo escojo.** I choose, I select.

escribir *v.* to write

escritorio *n.m.* desk

escuchar *v.* to listen (to)

ese, esa, esos, esas; ése, ésa, ésos, ésas See these words in the index.

eso *neuter dem.pron.* that; **¿Qué es eso?** What's that? See WU 9.

España *n.f.* Spain

espantar *v.* to chase away

especial *adj.* special

especie *n.f.* species, kind, type

espectáculo *n.m.* show (theater, cinema, circus, *etc.*)

esperar *v.* to hope, to wait (for)

espléndido *adj.* splendid

esposa *n.f.* wife

esposo *n.m.* husband

está *3d pers.,s., pres.indic. of* **estar**; see **estar** in the index and verb tables, p. 448

está comiendo *pres.prog. of* **comer**; is eating; see WU 1, 3 and 9.

esta, estas *dem.adj.* this, these; see **esta, estas** in the index.

ésta, éstas *dem.pron.* this one, these; see **ésta, éstas** in the index.

estaba *1st & 3d pers.,s., imperf. indic. of* **estar**; was

estar *v.* to be; see **estar** in the index and verb tables, p. 448.

este, estos *dem.adj.* this, these; see **este, estos** in the index.

éste, éstos *dem.pron.* this one, these; see **éste, éstos** in the index.

esto *dem.pron.,neuter* this; see WU 9.

estoy *1st pers.,sing., pres. indic. of* **estar**; see **estar** in the index and verb tables, p. 448.

estudiar *v.* to study

evening *n.* **la noche**; good evening **buenas noches**; every evening **todas las noches**

every day **todos los días**; every morning **todas las mañanas**; every night **todas las noches**

everybody *pron.* **todo el mundo**

everywhere *adv.* **en (por) todas partes**

example *n.* **el ejemplo**; for example **por ejemplo**

exclamar *v.* to exclaim

Excuse me **Dispénseme**

expect *v.* **esperar**

explain *v.* **explicar (qu)**; I explained it to you. **Yo se lo expliqué.**

extático *adj.* ecstatic

extranjero, extranjera *adj.* foreign; *n.* foreigner

extremely *adv.* **extremadamente**

eye *n.* **el ojo**; eyelid **el párpado**

eyeglasses **los anteojos, las gafas**; sun glasses **las gafas contra el sol, los anteojos oscuros**

F

face *n.* **la cara**

fair (bazaar) *n.* **la feria**

falda *n.f.* skirt

familia *n.f.* family

fantástico, fantástica *adj.* fantastic

far *adv.* **lejos**

fast *adv.* **pronto**

fat *adj.* **gordo, gorda**

father *n.m.* **el padre**

favor *n.m.* favor; **por favor** please

favorite *adj.* **favorito, predilecto**

fear, to dread *v.* **temer**; *n.* **el temor**; to be afraid **tener miedo**

feel *v.* **sentirse (ie, i); Yo me siento bien.** I feel well. Mary felt sick. **María se sintió mal**; see verb tables.

feliz *adj.* happy; **felices** *pl.*

feo, fea *adj.* ugly

few *adj.* **pocos, pocas**

field *n.* **el campo**; see **campo** in the index

fiesta *n.f.* holiday, celebration, party

fifty *num.* **cincuenta**; see WU 4

fila *n.f.* row; **la quinta fila** the fifth row

fill *v.* **llenar, rellenar**

film *n.* **la película**

finally *adv.* **finalmente**

find *v.* **hallar**

finger *n.* **el dedo**

finish *v.* **acabar, terminar**; see verb tables; see **acabar** in the index.

first *adj.* **primer, primero, primera**; see **primer** in the index.

fish *n.* **el pescado**; *v.* **pescar (qu)**; I fished. **Yo pesqué**; fish (swimming in water) **el pez, los peces**

five *num.* **cinco**; see numbers in the index.

float *v.* **flotar**

flower *n.f.* **la flor**

fly (insect) *n.* **la mosca**; *v.* **volar (ue); Yo vuelo.** I'm flying.

foods *n.* **los alimentos**

foolish *adj.* **tonto, tonta**; foolish thing *n.* **la tontería**

foot *n.* **el pie**

football *n.* **el fútbol americano**

for *prep.* **para, por**

forehead *n.* **la frente**

foreign *adj.* **extranjero**; foreigner **el extranjero, la extranjera**

form *n.* **la forma**

fortuna *n.f.* fortune, luck, chance; **¡Qué fortuna!** What luck!

four *num.* **cuatro**; see numbers in WU 4

freeze *v.* **helar (ie)**; Let it freeze! **¡Que hiele!** ice **el hielo**

frente *n.f.* forehead, brow

fried *adj.* **frito, frita, fritos, fritas**

friend *n.* **el amigo, la amiga**

from *prep.* **de**; from the **del, de la, de los, de las**; see **de** in index

fruit *n.* **la fruta**

fue *3d pers.,s., pret. of* **ir** and **ser**; **fui** *1st pers.,s., pret. of* **ir** and **ser**; see **ir, ser** in the index and verb tables, p. 448.

G

gain *v.* **ganar**

game *n.* **el juego; el partido** (sports)

ganar *v.* to gain, to win, to earn

garaje *n.m.* garage

garbage *n.* **la basura**

garden *n.* **el jardín, los jardines**

gaseosa *n.f.* soda (carbonated)

gastado *past part. of* **gastar**; spent; see *past part.* in WU 12.

gastando *pres.part. of* **gastar**; spending; see *pres.part.* in WU 3.

gastar *v.* to spend (money); **pasar** to spend (time)

generous *adj.* **generoso, generosa**

gente *n.f.* people; **mucha gente** many people

get *v.* **obtener, recibir**

get dressed *v.* **vestirse (i); Me visto.** I'm dressing.

get married *v.* **casarse**

get on (a train, bus) *v.* **subir a**

get up *v.* **levantarse**

gift *n.* **el regalo**

giggle *v.* **reírse sin motivo**

girl *n.* **la chica; la muchacha**

give *v.* **dar**; see **dar** in verb tables and index.

give a gift **regalar**

Give it to me! **¡Dámelo (tú)!; ¡Démelo (Ud.)!**

Give me... **Dame (tú)...; Deme (Ud.)...**

given *past part.* **dado**; see *past part.* in WU 12.

gladly **con mucho gusto**

go *v.* **ir**; see **ir** in the index and verb tables, p. 448; go down *v.* **bajar**; go out *v.* **salir**; go to bed *v.* **acostarse (ue) Me acuesto temprano.** I go to bed early; go up *v.* **subir a**; go for a walk **ir de paseo**

God **Dios**

gold *n.* **el oro**

good *adj.* **buen, bueno, buena, buenas**; good afternoon **buenas tardes**; good-bye **adiós**

good looking *adj.* **guapo, guapa**

grace *n.* **la gracia**

gracefully *adv.* **con gracia**

gracias *n.f.,pl.* thanks; **dar las gracias** to thank; **muchas gracias** thank you very much

gracioso, graciosa *adj.* gracious

grade (mark in studies) *n.* **la nota**

gran, grande *adj.* great, big; see index

grass *n.* **la hierba**

Great Britain *n.* **la Gran Bretaña**

grocer *n.* **el bodeguero, la bodeguera**

grocery store *n.* **la bodega; la tienda de comestibles**

grupo *n.m.* group

guapo *adj.* handsome

guardarropa *n.m.* wardrobe, clothes closet

guerra *n.f.* war

guiñar *v.* to wink; **Juana guiña el ojo.** Jane winks.

guitar *n.* **la guitarra**

gustar *v.* to please, to be pleasing (to), to like; see WU 2 and 11.

gusto *n.m.* taste, pleasure (synonyms: **el placer, la euforia, el júbilo, la satisfacción, la alegria**)

gym, gymnasium *n.* **el gimnasio**

H

ha *3d pers.,s., pres.indic. of* **haber**; see **haber** in the index and verb tables, p. 448.

haber *v.* to have (aux. v. to form the compound tenses)

había dado *1st & 3d pers.,s., pluperf.indic. of* **dar**; had given; see WU 13.

habitación *n.f.* room

hablando *pres.part. of* **hablar**; see *pres.part.* in WU 3.

hablar *v.* to talk, to speak; see **hablar** in the index

hacer *v.* to do, to make; see **hace, hacía, hacer** in the index and verb tables, p. 448.

hacia *prep.* toward, in the direction of; **hacia atrás** toward the back

haciendo *pres.part. of* **hacer**; see *pres. part.* in WU 3.

haga *3d pers.,s., imper. (command) Ud. of* **hacer**; make, do; see **hacer** in the verb tables, p. 448.

hair *n.* **el cabello, el pelo**

half *n.* **la mitad**

hallar *v.* to find

halló *3d pers.,s., pret. of* **hallar**; he/she/you found

hallway *n.* **el pasillo**

ham *n.* **el jamón**

hand *n.* **la mano**

handsome *adj.* **guapo**

hang *v.* **colgar (ue); Yo cuelgo.**

happen *v.* **pasar**

happy *adj.* **contento, contenta; feliz, felices**

has *2d pers.,s., pres.indic. of* **haber**; see **haber** in the verb tables, p. 448.

hasta *adv., prep.* up to, until; see **hasta** in the index.

hat *n.* **el sombrero**

have *v.* **tener; haber** (used as a helping verb to form the compound tenses); see **haber** and **tener** in the index.

Have a nice day **¡Pase muy buenos días!**

have breakfast **desayunar**

have dinner **cenar; tomar la cena**

have lunch **almorzar (ue, c); Yo almuerzo.** I have lunch; **Yo almorcé.** I had lunch.

hay there is..., there are..., (*idiomatic v. form of* **haber**); see **hay** in the index.

haz *2d pers.,s., (tú) imper. (command) of* **hacer**; do, make; see **hacer** in the verb tables, p. 448.

he *1st pers.,s., pres.indic. of* **haber**; see **haber** in the verb tables, p. 448.

He aquí ... Here is..., Here are ...

head *n.* **la cabeza**

headache *n.* **el dolor de cabeza; Me duele la cabeza.** I have a headache.

health *n.* **la salud**

hear *v.* **oír**

heart *n.* **el corazón**

heat *n.* **el calor**; to be warm (weather) **hacer calor**; to be warm (persons) **tener calor**

hecho *past part. of* **hacer**; see *past part.* in WU 12.

heladería *n.f.* ice cream shop

helado *n.m.* ice cream

helar (ie) *v.* to freeze; **Hiela.** It's freezing.

Hello! **¡Hola!**

help *n.* **la ayuda; v. ayudar**

hemos *1st pers.,pl. pres. indic. of* **haber**; see **haber** in the index and verb tables, p. 470.

her *poss.adj.* **su, sus**; see *poss.adj.* in WU 6.

here *adv.* **aquí**; here is ..., here are ... **aquí tiene Ud.; he aquí**

hermana *n.f.* sister; **la hermanita** little sister

hermano *n.m.* brother; **el hermanito** little brother

hermoso, hermosa *adj.* beautiful

Hi! **¡Hola!**

hice *1st pers.,s., pret. of* **hacer**; I did, made; see **hacer** in the index and verb tables, p. 448.

hide *v.* **esconder**; hidden **escondido**; see *past part.* in WU 12.

hierba *n.f.* grass

high *adj.* **alto, alta**

hija *n.f.* daughter

hijo *n.m.* son

hijos *n.m.* children, sons and daughters

him *pron.* **lo, le;** see *dir. & indir. obj. pron.* in WU 8, 9 and 10.

his *poss.adj.* **su, sus**; see *poss.adj.* in WU 6.

hizo *3d pers.,s., pret. of* **hacer**; he/she/you did, made; see **hacer** in the index and verb tables, p. 448.

hog *n.* **el cerdo**

hold *v.* **tener**; see **tener** in the index.

holiday *n.* **la fiesta**; holidays *n.* **los días festivos**

hombre *n.m.* man

hombro *n.m.* shoulder

home *n.* **el hogar**; at home **en casa**; I'm going home. **Voy a casa**; I am home. **Estoy en casa.**

homework *n.* **la tarea**

hope *v.* **esperar**; *n.* **la esperanza**

horóscopo *n.m.* horoscope

horse *n.* **el caballo**

hospital *n.* **el hospital**

hotel *n.* **el hotel;** hotel room *n.* **la habitación**

hour *n.* **la hora**; At what time? **¿A qué hora?** What time is it? **¿Qué hora es?**

house *n.* **la casa**; private residence **la casa particular**

how *adv.* **como**; How are you? **¿Cómo está (Ud.)? ¿Cómo estás (tú)?** How are things? **¿Qué tal?** See *how* in the index.

How many? How much? See **cuanto, cuánto** in the index.

How much does it cost? **¿Cuánto cuesta? ¿Cuánto vale?**

How old are you? **¿Cuántos años tienes (tú)? ¿Cuántos años tiene (Ud.)?** How old is he/she? **¿Cuántos años tiene él/ella?**

hoy *adv.* today

hube, hubo See index.

hugs *n.* **los abrazos**

hunger *n.* **el hambre**; to be hungry **tener hambre**; I am very hungry. **Tengo mucha hambre**; see **tener** in the index.

hurry *v.* **apresurarse**; *n.* **la prisa**; to be in a hurry **tener prisa**; I'm in a hurry. **Tengo prisa.**

hurt *v.* **doler (ue)**; My foot hurts. **Me duele el pie.**

husband *n.* **el esposo, el marido**

I

I am Juan/Juana López. **Soy Juan/Juana López.**

I am... **Soy..., Estoy...**; see **ser** and **estar** in the index and verb tables, p. 448.

I bought ... **Compré ...**

I deserve ... **Merezco ...;** see **merecer**

I detest ... **Detesto ...**

I don't know. **Yo no sé.**

I gave... **Yo dí ...**

I hate ... **Detesto ...**

I like it a lot. **Me gusta mucho.**

I love you a lot. **Te quiero mucho;** I love children. **Amo a los niños.**

I said ... **Yo dije ...**

I saw ... **Yo vi ...**

I went ... **Yo fui ...**

I would like ... **Me gustaría ... ; Quisiera ...**

I'm only looking. **Sólo estoy mirando.**

iba *1st & 3d pers.,s., imperf. indic. of* **ir**; I/he/she/you went, used to go, was going, were going; see **ir** in the index and verb tables, p. 448.

ice cream *n.* **el helado**

ice cream shop *n.* **la heladería**

idea *n.f.* idea

if *conj.* **si**; see If clause in WU 11.

ill, sick *adj.* **enfermo, enferma**

illness, sickness *n.* **la enfermedad**

imaginary *adj.* **imaginario, imaginaria**

immediately *adv.* **en seguida, inmediatamente**

importante *adj.* important

impresionante *adj.* impressive

in *prep.* **en**; in order to **para**; in front of **delante de**; in love with **enamorado de**; in place of **en lugar de**; see **en** in the index.

increíble *adj.* incredible, unbelievable

independencia *n.f.* independence

in front **al frente**; in front of **delante de**

infant *n.* **el nene**

ingrato *adj.* ungrateful

inside *adv.* **dentro**

insistir *v.* to insist

instead of **en lugar de**

inteligente *adj.* intelligent

interesante *adj.* interesting

intermission *n.* **el entreacto**

introduce *v.* **presentar**

invitación *n.f.* invitation

ir *v.* to go; **ir de paseo** to go for a walk; **ir a pie** to walk; see **ir** in the index and verb tables, p. 448.

irse *refl.v.* to go away; to leave; see **irse** in the index.

Isn't that so? **¿No es verdad?**

It costs ... **Cuesta ...**

It seems to me that ... **Me parece que ...**

J

jacket *n.* **la chaqueta**

jam *n.* **la confitura**

jamón *n.m.* ham

jester, joker *n.* **el burlador**

jewel *n.* **la alhaja, la joya**

job *n.* **el empleo**

joven, jóvenes *adj.* young; **el más joven** the younger

joy *n.* **la alegría, el gozo**

juego *n.m.* game

jugar (ue, gu) *v.* to play (game or sport); **Yo juego.** I play; **Yo jugué.** I played; see **jugar** in the verb tables.

juice *n.* **el jugo**

julio *n.m.* July

jump *v.* **saltar**

juntos *adj.,adv.* together, joined

K

keep *v.* **guardar**

key *n.* **la llave**

kick *v.* **patear, dar una patada**; *n.* **la patada**

kilómetro *n.m.* kilometer (about 0.62 mile)

kind (type, species) *n.* **la especie**; kind (gentle, amiable) *adj.* **amable, gentil**

kisses *n.* **los besos**

kitchen *n.* **la cocina**

kitten *n.* **el gatito**

knee *n.* **la rodilla**

knife *n.* **el cuchillo**

knock *v.* **tocar (qu); Yo toqué.** I knocked.

know *v.* **conocer** (to be acquainted); I know your friends. **Yo conozco a sus (tus) amigos**; to know how **saber + inf.**; I know how to swim. **Yo sé nadar;** see WU 3 and 13.

L

la *def.art.,f.s.* the; **la casa** the house; *dir.obj.pron.,f.s.* her, it; see WU 8, 9 and 10.

la cual *rel.pron.* which; see index and WU 10.

la de, la mía, la que, la suya, la tuya; see index.

lack *v.* **faltar**

lady *n.* **la dama**

lake *n.* **el lago**

lamb *n.* **el cordero**

lamp *n.* **la lámpara**

land *n.* **la tierra**

language *n.* **la lengua**

lanzar *v.* to throw

large *adj.* **gran, grande**; see these words in the index

large room *n.* **la sala**

largo, larga *adj.* long

las *def.art.,f.pl.* the **las casas**; *dir.obj.pron.,f.pl.* them; see WU 8, 9, 10 and the index.

las cuales, las de, las mías, las que, las suyas, las tuyas; see index.

last (ultimate) *adj.* **último, última**

last night *adv.* **anoche**; last week **la semana pasada**; last year **el año pasado**

lástima *n.f.* pity; **¡Qué lástima!** What a pity! Too bad!

late *adv.* **tarde**; later **más tarde**

laugh *v.* **reír, reírse**

lawyer *n.* **el abogado, la abogada**

lazy *adj.* **perezoso, perezosa**

le, les *indir.obj.pron.* to him, to her, to you, to them; see WU 8, 9 and 10.

learn *v.* **aprender**

least *adv.* **menos**; at least **a (por) lo menos**

leave *v.* **marcharse; partir, salir (de), irse; dejar**; see **dejar, salir** in the index.

lección *n.f.* lesson

leche *n.f.* milk

lectura *n.f.* reading

leer (y) *v.* to read; **Mi hermano leyó un libro.** My brother read a book; see **leer** in WU 7 and the verb tables.

left *n.* **la izquierda**; to (on) the left **a la izquierda**; *adj.* **izquierdo, izquierda**

leg *n.* **la pierna**

lemon *n.* **el limón**; lemonade **la limonada**

lend *v.* **prestar**

les, le *indir.obj.pron.* to them, to him, to her, to you; see WU 8, 9 and 10.

less *adv.* **menos**

lesson *n.* **la lección**

Let's begin! **¡Vamos a comenzar!**

Let's eat! **¡Vamos a comer!**

Let's see! **¡(Vamos) a ver!**

Let's sit down! **¡Vamos a sentarnos!**

Let's go! **¡Vamos!**

Let's search! **¡Vamos a buscar!**

letter *n.* **la carta; la letra** (of the alphabet)

levantar *v.* to raise; **levantarse** *refl.v.* to get up; **Me levanto a las seis.** I get up at six o'clock.

leyendo *pres.part. of* **leer (y)**; reading; see *pres.part.* in WU 3.

leyó *3d pers.,s., pret. of* **leer (y); ¿Quién leyó este libro?** Who read this book? See **leer** in WU 7.

libertad *n.f.* liberty, freedom

library *n.* **la biblioteca**

lie (opposite of truth) *n.* **la mentira**; *v.* **mentir (ie, i); Yo no miento.** I do not lie; He lied **Él mintió.**

life *n.* **la vida**

like (to be pleasing to) *v.* **gustar**; see WU 2 and 11.

lindo, linda *adj.* pretty

lips *n.* **los labios**

líquido *n.m.* liquid

listen (to) *v.* **escuchar**

listo, lista, listos, listas *adj.* ready

little (in size) *adj.* **pequeño, pequeña**; little (in quantity) **poco, poca**

little dog *n.* **el perrito**

little house *n.* **la casita**

live *v.* **vivir**

living room *n.* **la sala**

llamarse *refl.v.* to be named, to be called; see verb tables.

llegar (gu) *v.* to arrive; **Yo llegué tarde.** I arrived late.

llegaron *3d pers.,pl., pret. of* **llegar**; they arrived

llevar *v.* to wear, to carry

lo *dir.obj.pron., m.s.* him, it; see **lo** and *dir.obj.pron.* in the index.

lo que *pron.* what, that which; **lo que pasa** what

is going on, happening; see **lo que, los que** in the index.

loco, loca *adj.* crazy

long *adj.* **largo, larga**

Long live...! **¡Viva... !**

look (at) *v.* **mirar**

look for *v.* **buscar (qu)**; I looked for the money. **Busqué el dinero.**

Look! **¡Mira! ¡Miren!**

los *def.art.,m.pl.* the; **los pasteles** the pastries; *dir. obj.pron., m.pl.* them; **Los tengo.** I have them; see *dir.obj.pron.* in the index.

los cuales, los de, los míos, los que, los suyos, los tuyos; see these words in the index.

lose *v.* **perder (ie)**; Robert is losing his money. **Roberto pierde su dinero**; see **perder** in WU 3.

lost *past part.* **perdido**; see *past part.* in WU 12.

love *v.* **amar**; *n.* **el amor**; **querer a**; see **querer** in the verb tables.

lovely *adj.* **preciosa**

lovingly *adv.* **cariñosamente**

low *adv.* **baja**; in a low voice **en voz baja**

luck *n.* **la fortuna, la suerte**; What luck! **¡Qué fortuna!** Good luck! **¡Buena suerte!**

lugar *n.m.* place; **en lugar de** in place of, instead of

lunch *n.* **el almuerzo**; to have lunch **tomar el almuerzo, almorzar (ue, c)**; I have lunch. **Almuerzo**; I had lunch. **Almorcé.**

M

madam *n.* **la señora**

madre *n.f.* mother; **la madre de Juana** Jane's mother

madrugada *n.f.* dawn

magazine *n.* **la revista**

magnífico *adj.* magnificent

mail, post (a letter) *v.* **echar una carta al correo**; see letter writing in the index.

majestuoso *adj.* majestic

make *v.* **hacer**; see **hacer** in the index and verb tables, p. 471.

mal, malo *adj.* bad; see WU 6.

malgastar *v.* to squander, spend foolishly

mamá *n.f.* mom

man *n.* **el hombre**

mano *n.f.* hand

many *adj.* **mucho, mucha, muchos, muchas**; see WU 7.

many times **muchas veces**

map *n.* **el mapa**

marchar *v.* to walk; **marcharse** *refl.v.* to leave, to walk away

mark (grade in a course of study) *n.* **la nota**; to get a mark **sacar una nota**

market *n.* **el mercado**

married *adj.* **casados**

marry *v.* **casarse (con alguien)**

marvelous *adj.* **maravilloso**

más *adv.* more; see **más, menos, más ... que, más ... de** in the index.

match (sports) *n.* **el partido**

May *n.* **el mayo**

maybe *adv.* **tal vez**

mayor *adj.* older

me *pron.* **me, mí, yo**; see WU 8, 9, 10 and 14.

Me gusta mucho. I like it a lot.

Me llamo Juan/Juana. My name is Juan/Juana.

Me neither. **Ni yo tampoco.**

Me parece que ... It seems to me that ...

me, te, se, nos, os *pron.* See WU 8.

meal *n.* **la comida**

mean *v.* **significar (qu), querer decir**; What does it mean? **¿Qué quiere decir?**

meanwhile *adv.* **entretanto**

meat *n.* **la carne**

medianoche *n.f.* midnight; **Era medianoche.** It was midnight.

mejor, mejores *adj.* better, best; see **mejor, peor** in the index.

member *n.* **el miembro**

mend *v.* **reparar**

menor *adj.* younger

menos *adv.* less

menu *n.* **el menú, la lista de platos**

merecer (z) *v.* to merit, to deserve; **Yo merezco.** I deserve.

Merry Christmas **Feliz Navidad**

mes *n.m.* month; **los meses**

mesa *n.f.* table

Mexico *n.* **México, Méjico**

mí *pron.* me; see *prep. pron.* in WU 9.

mi, mis *poss.adj.* my; **mi lección** my lesson; **mis lecciones** my lessons; see WU 6.

middle *n.* **el medio**

midnight *n.* **la medianoche**

milk *n.* **la leche**

mine, yours, *etc.*; see index.

mineral water *n.* **el agua mineral**

minute *n.* **el minuto**

mío, mía, míos, mías, el mío, la mía, los míos, las mías See WU 6 and 10.

Mira! ¡Miren! Look!

mirar *v.* to look (at), to watch; **Miro el pájaro en el árbol.** I'm looking at the bird in the tree.

mismo *adj.* same; see **mismo** in the index.

Miss *n.* **la señorita**

miss, to be missing *v.* **faltar**

mistaken, to be *v.* **equivocarse (qu)**; I was mistaken. **Me equivoqué.**

Mister *n.* **el señor**

mitad *n.f.* half

modelo *n.m.* model

moderación *n.f.* moderation

modo *n.m.* way; **de todos modos** anyway, anyhow

mojado *adj.* moist, wet

mom *n.* **la mamá**

moment *n.* **el momento**

moneda *n.f.* coin

money *n.* **el dinero**

monkey *n.* **el mono**

monstrous *adj.* **monstruoso**

month *n.* **el mes, los meses**

monument *n.* **el monumento**

moon *n.* **la luna**

more *adv.* **más**

morir (ue, u) *v.* to die; see verb tables.

morning *n.* **la mañana**; good morning **buenos días**; in the morning **por la mañana**; see **mañana** in the index.

mosca *n.f.* fly (insect)

mostrar (ue) *v.* to show; **El vendedor me muestra los zapatos.** The salesman is showing me the shoes.

mother *n.* **la madre**

motivo *n.m.* motive; **reírse sin motivo** to giggle

motorcycle *n.* **la motocicleta, la moto**

mountains *n.* **las montañas**

mouth *n.* **la boca**

moverse (ue) *refl.v.* to move

movies (cinema) *n.* **el cine**; film **la película**

Mr. **Señor**; Mrs. **Señora**

muchacha *n.f.* girl

muchacho *n.m.* boy

muchísimo *adv.* very much; see this word in the index.

mucho, mucha *adj.* many, much, **Tengo mucho que hacer.** I have a lot to do.

muerte *n.f.* death; **muerto, muerta** *adj.* dead

mujer *n.f.* woman (synonym: **dama**)

mundo *n.m.* world; **todo el mundo** everybody

muro *n.m.* wall (outside)

museum *n.* **el museo**

mushroom *n.* **el hongo**

música *n.f.* music

must *v.* **deber**; see **deber** in the index.

muy *adv.* very

my *poss.adj.* **mi, mis; mío, mía**, *etc.* See WU 6 and 10.

My God! *excl.* **¡Dios mío!**

My name is Juan/Juana. **Me llamo Juan/Juana; Soy Juan/Juana.**

mysterious *adj.* **misterioso, misteriosa**

N

nación, campo, país, patria country; for differences in meaning, see WU 13.

nada *pron.* nothing; **nada más** nothing more; **nada que comer** nothing to eat; **de nada** you're welcome; see **nada** in WU 3.

nadar *v.* to swim

nadie *pron.* nobody; see **nadie** in WU 3.

name *n.* **el nombre**; What is your name? **¿Cómo te llamas (tú)? ¿Cómo se llama Ud.? ¿Cuál es tu (su) nombre?**

napkin *n.* **la servilleta**

naranja *n.f.* orange

near *adv.* **cerca (de)**

neat *adj.* **neto**

neck *n.* **el cuello**; necktie **la corbata**

need *v.* **necesitar**

neighbor *n.* **el vecino, la vecina**

neighborhood *n.* **la vecindad, el vecindario, el barrio**

neither, not either *adv.* **tampoco;** Me neither. **Ni yo tampoco.**

nene *n.m.* baby

nephew *n.* **el sobrino**

nervous *adj.* **nervioso, nerviosa**

never *adv.* **nunca**

new *adj.* **nuevo, nueva**

New York **Nueva York**

New Zealand **la Nueva Zelanda**

newspaper *n.m.* **el periódico**

next *adj.* **próximo, próxima**; next time **la próxima vez**; next week **la semana próxima, la semana que viene**

nice *adj.* **simpático, simpática** (person)

niece *n.* **la sobrina**

night *n.* **la noche**; good night **buenas noches**; last night **anoche**; every night **todas las noches**; at night **de noche**

ninety *num.* **noventa**; see numbers in WU 4.

ningún, ninguno, ninguna *adj.* not any; **ningún dinero** not any money; see WU 6.

niño, niña *n.,m.f.* child; **los niños** children; **nosotros los niños** we kids

no problem **no hay problema**

nobody, no one *pron.* **nadie**; see **nadie** in WU 3.

noche *n.f.* evening, night; **buenas noches** good evening, good night

noise *n.* **el ruido**

nombre *n.m.* name; noun

none, not any *pron., adj.* **ningún, ninguno, ninguna**; see WU 6.

noon *n.* **el mediodía**

nose *n.* **la nariz, las narices**

not either, neither *adv.* **tampoco**

not I, not me **yo no**

note (written) *n.* **la nota, el billete**

notebook *n.* **el cuaderno**

nothing *indef.pron.* **nada**; see WU 3; nothing more **nada más**; nothing to eat **nada que comer**

noun *n.* **el nombre, el sustantivo**

noventa *num.* ninety; see numbers in WU 4.

now *adv.* **ahora, ya**

nuestro, nuestra, nuestros, nuestras *poss.adj.* our; see these words in WU 6.

Nueva York New York

número *n.m.* number; **el número cardinal** cardinal number; see numbers in WU 4.

nurse *n.* **la enfermera, el enfermero**

O

o *conj.* or; if a word right after **o** begins with **o** or **ho**, use **u**: **septiembre u octubre** September or October; **muchachos u hombres** boys or men

obra *n.f.* work

obstáculo *n.m.* obstacle

ocasión *n.f.* occasion (time, opportunity)

occupy *v.* **ocupar**

ocho *num.* eight; see numbers in WU 4

of *prep.* **de**; of the, from the **del, de la, de los, de las**; see WU 1; see also **de** in the index; of course **por supuesto**

oferta *n.f.* offer; *v.* **ofrecer (z);** see orthographical changing verbs in WU 3.

office *n.* **la oficina**

often *adv.* **a menudo**

oigo *1st pers.,s., pres.indic. of* **oír**

oír *v.* to hear; see verb tables.

¡Ojalá que ... ! See this expression in the index.

ojo *n.m.* eye

okay **de acuerdo; está bien**

old *adj.* **viejo, vieja**

older *adj.* **mayor**

oler (hue) *v.* to smell; **oler a** to smell of; see **oler** in the verb tables.

olvidar *v.* to forget

omelet *n.* **la tortilla de huevos**

omit *v.* **omitir**

on *prep.* **en, sobre**

once, one time **una vez**

one *num.* **un, uno, una**; see WU 1 and 4.

one hundred *num.* **cien, ciento**; see these words in the index.

only *adv.* **solamente, sólo, único, única, únicamente**; I'm only looking. **Sólo estoy mirando.**

open *v.* **abrir**

opposite *adj.* **contrario, contraria;** the opposite **lo contrario**

or *conj.* **o, u**; if a word right after **o** begins with **o** or **ho**, use **u: septiembre u octubre** September or October; **muchachos u hombres** men or boys

orange *n.* **la naranja**; orange color **anaranjado, anaranjada**

orange juice *n.* **el jugo de naranja**

ordinary *adj.* **ordinario, ordinaria**

otra, otro *adj.,f.,m.* other, another; **en otra ocasión** at some other time

ought to *v.* **deber**; see verb tables.

our *poss.adj.* **nuestro, nuestra, nuestros, nuestras;** see WU 6.

outside *adv.* **afuera**

over *adv.* **sobre**

overcoat *n.* **el abrigo**

owe *v.* **deber**; see verb tables; see also **deber** in the index.

own *adj.* **propio, propia**

oyen *3d pers.,pl., pres.indic. of* **oír**; see verb tables.

P

paciencia *n.f.* patience

package *n.* **el paquete**

padre *n.m.* father

pagar (ue) *v.* to pay; **Yo pagué.** I paid.

page *n.* **la página**

pail *n.* **el cubo**

pain *v.* **doler (ue)**; *n.* **el dolor; Me duele el pie.** My foot hurts.

paint *v.* **pintar**

painting *n.* **la pintura, el cuadro**

país *n.m* country; see **país** in the index.

pájaro *n.m.* bird (synonym: **ave**, *n.f.*)

palace *n.* **el palacio**

pants (trousers) *n.* **los pantalones**

papá *n.m.* dad

papas fritas *n.f.* fried potatoes

paper *n.* **el papel**

para *prep.* for, in order (to); see **para** in the index.

parade *n.* **el desfile**

paragraph *n.* **el párrafo**

pardon *v.* **perdonar;** Pardon me. **Perdóneme.**

parecer (z) *v.* to seem, to appear; **Yo parezco.** I appear.

parents *n.* **los padres**; my parents **mis padres**

parque *n.m.* park

part *n.* **la parte**

participate *v.* **participar**

partir *v.* to leave

party *n.* **la fiesta**

pasar *v.* to happen; to pass by; to spend (time)

pasear *v.* to stroll

pass (by) *v.* **pasar**

past *n.* **el pasado**

pastel *n.m.* pastry; **los pasteles** pastries

patatas *n.f.* potatoes

patience *n.* **la paciencia**

patria, nación, campo, país country; for differences in meaning, see WU 13.

pay (for) *v.* **pagar (ue); Yo pagué la cuenta.** I paid the check (bill).

pear *n.* **la pera**

pedestrian *n.* **el peatón**

pedir (i) *v.* to ask for, to request; **Pido dinero a mi madre.** I'm asking my mother for money.

peligro *n.m.* danger; **peligroso** dangerous

pelo *n.m.* hair

pen *n.* **la pluma**

pencil *n.* **el lápiz, los lápices**; pencil sharpener **el sacapuntas**

pensar (ie) *v.* to think; **Yo pienso que...** I think that... see verb tables.

people *n.* **la gente**; many people **mucha gente**; many persons **muchas personas**

pepper *n.* **la pimienta**

pequeño, pequeña *adj.* small, little

perder (ie) *v.* to lose, to waste (time); **No pierdo mi tiempo.** I don't waste my time.

perdido *past part. of* **perder**; lost; see *past part.* in WU 12.

performance *n.* **la representación**

perhaps *adv.* **tal vez, acaso**

period *n.* **el punto** (at end of a sentence)

periódico *n.m.* newspaper

permission *n.* **el permiso**; Excuse me, with your permission. **Con permiso.**

permitir *v.* to permit

pero *conj.* but

perrito *n.m.* little dog

perro *n.m.* dog

persona *n.f.* person

pertenecer (z) *v.* to belong (to)

pesar *v.* to weigh; **a pesar de** in spite of

peseta *n.f.* peseta (monetary unit of Spain)

petición *n.f.* request, petition

pharmacy *n.* **la farmacia**

picture *n.* **la foto, la fotografía; el cuadro, el grabado**

pidió *3d pers.,s., pret. of* **pedir (i)**; he/she/you requested, asked for

pido *1st pers.,s., pres.indic. of* **pedir (i); Yo pido ayuda.** I'm asking for help; see verb tables.

pie *n.m.* foot

pie *n.* **la tarta**

pieza *n.f.* play (theater)

pig *n.* **el cerdo, el puerco**

pintura *n.f.* painting

pity *n.* **la lástima**; What a pity! **¡Qué lástima!**

pizarra *n.f.* chalkboard

place *n.* **el lugar, el sitio**

plant *n.* **la planta**

play *v.* **jugar (ue)**; I play. **Yo juego**; to play a game **jugar a, al, a la**; to play a musical instrument **tocar (qu)**; to play the piano **tocar el piano**; I played the piano. **Toqué el piano.**

player *n.* **el jugador, la jugadora**

plaything *n.* **el juguete**

pleasant *adj.* **agradable; simpático, simpática** (person)

please **por favor**

pleasure *n.* **el placer, el gusto**

pocket *n.* **el bolsillo**

poco, poca *adj.* little (in quantity); **poco trabajo** little work; see **poco** in the index.

poder (ue, u) *v.* to be able, can; **Puedo venir.** I can come; **Pude venir.** I was able to come; see verb tables.

polite *adj.* **cortés, corteses**

pollo *n.m.* chicken

poner *v.* to put, to place; see verb tables.

pool (swimming) *n.* **la piscina**

poor *adj.* **pobre**

por *prep.* for, by; **por ejemplo** for example; **por todas partes** everywhere; **por favor** please

pork *n.* **la carne de cerdo**

posesivo *adj.* possessive

possible *adj.* **posible**

post (mail) a letter *v.* **echar una carta al correo**

postage stamp *n.* **el sello postal, el sello de correo, la estampilla**

postre *n.m.* dessert

potatoes *n.* **las patatas, las papas**

pray *v.* **rogar (ue)**; I pray. **Yo ruego.**

precio *n.m.* price

preciosa *adj.* lovely, beautiful

prefer *v.* **preferir (ie, i)**; I prefer this blouse. **Prefiero esta blusa**; You preferred this restaurant. **Ud. prefirió este restaurante**; see verb tables.

preguntar *v.* to ask

preparar *v.* to prepare

preparations *n.* **los preparativos**

preposición *n.f.* preposition

present (gift) *n.* **el regalo**; *v.* **presentar**

pretty *adj.* **bonito, bonita, lindo, linda**

price *n.* **el precio**

primer, primero, primera *num.* first; see these words in WU 6; see also numbers in WU 4.

principal *n.* **el director, la directora**

printer (computer) *n.* **la impresora**

prize *n.* **el premio**

problem *n.* **el problema**; No problem! **¡No hay problema!**

pródigo *adj.* prodigal, wasteful, recklessly extravagant

professor *n.* **el profesor, la profesora**

programa *n.m.* program

prohibir *v.* to prohibit; see verb tables.

promise *v.* **prometer**; *n.* **la promesa**; to keep a promise **cumplir una promesa**

pronombre *n.m.* pronoun

pronounce *v.* **pronunciar**

pronunciation *n.* **la pronunciación**

pronto *adv.* quickly, fast

propia *adj.* own; **en mi propia cama** in my own bed

proverb *n.* **el proverbio, el refrán**; see proverbs in Spanish in the index.

pública *adj.,f.s.* public

pude *1st pers.,s., pret. of* **poder (ue, u)**; I could, was able to

puedo *1st pers.,s., pres. indic. of* **poder (ue, u)**; see verb tables.

puerta *n.f.* door

pues *adv.* well, then

punto *n.m.* period, dot

pupil *n.* **el alumno, la alumna**

purchase *v.* **comprar**

purse *n.* **la bolsa**

puse *1st pers.,s., pret. of* **poner; me puse a +** *inf.* I began to + *inf.*

put *v.* **poner, colocar (qu)**; see verb tables; to put on clothing **ponerse**

Q

quality *n.* **la calidad**

que *adj. & pron.* that, what, which; *rel.pron.* who; see *relative pronouns* in WU 10.

¡Qué fortuna! What luck!

¿Qué tal? How are things?

quedarse *refl.v.* to stay, to remain

quepo *1st pers., sing., pres. indic. of* **caber**

querer (ie) *v.* to want; **¿Quiere Ud. ...?** Do you want... ? **querer a** to love; **querer decir** to mean; **¿Qué quiere decir esta palabra?** What does this word mean?

querido *adj. & past part. of* **querer; querido mío (querida mía)** my dear, darling question *n.* **la pregunta**; to ask a question **hacer una pregunta**

quickly *adv.* **pronto**

quien *pron.* who, whom; see *pronouns* in WU 2, 8, 9 and 10.

quiere *3d pers.,s., pres. indic. of* **querer (ie); quiero** *1st pers.,s., pres. indic. of* **querer;** see **querer** in the verb tables.

quinta *num.* fifth; **la quinta fila** the fifth row; see ordinal numbers in WU 4.

Quisiera hacer una pregunta. I would like to ask a question; see **quisiera** in WU 11.

R

rabbit *n.* **un conejo**

race *n.* **correr**; race track **la pista**

railroad *n.* **el ferrocarril**

rain *n.* **la lluvia**; *v.* **llover (ue)**; It's raining. **Llueve. Está lloviendo.**

raise *v.* **levantar**

rasgados *adj.* torn

rastro *n.m.* store, market where used things are sold; flea market

read *v.* **leer (y)**; Did you read this book? **¿Leyó Ud. este libro?** see **leer** in WU 7 and in the verb tables.

reading *n.* **la lectura**; *pres. part. of* **leer (y); leyendo**; see *pres.part.* in WU 3.

ready *adj.* **dispuesto, listo**

really *adv.* **de veras, realmente**

rebajados *adj.* reduced

receipt *n.* **el acuse de recibo**

recibir *v.* to receive

recognize *v.* **reconocer (z)**; I recognize her. **Yo la reconozco.**

record (disk) *n.* **el disco**; record player **el tocadiscos**

red *adj.* **rojo, roja**

redondo, redonda *adj.,m.f.* round

reflexivo *adj.* reflexive

refreshment *n.* **el refresco**

refrigerator *n.* **el refrigerador**

regalar *v.* to give a gift

regalo *n.m.* gift, present

regresar *v.* to return

reír (i) *v.* to laugh; see **reír** in WU 7 and the verb tables.

rejoice *v.* **alegrarse (de)**

relative (family) *n.* **el pariente, la pariente**; relatives **los parientes**

reloj *n.m.* watch

remain *v.* **quedarse**

remember *v.* **acordarse (ue), recordar (ue)**; I remember. **Me acuerdo.**

rent *v.* **alquilar**; rental *n.* **el alquiler**

repeat *v.* **repetir (i)**; I repeat the question. **Repito la pregunta.**

reply *v.* **responder, contestar**; *n.* **la respuesta, la contestación**

request *n.* **la petición**; *v.* **pedir (i)**; see **pedir** in the verb tables.

responder *v.* to answer, respond, reply

respuesta *n.f.* answer

rest *v.* **descansar**

restaurant *n.* **el restaurante**

result *n.* **el resultado**

return (something) *v.* **devolver (ue)**; I'm returning the book to the library **Devuelvo el libro a la biblioteca.**

return (go back) *v.* **regresar, volver (ue)**; I'm returning at two o'clock **Vuelvo a las dos.**

review *v.* **repasar**; *n.* **el repaso**

rice *n.* **el arroz**

rich *adj.* **rico, rica**

riddle *n.* **la adivinanza**

ridiculous *adj.* **ridículo**

rieron *3d pers.,pl., pret. of* **reír (i)**; see **reír** in WU 7 and the verb tables.

right (as opposed to left) *n.* **la derecha**; to the right **a la derecha**; right (privilege) **el derecho**; Isn't that right? Isn't that so? **¿No es verdad?** to be right **tener razón**; see **tener** in the index.

ring *v.* **sonar (ue)**; it rings **suena**; *n.* ring (on finger) **el anillo**

river *n.* **el río**

road *n.* **el camino**

roast beef *n.* **el rosbif**

rogar (ue) *v.* to pray; **rogando** praying

romántico, romántica *adj.* romantic

roof *n.* **el techo**

room *n.* **el cuarto, la habitación**; bedroom **el dormitorio**; bathroom **el cuarto de baño**; living room **la sala, el cuarto de estar**; hotel room *n.* **la habitación**

rose *n.* **la rosa**

round *adj.* **redondo, redonda**

ruido *n.m.* noise

rule *n.f.* **la regla**

run *v.* **correr**

S

saber *v.* to know; **saber** + *inf.* to know how + *inf.*; **Yo sé nadar.** I know how to swim; see **saber** in the verb tables and index.

sabroso *adj.* tasty

sacar fotos to take pictures

sad *adj.* **triste**; sadness *n.* **la tristeza**

sala *n.f.* living room; large room

salad *n.* **la ensalada**

salary *n.* **el sueldo**

salchicha *n.f.* sausage

salchichón *n.m.* thick, large sausage

sale *n.* **la venta**

salir *v.* to go out, to leave; **Salgo a las tres.** I'm going out at three o'clock; see **salir** in WU 3 and 14, and the verb tables.

salt *n.* **la sal**

salud *n.f.* health

same *adj.* **mismo, misma**

San, Santo *n.* Saint; see WU 6.

sand *n.* **la arena**

sandwich *n.* **el bocadillo**; in some Latin American countries, **un sandwich**

Saturday *n.* **el sábado**; last Saturday **el sábado pasado**

saucer *n.* **el platillo**

sausage *n.* **la salchicha**; thick, large sausage **el salchichón**

say, to tell *v.* **decir**; How do you say ... in Spanish? **¿Cómo se dice ... en español?** See **decir** in the verb tables and index.

scare away *v.* **espantar**

scene *n.* **la escena**

school *n.* **la escuela**

scissors *n.* **las tijeras**

score a point (sports) *v.* **marcar (qu) un tanto**; I scored a point. **Marqué un tanto.**

scream *v.* **gritar**

sé *1st pers.,s., pres.indic. of* **saber**; **Yo no sé.** I don't know; see **saber** in the verb tables and index.

se habla, se cree, se dice, se sabe, se vende it is spoken, it is believed, it is said, it is known, it is sold, see **se** and its uses in WU 8 and 14.

se sientan *3d pers.,pl., pres.indic. of* **sentarse (ie)**; see verb tables.

se terminó *3d pers.,s., pret. of* **terminarse**; it has ended

sea *3d pers.,s., pres.sub. of* **ser**; be; see **ser** in WU 1 and the verb tables, p. 448.

sea *n.* **el (la) mar**

¡Seamos serios! Let's be serious!

search (for) *v.* **buscar (qu)**; I searched for the money. **Busqué el dinero.**

season *n.* **la estación**

seat *n.* **el asiento**

second *adj.* **segundo, segunda**; see numbers in WU 4.

secreto *n.m.* secret

see *v.* **ver**; see **ver** in verb tables; See you tomorrow! **¡Hasta mañana!**

seem *v.* **parecer (z)**; I seem... **Yo parezco...**

seguramente *adv.* surely

seguro *adj.* sure; **de seguro** surely; I am sure. **Estoy seguro (segura).**

select *v.* **elegir (i, j), escoger (j)**; I select, I choose. **Elijo, escojo.**

sell *v.* **vender**

send *v.* **enviar (í)**; I'm sending a letter. **Envío una carta;** see verb tables; to send for **enviar por**

señor *n.m.* sir, Mr., mister; **señora** *n.f.* madam, Mrs.; **señoras y señores** ladies and gentlemen.

sentarse (ie) *refl.v.* to sit (oneself) down; **Me siento aquí.** I'm sitting here; see verb tables.

sentence *n.* **la frase, la oración**

ser *v.* to be; see **ser** in the index and verb tables, p. 448.

serious *adj.* **serio, seria**

servicio *n.m.* service

servir (i) *v.* to serve; **El camarero nos sirve.** The waiter is serving us; see **servir** in the verb tables and WU 14.

sesenta *num.* sixty; see numbers in WU 4.

seventy *num.* **setenta**; see numbers in WU 4.

several *adj.* **varios, varias**

Shall we go to the movies? **¿Vamos al cine?**

shampoo *n.* **el champú**

shape *n.* **la forma**

sharpener, pencil *n.* **el sacapuntas**

shave oneself *refl.v.* **afeitarse**; My father shaves himself every morning. **Mi padre se afeita todas las mañanas**; see verb tables.

shellfish *n.* **el marisco**

shine *v.* **brillar**

ship *n.* **un barco, un buque**

shirt *n.* **la camisa**

shoes *n.* **los zapatos**; shoe shop **la zapatería**

shopping, go *v.* **ir de compras;** see **ir** in the index.

shore *n.* **la orilla, la costa, la playa** (beach)

short *adj.* **corto, corta; bajo, baja; pequeño, pequeña**

short story *n.* **el cuento**

shoulder *n.* **el hombro**

shout *v.* **gritar**

show *v.* **enseñar, mostrar (ue)**; I am showing you the photo. **Yo te (le) muestro la foto;** *n.* **el espectáculo, la representación** (theater, cinema)

si *conj.* if; see **si** clause in WU 11.

sick, ill *adj.* **enfermo, enferma**; to be sick **estar enfermo, enferma**

sickness *n.* **la enfermedad**

sidewalk café-restaurant *n.* **la terraza de café-restaurante**

siempre *adv.* always

sientan *v.form of* **sentarse**; see **se sientan** in this list

sightseeing bus *n.* **el autobús turístico**

silla *n.f.* chair

sillón *n.m.* armchair

silly *adj.* **tonto, tonta**

simpático, simpática *adj.* nice, pleasant (person)

simple *adj.* **sencillo, sencilla; easy fácil**

sin *prep.* without; see **sin** in WU 7

sing *v.* **cantar**

sinónimo *n.m.* synonym

sir *n.* **el señor**

sister *n.* **la hermana**; little sister **la hermanita**

sit down *v.* **sentarse (ie)**; see verb tables; Sit down! *imper.* **¡Siéntese (Ud.)! ¡Siéntate (tú)!**

sixty *num.* **sesenta**; see numbers in WU 4.

ski *v.* **esquiar**

skirt *n.* **la falda**

sky *n.* **el cielo**

sleep *v.* **dormir (ue, u)**; I sleep well. **Duermo bien;** Mary slept eight hours. **María durmió ocho horas;** see verb tables; to be sleepy **tener sueño**

slender, slim *adj.* **delgado, delgada**

497

slow *adj.* **lento, lenta**; slowly *adv.* **lentamente**

small *adj.* **pequeño, pequeña**

smell *v.* **oler (hue)**; see **oler** in the verb tables.

smile *n.* **la sonrisa**; *v.* **sonreír (i)**; see **reír** in the verb tables.

smoke *n.* **el humo**; *v.* **fumar**; I don't smoke. **No fumo.**

snack *n.* **el bocadillo**

snatch *v.* **arrancar (qu)**; I snatched... **Arranqué...**

snow *n.* **la nieve**; *v.* **nevar (ie)**; it snows **nieva**; it's snowing **está nevando**

so *adv.* **tan**; so, so **así, así**; so much **tanto**; see **tan, tanto** in the index.

So long! See you later! **¡Hasta luego!**

so many, so much *adj.* so many books **tantos libros**; so much money **tanto dinero**; see **tan, tanto** in WU 6.

so, so *adv.* **así, así**

sobre *prep.* on; *n.* envelope; The envelope is on the table. **El sobre está sobre la mesa**; I need an envelope for this letter. **Necesito un sobre para esta carta.**

soccer *n.* **el fútbol**

soccer player *n.* **el (la) futbolista**

social gathering *n.* **la tertulia**

socks *n.* **los calcetines**

soda (carbonated) *n.* **la gaseosa**

sofa *n.* **el sofá**

soft boiled egg *n.* **un huevo pasado por agua**

solamente *adv.* only

sold *past part.* **vendido**; see *past part.* in WU 12.

soldado *n.m.* soldier

sólo *adv.* only; **Sólo estoy mirando.** I'm only looking.

solo, sola *adj.* alone

solution *n.* **la solución**

sombrero *n.m.* hat

some, any *adj.* **algún, alguno, alguna, algunos, algunas**; see WU 3 and 6.

someone, somebody *pron.* **alguien**

something *pron.* **algo**

sometimes *adv.* **algunas veces**; one time **una vez**

somos *1st pers.,pl., pres. indic. of* **ser**; **son** *3d pers.,pl., pres.indic. of* **ser**; see **ser** in the index and verb tables, p. 448.

son *n.* **el hijo**; sons and daughters **los hijos**

song *n.* **la canción**

sonreír (i) *v.* to smile; see **reír** in the verb tables.

sonrisa *n.f.* smile

soon *adv.* **pronto**; as soon as possible **lo más pronto posible**; sooner or later **tarde o temprano**

sótano *n.m.* cellar

sound *n.m.* **el sonido**

soup *n.* **la sopa**

South America *n.* **la América del Sur, la Sudamérica**; South American *adj.* **sudamericano, sudamericana**

soy *1st pers.,sing., pres. indic. of* **ser**; see **ser** in the index and verb tables, p. 448.

Spain *n.* **la España**; Spaniard **el español, la española**

speak *v.* **hablar**

special *adj.* **especial**

species *n.* **la especie**

spectator *n.* **el espectador, la espectadora**

speed *n.* **la velocidad**; at full speed **a toda velocidad**

spend (time) *v.* **pasar**; spend (money) **gastar**; to spend money foolishly **malgastar**

splendid *adj.* **espléndido**

sponge cake *n.* **el bizcocho**

spoon *n.* **la cuchara**

sport *n.* **el deporte**

spring (season) *n.* **la primavera**

stadium *n.* **el estadio**

stairs *n.* **la escalera**

stamp (postage) *n.* **el sello, la estampilla**

stand *v.* **estar de pie**

star *n.* **la estrella**

start *v.* **comenzar (ie, c), empezar (ie, c); principiar;**

Now I'm starting. **Ahora comienzo, ahora empiezo**; I started. **Comencé, empecé.**

statue *n.* **la estatua**

stay *v.* **quedarse** *refl.v.*; to stay in bed **guardar cama**

steak *n.* **el bistec, el biftec**

steamship *n.* **el vapor**

stick *v.* **pegar**; to stick out **sacar (qu)**; I stuck out my tongue. **Saqué la lengua.**

stockings *n.* **las medias**

stomach *n.* **el estómago**; stomach ache **el dolor de estómago**

stone *n.* **la piedra**

stop (someone or something) *v.* **parar**; bus stop **la parada del autobús**; to stop oneself **detenerse**

store *n.* **la tienda**

story *n.* **el cuento, la historia**

stove *n.* **la estufa**

strange *adj.* **extraño, extraña**

straw *n.* **la paja**

street *n.* **la calle**

stroll *v.* **pasear**

strong *adj.* **fuerte**

student *n.* **el (la) estudiante**; pupil **el alumno, la alumna**

study *v.* **estudiar**

stupid *adj.* **tonto, tonta**

su, sus *poss.adj.* his, her, its, your, their; see WU 6.

subasta *n.f.* auction sale

subastador *n.m.* auctioneer

subir a *v.* to go up, to get on (a train, bus); see verb tables.

subject (course of study) *n.* **la asignatura**

subway *n.* **el subterráneo, el metropolitano, el metro**

such *adj.* **tal**; such as, like **tal como**

sucio *adj.* dirty

suddenly *adv.* **de repente**

suffering *n.* **el sufrimiento**

sufrir *v.* to suffer, to endure; see verb tables.

sugar *n.* **el azúcar**

suit (outfit) *n.* **el traje**

summer *n.* **el verano**; summer vacation **las vacaciones de verano**

sumo *adj.* highest, greatest (synonym: **supremo**)

sun *n.* **el sol**; to be sunny **hacer sol**; to take a sun bath **tomar el sol**

sunglasses *n.* **las gafas contra el sol; las gafas de sol; los anteojos oscuros**

supermercado *n.m.* supermarket

superstitious *adj.* **supersticioso**

supper *n.* **la cena**

supuesto *adj.* supposed; **por supuesto** of course

sure *adj.* **seguro**; I'm sure. **Estoy seguro (segura)**; Sure! **¡Claro!**

surely *adv.* **seguramente; de seguro**

surprise *n.* **la sorpresa**; *v.* **sorprender**; surprised *adj.* **sorprendido, sorprendida**

sus, su *poss.adj.* his, her, its, your, their; see WU 6.

sustantivo *n.m.* noun

suyo, suya, suyos, suyas See WU 6 and 10.

sweep *v.* **barrer, escobar**

sweetheart *n.* **el novio, la novia**

sweets, candies *n.* **los dulces**

swim *v.* **nadar**; swim suit *n.* **el traje de baño**

swimming *n.* **la natación**; swimming pool **la piscina**; I like swimming. **Me gusta la natación.**

T

table *n.* **la mesa**; little table **la mesita**; to set the table **poner la mesa**

tablecloth *n.* **el mantel**

tailor *n.* **el sastre**

take *v.* **tomar**; to take a walk **dar un paseo**; to take a bath **bañarse**; to take away **llevar**; to take a trip **hacer un viaje**; to take a sun bath **tomar el sol**; to take out (something), to stick out **tocar (qu)**; to take place **tener lugar**; to take a horseback ride **dar un paseo a caballo**; to

take a car ride **dar un paseo en automóvil**; to take pictures **sacar fotos**

tal *adj., adv.* such; **tal como** such as, like; **tal vez** perhaps; **¿Qué tal?** How are things?

talent *n.* **el talento**

talk *v.* **hablar**

tall *adj.* **alto, alta**

también *adv.* also, too

tampoco *adv.* neither, nor; **Ni yo tampoco.** Me neither. Nor I, either.

tan *adv.* so; **tan hermosa** so beautiful; **tan ... como** as ... as; **tanto ... como** as much ... as; see WU 6 and **tan** in the index.

tañer *v.* to pluck a stringed musical instrument

tanto, tanta, tantos, tantas *adj.* as (so) much, as (so) many; see WU 6 and **tanto** in the index.

tarde *n.f.* afternoon; **buenas tardes** good afternoon; *adv.* late; **más tarde** later

tarea *n.f.* homework

taste *v.* **saborear**; *n.* **el gusto**

tasty *adj.* **sabroso, gustoso**

taxi *n.* **el taxi**

te *refl.pron., dir. & indir. obj. pron. (tú form)* you, to you, yourself; see WU 8, 9 and 10.

tea *n.* **el té**

teach *v.* **enseñar**; teaching (profession) **la enseñanza**

teacher *n.* **el maestro, la maestra, el profesor, la profesora**

team *n.* **el equipo**

teaspoon **la cucharita**

teatro *n.m.* theater

telefonear *v.* to telephone

telephone *n.* **el teléfono**; cellular telephone **el teléfono inalámbrico**; rotary dial **el disco**; touch tone telephone **el teléfono a botones**; pick up the receiver **descolgar (ue)**; hang up **colgar (ue)**; to dial a number **marcar (qu)**; dial tone **el tono**; to tele-

phone someone **llamar a alguien por teléfono**

television *n.* **la televisión**; television set **el televisor**

tell *v.* **decir**; see verb tables; Tell me! **¡Dígame (Ud.)! ¡Dime (tú)!**

teller's window (bank, station, post office) *n.* **la ventanilla**

tenderly *adj.* **cariñosamente**

tener *v.* to have; see **tener** in WU 3, the verb tables, and index.

tengo *1st pers.,sing., pres. indic.* of **tener**

tennis *n.* **el tenis**

tent *n.* **la tienda**

tercer, tercero, tercera *num.* third; see WU 6 and numbers in WU 4.

terminar *v.* to terminate, to end, to complete

terminarse *refl.v.* to end (itself)

terminó *3d pers.,s., pret.* of **terminar**

ternera *n.f.* veal; **las chuletas de ternera** veal chops

terrible *adj.* terrible, awful

tertulia *n.f.* chat, social gathering; evening party

test *n.* **la prueba**

thank you, thanks **gracias**; thank you very much **muchas gracias**; thanks to **gracias a**

that *dem.adj.* **ese, esa, aquel, aquella;** see these words in Index; that *dem.pron.neuter* **eso**; What's that? **¿Qué es eso?** that one, those *dem.pron.* **aquél, aquélla, aquéllos, aquéllas**; that, those *dem.adj.* **aquel, aquella, aquellos, aquellas**; see WU 6 and 9.

that, which *pron.* **que**; see *pronouns* in WU 2, 8, 9 and 10.

That's right! **¡Eso es!**

the *def.art.* **el, los; la, las**; see WU 1.

theater *n.* **el teatro**

their *poss.adj.* **su, sus**; see WU 6.

499

them *dir.obj.pron.* **los, las**; to them *indir.obj.pron.* **les**; see WU 8, 9 and 10; see also *prep.pron.* in WU 9.

theme *n.* **el tema**

then *adv.* **entonces, luego**

there *adv.* **allí, allá**

there is..., there are... **hay**; there was, there were **había**; see **haber** in the verb tables, p. 448.

therefore (for that reason) *adv.* **por eso**

these *dem.adj.* **estas, estos**; see index.

thin *adj.* **delgado, delgada, flaco, flaca**

thing *n.* **la cosa**

think *v.* **pensar (ie)**; to think of (about) **pensar en**; see **pensar** in the verb tables.

thirst *n.* **la sed**; to be thirsty **tener sed**

this *dem.adj.* **este, esta**; see these words in the index; this *dem.pron.,neuter* **esto**; see WU 9.

those *dem.adj.* **esos, esas, aquellos, aquellas**; see index; those, that *dem.adj.* **aquellos, aquellas, aquel, aquella**; see WU 6; those, that one *dem.pron.* **aquéllos, aquéllas, aquél, aquélla**; see WU 9.

thousand *num.* **mil**; see WU 4.

throat *n.* **la garganta**

throw *v.* **lanzar, echar, tirar**; throw away **botar**

tie, necktie *n.* **la corbata**

tienes *2d pers.,s. (tú), pres.indic. of* **tener**; see **tener** in WU 3, the verb tables, and index.

tierra *n.f.* land, earth

time *n.* **la hora, el tiempo, la vez**; What time is it? **¿Qué hora es?** It's one o'clock. **Es la una**; It's two o'clock **Son las dos**; At what time? **¿A qué hora?**; at one o'clock **a la una**; at two o'clock **a las dos**; on the dot **en punto**; I have lots of time **Tengo mucho tiempo**; at the same time **al mismo tiempo**; on time

a tiempo; one time **una vez**; two times, twice **dos veces**; many times **muchas veces**

tired *adj.* **cansado, cansada; fatigado, fatigada**; to be tired **estar cansado**

tiza *n.f.* chalk

to *prep.* **a**; to the **al, a la, a los, a las**; see WU 1 and 5.

to him, to her, to you, to them **le, les**; see *indir.obj.pron.* in WU 8, 9 and 10.

to where? **¿adónde?**

toasted *adj.* **tostado**

tocador *n.m.* dresser, chest of drawers

todas *adj.* all; **todas las noches** every night, every evening

today *adv.* **hoy**

todo el mundo everybody; **todo mi dinero** all my money

todo, toda, todos, todas *adj.* all; **todo el mundo** everybody; **todas las noches** every night, every evening

together *adv.* **junto, juntos**

tomar *v.* to take

tomorrow *adv.* **mañana**; tomorrow morning **mañana por la mañana**; until tomorrow **hasta mañana**

tongue *n.* **la lengua**

tontería *n.f.* foolish thing

tonto, tonta *adj.* foolish, silly, stupid

too (also) *adv.* **también**; too much **demasiado**

tooth *n.* **el diente**

torn *adj.* **rasgados**

touch *v.* **tocar (qu); Yo toqué el piano.** I played the piano.

town *n.* **el pueblo, la aldea**

toy *n.* **el juguete**

trabajado *past part. of* **trabajar**; see *past part.* in WU 12.

trabajar *v.* to work; **trabajo** *n.m.* work; (synonym: **la obra**)

track *n.* **la pista**

traffic (vehicles) *n.* **la circulación**

train *n.* **el tren**; dining car **el coche-comedor**; sleeping car **el coche dormitorio, el coche cama**

transparante *adj.* transparent

travel *v.* **viajar**; by plane **por avión**; travel agency **la agencia de viajes**; see **viajar** in the verb tables.

tree *n.* **el árbol, los árboles**

trip *n.* **la excursión, el viaje**; to take a trip **hacer un viaje**

truck *n.* **el camión**

truly *adv.* **de veras**

truth *n.* **la verdad**

tu, tus *poss.adj. (fam.)* your; see WU 6.

tuyo, tuya, tuyos, tuyas *poss.pron.* yours; see *poss.pron.* in WU 10.

type (kind, sort) *n.* **el tipo**

U

u *conj.* or; if a word right after **o** (or) begins with **o** or **ho,** use **u: septiembre u octubre** September or October; **muchachos u hombres** boys or men

ugly *adj.* **feo, fea**

último, última *adj.* last

umbrella *n.* **el paraguas**

unbelievable *adj.* **increíble**

uncle *n.* **el tío**

under, underneath *adv.* **debajo (de)**

understand *v.* **comprender, entender (ie)**; I understand. **Yo comprendo, yo entiendo.**

underwear *n.* **la ropa interior**

unfortunately *adv.* **desafortunadamente**

ungrateful *adj.* **ingrato, ingrata**

únicamente *adv.* only

United Nations *n.* **las Naciones Unidas**

United States *n.* **los Estados Unidos**

until *adv.* **hasta**; until I see you again **hasta la vista**; until then **hasta luego** up *adv.* **arriba**; upstairs **en el piso de arriba**; to go up **subir a**; upon entering **al entrar**; upon arriving **al llegar**; upon seeing **al ver**; see WU 13.

us *pron.* **nosotros, nosotras**; with us **con nosotros;** for us **para nosotros**; see WU 8, 9 and 10.

usar *v.* to use

useful *adj.* **útil, útiles**

utilize *v.* **utilizar, usar**

V

vacation *n.* **las vacaciones**

valer *v.* to be worth

value *n.* **el valor**

vamos *1st pers.,pl., pres. indic. & imper. of* **ir**; see **ir** in the index and verb tables, p. 448.

¡Vamos a comenzar! Let's begin! **¡Vamos a comer!** Let's eat! **¡Vamos a sentarnos!** Let's sit down!

vas *2d pers.,s., pres indic. (tú) of* **ir**; see **ir** in the index and verb tables, p. 448.

vase *n.* **el jarrón**

veal *n.* **la ternera**; veal chops **las chuletas de ternera**

vegetables *n.* **las legumbres, los vegetales**

velocidad *n.f.* velocity

vender *v.* to sell; see **vender** in the verb tables.

vendido *adj. & past part. of* **vender**; sold; see *past part.* in WU 12.

vendrá *3d pers.,s., fut. of* **venir**; will come; see **venir** in WU 8 and the verb tables.

¡Vengan! *3d pers.,pl. (Uds.), imper. of* **venir**; Come!

venir *v.* to come; see **venir** in WU 3, 7, 8 and the verb tables.

venta *n.f.* sale

ventana *n.f.* window

ver *v.* to see; see **ver** in the verb tables.

verá *3d pers.,s., fut. of* **ver**; he/she/you will see

veras *n.f.,pl.* reality, truth; **de veras** really, truly

very *adv.* **muy**; very much **muchísimo**; see index.

vestíbulo *n.m.* vestibule, entrance hallway

vestidos *n.m.* clothes

¡Vete! *2d pers.,s. (tú), imper. of* **irse**; Go away! Shoo! Scat!

vez *n.f.* time; **una vez** one time, once; **dos veces** two times, twice; **otra vez** again

viajar *v.* to travel; see verb tables

viaje *n.m.* trip; **hacer un viaje** to take a trip

vida *n.f.* life

vienen *3d pers.,pl., pres. indic. of* **venir**; see **venir** in WU 3 and the verb tables.

viento *n.m.* wind (air); **la brisa** breeze

vieron *3d pers.,pl., pret. of* **ver**; they saw; see **ver** in WU 7 and the verb tables.

vio *3d pers.,s., pret. of* **ver**; he/she/you saw

visit *v.* **visitar**; *n.* **la visita**

¡Viva ... ! Long live ... ! **viva** *3d pers.,sing., imper. (command) of* **vivir**; see the verb tables.

vivir *v.* to live

voice *n.* **la voz, las voces**; in a low voice **en voz baja**

volver (ue) *v.* to return; **Vuelvo a las tres.** I'm returning at three o'clock; see verb tables.

voy *1st pers.,s., pres.indic. of* **ir**; see **ir** in WU 3, the index and verb tables, p. 448.

voz *n.f.* voice; **en voz baja** in a low voice, in a whisper

W

wait (for) *v.* **esperar**

waiter *n.* **el camarero, el mozo**

wake up *v.* **despertarse (ie)**; I wake up at seven. **Me despierto a las siete.**

walk *v.* **caminar, andar, marchar, ir a pie**; to walk away

marcharse; *n.* **el paseo**; to go for a walk **ir de paseo**; to take a walk **dar un paseo**

wall *n.* **la pared** (inside); **el muro** (outside)

wallet *n.* **la cartera**

walnut *n.* **la nuez, las nueces**

want *v.* **desear, querer (ie)**; I want to go to Spain. **Quiero ir a España.** See verb tables.

war *n.* **la guerra**

wardrobe *n.* **el guardarropa**

warm *adj.* **caliente**; warmth **el calor**; It's warm today. **Hace calor hoy.**

wash *v.* **lavar**; wash oneself **lavarse**; I'm washing my car. **Lavo mi coche**; I wash myself every day. **Me lavo todos los días.**

waste *v.* **gastar**

watch *v.* **mirar**; I watch television. **Miro la televisión**; *n.* **el reloj**

water *n.* **el agua** *(fem.)***, las aguas**; fresh water **el agua fresca**

we *pron.* **nosotros, nosotras**; see *subject pron.* in WU 2.

weak *adj.* **débil**

wear *v.* **llevar, usar**

weather *n.* **el tiempo**; to be good (bad) weather **hacer buen (mal) tiempo**; to be warm (cold) **hacer calor (frío)**; to be sunny (windy) **hacer sol (viento)**; to be cool **hacer fresco**

week *n.* **la semana**; last week **la semana pasada**; next week **la semana próxima, la semana que viene**

weekend *n.* **el fin de semana**; Have a nice weekend! **¡Pase un buen fin de semana!**

weep *v.* **llorar**

weigh *v.* **pesar**

weight lifting *n.* **el levantamiento de pesas**

welcome *adj.* **bienvenido, bienvenida**; to welcome someone **dar la bienvenida a alguien**; you're welcome **de nada, no hay de qué**

501

well *adv.* **bien**; well, then **pues, pues bien**

wet *adj.* **mojado**

what *pron.* **que**; What did you say? **¿Qué dijo Ud.?** What do you want? **¿Qué quiere Ud.? ¿Qué desea Ud.?** What's going on? **¿Qué pasa?** What's the matter? **¿Qué hay?** What's the matter with you? **¿Que tienes (tú)? ¿Qué tiene (Ud.)?** What's the matter with him (her)? **¿Qué tiene él (ella)?** See *pronouns* in WU 2, 8, 9 and 10.

What a day! **¡Qué día!**

What luck! **¡Qué fortuna!**

whatever, whichever *adj.* **cualquier, cualquiera**

when *adv.* **cuando**; when? **¿cuándo?**

where *adv.* **donde**; where? **¿dónde?** where to? to where? **¿adónde?**

whether ... or *conj.* **ya ... ya; ya sea ... o**

which *rel.pron.* **el cual, la cual, los cuales, las cuales, que**; see these words in WU 10 and index.

while *adv.* **mientras**; *conj.* **mientras que**; after a little while **al poco rato**

whistle *v.* **silbar, chiflar**; *n.* **el silbido, el silbato, el chiflo**

white *adj.* **blanco, blanca, blancos, blancas**

who, whom *pron.* **que, quien, quienes; el cual, los cuales; el que**; see *pronouns* in WU 2, 8, 9 and 10.

Whose is...? Whose are...? **¿De quién es...? ¿De quiénes son...?** See WU 10.

why *adv.* **¿por qué? ¿para qué?** See WU 11.

wide *adj.* **ancho, ancha**

wife *n.* **la esposa**

win *v.* **ganar**

wind *n.* **el viento**; to be windy **hacer viento**

window *n.* **la ventana**; teller's window (bank, station) *n.* **la ventanilla**

wine *n.* **el vino**

wings *n.* **las alas (el ala)**

wink *v.* **guiñar**; Jane winks. **Juana guiña el ojo.**

winter *n.* **el invierno**

wipe dry *v.* **secar (qu)**; I wiped the table dry. **Sequé la mesa.**

wish *v.* **desear, querer (ie)**

with *prep.* **con**; with me **conmigo**; see **conmigo, contigo, consigo** in the index.

without *prep.* **sin**

woman *n.* **la mujer**

wood *n.* **la madera**; wooden **de madera**; in the woods **en el bosque**

wool *n.* **la lana**

word *n.* **la palabra**

work *v.* **trabajar**; *n.* **el trabajo, la obra**

worried *adj.* **preocupado, preocupada**; I'm worried. **Estoy preocupado (preocupada)**; Don't worry! **¡No te preocupes (tú)! ¡No se preocupe (Ud.)!**

worth, to be *v.* **valer**; *n.* **el valor**; How much is it worth? **¿Cuánto vale?**

Wow! **¡Ay!**

write *v.* **escribir**; written **escrito, escrita**; see *past part.* in WU 12.

Y

y *conj.* and; see **y** and **e** in the index.

ya *adv.* already, now; **ya no** no longer; **Ya lo sé.** I already know it; **¡Ya lo creo!** I should say so! **Ya entiendo.** Now I understand.

ya ... ya *conj.* whether ... or

year *n.* **el año**; last year **el año pasado**; next year **el año próximo, el año que viene**

yellow *adj.* **amarillo, amarilla**

yendo *pres.part.* **(gerundio)** of **ir**; going; see *pres.part.* in WU 3.

yesterday *adv.* **ayer**; day before yesterday **anteayer**; yesterday afternoon **ayer por la tarde**; yesterday evening **ayer por la noche**; last night **anoche**

yet *adv.* **todavía**; not yet **todavía no**

you *pron.* **tú, vosotros, vosotras, usted, ustedes**; see *subject pron.* in WU 2

you are ... **(tú) eres...; (tú) estás...; (Ud.) es...; (Ud.) está....**; see **estar** and **ser** in the index and verb tables, p. 448.

You don't say! **¡No me diga (Ud.)! ¡No me digas (tú)!**

young *adj.* **joven, jóvenes**; young man **el joven**; young woman **la joven**

younger *adj.* **menor; más joven**

your *poss.adj.* **su, sus; tu, tus** (fam.); see *possessive adjectives* in WU 6.

yours *poss.pron.* See *possessive pronouns* in WU 10.

Z

zapatería *n.f.* shoe store

zapatero *n.m.* shoemaker

zapato *n.m.* shoe

Zodiaco *n.m.* Zodiac

zoo *n.* **el parque zoológico**

Index

503